White-Collar Crime

White-Collar Crime

Crime

Classic and Contemporary Views

THIRD EDITION

GILBERT GEIS, ROBERT F. MEIER,
and
LAWRENCE M. SALINGER
editors

THE FREE PRESS
New York London Toronto Sydney Tokyo Singapore

The Free Press
A Division of Simon & Schuster Inc.
866 Third Avenue, New York, N. Y. 10022

Printed in the United States of America

printing number
1   2   3   4   5   6   7   8   9   10

Library of Congress Cataloging-in-Publication Data

White-collar crime: classic and contemporary views/ Gilbert Geis,
    Robert F. Meier, and Lawrence M. Salinger, editors. —3rd ed.
        p.   cm.
    Includes bibliographical references and index.
    ISBN 0-02-911601-5
        1. White-collar crimes.   2. White-collar crimes—United States.
I. Geis, Gilbert.   II. Meier, Robert F. (Robert Frank).
III. Salinger, Lawrence M.
HV6635.W45   1995
364. 1'68—dc20   94-31736
                                                                           CIP

For Dolores, Lee, and Denise

and in memory of
Robley Elizabeth Geis and
Michelle Smith Pontell

Contents

Acknowledgments

A number of people have helped with substantive advice and technical assistance. We want to express our appreciation to Charles Lieber, then president of Atherton Press, who was the moving force in the preparation of the first edition of this book, and Gladys Topkis, now a senior editor at Yale University Press, who encouraged the revision. At The Free Press, Bruce Nichols, our editor, has been a pleasure to work with on this third edition; and we also wish to thank Loretta Denner for supervising its production, as well as Ann E. Hirst for copyediting it.

Colin Goff of the University of Winnipeg helped us construct the roster of those pieces included in the volume. Assistance at the University of California, Irvine, was provided by Judy Omiya and Carol Wyatt, and collegial support by Arnie Binder, Kitty Calavita, Joe DiMento, Paul Jesilow, and Henry Pontell. Special thanks also are due to Steve Reynard and to Joseph T. Wells.

There are three people at Iowa State University whom we want to thank as well. Lynnell Simonson was extremely effective in her library and editorial work. Her contributions were essential to the completion of the book. Ramona Wierson and Deb McKay handled a variety of administrative chores that would have taken time away from the book. Their professionalism and support are very much appreciated.

At Arkansas State University, assistance was provided by Kristy Scarbrough and Rena Bradley, who assiduously helped to gather in copies of the articles we considered for inclusion in the volume. Susan Rainwaiter also was very helpful with a variety of assignments. Thanks also go to the students in the Graduate Seminar on White-Collar Crime and to colleagues in the Department of Criminology, Sociology, Social Work, and Geography. Loving thanks are due to Denise and Jeremy "Bear" Salinger who lived with the turbulence and disruption caused by the preparation of this volume, and to Dr. Gerard and Ursel Salinger, who have supported a third of the editors through thick and thin.

Introduction

I

There have been sharp swings in both public and scholarly concern with the subject of white-collar crime. Today, interest is intense, though for the moment it is being overshadowed by a focus on street violence, gang behavior, and transactions in illegal drugs. It is rare that the political and lay agenda can simultaneously make the same emotional and fiscal investment in both the traditional forms of lawbreaking that the public most commonly associates with the word "crime" and the more complex and remote violations that constitute the realm of "white-collar crime." Street crimes overwhelmingly are the work of the disenfranchised—the poor and those in the dispossessed segments of society. In times of economic stress, marked most notably by high unemployment, the public tends to focus on street offenders, often using hostility to their depredations to camouflage socially unacceptable anger about those who are new to the country and those who exist marginally, people who are defined as a threat to mainstream members of the middle class.

Nonetheless, there is no returning to those halcyon days for entrepreneurs when their exploitation of customers and the public purse went almost totally unattended. Reformers today persistently denounce "crime in the suites" and point out that the toll it exacts is far worse than that inflicted on us by "crime in the streets," the robberies, gang shootings, and rapes that preoccupy the public mind. Citizens are worried about the quality of their life, the safety of the cars they drive, the legal drugs and food they ingest, the places where they work, and even the air they breathe. Note the concern with diet, the streets dotted with joggers, the proliferation of health centers where the faithful puff and frolic with ingenious devices whose use they anticipate will make their life better and longer. Little of this was in evidence fewer than twenty years ago.

Scholarly work on white-collar crime today has reached the point where it is no longer in jeopardy of being upstaged and displaced by newer trends in academic inquiry. The enormous growth in the past three decades in persons pursuing careers in criminology and criminal justice inevitably led some of these recruits to seek relatively uncluttered and undercultivated research pastures that offered a reasonable prospect for a high-quality scholarly yield. Besides, social science has always attracted a disproportionate number of students and professionals with sympathy for the underdog. Working to rid the streets of the menace of lower-class offenders

1

certainly has social value, but there must exist in those who do such work some uncertainty that they are merely dealing with the consequences of mean and discriminatory social policies and that their efforts will have little or no impact on the true underlying causes of the criminal behaviors they study. Little such moral malaise is associated with endeavors in white-collar crime. Here what is seen most often is greed for more—power and money, in particular—by those who usually have plenty already. It is true, of course, that pressures on suite and street offenders may seem comparably demanding to those committing the crimes. But it is much more difficult to generate sympathy for chief executive officers who earn a million or more each year and nonetheless agree to market a product they know is dangerous rather than to risk a decline in corporate profits, than it is to feel some empathy for slum youngsters who spend their days mindlessly sandpapering furniture for minimum wages and decide to commit a burglary to obtain money for a pleasurable spree.

Firmly entrenched, the study of white-collar crime travels under a number of criminological identities. Some prefer the term "upperworld crime," while others favor "crimes of the powerful," "avocational crime," "economic crime," or "abuse of power," the last the designation used by the United Nations. No matter what they are called, the behaviors being classified have a similar core: they include rip-offs of savings and loan institutions; antitrust violations; health-care frauds; misrepresentation in financial statements; and unnecessary surgery or bills for services not rendered by physicians. White-collar crimes can be crimes of violence—hundreds of people die each year from illegally unsafe working conditions and from surgery performed only to collect a hefty fee. More commonly, white-collar crimes involve frauds in which unwitting and unwary customers and consumers are cheated.

The academic study of white-collar crime has had an erratic history. It was forcefully brought to the attention of the scholarly community by Edwin H. Sutherland, then a 56-year-old sociologist at Indiana University, in his presidential address to the American Sociological Society in Philadelphia in 1939. Sutherland coined the term "white-collar crime," and denounced in no uncertain terms those who engaged in what he saw as evil machinations at the expense of the public well-being.

Yet, at the same time as he castigated what he saw as malevolent politicians, professionals, and businessmen (for, at the time, they were almost exclusively men), Sutherland disingenuously maintained that he was not interested in social reform, but only in alerting criminological theorists to the fact that, unless they attended to the crimes committed by the well-heeled in the course of their work, they would derive woefully inadequate conceptions of the causes of crime.

Among the more pointed and pungent of Sutherland's observations, which the reader will encounter in the first selection in this volume, were:

• "White-collar criminality in business is similar to what Al Capone called 'the legitimate rackets.' "

- "White-collar criminals are relatively immune because of the class bias of the courts and the power of their class to influence the implementation and administration of the law."
- "Political graft almost always involves collusion between politicians and businessmen, but prosecutions are generally limited to the politicians."

The hostility toward business in Sutherland's pioneering polemic on white-collar crime has ever after permeated criminological studies and statements on the subject. It reflects a belief among many social scientists that the conduct of business is an endemically corrupt enterprise. Any endeavor whose basic goal is profit maximization, it is felt, will be tainted and twisted. Most social scientists would undoubtedly reflexively endorse the stark judgment of Micah of Moresheth, a prophet of the biblical period, regarding commercial activity: "A merchant shall hardly keep himself from doing wrong and a huckster shall not be freed from sin. . . . As a nail sticketh between the joinings of a stone, so doth sin stick close to buying and selling."[1] Illegal acts are particularly likely to occur, the formula goes, when the profit-seeker is powerful, and the agents of control and the means at their disposal are weak.

Perhaps the most puzzling phenomenon is that there is not a great deal more corporate crime than there seems to be, given the minimum risks involved. This situation reinforces the commonplace observation that all of us are capable of resisting the temptation to incessantly pursue self-interest, even outside the law, if certain conditions prevail. Scholars of white-collar crime have not as yet adequately scrutinized conditions creating conformity: for those with power, they could include, among other things, a sense of morality and justice, inertia, or a belief that what they have is enough.

The bias in social science regarding business conduct, a bias with considerable support among the general public, has been addressed by Robert Heilbroner, a notably perceptive analyst of the social aspects of economic life, in the following terms:

> What . . . explains the fury with which we turn on the corporation for despoiling the air and water, and for vending shoddy or dangerous wares? I suspect that the answer lies more in our resentment of the kind of presence the corporation represents than in the particular crimes it commits (which . . . I have no wish to condone or minimize). What fuels the public protest against corporate misbehavior is the same animus that fuels the protest against the Teamsters Union or against "Welfare." It is an aspect of a widely shared frustration with respect to all bastions of power that are immense, anonymous and impregnable, and yet inextricably bound up with the industrial society that few of us wish to abandon.[2]

The "crime" of business, after all, is that it perpetuates a culture of self-interest through its ethos of self-realization. It is natural for people to be suspicious of business. Business is not a team player in the same way that other social institutions are supposed to be. Although there is more than enough at times to be suspicious about regarding education, medicine, and religion, these institutions are oriented around the needs and interests of others, not themselves. When professors, physicians, and ecclesiastical officials violate others' trust, it is occasion for much disapproval; when people in business violate trust, they are merely "doing their job."

II

A few quick brush strokes are necessary to review research on white-collar crime from the time when Sutherland's work burst upon the sociological scene until the present. Such work can roughly be divided into three periods. The first ran from 1939 to 1963 and saw a considerable outpouring of pioneering work. During the 1964–1975 period there was a sharp decline in scholarly work on white-collar crime. Since about 1975, however, there has been a dramatic revival of interest in the subject.

The 1939–1963 Period

Sutherland's vivifying presidential address and his groundbreaking monograph, *White Collar Crime,* which appeared in 1949, ten years following the address, were the spurs for a spate of work on white-collar crime. Much of it involved somewhat sterile jousting about the proper definition and embrace of the term itself, including charges (significantly mostly from sociologists who also possessed law degrees) that criminologists were branding innocent businessmen as crooks merely because they did not approve of them.[3] Ernest W. Burgess, one of the renowned sociologists of the period, also argued that there was something inherently wrong with labeling persons "criminals" who did not so regard themselves. This was perhaps the low point intellectually in the semantic sorties.

There also emerged during this period a rich lode of field research on white-collar crime, virtually all of it carried out by persons who had been Sutherland's students or who had academic ties to him, indicating that the concept had not truly entered into the mainstream of the criminological enterprise.

Representative of such work was Marshall Clinard's study of wartime black market operations. Clinard suggested that the most useful explanation of such white-collar crime might be established in terms of the personalities of the particular offenders.[4] Such a suggestion has rarely found favor with later scholars, who tend to seek structural explanations. Additional seminal studies during the period were contributed by Richard Quinney on pharmacists,[5] Donald Newman on public attitudes regarding pure food and drug laws,[6] and Frank Hartung on wartime rationing violations in the meat industry.[7] Quinney found that pharmacists whose orientation is more businesslike than professional are most likely to violate the laws regulating their trade. Newman discovered that the general public felt that persons breaking pure food and drug laws should be punished more severely than they were, but not as harshly as the law permitted. Hartung established that price violations at one point in the retail process were duplicated throughout the sales chain until ultimately the consumer was forced to pay the illegally high cost of the product.

A prominent feature of the early work done on the topic was that it concentrated on documenting the nature of the offenses, rather than on more theoretical explanations or policy conclusions. These early studies were mainly descriptive. Their empiricism was confined within a narrow vision provided by hypotheses derived from specific theoretical perspectives. What theory they considered generally was post hoc and applied only to the form of illegality under review.

It is notable that none of the major studies dealt with *corporate* crime. Robert Lane had conducted research indicating that New England shoe manufacturing companies in financial difficulty were more likely to violate the regulatory laws than those with a healthier balance sheet.[8] Except for this inquiry, conducted by a political scientist interested in organizational behavior, the corporate world remained untouched by social scientists concerned about white-collar crime. In large measure, this was because access was strictly limited—or thought to be. "Private enterprise remains extraordinarily private," Roy Lewis and Rosemary Stewart wrote. "We know more about the motives, habits, and most intimate arcana of primitive peoples in New Guinea . . . than we do of the denizens of executive suites in Unilever, Citroen, or General Electric."[9]

The 1964–1975 Period

By 1964, it appeared that the study of white-collar crime was well established. During the next decade, however, work on the subject came to a virtual standstill. A case study of the General Electric heavy equipment antitrust case represented the only major academic contribution to emerge.[10] That study was made possible largely because of the extensive Congressional investigations prompted by the celebrity of the case and by Senator Estes Kefauver's political ambitions.[11]

The abrupt disappearance of social science interest in white-collar crime is not easily explained. Economic conditions were both good and poor during the period. It seems most likely that the dearth of scholarly work on the subject represented an aftermath of earlier times, when challenges to established centers of power could prove hazardous, especially during the reign of Senator Joseph McCarthy.[12] As novelist Raphael Yglesias noted recently: "McCarthy was sort of a simplistic Hitler. But it only seemed farcical in retrospect. At the time, with people losing their jobs, committing suicide, with the Rosenbergs dying in the electric chair, there was little of the black comedy that now remains when seeing those black and white t.v. hearings."[13]

The cold war standoff between the United States and the Soviet Union also produced a patriotic acceptance at home of the status quo. Academic work, it seems, requires an incubation period: It had been stifled during the cold war years in regard to what might be seen as iconoclastic ventures. It would be reborn with the turmoil of Vietnam and Watergate and bear fruit in a later time.

The Contemporary Scene

Work in criminology in the mid- to late 1950s had shifted to juvenile delinquency and the nature of delinquent subcultures. Much attention was paid throughout the 1960s and 1970s to labeling theory, but the focus of interest tended to be on youngsters and, in particular, drug users. When applied to criminal acts, labeling theory denounced the consequences of official sanctions on nonthreatening offenders. No one was concerned about possible negative effects of official labels on powerful people. The problem seemed to be quite the reverse; how to get them labeled at all.

By the mid-1970s, criminologists were looking to conflict theories for intellectual support. They turned their attention to the importance of power as influential in defining crime. Conflict theorists pointed out that the misbehavior of the socially marginal was considered illegal, while misbehavior of the powerful was protected behind a screen of secretaries, paperwork, ledgers, lawyers, and administrative law procedures that produced the belief that any wrongs were only technical errors and nonthreatening. It was against this conventional wisdom that attention to the crimes of the powerful began to increase. The study of white-collar crime had become popular again.

The social unrest that reached its peak in the early 1970s apparently contributed most to the revival of interest in the study of white-collar crime. Students at universities turned militant, daring the power of the authorities. The Vietnam War fueled beliefs that elected officials were deceitful. Underdog groups, such as blacks, women, and homosexuals, demanded fair and equal treatment. Poor persons demanded that wealth should be more equitably shared, and criminal offenders became politicized, insisting that social injustice, not personal pathologies, lay at the root of their lawbreaking.

The uncovering of the Watergate scandals and the subsequent resignation of President Richard M. Nixon further undermined public confidence in leaders, particularly as his vice president, Spiro Agnew, had only recently been forced from office in the face of allegations that he had accepted bribes while governor of Maryland, and that bribe money was still being delivered to him in his White House office.

The widely publicized work of Ralph Nader and his associates indicated that bureaucracies were penetrable, and that rot, real or perceived, could be readily found.[14] The government, responding to President Jimmy Carter's own populism, began to allocate sizable sums of money for research on white-collar crime; changing priorities in the federal Department of Justice reflected his turn of focus.[15] Finally, the incursion into criminological thinking of Marxist doctrine carried with it a strong condemnation of upper-class privilege and a categoric assumption that such privilege was being abused.[16]

A measure of recent developments can be derived from a comparison of the present and earlier editions of this book. The first edition, published in 1968, specifically called attention to the rather small amount of scholarly material on white-collar crime and noted that a student absorbing the volume's contents would be in command of virtually everything of significance written to that date on the subject. The Introduction predicted that "this encapsulated state of affairs is not likely to last for long." It singled out the work on white-collar crime in the 1967 report of the President's Commission on Law Enforcement and Administration of Justice as presaging an upsurge of interest in the subject. The bibliography of related writings in this first edition, which represented pretty much all of what was in print, ran to little more than four pages.

Almost a decade later, in 1977, the Preface to the revised edition lamented that the earlier prediction of a renaissance of research "went astray, for social scientists have been relatively inactive in their investigation of white-collar crime" and that "the challenge offered by white-collar crime . . . has continued to be unanswered."[17] Only a third of the articles reprinted in the 1977 edition had been published since the reader's first appearance in 1968. The Reference section had almost doubled, but this largely reflected law review articles providing technical analyses of federal statutes concerning white-collar offenses.

In the 1977 edition attention was again called to signs that there would shortly be renewed interest in the subject. These included the appearance of a militant consumer constituency, and a survey of criminal justice researchers indicated they believed that legislatures would soon begin to devote more attention to white-collar than to any other forms of crime.

This time the nascent signs proved to be true heralds of a strong growth of public and academic concern with white-collar crime. A great majority of the articles included in the present volume first saw the light of day since the previous edition: only a handful of basic, classic pieces have been retained. No longer is it possible to say that everything of scholarly merit has found its way between the covers of this book. Very difficult decisions were involved in selecting what we would reprint from amongst a mass of important and sophisticated publications. The present bibliography, vastly expanded, nonetheless had to omit many references in order to keep it within reasonable bounds.

III

Behavior duplicating in form and spirit what is now regarded as white-collar crime can be found throughout recorded history. People have always been suspicious of power. As far back as 1635, a satirist had a businessman proclaim: "I love churches. I mean to turn pirate, rob my countrymen and build one."[18] In recent times, a U.S. Senator told the story of a corporation officer who, asked if he were not ashamed of double-dealing persons who trusted him, was puzzled: "Who else can you cheat?" he wanted to know.[19]

Three marketplace offenses in medieval and early modern England—called regrating, engrossing, and forestalling—illustrate early concern with the use of commercial power to harm ordinary citizens. In periods of terrible food shortages caused by crop failures and inadequate means to transfer produce from a bountiful site to a site in dire need, the authorities cracked down on these crimes. The laws were invoked for at least 500 years, more than twice as long as the history of the United States.

Regrating refers to the practice of buying up market commodities, especially foodstuffs, in order to resell them at a profit before they reach the public market, especially buying them privately with a view to enhancing their price. Engrossing is concerned with wholesale purchasing, especially buying up the entire stock for the purpose of reselling it at a monopoly price;[20] it stands as an important precursor of the Sherman antitrust law, enacted in the United States in 1890.

Forestalling was the umbrella term for the offenses, derived etymologically from the Anglo-Saxon *foresteal.* Its lineage is biblical; jeremiads concerning marketplace duplicity are common in Judeo-Christian theology. Proverbs (11:25) admonishes: "He that holdeth corn, the people will curse him: But blessing shall be upon the head of him that selleth it." Deuteronomy (25:13) proclaims: "For every one practicing unfairness is abominable to the Lord your God."

English market control laws drew upon these theological precepts. Forestalling was forbidden as early as the reign of Henry II (1216–1272), and there are surviving records from the town of Norwich in 1278 reporting court fines against local citizens for selling shoddy products and charging excessive prices.[21] By law, corn could not be sold in sheaves before it was threshed and measured; in this way attempts to forestall were frustrated. When starvation threatened, grain was not to be used to make malt products, such as ale. Near-starvation was said to provoke "the poorer sort," especially those "dysordred and lewd dysposed persons" to unrest. So uneasy were the authorities that a 1549 proclamation decreed that persons who sought revenge against profiteers by force, riot, menace, or unlawful assembly were to be regarded as high traitors and suffer death.[22] Following the 1597 drought, when starvation was rampant, the king's advisors reflected on what they had learned:

> There are seene and fownde a number of wycked people in condicions more lyke to wolves or cormerants than to naturall men, that doe moste covetusly seeke to hold up the late great pryces of corne and other victuells by ingrossing the same into theire private hands berganynge beforehand. . . . Against which fowle, corrupt, fraude and malycious greedyness therre are bothe manie good lawes and sondry orders of late yeres given to all Justices.[23]

The rich were told to modify their diets; their excessive consumption of food was regarded as a particular cause of scarcity. The poor were told to keep their "ydle brains" on the "humble duties of good subjects." Joel Samaha documents a striking increase in theft during this period, underlying the lesson that white-collar crime can feed into traditional forms of lawbreaking.[24]

The hoarders and cheaters, however, had sufficient wit to reconcile their self-interest with their self-esteem, a matter of considerable present-day importance for the understanding of white-collar crime. One hoarder insisted that it was not covetousness that made the rich hoard grain, but rather foresightedness and their provident nature. Others thought that the blame for scarcity and for the consequent soaring prices ought to be placed in God's lap, where it properly belonged, and not on the heads of forestallers and other market manipulators.

A decay in the policy of market regulation began at the end of the seventeenth century. Enclosure rendered arable land more productive and population growth slowed. The laws against forestalling and its quaint lexical companions were finally repealed by 12 Geo. III, c. 7, which would place their demise in 1772. What remained was an ethos—however much it waxed and waned over the centuries—that marketplace forces can and should be monitored.

It may be argued that control of the market through the imposition of criminal sanctions was necessary to keep the upper class from being slaughtered by the riotous actions of starving peasants and that a marginally contented population was essential to maintain the lifestyle of those with power. In any case, persons with no significant voice in the government nonetheless gained the support of law in a righteous cause against those who would exploit them. It was—and remains—an important achievement and a significant lesson.

As feudalism gave way to capitalism, and particularly as industrialization progressed, exploitation moved into the shadows, camouflaged by its remoteness, the diffuse nature of the harm it inflicted, and the obscurity of the source of the harm. R. H. Tawney has captured the essence of the attitude which prevailed and which persists today, though perhaps to a lesser extent:

> The secret of industrialism's triumph is obvious. . . . It concentrates attention upon the right of those who possess or can acquire power to make the fullest use of it for their own self-advancement. By fixing men's minds not upon the discharge of social obligations, . . . but upon the exercise of the right to pursue their own self-interest, it offers unlimited scope for the acquisition of riches, and therefore gives free play to one of the most powerful of human instincts. To the strong it promises unfettered freedom for the exercise of their strength; to the weak the hope that they too one day may be strong. Before the eyes of both it suspends a golden prize, the enchanting vision of infinite expansion. It assures men that there are no ends other than their own ends, no law other than their desires, no limit other than that which they think advisable. . . . It relieves communities of the necessity of discriminating . . . between enterprise and avarice, energy and unscrupulous greed, property which is legitimate and property which is theft . . . because it treats all economic activities as standing upon the same level, and suggests that excess or defect, waste or superfluidity, require no conscious effort of social will to avert them.[25]

The South Sea Bubble case in England in the early 1700s was the landmark episode that initiated state attempts to defuse somewhat the ethos of industrialism depicted by Tawney.

The South Sea Company, chartered in 1711, was one of a handful of state-recognized business corporations at the time. It proposed to reward stockholders with anticipated heady profits from trade in what was called the "South Seas," by which was meant South America from the Orinoco River to the south of Tierra del Fuego. The company prospered at first, primarily because huge bribes were slipped to members of Parliament to support it.

Stockholders were misled throughout the life of the Scheme (as it was called) about the company's true financial condition. The price of South Sea stock surged wildly because of a snowball effect created by clever manipulation of the atmosphere surrounding the company and because of the greed of the public scenting huge profits. The managers of the stock made it easy to invest, allowing purchases for amounts as low as 10 percent of the total stock value, contingent upon higher payments over the later years. On the basis of what had been happening, customers presumed that they would be able to raise the money due later by selling at a magnificent profit just a small portion of the stock they then were purchasing.

When the stock first came onto the market in 1711 it was quoted at a price of between 73 and 76 pounds a share. Near the end, nine years later, it reached its peak, selling at nearly 2,000 pounds for each share. By the end of 1720, however, it had dropped back to 190.

Ironically, part of the company's difficulty was created by passage of the Bubble Act (6 Geo. I, c. 18), which was sponsored by South Sea directors. The success being enjoyed by South Sea investors had prompted the incorporation of numerous other enterprises, some of them wildly improbable, such as one that solicited funds to construct a perpetual motion machine. The money the other corporations attracted reduced significantly the funds available for investment in the South Sea enterprise; its directors therefore sought to dry up diversionary founts by severely controlling the formation and activities of other enterprises competing for investment funds. The unexpected upshot was that when the other corporations went downhill because of the new limitations, they had to call for further money from those who had speculated on margin, leading to withdrawals from South Sea holdings, and thereby further jeopardizing the company's already precarious financial position.

The falling apart of the South Sea Company, as Viscount Erleigh has noted, was "not merely one of a long process of financial crises, but the first great crisis in the modern manner."[26] King George I sounded a particularly loud blast against the company when things began going sour, referring to the "unwarrantable practices" and berating the speculative fever that he insisted was diverting people from more practical pursuits. The stock swindle, the King declared, had involved "ensnaring and defrauding unwary persons to their utter impoverishment and ruin" and "taking off the minds of many our subjects from attending [to] their lawful employments and by introducing a general neglect of trade and commerce."[27]

Despite this setback, laissez-faire capitalism triumphed in the nineteenth century, which saw the entrenchment of doctrines establishing the supremacy of property rights. Writers of this period employ terms from the criminal law to defend what they regard as the right of capitalists to make unchecked use of their holdings. Thus Lord Gainford wrote that it was nothing other than "sheer robbery" to limit the profit on coal mines,[28] and Lord Hugh Cecil insisted that even if private property was employed mischievously, society could not interfere because to do so would be "theft."[29] Such views were endorsed as early as the thirteenth century by English courts which had ruled, for example, that there was to be "no remedy for that man who to his damage had trusted the word of a liar."[30] Even in the eighteenth century, a British chief justice could ask rhetorically: "When A got money from B by pretending that C had sent for it, shall we indict one man for making a fool of another?"[31] It was only in 1757 that a statutory provision for the punishment of "mere private cheating" was placed into the English law. It was the earlier line of class-related and self-serving judicial pronouncements that led the eighteenth-century English satirist, Jonathan Swift, to locate an ancient Hebrew tradition in a land visited by Gulliver:

> The Lilliputians look upon fraud as a greater crime than theft, and therefore seldom fail to punish it with death, for they allege that care and vigilance, with a very common understanding, may preserve a man's goods from theft, but honesty has no defense against superior cunning.[32]

In the United States by the 1920s, the tide began to turn slightly, fueled by a crusade against the more glaring abuses of big business. The shift was pinpointed by the eminent U.S. Supreme Court judge Oliver Wendell Holmes in a trenchant observation:

> When we read in the old books that it is the duty of one exercising a common calling to do his work upon demand and do it with reasonable skill, we shall see that the gentleman is in the saddle and means to have the common people kept up to the mark for his convenience. We recognize the imperative tone which in our day has changed sides, and is oftener to be heard from the hotel clerk than from the guest.[33]

While Holmes's observation documents a shift in power, it hardly signals the crashing triumph of the customer over the capitalist or the underdog over the mastiff. It does, though, accurately signify that the tune may be called by different pipers, depending upon the circumstances of a particular time. But few would dispute that those with power more often than others get to have their way; indeed, this is the common understanding of what power is about.

The shift marked by Holmes was in considerable part the product of the muckrakers, a fervent and articulate group of American writers, who stand as the obvious precursors of academic concern with white-collar crime. The muckraking period in the United States ran from about 1903 to 1912. During it, crusading writers published some 90 books and more than 2,000 articles in mass circulation magazines that had been made inexpensive by new techniques of printing and distribution. About a third of this writing was by a dozen leading figures, persons such as Ida Tarbell, David Graham Phillips, Upton Sinclair, and Lincoln Steffens.

The term "muckrake" had been coined by Arthur Dent, a Puritan clergyman, in his devotional guide *The Plain Mans Pathway To Heaven,* written in 1601. This book was one of the pitifully few possessions brought to her marriage by John Bunyan's first wife. Subsequently imprisoned for his feisty unwillingness to abandon nonconformist preaching, Bunyan, while confined in prison, wrote *The Pilgrim's Progress* (1678), an allegorical treatise that would become one of the two or three most widely read prose works in the world. In it Bunyan told of the man so preoccupied with his muckrake, gathering up the world's filth, that he failed to look upward at celestial glories.

Centuries later, President Theodore Roosevelt appropriated from Bunyan the term "muckrakers" to label reformist writers. These writers focused most particularly on close alliances between business and politics, especially the bribing of "public servants." A particularly good illustration is the work of Ida Tarbell, who discovered that the Standard Oil Company produced one-third and controlled all but 10 percent of the nation's petroleum supply. Standard Oil would undersell rivals, cut off their supplies, or otherwise make it virtually impossible for them to conduct business. Central to Standard's power was its control of the railroads. It was a relentless competitor, as it deployed part of its huge profits into continuous absorption of rivals and purchase of whatever resources were deemed necessary to attain its sensational level of prosperity.[34]

Most of the muckraking writers believed that if unfettered competition were allowed to operate, things would straighten out. Another part of their message was that responsibility for what was wrong lay in the indifference of citizens; everybody was cheating in a society based on cheating.

The demise of the muckraking effort not long after the beginning of the second decade of the twentieth century carries instructive lessons. Part, but only a very minor part, of the problem resulted from effective pressures exercised against the muckraking magazines by those they were attacking.[35] Wounded corporations curtailed advertising and, more effectively, brought out and buried some of the muckraking publications. More significant, however, was a growing tendency toward sensationalism and shrillness as the magazines, having mined the most promising fields, became more frantic about outdoing competitors and capturing public attention. The public, for its part, apparently became bored with what seemed an endless diet of social criticism. Muckraking had virtually disappeared when the advent of the First World War conclusively turned citizens' attention to other business. The summary judgment by Cornelius Regier does not seem unreasonable: "Muckraking, however necessary and however valuable it might have been for the time being, was essentially a superficial attack upon a problem which demanded—and demands—fundamental analysis and treatment."[36]

Muckraking brought home the lesson that unharnessed power is not to be trusted, at least not in social systems where the desire for personal gain operates strongly and where the opportunity to secure such gain at the expense of others is readily available to those with such power. Human beings, particularly those with strong organizational force behind them, are much too artful in constructing benign, personally lulling explanations for evil actions to be allowed to operate beyond scrutiny. It seems essential that efforts be directed toward encouraging countervailing centers of power, so that the aggrieved and the victimized have access to influential champions of their cause, whether in the courts, in the legislature, in the executive branch, or in the forum of public opinion.

IV

The record of scholarship on white-collar crime shows rather clearly how close academic work can parallel political and social climates. Sutherland, who thrust sociology into the study of white-collar crime, was a child of populism. Thereafter, the ebb and flow of research and theory regarding white-collar crime was dictated largely by the priorities of the federal government and the spirit of the times, which themselves interacted. Yet individuals occasionally nudged the academic agenda in one direction or another. Lloyd Ohlin, for example, inserted a brief review of white-collar crime into the report of the President's Commission on Law Enforcement and Administration of Justice in the mid-1960s. This helped to begin the movement to resurrect academic concern, and in time it brought back to work on the subject eminent scholars such as Marshall Clinard and Donald Cressey, who had begun their careers studying white-collar crime but had shifted their attention to other research issues.

Where do we stand today and where are we likely to be heading in regard to the study of white-collar crime? Several matters may be noted:

First, the question of the most appropriate definition of the term, while it undoubtedly will continue to command attention, seems to have reached—and perhaps passed—the point of diminishing returns. Cynics are wont to view the jousting about the "best" definition of white-collar crime the same way some people regard disputes about the proper definition of pornography: We all can recognize it when we see it, so why bother overmuch with attempting to pinpoint precise parameters? Those rejecting this viewpoint maintain that it is vital to establish an exact meaning for a term so that everyone employing it is talking about the same thing, and so that scientific investigations can be built one upon the other rather than going off in disparate directions because of incompatible definitions of their subject matter.

In a rousing bit of rhetoric, Susan Shapiro called for a focus on violations of trust as the most fruitful path for the study of white-collar lawbreaking, concluding that the present definitions are "creating an imprisoning framework for contemporary scholarship, impoverishing theory, distorting empirical inquiry, oversimplifying policy analysis, inflaming our muckraking instincts, and obscuring fascinating questions about the relationship between social organizations and crime."[37] Her statement offers an invigorating challenge to reexamine traditional ways of looking at the subject. On the other hand, Robert Nisbet claims that such debate can be diversionary: "Beyond a certain point, it is but a waste of time to seek tidy semantic justifications for concepts used by creative minds," Nisbet writes. "The important and all-too neglected task in philosophy and social theory is that of observing the ways in which abstract concepts are converted by their creators into methodologies which provide new illumination of the world."[38]

Second, there is a need for sharper theoretical focus to be brought to bear upon the analysis of white-collar crime. Most causal explanations derive from an "evil causes evil" view based on the belief that only deplorable conditions of person and place can give rise to criminal behavior. There is neglect of the fact that perfectly adequate human beings and perfectly adequate social situations, judged by reasonable criteria, may produce untoward consequences, in the manner that both kindness and murder kill.

One of the earliest and hardiest explanations of white-collar crime was suggested by Aristotle in *Politics*. "Men desire superfluities in order to enjoy pleasure unaccompanied with pain, and therefore they commit crimes," he noted. "The greatest crimes are caused by excess and not by necessity."[39] Sutherland, however, in perhaps the most telling of his observations on crime causation, challenged the Aristotelian postulate and its contemporary kin. "Though criminal behavior is an expression of general needs and values," he emphasized, "it is not explained by those general needs and values, since non-criminal behavior is an expression of the same needs and values."[40] The financially pressed corporate executive, Sutherland's position points out, may embezzle, may move to a cheaper home, take a weekend job, or borrow money from an uncle. The need alone does not suffice to explain the method that will be selected for its satisfaction.[41]

It is necessary to remind ourselves that white-collar crime may arise more from ordinary than special desires. The temptation to steal may be greatest among those who have little as well as among those who think they have little compared to those in even more affluent positions. Both the temptations and the rate of theft may be highest in the lowest and the highest classes. What may vary is the specific motivation.

Questions such as the following remain unanswered in regard to white-collar crime: What are the implications of labeling theory for white-collar crime; that is, what does status degradation and loss of self-esteem mean for a white-collar criminal? How do the concepts of socialization, criminal subculture, self-concept, and criminal motivation apply to white-collar crime? David Ermann suggests that corporate offenders often drift innocently into lawbreaking and find that they are at a point of no return when they ultimately realize that what they are engaged in has criminal consequences.[42] This insight offers a particularly promising exploratory route. There also appears to be a need for further case studies, statistical comparisons, personality profiles, and historical analyses of industrial growth and concentration and its crimogenic implications.

Third is the necessity to express openly the value premises that underlie work on white-collar crime, and to confront some striking differences between the manner in which scholars in the field often view traditional offenses and white-collar offenses. Some support the position that street criminals are the victims of the political process: as "political prisoners" they are seen as having little, if any, control over their social conditions and the acts of law violation in which they indulge. Why, then, is it alleged that white-collar offenders should be held totally responsible for their acts, and why should they be regarded as nefarious and dangerous enemies of society when, perhaps, they have as little control over the wellsprings of their behavior as do traditional offenders? Or, alternatively, if it is suggested that white-collar criminals deserve to be punished severely for what they have done, why should it not also be held that traditional offenders merit the same fate?

It is not that these inconsistencies cannot be resolved, but that few attempts have been made to do so. The idea that the rich ought to be held to higher standards than the poor offers one possible resolution. Another resolution resides in the view that the amount of free will (and, thus, responsibility) a person has is directly related to the wherewithal that person possesses. A third possible approach is to maintain that white-collar crime causes more social disruption than traditional crime, and that therefore white-collar offenders deserve to be treated more harshly. Which, if any, of these rationales will hold up when scrutinized carefully and fleshed out with research data remains an open question.

Current theoretical perspectives need to be applied to the study of white-collar crime; there is a relatively small theoretical literature on the subject, perhaps because of the large scope of the subject. For one thing, white-collar and corporate criminality are global phenomena tied into economic and political structures throughout the world.[43] Robbery and murder almost invariably are more confined practices, taking place at a particular time and in a particular place. There are identifiable victims and offenders. But a banking fraud can involve massive amounts of money, time, and geography. The sheer complexity makes the going slow.

White-collar crime is an area of study in which much material remains to be mined. It also is a realm of inquiry that sheds considerable light on some of the more significant aspects of contemporary life. Among the social and criminological issues that further work on white-collar crime can illuminate, the following seem notable:

1. White-collar crime challenges the more banal kinds of explanations of criminal activity. To say that poverty "causes" crime, for instance, fails utterly to account for widespread lawbreaking by persons who are extraordinarily affluent. To suggest that criminals lack "self-control" similarly ignores offenders such as antitrust violators and insider traders whose lives and achievements represent models of success through the exhibition of self-control.

2. White-collar crime indicates the distribution of power in our society. An examination of the statute books shows what kinds of corporate and occupational acts have come to be included within the criminal code and regulatory laws and what kind go unproscribed. The enactment of laws curbing the activities of certain persons and businesses demonstrates that, at least for the moment, other persons with other interests hold the power to prevail legislatively.

3. White-collar crime portrays the manner in which power is exercised illegitimately in our society. A review of upperworld violations and the manner in which they are (and are not) prosecuted and punished tells who is able to control what in American society and indicates the extent to which such control is effective.

4. White-collar crime provides an indication of the degree of hypocrisy present in a society. Such hypocrisy may be seen as leverage by means of which the society may be forced toward congruence between its verbal commitments and its actual conduct, much as Gunnar Myrdal insisted that the "dilemma" in the United States between democratic ideas and the actual treatment of minorities exerted incessant pressure for reconciliation in terms of the values.[44] In regard to white-collar crime, hypocrisy exists when crime among the lower class is viewed with distaste and punished severely, while upper-class depredations are countenanced and defined as nothing more than "shrewd business practice."

5. White-collar crime illustrates changes in social and business life. Thus, the old-time grocer, weighing merchandise by hand and dealing with customers on a personal basis, probably had less inclination and less opportunity to defraud. Today's supermarkets, engaged essentially in the rental of shelf space to manufacturers and producers, epitomize impersonality, with consequences for a new form of crime, that involving consumer fraud and deception.

6. White-collar crime furnishes material helpful for an understanding of changes in social values. Present-day laws demanding that foods be uncontaminated and that pollution be controlled reflect an emerging ethos that insists that every person be accorded every reasonable opportunity to remain alive and healthy until cut down by uncontrollable forces. In the future, if support cements for the right of all human beings to achieve their full potential, new forms of white-collar crime will be legislated.

These postulates, as well as those noted earlier, constitute the kinds of general propositions that will demand closer attention—with additional refinements—as white-collar crime comes to be studied as thoroughly as most traditional crime forms now are scrutinized.

There are indications that such changes will be forthcoming, but they require, among other things, a level of public support that has not as yet been mobilized. The amount of concern and understanding of white-collar crime is small compared to conventional crimes. Criminologists have known for some time that white-collar and corporate crimes rarely have the "brimstone smell"; not the lack of urgency and anger that arose in the wake of the multibillion dollar losses suffered by immediate victims and the society as a whole in the wake of the savings and loan scandals.

Notes

1. Micah 1:1–6 and 2:1–12. See also Hans Walter Wolff, *Micah the Prophet,* trans. Ralph D. Gehrke. Philadelphia: Fortress Press, 1981.
2. Robert Heilbroner, ed. *In the Name of Profit.* Garden City, NY: Doubleday, 1972, p. 200.
3. See, e.g., Robert Caldwell, "A Re-examination of the Concept of White-Collar Crime," *Federal Probation,* 22 (March 1958):30–36.
4. Marshall B. Clinard, *The Black Market: A Study of White-Collar Crime.* New York: Holt, 1952.
5. Richard Quinney, "Occupational Structure and Criminal Behavior: Prescription Violation by Retail Pharmacists," *Social Problems,* 11 (1963):170–185.
6. Donald J. Newman, "Public Attitudes toward a Form of White-Collar Crime," *Social Problems,* 4 (1957):228–232.
7. Frank E. Hartung, "White-Collar Offenses in the Wholesale Meat Industry," *American Journal of Sociology,* 56 (1953):25–34.
8. Robert E. Lane, "Why Businessmen Violate the Law," *Journal of Criminal Law, Criminology, and Police Science,* 44 (1953):151–165.
9. Roy Lewis and Rosemary Stewart, *The Managers.* New York: New American Library, 1961, pp. 161–162.
10. Gilbert Geis, "White Collar Crime: The Heavy Electrical Equipment Antitrust Cases of 1961." In Marshall B. Clinard and Richard Quinney, eds., *Criminal Behavior Systems: A Typology.* New York: Holt, Rinehart & Winston, 1967, pp. 139–150.
11. U.S. Senate, Subcommittee on Antitrust and Monopoly, Committee on the Judiciary, 87th Cong., 2d Sess., "Administered Prices," *Hearings, Part 27 and 28,* 1961; Joseph B. Gorman, *Kefauver: A Political Biography.* New York: Oxford University Press, 1971.
12. Ellen W. Schrecker, *No Ivory Tower: McCarthyism and the Universities.* New York: Oxford University Press, 1986.
13. Raphael Yglesias, *Hot Properties.* New York: Dutton, 1986, pp. 42–43.
14. See, e.g., James S. Turner, *The Chemical Feast.* New York: Grossman, 1970; John C. Esposito, *The Vanishing Air.* New York: Grossman, 1970; Ralph Nader and Mark J. Green, eds., *Corporate Power in America.* New York: Grossman, 1973.
15. U.S. Department of Justice, *National Priorities for the Investigation and Prosecution of White-Collar Crime.* Washington, DC: Office of the Attorney General, 1980.
16. See, e.g., Frank Pearce, "Crime, Corporations, and the American Social Order." In Ian Taylor and Laurie Taylor, eds., *Politics and Deviance.* Baltimore: Penguin, 1973, pp. 13–41.
17. Gilbert Geis and Robert F. Meier, eds., *White-Collar Crime: Offenses in Busi-*

ness, Politics, and the Professions. Revised ed. New York: Free Press, 1977, p. xi.

18. Christopher Hill, *Society and Puritanism in Pre-Revolutionary England.* London: Secker & Warburg, 1964, p. 267.
19. John T. Noonan, *Bribes.* New York: Macmillan, 1984, p. 660.
20. Mildred Campbell, *The English Yeoman under Elizabeth and the Early Stuarts.* New Haven: Yale University Press, 1942, p. 187; John Patten, *English Towns, 1500–1700.* Folkestone: William Dawson, 1978, p. 203.
21. John P. Dawson, *A History of Lay Judges.* Cambridge: Harvard University Press, 1960, p. 190.
22. John G. Bellamy, *Criminal Law and Society in Late Medieval and Tudor England.* Gloucester: Alan Sutton, 1984, p. 53.
23. Andrew B. Appleby, *Famine in Tudor and Stuart England.* Stanford: Stanford University Press, 1978, p. 143.
24. Joel Samaha, *Law and Order in Historical Perspective: The Case of Elizabethan Essex.* New York: Academic Press, 1974.
25. Richard H. Tawney, *The Acquisitive Society.* New York: Harcourt, Brace, 1920, pp. 30–31.
26. G. R. Erleigh, *The South Sea Bubble.* New York: Putnam's, 1933, p. 10. See also John Carswell, *The South Sea Bubble.* Stanford: Stanford University Press, 1960; V. Cowles, *The Great Swindle: The Story of the South Sea Bubble.* New York: Harper, 1960.
27. Cowles, *op. cit.,* p. 138. See generally Gilbert Geis, "The Evolution of the Study of Corporate Crime." In Michael Blankenship, ed., *Understanding Corporate Criminality.* New York: Garland, 1993, pp. 6–11.
28. Quoted in Tawney, *op. cit.,* p. 26.
29. *Ibid.,* p. 23.
30. Frederic Pollock and Frederic W. Maitland, *History of English Law.* Boston: Little Brown, 1909, vol. 2, p. 535.
31. Quoted in Hermann Mannheim, *Criminal Justice and Social Reconstruction.* London: Routledge & Kegan Paul, 1946, p. 121.
32. Jonathan Swift, "A Voyage to Lilliput," in *Gulliver's Travels,* part 1, chap. 6 (1735).
33. Oliver Wendell Holmes, "Law in Science and Science in Law," in *Collected Papers.* New York: Harcourt, Brace, 1921, p. 212.
34. Ida M. Tarbell, *The History of the Standard Oil Company.* New York: McClure, Phillips, 1904.
35. Michael D. Maraccio, "Did a Business Conspiracy End Muckraking?" *Historian,* 47 (1985):58–71.
36. Cornelius C. Regier, *The Era of the Muckrakers.* Chapel Hill: University of North Carolina Press, 1932, p. 212.
37. Susan Shapiro, "Collaring the Crime, Not the Criminal: Reconsidering the Concept of White-Collar Crime," *American Sociological Review,* 55 (1990): 362.

38. Robert A. Nisbet, *Makers of Modern Social Science: Emile Durkheim.* Englewood Cliffs, NJ: Prentice-Hall, 1965, p. 39.
39. Aristotle, *Politics,* trans. J. E. C. Weldon. London: Macmillan, 1932, book II, chap. 7, p. 65.
40. Edwin H. Sutherland and Donald R. Cressey, *Principles of Criminology,* 7th ed. Philadelphia: Lippincott, 1966, p. 82.
41. See further Francis T. Cullen, *Rethinking Crime and Deviance Theory: The Emergence of a Structuring Tradition.* Totowa, NJ: Rowman and Allanheld, 1983.
42. M. David Ermann. Newark: Department of Sociology, University of Delaware, 1989.
43. See John Hagan, *Crime and Disrepute.* Thousand Oaks, CA: Pine Forge Press, 1984, chap. 4.
44. Gunnar Myrdal, *An American Dilemma.* New York: Harper, 1944.

PART I

The Realm of White-Collar Crime

Introduction to Part I

What is meant by white-collar crime, what are its consequences, what role do women play in the commission of such offenses, and how is white-collar crime treated by the media, in particular by television newscasts and national news magazines? The seven articles in this section address these issues.

The first article, "White Collar Criminality," is the text of the landmark presidential address that Edwin H. Sutherland presented to a joint meeting of the American Sociological Society and the American Economics Association at the Benjamin Franklin Hotel in Philadelphia during the Christmas academic recess in 1939. Sutherland's talk was hailed both in professional circles and in the media as a monumental breakthrough in sociological criminology. Hermann Mannheim, a noted British criminologist, has suggested that if there were a Nobel Prize for criminology, Sutherland would surely earn it for his work on white-collar crime.[1] Writing about Sutherland's speech at the time, a reporter for the *Philadelphia Inquirer* portrayed the audience as "astonished" when "Dr. Sutherland figuratively heaved scores of sociological textbooks into the waste basket."[2] The *New York Times* noted that Sutherland had "discarded accepted conceptions and explanations of crime."[3] In fundamental ways, though, Sutherland was following a traditional scholarly path: describe a behavior, identify some concepts around which hypotheses could be constructed, and apply or develop a theory to explain the behavior by use of the concepts. The phrase "white-collar crime" was what was new as was the clarion call to attend to the illegalities of the upper class. Despite Sutherland's disclaimers that he was interested only in theory, the reporters also attended to the strong attack that Sutherland launched against business behavior.

Among the more remarkable aspects of the presentation was the fact that Sutherland's scholarly career to that point offered not the slightest suggestion that he harbored such strong moral repulsion for the criminal acts of persons in positions of power. Sutherland was the product of the midwestern frontier. His father was a Baptist minister who later became president of Grand Island College in Nebraska, where Sutherland obtained his undergraduate education. The milieu in which Sutherland was raised was permeated with intense populist concern over the increasing dominance of business and the growing concentration of economic power and wealth. He regarded with nostalgia and regret the shift in the United States from the personal, close-knit, and interdependent relationships of the small town to the more anonymous and formal relationships of the city. But Sutherland was not a political revolutionary. He believed that white-collar crime undermined basic American principles of economic competition and free trade and feared that socialism might prevail unless the monopolistic power of industrial giants and the corruption of politicians were curbed. Sutherland might best be seen as defending the existing economic system from being undermined by those seeking their own advantage by the use of criminal means.

Sutherland's focus on white-collar crime was influenced by his earlier investigation of professional theft.[4] He came to regard white-collar criminals as the upperworld counterparts of professional thieves. In both groups, Sutherland maintained, illegal activity was an integral part of occupational efforts, and for both groups there was no loss of prestige among colleagues because of such activity. Both kinds of crime required training, tutelage, and specialized skills. A significant difference between professional theft and white-collar crime, Sutherland believed, lay in the self-conception of the violators. "Professional thieves, when they speak honestly, admit that they are thieves," Sutherland observed, whereas white-collar criminals "think of themselves as honest men."[5] It is evident that in some ways Sutherland came to admire and glamorize the professional thief and to loathe the white-collar offender, a loathing that translated into his claim in his later monograph *White Collar Crime* that businessmen are the most subversive force in America and his equating the advertising tactics of the power and light utilities with the propaganda of the German Nazis.[6]

Sutherland's definition of white-collar crime in this first reading is unacceptably vague. He calls it "crime in the upper, white-collar class, which is composed of respectable, or at least respected, business and professional men." In several subsequent stabs, he never offered a more precise characterization of his subject matter. Semantic debates, fueled by Sutherland's imprecision have, as we noted in the Introduction, continued to plague the study of white-collar crime.

The second reading, also by Sutherland, represents his attempt to protect his concept against scholars, usually with law backgrounds, who accused him of mounting a campaign against the elite that was based in moral distaste rather than rooted in the solid footings of criminal law. Sutherland argues effectively that whether a person is arrested or convicted of a criminal act is of secondary importance to the issue of whether that person has committed an act which reasonably could be regarded as a violation of the criminal law. For a brief period, Sutherland was willing to extend his definition to embrace all elite behaviors which because of the harm they caused *ought* to have been declared criminal offenses. But he backed away from this position, largely under the influence of law professor Jerome Michael and philosopher Mortimer J. Adler's penetrating examination of the scientific aspirations of criminology which insisted that "the most precise and least ambiguous definition of crime is that which defines it as behavior which is prohibited by the criminal code" and continued with the observation that "this is the only possible definition of crime."[7]

The third reading, by Paul Tappan, a lawyer-sociologist, who first taught at New York University and finished his career at the School of Criminology, University of California, Berkeley, sets out the author's claim that the concept of white-collar crime is insufficiently sensitive to legal norms and that it fails to draw essential juridical distinctions between civil and criminal law. Artfully, Tappan avoids direct criticism of Sutherland, but rather concentrates his fire on two lesser criminological figures—textbook writers Negley Teeters and Harry Elmer Barnes. Perhaps Sutherland was too prominent a figure to risk alienating; Teeters and Barnes were lower in the academic pecking order.

Tappan's article has an interesting background. He had submitted it to the *American Journal of Sociology* in 1946; the journal's editor sent it to Sutherland for review. Sutherland deplored Tappan's idea that only convicted persons ought to be called "criminals" and be part of studies of crime and thought that the article did not make a sufficient contribution. But Sutherland stressed that since he was personally involved in the intellectual dispute, the editor should ask for further appraisals. Tappan's article was rejected by *AJS* but subsequently accepted by the *American Sociological Review.*

Kathleen Daly's report of data on the participation of women in white-collar crime contributes both to empirical understanding of a neglected area of inquiry and to the definitional difficulties associated with the concept of white-collar crime. Daly employs legal charges against them to identify women who commit what are held to be white-collar offenses. A major conclusion is that occupational marginality explains women's white-collar crime. Had her definition been restricted to abuses of power, by definition that conclusion could not have been reached. On the other hand, Daly's approach democratizes white-collar crime and provides it with a behavioral rather than a structural basis. Herbert Edelhertz, a federal prosecutor who subsequently wrote extensively about white-collar crime, made the point well. "No prosecutor could accept, as a basis for a criminal charge, that embezzlement by a bank president was white-collar crime, and that the same act by a low-paid bank teller was not," Edelhertz observed, adding: "It is fair to speculate that the long hiatus in research in white-collar crime . . . stemmed in part from this gulf." Sutherland's perspective, Edelhertz claimed, "was responsible for a barrier between academic, or research investigators, and practitioners and legislators in the field."[8]

Daly also calls her reader's attention to one of the more interesting findings about gender and white-collar crime. In a study of women embezzlers incarcerated in California, Dorothy Zietz found that they explained their offenses as attempts to resolve family problems, whereas men explained theirs as motivated by self-interest.[9]

Daly's work was part of a large and very important research program on white-collar crime carried out at the Yale Law School under the leadership of

Stanton Wheeler. Besides Wheeler and Daly, the effort involved, among others, David Weisburd, Susan Shapiro, Jack Katz, Kenneth Mann, Elin Waring, and Nancy Bode, all of whom individually and collectively have made significant contributions to the field. Not only their research itself, but the drawing into the realm of work on white-collar crime of a talented group of young scholars was a significant contribution. The full body of publications produced by the Yale group is listed in a 1993 article by Wheeler in *Law and Social Inquiry* (see the bibliography at the end of this volume).

White-collar crime, those who write about the issue consistently maintain, costs more, and maims and kills more, than traditional forms of crime. It also saps social morale, because it brings into question the legitimacy of those who are supposed to lead. These views are typically employed as an attempt to stir up public concern with white-collar crime. Robert F. Meier and James F. Short, Jr., offer a comprehensive examination of such claims in the fifth article in this section. They note that any social activity carries some element of harm and that the notion of "minimally acceptable level of risk" provides a more satisfactory measuring with which to judge the consequences of various forms of white-collar and street crime. The position that white-collar crime ruptures the social fabric of a society, Meier and Short note, is likely the most important outcome of the behavior, but one that will require a great deal of more and more sophisticated research to demonstrate satisfactorily.

The failure of the media to react to white-collar crime, presuming that it has as serious consequences as are said to ensue from it, may reflect the affiliation of the corporate world that controls information with the elite who commit white-collar crimes. Certainly, part of the explanation also undoubtedly lies in the more dramatic nature of murders and muggings; for television, photo opportunities are crucial. It is difficult for television to get something onto film that portrays bribery or a business scam carried out in secret. As Donna Randall notes in the sixth article in this section, the focus tends to be on the sentencing of white-collar offenders, where there is a bustling courthouse scene and the defendant and attorneys can make statements into a microphone amidst jostling crowds. Here is at least some semblance of the kind of drama on which television thrives.

In his presidential address, Sutherland noted that there was more white-collar crime news on the financial pages of the papers than on the front pages, where he thought it properly belonged. In a classic early article, Alan Dershowitz, then a student at Yale Law School, pointed out what he saw as systemic neglect of white-collar crime in the coverage by newspapers of the day of the General Electric heavy equipment antitrust conspiracy,[10] a finding duplicated by Sandra Evans and Richard Lundman in regard to a later antitrust crime in the folding cartoon industry.[11] Randall analyzes newsmagazines and network news reports over a decade, and compares how each treat individuals who commit business crime as well as corporate violations.

The concluding contribution, by John Braithwaite, offers a comprehensive overview of white-collar crime research during the more than fifty years since the concept was introduced. Braithwaite, a professor at the Australian National University in Canberra, observes, among other things, that more than in most fields of criminological inquiry, the study of white-collar crimes appears to have exercised significant influence on public policy.

Notes

1. Hermann Mannheim, *Comparative Criminology*. Boston: Houghton Mifflin, 1965, p. 470.
2. "Poverty Belittled as Crime Factor," *Philadelphia Inquirer,* December 28, 1939, p. 17.
3. "Hits Criminality in White Collars," *New York Times,* December 28, 1939, p. 12.
4. Edwin H. Sutherland, *The Professional Thief.* Chicago: University of Chicago Press, 1937.
5. Edwin H. Sutherland, "Crimes of Corporations." In Karl Schuessler, ed., *On Analyzing Crime.* Chicago: University of Chicago Press, 1973, pp. 95–96.
6. Edwin H. Sutherland, *White Collar Crime.* New York: Dryden Press, 1949, p. 210.
7. Jerome Michael and Mortimer J. Adler, *Crime, Law and Social Science.* New York: Harcourt Brace, 1933, p. 2.
8. Herbert Edelhertz, "White-Collar and Professional Crime," *American Behavioral Scientist,* 27 (1983): 110.
9. Dorothy Zietz, *Women Who Embezzle or Defraud: A Study of Convicted Felons.* New York: Praeger, 1981.
10. Alan M. Dershowitz, "Increasing Community Control over Corporate Crime," *Yale Law Journal,* 71 (1961): 289–306.
11. Sandra S. Evans and Richard J. Lundman, "Newspaper Coverage of Corporate Price-Fixing," *Criminology,* 21 (1983):529–541.

1

White-Collar Criminality

Edwin H. Sutherland

This paper is concerned with crime in relation to business. The economists are well acquainted with business methods but not accustomed to consider them from the point of view of crime; many sociologists are well acquainted with crime but not accustomed to consider it as expressed in business. This paper is an attempt to integrate these two bodies of knowledge. More accurately stated, it is a comparison of crime in the upper, or white-collar, class, which is composed of respectable, or at least respected, business and professional men; and crime in the lower class, which is composed of persons of low socioeconomic status. This comparison is made for the purpose of developing the theories of criminal behavior, not for the purpose of muckraking or of reforming anything except criminology.

The criminal statistics show unequivocally that crime, as *popularly conceived and officially measured,* has a high incidence in the lower class and a low incidence in the upper class; less than 2 percent of the persons committed to prisons in a year belong to the upper class. These statistics refer to criminals handled by the police, the criminal and juvenile courts, and the prisons, and to such crimes as murder, assault, burglary, robbery, larceny, sex offenses, and drunkenness; it does not include traffic violations.

The criminologists have used the case histories and criminal statistics derived from these agencies of criminal justice as their principal data. From them, they have derived general theories of criminal behavior. These theories are that, since crime is concentrated in the lower class, it is caused by poverty or by personal and social characteristics believed to be associated statistically with poverty, including feeble-mindedness, psychopathic deviations, slum neighborhoods, and "deteriorated" families. This statement, of course, does not do justice to the qualifications and variations in the conventional theories of criminal behavior, but it presents correctly their central tendency.

The thesis of this paper is that the conception and explanations of crime which have just been described are misleading and incorrect, that crime is, in fact, not closely correlated with poverty or with the psychopathic and sociopathic conditions

Reprinted from *American Sociological Review,* 5 (February 1940), pp. 1–12, by permission of The American Sociological Association.

associated with poverty, and that an adequate explanation of criminal behavior must proceed along quite different lines. The conventional explanations are invalid principally because they are derived from biased samples. The samples are biased in that they have not included vast areas of criminal behavior of persons not in the lower class. One of these neglected areas is the criminal behavior of business and professional men, which will be analyzed in this paper.

The "robber barons" of the last half of the nineteenth century were white-collar criminals, as practically everyone now agrees. Their attitudes are illustrated by these statements: Colonel Vanderbilt asked, "You don't suppose you can run a railroad in accordance with the statutes, do you?" A. B. Stickney, a railroad president, said to sixteen other railroad presidents in the home of J. P. Morgan in 1890, "I have the utmost respect for you gentlemen, individually; but as railroad presidents I wouldn't trust you with my watch out of my sight." Charles Francis Adams said, "The difficulty in railroad management . . . lies in the covetousness, want of good faith, and low moral tone of railway managers, in the complete absence of any high standard of commercial honesty."

The present-day white-collar criminals, who are more suave and deceptive than the "robber barons," are represented by Krueger, Stavisky, Whitney, Mitchell, Foshay, Insull, the Van Sweringens, Musica-Coster, Fall, Sinclair, the many other merchant princes and captains of finance and industry, and by a host of lesser followers. Their criminality has been demonstrated again and again in the investigations of land offices, railways, insurance, munitions, banking, public utilities, stock exchanges, the oil industry, real estate, reorganization committees, receiverships, bankruptcies, and politics. Individual cases of such criminality are reported frequently, and in many periods more important crime news may be found on the financial pages of newspapers than on the front pages. White-collar criminality is found in every occupation, as can be discovered readily in casual conversation with a representative of an occupation by asking him, "What crooked practices are found in your occupation?"

White-collar criminality in business is expressed most frequently in the form of misrepresentation in financial statements of corporations, manipulation in the stock exchange, commercial bribery, bribery of public officials directly or indirectly in order to secure favorable contracts and legislation, misrepresentation in advertising and salesmanship, embezzlement and misapplication of funds, short weights and measures and misgrading of commodities, tax frauds, misapplication of funds in receiverships and bankruptcies. These are what Al Capone called "the legitimate rackets." These and many others are found in abundance in the business world.

In the medical profession, which is here used as an example because it is probably less criminalistic than some other professions, are found illegal sale of alcohol and narcotics, abortion, illegal services to underworld criminals, fraudulent reports and testimony in accident cases, extreme cases of unnecessary treatment, fake specialists, restriction of competition, and fee splitting. Fee splitting is a violation of a specific law in many states and a violation of the conditions of admission to the practice of medicine in all. The physician who participates in fee splitting tends to send his patients to the surgeon who will give him the largest fee rather than to the surgeon who will do the best work. It has been reported that two-thirds of the surgeons in New York City split fees and that more than one-half of the physicians in a central western city who answered a questionnaire on this point favored fee splitting.

These varied types of white-collar crimes in business and the professions consist principally of violation of delegated or implied trust, and many of them can be reduced to two categories: (1) misrepresentation of asset values and (2) duplicity in the manipulation of power. The first is approximately the same as fraud or swindling; the second is similar to the double-cross. The latter is illustrated by the corporation director who, acting on inside information, purchases land which the corporation will need and sells it at a fantastic profit to his corporation. The principle of this duplicity is that the offender holds two antagonistic positions, one of which is a position of trust that is violated, generally by misapplication of funds, in the interest of the other position. A football coach, permitted to referee a game in which his own team is playing, would illustrate this antagonism of positions. Such situations cannot be completely avoided in a complicated business structure, but many concerns make a practice of assuming such antagonistic functions and regularly violating the trust thus delegated to them. When compelled by law to make a separation of their functions, they make a nominal separation and continue by subterfuge to maintain the two positions.

An accurate statistical comparison of the crimes of the two social classes is not available. The most extensive evidence regarding the nature and prevalence of white-collar criminality is found in the reports of the larger investigations to which reference was made. Because of its scattered character, that evidence is assumed rather than summarized here. A few statements will be presented as illustrations rather than as proof of the prevalence of this criminality.

The Federal Trade Commission in 1920 reported that commercial bribery was a prevalent and common practice in many industries. In certain chain stores, the net shortage in weights was sufficient to pay 34 percent on the investment in those commodities. Of the cans of ether sold to the Army in 1923 to 1925, 70 percent were rejected because of impurities. In Indiana, during the summer of 1934, 40 percent of the ice-cream samples tested in a routine manner by the Division of Public Health were in violation of law. The Comptroller of the Currency in 1908 reported that violations of law were found in 75 percent of the banks examined in a three-month period. Lie detector tests of all employees in several Chicago banks, supported in almost all cases by confessions, showed that 20 percent of them had stolen bank property. A public accountant estimated, in the period prior to the Securities and Exchange Commission, that 80 percent of the financial statements of corporations were misleading. James M. Beck said, "Diogenes would have been hard put to it to find an honest man in the Wall Street which I knew as a corporation lawyer" (in 1916).

White-collar criminality in politics, which is generally recognized as fairly prevalent, has been used by some as a rough gauge by which to measure white-collar criminality in business. James A. Farley said, "The standards of conduct are as high among officeholders and politicians as they are in commercial life," and Cermak, while mayor of Chicago, said, "There is less graft in politics than in business."

John Flynn wrote, "The average politician is the merest amateur in the gentle art of graft compared with his brother in the field of business." And Walter Lippmann wrote, "Poor as they are, the standards of public life are so much more social than those of business that financiers who enter politics regard themselves as philanthropists."

These statements obviously do not give a precise measurement of the relative criminality of the white-collar class, but they are adequate evidence that crime is not so highly concentrated in the lower class as the usual statistics indicate. Also, these statements obviously do not mean that every business and professional man is a criminal, just as the usual theories do not mean that every man in the lower class is a criminal. On the other hand, the preceding statements refer in many cases to the leading corporations in America and are not restricted to the disreputable business and professional men who are called quacks, ambulance chasers, bucket-shop operators, dead-beats, and fly-by-night swindlers.*

The financial cost of white-collar crime is probably several times as great as the financial cost of all the crimes which are customarily regarded as the "crime problem." An officer of a chain grocery store in one year embezzled $600,000, which was six times as much as the annual losses from five hundred burglaries and robberies of the stores in that chain. Public enemies numbered one to six secured $130,000 by burglary and robbery in 1938, while the sum stolen by Krueger is estimated as $250,000,000, or nearly two thousand times as much. The *New York Times* in 1931 reported four cases of embezzlement in the United States with a loss of more than $1 million each and a combined loss of $9 million. Although a million-dollar burglar or robber is practically unheard of, these million-dollar embezzlers are small-fry among white-collar criminals. The estimated loss to investors in one investment trust from 1929 to 1935 was $580,000,000, due primarily to the fact that 75 percent of the values in the portfolio were in securities of affiliated companies, although it advertised the importance of diversification in investments and its expert services in selecting safe securities. In Chicago, the claim was made six years ago that householders had lost $54,000,000 in two years during the administration of a city sealer who granted immunity from inspection to stores which provided Christmas baskets for his constituents.

The financial loss from white-collar crime, great as it is, is less important than the damage to social relations. White-collar crimes violate trust and therefore create distrust, which lowers social morale and produces social disorganization on a large scale. Other crimes produce relatively little effect on social institutions or social organization.

---

* Perhaps it should be repeated that "white-collar" (upper) and "lower" classes merely designate persons of high- and low-socioeconomic status. Income and amount of money involved in the crime are not the sole criteria. Many persons of "low" socioeconomic status are "white-collar" criminals in the sense that they are well dressed, well educated, and have high incomes, but "white-collar" as used in this paper means "respected," "socially accepted and approved," "looked up to." Some people in this class may not be well dressed or well educated or have high incomes, although the "upper" classes usually exceed the "lower" classes in these respects, as well as in social status.

White-collar crime is real crime. It is not ordinarily called crime, and calling it by this name does not make it worse, just as refraining from calling it crime does not make it better than it otherwise would be. It is called crime here in order to bring it within the scope of criminology, which is justified because it is in violation of the criminal law. The crucial question in this analysis is the criterion of violation of the criminal law. Conviction in the criminal court, which is sometimes suggested as the criterion, is not adequate because a large proportion of those who commit crimes are not convicted in criminal courts. This criterion, therefore, needs to be supplemented. When it is supplemented, the criterion of the crimes of one class must be kept consistent in general terms with the criterion of the crimes of the other class. The definition should not be the spirit of the law for white-collar crimes and the letter of the law for other crimes, or in other respects be more liberal for one class than for the other. Since this discussion is concerned with the conventional theories of the criminologists, the criterion of white-collar crime must be justified in terms of the procedures of those criminologists in dealing with other crimes. The criterion of white-collar crimes, as here proposed, supplements convictions in the criminal courts in four respects, in each of which the extension is justified because the criminologists who present the conventional theories of criminal behavior make the same extension in principle.

First, other agencies than the criminal court must be included, for the criminal court is not the only agency which makes official decisions regarding violations of the criminal law. In many states, the juvenile court, dealing largely with offenses of the children of the poor, is not under the criminal jurisdiction. The criminologists have made much use of case histories and statistics of juvenile delinquents in constructing their theories of criminal behavior. This justifies the inclusion of agencies other than the criminal court that deal with white-collar offenses. The most important of these agencies are the administrative boards, bureaus, or commissions; and much of their work, although certainly not all, consists of cases that are in violation of the criminal law. The Federal Trade Commission recently ordered several automobile companies to stop advertising their interest rate on installment purchases as 6 percent, since it was actually 11½ percent. Also it filed complaint against *Good Housekeeping,* one of the Hearst publications, charging that its seals led the public to believe that all products bearing those seals had been tested in their laboratories, which was contrary to fact. Each of these involves a charge of dishonesty, which might have been tried in a criminal court as fraud. A large proportion of the cases before these boards should be included in the data of the criminologists. Failure to do so is a principal reason for the bias in their samples and the errors in their generalizations.

Second, for both classes, behavior that would have a reasonable expectancy of conviction if tried in a criminal court or substitute agency should be defined as criminal. In this respect, convictability rather than actual conviction should be the criterion of criminality. The criminologists would not hesitate to accept as data a verified case history of a person who was a criminal but who had never been convicted. Similarly, it is justifiable to include white-collar criminals who have not been convicted, provided reliable evidence is available. Evidence regarding such cases appears in many civil suits, such as stockholders' suits and patent-infringement suits. These cases might have been referred to the criminal court but they were referred to the civil court because the injured party was more interested in securing damages than in seeing punishment inflicted. This also happens in embezzlement cases, regarding which surety companies have much evidence. In a short consecutive series of embezzlements known to a surety company, 90 percent were not prosecuted because prosecution would interfere with restitution or salvage. The evidence in cases of embezzlement is generally conclusive and would probably have been sufficient to justify conviction in all cases in this series.

Third, behavior should be defined as criminal if conviction is avoided merely because of pressure which is brought to bear on the court or substitute agency. Gangsters and racketeers have been relatively immune in many cities because of their pressure on prospective witnesses and public officials; professional thieves, such as pickpockets and confidence men who do not use strong-arm methods, are even more frequently immune. The conventional criminologists do not hesitate to include the life histories of such criminals as data, because they understand the generic relation of the pressures to the failure to convict. Similarly, white-collar criminals are relatively immune because of the class bias of the courts and the power of their class to influence the implementation and administration of the law. This class bias affects not merely present-day courts, but also, to a much greater degree, affected the earlier courts which established the precedents and rules of procedure of the present-day courts. Consequently, it is justifiable to interpret the actual or potential failures of conviction in the light of known facts regarding the pressures brought to bear on the agencies which deal with offenders.

Fourth, persons who are accessory to a crime should be included among white-collar criminals as they are among other criminals. When the Federal Bureau of Investigation deals with a case of kidnapping, it is not content with catching the offenders who carried away the victim; they may catch and the court may convict twenty-five other persons who assisted by secreting the victim, negotiating the ransom, or putting the ransom money into circulation. On the other hand, the prosecution of white-collar criminals frequently stops with one offender. Political graft almost always involves collusion between politicians and businessmen, but prosecutions are generally limited to the politicians. Judge Manton was found guilty of accepting $664,000 in bribes, but the six or eight important commercial concerns that paid the bribes have not been prosecuted. Pendergast, the late boss of Kansas City, was convicted for failure to report as a part of his income $315,000 received in bribes from insurance companies, but the insurance companies which paid the bribes have not been prosecuted. In an investigation of an embezzlement by the president of a bank, at least a dozen other violations of law which were related to this embezzlement and which involved most of the other officers of the bank and the officers of the clearing house were discovered, but none of the others was prosecuted.

This analysis of the criterion of white-collar criminality results in the conclusion that a description of white-collar criminality in general terms will be also a description of the criminality of the lower class. The respects in which the crimes of the two classes differ are the incidentals rather than the essentials of criminality. They differ principally in the implementation of the criminal laws that apply to them. The crimes of the lower class are handled by policemen, prosecutors, and judges with penal sanctions in the form of fines, imprisonment, and death. The crimes of the upper class either result in no official action at all, or result in suits for damages in civil courts, or are handled by inspectors and by administrative boards or commissions with penal sanctions in the form of warnings, orders to cease and desist, occasionally the loss of a license, and only in extreme cases by fines or prison sentences. Thus, the white-collar criminals are segregated administratively from other criminals and, largely as a consequence of this, are not regarded as real criminals by themselves, the general public, or the criminologists.

This difference in the implementation of the criminal law is due principally to the difference in the social position of the two types of offenders. Judge Woodward, when imposing sentence upon the officials of the H. O. Stone and Company, bankrupt real estate firm in Chicago, who had been convicted in 1933 of the use of the mails to defraud, said to them, "You are men of affairs, of experience, of refinement and culture, of excellent reputation and standing in the business and social world." That statement might be used as a general characterization of white-collar criminals, for they are oriented basically to legitimate and respectable careers. Because of their social status they have a loud voice in determining what goes into the statutes and how the criminal law as it affects themselves is implemented and administered. This may be illustrated from the Pure Food and Drug Law. Between 1879 and 1906, 140 pure food and drug bills were presented in Congress and all failed because of the importance of the persons who would be affected. It took a highly dramatic performance by Dr. Wiley in 1906 to induce Congress to enact the law. That law, however, did not create a new crime, just as the federal Lindbergh kidnapping law did not create a new crime; it merely provided a more efficient implementation of a principle which had been formulated previously in state laws. When an amendment to this law, which would bring within the scope of its agents fraudulent statements made over the radio or in the press, was presented to Congress, publishers and advertisers organized support and sent a lobby to Washington which successfully fought the amendment principally under the slogans of "freedom of the press" and "dangers of bureaucracy." This proposed amendment also would not have created a new crime, for the state laws already prohibited fraudulent statements over the radio or in the press; it would have implemented the law so it could have been enforced. Finally, the administration has not been able to enforce the law as it has desired because of the pressures by the offenders against the law, sometimes brought to bear through the head of the Department of Agriculture, sometimes through congressmen who threaten cuts in the appropriation, and sometimes by others. The statement of Daniel Drew, a pious old fraud, describes the criminal law with some accuracy: "Law is like a cobweb; it's made for flies and the smaller kinds of insects, so to speak, but lets the big bumblebees break through. When technicalities of the law stood in my way, I have always been able to brush them aside easy as anything."

The preceding analysis should be regarded neither as an assertion that all efforts to influence legislation and its administration are reprehensible nor as a particularistic interpretation of the criminal law. It means only that the upper class has greater influence in molding the criminal law and its administration to its own interests than does the lower class. The privileged position of white-collar criminals before the law results to a slight extent from bribery and political pressures, but principally from the respect in which they are held and without special effort on their part. The most powerful group in medieval society secured relative immunity by "benefit of clergy," and now our most powerful groups secure relative immunity by "benefit of business or profession."

In contrast with the power of the white-collar criminals is the weakness of their victims. Consumers, investors, and stockholders are unorganized, lack technical knowledge, and cannot protect themselves. Daniel Drew, after taking a large sum of money by sharp practice from Vanderbilt in the Erie deal, concluded that it was a mistake to take money from a powerful man on the same level as himself and declared that in the future he would confine his efforts to outsiders, scattered all over the country, who wouldn't be able to organize and fight back. White-collar criminality flourishes at points where powerful business and professional men come in contact with persons who are weak. In this respect, it is similar to stealing candy from a baby. Many of the crimes of the lower class, on the other hand, are committed against persons of wealth and power in the form of burglary and robbery. Because of this difference in the comparative power of the victims, the white-collar criminals enjoy relative immunity.

Embezzlement is an interesting exception to white-collar criminality in this respect. Embezzlement is usually theft from an employer by an employee, and the employee is less capable of manipulating social and legal forces in his own interest than is the employer. As might have been expected, the laws regarding embezzlement were formulated long before laws for the protection of investors and consumers.

The theory that criminal behavior in general is due either to poverty or to the psychopathic and sociopathic conditions associated with poverty can now be shown to be invalid for three reasons. First, the generalization is based on a biased sample which omits almost entirely the behavior of white-collar criminals. The criminologists have restricted their data, for reasons of convenience and ignorance rather than of principle, largely to cases dealt with in criminal courts and juvenile courts, and these agencies are used principally for criminals from the lower economic strata. Consequently, their data are grossly biased from the point of view of the economic status of criminals and their generalization that criminality is closely associated with poverty is not justified.

Second, the generalization that criminality is closely associated with poverty obviously does not apply to white-collar criminals. With a small number of exceptions, they are not in poverty, were not reared in slums or badly deteriorated families, and are not feebleminded or psychopathic. They were seldom problem children in their earlier years and did not appear in juvenile courts or child-guidance clinics.

The proposition, derived from the data used by the conventional criminologists, that "the criminal of today was the problem child of yesterday" is seldom true of white-collar criminals. The idea that the causes of criminality are to be found almost exclusively in childhood is similarly fallacious. Even if poverty were extended to include the economic stresses which afflict business in a period of depression, it is not closely correlated with white-collar criminality. Probably at no time within the last fifty years have white-collar crimes in the field of investments and of corporate management been so extensive as during the boom period of the twenties.

Third, the conventional theories do not even explain lower-class criminality. The sociopathic and psychopathic factors which have been emphasized doubtless have something to do with crime causation, but these factors have not been related to a general process that is found both in white-collar criminality and lower-class criminality; therefore, they do not explain the criminality of either class. They may explain the manner or method of crime—why lower-class criminals commit burglary or robbery rather than false pretenses.

In view of these defects in the conventional theories, a hypothesis is needed that will explain both white-collar criminality and lower-class criminality. For reasons of economy, simplicity, and logic, the hypothesis should apply to both classes, for this will make possible the analysis of causal factors freed from the encumbrances of the administrative devices which have led criminologists astray. Shaw and McKay and others, working exclusively in the field of lower-class crime, have found the conventional theories inadequate to account for variations within the data of lower-class crime and from that point of view have been working toward an explanation of crime in terms of a more general social process. Such efforts will be greatly aided by the procedure which has been described.

The hypothesis which is here suggested as a substitute for the conventional theories is that white-collar criminality, just as other systematic criminality, is learned; that it is learned in direct or indirect association with those who already practice the behavior; and that those who learn this criminal behavior are segregated from frequent and intimate contacts with law-abiding behavior. Whether a person becomes a criminal or not is determined largely by the comparative frequency and intimacy of his contacts with the two types of behavior. This may be called the "process of differential association." It is a genetic explanation both of white-collar criminals and lower-class criminality. Those who become white-collar criminals generally start their careers in good neighborhoods and good homes, graduate from colleges with some idealism, and, with little selection on their part, get into particular business situations in which criminality is practically a folkway, becoming inducted into that system of behavior just as into any other folkway. The lower-class criminals generally start their careers in deteriorated neighborhoods and families, find delinquents at hand from whom they acquire the attitudes toward, and the techniques of, crime through association with delinquents and through partial segregation from law-abiding people. The essentials of the process are the same for the two classes of criminals. This is not entirely a process of assimilation, for inventions are frequently made, perhaps more frequently in white-collar crime than in lower-class crime. The inventive geniuses for the lower-class criminals are generally professional criminals, while the inventive geniuses for many kinds of white-collar crime are generally lawyers.

A second general process is social disorganization in the community. Differential association culminates in crime because the community is not organized solidly against that behavior. The law is pressing in one direction and other forces are pressing in the opposite direction. In business, the "rules of the game" conflict with the legal rules. A businessman who wants to obey the law is driven by his competitors to adopt their methods. This is well illustrated by the persistence of commercial bribery in spite of the strenuous efforts of business organizations to eliminate it. Groups and individuals are individuated; they are more concerned with their specialized group or individual interests than with the larger welfare. Consequently, it is not possible for the community to present a solid front in opposition to crime. The better business bureaus and crime commissions, composed of businessmen and professional men, attack burglary, robbery, and cheap swindles but overlook the crimes of their own members. The forces which impinge on the lower class are similarly in conflict. Social disorganization affects the two classes in similar ways.

I have presented a brief and general description of white-collar criminality on a framework of argument regarding theories of criminal behavior. That argument, stripped of the description, may be stated in the following propositions:

1. White-collar criminality is real criminality, being in all cases in violation of the criminal law.
2. White-collar criminality differs from lower-class criminality principally in an implementation of the criminal law, which segregates white-collar criminals administratively from other criminals.
3. The theories of the criminologists that crime is due to poverty or to psychopathic and sociopathic conditions statistically associated with poverty are invalid because, first, they are derived from samples which are grossly biased with respect to socioeconomic status; second, they do not apply to the white-collar criminals; and third, they do not even explain the criminality of the lower class, since the factors are not related to a general process characteristic of all criminality.
4. A theory of criminal behavior which will explain both white-collar criminality and lower-class criminality is needed.
5. A hypothesis of this nature is suggested in terms of differential association and social disorganization.

2

Is "White-Collar Crime" Crime?

Edwin H. Sutherland

The argument has been made that business and professional men commit crimes which should be brought within the scope of the theories of criminal behavior.[1] In order to secure evidence as to the prevalence of such white-collar crimes, an analysis was made of the decisions by courts and commissions against the seventy largest industrial and mercantile corporations in the United States under four types of laws: namely, antitrust, false advertising, National Labor Relations, and infringement of patents, copyrights, and trademarks. This resulted in the finding that 547 such adverse decisions had been made, with an average of 7.8 decisions per corporation and with each corporation's having at least one.[2] Although all of these were decisions that the behavior was unlawful, only forty-nine, or 9 percent, of the total were made by criminal courts and were *ipso facto* decisions that the behavior was criminal. Since not all unlawful behavior is criminal behavior, these decisions can be used as a measure of criminal behavior only if the other 498 decisions can be shown to be decisions that the behavior of the corporations was criminal.

This is a problem in the legal definition of crime and involves two types of questions: May the word "crime" be applied to the behavior regarding which these decisions were made? If so, why is it not generally applied and why have not the criminologists regarded white-collar crime as cognate with other crime? The first question involves semantics, the second interpretation or explanation.

A combination of two abstract criteria is generally regarded by legal scholars as necessary to define crime; namely, legal description of an act as socially injurious and legal provision of a penalty for the act.[3]

When the criterion of legally defined social injury is applied to these 547 decisions, the conclusion is reached that all of the classes of behaviors regarding which the decisions were made are legally defined as socially injurious. This can be readily determined by the words in the statutes—"crime" or "misdemeanor" in some, and "unfair," "discrimination," or "infringement" in all the others. The persons injured may be divided into two groups: first, a relatively small number of persons engaged in the same occupation as the offenders or in related occupations; and, second, the

Reprinted from *American Sociological Review,* 10 (April 1945), pp. 132–139, by permission of The American Sociological Association.

general public either as consumers or as constituents of the general social institutions which are affected by the violations of the laws. The antitrust laws are designed to protect competitors; they are also designed to protect the institution of free competition as the regulator of the economic system and thereby to protect consumers against arbitrary prices, as well as being designed to protect the institution of democracy against the dangers of great concentration of wealth in the hands of monopolies. Laws against false advertising are designed to protect competitors against unfair competition and also to protect consumers against fraud. The National Labor Relations Law is designed to protect employees against coercion by employers and also to protect the general public against interferences with commerce due to strikes and lockouts. The laws against infringements are designed to protect the owners of patents, copyrights, and trademarks against deprivation of their property and against unfair competition, and also to protect the institution of patents and copyrights which was established in order to "promote the progress of science and the useful arts." Violations of these laws are legally defined as injuries to the parties specified.

Each of these laws has a logical basis in the common law and is an adaptation of the common law to modern social organization. False advertising is related to common-law fraud, and infringement to larceny. The National Labor Relations Law, as an attempt to prevent coercion, is related to the common-law prohibition of restrictions on freedom in the form of assault, false imprisonment, and extortion. For at least two centuries prior to the enactment of the modern antitrust laws, the common law was moving against restraint of trade, monopoly, and unfair competition.

Each of the four laws provides a penal sanction and thus meets the second criterion in the definition of crime, and each of the adverse decisions under these four laws (except certain decisions under the infringement laws to be discussed later) is a decision that a crime was committed. This conclusion will be made more specific by analysis of the penal sanctions provided in the four laws.

The Sherman antitrust law states explicitly that a violation of the law is a misdemeanor. Three methods of enforcement of this law are provided, each of them involving procedures regarding misdemeanors. First, it may be enforced by the usual criminal prosecution, resulting in the imposition of a fine or imprisonment. Second, the Attorney General of the United States and the several district attorneys are given the "duty" of "repressing and preventing" violations of the law by petitions for injunctions, and violations of the injunctions are punishable as contempt of court. This method of enforcing a criminal law was an invention and, as will be described later, is the key to the interpretation of the differential implementation of the criminal law as applied to white-collar criminals. Third, parties who are injured by violations of the law are authorized to sue for damages, with a mandatory provision that the damages awarded be three times the damages suffered. These damages in excess of reparation are penalties for violation of the law. They are payable to the injured party in order to induce him to take the initiative in the enforcement of the criminal law and in this respect are similar to the earlier methods of private prosecutions under the criminal law. All three of these methods of enforcement are based on decisions that a criminal law was violated and, therefore, that a crime was committed; the decisions of a civil court or a court of equity as to these violations are as good evidence of criminal behavior as is the decision of a criminal court.

The Sherman Antitrust Act has been amended by the Federal Trade Commission Law, the Clayton Law, and several other laws. Some of these amendments define violations as crimes and provide the conventional penalties, but most of the amendments do not make the criminality explicit. A large proportion of the cases which are dealt with under these amendments could be dealt with instead under the original Sherman Act, which is explicitly a criminal law. In practice, the amendments are under the jurisdiction of the Federal Trade Commission, which has authority to make official decisions as to violations. The commission has two principal sanctions under its control: the stipulation and the cease and desist order. The commission may, after the violation of the law has been proved, accept a stipulation from the corporation that it will not violate the law in the future. Such stipulations are customarily restricted to the minor or technical violations. If a stipulation is violated or if no stipulation is accepted, the commission may issue a cease and desist order; this is equivalent to a court's injunction except that violation is not punishable as contempt. If the commission's desist order is violated, the commission may apply to the court for an injunction, the violation of which is punishable as contempt. By an amendment to the Federal Trade Commission Law in the Wheeler-Lea Act of 1938, an order of the commission becomes "final" if not officially questioned within a specified time and thereafter its violation is punishable by a civil fine. Thus, although certain interim procedures may be used in the enforcement of the amendments to the antitrust law, fines or imprisonment for contempt are available if the interim procedures fail. In this respect, the interim procedures are similar to probation in ordinary criminal cases. An unlawful act is not defined as criminal by the fact that it is punished, but by the fact that it is punishable. Larceny is as truly a crime when the thief is placed on probation as when he is committed to prison. The argument may be made that punishment for contempt of court is not punishment for violation of the original law and that, therefore, the original law does not contain a penal sanction. This reasoning is specious, since the original law provides the injunction with its penalty as a part of the procedure for enforcement. Consequently, all of the decisions made under the amendments to the antitrust law are decisions that the corporations committed crimes.[4]

The laws regarding false advertising, as included in the decisions under consideration, are of two types. First, false advertising in the form of false labels is defined in the Pure Food and Drug Act as a misdemeanor and is punishable by a fine. Second, false advertising generally is defined in the Federal Trade Commission Act as unfair competition. Cases of the second type are under the jurisdiction of the Federal Trade Commission, which uses the same procedures as in antitrust cases. Penal sanctions are available in antitrust cases, as previously described, and are similarly available in these cases of false advertising. Thus, all of the decisions in false advertising cases are decisions that the corporations committed crimes.

The National Labor Relations Law of 1935 defines a violation as "unfair labor practice." The National Labor Relations Board is authorized to make official deci-sions as to violations of the law and, in case of violation, to issue desist orders and also to make certain remedial orders, such as reimbursement of employees who had been dismissed or demoted because of activities in collective bargaining. If an order is violated, the board may apply to the court for enforcement and a violation of the order of the court is punishable as contempt. Thus, all of the decisions under this law, which is enforceable by penal sanctions, are decisions that crimes were com-mitted.

The methods for the repression of infringements vary. Infringements of a copy-right or a patented design are defined as misdemeanors, punishable by fines. No case of this type has been discovered against the seventy corporations. Other infringe-ments are not explicitly defined in the statutes on patents, copyrights, and trade-marks as crimes, and agents of the state are not authorized by these statutes to initiate actions against violators of the law. Nevertheless, infringements may be pun-ished in either of two ways: First, agents of the state may initiate action against infringers under the Federal Trade Commission Law as unfair competition and they do so, especially against infringers of copyrights and trademarks; these infringe-ments are then punishable in the same sense as violations of the amendments to the antitrust laws. Second, the patent, copyright, and trademark statutes provide that the damages awarded to injured owners of those rights may be greater than (in one statute as much as threefold) the damages actually suffered. These additional dam-ages are not mandatory, as in the Sherman Antitrust Law, but on the other hand they are not explicitly limited to wanton and malicious infringements. Three decisions against the seventy corporations under the patent law and one under the copyright law included awards of such additional damages and on that account were classified in the tabulation of decisions as evidence of criminal behavior of the corporations. The other decisions, seventy-four in number, in regard to infringements were classi-fied as not conclusive evidence of criminal behavior and were discarded. However, in twenty of these seventy-four cases the decisions of the court contain evidence which would be sufficient to make a *prima facie* case in a criminal prosecution; evi-dence outside these decisions, which may be found in the general descriptions of practices regarding patents, copyrights, and trademarks, justifies a belief that a very large proportion of the seventy-four cases did, in fact, involve willful infringement of property rights and might well have resulted in the imposition of a penalty if the injured party and the court had approached the behavior from the point of view of crime.

In the preceding discussion, the penalties that are definitive of crime have been limited to fine, imprisonment, and punitive damages. In addition, the stipulation, the desist order, and the injunction, without references to punishment for contempt, have the attributes of punishment. This is evident both in that they result in some suffering on the part of the corporation against which they are issued and also in that they are designed by legislators and administrators to produce suffering. The suffer-ing is in the form of public shame, as illustrated in more extreme form in the colo-nial penalty of sewing the letter *T* on the clothing of the thief. The design is shown in the sequence of sanctions used by the Federal Trade Commission. The stipulation involves the least publicity and the least discomfort, and it is used for minor and technical violations. The desist order is used if the stipulation is violated and also if the violation of the law is appraised by the commission as willful and major. This involves more public shame; this shame is somewhat mitigated by the statements made by corporations, in exculpation, that such orders are merely the acts of bureaucrats. Still more shameful to the corporation is an injunction issued by a court. The shame resulting from this order is sometimes mitigated and the corporation's face saved by taking a consent decree.[5] The corporation may insist that the consent decree is not an admission that it violated the law. For instance, the meat packers took a consent decree in an antitrust case in 1921, with the explanation that they had not knowingly violated any law and were consenting to the decree without attempting to defend themselves because they wished to cooperate with the government in every possible way. This patriotic motivation appeared questionable, however, after the packers fought during almost all of the next ten years for a modification of the decree. Although the sequence of stipulation, desist order, and injunction indicates that the variations in public shame are designed, these orders have other functions as well, especially a remedial function and the clarification of the law in a particular complex situation.

The conclusion in this semantic portion of the discussion is that 473 of the 547 decisions are decisions that crimes were committed. This conclusion may be questioned on the ground that the rules of proof and evidence used in reaching these decisions are not the same as those used in decisions regarding other crimes, especially that some of the agencies which rendered the decisions did not require proof of criminal intent and did not presume the accused to be innocent. These rules of criminal intent and presumption of innocence, however, are not required in all prosecutions under the regular penal code and the number of exceptions is increasing. In many states a person may be committed to prison without protection of one or both of these rules on charges of statutory rape, bigamy, adultery, passing bad checks, selling mortgaged property, defrauding a hotel keeper, and other offenses.[6] Consequently, the criteria that have been used in defining white-collar crimes are not categorically different from the criteria used in defining other crimes, for these rules are abrogated both in regard to white-collar crimes and other crimes, including some felonies. The proportion of decisions rendered against corporations without the protection of these rules is probably greater than the proportion rendered against other criminals, but a difference in proportions does not make the violations of law by corporations categorically different from the violations of law by other criminals. Moreover, the difference in proportion, as the procedures actually operate, is not great. On the one side, many of the defendants in usual criminal cases, being in relative poverty, do not get good defense and consequently secure little benefit from these rules; on the other hand, the commissions come close to observing these rules of proof and evidence although they are not required to do so. This is illustrated by the procedure of the Federal Trade Commission in regard to advertisements. Each year it examines several hundred thousand advertisements and appraises about

50,000 of them as probably false. From the 50,000 it selects about 1,500 as patently false. For instance, an advertisement of gum-wood furniture as "mahogany" would seldom be an accidental error and would generally result from a state of mind which deviated from honesty by more than the natural tendency of human beings to feel proud of their handiwork.

The preceding discussion has shown that these seventy corporations committed crimes according to 473 adverse decisions and has also shown that the criminality of their behavior was not made obvious by the conventional procedures of the criminal law, but was blurred and concealed by special procedures. This differential implementation of the law as applied to the crimes of corporations eliminates, or at least minimizes, the stigma of crime. This differential implementation of the law began with the Sherman Antitrust Law of 1890. As previously described, this law is explicitly a criminal law and a violation of the law is a misdemeanor no matter what procedure is used. The customary policy would have been to rely entirely on criminal prosecution as the method of enforcement But a clever invention was made in the provision of an injunction to enforce a criminal law; this was not only an invention, but also a direct reversal of previous case law. Also, private parties were encouraged by treble damages to enforce a criminal law by suits in civil courts. In either case, the defendant did not appear in the criminal court, and the fact that he had committed a crime did not appear in the face of the proceedings.

The Sherman Antitrust Act, in this respect, became the model in practically all the subsequent procedures authorized to deal with the crimes of corporations. When the Federal Trade Commission Bill and the Clayton Bill were introduced in Congress, they contained the conventional criminal procedures; these were eliminated in committee discussions, and other procedures which did not carry the external symbols of criminal process were substituted. The violations of these laws are crimes, as has been shown above, but they are treated as though they were not crimes, with the effect and probably the intention of eliminating the stigma of crime.

This policy of eliminating the stigma of crime is illustrated in the following statement by Wendell Berge, at the time assistant to the head of the antitrust division of the Department of Justice, in a plea for abandonment of the criminal prosecution under the Sherman Antitrust Act and the authorization of civil procedures with civil fines as a substitute.

> While civil penalties may be as severe in their financial effects as criminal penalties, yet they do not involve the stigma that attends indictment and conviction. Most of the defendants in antitrust cases are not criminals in the usual sense. There is no inherent reason why antitrust enforcement requires branding them as such.[7]

If a civil fine were substituted for a criminal fine, a violation of the antitrust law would be as truly a crime as it is now. The thing which would be eliminated would be the stigma of crime. Consequently, the stigma of crime has become a penalty in itself, which may be imposed in connection with other penalties or withheld, just as it is possible to combine imprisonment with a fine or have a fine without imprisonment. A civil fine is a financial penalty without the additional penalty of stigma, while a criminal fine is a financial penalty with the additional penalty of stigma.

When the stigma of crime is imposed as a penalty, it places the defendant in the category of a criminal and he becomes one according to the popular stereotype of "the criminal." In primitive society "the criminal" was substantially the same as "the stranger,"[8] while in modern society "the criminal" is a person of less-esteemed cultural attainments. Seventy-five percent of the persons committed to state prisons are probably not, aside from their unesteemed cultural attainments, "criminals in the usual sense of the word." It may be excellent policy to eliminate the stigma of crime in a large proportion of cases, but the question at hand is why the law has a different implementation for white-collar criminals than for others.

Three factors assist in explaining this differential implementation of the law: the status of the businessman, the trend away from punishment, and the relatively unorganized resentment of the public against white-collar criminals. Each of these will be described.

First, the methods used in the enforcement of any law are an adaptation to the characteristics of the prospective violators of the law, as appraised by the legislators and the judicial and administrative personnel. The appraisals regarding businessmen, who are the prospective violators of the four laws under consideration, include a combination of fear and admiration. Those who are responsible for the system of criminal justice are afraid to antagonize businessmen; among other consequences, such antagonism may result in a reduction in contributions to the campaign funds needed to win the next election. Probably much more important is the cultural homogeneity of legislators, judges, and administrators with businessmen. Legislators admire and respect businessmen and cannot conceive of them as criminals; that is, businessmen do not conform to the popular stereotype of "the criminal." The legislators are confident that these businessmen will conform as a result of very mild pressures.

This interpretation meets with considerable opposition from persons who insist that this is an egalitarian society in which all men are equal in the eyes of the law. It is not possible to give a complete demonstration of the validity of this interpretation but four types of evidence are presented in the following paragraphs as partial demonstration.

The Department of Justice is authorized to use both criminal prosecutions and petitions in equity to enforce the Sherman Antitrust Act. The department has selected the method of criminal prosecution in a larger proportion of cases against trade unions than of cases against corporations, although the law was enacted primarily because of fear of the corporations. From 1890 to 1929, the Department of Justice initiated 438 actions under this law with decisions favorable to the United States. Of the actions against business firms and associations of business firms, 27 percent were criminal prosecutions; while of the actions against trade unions, 71 percent were criminal prosecutions. This shows that the Department of Justice has been comparatively reluctant to use a method against business firms which carries with it the stigma of crime.

The method of criminal prosecution in enforcement of the Sherman Antitrust Act has varied from one presidential administration to another. It has seldom been used in the administrations of the presidents who are popularly appraised as friendly toward business; for example, McKinley, Harding, Coolidge, and Hoover.

Businessmen suffered their greatest loss of prestige in the Depression which began in 1929. It was precisely in this period of low status of businessmen that the most strenuous efforts were made to enforce the old laws and enact new laws for the regulation of businessmen. The appropriations for this purpose were multiplied several times and persons were selected for their vigor in administration of the laws. Of the 547 decisions against the seventy corporations during their life careers (which have averaged about forty years) 63 percent were rendered in the period of 1935 to 1943, that is, during the period of the low status of businessmen.

The Federal Trade Commission Law states that a violation of the antitrust laws by a corporation shall be deemed to be, also, a violation by the officers and directors of the corporation. However, businessmen are practically never convicted as persons, and several cases have been reported (such as the "6 percent case" against the automobile manufacturers) in which the corporation was convicted and the persons who direct the corporation were all acquitted.[9]

A second factor in the explanation of the differential implementation of the law as applied to white-collar criminals is the trend away from reliance on penal methods. This trend advanced more rapidly in the area of white-collar crime than of other crime because—due to the recency of the statutes—it is least bound by precedents and also because of the status of businessmen. This trend is seen in the almost complete abandonment of the most extreme penalties of death and physical torture; in the supplanting of conventional penal methods by nonpenal methods, such as probation and the case work methods which accompany probation. These decreases in penal methods are explained by a series of social changes: the increased power of the lower socioeconomic class upon which most of the penalties were previously inflicted; the inclusion within the scope of the penal laws of a large part of the upper socioeconomic class, as illustrated by traffic, resulted in increased understanding and sympathy; the failure of penal methods to make substantial reductions in crime rates; and the weakening hold on the legal profession and others of the individualistic and hedonistic psychology, which had placed great emphasis on pain in the control of behavior. To some extent overlapping those just mentioned is the fact that punishment, which was previously the chief reliance for control in the home, the school, and the church, has tended to disappear from those institutions, leaving the state without cultural support for its own penal methods.[10]

White-collar crime is similar to juvenile delinquency in respect to the differential implementation of the law. In both cases, the procedures of the criminal law are modified so that the stigma of crime will not attach to the offenders. The stigma of crime has been less completely eliminated from juvenile delinquents than from white-collar criminals because the procedures for the former are a less complete departure from conventional criminal procedures, since most juvenile delinquents come from a class with low social status, and because the juveniles have not organized to protect their good names. Because the juveniles have not been successfully freed from the stigma of crime, they have been generally held to be within the scope of the theories of criminology and, in fact, provide a large part of the data for criminology; because the external symbols have been more successfully eliminated from white-collar crimes, white-collar crimes have generally not been included within these theories.

A third factor in the differential implementation of the law is the difference in the relation between the law and the mores in the area of white-collar crime. The laws under consideration are recent and do not have a firm foundation in public ethics or business ethics; in fact, certain rules of business ethics, such as the contempt for the "price chiseler," are generally in conflict with the law. These crimes are not obvious, as is assault and battery, and can be appreciated readily only by persons who are expert in the occupations in which they occur. A corporation often violates a law for a decade or longer before the administrative agency becomes aware of the violation; in the meantime the violation may have become accepted practice in the industry. The effects of a white-collar crime upon the public are diffused over a long period of time and perhaps over millions of people, with no person's suffering much at a particular time. The public agencies of communication do not express and organize the moral sentiments of the community as to white-collar crimes in part because the crimes are complicated and not easily presented as news, but probably in greater part because these agencies of communication are owned or controlled by the businessmen who violate the laws and because these agencies are themselves frequently charged with violations of the same laws. Public opinion in regard to picking pockets would not be well organized if most of the information regarding this crime came to the public directly from the pick-pockets themselves.

This third factor, if properly limited, is a valid part of the explanation of the differential implementation of the law. It tends to be exaggerated and become the complete explanation in the form of a denial that white-collar crimes involve any moral culpability whatever. On that account it is desirable to state a few reasons why this factor is not the complete explanation.

The assertion is sometimes made that white-collar crimes are merely technical violations and involve no moral culpability (i.e., violation of the mores) whatever. In fact, these white-collar crimes, like other crimes, are distributed along a continuum in which the *mala in se* are at one extreme and the *mala prohibita* at the other.[11] None of the white-collar crimes is purely arbitrary, as is the regulation that one must drive on the right side of the street, which might equally well be that one must drive on the left side. The Sherman Antitrust Law, for instance, is regarded by many persons as an unwise law and it may well be that some other policy would be preferable. It is questioned principally by persons who believe in a more collectivistic economic system; namely, the communists and the leaders of big business, while its support comes largely from an emotional ideology in favor of free enterprise which is held by farmers, wage-earners, small-business men, and professional men. Therefore, as appraised by the majority of the population it is necessary for the preservation of American institutions and its violation is a violation of strongly entrenched moral sentiments.

The sentimental reaction toward a particular white-collar crime is certainly different from that toward some other crimes. This difference is often exaggerated, especially as the reaction occurs in urban society. The characteristic reaction of the average citizen in the modern city toward burglary is apathy, unless he or his immediate friends are victims or unless the case is very spectacular. The average citizen, reading in his morning paper that the home of an unknown person has been burglarized by another unknown person, has no appreciable increase in blood pressure. Fear and resentment develop in modern society primarily as the result of the accumulation of crimes as depicted in crime rates or in general descriptions, and this develops both as to white-collar crimes and other crimes.

Finally, although many laws have been enacted for the regulation of occupations other than business, such as agriculture or plumbing, the procedures used in the enforcement of those other laws are more nearly the same as the conventional criminal procedures, and law-violators in these other occupations are not so completely protected against the stigma of crime as are businessmen. The relation between the law and the mores tends to be circular. The mores are crystallized in the law and each act of enforcement of the laws tends to reenforce the mores. The laws regarding white-collar crime, which conceal the criminality of the behavior, have been less effective than other laws in reenforcement of the mores.

Notes

1. Edwin H. Sutherland, "White-Collar Criminality," *American Sociological Review,* 5 (1940):1–12; and "Crime and Business," *Annals of the American Academy of Political and Social Science,* 217 (1941):112–118.
2. Cf. Edwin H. Sutherland, *White Collar Crime.* New York: Dryden, 1949, pp. 15–182.
3. The most thorough analysis of crime from the point of view of legal definition is Jerome Hall, *Principles of Criminal Law.* Indianapolis: Bobbs-Merrill, 1947.
4. Some of the antitrust decisions were made against meat packers under the Packers and Stockyards Act. The penal sanctions of the act are essentially the same as in the Federal Commission Act.
5. The consent decree may be taken for other reasons, especially because it cannot be used as evidence in other suits.
6. Livingston Hall, "Statutory Law of Crimes, 1887–1936," *Harvard Law Review,* 50 (1937):616–653.
7. Wendell Berge, "Remedies Available to the Government under the Sherman Act," *Law and Contemporary Problems,* 7 (1940): 111.

8. On the role of the stranger in punitive justice, see Ellsworth Faris, "The Origin ·of Punishment," *International Journal of Ethics,* 25 (1914):54–67; George H. Mead, "The Psychology of Punitive Justice," *American Journal of Sociology,* 23 (1918):577–602.

9. The question may be asked, "If businessmen are so influential, why did they not retain the protection of the rules of criminal procedure?" The answer is that they lost this protection, despite their status, on the principle, "You can't eat your cake and have it, too."

10. This trend away from penal methods suggests that the penal sanction may not be a completely adequate criterion in the definition of crime.

11. An excellent discussion of this continuum is presented by Jerome Hall, "Prolegomena to a Science of Criminal Law," *University of Pennsylvania Law Review,* 89 (1941): 563–569.

3

Who Is the Criminal?

Paul W. Tappan

What is crime? As a lawyer-sociologist, the writer finds perturbing the current confusion on this important issue. Important because it delimits the subject matter of criminological investigation. A criminologist who strives to aid in formulating the beginnings of a science finds himself in an increasingly equivocal position. He studies the criminals convicted by the courts and is then confounded by the growing clamor that he is not studying the real criminal at all, but an insignificant proportion of nonrepresentative and stupid unfortunates who happened to have become enmeshed in technical legal difficulties. It has become a fashion to maintain that the convicted population is no proper category for the empirical research of the criminologist. Ergo, the many studies of convicts which have been conducted by the orthodox, now presumably outmoded criminologists, have no real meaning for either descriptive or scientific purposes. Off with the old criminologies, on with the new orientations, the new horizons!

This position reflects in part at least the familiar suspicion and misunderstanding held by the layman sociologist toward the law. To a large extent it reveals the feeling among social scientists that not all antisocial conduct is proscribed by law (which is probably true), that not all conduct violative of the criminal code is truly antisocial, or is not so to any significant extent (which is also undoubtedly true). Among some students the opposition to the traditional definition of crime as law violation arises from their desire to discover and study wrongs which are absolute and eternal rather than mere violations of a statutory and case law system which vary in time and place; this is essentially the old metaphysical search for the law of nature. They consider the dynamic and relativistic nature of law to be a barrier to the growth of a scientific system of hypotheses possessing universal validity.[1]

Recent protestants against the orthodox conceptions of crime and criminal are diverse in their views; they unite only in their denial of the allegedly legalistic and arbitrary doctrine that those convicted under the criminal law are the criminals of our society and in promoting the confusion as to the proper province of criminology.

Reprinted from *American Sociological Review,* 12 (February 1947), pp. 96–102, by permission of The American Sociological Association.

It is enough here to examine briefly a few of the current schisms with a view to the difficulties at which they arrive.

I

A number of criminologists today maintain that mere violation of the criminal law is an artificial criterion of criminality, that categories set up by the law do not meet the demands of scientists because they are of a "fortuitous nature" and do not "arise intrinsically from the nature of the subject matter."[2] The validity of this contention must depend, of course, upon what the nature of the subject matter is. These scholars suggest that, as a part of the general study of human behavior, criminology should concern itself broadly with all antisocial conduct, behavior injurious to society. We take it that antisocial conduct is essentially any sort of behavior which violates some social interest. But what are these social interests? Which are weighty enough to merit the concern of the sociologist, to bear the odium of crime? What shall constitute a violation of them—particularly where, as is so commonly true in our complicated and unintegrated society, these interests are themselves in conflict? Roscoe Pound's suggestive classification of the social interests served by law is valuable in a juristic framework, but it solves no problems for the sociologist who seeks to depart from legal standards in search of all manner of antisocial behavior.

However desirable may be the concept of socially injurious conduct for purposes of general normation or abstract description, it does not define what is injurious. It sets no standard. It does not discriminate cases, but merely invites the subjective value judgments of the investigator. Until it is structurally embodied with distinct criteria or norms—as is now the case in the legal system—the notion of antisocial conduct is useless for purposes of research, even for the rawest empiricism. The emancipated criminologist reasons himself into a *cul de sac:* having decided that it is footless to study convicted offenders on the ground that this is an artificial category—though its membership is quite precisely ascertainable, he must now conclude that, in his lack of standards to determine antisociality, though this may be what he considers a real scientific category, its membership and its characteristics are unascertainable. Failing to define antisocial behavior in any fashion suitable to research, the criminologist may be deluded further into assuming that there is an absoluteness and permanence in this undefined category, lacking in the law. It is unwise for the social scientist ever to forget that all standards of social normation are relative, impermanent, variable, and that they do not, certainly the law does not, arise out of mere fortuity or artifice.[3]

II

In a differing approach certain other criminologists suggest that "conduct norms" rather than either crime or antisocial conduct should be studied.[4] There is an unques-

tionable need to pursue the investigation of general conduct norms and their violation. It is desirable to segregate the various classes of such norms, to determine relationships between them, and to understand similarities and differences between
them as to the norms themselves, their sources, methods of imposition of control,
and their consequences. The subject matter of this field of social control is in a
regrettably primitive state. It will be important to discover the individuals who
belong within the several categories of norm-violators established and to determine
then what motivations operate to promote conformity or breach. So far as it may be
determinable, we shall wish to know in what way these motivations may serve to
insure conformity to different sets of conduct norms, how they may overlap and
reinforce the norms or conflict and weaken the effectiveness of the norms.

We concur in the importance of the study of conduct norms and their violation
and, more particularly, if we are to develop a science of human behavior, in the need
for careful research to determine the psychological and environmental variables
which are associated etiologically with nonconformity to these norms. However, the
importance of the more general subject matter of social control or "ethology" does
not mean that the more specific study of the law-violator is nonsignificant. Indeed,
the direction of progress in the field of social control seems to lie largely in the
observation and analysis of more specific types of nonconformity to particular,
specialized standards. We shall learn more by attempting to determine *why* some
individuals take human life deliberately and with premeditation, *why* some take
property by force and others by trick than we shall in seeking at the start a universal
formula to account for any and all behavior in breach of social interests. This
broader knowledge of conduct norms may conceivably develop through induction,
in its inevitably very generic terms, from the empirical data derived in the study of
particular sorts of violations. Also, our more specific information about the factors
which lie behind violations of precisely defined norms will be more useful in the
technology of social control. Where legal standards require change to keep step with
the changing requirements of a dynamic society, the sociologist may advocate—
even as the legal profession does—the necessary statutory modifications, rather than
assume that for sociological purposes the conduct he disapproves is already criminal, without legislative, political, or judicial intervention.

III

Another increasingly widespread and seductive movement to revolutionize the concepts of crime and criminal has developed around the currently fashionable dogma of
"white-collar crime." This is actually a particular school among those who contend
that the criminologist should study antisocial behavior rather than law violation. The
dominant contention of the group appears to be that the convict classes are merely
our "petty" criminals, the few whose depredations against society have been on a
small scale, who have blundered into difficulties with the police and courts through
their ignorance and stupidity. The important criminals, those who do irreparable dam-

age with impunity, deftly evade the machinery of justice, either by remaining "techni-cally" within the law or by exercising their intelligence, financial prowess, or politi-cal connections in its violation. We seek a definition of the white-collar criminal and find an amazing diversity, even among those flowing from the same pen, and observe that characteristically they are loose, doctrinaire, and invective. When Professor Sutherland launched the term, it was applied to those individuals of upper socioeco-nomic class who violate the criminal law, usually by breach of trust, in the ordinary course of their business activities.[5] This original usage accords with legal ideas of crime and points moreover to the significant and difficult problems of enforcement in the areas of business crimes, particularly where those violations are made criminal by recent statutory enactment. From this fruitful beginning, the term has spread into vacuity, wide and handsome. We learn that the white-collar criminal may be the suave and deceptive merchant prince or "robber baron," that the existence of such crime may be determined readily "in casual conversation with a representative of an occupation by asking him, 'What crooked practices are found in your occupation?' "[6]

Confusion grows as we learn from another proponent of this concept that, "There are various phases of white-collar criminality that touch the lives of the common man almost daily. The large majority of them are operating within the letter and spirit of the law" and that "In short, greed, not need, lies at the basis of white-collar crime."[7] Apparently, the criminal may be law-obedient but greedy; the specific qual-ity of his crimes is far from clear.

Another avenue is taken in Professor Sutherland's more recent definition of crime as a "legal description of an act as socially injurious and legal provision of penalty for the act."[8] Here he has deemed the connotation of his term too narrow if confined to violations of the criminal code; he includes by a slight modification con-duct violative of any law, civil or criminal, when it is "socially injurious."

In light of these definitions, the normative issue is pointed. Who should be con-sidered the white-collar criminal? Is it the merchant who out of greed, business acu-men, or competitive motivations, breaches a trust with his consumer by "puffing his wares" beyond their merits, by pricing them beyond their value, or by ordinary advertising? Is it he who breaks trust with his employees in order to keep wages down, refusing to permit labor organization or to bargain collectively, and who is found guilty by a labor relations board of an unfair labor practice? May it be the white-collar worker who breaches trust with his employers by inefficient perfor-mance at work, by sympathetic strike or secondary boycott? Or is it the merchan-diser who violates ethics by undercutting the prices of his fellow merchants? In general these acts do not violate the criminal law. All in some manner breach a trust for motives which a criminologist may (or may not) disapprove for one reason or another. All are within the framework of the norms of ordinary business practice. One seeks in vain for criteria to determine this white-collar criminality. It is the con-duct of one who wears a white collar and who indulges in occupational behavior to which some particular criminologist takes exception. It may easily be a term of pro-paganda. For purposes of empirical research or objective description, what is it?

Whether criminology aspires one day to become a science or a repository of reasonably accurate descriptive information, it cannot tolerate a nomenclature of such loose and variable usage. A special hazard exists in the employment of the term, "white-collar criminal," in that it invites individual systems of private values to run riot in an area (economic ethics) where gross variation exists among criminologists as well as others. The rebel may enjoy a veritable orgy of delight in damning as criminal most anyone he pleases; one imagines that some experts would thus consign to the criminal classes any successful capitalistic businessman; the reactionary or conservative, complacently viewing the occupational practices of the business world, might find all in perfect order in this best of all possible worlds. The result may be fine indoctrination or catharsis achieved through blustering broadsides against the "existing system." It is not criminology. It is not social science. The terms "unfair," "infringement," "discrimination," "injury to society," and so on, employed by the white-collar criminologists cannot, taken alone, differentiate criminal and non-criminal. Until refined to mean certain specific actions, they are merely epithets.

Vague, omnibus concepts defining crime are a blight upon either a legal system or a system of sociology that strives to be objective. They allow judge, administrator, or—conceivably—sociologist, in an undirected, freely operating discretion, to attribute the status "criminal" to any individual or class which he conceives nefarious. This can accomplish no desirable objective, either politically or sociologically.[9]

Worse than futile, it is courting disaster, political, economic, and social, to promulgate a system of justice in which the individual may be held criminal without having committed a crime, defined with some precision by statute and case law. To describe crime the sociologist, like the lawyer-legislator, must do more than condemn conduct deviation in the abstract. He must avoid definitions predicated simply upon state of mind or social injury and determine what particular types of deviation, in what directions, and to what degree shall be considered criminal. This is exactly what the criminal code today attempts to do, though imperfectly of course. More slowly and conservatively than many of us would wish—that is in the nature of legal institutions, as it is in other social institutions as well. But law has defined with greater clarity and precision the conduct which is criminal than our antilegalistic criminologists promise to do; it has moreover promoted a stability, a security and dependability of justice through its exactness, its so-called "technicalities," and its moderation in inspecting proposals for change.

IV

Having considered the conceptions of an innovating sociology in ascribing the terms "crime" and "criminal," let us state here the juristic view: Only those are criminals who have been adjudicated as such by the courts. Crime is an intentional act in violation of the criminal law (statutory and case law), committed without defense or excuse, and penalized by the state as a felony or misdemeanor. In studying the offender there can be no presumption that arrested, arraigned, indicted, or prosecuted persons are criminals unless they also be held guilty beyond a reasonable doubt of a particular offense.[10] Even less than the unconvicted suspect can those individuals be considered criminal who have violated no law. Only those are criminals who have been selected by a clear substantive and a careful adjective law, such as obtains in our courts. The unconvicted offenders of whom the criminologist may wish to take cognizance are an important but unselected group; it has no specific membership presently ascertainable. Sociologists may strive, as does the legal profession, to perfect measures for more complete and accurate ascertainment of offenders, but it is futile simply to rail against a machinery of justice which is, and to a large extent must inevitably remain, something less than entirely accurate or efficient.

Criminal behavior as here defined fits very nicely into the sociologists' formulations of social control. Here we find *norms* of conduct, comparable to the mores, but considerably more distinct, precise, and detailed, as they are fashioned through statutory and case law. The agencies of this control, like the norms themselves, are more formal than is true in other types of control: The law depends for its instrumentation chiefly upon police, prosecutors, judges, juries, and the support of a favorable public opinion. The law has for its *sanctions* the specifically enumerated punitive measures set up by the state for breach, penalties which are additional to any of the sanctions which society exerts informally against the violator of norms which may overlap with laws. Crime is itself simply the breach of the legal norm, a violation within this particular category of social control; the criminal is, of course, the individual who has committed such acts of breach.

Much ink has been spilled on the extent of deterrent efficacy of the criminal law in social control. This is a matter which is not subject to demonstration in any exact and measurable fashion, any more than one can conclusively demonstrate the efficiency of a moral norm.[11] Certainly the degree of success in asserting a control, legal or moral, will vary with the particular norm itself, its instrumentation, the subject individuals, the time, the place, and the sanctions. The efficiency of legal control is sometimes confused by the fact that, in the common overlapping of crimes (particularly those *mala in se*) with moral standards, the norms and sanctions of each may operate in mutual support to produce conformity. Moreover, mere breach of norm is no evidence of the general failure of a social control system, but indication rather of the need for control. Thus, the occurrence of theft and homicide does not mean that the law is ineffective, for one cannot tell how frequently such acts might occur in the absence of law and penal sanction. Where such acts are avoided, one may not appraise the relative efficacy of law and mores in prevention. When they occur, one cannot apportion blame, either in the individual case or in general, to failures of the legal and moral systems. The individual in society does undoubtedly conduct himself in reference to legal requirements. Living "beyond the law" has a quality independent of being nonconventional, immoral, sinful. Mr. Justice Holmes has shown that the "bad man of the law"—those who become our criminals—are motivated in part by disrespect for the law or, at the least, are inadequately restrained by its taboos.

From introspection and from objective analysis of criminal histories one can not but accept as axiomatic the thesis that the norms of criminal law and its sanctions do exert some measure of effective control over human behavior; that this control is increased by moral, conventional, and traditional norms; and that the effectiveness of control norms is variable. It seems a fair inference from urban investigations that in our contemporary mass society, the legal system is becoming increasingly important in constraining behavior as primary group norms and sanctions deteriorate. Criminal law, crime, and the criminal become more significant subjects of sociological inquiry, therefore, as we strive to describe, understand, and control the uniformities and variability in culture.

We consider that the "white-collar criminal," the violator of conduct norms, and the antisocial personality are not criminal in any sense meaningful to the social scientist unless he has violated a criminal statute. We cannot know him as such unless he has been properly convicted. He may be a boor, a sinner, a moral leper, or the devil incarnate, but he does not become a criminal through sociological name calling unless politically constituted authority says he is. It is footless for the sociologist to confuse issues of definition, normation, etiology, sanction, agency and social effects by saying one thing and meaning another.

V

To conclude, we reiterate and defend the contention that crime, as legally defined, is a sociologically significant province of study. The view that it is not appears to be based upon either of two premises: first, that offenders convicted under the criminal law are not representative of all criminals and, second, that criminal law violation (and, therefore, the criminal himself) is not significant to the sociologist because it is composed of a set of legal, nonsociological categories irrelevant to the understanding of group behavior and/or social control. Through these contentions to invalidate the traditional and legal frame of reference adopted by the criminologist, several considerations, briefly enumerated below, must be met.

1. *Convicted criminals as a sample of law violators:*
   a. Adjudicated offenders represent the closest possible approximation to those who have in fact violated the law, carefully selected by sieving of the due process of law; no other province of social control attempts to ascertain the breach of norms with such rigor and precision.
   b. It is as futile to contend that this group should not be studied on the grounds that it is incomplete or nonrepresentative as it would be to maintain that psychology should terminate its description, analysis, diagnosis, and treatment of deviants who cannot be completely representative as selected. Convicted persons are nearly all criminals. They offer large and varied samples of all types; their origins, traits, dynamics of development, and treatment influences can be studied profitably for purposes of description, understanding, and control. To

be sure, they are not necessarily representative of all offenders; if characteristics observed among them are imputed to law-violators generally, it must be with the qualification implied by the selective processes of discovery and adjudication.
c. Convicted criminals are important as a sociological category, furthermore, in that they have been exposed and respond to the influences of court contact, official punitive treatment, and public stigma as convicts.
2. *The relevance of violation of the criminal law:*
a. The criminal law establishes substantive norms of behavior, standards more clear-cut, specific, and detailed than the norms in any other category of social controls.
b. The behavior prohibited has been considered significantly in derogation of group welfare by deliberative and representative assembly, formally constituted for the purpose of establishing such norms; nowhere else in the field of social control is there directed a comparable rational effort to elaborate standards conforming to the predominant needs, desires, and interests of the community.
c. There are legislative and juridical lags which reduce the social value of the legal norms; as an important characteristic of law, such lag does not reduce the relevance of law as a province of sociological inquiry. From a detached sociological view, the significant thing is not the absolute goodness or badness of the norms but the fact that these norms do control behavior. The sociologist is interested in the results of such control, the correlates of violation, and in the lags themselves.
d. Upon breach of these legal (and social) norms, the refractory are treated officially in punitive and/or rehabilitative ways, not for being generally antisocial, immoral, unconventional, or bad, but for violation of the specific legal norms of control.[12]
e. Law becomes the peculiarly important and ultimate pressure toward conformity to minimum standards of conduct deemed essential to group welfare as other systems of norms and mechanics of control deteriorate.
f. Criminals, therefore, are a sociologically distinct group of violators of specific legal norms, subjected to official state treatment. They and the noncriminals respond, though differentially, of course, to the standards, threats, and correctional devices established in this system of social control.
g. The norms, their violation, the mechanics of dealing with breach constitute major provinces of legal sociology. They are basic to the theoretical framework of sociological criminology.

Addendum

A special class of cases that illustrates very well both the problem of definition and of legal policy is that of so-called "white-collar crime." Much attention has been devoted to such "crime" in recent years, and properly so, for peculiarly difficult problems of public policy as well as causation and treatment are involved in this area.[13] However, there is possibly less consistency involved in analyses of white-collar "criminality" than there is in any other category of crime. The white-collar criminologists represent one particular group among those who contend that the criminologist should study antisocial behavior rather than criminal law violation as such.[14] In seeking definitions of white-collar crime, one finds a rather remarkable diversity, but characteristically the definitions are loose and sometimes doctrinaire.

Unfortunately, norms of proper behavior in the economic fields of production, distribution, and advertising have been difficult to develop, partly because the commercial revolution took place so rapidly. Drawing lines between efficient and practical competitive behavior by the sharp but skilled and honest businessman, on the one hand, and the criminal practices of the dishonest and overpowerful, on the other, has proved extremely difficult. Interpretations and enforcement of the modern laws directed against various forms of white-collar crime have revealed the complex and controversial character of such policy, in part but not entirely by any means, because of the wealth and power of many of those who are brought to trial. The excessive tolerance that has developed for a loose economic and political morality is also at fault to a great extent. Unlike most forms of crime, white-collar depredations commonly have a diffused impact upon many in the society but little direct or obvious injury to single individuals. Moreover, and this is a peculiarly subtle problem, much of the white-collar conduct disapproved by some criminologists does have economic value. Often the policy question is one of balancing gain and loss from the behavior involved. Finally, it should be noted that our court and correctional systems have little to offer in the way of effective treatment, training, or even of deterrence in the handling of individuals of the sort here involved.

Our definitions of crime cannot be rooted in epithets, in minority value judgments or prejudice, or in loose abstractions. Within a system of justice under law, crime must be defined quite precisely and in accordance with the explicit formulations of the legislature. Such crime will not include all behavior that is antisocial, for reasons that we have noted, nor even all conduct that should be made criminal.

Notes

1. For the manner in which the legal definition of the criminal is avoided by prominent sociological scholars through amazingly loose, circumlocutory description, see, for instance, Florian Znaniecki, "Social Research in Criminology," *Sociology and Social Research,* 12 (1928):307.
2. See, for example, Thorsten Sellin, *Culture Conflict and Crime.* New York: Social Science Research Council, 1938, pp. 20–21.
3. An instance of this broadening of the concept of the criminal is the penchant among certain anthropologists to equate crime with taboo. See, especially, Bronislaw Malinowski, *Crime and Custom in Savage Society.* New York: Harcourt Brace, 1926, and "A New Instrument for the Interpretation of Law— Especially Primitive," *Yale Law Journal,* 51 (1942):1237–1254.
4. Sellin, *op. cit.,* pp. 25ff.
5. Edwin H. Sutherland, "Crime and Business," *Annals of the American Academy of Political and Social Science,* 217 (1941):112–118.
6. Edwin H. Sutherland, "White-Collar Criminality," *American Sociological Review,* 5 (1940):1–12.
7. Harry Elmer Barnes and Negley K. Teeters, *New Horizons in Criminology.* Englewood Cliffs, NJ: Prentice-Hall, 1943, pp. 42–43.
8. Edwin H. Sutherland, "Is 'White Collar Crime' Crime?" *American Sociological Review,* 10 (1945):132–139.
9. In the province of juvenile delinquency we may observe already the evil that flows from this sort of loose definition in applied sociology. See Roscoe Pound, "Introduction," in Pauline V. Young, *Social Treatment in Probation and Delinquency.* New York: McGraw-Hill, 1937, pp. xxiii-xxxi.
10. The unconvicted suspect cannot be known as a violator of the law; to assume him so would be in derogation of our most basic political and ethical philosophies. In empirical research it would be quite inaccurate, obviously, to study all suspects or defendants as criminals.
11. For a detailed consideration of the efficacy of legal norms, see Jerome Michael and Herbert Wechsler, "A Rationale of the Law of Homicide," *Columbia Law Review,* 37 (1937):701–761, and 37 (1937):1261–1325.
12. For another exposition of this view, see Jerome Hall, "Prolegomena to a Science of Criminal Law," *University of Pennsylvania Law Review,* 89 (1941):549–580.
13. The author wishes to make it clear here, since there have been some misconceptions of his view in the literature on the subject, that he believes white-collar crime, properly and precisely defined, to be not only a legitimate but an important phase of criminological inquiry. He deplores the loosely normative connotations that have been attached to the concept by some of Sutherland's interpreters, and he believes that they have resulted in some confusion so far as needed empirical research in this area is concerned.
14. Barnes and Teeters, *op. cit.,* 3d ed. (1959).

4

Gender and Varieties
of White-Collar Crime

Kathleen Daly

S tudies of gender and crime draw primarily on official arrest statistics. From such studies we learn a good deal about the frequency, but almost nothing of the nature, of men's and women's illegalities.[1] These gaps are especially acute for white-collar crime.

Scholars typically use Uniform Crime Reports (UCR) or Offender-Based Transaction Statistics (OBTS) arrest data on embezzlement, fraud, and forgery when assessing gender- or race-based rates of white-collar crime,[2] but their analyses are based on questionable assumptions. Simon argues, for example, that the increasing female share of embezzlement, forgery, and fraud arrests during the 1960s and early 1970s may be explained by increases in women's labor force participation rate. She assumes that all three offenses are occupationally related.[3] Hirschi and Gottfredson assert that "by definition one must be in the white-collar world to be a white-collar offender."[4] They apparently assume that all those arrested for fraud and embezzlement are white-collar workers.[5] Most research on the sentencing of white-collar offenders focuses on class-based disparities; however important that question, more basic questions are overlooked. Who are these white-collar offenders and what is the nature of their acts? Is there any relationship between celebrated cases of white-collar crime described in case studies,[6] and most defendants prosecuted for white-collar crime in the courts?

It is imperative that we understand the characteristics of acts falling in the presumptive "white-collar" statutory domain, how they are organized both within and outside workplace settings, and their class-, gender-, and race-specific nature. The aim of this paper is to begin that process. The focus of the analysis is 1,342 defendants (14% female) who were convicted of white-collar offenses in U.S. federal district courts during the late 1970s. This is a select group of white-collar offenders, those who were prosecuted and convicted; thus, the generalizations that can be drawn are limited. Despite these restrictions, which are addressed below, the data are useful for contrasting varieties of men's and women's white-collar crime.

Reprinted from *Criminology*, 27 (1989), pp. 769–793.

RESEARCH LITERATURE AND HYPOTHESES

Disputes over defining white-collar have been with us for half a century.[7] Rather than entering into the dissension over when an illegality is a white-collar offense, this section highlights the links between different definitions and themes in the literature on gender and white-collar crime.

The disagreement in defining white-collar crime revolves around whether characteristics of the offense or the offender should be primary. An offense-related approach focuses on how a crime is committed, while an offender-related approach focuses on a particular group of people—those in high-status or "respected" occupations or in positions of power. If one takes an offender-related approach, a Medicaid fraud is considered a white-collar crime if it is carried out by a doctor or nursing home owner, but not if it is carried out by a clerical worker or poor person. If one uses an offense-related approach, that distinction is not important.

The different definitions affect how scholars conceptualize gender and white-collar crime. One line of research is to analyze state- or federal-level arrest data for embezzlement, fraud, and forgery, a method using an offense-based definition of white-collar crime, that is, a crime committed by fraud or deception. State data show that the female share of arrests for these three white-collar offenses is 35 to 40%.[8] At the federal level the female share of arrests for embezzlement and forgery is 30 to 40%.[9] Because the female share of arrests has increased in the past two decades, some believe that men's and women's white-collar crime rates are converging.

Women's visibility in arrest data is not reflected in the second line of research, which focuses on major forms of organizational crime, workplace crime, or crimes committed by professional workers, such as doctors or lawyers. Few of these studies have a single woman in them. One explanation is that, relative to men, few women are in positions of power. But there are other reasons for women's invisibility in this body of research: few researchers thought it important to interview female managers, professional workers, or business owners, or to pursue questions of how gender relations in the workplace may structure occupational or organizational crime.

These two lines of inquiry produce radically opposite images of gender and white-collar crime. The offense-based approach suggests a rising tide of "new" female white-collar criminals; the offender-based approach suggests that white-collar crime is a male-only domain. And in a nimble feat of journalistic ingenuity, selected cases of major embezzlements and frauds carried out by women are juxtaposed against female arrest rates for these crimes.[10]

A review of the research literature reveals the paucity of evidence beyond statistical analyses of arrest data or sensational media stories. With the exception of some small-scale case studies,[11] Zietz's research offers the only sustained inquiry.[12] Zietz wanted to determine if Cressey's generalizations for men who had "violated a position of financial trust"[13] applied to women imprisoned for fraud and embezzlement. She found that the circumstances precipitating crime for her group of women differed from those of Cressey's men. The women were more often motivated by a need to meet their responsibilities as wives or mothers. Zietz says that women had a "Joan of Arc quality . . . a willingness to be burned at the stake" to obtain medical care for a loved one or to preserve a marital relationship, and that they rationalized the crime on the basis of family need or maintaining relations with spouses.[14] Cressey's men, in contrast, had a "non-shareable" financial problem stemming from business or gambling debts, poor judgment, or spending beyond their means. Virtually all rationalized their illegalities as "borrowing"; none of Zietz's women used that rationale.

What remains in the literature are hypotheses, speculations, and a debate over interpreting white-collar arrest data. Drawing from studies of sex segregation in corporations[15] and in "underworld" crime, Steffensmeier outlines these hypotheses for men's and women's "upperworld" crime: an absence of women in corporate (or organizational) crime, a lower likelihood that women will work in organized groups or with others in comparison with men, and less lucrative economic gains from women's crimes.[16] Steffensmeier suggests that men's sexism toward women in the "underworld" should also be seen in the "upperworld": men do not like having women as crime partners; they neither trust women nor think them capable in a jam.

But if men exclude women from upperworld crime groups, why don't women form their own groups? Messerschmidt attempts to answer this question by pointing to a "masculine ethic" in the corporate world.[17] This ethic of success and achievement at all costs may propel more men than women who are in the middle and managerial ranks to become involved in corporate crime. Messerschmidt's explanation is echoed in Ghiloni's study of gender differences in the use of organizational power. Ghiloni finds that corporate women are more inclined toward a "morality of positive change" and more concerned with issues of social responsibility in comparison with men in similar corporate positions.[18]

Sex segregation in the labor market or within work organizations is the basis for Box's assertion that the female share of occupational crime (crime against one's employer or that uses one's technical expertise) should also be low. Specifically, Box speculates that because women are subject to greater supervision in their jobs, their opportunities to engage in white-collar crime are restricted. He also points to women's shorter history of "collectivist" experiences in the workplace.[19] One implication may be that workplace social bonds are stronger for men than for women, and thus occupational crime as a group activity is more likely for men.

The issue of gender differences in "workplace opportunities" to commit white-collar crime has sparked debate over interpreting UCR arrest data. Simon argues that as women move into "those types of jobs that will provide them with the opportunities to commit offenses that are important enough to report," the female share of arrests for forgery, fraud, and embezzlement will increase.[20] Critics take Simon to task on several grounds. Chapman as well as Messerschmidt say that the increasing female share of UCR white-collar arrests reflects women's economic and occupational marginality, not mobility;[21] and Steffensmeier suggests that women's frauds and forgeries may not be occupationally related at all.[22]

Plainly, the literature on gender and white-collar crime is long on speculation and short on evidence. Hence, five hypotheses that consolidate some of the major themes reviewed are explored in this paper:

H1: The female share of corporate (or organizational) crime is very low.
H2: The female share of occupational crime is low.
H3: Women are less likely to work in crime groups than men.
H4: Women's economic gains from crime are less than men's.
H5: Men's and women's motives for criminal involvement differ.

But to analyze the data with only these hypotheses in mind is insufficient. We need a descriptive portrait of the defendants and the nature of their acts. Thus, also sketched are the defendants' socioeconomic profiles, occupations, and occupational roles in the crimes, and how their crimes are organized.

THE DATA

The Wheeler et al. data set[23] used in this analysis was gathered in the following way. At seven federal district courts a sample of cases was drawn for defendants convicted during 1976–1978 of bank embezzlement, income tax fraud, postal fraud, credit fraud, false claims and statements, and bribery. In addition, all antitrust and securities fraud convictions in these and other federal districts were selected.[24] The presentence investigation (PSI) report was obtained for each defendant, and a coding scheme was developed to quantify information in the PSI narrative.[25] In selecting cases, Wheeler et al. took an offense-based approach and defined white-collar crime as "economic offenses committed through the use of some combination of fraud, deception, or collusion."[26] Thus, the sample is not restricted by any offender-based criteria.

Selection Bias and Generalization

Several features of the data warrant caution in the generalizations that can be drawn. First, these white-collar offenders have been subject to criminal prosecution and conviction. Katz, Rabin, and Shapiro show that the desire and investigative ability of federal agencies, departments, and attorneys to pursue cases as criminal matters are important questions.[27] Sample selection bias looms large, but, at present, we do not know how this sample of cases differs from others in which civil or administrative action or no legal action was taken.

Second, because the cases were selected by a stratified random sampling procedure, the structure of offenses in the sample does not reflect the structure of white-collar convictions in federal courts during 1977. A comparison of the data with statistics compiled by the Administrative Office of the U.S. Courts shows the sample has proportionally fewer convictions for income tax fraud, and to some extent, postal fraud and bank embezzlement; antitrust violations and, especially, securities fraud are overrepresented.[28] Thus one can draw generalizations from the sample by using a weighting procedure or by analyzing each offense separately. The latter approach is taken here.

Third, the sample is bounded in time and place. The defendants were prosecuted in major urban areas in 1976 through 1978. Benson and Walker argue that the cases differ from those prosecuted in less urban federal districts.[29] A comparison of conviction statistics compiled by the Administrative Office of the U.S. Courts for 1977 and 1985, however, reveals no major temporal shifts. During this period, there were increases in false claims convictions and decreases in tax fraud convictions; the remaining six offenses had about the same share in both years.[30]

Offense Variability

Each of the eight crimes encompasses diverse illegalities.[31] The proscribed activities are outlined in the appendix, but because the offense categories are broad, they can be misleading. For example, postal fraud is a residual category because it includes any activity in which the U.S. mail or other federal communication systems are used to defraud persons, businesses, or state and federal agencies. Some drug traffickers may be convicted of tax fraud because prosecutors have insufficient evidence for a drug conviction, and bribery cases may be related to income tax fraud.

RESULTS

Features of the Eight Offenses

Sociodemographic measures are shown in Table 4.1. The proportion of female defendants in each offense category varies dramatically: women were 45% of convicted bank embezzlers, but their numbers were negligible for antitrust violations, bribery, and securities fraud (N's of 1, 4, and 5, respectively). Offense categories in which there was a moderate share of women were postal fraud (18%), credit fraud (15%), and false claims and statements (15%). Generally, the higher the percentage

Table 4.1
SOCIODEMOGRAPHIC FEATURES OF THE SAMPLE

	Bank Emb (N = 201)	Postal Fraud (N = 190)	Credit Fraud (N = 158)	False Claims (N = 157)	Tax Fraud (N = 210)	Bribe (N = 84)	Sec Fraud (N = 225)	Antitrust (N = 117)
Female	45%	18%	15%	15%	6%	5%	2%	0.5%
White	74	77	72	62	87	82	99.5	97
Completing 4-yr College	13	22	18	29	27	29	41	40

of women in each offense, the higher the fraction of nonwhites (predominantly Black) and those not completing four years of college. In fact, the results for the education variable are startling. If completing college is an indication of status or occupational power, then most of the defendants, including those convicted of securities fraud and antitrust violations do not fit a high-status profile.

Table 4.2 reports the offenders' occupations, whether an occupational role was used in some way to carry out the crime, and the corporate nature of the defendants' illegalities. The occupations held by men and women when they committed the white-collar crimes are compressed into four groups: professional and managerial, other workers (sales, clerical, craft, operatives, laborers, service, and farm workers),

Table 4.2

OFFENDERS' OCCUPATIONS,* OCCUPATIONAL ROLES IN OFFENSES,** AND THE CORPORATE NATURE OF THEIR CRIMES

	Bank Emb (N = 90)	Postal Fraud (N = 34)	Credit Fraud (N = 24)	False Claims (N = 24)	Tax Fraud (N = 12)	Bribe (N = 4)	Sec Fraud (N = 5)	Antitrust (N = 1)
Women								
Prof & Mgr	7%	12%	12%	12%	59%	50%	60%	100%
All Other Workers	91	44	59	59	33	25	40	0
Unemployed	0	35	20	21	0	25	0	0
Illegal or Unknown	2	9	9	8	8	0	0	0
Occupational Role Used								
% Yes	100	9	58	29	33	50	100	100
Corporate Indictment								
% Yes	0	0	0	0	0	0	20	100
	(N = 111)	(N = 156)	(N = 134)	(N = 133)	(N = 198)	(N = 80)	(N = 220)	(N = 116)
Men								
Prof & Mgr	51	43	45	39	59	66	62	84
All Other Workers	45	34	31	40	32	23	31	12
Unemployed	2	14	12	14	2	6	0	0
Illegal or Unknown	2	9	12	7	7	5	7	4
Occupational Role Used								
% Yes	89	54	43	54	14	61	91	99
Corporate Indictment								
% Yes	0	3	1	5	0	9	15	93

* The occupational classifications are professional, technical, managerial, and administrative workers; all other workers (sales, clerical, service, operatives, laborers, craft, and farm); unemployed; and illegal or unknown occupation. In Table 4.4 and the text, those not employed or having an illegal or unknown occupation are defined as having no labor force ties.

** Occupational role includes using a business identity or position of power, or using an occupational role in a workplace organization, to carry out the crime.

unemployed, and illegal or unknown occupation. To simplify the discussion, defendants in the last two groups are described as having "no labor force ties."

Four findings are noteworthy. First, a high percentage of women (30 to over 40%) and about one-fourth of the men convicted of postal fraud, credit fraud, and false claims and statements had no labor force ties. Second, 40 to 85% of the male offenders were professional or managerial workers, but only a majority of the very small number of women convicted for tax fraud, bribery, securities fraud, and antitrust violations were professionals or managers. Third, there is offense- and gender-specific variability in whether an offender used an occupational role to carry out the offense. As one would expect, bank embezzlement, securities fraud, and antitrust violations were occupationally related. Postal fraud and false claims, however, were more likely to be occupationally related for men than for women, and credit fraud was somewhat more likely to be occupationally related for women than for men.

Finally, a higher percentage of men's (14%) than women's (1%) cases involved indictments against corporations or businesses. The corporate nature of defendants' illegalities is moderate to low for men, and almost negligible for women. Of the 194 women, only two cases had corporate indictments: the one woman convicted of antitrust violations and one of the five convicted of securities fraud. For the 162 men's cases involving corporate indictments, most were concentrated, not surprisingly, among the antitrust violators, and to a lesser degree, securities fraud offenders.

Gender Comparisons for Four Offenses

Because there are so few women in the sample who were convicted of tax fraud, bribery, securities fraud, and antitrust violations, this section draws gender comparisons for the remaining four offenses: bank embezzlement, postal fraud, credit fraud, and false claims.

Socioeconomic Profile. Table 4.3 shows that there are substantially higher proportions of nonwhite women than men for all but one offense, false claims. The women are somewhat younger than the men, they are much less likely to have completed four years of college, and they are more likely to have familial dependents outside a marital context. The economic circumstances of both the men and women are far from affluent. The median value of assets owned for women ranged from no assets to $2,500; and for the men, from $5,500 to $8,500. When they committed the offense, most men and women supported themselves by their own earnings. However, the primary means of support for about one-fifth of the women convicted of postal fraud and false claims was welfare or unemployment benefits. This and other tables report the percentage of data or number of cases "not in the PSI." This enables accurate interpretations of the data and flags those variables with gender differences in "missing data," which, as discussed below, bears on the analysis of men's and women's motives.

Table 4.3
SOCIODEMOGRAPHIC AND ECONOMIC INDICATORS

	Embezzlement		Postal Fraud		Credit Fraud		False Claims	
	Men (N = 111)	Women (N = 90)	Men (N = 156)	Women (N =34)	Men (N = 134)	Women (N = 24)	Men (N = 133)	Women (N = 24)
Race (%)								
White	86	59	83	47	75	54	62	63
Nonwhite*	14	41	17	53	25	46	38	37
Age (Yrs)								
Median	31	26	41	30	38	31	38	32
Range	18–62	19–50	20–69	20–36	21–64	22–38	21–70	22–68
Education (%)								
Did Not Complete High School	11	11	28	38	25	21	12	33
Completed High School	69	85	47	56	54	79	55	63
4-year College Degree or More	20	4	25	6	21	0	33	4
Family Circumstances (%)								
Married, Dependent(s)	55	24	55	18	51	29	52	25
Not Married, Dependent(s)	12	23	16	55	24	41	20	33
Married, No Dependents	5	18	2	3	1	4	1	8
Not Married, No Dependents	28	35	27	24	24	26	27	34
Value of Assets Owned ($) (can be determined from PSI)	(N = 95)	(N = 69)	(N = 113)	(N = 29)	(N = 106)	(N = 19)	(N = 113)	(N = 20)
Median Value Men	7,500		5,500		7,500		8,500	
Women		1,000		none		2,500		1,500
Primary Means of Support (%)								
Own Earnings	73	82	58	53	53	54	62	42
Welfare, Unemployment Benefits	0	1	3	18	2	4	5	17
Other (pension, social security, friends, relatives, uncertain)	2	1	10	6	8	8	5	4
Not in PSI	25	16	29	23	37	34	28	37

* Predominantly Black, but includes some Latinos and Asians.

Occupation and Occupational Role in the Offense. Table 4.4 provides detail on men's and women's occupations and whether and how they used their job to commit the crime. Turning first to the women, no matter what the offense, most employed women were clerical workers. Over 90% of the bank embezzlers were clerical workers, as were over half of the employed women in the remaining offenses. Few women were self-employed or owned a business; of the employed women, most worked in the private sector, with the exception of postal fraud offenders. For two offenses that are job related—bank embezzlement and, to a lesser extent, credit fraud—women used their access to documents to carry out the crime. It appears, however, that many women supplemented wage-earning income by engaging in illegalities that were not related to their jobs. This pattern holds for men, as well.

The majority of employed men were managers or administrators, and about 10 to 20% were sales workers. Like the women, but to a lesser degree, many men (about 20 to 25%) convicted of postal fraud, credit fraud, and false claims had no labor force ties. The proportion of men who were self-employed or owned their own business ranged from 10% of bank embezzlers to about 40% of postal fraud and credit fraud offenders. With the exception of false claims and statements, men were more likely than women to have used a business identity or position of authority to carry out their crimes.

Table 4.4
OCCUPATIONS AND OCCUPATIONAL ROLES IN OFFENSES

	Embezzlement		Postal Fraud		Credit Fraud		False Claims	
	Men (N = 111)	Women (N = 90)	Men (N = 156)	Women (N =34)	Men (N = 134)	Women (N = 24)	Men (N = 133)	Women (N = 24)
Occupation Category								
Professional and Technical	0%	0%	9%	6%	7%	4%	17%	0%
Managerial and Administrative	51	7	34	6	38	8	22	12.5
Sales	5	0	18	0	17	13	12	8
Clerical	36	90	5	29	5	42	11	38
Other (service, operatives, laborer, craft or farm)	4	1	11	15	9	4	17	12.5
No Labor Force Ties*	4	2	23	44	24	29	21	29
Class of Worker								
Employee in Private Company	84	99	31	24	37	63	37	59
Government Employee	1	0	8	32	3	8	10	8
Self-employed or Owns Business	11	0	40	0	38	4	29	4
No Labor Force Ties*	4	1	21	44	22	25	24	29
How Occupational Role Was Used								
Had Access to Documents; Job Facilitated Access to Documents	80	100	12	6	18	42	23	4
Used Business Identification or Position of Power	4	0	31	3	17	12	22	21
Combinations of Above	5	0	10	0	8	4	9	4
No Role, Not Employed, Not Known	11	0	47	91	57	42	46	71

* No labor force ties include those not employed, illegal occupations, or occupation is not known. Small discrepancies in this category for occupation and class of worker reflect the fact that occupation but not class of worker is known or vice versa.

Of the four offenses, bank embezzlement was the only one that was clearly occupationally related. Thus, the particular type of bank worker and how he or she embezzled funds is of interest (Table 4.5). In this sample, 60% of the convicted female embezzlers were bank tellers; few were bank officers or financial managers (7%). Thus, most women embezzled funds by taking cash or negotiable instruments or by manipulating bank accounts. For the men, about 40% were bank officers or financial managers, and 14% were bank tellers. Thus, in addition to taking cash and manipulating bank accounts, the men also manipulated documents.

Organization of the Offense and Attempted Economic Gain. There is a good deal of diversity within and across the four crime categories (Table 4.6). This occurs, in part, because each offense (except bank embezzlement) contains a mix of occupationally related and unrelated crime. Also, for the men's offenses there is an admixture of those using (or not using) their business or self-employment status as a conduit for crime.

The first variable in Table 4.6, resources used, reveals gender-based variability in offense organization. One or more individuals using "personal" resources means that the crime was accomplished without the expertise of other workplace personnel or without using a business entity, whether one's employer or another business. One or more individuals using "organizational" resources is a more heterogenous category; it includes a business entity formed to sell nonexistent land to unwitting customers, as well as a bank manager who embezzled funds by seeking assistance from one of the bank's accountants.

For all four offenses, the majority of men and women did not use organizational

Table 4.5

BANK EMBEZZLEMENT: OCCUPATIONAL DETAIL AND HOW THE EMBEZZLEMENT WAS CARRIED OUT

	Men (N = 111)	Women (N = 90)
Specific Job		
Bank Officer or Financial Manager	39%	7%
Other Type of Manager	12	0
Bank Teller	14	60
Bookkeeper	7	11
Other Type of Clerical Worker	15	19
All Other Types of Workers or Unknown	13	3
How the Offender Embezzled		
Took Cash	21	37
Stole Negotiable Instruments	3	14
Manipulated Bank Accounts	38	39
Manipulated Documents	29	8
Other Method	5	2
Not in PSI	4	0

resources, although more men than women did. Interpreting this finding for women is straightforward. When women used organizational resources, they did so in the context of wage-earning employment. But when men used organizational resources, they did so in one of two ways: either they used their own business or professional enterprise as a front or conduit for crime, or they drew from organizational resources in the context of wage-earning employment.

As for crime group size, most women worked alone in committing the offense, although the percentage varied from 50% of women convicted of false claims to almost 90% of bank embezzlers. For the men, with the exception of postal fraud, 50 to 60% worked alone. In general, men were more likely than women to have carried out their crimes with at least two other persons. In comparing the results for group size with the defendant's role in a group, the percentages for "worked alone" and "acted alone—no coordination with others" are slightly discrepant because some

Table 4.6
OFFENSE ORGANIZATION AND ATTEMPTED GAINS

	Embezzlement		Postal Fraud		Credit Fraud		False Claims	
	Men (N = 111)	Women (N = 90)	Men (N = 156)	Women (N =34)	Men (N = 134)	Women (N = 24)	Men (N = 133)	Women (N = 24)
Resources Used								
Personal Resources	86%	98%	61%	94%	74%	87%	71%	79%
Organizational Resources	14	2	39	6	26	13	29	21
Size of Crime Group								
Worked Alone	63	87	29	61	50	63	49	50
Worked with One Other	11	4.5	20	6	11	12	14	13
Small to Moderate (2–10 others)	13	6.5	27	27	18	8	12	8
Large (11 or more others)	13	2	24	6	21	17	25	29
Role Relative to Others								
Acted Alone—No Coordination	70	92	44	71	56	71	53	54
Acted with Others—Subordinate Role	14	3	21	14	16	12.5	12	30
Acted with Others—Primary Role	11	3	21	6	15	12.5	25	8
Uncertain or Not in PSI	5	2	14	9	13	4	10	8
Attempted Economic Gain (can be determined from PSI)	(N = 100)	(N = 82)	(N = 117)	(N = 23)	(N = 98)	(N = 19)	(N = 82)	(N = 15)
$1,000 or less	8	26	6	4.5	5	16	13	7
$1,001 to $10,000	40	55	29	78	35	37	46	73
$10,001 to $100,000	36	18	26	13	36	42	27	7
$100,001 to $500,000	8	0	17	0	17	5	5	13
$500,000 or more	8	1	22	4.5	7	0	9	0
Median (in thousands)								
Men	$10–25		$25–100		$10–25		$5–10	
Women		$1–2.5		$5–10		$5–10		$2.5–5

offenders knew that others were involved in the same illegal activity, but they did not plan or coordinate the activity with them.

When women worked in groups, their leadership and subordinate roles varied by offense. For credit fraud, women were just as likely to be leaders as subordinates, but for false claims, more took a subordinate role. By contrast, more men took a primary role in false claims offenses; but for the remaining offenses, men were just as likely to be leaders as subordinates. There is no variable in the data file for the gender (or race) composition of crime groups; thus, the proportions of men and women working in same- or mixed-gender (or race) groups cannot be determined.

For each offense, the men's attempted economic gain was higher than the women's: by a factor of ten for bank embezzlement, five for postal fraud, and two for credit fraud and false claims. Note that the attempted economic gain variable is based on the whole offense, not on an individual's "take" when two or more persons were involved.[32]

The more grouped nature of men's bank embezzlements, coupled with the higher numbers of male bank officers and financial managers, likely explains men's substantially greater economic gains from embezzlement. Yet group size alone cannot explain why men's monetary gains from credit fraud, postal fraud, and false claims were higher than women's. An added ingredient is men's more frequent use of organizational resources to carry out their crimes. As one would expect, when organizational resources are used, the magnitude of white-collar crime is greater.[33] On average, the attempted gains for these four white-collar offenses are much higher than those for common crime, ranging from $1,000 to 10,000 for women and $2,500 to 25,000 for men. Compared with the gains from antitrust or securities fraud violations, however, they are trivial.[34]

Motives. Before examining men's and women's motives for criminal involvement (Table 4.7), several issues must be addressed: the higher proportion of "missing data" for men than women on this variable, the relationship between motive and rationalization, and interpretive problems.

Information on defendants' motives is missing for a higher proportion of male (about one-third) than female offenders (about one-fifth). Did the women more frequently give a motive or "explain themselves"? We cannot know from the data set, but a qualitative study of the same PSI reports by Rothman and Gandossy sheds some light. They found that in comparison with men, women more often admitted guilt, more readily acknowledged personal responsibility for the offense, provided stronger justifications for their crimes, and were more likely to express remorse. Their study suggests that women's accounts were more compelling than men's, and that a sense of shame or stigma was felt more deeply by women.[35]

In the discussion of the defendants' stated motives, the words motive, justification, and rationalization are used interchangeably, but the imprecision is deliberate. It is simply the best way to represent what probation officers recorded from their interviews with defendants.

Finally, the interpretive layers in the PSI reports are many: the defendant's portrayal of his or her motives, the probation officer's account of what the defendant said, potential differences in what probation officers remember male or female defendants saying, and the like. To avoid convoluted sentence constructions, the defendants' motives are represented as what defendants said.[36]

Women's Motives. For the women giving motives, the most frequent was financial need for their families—30 to 35% of women gave this motive. In addition, 10 to 15% cited financial gain without any reference to need, and 15 to 20% gave non-financial personal reasons, such as frustration or some kind of distress. Different motives are apparent for women convicted of embezzlement and credit fraud and those convicted of postal fraud and false claims. More women in the first group said they were motivated from a financial need for themselves, while more in the second group said they were influenced by others, whether by coercion, following orders, or doing a favor. None of the women rationalized their crimes as stemming from "normal business practices."

Men's Motives. Need-based motives (financial need for their families or for themselves) were 25 to 40% of men's motives across the four offenses. For each offense, about 15 to 20% of men said they were influenced by others; financial gain (no need stated) and nonfinancial personal reasons each accounted for 10 to 20% of men's motives. Financial need for a business was the motive for about 20% of men convicted of credit fraud, but only 3 to 8% of men convicted of the other offenses.

Gender Differences in Motives. Men's and women's motives differ in two areas: (1) the relative importance of self and family in need-based justifications and (2) the degree to which being influenced by others varies by offense for women.

Although financial need for themselves or their families was the modal justifica-

Table 4.7
OFFENDERS' STATED MOTIVES

	Embezzlement		Postal Fraud		Credit Fraud		False Claims	
	Men (N = 111)	Women (N = 90)	Men (N = 156)	Women (N =34)	Men (N = 134)	Women (N = 24)	Men (N = 133)	Women (N = 24)
No Motive Stated or Not in PSI (can be determined	26%	20%	39%	21%	33%	21%	34%	13%
from PSI) Financial Need for:	(N = 82)	(N = 72)	(N = 95)	(N = 27)	(N = 90)	(N = 19)	(N = 88)	(N = 21)
Self	22	29	13	4	15.5	21	16	9
Family	18	36	12	37	15.5	37	14	29
Business	6	0	8	0	18	0	3	0
Other need	3	1	3	4	4	5	7	5
Financial Gain (no need stated)	18	11	21	15	17	16	11	9
Influenced by Others (coerced, following orders, or doing a favor)	20	5	21	25	15	5	20	29
Following Normal Business Practice	1	0	9	0	7	0	11	0
Nonfinancial Personal Reason	12	18	13	15	8	16	18	19

tion for men and women, family need dominated women's need-based motives more than men's (about 35% and 15%, respectively). By comparison, men were just as likely to say they needed money for themselves or for their families.

For each offense, similar proportions (15 to 20%) of men said they were influenced by others. But for the women, the influence of others varied by offense: it was a more frequent rationale for postal fraud and false claims offenders (25 to 30%) than for the bank embezzlers and credit fraud offenders (5%). To interpret this finding, we must consider the organization of men's and women's bank embezzlements and credit frauds.

Recall that women's embezzlements were less likely to be coordinated with others than men's (6% and 25%, respectively), and men more often played a subordinate role (14%) than women (3%). Thus, one would expect fewer women to say they were influenced by others. But this explanation does not satisfy for credit fraud. Similar proportions of men's and women's credit frauds were coordinated with others (25 to 30%), and similar proportions of men and women played a subordinate role (13 to 16%). Yet, few female credit fraud offenders said they were influenced by others. Although the number of cases is small, I would speculate that women's credit frauds are organized more along egalitarian lines than men's. Put another way, the composition of men's crime groups in workplace settings may be more hierarchical in nature, perhaps reflecting a mix of managers and clerical workers.

"His" and "Her" White-Collar Crime

The variable patterns in these four white-collar crimes defy any simple characterization of men's and women's crimes. It is possible, however, to identify some gender-specific elements. Three offenses—postal fraud, credit fraud, and false claims and statements—have a distinctive "his" and "her" flavor. Although men's and women's bank embezzlements differ, much of the variability is related to occupational location and, perhaps, to a cross-occupational composition of men's crime groups.

The crime patterns for men's and women's postal frauds are distinctive in the following ways. The men coordinated with others to defraud businesses and individuals; many of their offenses seemed to be fraudulent sales scams to unwitting investors. The women's postal frauds were not job- or business-related nor carried out with others; they involved receiving credit cards or government checks under false pretenses. Although postal fraud is known as a residual "garbage can" offense category, these differences are noteworthy.

The women convicted of credit fraud and embezzlement share similar crime patterns. Most were clerical workers who used their occupational access to documents to carry out the fraud or to embezzle. Women's credit frauds were more likely than men's to be carried out by insiders in financial institutions. Men, on the other hand, more frequently tried to defraud as outsiders to lending institutions.

In contrast to credit fraud, men's false claims offenses were more likely to be occupationally related than women's. For these illegalities, the pattern for men was to inflate or falsify claims for reimbursement of goods and services; the pattern for women was fraudulently obtaining government benefits or loans.

DISCUSSION

It bears repeating that these white-collar offenders are a select group. They were criminally prosecuted and convicted in urban federal district courts during 1976–1978. Skeptical readers may question the utility of describing white-collar crime from this sample, but there are good reasons for doing so. Until we understand what offenses and people are subject to criminal proceedings, the parameters of discretion and selection bias will not be known. And until we have a grasp of the variable nature of crime in the statutory white-collar domain, theoretical efforts will founder.

This sample of white-collar cases supports hypothesis 1 that the female share of corporate (or organizational) crime is low. Only 1% of women's cases, but 14% of men's involved indictments against corporations or businesses. The rare presence of female corporate crime defendants can be interpreted in several ways. Women may be more averse than men to abusing positions of organizational power, or they may be excluded from men's corporate crime groups, or perhaps both. It is also possible that more women are in fact involved in corporate crime, but fewer are caught or criminally prosecuted.

As for the hypothesis that the female share of occupational crime is low, the results are mixed; hypothesis 2 cannot be supported fully. If occupational crime is defined broadly as crime committed for personal gain in the course of an "otherwise respected and legitimate occupation or financial activity,"[37] all but one of the eight offenses (antitrust violations) include forms of occupational crime. The female share was low or negligible for six of these seven offenses. But for bank embezzlement— an archetypal occupational crime—the female share was close to 50%. In suggesting that women's workplace jobs have a higher degree of surveillance than men's, Box ignored the possibility that enhanced surveillance may increase the likelihood of being caught for some occupational crimes, especially in banks or other work settings where there are daily checks of cashiers' or tellers' transactions.[38] With 60% of the female bank embezzlers working as tellers, and 90% working in clerical jobs of some kind, the image of embezzlers as "aristocrats of chiseling employees"[39] does not suit most female offenders.

The hypothesis that women are less likely than men to work in crime groups is supported for three of four offenses examined. With the exception of false claims, women were more likely to work alone and to not coordinate their illegalities with others. The average attempted gain from women's crime was less than men's, which confirms hypothesis 4. Gender differences in group size, occupational location, and the greater use of organizational resources in men's crime likely explain the lower monetary gains in women's crime. But gender differences in need or greed cannot be discounted.

Finally, financial need for themselves or their families were more frequent rationales for women's involvement in crime than men's: over twice as many women as men cited financial need for families. Despite these differences, hypothesis 5 is only partially supported. Men's and women's motives do differ to some degree, but not as starkly as Cressey's and Zietz's studies suggest.[40] For example, although 30 to 40% of the women said their offenses were motivated by financial need for their families, most women gave a combination of other motives, including financial need for themselves and nonfinancial personal reasons. A good way to compare Cressey's and Zietz's findings with those presented here is to examine only those men and women convicted of bank embezzlement, the offense closest to what Cressey's men and Zietz's women were convicted of (and imprisoned for). Half the male embezzlers in this study cited motives that reflect a "non-shareable" financial problem, but about 40% of the female embezzlers also gave such motives.[41] Family need, though a more frequently stated motive for the female bank embezzlers (36%), was also a motive among their male counterparts (18%).

SUMMARY AND IMPLICATIONS

In this group of white-collar offenders, some men are "big fish," but most are "little fish" and do not comport with images of highly placed or powerful white-collar criminals. Men's white-collar crimes were both petty and major, but almost all the women's were petty. Although half or more of the employed men were managerial or professional workers, most employed women were clerical workers. Higher proportions of women were Black and had no ties to the paid labor force; fewer women had a four-year college degree. The women's socioeconomic profile, coupled with the nature of their crimes, makes one wonder if "white-collar" aptly describes them or their illegalities.

The results help to fill some gaps in our knowledge of gender-based variability in white-collar crime. Although the profile of offenses and offenders answers some questions, many others are raised. Three implications for theory and research on white-collar crime are highlighted.

First, state or federal data for embezzlement, fraud, and forgery should be used with great caution, if at all, as measures of white-collar crime.[42] Of these offenses, embezzlement is the only one that is clearly occupationally related, and the sole requirement to embezzle is that a person be in a position of financial trust. Such positions are widespread in female-dominated "pink-collar" jobs,[43] such as bookkeeper, bank teller, and cashier. The average attempted gain for female embezzlers in the sample ($1,000 to $2,500) bears no resemblance to celebrated cases of female embezzlement touted in the media. In short, one need not be in the white-collar world to commit embezzlement, fraud, or forgery. The "pink-collar" world suffices, as does having no ties to the labor market. Scholars would do well to heed Wheeler et al.'s advice: "it [is] dangerous to infer the 'white collarness' of an offense from its statutory category alone."[44]

Second and relatedly, efforts to link changing rates of female arrests for embezzlement, fraud, or forgery to increases in women's labor force participation rates are dubious. The results of this analysis lend more support to Chapman's and Messerschmidt's claims than to Simon's.[45] Women's economic marginality, not liberation or occupational mobility, better describes the form of female white-collar crime in this sample. Specifically, these data suggest that if women's share of white-collar arrests increases, it will stem from (1) increasing numbers of women in highly monitored, money-changing types of clerical, sales, or service jobs and (2) increasing numbers of poor or unemployed women attempting to defraud state and federal governments or banks by securing loans, credit cards, or benefits to which they are not legally entitled.

Finally, in building theories of white-collar crime, scholars should be cognizant of the points of gender difference found in this study. *The* white-collar crime offender is rarely named the *male* offender, suggesting a repeat of the past in explaining common crime.[46] Men's white-collar crime, though more frequent than women's and exacting more social injury or harm, should not be used as the "norm" from which women's white-collar crime is thought to deviate. Women's illegalities should be explored on their own terms. The multiple influences of gender, class, and race relations, both within and outside work organizations and occupations, should also be investigated. These relations not only generate many varieties of white-collar crime, they also undoubtedly play a role in who is caught and prosecuted for white-collar crime.

Notes

1. See, e.g., Rita J. Simon, *Women and Crime.* Lexington, MA: Lexington Books, 1975.
2. Travis Hirschi and Michael Gottfredson, "Causes of White-Collar Crime," *Criminology,* 25 (1987):949–974; Donald A. Manson, "Tracking Offenders: White-Collar Crime," *Bureau of Justice Statistics Special Report NCH-102867.* Washington, DC: U.S. Department of Justice, 1986; Simon, *op. cit.*
3. Simon, *op. cit.*
4. Hirschi and Gottfredson, *op. cit.,* p. 967.
5. Travis Hirschi and Michael Gottfredson, "The Significance of White-Collar Crime for a General Theory of Crime," *Criminology,* 27 (1989):359–371. Hirschi and Gottfredson are inconsistent on this point. In their 1987 article they suggest that "white-collar crimes are events that take place in an occupational setting" and that "obviously, only white-collar workers can commit white-collar crimes . . ." (*op. cit.,* p. 961). But in their 1989 article, they say "we did

not define for the purposes of empirical work 'white-collar crimes' as crimes committed by employees" (*op. cit.,* p. 302).

6. Gilbert Geis and Robert F. Meier, eds., *White-Collar Crime.* New York: Free Press, 1977; Geis and Ezra Stotland, eds., *White-Collar Crime: Theory and Research.* Beverly Hills: Sage, 1980.

7. See James W. Coleman, *The Criminal Elite: The Sociology of White Collar Crime.* New York: St. Martin's Press, 1989; Gilbert Geis and Colin Goff, Introduction, Edwin H. Sutherland, *White Collar Crime: The Uncut Version.* New Haven: Yale University Press, 1983.

8. Bureau of Justice Statistics, *Sourcebook of Criminal Justice Statistics.* Katherine Jamieson and Timothy J. Flanagan, eds. Washington, DC: U.S. Department of Justice, 1987, p. 298; Manson, *op. cit.,* p. 3.

9. Bureau of Justice Statistics, *White Collar Crime.* Special Report, NCJ-106876. Washington, DC: U.S. Department of Justice, 1987, p. 7.

10. Freda Adler, *Sisters in Crime.* Prospect Heights, IL: Waveland Press, 1975; Bryan Burrough, "Broken Barriers: More Women Join Ranks of White-Collar Criminals," *Wall Street Journal,* May 2, 1987, p. 29; Carol Kirschenbaum, "White Collar Criminals," *Glamour Magazine,* March 1987, p. 306.

11. Pat Carlen, ed., *Criminal Women.* Cambridge, MA: Polity Press, 1985; Alice Franklin, "Criminality in the Work Place: A Comparison of Male and Female Offenders." In Freda Adler and Rita James Simon, eds., *The Criminality of Deviant Women.* Boston, MA: Houghton Mifflin, 1979; Sue Mayan, "Opportunities for Women in White Collar Crime," Paper presented at the Annual Meeting of the American Society of Criminology, Montreal, Canada, 1987.

12. Dorothy Zietz, *Women Who Embezzle or Defraud: A Study of Convicted Felons.* New York: Praeger, 1981.

13. Donald R. Cressey, *Other People's Money: A Study in the Social Psychology of Embezzlement.* Glencoe, IL: Free Press, 1953.

14. Zeitz, *op. cit.,* p. 58.

15. Rosabeth Moss Kanter, *Men and Women of the Corporation.* New York: Basic Books, 1977.

16. Darrell J. Steffensmeier, "Organization Properties and Sex-Segregation in the Underworld: Building a Sociological Theory of Sex Differences in Crime," *Social Forces,* 61 (1983):1011–1032.

17. James W. Messerschmidt, *Capitalism, Patriarchy, and Crime: Toward a Socialist Feminist Criminology.* Totowa, NJ: Rowman and Littlefield, 1986, pp. 116–121.

18. Beth W. Ghiloni, "Power Through the Eyes of Women," Paper presented at the Annual Meeting of the American Sociological Association, Chicago, 1987.

19. Steven Box, *Power, Crime and Mystification.* New York: Tavistock, 1983, pp. 181–182.

20. Simon, *op. cit.,* p. 106.

21. Jane Roberts Chapman, *Economic Realities and the Female Offender.* Lexington, MA: Lexington Books, 1980; Messerschmidt, *op. cit.*

22. Darrell J. Steffensmeier. "Crime and the Contemporary Woman: An Analysis of Changing Levels of Female Property Crime," *Social Forces,* 57 (1978): 566–584.

23. Stanton Wheeler, David Weisburd, and Nancy Bode, "Sentencing the White-Collar Offender: Rhetoric and Reality." *American Sociological Review,* 47(1982):641–659; Wheeler, Weisburd, Bode, and Elin Waring, "White Collar Crime and Criminals," *American Criminal Law Review,* 25 (1988):331–357.

24. The federal districts and cities are Central California (Los Angeles), Northern Georgia (Atlanta), Northern Illinois (Chicago), Maryland (Baltimore), Southern New York (Manhattan and the Bronx), Northern Texas (Dallas), and Western Washington (Seattle). Unlike the analysis in Wheeler et al., 1982, but like Wheeler et al., 1988, the sample here analyzed includes all securities fraud and antitrust cases.

25. A PSI report is written by a probation officer and describes the nature of the offense and characteristics of the offender. It includes the prosecuting attorney's and the defendant's description of the offense; the defendant's current and previous family history, occupational and financial status, physical and mental health, and other biographical elements. It also contains the probation officer's evaluation of the case and sentencing recommendations.

26. Wheeler et al., 1982, *op. cit.,* p. 642.

27. Jack Katz, "Legality and Equality: Plea Bargaining in the Prosecution of White-Collar and Common Crimes," *Law and Society Review,* 13 (1979): 431–460; Robert L. Rabin, "Agency Criminal Referrals in the Federal System: An Empirical Study of Prosecutorial Discretion," *Stanford Law Review,* 24 (1972):1036–1091; Susan P. Shapiro, "The Road Not Taken: The Elusive Path to Criminal Prosecution for White-Collar Offenders," *Law and Society Review,* 19 (1985):179–217.

28. Administrative Office of the U.S. Courts, *Annual Report of the Director.* Washington, DC: Government Printing Office, 1977, pp. 370–373.

29. Michael L. Benson and Esteban Walker, "Sentencing the White-Collar Offender," *American Sociological Review,* 53 (1988):294–302.

30. One cannot know the mix of convicted offenses if the characteristics of acts prosecuted in 1977 differ from those prosecuted in 1985 or today. However, the analysis of federal court conviction statistics for 1977 and 1985 does not support the perception that U.S. attorneys are prosecuting more "real" white-collar crime (securities fraud or antitrust violations) in the 1980s than in the 1970s. My thanks to one reviewer who cites contradictory evidence from the Justice Department and insiders on this issue.

31. David Weisburd, Stanton Wheeler, Elin Waring, and Nancy Bode, *Middle-Class Criminals: White-Collar Crime in the Federal Courts.* New Haven: Yale University Press, 1991; Wheeler et al., 1988, *op. cit.*

32. It is not possible to construct a precise measure of an individual's take in an offense because the group size and attempted gain variables are coded in range

form. The conceptual basis for the attempted economic gain measure is total impact or harm to victims, not the avarice of individual offenders.

33. Stanton Wheeler and Mitchell L. Rothman, "The Organization as Weapon in White-Collar Crime," *University of Michigan Law Review,* 80 (1982):1403–1426.

34. The magnitude of attempted economic gain could not be determined for most antitrust violators, but in the cases for which it could (N = 16), all cases exceeded $500,000. For the securities fraud cases in which attempted economic gain could be determined (N = 143), half exceeded $500,000.

35. Mitchel Rothman and Robert P. Gandossy, "Sad Tales: The Accounts of White-Collar Defendants and the Decision to Sanction," *Pacific Sociological Review,* 25 (1982):449–473.

36. When a probation officer described a defendant's motive but then challenged its veracity, the coders were instructed to code what the defendant said. The results therefore reflect what the defendant said even when probation officers believed other motives were central.

37. Coleman, *op. cit.,* p. 5.

38. Box, *op. cit.*

39. Coleman, *op. cit.,* p. 83.

40. Cressey, *op. cit.;* Zietz, *op. cit.;* Mahan, *op. cit.*

41. To estimate the proportion of defendants whose motives fit Cressey's concept of a "non-shareable financial problem," the percentage of offenders who said financial need for self, business, other than family, and financial gain (no need stated) were summed.

42. Steffensmeier, *op. cit.,* pp. 347–348, 355.

43. Louise Kapp Howe, *Pink Collar Workers.* New York: Avon, 1977.

44. Wheeler et al., 1988, *op. cit.,* p. 334.

45. Chapman, *op. cit.;* Messerschmidt, *op. cit.;* Simon, *op. cit.*

46. Kathleen Daly and Meda Chesney-Lind, "Feminism and Criminology," *Justice Quarterly,* 5 (1988):497–538; Anthony Harris, "Sex and Theories of Deviance: Toward a Functional Theory of Deviant Type-Scripts," *American Sociological Review,* 42 (1977):3–15; Carol Smart, *Women, Crime and Criminology: A Feminist Critique.* Boston, MA: Routledge and Kegan Paul, 1976.

5

The Consequences of White-Collar Crime

Robert F. Meier and James F. Short, Jr.

W hite-collar and corporate criminality are commonly viewed by observers as among the most serious—for some, indeed, *the* most serious—forms of crime.[1] These views appear to be related to the impact of this form of criminality on society, an impact so substantial that it equals or surpasses that of homicide, robbery, forcible rape, and mass murders. One might be tempted to challenge such opinions as conjectural and the result of personal idiosyncrasies were they not so widely held and so ardently defended among criminologists. How are such judgments made? This is the central question addressed in this chapter in which a variety of issues of crime impact and its measurement are discussed. Because so little is known, however, special attention is given to kinds of data and substantive topics that future research concerned with this subject might consider.

CRITERIA OF CRIMINAL HARM

Although we wish to avoid the many conceptual problems associated with the definition of white-collar criminality,[2] it is necessary to provide a preliminary definition of the phenomenon under discussion. We have decided to follow, but not to defend here, the definition of white-collar crime adopted in a recent survey of data sources of white-collar lawbreaking. Reiss and Biderman define white-collar crime in terms of "1) the violator's use of a significant position of power for 2) illegal gain." These authors continue by noting that:

> The corollary condition that there be damage or harm to victims is an essential condition for all torts as well as crimes. . . . Although calculations of probable harm are implicit in the definition and classification of types of law violation and in the range of possible penalties attached to each violation, in practice the

Reprinted from Herbert Edelhertz, ed., *White-Collar Crime: An Agenda for Research.* Lexington, MA: Lexington Books, 1983, pp. 23–49.

actual harm done to victims is more often than not the principal element in determining the offense alleged and, later, of sanctions.[3]

This makes an evaluation of the impact of crime all the more important.

Three criteria are most often mentioned in determining the degree of harm from crime: financial loss, physical harm, and damage to the moral climate of the community. This abbreviated list does not exhaust the potential standards by which one can judge an act socially injurious, but it does seem to capture the dimensions on which observers rate white-collar and corporate criminality as harmful. Unfortunately, different definitions of white-collar crime make strict comparisons between white-collar and ordinary crime spurious. Moreover, the nature of these crimes makes complete detection and assessment impossible. This is compounded by the fact that each of the standards of criminal harm is difficult to evaluate unambiguously, making comparative statements between precise levels of harm among different categories of crime impossible.

Financial Harm

Although precise financial estimates of the economic impact of white-collar and corporate criminality do not exist, several estimates of such impact have been offered.

In 1974 the U.S. Chamber of Commerce estimated the short-run direct cost of white-collar crime to the U.S. economy at no less than $40 billion annually,[4] an estimate that is consistent with that quoted by Congressman John Conyers in hearings before the Subcommittee on Crime of the Committee on the Judiciary in 1978.[5] In 1976 the Joint Economic Committee of the U.S. Congress put the figure at $44 billion annually. Several observers since that time have pointed out that this estimate is very conservative and excludes a number of offenses.[6] Senator Philip Hart, as chair of the Judiciary Subcommittee on Antitrust and Monopoly, estimated that antitrust-law violations may illegally divert as much as $200 billion annually from the U.S. economy.

Congressman Peter Rodino, in hearings conducted in 1978, informed the Conyers committee that the Justice Department estimated in 1968 that the estimated loss due to violations of the Sherman Act alone was $35 billion, and a 1977 GAO study estimated that frauds against government programs in seven federal agencies alone cost the taxpayers roughly $25 billion.[7] Rodino placed the estimated loss from all forms of white-collar criminality as closer to $100 billion annually.

Estimates of total financial loss from white-collar crimes are in the billions of dollars each year, and estimates of financial loss from specific white-collar crimes are similarly high. The American Management Association has estimated that the loss due to employee pilferage—arguably a white-collar crime, but one that is not typically discussed as such—costs the business community $5 billion a year.[8]

The difficulty with estimates of specific white-collar crimes parallels that with estimates for white-collar criminality in general: The definition of white-collar crime varies from observer to observer, making such estimates impossible to reconcile. For example, the U.S. Chamber of Commerce estimate mentioned previously includes the estimated cost of shoplifting, but not that of price-fixing. That report does not provide a strenuous defense of such a debatable choice of crimes.

Most observers are quick to point out that the estimates they provide are conservative, and that the actual loss is probably far greater. There is agreement, however, that the annual cost from white-collar and corporate crimes is far greater than that from ordinary crime. As we shall see, measurement of these costs is extremely complex. Data sources are inconsistent and plagued by problems of reliability and validity. A beginning has been made,[9] but many problems remain. It seems safe to say that statistics on white-collar crime are at a more-primitive stage than were statistics on street crime prior to the initiation of the Uniform Crime Reporting system.

Physical Harm

As high as financial estimates are, by most standards, they do not include the total losses that accrue from these offenses. For example:

> They do not cover the losses due to sickness and even death that result from the environmental pollution of the air and water, and the sale of unsafe food and drugs, defective autos, tires, and appliances, and of hazardous clothing and other products. They also do not cover the numerous disabilities that result from injuries to plant workers, including contamination by chemicals that could have been used with more adequate safeguards, and the potentially dangerous effects of work-related exposures that might result in malignancies, lung diseases, nutritional problems, and even addiction to legal drugs and alcohol.[10]

Physical harm, like financial losses, can be directed toward at least three different groups: employees of offending firms, consumers, and the community at large.[11] Physical harm to employees includes unsafe working conditions, such as those found in many mining operations and in fiberglass plants. The effects of black-lung disease and asbestos poisoning, although relatively slow to develop, can result in death.

Harm experienced by consumers includes the sale of unsafe products (such as flammable clothing for children), food, and drugs. Perhaps the most dramatic and significant case of consumer harm in recent history arose over the manufacture and sale of an automobile, the Ford Pinto, which had been linked with a number of driver and passenger deaths due to an unsafe fuel tank. Although the criminal trial related to this case resulted in acquittal of the Ford Motor Company, commentators have been quick to point out that the principle of manufacturers' criminal liability for their products was more firmly established by the trial. Many other instances of severe physical harm might be cited, although they have not always resulted in criminal prosecution and conviction. For several years the Beechcraft Company allegedly used a fuel pump with a faulty design that caused a number of deaths of pilots and passengers in the Beechcraft "Bonanza" series of aircraft; the engine would often stall when the plane was banking lightly shortly after takeoff, causing a loss of power and control.[12]

Harm to the community at large can take many forms, such as pollution—air, water, and noise. A recent report estimated that 14,000 persons in the United States who would have died in 1978 of lung cancer and other diseases related to air pollution were spared because of improvements in air quality since the enactment of the Clean Air Act of 1970.[13] The estimate was derived from previous studies of the impact of air pollution.

Perhaps because physical injuries are not readily quantifiable in terms of dollars and cents, these consequences of white-collar and corporate criminality are viewed as more serious by citizens than are financial or property losses.[14] One problem is that it is often impossible to demonstrate that actions leading to physical injuries were intentional or were the result of faulty decision making or other "human-like" qualities. This, evidently, accounted for the recent court decision that found Ford Motor Company not guilty of the deaths of persons resulting from a Pinto fuel-tank explosion and fire. To cite the lack of complete documentation concerning corporate liability in such matters is not to deny that there are physical injuries; nor is it to argue against the notion that the public, regardless of strict legal criteria, may blame corporations and their officers for such acts. Nevertheless, it must be recognized that all the cautions concerning data sources regarding economic harm apply with even greater force in the case of physical harm.

Another difficulty in assessing this consequence is the absence of clear criteria or standards by which physical harm from criminal means can be evaluated. Life itself is physically risky in many respects; to claim that such risks are due to criminal conduct is quite another matter. The best-designed aircraft and the most intensively trained pilots still cannot eliminate completely the risk of flying. Until the idea of *minimum acceptable level of risk* is explicated and put into practice, discussions of physical harm from white-collar crimes are likely to be widely speculative. The idea of minimum acceptable levels of risk is not new, having been employed, for example, in determining unacceptable health risks for air and water pollution. Airborne particulates or water contaminates above specified medically determined levels are deemed unacceptable. If high levels of particulates or contaminants can be traced to a manufacturing concern, then state or federal sanctions can be imposed. Acceptable levels of risk for many types of pollution have not yet been determined, and they often shift as knowledge is expanded. This further complicates assessments of physical impacts of corporate behavior.

Damage to Moral Climate

Although few dispute that the financial loss and physical harm due to white-collar crime are enormous, perhaps the criterion of harm that has been stressed most strongly by sociologists is the set of broader social consequences of crimes committed by persons of high social status. Persons of wealth and high social standing are often held to very high standards of accountability for their conduct. As one observer put it: "It can be argued, convincingly I think, that social power and prestige carry heavier demands for social responsibility, and that the failure of corporation executives to obey the law represents an even more serious problem than equivalent failure by persons less well-situated in the social structure."[15]

The notion that prestige carries with it greater responsibility toward the community is objectionable to some on the grounds that it may lead to standards of seriousness of crime that depend on characteristics of persons such as socioeconomic status, race, or gender. One of the charges against the traditional criminological focus on ordinary crime is that it does precisely this, since the most-serious crimes of this sort are heavily concentrated among those segments of the population of lower socioeconomic status. Still, it is unmistakable that some crimes *are* more serious than others, and more-serious crimes may indeed be those committed by persons in positions of power and prestige. In fact, one of the characteristics of white-collar crimes—that victimization patterns are spread over many more persons than with most conventional crimes—suggests that crimes by persons in power may have more impact precisely for this reason.

Because of the high social standing of white-collar offenders, some observers have maintained that these violations create cynicism and foster the attitude that "if others are doing it, I will too."[16] Tax authorities have used this interpretation of the fact that after exposure of former President Nixon's tax deceits, false reporting of taxes increased substantially.[17] More fundamentally, it is held that white-collar crime threatens the trust that is basic to community life—for example, between citizens and government officials, professionals and their clients, businesses and their customers, employers and employees, and—even more broadly—among members and between members and nonmembers of the collectivity. Thus, Cohen argues that "the most destructive impact of deviance on social organization is probably through its impact on *trust*, or confidence that others *will*, by and large, play by the rules."[18] Because both the offenders and the offenses are "high placed," this is a particularly troublesome feature of white-collar crime.

The relationship between white-collar crime and prevailing public attitudes about trust has never been explored systematically. Yet it is precisely public trust—trust in social institutions, groups, and particular persons—that may provide the social glue that is social cohesion in the community. Once that cohesiveness is weakened or broken, the social fabric itself suffers. (We will return presently to these considerations, which deserve more than passing mention.)

These consequences, however, rest to a large extent on some unstated and untested assumptions, namely, (1) that high-status persons serve as moral role models for the rest of the population, who, in turn, pattern their behavior after those they emulate; and (2) that the public generally views such conduct as relatively serious, at least compared with street crime. The former assumption has never been tested empirically, and one could generate arguments both for and against it. The second assumption has received more empirical attention, both because public perceptions of crime seriousness may be important criteria of harm, and because these perceptions may be related to other criteria mentioned earlier. However, none of these studies can be considered definitive. Paradoxically, the accepted social-science view has been that the public does not view white-collar crime as serious in comparison with ordinary or street crime. This view may be related to the inconclusiveness of the research; if so, however, it is odd that the second assumption has been implied at all.

PUBLIC REACTIONS TO WHITE-COLLAR CRIME

The conventional wisdom that members of the public do not view white-collar violations as terribly serious, compared with ordinary crimes, was succinctly summarized by the President's Commission on Law Enforcement and Administration of Justice:[19] "The public tends to be indifferent to business crime or even to sympathize with the offenders when they have been caught."

This argument dates back at least to Ross, who claimed that

the real weakness in the moral positions of Americans is not their attitude toward the plain criminal, but their attitude toward the quasi-criminal. The shocking leniency of the public in judging conspicuous persons who have thriven by antisocial practices is not due, as many imagine, to sycophancy . . . but the fact that the prosperous evildoers that bask undisturbed in popular favor have been careful to shun—or seem to shun—the familiar types of wickedness.[20]

Sutherland maintained this view in his major work on white-collar crime when he claimed that "the public . . . does not think of the businessman as a criminal; the businessman does not fit the stereotype of 'criminal.' "[21] However, Sutherland, like Ross before him, did not support his claim with reference to data. Work subsequent to Sutherland has perpetuated this view. Clinard and Aubert both subscribed to this view. According to Aubert, "The public has customarily a condoning, indifferent or ambivalent attitude," although he does admit that this conclusion is not based on systematic surveys.[22]

Supporters of this conventional wisdom have often attributed this fact to the influence of white-collar violators in manipulating stereotypes and images of "the criminal" so as to exclude themselves. As Sutherland observed: "Public opinion in regard to picking pockets would not be well organized if most of the information regarding this crime came to the public directly from the pickpockets themselves."[23] Still other writers have quarreled with the reason for public indifference while at the same time maintaining its existence. Kadish takes as given the public's nonserious perception of white-collar crimes and uses it to support his argument that white-collar crimes must be processed differently (that is, administratively, not criminally).[24]

The Evidence

What is the empirical evidence with respect to this conventional wisdom? Actually, there is very little. One small-scale study (one that was conducted as part of a larger survey on a topic quite removed from white-collar crime) is often cited in support of this view. Newman found that 78 percent of his 178 respondents did not rate violations of pure food and drug laws as comparable in seriousness to street crimes; but the respondents did favor stiffer penalties than the courts usually gave out for such violations.[25] Aside from these findings, most of the research on perceived crime seriousness has suggested a far different conclusion: Members of the public do make discriminations among types of white-collar crime (as they do for street crime), rating some as more serious, some as less. Moreover, white-collar violations as a group are generally ranked as quite serious.

Reed and Reed found that 305 freshmen at a southern university rated a number of white-collar crimes as being at least as serious as street crimes.[26] Rettig and Passamanick questioned respondents about the rightness and wrongness of fifty different acts, five of which involved business crime. Four of these business crimes were among the twenty-five eliciting the severest moral condemnation.[27] (A follow-up showed, however, that most of these white-collar offenses elicited less condemnation with increasing age of the respondents.)

Gibbons questioned 320 San Francisco residents about their preferred punishments for a variety of offenses. Of the respondents, 70 percent preferred prison sentences for an antitrust violator, about the same percentage that preferred imprisonment for an auto thief. Forty-three percent preferred imprisonment for an advertiser who misrepresents his product, a figure similar to that for the imprisonment of one who assaults another person.[28]

A 1969 Harris poll concluded that analysis of this list of white-collar and street crimes and rankings of seriousness leaves little doubt that immoral acts committed by "establishment" figures are viewed as much worse, by and large, than those of the antiestablishment figures who have caused all the recent flurry of public indignation.[29]

Clinard, in spite of his view that the public does not condemn white-collar crimes to the same extent as street crimes, indicated that polls conducted at the time of his study of Office of Price Administration (OPA) violations during World War II found that most persons (between two-thirds and 97 percent, depending on the specific poll of a national sample) favored OPA controls.[30]

Hartung asked forty meat company managers and 322 citizens to express their disapproval of ten different acts (five criminal, five civil and of the white-collar-crime variety). Citizens disapproved of the civil acts to the same extent—not more, but certainly not less—as the criminal acts; the meat managers, perhaps expectedly, disapproved more of the criminal acts.[31]

A 1968 survey of U.S. citizen attitudes also found relatively high condemnation for one specific white-collar offender: the embezzler. Samples of 1,000 adults and 200 adolescents rated the embezzler as a less-serious criminal than the armed robber, murderer, or narcotics seller to minors, but as more serious than the burglar, prostitute, or rioter who engages in looting. There was no difference by sex of respondent in these ratings, but more highly educated and white respondents were more likely to favor lesser penalties for the embezzler (however, even here the degree of condemnation was high). In another part of the survey, respondents were asked how uneasy they would be working with a parolee who had been convicted of a crime. Only the armed robber provoked more anxiety than the embezzler who stole from a charity; much less anxiety was expressed over the prospect of working with a check forger, an auto thief, an income-tax defrauder, or a shoplifter. When asked about specific dispositions, 7 percent of the respondents were willing to place the embezzler on probation; but 43 percent favored a short period of confinement, and 42 percent a longer sentence. More-lenient handling was favored by the respondents for a 25-year-old burglar, with 20 percent favoring probation, 57 percent a short period of confinement, and 15 percent a longer sentence.[32]

More-recent surveys show similar results. In a survey of Baltimore residents, Rossi et al. found that manufacturing drugs known to be harmful to users and knowingly selling contaminated food that causes a death were rated as more serious than armed robbery, child abuse, selling secret documents to a foreign government, arson, deserting the army in time of war, spying for a foreign government, or child molesting. Of the 140 offenses on this list, 20 could reasonably be considered white-collar crimes. Taken together, the white-collar offenses as a group were rated as more serious than spouse abuse, burglary of a factory, resisting arrest, bribing a public official, simple assault, or killing a suspected burglar in one's home.[33]

Cullen, Link, and Polanzi replicated the rankings of Rossi et al. in a rural area in Illinois. On the basis of 105 responses, they conclude that citizens do view white-collar criminality as serious (more so, in fact, than did Rossi's respondents), although, as expected, they make distinctions in terms of relative seriousness on the basis of different kinds of white-collar crimes. Violent corporate offenses, in particular, were rated as highly serious. Knowingly selling contaminated food that causes death, for example, was rated as more serious than forcible rape, aggravated assault, or selling secret documents to a foreign government. Causing the death of an employee by neglecting to repair machinery was rated by the Illinois respondents as more serious than child abuse, making sexual advances to small children, and kidnapping for ransom.[34]

Hawkins surveyed 662 undergraduates at the University of North Carolina. Students were asked to rank the seriousness of twenty-five different acts presented in scenarios that altered the nature of the acts and the actors. Six of the scenarios depicted white-collar offenses. One such act, that of a hotel owner who refuses to install a fire alarm, as a result of which one hundred persons die in a fire, was rated as more serious than the crimes of a 50-year-old man who rapes a babysitter, a young man who kills his parents, or a woman who shoots and injures her husband. The other white-collar crimes received differential ratings, although the lowest-rated white-collar crime—that of a man who fails to pay income tax—was rated sixteenth out of the list of twenty-five.[35]

A preliminary analysis of data collected in a nationwide sample of 60,000 households by Marvin Wolfgang found that the public does indeed view white-collar crimes as serious. Wolfgang's data show that the crime of a legislator who takes a bribe of $10,000 was rated as more serious than a burglary of a bank that netted the burglar $100,000. The polluting of a city's water supply by a factory, resulting in the illness of only one person, was rated as more than twice as serious as the burglary of a private home in which the burglar steals $100.[36] Consistently, certain white-collar violations—particularly those that result in injury or death—are rated as very serious, a view that is supported by a reanalysis of Rossi's data by Schrager and Short, who found that white-collar crimes involving violence are rated as being as serious as street crimes of violence and more serious than nonviolent crimes of either variety.[37]

The Confrontation of Empirical Evidence and Conventional Wisdom

One must wonder on what basis criminologists have maintained the view that the public is indifferent to white-collar crimes. Virtually all the research done so far suggests quite another conclusion: The public does condemn white-collar crimes, many of them as much as or more than forms of ordinary crime. Yet the conventional wisdom persists: "One must, of course, recognize that the public is far less fearful of dying a slow death as a result of air pollution, or of a disease caused by their occupation, than they fear being robbed or burglarized."[38]

One could argue, we suppose, that the findings reviewed indicate increased awareness of such crimes on the part of the public, perhaps a shift in public knowledge; that is, the more one knows about these crimes—particularly about their harmful consequences—the more one condemns them. The problem with comparing the public with criminologists in this respect is that the latter have done very little research on white-collar crime compared with ordinary crime. At this point, it is questionable whether criminologists are better armed with scientific knowledge about white-collar crime than is the public. In this sense, the protestations of criminologists appear to be a case of "Do as I say, not as I do." Further, one could argue that increased public awareness and knowledge are products of the consumer movement, which has taken as its objective precisely this sort of public information dissemination. Yet even those studies done prior to the existence of the current consumer movement suggest that the public has hardly been indifferent to white-collar crimes. In any case, there are other plausible explanations for public awareness.

Heightened Social Consciousness. There seem to us to be at least three possible explanations for the discrepancy between the empirical evidence and criminologists' interpretation of that evidence. First, the moral condemnation displayed by criminologists is so intense, compared with that of the public, that anything less than total public outrage will be interpreted by criminologists as indifference. Such a hypothesis is clearly plausible and is, in fact, suggested by the work of many criminologists who have studied white-collar crime. Meier and Geis, for example, have recently argued that criminologists have adopted a strict "correctionalist" stance with respect to white-collar crime.[39] The works of Ross, Sutherland, Clinard, and many others seem to have been oriented more toward control and regulation than toward increasing social understanding of this form of criminality, an orientation that is often quite divergent from that which criminologists bring to the study of ordinary crime.

Whereas the ideological position of, say, Sutherland was masked by statements indicating that he viewed his contribution as "reforming criminological theory, and nothing else,"[40] criminologists have recently been less subtle. Donald Cressey, a collaborator with Sutherland and himself a contributor to the literature on white-collar crime, has noted Sutherland's strong reformist inclinations with respect to the conditions he was studying.[41] Recently, Cressey himself illustrated this tendency in testimony before the Subcommittee on Crime of the Committee of the Judiciary: "I am glad you invited me back because, among other things, my testimony in June didn't show enough *indignation.* I am quite indignant about white-collar crime, and my prepared statement this time expresses a little of that indignation. I am looking for solutions to our white-collar crime problem that involve something other than mere deterrence and defense."[42]

Such indignation, of course, may simply reflect the greater consciousness among criminologists of the nature and extent of white-collar crime. It is true that many citizens do not realize that they are being victimized by some white-collar crimes (such as price-fixing or restraint of trade) and, under those circumstances, the public cannot be expected to react to such behavior. Yet the evidence reviewed suggests that the public does react negatively to white-collar offenses in its ratings of seriousness (for example, according to the consequences of the act and, perhaps, the characteristics of the actor). The public does not lump all white-collar crimes into the same cognitive category, as criminologists often do. Of course, there is nothing inherently improper about being indignant about white-collar crime as long as this attitude does not interfere with the scientific task.

What People Say and What They Do. Another possible explanation for the divergence of the empirical literature on public perceptions of seriousness and criminologists' interpretations of that literature is that criminologists are acutely aware that what people say is often different from what they do.[43] Finding that people regard some white-collar crimes as being as serious as some ordinary crimes may tell us nothing, for example, about the willingness of those same people to support legislation dealing more harshly with white-collar criminals; or to convict white-collar crimes from a safe distance, yet to accord white-collar criminals differential treatment at the hands of the law (or tolerate such treatment).

One reason for this apparent discrepancy between attitudes and actions may be

that the kinds of contingencies that often mitigate criminal penalties are more prevalent among white-collar criminals (for example, no prior record or no record of violent acts, steady employment, ability to meet other social and financial obligations,
few prospects for recidivism, and so forth). Moreover, one must consider that most
white-collar criminals are not tried by juries (neither are most ordinary criminals, of
course), but are dealt with by officials of regulatory agencies; the public seldom has
an opportunity to influence directly either the nature of the penalties for these crimes
or the application of those penalties that do exist with respect to specific violations.

Even if citizens were deeply sincere in condemning white-collar crimes, it could
be that their outrage has no collective expression in the form of citizen groups and
lobbyists. However, the tremendous increase in consumer advocacy suggests precisely the opposite—that citizens are not only concerned, but are finding political
means to express their opinions,[44] even if some recent evidence has indicated that
public opinion does not directly affect either the content or the administration of the
criminal law.[45]

Flaws in the Research. A third explanation for criminologists' interpretations of
research concerning public reactions to white-collar crimes concerns various
methodological defects of the research that render it implausible. One could ask
whether respondents are willing to respond to an investigator's questions about the
seriousness of white-collar crimes in a manner that is socially acceptable (at least to
the investigator), and still regard white-collar crimes as less serious, on the whole,
than ordinary crime. Moreover, it is true that some studies of public perceptions of
crime seriousness have used nonrandom samples of citizens making generalizations
of results questionable.[46]

Rossi et al. used a representative sample of Baltimore, Maryland, respondents
(who may be atypical of citizens elsewhere);[47] several other problems also limit
complete confidence in their findings:

1. The method of rating crime seriousness is that suggested by Wolfgang and
Sellin, which presents respondents with a crime description and asks them to rate
the crime from 1 to 9 (with 9 representing the most serious).[48] This technique has
proved troublesome in some respects;[49] consequently, investigators increasingly
have used a technique known as *magnitude estimation,* whereby an arbitrary value
(such as 100) is assigned to a criterion crime, and respondents are asked to rate other
offenses as more or less serious (by assigning higher or lower values) than the criterion offense.[50] This method greatly increases the potential range of expressed seriousness, thus permitting more variability in seriousness ratings; moreover, one can
most easily make comparative judgments about the relative positions of offenses,
since this technique produces a ratio scale.

2. The number of persons who rated each of Rossi's crimes varied from crime to
crime (each crime was rated by at least 100 persons). Thus, although the total sample may have been representative of Baltimore citizens, the representativeness of the
sample for *each* crime varied. Rossi and his colleagues do not provide sufficient
information about the sample for each crime to satisfy this nagging doubt.

3. Perhaps because of these difficulties, there appears to be a serious problem of response reliability in Rossi's findings. One crime, assault with a gun on a stranger, was inadvertently repeated in the survey. The first time it was asked, this crime was rated as eighteenth most serious out of the 140 total offenses. The second time it was asked, this crime fell to twenty-fourth position.[51] Moreover, the standard deviation for this offense does not appear much larger than those for other offenses in the study, suggesting that reliability may be a problem for other offenses as well. In a subsequent publication, Berk and Rossi[52] address some of these issues, but not in a completely satisfying manner. Moreover, the subsequent discussion raises yet another question, that of the possibility of low test-retest reliability.

This third problem of Rossi's study was evident in the replication of that study as well. Cullen, Link, and Polanzi indicate that they inadvertently repeated three offenses, and that respondents rated the same crimes differently the second time. Armed robbery of a company payroll dropped from the twenty-ninth position to the thirty-sixth; burglary of a home with stealing of a color television set was ranked both seventy-seventh and eighty-second; and assault with a gun on a spouse was ranked twenty-seventh and thirty-seventh.[53] Such differences in ranks for the same offenses cannot but raise questions about other crime rankings.

ALIENATION, SOCIAL CONFIDENCE, AND THE MORAL CLIMATE

If social scientists have misinterpreted (or do not accept) the evidence on perceived seriousness and public concern with white-collar crime, they have left virtually unexamined their own stress on damage to the moral climate and the social fabric. The complexity of these phenomena undoubtedly contributes to the lack of empirical work. Yet relevant theory and research exist, although the concepts and methods of inquiry of the body of this work have not been applied to the study of white-collar crime. In this section we discuss two areas of inquiry that seem especially relevant to our concerns, and the implications of these for the study of white-collar crime. Following this, we discuss research strategies suggested by these implications, as well as strategies designed to permit greater precision concerning seriousness ratings.

Alienation

The "alienation syndrome" is based on "root ideas concerning personal control and comprehensible social structures."[54] Some of the varieties of alienation that scholars in this tradition delineate relate directly to the lack of trust that is hypothesized to result from white-collar crime. The most obviously relevant variety of alienation in this respect is normlessness, which is prominent in both structural and social-psychological theories. Here, the focus is on standards of behavior, not on the behavior of individuals. The relationship between the two may be regarded as problematic. Structurally, the concept of normlessness refers to "the condition in which norms have lost their regulatory powers"; at the individual level, the concept "refers to expectations or commitments concerning the observance of established norms of behavior."[55] Operationally, attempts to measure normlessness suggest the concept's affinity to trust; for example, in "Dean's usage (his item: 'Everything is relative and there just aren't any definite rules to live by')[56] or McClosky and Schaar's measure of 'anomy'[57] (item: 'People were better off in the old days when everyone knew just how he was expected to act')."[58] Trust has also been a major focus of recent work on political issues[59] and on interpersonal trust.[60]

Studies of normlessness suggest, as Seeman notes, that trust is not a "unitary personality feature, a thread which binds attitudes toward oneself, toward others, and toward the polity into a generally positive (or negative) orientation."[61] A clear implication for study of the impact of white-collar crime is that interpersonal referents of trust must be differentiated from institutional ones. Institutions, broadly conceived, have been differentiated in the next body of research to be considered. Before turning to this research, however, mention should be made of other possibly relevant varieties of alienation.

Powerlessness is the dimension of alienation most extensively studied by social scientists. Defined as "a low expectancy that one's own behavior can control the occurrence of personal and social rewards,"[62] powerlessness might be expected to result from white-collar crime to the extent that trust in large corporations, government, or other seemingly responsible organizations is eroded by its occurrence. A less-studied dimension, "cultural estrangement"—"the perceived gap between the going values in a society . . . or subunit thereof . . . and the individual's own standards," again following Seeman[63]—might be expected to rise in response to the crimes of apparently responsible officials in business, government, and other offending institutions.

Another dimension of alienation delineated by Seeman and others is *meaninglessness*. "Things have become so complicated in the world today, that I really don't understand just what is going on" is an item on Middleton's alienation scale.[64] Yet another is *self-estrangement,* perhaps the alienation theme with the most-venerable history, from Marx to the present. Finally, there is *social isolation,* which, in Wilson's usage, has a strong trust component, being based on "a desire for the observance of standards of right and seemly conduct."[65] These are also important to consider as we study the impact of white-collar crime on moral climate and the social fabric.

Although alienation relates in a general way to the moral-climate and social-fabric impacts of white-collar crime, Seeman's cautions suggest the desirability of differentiating trust and other types of impact into more-specific institutional areas than has been customary in the alienation literature. Alienation scales have tended to concentrate on *interpersonal* and *political* trust, and on disaffection in these areas and in one's *work* situation,[66] areas that may or may not be affected by one's experience with and/or perceptions of white-collar crime. Both general and more specifically directed effects require investigation, as the next body of research to be examined suggests.

Confidence in Institutions

Since 1972, the General Social Survey (GSS), a project of the National Opinion Research Center (NORC), and the Louis Harris polling organization have been questioning samples of the U.S. population about their confidence in major institutions. The form of the questions occasionally varies, but the following GSS version is representative and has remained constant throughout the history of GSS (1973–1980):

> I am going to name some institutions in this country. As far as the *people running* these institutions are concerned, would you say you have a great deal of confidence, only some confidence, or hardly any confidence at all in them?

Similarly, precise descriptors have varied between GSS and Harris, with GSS being more consistent. GSS descriptors, since 1973, were the following: major companies, organized religion, education, executive branch of the federal government, organized labor, press, medicine, television, U.S. Supreme Court, scientific community, Congress, and the military. In 1975, banks and financial institutions were added. Harris descriptors have been identical in many instances, and very similar in most others. Smith has examined at length the impact of these and other differences between GSS and Harris.[67] His conclusion is that, with proper caution, the confidence items used by GSS and Harris can be used "as measures of the fluctuating state of trust in major institutions."[68] Trust was the single most frequently given definition of confidence by a randomly chosen subsample of the 1978 GSS sample. "In general . . . confidence means to the vast majority of people trusting or having faith in the leadership, while a secondary group emphasizes competence, and a much smaller group stresses the concepts of serving either the common good or personal interests."[69] These differences in definition of confidence were not found to be related to the *level* of confidence expressed by respondents.

Smith suggests that a major problem that lends instability to confidence measures relates to the abstract nature of the items. "This can make it harder for items to become crystalized and, as a result, make changes in responses easier and more common."[70] Again,

> Attitudes about confidence are not usually consciously preformulated in a summary and coherent fashion and cannot be simply or automatically plugged into *any* scale of responses. In essence, the nature of the topic of confidence in institutions probably helps to keep many attitudes uncrystalized and thus makes them more susceptible than average to changes.[71]

It thus appears that confidence is a viable concept, in the sense of being widely and correctly understood, but that the particular institutional items studied are ambiguous enough to introduce an element of instability. It is possible—and, we think, probable—that more specific institutional referents, related to more-specific events, might elicit more sharply focused, reliable, and valid responses. Such a strategy would require detailed questioning about knowledge, awareness, and concern before respondents were questioned about confidence and the meaning of the concept. Such a procedure is well worth the effort, given the potentially important relationship between the concept of confidence and white-collar criminality.

THE IMPACT OF WHITE-COLLAR CRIME: A PROPOSAL

The impact of white-collar crime may now be restated in terms of the issues discussed earlier. Impact is of three types: (1) economic harm, (2) physical harm, and (3) damage to the social fabric (including moral climate or climates). The first two of these may be identified with objective—although difficult to measure—criteria, such as monetary costs and health hazards associated with white-collar crime. Economic and physical harm depend to some extent on each other, most typically in the form of economic costs associated with physical damage (to health, as a result of disease or injury, and, in the extreme case, death). Similarly, damage to moral climate or social fabric is presumably partly a function of perceived and experienced economic and physical harm. By its very nature, however, the social fabric represents more than individual experiences or perceptions of harm, or their accumulation. Although debate about precise meanings is unlikely to be stilled by any definition—nor should it be—based on the "alienation" and "confidence" literature, the notion of *trust* appears to be crucial.

Trust is an element of both normlessness and social isolation, as they have been measured. Its relationship with other types of alienation, and the relationship of white-collar crime to each type of alienation, are problems worthy of attention. Trust has been defined as a "generalized expectancy held by another individual that the word, promise, oral or written statement of another individual or group can be relied on."[72] This suggests that an institutional or collective counterpart to interpersonal trust could be defined as the expectancy that institutions can be relied on to meet the expectations constituents have for them. To the extent that expectations are not met, constituents may become alienated from these institutions, and may reduce or eliminate participation in them. Thus the inability of political institutions to produce effective and meaningful majorities through elective procedures, such that persons can readily identify the most-effective means by which they can attempt to satisfy their political self-interest, may reduce the percentage of persons who vote in elections.[73] Similarly, the inability of economic institutions to produce high-quality goods at "fair" prices without resorting to deceptive and illegal means, may lead to economic boycotts, consumer advocacy, and suspicion of the business community.

The rest of this chapter examines problems associated with the measurement of each of the types of impact. Since our own research is focused on public assessments of white-collar crime, and on damage to the social fabric, we will concentrate on these areas and will devote less attention to the assessment of economic and physical harm. We will, however, begin our discussion with the latter.

Data Sources on White-Collar Lawbreaking

Until recently, no attention has been given to the problem of data sources on white-collar and corporate criminality, aside from the plaintive suggestions of criminologists that current sources are inadequate. Toward that end, Reiss and Biderman and their associates have surveyed public and private data sources on white-collar lawbreaking. Their state-of-the-art survey reveals a multitude of data sources, as well as problems in their interpretation. Their concluding observations, although focused on social indicators and substantive theories of white-collar crime, are no less applicable to the problem of assessing many of the consequences of such crime. They indicate that

> the current state of federal agencies' information systems makes it difficult to develop a system of social indicators on white-collar law-breaking without substantial alteration in their data collection, processing, and reporting subsystems. . . . Quite often the current data cannot provide satisfactory tests of substantive theory, yet they are nonetheless put to it. The result is a body of empirical investigations that are inappropriate and inaccurate tests of theory.[74]

This is true also with respect to assessment of the consequences of white-collar crime. Reliable and valid social indicators of white-collar crime are crucial to any such assessment. Yet, just as the Uniform Crime Reports provide little information about the consequences of even Class I crimes, social indicators of white-collar crimes are unlikely to provide complete information about its consequences. Reiss and Biderman acknowledge that seriousness often enters into measurement considerations in a variety of ways, but conclude that "it seems premature . . . to attempt any classification of illegal gains or harms" and that such problems are "worthy of systematic investigation."[75]

At present, there are substantial problems with virtually every known data source on the consequences of white-collar crimes. Records and statistics maintained by offending organizations, for example, are unlikely to have this sort of information; and, if such information is maintained, it is unlikely to be available to outsiders. Records of enforcement and sanctioning agencies are more likely to have information about the nature of the offense than about its impact (except, perhaps, in very general terms). Moreover, those who would attempt victimization surveys that concentrate on white-collar crimes would somehow have to compensate for the fact that victims are often unaware of their victimization, a situation that is very different from that for street crime. Yet until such work is attempted, discussions of the physical and economic impact of white-collar crime are doomed to be shrouded in controversy and speculation.

Public Assessment

Public assessment of the impact of crime has most often been studied by means of seriousness ratings. Contingencies of perceived seriousness have seldom been studied directly. Rather, they have been inferred from variations in ratings of crimes associated with, for example, age, sex, and other characteristics of the victim and the offender, and the relationship between the victim and the offender. We propose to study these relationships directly by inquiring about the influence on perceived seriousness of dimensions of harm, such as those suggested by Reiss and Biderman.[76] We propose, further, to study the effect on perceived seriousness of the *degree of harm* associated with crimes, that is, the economic, physical, and "community" (social fabric and moral climate) criteria, as noted earlier.

Earlier research suggests strongly that physical harm is perceived as more serious than is economic harm, for both white-collar and ordinary crime. However, the range of such variation, and the influence of victim-offender relationships, has hardly been studied at all. This is particularly true with respect to white-collar crime in which such relationships may be critical, as between employers and employees; between producers of products and consumers of those products; or between the general public or segments thereof and those who offend against them, such as polluters of the environment or corrupters of common trust.[77]

Little systematic research of this sort has been undertaken—none, to the best of our knowledge, concerning white-collar crime. Sykes and West report exploratory research concerning "how people perceive various crimes and how the elements composing these images influence their evaluations."[78] Fifty respondents from randomly selected households in Charlottesville, Virginia, were interviewed concerning their images of ten crimes (none, unfortunately, white-collar crimes) selected from the Rossi et al. study.[79] Asked "what factors would, in their judgment, make each crime more or less serious," respondents volunteered "at least eight major factors at work":

First, as might be expected, the degree of bodily hurt and the degree of economic damage or loss a crime caused were both cited. In addition, however, many respondents also pointed to the degree of psychological or emotional damage caused by a crime; the degree to which a crime posed a threat to persons other than the victim or its *potential* for harm; the presence or absence of intent—that is, the extent to which the crime was "voluntary"; what the offender expected to achieve by the crime, which can be called *purpose;* why the offender had that purpose, which can be called *motive;* and finally the presence or absence of something that can be called *fair play.* Judgments concerning the seriousness of crimes are apparently based not simply on some concept of financial or physical injury, but represent instead a complex set of evaluations in which the character or nature of the criminal is no less important than the consequences for the victim. [Emphasis in original.]

These findings are suggestive, but hardly (as Sykes and West readily acknowledge) definitive, again particularly with respect to white-collar crimes in which both perpetrators and victims often are organizational, or at least are far more numerous than is the case for the common crimes studied. Such findings, in any case, call even more strongly for the inclusion of possibly relevant contingencies in determining public perceptions of white-collar crimes.

Measuring Social Impact: Seriousness and Harm

No social impact of white-collar crime involves all the complexities of the phenomena so labeled, as these are understood and reacted to by citizens, both individually and in a variety of collectivities. Experienced and perceived economic and physical harm, however measured, are both related to social impact, but in largely unknown ways. As we have seen, studies of perceived seriousness yield impressive empirical regularities with respect to the relative seriousness of particular crimes and combinations of victim and offender characteristics. Yet little is known of the precise bases for perceived seriousness, that is, the characteristics of crimes that are associated with assigned seriousness ratings. We know that, *in general,* crimes resulting in physical harm are rated as more serious than are crimes resulting in economic harm, and that the degree of each type of harm is associated with perceived seriousness. Yet this knowledge is quite limiting and is unlikely to generate any new insights about public perceptions of crime seriousness or, more grandly, public perceptions of trust and confidence in social institutions.

This insight, however, does not take us very far unless we take other sources of complexity into account. Two such factors that are worthy of attention include personal experience with crime, and the relationship between white-collar crime and values. Instances of white-collar crimes may result in trivial individual harm (for example, persons victimized by a price-fixing conspiracy may be charged only one cent more for a product as a result of that crime); yet those small individual harms can be aggregated into losses that are indeed substantial.[80] Given the literature reviewed earlier, individual perceptions of crime seriousness may rely less on *personal experience* with crime—such as being victimized directly and substantially—than on other bases. Moreover, values such as those placed on private ownership of property and enterprise (and its uses), as well as other fundamental values,[81] seem likely to be related in more-complex ways to white-collar than to ordinary crime.

A second aspect of measuring social impact concerns various dimensions of trust, drawing on the literature of alienation and on confidence in major social institutions. Here, the focus is on the social fabric. The rich literature on alienation and institutional confidence unfortunately has little reference to white-collar crime. Substantive findings in both literature and research on political efficacy are of considerable interest and relevance, however. It is known, for example, that better-educated persons and those of high socioeconomic status generally have lower scores on powerlessness and normlessness scales, and higher scores on scales of political efficacy. These same persons seem more likely to be knowledgeable about white-collar crime both in general and with respect to particular instances that have achieved notoriety, such as the Thalidomide and Love Canal disasters, and price-fixing by major electrical companies. Nisbet, among others, has pointed to the great difference between public understanding and reaction to widely publicized events such as the accident at Three Mile Island, and reaction to less-publicized but perhaps even more-serious conditions, such as contamination of waterways by chemical dumps.[82] It will be important, therefore, to study carefully a variety of segments of the population, and *general* perceptions of economic and physical harm caused by white-collar violations, as well as knowledge of and reactions to particular events.

In general, powerlessness and normlessness are positively related to one another, and both are negatively related to political efficacy. But the relationship of these to the phenomena of white-collar crime is not known. The politically and economically powerful are *less* likely to suffer personally devastating consequences of white-collar crime—and, by definition, are more likely to be engaged in such crime than are the less powerful. Awareness of the seriousness of violations that threaten the environment—air, water, and esthetic quality, for example—may make them *more* concerned than others who are less aware and less knowledgeable. However, beliefs in political efficacy—confidence in their ability to control events—may lead them to be less alienated from the system. Because white-collar violations so often involve corporate enterprise and its relationship with government, political philosophies become involved in attitudes toward such phenomena. This is evident in lobbying efforts related to legislation that affects corporate behavior as well as enforcement. A prime example is Occupational Safety and Health legislation (OSHA), about which labor and business groups hold strongly opposing views. At issue are activities to be defined as in violation of law, as well as policies and practices of law enforcement and how these are to be reported and, therefore, understood by interested groups.

Political and economic issues involved in the assessment of the impact of white-collar crime are illustrated by recent polls concerning confidence in business and government regulation. Defenders of private enterprise have been quick to point out that declining confidence in corporate business has not been paralleled by beliefs that government regulation of business should be increased. If the polls are to be believed, in fact, quite the opposite has occurred. Majorities of those questioned express the opinion that government regulation of business should be decreased. The polls also show, however, that confidence in government has eroded in recent years. Lack of support for government regulation may, therefore, reflect a lack of trust in government rather than, as some have suggested, a lack of faith in the efficacy of government regulation or in the system in general.

These interpretations also are clouded by finding that confidence in business varies a good deal by broad product categories. Confidence in the drug industry, for example, has been found to be relatively low compared with that in most other industries.[83] Although it is possible that the drug industry is tainted by association in the minds of some with illegal drugs, such as heroin, it is also true that the industry has been involved in some of the more-notorious cases of widespread physical harm, such as the use of thalidomide and diethyl stilbestrol (DES), for which large court penalties have been assessed. Clearly, there is a need for careful assessment of public knowledge and opinions about the behavior of specific industries, and perhaps of specific companies.

In addition to targeting specific categories of white-collar offenders, it is necessary to target segments of the population according to their status, or potential status, as victims. This can be done both by identifying "known groups" of victims and by specifying groups in the general population with differing probabilities of victimization. In each case, there is reason to believe that *classes* of victims should be distinguished. It has been suggested that individuals may be victimized by virtue of their status as employees, consumers, or members of the general public; that is, white-collar violators may victimize persons in the workplace, as consumers of products, or as members of the general public by virtue of common dependence on air, water, and soil. To this list can be added the possibility of victimization as coowners, as in the case of stockholders of companies who are defrauded or are victims of embezzlement.

In spite of all this, however, the precise relation of victimization to perceptions of crime seriousness and/or trust and confidence in institutions is troublesome. Thus, although personal experience may be less important than previously thought, one's relation to a *class* of potential or real victims may be very important in determining such attitudes.

These considerations all point to a research design that is sensitive to different populations; that employs multiple indicators of concepts such as social trust, perceived seriousness of different crimes, and value positions, and that attempts to examine the consequences of white-collar and corporate criminality within the larger context of "community." For some time, sociologists have maintained that the most-devastating impact of white-collar crime lies in the nature of social relationships that may be altered as a result of declining trust and confidence in institutions, which provide the setting for most interaction. Up to now, there has been little empirical work to generate a more-refined statement of this impact. This is precisely what we call for here. At this point there is ample reason to believe that white-collar and corporate criminality may have consequences that are far more harmful to the nature of communities than those of ordinary crime. Hence, the sociological agenda seems self-evident.

SUMMARY AND CONCLUSIONS

The impact of white-collar crime in economic and physical terms has occupied most of the attention of criminologists, although the estimates of such harms are imprecise. Increased precision might be achieved with more attention to the notion of "minimally acceptable level of risk," devising standards of such risks, and applying these standards across a broad number of behavioral areas. It seems likely that until such criteria can be developed, estimates of the extent to which white-collar crime constitutes socially injurious conduct will continue to be speculative.

The impact of white-collar crime on the social fabric of the community is perhaps the most-serious harm discussed by sociologists; but no one has yet devised a method by which such an impact can be determined empirically beyond very general statements of "social harm." We propose that (1) the impact of white-collar crime on the social fabric is perhaps the most important, long-term harm caused by such offenses; (2) sociologists need to devote a good deal more conceptual and theoretical attention to the nature of the social fabric, as well as to begin to explore such concepts empirically; and (3) a reasonable starting point for such work would lie in the notions of alienation, confidence in major institutions, and collective trust. The research that has been devoted to these areas so far has not recognized their possible relationship with white-collar crime, although the implications of these relationships pose intriguing and seemingly fruitful areas of inquiry.

The research program envisaged here is one that studies directly the nature of this impact, with attention to individual perceptions of the seriousness of white-collar and corporate criminality, one's relationship with major institutions, and the extent to which those institutions (and subunits within them) are able to generate trust and confidence in their performance. Until such questions are posed directly, discussions of the consequences of white-collar crime will suffer from the narrow focus that presently characterizes them.

Notes

1. David Ermann and Richard Lundman, eds., *Corporate and Government Deviance.* New York: Oxford University Press, 1978; Miriam Saxon, *White-Collar Crime: The Problem and the Federal Response.* Washington, DC: Congressional Research Service, Library of Congress Report No. 80-84 EPW, 1980; Marshall B. Clinard, *Illegal Corporate Behavior.* National Institute of Law Enforcement and Criminal Justice. Washington, DC: U.S. Government Printing Office, 1979.
2. Gilbert Geis and Robert F. Meier, *White-Collar Crime: Offenses in Business, Politics and the Professions.* New York: The Free Press, 1977.
3. Albert J. Reiss, Jr., and Albert D. Biderman, *Data Sources on White-Collar Law-Breaking.* Washington, DC: U.S. Department of Justice, 1980, pp. 51–52.
4. Chamber of Commerce, *A Handbook on White Collar Crime: Everyone's Problem, Everyone's Loss.* Washington, DC: Chamber of Commerce of the United States, 1974, p. 5.

5. Congressman John Conyers, *Testimony.* Subcommittee on Crime, *White Collar Crime.* Hearings, 21 June, 12 July, 1 December, 1978. U.S. House of Representatives, Committee on the Judiciary. Washington, DC, 1978, p. 93.

6. Richard Sparks, *Testimony.* Subcommittee on Crime, *op. cit.,* p. 172. Congressman Peter W. Rodino, Jr., *Testimony.* Subcommittee on Crime, *op. cit.,* p. 146.

7. Rodino, *op. cit.,* p. 138.

8. Ramsey Clark, *Testimony.* Subcommittee on Crime, *op. cit.,* p. 143.

9. Reiss and Biderman, *op. cit.*

10. Clinard, *op. cit.*

11. Laura Shill Schrager and James F. Short, Jr., "Toward a Sociology of Organizational Crime," *Social Problems,* 25 (1978):407–419.

12. Gilbert Geis and John Monahan, "The Social Ecology of Violence." In Thomas Lickona, ed., *Moral Development and Behavior.* New York: Holt, Rinehart & Winston, 1976, pp. 342–356.

13. *Lewiston (Idaho) Morning Tribune,* April 22, 1980, p. 4A.

14. Laura Shill Schrager and James F. Short, "How Serious a Crime? Perceptions of Organizational and Common Crimes." In Gilbert Geis and Ezra Stotland, eds., *White-Collar Crime: Theory and Research.* Beverly Hills: Sage, 1980, pp. 14–31.

15. Gilbert Geis, "Criminal Penalties for Corporate Criminals," *Criminal Law Bulletin,* 8 (1972):279–292.

16. Saxon, *op. cit.,* p. 12.

17. Gilbert Geis, "White Collar Crime: It Pays," *Washington Post,* September 16, (1977), p. 11.

18. Albert K. Cohen, *Deviance and Control.* Englewood Cliffs, NJ: Prentice-Hall, 1966, pp. 4–5.

19. President's Commission on Law Enforcement and Administration of Justice, *The Challenge of Crime in a Free Society.* Washington, DC. Government Printing Office, 1967, p. 48.

20. Edward A. Ross, *Sin and Society.* Boston: Houghton Mifflin, 1907, p. 46.

21. Edwin H. Sutherland, *White Collar Crime.* New York: Dryden, 1949, p. 224.

22. Marshall B. Clinard, *The Black Market.* New York: Holt, Rinehart & Winston, 1952, p. 355; Vilhelm Aubert, "White-Collar Crime and Social Structure," *American Journal of Sociology,* 58 (1952):263–271.

23. Edwin H. Sutherland, "Is 'White-Collar Crime' Crime?" *American Sociological Review,* 10 (1949), 270.

24. Sanford H. Kadish, "Some Observations on the Use of Criminal Sanctions in Enforcing Economic Regulations," *University of Chicago Law Review,* 30 (1963):423–449.

25. Donald J. Newman, "Public Attitudes toward a Form of White-Collar Crime," *Social Problems,* 4 (1953):228–232.

26. John P. Reed and Robin S. Reed, "Doctor, Lawyer, Indian Chief: Old Rhymes and New on White-Collar Crime," *International Journal of Criminology and Penology,* 3 (1975):279–293.

27. Solomon Rettig and Benjamin Passamanick, "Changes in Moral Values over Three Decades," *Social Problems,* 6 (1959): 320–328.
28. Don C. Gibbons, "Crime and Punishment: A Study in Social Aptitudes," *Social Forces,* 47 (1969): 391–397.
29. *Time,* June 6, 1969, p. 26.
30. Clinard, *op. cit.,* pp. 89–114.
31. Frank E. Hartung, "Common and Discrete Values," *Journal of Social Psychology,* 38 (1953):3–22.
32. Joint Commission on Correctional Manpower and Training, *The Public Looks at Crime and Corrections,* Washington, DC: U.S. Government Printing Office, 1968.
33. Peter H. Rossi, Emily Waite, Christine E. Bose, and Richard E. Berk, "The Seriousness of Crimes: Normative Structure and Individual Differences," *American Sociological Review,* 39 (1974):224–237.
34. Francis T. Cullen, Bruce G. Link, and Craig W. Polanzi, "The Seriousness of Crime Revisited: Have Attitudes toward White-Collar Crime Changed?" Unpublished paper, Department of Sociology, Western Illinois University, Macomb, 1980.
35. Darnell Hawkins, "Perceptions of Punishment for Crime," *Deviant Behavior,* 1 (1980):193–215.
36. Marvin E. Wolfgang, "Crime and Punishment," *New York Times,* March 2, 1980, p. 4E.
37. Schrager and Short, 1980, *op. cit.*
38. Clinard, 1979, *op. cit.*
39. Robert F. Meier and Gilbert Geis, "The White Collar Offender." In Hans Toch, ed., *Psychology of Crime and Criminal Justice.* New York: Holt Rinehart & Winston, 1979, pp. 427–443.
40. Sutherland, *op. cit.,* p. 1.
41. Donald R. Cressey, "Restraint of Trade, Recidivism, and Delinquent Neighborhoods." In James F. Short, Jr., ed., *Delinquency, Crime, and Society.* Chicago: University of Chicago Press, 1976, pp. 113–114.
42. Donald R. Cressey, *Testimony.* Subcommittee on Crime, *op. cit.,* pp. 113–114.
43. Irwin Deutscher, *What We Say/What We Do: Sentimental Acts.* Glenview, IL: Scott Foresman, 1973.
44. Gilbert Geis, "Avocational Crime." In Daniel Glaser, ed., *Handbook of Criminology.* Chicago: Rand-McNally, 1974.
45. Richard E. Berk, H. Brackman, and S. Lesser, *A Measure of Justice.* New York: Academic Press, 1977.
46. Newman, *op. cit.;* Reed and Reed, *op. cit.;* Hawkins, *op. cit.*
47. Rossi et al., *op. cit.*
48. Marvin E. Wolfgang and Throsten Sellin, *The Measurement of Delinquency.* New York: Wiley, 1964.
49. G. N. G. Rose, "Concerning the Measurement of Delinquency," *British Journal of Criminology,* 14 (1966):256–263.

50. Maynard L. Erickson and Jack P. Gibbs, "On the Perceived Severity of Legal Penalties," *Journal of Criminal Law and Criminology,* 70 (1979):102–116; see also Wolfgang, *op. cit.*

51. Rossi et al., *op. cit.,* p. 229.

52. Richard E. Berk, and Peter H. Rossi, *Prison Reform and State Elites.* Cambridge, MA: Ballinger, 1977.

53. Cullen et al., *op. cit.,* p. 16.

54. Melvin Seeman, "Alienation Studies," *Annual Review of Sociology,* 1 (1975):91.

55. *Ibid.,* p. 102.

56. Dwight G. Dean, "Alienation: Its Meaning and Measurement." *American Sociological Review,* 26 (1961):753–768.

57. Herbert McClosky and John H. Schaar, "Psychological Dimensions of Anomy." *American Sociological Review,* 30 (1965):14–40.

58. Seeman, *op. cit.,* p. 103.

59. Ada W. Finifter, "Dimensions of Political Alienation." *American Political Science Review,* 64 (1970):389–410; Philip E. Converse, "Changes in the American Electorate." In Angus Campbell and Philip E. Converse, eds., *The Human Meaning of Social Change.* New York: Russell Sage Foundation, 1972, pp. 263–337.

60. Julian B. Rotter, "Interpersonal Trust, Trustworthiness, and Gullibility." *American Psychologist,* 35 (1980):1–7.

61. Seeman, *op. cit.,* p. 104.

62. Melvin Seeman, "Alienation and Engagement." In Angus Campbell and Philip E. Converse, eds., *The Human Meaning of Social Change.* New York: Russell Sage Foundation, 1972, p. 473.

63. *Ibid.,* p. 473.

64. Russell Middleton, "Alienation, Race and Education." *American Sociological Review,* 22 (1963):670–677.

65. James Q. Wilson, "The Urban Unease." *The Public Interest,* 12 (1968):27.

66. John P. Robinson and Phillip R. Shaver, *Measures of Social Psychological Attitudes.* Ann Arbor, MI: Institute for Social Research, 1973. See chapters 4 and 5.

67. Tom Smith, "Can We Have Confidence in Confidence? Revisited." In Dennis F. Johnston, ed., *The Measurement of Subjective Phenomenon.* Washington, DC: Government Printing Office, 1979.

68. *Ibid.,* p. 93.

69. *Ibid.,* p. 76.

70. *Ibid.,* p. 87.

71. *Ibid.,* p. 88.

72. Rotter, *op. cit.,* p. 1.

73. Morris Janowitz, *The Last Half-Century.* Chicago: University of Chicago Press, 1978.

74. Reiss and Biderman, *op. cit.*

75. *Ibid.*, p. 697.
76. *Ibid.*
77. Schrager and Short, 1978 and 1980, *op. cit.*
78. Gresham Sykes and Stephen R. West, "The Seriousness of Crime: A Study of Popular Morality." Paper presented at the annual meeting of the Eastern Sociological Society, 1978, p. 3.
79. Rossi et al., *op. cit.*
80. Reiss and Biderman, *op. cit.*
81. Milton Rokeach, ed., *Understanding Human Values.* New York: The Free Press, 1979.
82. Robert Nisbet, "The Rape of Progress." *Public Opinion* (June–July 1979):2–6.
83. Seymour Martin Lipset and William Schneider, "The Public View of Regulation." *Public Opinion* (January–February 1979):8.

6

The Portrayal of Business Malfeasance in the Elite and General Media

Donna Randall

Research by Clinard and Yeager revealed that publicity about law violations is one of the most feared sanctions that can be imposed on a corporation.[1] A tarnished corporate image may have a variety of consequences, such as a loss of present or future customers, stockholders, and employees or a public outcry for more stringent governmental regulation.[2]

From the research available, it is clear that the media play a particularly important role in the dissemination of information about business crime to the general public. It is relatively difficult for the general public to learn about forms of business malfeasance from any other source. The general public, the 70–90 percent of the population whose knowledge of events is predicated neither on substantive knowledge of events nor firsthand experience,[3] typically has little or no personal or direct exposure with business misconduct.[4] The public is prone to accept media views because there are no competing sources of information and no personal stake in resisting an appeal or disbelieving information.[5] Indeed, in the area of crime and crime control, the media possess a "near monopoly" over social knowledge.[6]

In providing information to the public about incidents of business malfeasance which have occurred, media organizations do not function as "mirrors" and crime coverage does not closely follow crime statistics.[7] Rather, the media assume roles of producers, even creators, of social reality by actively selecting and publicizing a limited range of events.[8] According to the theory of agenda setting, through their selectivity the media provide an order of importance and structure to the world they portray.[9] The priorities established by the media become to some degree the priorities adopted by the public and public officials.[10]

The possibility that different media may be setting different agendas and may be portraying different realities of business impropriety has not yet been explored. Past research has consistently shown that the same media are not relied upon across all

Reprinted from *Social Science Quarterly,* 68 (1987), pp. 281–293.

segments of society.[11] For instance, the elite, the 20–25 percent of the population who are usually better educated and in the higher economic strata,[12] tend to use the print media more and television less than the rest of the population.[13] A study by Weiss of mass media use by influential Americans revealed that for law and order questions the print media were most frequently mentioned as the most valuable source of information.[14] Newsmagazines are one type of print media, in particular, heavily relied upon by the elite,[15] possibly because newsmagazines seek to provide a less sensationalistic, more complete, coverage of issues.

On the other hand, national network news is most heavily relied upon by the general public.[16] Television enters almost every home in the nation, with nearly half of the U.S. population, approximately 100 million people, watching it on a typical evening.[17] People who rely on TV news as their primary source of information tend to have less education, to be in lower-status occupations, and to have lower household incomes than readers of newsmagazines.[18] For individuals in the lower socio-economic strata, TV is perceived as much more appealing than the print media due to the entertainment value TV provides.[19] Further, television was viewed by a wide margin of the general public as providing intelligent, complete, and impartial news coverage.[20]

Thus, through selective use of media sources, different audiences may be developing different views of business malfeasance. It is the purpose of this paper to describe the images of business malfeasance set forth by elite and general public media and to explore the implications of any divergence.

HYPOTHESES

Through their reliance upon TV as a primary source of information, the general public is likely to receive a quite different picture of business crime than the elite who rely more heavily upon newsmagazines. Box maintained that the general public is given a distorted view of business crime in that the mass media are too cautious in their coverage of business criminality, leaving the public uninformed about the truly pervasive, injurious nature of such offenses.[21] For instance, previous research revealed that TV networks "shrink" coverage of corporate illegalities substantially by presenting information on a limited range of crimes.[22]

Thus, one might hypothesize:

HYPOTHESIS 1: The elite media will devote a larger proportion of news coverage to business crime than will the general public media.

To operationalize the hypothesis, the proportion of news coverage in the general public media can be measured by comparing total seconds devoted to business crime on network news to total seconds available during the newscast. For elite media coverage, total column inches devoted to business crime in newsmagazines can be compared to total column inches available in the newsmagazine (excluding all advertisements), following Budd[23] and Meyer.[24]

The alleged inadequate coverage of business crime in the general public media can be partially explained by certain structural features of TV news coverage: complex stories are simplified and standardized because of time limitations, background information must be repeated for every story (because the media audience may not have been present for previously broadcast stories), thus consuming additional time; and TV media feel constrained to tell stories interestingly, an additional source of oversimplification, stereotypes, and emphasis on sensational human interest features.[25] Due to these constraints, network news may rely on stereotypes rather than presenting more complex information, may omit stories requiring lengthy description or explanation, and thus may highlight only a limited number of different types of business malfeasance. Hence,

HYPOTHESIS 2: The elite media will cover a greater variety of business crimes than will the general public media.

Edelhertz[26] and Clinard et al.[27] have provided a detailed categorization scheme of business crimes. This scheme can be used to identify and compare the variety of business crimes portrayed in each medium.

In the interest of simplicity, network news may tend to focus on the early steps in criminal justice processing (e.g., capture) as the latter steps (e.g., appeal) can be long, drawn out, complex affairs. The print media, not subject to the same constraints, are structurally able to provide greater coverage of the often complex latter steps of the adjudication process and to convey any necessary background information. It follows:

HYPOTHESIS 3: The elite media will focus more on the latter stages of the processing of business offenders, and the general public media will focus more on the earlier stages in the processing of business offenders.

Following Sherizen,[28] a number of steps in criminal justice processing can be identified in each newscast/broadcast: discovery, suspect follow-up, capture, arrest, arraignment, charge, plea, indictment, trial, verdict, sentence, appeal, commitment, and post-commitment follow-up. For purposes of analysis, the first four steps can be grouped into the investigative stage; the next five into the trial stage; and the last five into the sentencing stage.

Finally, the two media sources may emphasize different types of business malfeasance. Business malfeasance can be aggregated into two broad categories: white-collar and corporate crime. White-collar crimes can be defined as those business offenses committed by individuals acting on an ad hoc basis or within their occupation with the primary intent of benefiting themselves. Examples of white-collar crime include home improvement fraud, insurance fraud, stock fraud, computer fraud, commercial bribery, and embezzlement. The category of corporate crime consists of those business crimes typically committed by often unidentifiable corporate employees with the primary intent of benefiting the corporation. Examples of corporate crime include administrative, environmental, financial, labor, manufacturing, and unfair trade practices.

Researchers note that individuals are not accustomed to viewing corporations as capable of criminality because crime is more typically associated with natural rather than juristic persons.[29] Individual business offenders, not corporate entities, are stereotyped as offenders. Hence, in the interest of simplicity, TV news may be more likely to portray white-collar offenses, typically committed by specific and easily identifiable individuals. Less susceptible to stereotyping, the elite media would be expected to cover relatively more corporate crimes, committed by actors deeply imbedded within the corporate structure. It follows:

HYPOTHESIS 4a: White-collar crime coverage will be portrayed with greater proportionate coverage and greater variety of offense in the general public media than in the elite media.

HYPOTHESIS 4b: Corporate crime coverage will be portrayed with greater proportionate coverage and greater variety of offense in the elite media than in the general public media.

To operationalize the hypotheses, a categorization scheme developed by Edelhertz can be used to code white-collar crimes into 19 categories (18 specific categories and 1 "other" category).[30] Following Clinard et al., corporate crimes can be coded into 57 categories (56 specific categories and 1 "other" category).[31] In the present study, organized crime and political crimes (e.g., Watergate) are not considered business crimes and are excluded from analysis.

DATA AND METHODS

Network and newsmagazine coverage of business crime over a decade was analyzed using content analysis.[32] News coverage of the three major networks—CBS, NBC, and ABC—was content analyzed using the *Vanderbilt News Index and Abstracts.* The elite media selected for study were *U.S. News & World Report, Time,* and *Newsweek* because previous research revealed substantial newsmagazine readership by America's influential leaders.[33]

To explore media coverage in the identified media sources, a decade of news coverage was analyzed. The longitudinal nature of the study was a significant improvement over past research in the area as the large majority of designs for research on media effects have been single cross-sectional studies even though designs using time order provide more powerful evidence for media effects.[34]

Thirteen weeks were randomly selected from every year from January 1974 to December 1984. The coverage for each week, in all 15 weekday newscasts (five newscasts per week per network) and in the weekly newsmagazines, were content analyzed. Selection of a week as the sampling period allowed direct comparison between a week's broadcasts over national networks and coverage in weekly newsmagazines. The sampling procedure resulted in a random sample of 143 weeks over the entire ten-year period including 2,145 nightly network news broadcasts (715 nights of coverage per network) and 429 issues of newsmagazines (143 weekly magazines per publisher).

Two graduate research assistants coded all the offenses. The principal investigator trained the coders and provided each with a detailed codebook and list of decision rules. During the training period each research assistant coded a random selection of articles and newscasts and the coding was compared with that of the principal investigator. The training continued until consensus was reached with the principal investigator's coding scheme. At the completion of the coding, the principal investigator randomly rechecked the coding to ensure consistency with the codebook and decision rules.

For each instance of media coverage of business malfeasance, data were collected on the year, month, day, and day of the week of coverage; the network or newsmagazine, total minutes and seconds devoted on network broadcasts, and total column inches devoted in newsmagazine articles; the stage of criminal justice system processing that was covered; and the specific type of business crime being discussed. Pearson correlation coefficients, with one-tailed tests of significance, were used to determine the relationships between pairs of interval-level variables.

FINDINGS

Between 1974 and 1984, a total of 1,615 business crime stories were reported with 1,336 stories on network news and 279 in newsmagazines. Each week network news covered an average of 9.34 stories per week on business crime, whereas newsmagazines carried an average of only 1.95 stories per week.

Proportion of Coverage. The first hypothesis set forth that newsmagazines would devote a greater proportion of available space to business crime than the networks. This hypothesis was not supported. Neither type of medium devoted extensive space to business crime. However, network news, on the average, devoted twice the proportionate space of newsmagazines to business crime.

Over time a moderate decline can be detected in space devoted to business crime in newsmagazines, but not in network news. The correlation between space devoted to business malfeasance on network news and in newsmagazines each year is weak.

Variety of Coverage. The second hypothesis predicted that newsmagazines would present a greater variety of business crime than would network news. This hypothesis was not supported. Table 6.1 reflects that network news presented stories on 49 different types of business crime, whereas newsmagazines presented stories on only 38 types. The variety of coverage appearing on network news and in newsmagazines was fairly consistent over time and, again, the number of different types

Table 6.1
VARIETY OF COVERAGE ON TELEVISION NEWS AND IN
NEWSMAGAZINES BETWEEN 1974 AND 1984

Different Types of Crime Identified	Television	Newsmagazines
Corporate Crime	33	26
White-Collar Crime	16	12
Total Offenses	49	38
Ratio of Corporate Crime to White-Collar Crime Categories	2.06:1	2.17:1

of business crimes presented on network news was unrelated to the number of different types of business crimes portrayed in newsmagazines each year.

Stages of Criminal Justice Processing. The third hypothesis predicted that network news would cover more extensively the early investigative stage of criminal justice processing and less extensively the latter sentencing stage of processing than would newsmagazines. Contrary to expectation, newsmagazines covered more extensively the early investigative stage and less extensively the latter sentencing stage. Moreover, out of 14 possible steps, television news covered all 14 steps, while newsmagazines covered only 10 out of the possible 14. Hence, the third hypothesis was also rejected (Table 6.2).

Unlike the proportion of coverage and variety of coverage, coverage of the criminal justice stages on network news and in newsmagazines was highly correlated over time. It appears that each year newsmagazines and network news tend to mirror the same steps in the criminal justice process.

White-Collar and Corporate Crime Differences. Finally, it was hypothesized that there would be greater proportionate coverage and greater variety of white-collar crimes on network news, whereas there would be greater proportionate coverage and greater variety of corporate crime coverage in newsmagazines. Each type of medium does appear to have a specific focus, but not as predicted.

Corporate crime was given more space on network news than in newsmagazines by a ratio of 1.8 to 1, while white-collar crime had greater proportionate coverage in newsmagazines than on network news by a ratio of 3 to 1. Again, a pattern similar to that observed for total business crime coverage was detected, with the proportion of space devoted to corporate crime in network news and newsmagazines very lowly correlated over time, and proportionate space devoted to white-collar crime stories in network news and newsmagazines even slightly negatively correlated over time.

As predicted, there was greater variety of white-collar crime coverage on network news, but, contrary to prediction, there also was greater variety of corporate crime coverage on network news (Table 6.1). The variety of corporate crime on television news and in newsmagazines was not significantly correlated, nor was variety of white-collar crime on television news and in newsmagazines.

Table 6.2
STAGES OF CRIMINAL JUSTICE PROCESSING

	Television			Newsmagazines		
	Corporate Crime (%)	White Collar Crime (%)	Total (%)	Corporate Crime (%)	White-collar Crime (%)	Total (%)
Investigative stage						
1. Discovery	137	19	156	35	17	52
	(13)	(8)	(12)	(27)	(15)	(21)
2. Follow-up	332	48	380	27	31	58
	(31)	(20)	(29)	(21)	(27)	(24)
3. Capture	1	2	3	—	—	—
	(1)	(1)	(1)			
4. Arrest	10	6	16	—	1	1
	(1)	(3)	(1)		(1)	(1)
	480	75	555	62	49	111
	(45)	(32)	(42)	(48)	(43)	(46)
Trial stage						
5. Arraignment	3	4	7	1	—	1
	(1)	(1)	(1)	(1)		(1)
6. Charge	141	15	156	14	7	21
	(13)	(6)	(12)	(11)	(6)	(9)
7. Plea	9	22	31	1	—	1
	(1)	(9)	(2)	(1)		(1)
8. Indictment	34	33	67	—	6	6
	(3)	(14)	(5)		(5)	(2)
9. Trial	56	31	87	15	29	44
	(5)	(13)	(7)	(12)	(26)	(18)
	243	105	348	31	42	73
	(23)	(45)	(27)	(24)	(37)	(31)
Sentencing stage						
10. Verdict	30	2	32	12	5	17
	(3)	(1)	(2)	(9)	(4)	(7)
11. Sentence	298	38	336	21	8	29
	(28)	(16)	(26)	(16)	(7)	(12)
12. Appeal	1	2	3	—	—	—
	(1)	(1)	(1)			
13. Commitment	3	2	5	—	2	2
	(1)	(1)	(1)		(1)	(2)
14. Post-sentence	17	11	28	3	7	10
	(2)	(5)	(2)	(2)	(6)	(4)
	349	55	404	36	22	58
	(33)	(23)	(31)	(28)	(19)	(24)
TOTAL	1,072	235	1,307	129	113	242

NOTE: Not included are 29 network editorials and 37 newsmagazine editorials on the processing of offenders. Cell entries represent the number of stories, with percentages given in parentheses.

DISCUSSION AND IMPLICATIONS

Overall, it appears that two very different images of business malfeasance are being portrayed, side by side, in the national media. Network television and news-magazines do present roughly the same stages in the processing of business offend-ers, but generally fail to agree on the proportion of available space to be devoted to

white-collar and corporate crime stories and on the variety of offenses to be presented. It is clear that the different media are not reflecting a commonly shared
image of the world, but instead appear to be creating and producing very different
pictures of business malfeasance.

The most surprising finding in the present study concerns the image of business
malfeasance set forth by the different media. A wider variety of coverage and a
greater focus on the latter stages of criminal justice processing of business crime is
occurring on TV news rather than in newsmagazines as hypothesized. It appears
that the general public audience is getting much more information about business
malfeasance and the elite audience much less from the media than commonly
believed. Moreover, when the general public sees business malfeasance, it typically
sees corporations, not individuals, as the perpetrators.

This unexpected focus of television news could be in part due to time and audience preference constraints. Due to the necessity of making stories brief but entertaining, television news may find the topic of corporate crime more appealing than
newsmagazines. To gain and retain the public's attention, television news may need
to present a wide variety of white-collar and corporate crimes and highlight the sentencing of business offenders. Moreover, just as big business misbehavior has been
determined to be more newsworthy than smaller business misbehavior,[35] big business misbehavior might also be perceived by the networks as more newsworthy and
entertaining than individual misbehavior.

For their part, newsmagazines may find white-collar and corporate crime stories
as somewhat threatening for their elite audiences and thus give the stories less proportionate coverage over time (whereas network news has not significantly reduced
coverage over time) and fail to follow through on the processing of business offenders as much as network news does. Furthermore, not faced with the same audience
preferences as network news, the elite media may not be under as much pressure to
be entertaining in the presentation of business malfeasance. They may therefore feel
little need to emphasize the more sensational corporate crimes over white-collar
crimes, to present a wide variety of white-collar and corporate offenses, and to cover
a wide variety of steps in the processing of corporate and white-collar offenders.

The focus of general public media coverage on corporate crime can have important policy implications. The priorities of the public may very well depend upon patterns of media exposure. Over time, constant exposure of the general public to
instances of business malfeasance may lead to feelings of antipathy toward business
as an institution. As Robinson has observed, "because the networks are too credible
to be dismissed in their message, . . . viewers respond to the content by growing
more cynical, more frustrated, more despairing; they become increasingly less
enamored of their social and political institutions."[36]

Cognizant of the policy implications of media coverage of business illegality,
corporations have been concerned over their public image. However. media coverage of business crime may not be as much a threat to business as commonly
assumed. Relatively little attention is directed to business offenses. It is important to
note that a maximum of only 5 percent of available news time was devoted to busi-

ness crime and 4.4 percent, specifically, to corporate crime over the decade. Coverage of business illegality thus tends to be largely "buried" among many other news items.

Further, in practice, the coverage of business crime in the media may have even less impact on readers than the figures would indicate. Television news watchers only selectively watch TV and retain little of what they see.[37] The views of the elite are also more important as opinion leaders. For, as Paletz and Entman claimed, "the elite substantially influence, if they do not establish, public opinion."[38]

Finally, when business crimes were portrayed, network news typically portrayed the offenses as being processed through the full spectrum of the criminal justice system. In the end, the general public is presented with an image of business offenders as getting "their due." Thus, while the agenda set in the general public media clearly appears to be more damaging to corporate images, it appears likely that business may only suffer from public disdain but not greater governmental control in the future.

Notes

1. Marshall B. Clinard and Peter C. Yeager, *Corporate Crime.* New York: Free Press, 1980.
2. Jeff Blyskal and Marie Blyskal, "Making the Best of Bad News," *Washington Journalism Review,* 7 (December 1985):51–55; Comment, "Notes on Corporate Crime," *Yale Law Journal,* 71 (1961):280–306.
3. Herbert Gans, *Deciding What's News.* New York: Pantheon, 1979.
4. Steven Box, *Power, Crime, and Mystification.* New York: Methuen, 1984.
5. Denis McQuail, "The Influence and Effects of Mass Media." In Doris Graber, ed., *Media Power in Politics.* Washington, DC: Congressional Quarterly Press, 1984, pp. 36–53; Doris A. Graber, *Media Power in Politics.* Washington, DC: Congressional Quarterly Press, 1984.
6. Stuart Hall, Chas Chritner, Tony Jefferson, John Clarke, and Brian Roberts, "The Social Problem of News: Mugging in the Media." In Stanley Cohen and Jock Young, eds., *The Manufacture of News: Deviance, Social Problems and the Mass Media.* Beverly Hills: Sage, 1981, pp. 335–367.
7. Bob Roshier, "The Selection of Crime News by the Press." In Stanley Cohen and Jock Young, eds., *The Manufacture of News: Deviance, Social Problems and the Mass Media.* Beverly Hills: Sage, 1981, pp. 28–39; E. T. Jones, "The Press as Metropolitan Monitor," *Public Opinion Quarterly,* 40 (1976):239–249; Emilio Viano, *Victims and Society.* Washington, DC: Visage, 1976.
8. Gans, *op. cit.*
9. McQuail, *op. cit.*
10. Shanto Iyengar and Donald Kinder, "Psychological Accounts of Agenda-

Setting." In Sidney Kraus and Richard M. Perloff, eds., *Mass Media and Political Thought.* Beverly Hills: Sage, 1985, pp. 117–140.

11. Gans, *op. cit.*

12. Charles D. Elder and Roger W. Cobb, *The Political Uses of Symbols.* New York: Longman, 1983.

13. Graber, *op. cit.*

14. Carol Weiss, "What America's Leaders Read," *Public Opinion Quarterly,* 38 (1974):1–22.

15. Gans, *op. cit.*

16. Guy Cumberbatch and A. Beardsworth, "Criminals, Victims, and Mass Communications." In Emilio Viano, ed., *Victims and Society.* Washington, DC: Visage, 1976, pp. 72–90.

17. Graber, *op. cit.*

18. Gans, *op. cit.;* Lawrence Lichty, "Video vs. Print," *Wilson Quarterly,* 38 (1974):49–57.

19. Graber, *op. cit.*

20. Robert T. Bower, *Television and the Public.* New York: Holt, Rinehart, & Winston, 1973; Michael Robinson, "Public Affairs Television and the Growth of Political Malaise: The Case of 'The Selling of the Pentagon,'" *American Political Science Review,* 70 (1976):409–432.

21. Box, *op. cit.*

22. J. R. Dominick, "Business Coverage in Network Newscasts." In Doris A. Graber, ed., *Media Power in Politics.* Washington, DC.: Congressional Quarterly Press, 1984, pp. 101–108.

23. Richard W. Budd, "Attention Score: A Device for Measuring News 'Play,'" *Journalism Quarterly,* 41 (1964):259–262.

24. J. C. Meyer, "Newspaper Reporting of Crime and Justice: Analysis of an Assumed Difference," *Journalism Quarterly,* 52 (1975):731–734.

25. Graber, *op. cit.;* R. L. Bartley, "The News Business and Business and Business News." In Elie Abel, ed., *What's News: The Media in American Society.* San Francisco: Institute for Contemporary Studies, 1981, pp. 87–210.

26. Herbert Edelhertz, *The Nature, Impact and Prosecution of White-Collar Crime.* Washington, DC: United States Government Printing Office, 1970.

27. Marshall B. Clinard, Peter Yeager, Jeanne Brissette, David Petrashek, and Elizabeth Harries, *Illegal Corporate Behavior.* Washington, DC: United States Government Printing Office, 1979.

28. Sanford Sherizen, "Social Creation of Crime News: All the News Fitted to Print." In Charles Winick, ed., *Deviance and Mass Media.* Beverly Hills: Sage, 1978, pp. 203–224.

29. Sandra S. Evans and Richard J. Lundman, "Newspaper Coverage of Corporate Price-Fixing," *Criminology* 21 (1983):529–541.

30. Edelhertz, *op. cit.*

31. Clinard et al., *op. cit.*

32. Joseph R. Dominick, "Crime and Law Enforcement in the Mass Media." In

Charles Winick, ed., *Deviance and Mass Media.* Beverly Hills: Sage, 1978, pp. 105–128.

33. David G. Weaver, Cleveland Wilhoit, Sharon Dunwoody, and Paul Hagner, "Sensational News Coverage: Agenda-Setting for Mass and Elite Media in the United States." In *Senate Communications with the Public,* 94th Congress, 2d session. Washington, DC: United States Government Printing Office, 1977, pp. 41–62; Weiss, *op. cit.*

34. Lee B. Becker, Maxwell E. McCombs, and J. M. McLeod, "The Development of Political Cognitions." In Steven H. Chaffee, ed., *Political Communication: Issues and Strategies for Research.* Beverly Hills: Sage, 1975, pp. 21–64.

35. Frederick Randall and Michael Duerr, *Private Enterprise Looks at Its Image.* New York: Conference Board, 1971.

36. Robinson, *op. cit.,* p. 426.

37. Mark Levy, "The Audience Experience with Television News," *Journalism Monographs,* 55 (1978):10–19.

38. David Paletz and Robert Entman, *Media, Power, and Politics.* New York: The Free Press, 1981, p. 184.

7

White Collar Crime

John Braithwaite

The number of scholars who have worked on white collar crime has been modest, and the impact of white collar crime research on mainstream sociological theory unimportant. But we will see that white collar crime research marks a rare case of sociological scholarship having a substantial impact on public policy and public opinion. Even more unusual, this impact is largely attributable to the work of one great sociologist—Edwin H. Sutherland.

WHITE COLLAR CRIME RESEARCH BEFORE SUTHERLAND

There were great scholars on whose shoulders Sutherland could stand. The Dutch Marxist, Willem Bonger, in his *Criminality and Economic Conditions* (1916), was the first to develop a theory of crime which incorporated both "crime in the streets" and "crime in the suites." Bonger's contention was that capitalism "has developed egoism at the expense of altruism." Bonger argued that a criminal attitude is engendered by the conditions of misery inflicted on the working class under capitalism, and that a similar criminal attitude arises among the bourgeoisie from the avarice fostered when capitalism thrives.[1]

Influential criminological theory between Bonger and Sutherland continued to focus on class as the critical variable, but it was a truncated focus concerned with explaining why the poor seemed to commit more crime than the rest of us. Bonger's insight—that to assume poverty causes crime is to neglect the widespread nature of ruling class crime—was largely ignored until Sutherland revived it.

The important American antecedents in the early part of the century were the sociologist E. A. Ross (1907)[2] and the muckrakers—e.g. Tarbell;[3] Steffens;[4] Norris;[5] Sinclair.[6] In journalistic exposés and fictionalized accounts, these writers laid bare the occupational safety abuses of mining magnates, the flagrant disregard for consumer

Reprinted from *Annual Review of Sociology*, 11 (1985):1–21.

health of the meat packing industry, the corporate bribery of legislatures, and many other abuses. The muckrakers were responsible for some of the important statutes, like the US Federal Food, Drug, and Cosmetic Act of 1906, which criminalized many forms of corporate misconduct that Ross had been forced to label as "criminaloid." Sutherland's mission was to turn muckraking into sociology.

SUTHERLAND

White collar crime became part of the English language when Edwin Sutherland gave his Presidential Address to the American Sociological Society in 1939.[7] Sutherland's talk, "White-Collar Criminality," scorned traditional theories of crime which blamed poverty, broken homes, and disturbed personalities. He noted that many of the law breakers in business were far from poor, from happy family backgrounds, and all too mentally sound. After ten years of further research, Sutherland published *White Collar Crime*.[8] The book was a devastating documentation of crimes perpetrated by America's 70 largest private companies and 15 public utility corporations. His publisher, Dryden, insisted that all references to the companies by name be deleted for fear of libel suits. It was another 34 years before the uncut version was published.[9]

Sutherland defined white collar crime as "a crime committed by a person of respectability and high social status in the course of his occupation."[10] The definition has its problems. The concept of "respectability" defies precision of use. The requirement that a crime cannot be a white collar crime unless perpetrated by a person of "high social status" is an unfortunate mixing of definition and explanation, especially when Sutherland used the widespread nature of white collar crime to refute class-based theories of criminality.

These deficiencies have rendered white collar crime an impotent construct for theory building in sociology. No influential theory of white collar crime has developed, let alone an attempt to link such work to wider sociological theory. Sutherland's theory of differential association in *White Collar Crime* was a general theory of all crime, one whose generality borders on a platitudinous restatement of social learning theory.[11]

As Swigert and Farrell point out,[12] while there have been those who dabbled with differential association,[13] anomie theory,[14] labelling theory,[15] and social psychological and personality theories,[16] theoretical progress began only in the late 1970s when the individualistic theorizing spawned by the Sutherland tradition was rejected in favor of applying organization theory paradigms to the phenomenon. Ironically, it was lawyers who led this theoretical reorientation rather than sociologists.[17] The reorientation became possible only when ties to the Sutherland definition were cut in favor of a focus on the narrower domains of organizational or corporate crime.

The only justification for locating contemporary research in the white collar crime construct is phenomenological. The concept is shared and understood by ordinary folk as more meaningful than occupational crime, corporate deviance, commercial offenses, economic crime or any competing concept. Moreover, as Geis and Goff point out, Sutherland's Americanism soon became "crime en col blanc" in France, "criminalità in colletti bianchi" in Italy and "weisse-kragen-kriminalität" in Germany.[18]

Most researchers have dealt with the problem of definition by simply studying violations of particular laws (tax, environmental, antitrust, consumer protection, fraud). Patterns and processes of violations of such laws are all phenomena worthy of study in their own right, yet it is a pity that the phenomena do not comfortably sit as building blocks for theorizing around a more all-encompassing concept. In the conclusion to this review, I argue that we should cling to Sutherland's overarching definition, but then partition the domain into major types of white collar crime which do have theoretical potential.

Sutherland's operationalizing of the new concept also came under attack from lawyers. Sutherland was content to consider illegal behavior as white collar crime if it were punishable, even if not punished. and if the potential penalties for infringement were civil rather than provided for in a criminal code.[19] Tappan led a tradition insisting on proof beyond reasonable doubt in a criminal court before anything could be called a crime.[20] Sutherland's counter is today accepted by most sociologists—that to do this would be to sacrifice science to a class-biased administration of criminal justice that neglects the punishment of white collar offenders, often giving them the benefit of civil penalties for offenses that in law could equally be punished criminally. Sutherland was right in principle, but in practice he and his disciples often counted actions that were not violations of law (e.g. recalls of hazardous consumer products) as instances of white collar crime.

THE LEGACY OF SUTHERLAND

Two young scholars who later became preeminent in criminology quickly followed in Sutherland's footsteps—Marshall Clinard and Donald Cressey. Clinard produced a book on price control violations during World War II,[21] and Cressey wrote *Other People's Money,* a study of embezzlement.[22] There followed a twenty year hiatus during which a few diehards, notably Gilbert Geis and Herbert Edelhertz, kept the flickering flame of white collar crime research alight.[23] As a result, white collar crime continued to penetrate criminological textbooks and sociological teaching on crime.

When Watergate and then the foreign bribery scandal took America and the world by storm in the mid 1970s, a generation of students had been educated in the vocabulary of white collar crime. Public interest in the subject overflowed; American research dollars were for the first time unleashed in significant quantities. By the late 1970s, an international community of white collar crime scholars had been established.

STYLES OF CONTEMPORARY RESEARCH

The Search for Generalizations

Who engages in white collar crime and why? An unimpressive tradition of positivist criminology has developed around these two questions. The only generalizations that can reasonably be made about the characteristics of white collar criminals are banal. White collar criminals are not likely to be juveniles and are not likely to be female or poor. These generalizations are virtually true by definition, since juveniles, women, and the poor do not generally occupy the occupational roles required for white collar offending.

The only answers to "why" questions that can be made safely are also of no explanatory power. As Shichor suggests, "The most obvious explanation—that greed is the major causal factor of white collar crime—is very probable but it is too general."[24] The same can be said of Sutherland's differential-association explanation, that "criminal behavior is learned in association with those who define such criminal behavior favorably and in isolation from those who define it unfavorably."[25]

What of more tantalizing questions about which cultures, which periods of history, what types of organizations are associated with high rates of white collar crime? There is a tradition of comparative politics which persuasively concludes that as nations become more economically developed, corruption of public officials decreases.[26] These scholars interpret the historical decline of corruption in countries such as Britain in essentially Weberian terms—as legitimacy shifts from loyalty to family and tribe to authority for a national administrative order, new national elites mobilize public disapproval against the determination of administrative priorities by bribes.

But few other credible claims to this kind of generalization can be made, largely because of the elusiveness of adequate data. The nature of white collar crime—its complexity, the power of its perpetrators—means that only an unrepresentative minority of offenses is detected and officially recorded. Not only is the problem of nonreporting less severe with regard to common offenses, but there are alternative measures—self-reports and victim surveys. The latter are ruled out because victims of white collar crime are rarely aware that they have been so victimized, the former because company directors do not respond to questionnaires about their criminal activities. Reiss and Biderman in their encyclopedic study for the US Justice Department have demonstrated the enormous difficulties of assessing the level of white collar crime in one country at one point in time.[27]

Questions as to which types of organizations generate greater white collar criminality are somewhat more manageable and consequently have attracted significant empirical work. I am aware only of one data set in the world that would be adequate to address such questions and this is a very narrow one. Approximately 140,000 health and safety violations are recorded each year against American coal mining companies. Systematic bias is less than in other data sets because the US Mine

Safety and Health Act requires four random inspections of each coal mine per year and, unlike most regulatory statutes, it requires the inspector to cite every violation observed. Since the source of data is semirandom patrol by the agency rather than nonrandom reporting to the agency, and since the policy of nondiscretionary citation, while frequently ignored in practice, at least substantially reduces selective bias by inspectors, the US Mine Safety and Health Administration data are the closest we can approach to an indication of offending rates for organizations of different types. While there has been work on which kinds of companies have lower accident rates,[28] no criminologist has yet explored the characteristics of companies with high violation rates and the settings and other variables that seem to bear on such rates.

Use of other, more doubtful data sets has failed to yield a crop of generalizations about criminogenic organizations. It has been common for reviews, on the basis of limited studies by Lane,[29] and Staw and Szwajkowski,[30] to assert that firms in financial difficulty are more likely to offend than profitable ones. However, the two studies on the most substantial samples both found no association between company profitability and corporate crime; Clinard found a slight negative association between firm liquidity and corporate crime.[31] Review of the literature on industry concentration, company size, and similar economic variables yields highly conflicting findings.[32] Moreover, there is some evidence suggesting that regulatory stereotypes of large firms as law-abiding leads to less punitive treatment of them in comparison to smaller companies.[33] Contrary to the perceptions of many casual readers of the white collar crime literature, we may ultimately find that Aristotle was right all along, that "The greatest crimes are caused by excess and not by necessity."[34]

It may seem odd to argue that quantitative comparisons of offending rates for different companies are the kinds of research least needed when the two most influential studies of white collar crime—those of Sutherland and Clinard and Yeager—were precisely of this kind.[35] There are three answers to this. First, the quantification of white collar crimes in both works was important in demonstrating to a disbelieving world that the biggest and best companies are widely involved in criminality; it was not, however, very important for correlational analysis. Second, the major intellectual contributions of both works concerned their syntheses of theory and qualitative data. Third, even if the quantitative aspect of their work did have substantial intellectual as opposed to polemical significance, it is doubtful, given the problems outlined above, that future scholars will be able to advance much upon it.

It is remarkable that a reviewer can say so little about what quantitative and motivational studies of white collar crime have established. Ideas that at first seemed fruitful, such as Cressey's explanation of embezzlement in terms of "nonsharable financial problems,"[36] have failed to attract a body of literature to support them.[37] American sociologists have dominated the first forty years of white collar crime research, and their continued attachment to "who" and "why" questions has slowed progress. "In their obsession with the motivational issues surrounding why people do what they do, criminological theorists have tended to neglect the equally (if not more) important issue of *how* they are able to do what they do."[38]

There may be some further progress with motivational research. To make strides, however, this work would have to stop asking "Why do people commit white collar crime?" and begin to ask, "Given the great rewards and low risks of detection, why do so many business people adopt the 'economically irrational' course of obeying the law?"

Modus Operandi Studies

A number of recent studies, both scholarly and journalistic, of how people and organizations offend have enhanced our understanding of white collar crime.[39] Levi's study of long-firm fraud showed the low likelihood of legal control when frauds cross several national boundaries; it also showed the trade-offs enforcement agencies must make between stopping fraud to protect creditors and waiting until there is evidence for a conviction.[40] The modus operandi literature repeatedly demonstrates international law evasion strategies that utilize Swiss banks, tax havens, pollution havens, or international dumping of banned products. This points up the limitations of both research and control strategies confined to behavior within one set of national boundaries.[41]

The modus operandi literature demonstrates the existence of consistent pressures to pass blame for white collar crime downward in the class structure. It is not difficult for powerful actors to structure their affairs so that all of the pressures to break the law surface at a lower level of their own organization or in a subordinate organization. Examples include company presidents appointing "vice-presidents responsible for going to jail," respectable companies engaging contractors to do illegal dirty work such as disposing of toxic wastes or producing fraudulent scientific data about the safety of a product, or hiring agents to pay bribes.[42]

Combined with the recurrent demonstration of the capacity of organizations to manufacture an impression of confused accountability for wrongdoing, the scapegoating literature has underpinned a tradition of legal scholarship defending the need for a capacity to impose criminal liability on corporations.[43]

Vaughan's study of Medicaid fraud by the Revco drug store chain illustrated how complexity in a regulatory system can increase risks of noncompliance. It also showed how organizations are less easily controlled when governments are dependent on them for a service, more easily controlled when the organization is dependent on the government.[44] Reisman's work on corporate bribery showed that while bribes are deviations from a "myth system," they may be deemed appropriate under the "operational code"—the private and unacknowledged set of rules that selectively tolerates bribery as an ordinary and necessary form of business. Reisman warns that unless we realize that not only business people but also Presidents of the United States subscribe to both the "myth system" and the "operational code," we will never understand the social realities of bribery.[45] Studies of the Ford Pinto homicide prosecution have illuminated how intra- and inter-organizational struggles occur between those who wish to put human lives into a cost-benefit calculus and those who wish to treat human life as sacrosanct.[46]

The literature documents criminality on such a scale among public organizations[47]—from corruption of police departments,[48] to massive illegal mail intercep-
tion programs by the CIA,[49] to the US army intentionally exposing soldiers to fallout
from nuclear explosions[50]—that the profit motive must be questioned as the
supreme cause of white collar crime. All organizations, capitalist or socialist, experience pressure to resort to illegitimate means of goal attainment when legitimate
means are blocked.[51] As Gross points out: "Some organizations seek profits, others
seek survival, still others seek to fulfill government-imposed quotas, others seek to
service a body of professionals who run them, some seek to win wars, and some
seek to serve a clientele. Whatever the goals might be, it is the emphasis on them
that creates the trouble."[52]

Sherman's study of corruption in police departments concluded that a scandal
might cause corruption to be submerged while media coverage of the scandal runs
its course, but that the corruption resurfaces unless the adverse publicity produces
internal organizational countermeasures, such as a proactive internal affairs branch
which uses anticorruption techniques verging on entrapment.[53]

The modus operandi literature merges with a literature on what organizations do
when their misconduct reaches public attention. This research has significant implications. Demonstrating the importance of adverse publicity as a control mechanism
raises the question of regulatory strategies that mobilize adverse publicity and of
publicity orders by courts that are used as sanctions against white collar offenders.
Empirical findings that newspapers often do not take up stories of white collar crime
imply reliance on formal court-ordered rather than informal publicity.[54] And Sherman's finding that white collar crime just bobs up again once the heat is off unless
internal controls are introduced suggests consideration of management restructuring
orders to guarantee that the impact of reforms is enduring.[55]

On the other hand, Fisse and Braithwaite showed with their 17 case studies that
white collar crime scandals often produced substantial preventive reform prior to or
even in the absence of conviction.[56] Waldman's studies of the impact of antitrust
prosecution showed that some of the most dramatic changes in the competitiveness
of markets occurred where the government failed to secure convictions. When companies had the threat of divestiture or prosecution hanging over their heads throughout the many years during which an antitrust case incubates, they generally
improved their antitrust compliance. To be able to present themselves more favorably to the court they may, for example, pull down barriers to entry, cease retaliating
(as by predatory pricing) against competing firms, or even become industry leaders
in the development of antitrust compliance codes,[57] as IBM did during its years of
antitrust litigation.[58] They may even actively recruit a competitor into the industry.
Thus, du Pont, acquitted in 1956 for monopolizing the cellophane market, during
the nine-year court battle recruited the Olin corporation to enter the industry as a
competing cellophane manufacturer. Substantial white collar crime control often
occurs in cases prosecutors lose.

Similarly, qualitative empirical studies of regulatory agencies (to be reviewed in
the next section) show that most of the compliance with the law achieved by such

agencies is without recourse to criminal conviction. Qualitative research of a variety of kinds therefore suggests the need for a theory of organizational crime control without conviction—a theory which incorporates the significance of the reaction of white collar offenders to informal publicity, prosecutorial threats and negotiation with inspectors. This would involve a major shift from the current preoccupation with deterrence and incapacitation following conviction.

Control Agency Studies

Until the 1970s, sociologists had a simplistic conception of business regulatory agencies as "captured" law enforcement bodies, the members of which were responsible for the inequality of a justice system which turned a blind eye to the crimes of the powerful while bludgeoning those of the poor. The only systematic empirical investigations of the "capture" thesis lend little support to this conception.[59]

A proliferation of studies since 1970 tend to show that from the top administrator to the junior inspector, most officers of regulatory agencies never saw themselves as law enforcers.[60] Beyond the control agency studies mentioned in this review, Hawkins has cited an additional 35 which sustain the conclusion that regulatory agencies that deal with pollution, occupational health and safety, consumer protection, housing, discrimination, wage and price control, forestry, meat inspection, and agriculture all tend to conciliatory compliance styles rather than a punitive law enforcement approach.[61] Regulators are mystified by the sociologists' charge that their role creates structural inequality in the criminal justice system because they had never thought of themselves as part of the criminal justice system. Some of them have a tougher, more adversarial stance toward business than their critics in criminology textbooks. It is just that often they reject prosecution as the best way of getting tough.

Perhaps the most powerful of the early control agency studies was Schrag's account of what happened when he took over the enforcement division of the New York City Department of Consumer Affairs. When Schrag began in the job he adopted a prosecutorial stance. In response to a variety of frustrations, however, especially the use of delaying tactics by company lawyers, a direct action model was eventually substituted for the judicial model. Nonlitigious methods of achieving restitution, deterrence, and incapacitation were increasingly used. These included threats and use of adverse publicity, revocation of license, writing directly to consumers to warn them of company practices, and exerting pressure on reputable financial institutions and suppliers to withdraw support for the targeted company.[62]

The studies of business regulatory agencies cited above showed that regulatory officials view their primary objective as achieving substantive regulatory goals (safer factories, cleaner air, stronger competition); the fact that they were creating an inequitable criminal justice system by rejecting prosecution as the way to achieve those goals hardly occurred to them. Reiss dubbed the predominant regulatory strategy revealed in the literature as "compliance" rather than "deterrence" law enforcement systems: "The principal objective of a compliance law enforcement system is to secure conformity of law without the necessity to define, process, and penalize violations."[63] Optimism about the efficacy of compliance systems should be tempered by McCormick's conclusions concerning nonenforcement of US antitrust law. He argues that the lack of a continuously identifiable body of criminal violations symbolizing and reinforcing reaction has led to a "neutralization of indignation," which in turn has permitted some legitimation of illegality.[64]

If the regulators are right and the public best protected when regulators deal with most business crime by negotiation, bluff, adverse publicity, and other informal sanctions, then what of sociological theories which assume that nonprosecution reflects the unwillingness of the state to confront ruling class interests? What of jurisprudential theories that insist it is right to deploy the criminal law equally against rich and poor? Will it still be right if it is shown that the poor are left worse off in more dangerous factories, marketplaces, and environments when compliance strategies are rejected in favor of less effective retributive strategies? Should resources for policy evaluation research now be directed away from the effectiveness of law reform, of various court-ordered sanctions and remedies, in favor of evaluating different regulatory negotiation strategies?[65]

It will be some time before we are ready to hazard answers to these policy questions. The point here is that the qualitative studies of control agencies have prompted a fundamental rethinking of theory and policy implied by the questions. I suspect that some of the sociologists enraptured with the proposition that regulatory agencies opt for compliance law enforcement systems because this is the only way to achieve their mission are too quick to explain away capture. Nor is there really any evidence to support the reverse-capture views of scholars such as James Q. Wilson who see regulatory agencies as captured by "the new class."[66] As I have argued elsewhere, no matter what view one has of the efficacy of compliance law enforcement systems, that efficacy might be enhanced when it is complemented by criminal punishment.[67]

We need more studies of what regulatory agencies actually do. In addition to the intensive single agency studies that have been so important in beginning to reshape our thinking about crimes of the powerful, we need some more adventurous studies that paint a broad canvas, comparing a large number of agencies. Cross-cultural studies are also needed, given what we already know about how much regional cultures can affect the enforcement strategy of a single agency.[68] Kelman's research, which showed a more negotiated style of occupational health and safety enforcement in Sweden, compared with a more punitive style in the United States, is a promising beginning to this type of work.[69]

Another dimension coming into focus from the control agency studies is the importance of private justice systems. As Reiss points out,[70] we know more about the way the Securities and Exchange Commission controls illegal behavior in marketing securities[71] than we know about the role of the New York Stock Exchange in detecting such behavior. It is becoming clear that many regulatory agencies attempt

to maximize their impact for the tax-payer's dollar by effectively delegating important areas of enforcement to private justice systems, some of which may be puny in
the extreme, others of which may invoke draconian sanctions such as withdrawing a
doctor's right to practice with minimum due process protections. A few scholars are
now beginning to grapple with the implications of the staggering growth of private
law enforcement systems in modern societies.[72]

THE WIDER IMPLICATIONS OF
WHITE COLLAR CRIME RESEARCH

The literature on white collar crime has contributed significantly to our understanding of how enormous class inequalities are maintained even in welfare states with
nominally progressive taxation systems. The billions of dollars transferred annually
from the poor to the rich by antitrust offenses[73] and tax evasion[74] are particularly
important. For example, some data suggest that illegal returns to monopoly power
may account for perhaps one-quarter of the total value of corporate stock held by the
four million top wealth holders in the United States.[75]

The study of white collar crime probably also contributed a little to rendering
some reality to the sociology of law. There was a time when it was common for
Marxists to argue that "law is a tool of the ruling class."[76] The reified class interest
analysis that one sees in the earlier work of scholars like Quinney has been demol-
ished by both liberal and Marxist scholars who grant some autonomy to social control agencies.[77] In modern capitalist societies there are many more statutes which
criminalize the behavior of corporations (antipollution laws, occupational health and
safety laws, antitrust laws, laws to enforce compliance with standards for everything
from elevators to cleaning animal cages in laboratories) than there are laws which
criminalize the behavior of the poor. Moreover, under many of the business statutes,
mens rea is not required for proof of guilt; self-incrimination can be forced on
defendants; search and seizure without warrant are provided for; and due process
protections are generally weak.[78]

None of this is to deny the existence of profound class bias in the way laws are
often administered. The common disjunction between tough laws against business
and weak enforcement of them indicates a need to separate the instrumental and
symbolic effects of legislation.[79] Edelman is undoubtedly correct that unorganized
and diffuse publics tend to receive symbolic rewards, while organized professional
ones reap tangible rewards.[80] Equally, it is true that traditionally unorganized interests—consumers, women, environmentalists, workers—are becoming organized.
Even if the failure of regulatory agencies to mobilize available laws against business
can be justified on grounds that this is not the most effective way of safeguarding the
public, the fact of unequal enforcement of the law in ruling class interests cannot be
escaped. Note also Hagan's findings that the justice system gives greater assistance
to corporate than to individual victims of crime.[81]

The fundamental class bias in the criminal justice system is that white collar offenders, if they get to court at all, are punished less severely than traditional criminals.[82] Notwithstanding that, two major studies have now found that higher status individuals who are white collar offenders do not tend to be treated more leniently by US courts than lower status white collar offenders.[83] Indeed, the study by Wheeler et al. surprisingly found a positive correlation between the socioeconomic status of white collar offenders and the probability of imprisonment.[84]

The white collar crime literature does have important implications for jurisprudence. Three elements of the literature come together to establish this relevance. The first of these is the literature demonstrating the massive numbers of unpunished white collar offenders in the community and the enormous damage to persons and property caused by their offending.[85] Second is the literature arguing that protection of the public from white collar crime is better achieved by compliance law enforcement systems than by deterrence law enforcement systems. The third is the literature showing that ordinary citizens have had remarkably punitive attitudes recently toward white collar crime.[86]

This third stream of the literature is most interesting because it refutes a major plank of Sutherland's original work—that white collar crime is allowed to flourish because of permissive community attitudes toward it. Sutherland of course probably was correct in saying that community attitudes were tolerant in his time. Public interest crusades against white collar crime that drew inspiration from Sutherland possibly were responsible for changing the very community tolerance toward the phenomenon that Sutherland lamented. What this literature shows, in summary, is that the community perceives many forms of white collar crime as more serious and deserving of longer prison sentences than most forms of common crime. There are exceptions to this pattern. Tax offenses and false advertising in most studies are not viewed as serious crimes, and most types of individual homicide are perceived as more serious than all types of white collar crime. Nevertheless, white collar crimes that cause severe harm to persons are generally rated as more serious than all other types of crime and even some types of individual homicide. Meier and Short have shown that not only do citizens view white collar crime as serious, they rate being victimized by white collar offenses as more likely than being victimized by other life hazards, including common crime.[87]

The importance of these three elements of the literature for jurisprudence is that they show the political, fiscal, and moral impossibility of fidelity to a pure retributive philosophy of punishment. Whether the deserved punishment is determined by community attitudes toward the offense or by objective harm, retributivists, because of this literature, must judge white collar crimes to deserve heavy punishment. Add this fact together with the literature that concludes there are more white collar offenses and offenders in the community than common criminals, and it follows that equitable application of a retributive philosophy would see more white collar offenders in prison than common criminals. Given the minuscule numbers of prison spaces currently occupied by white collar criminals and the enormous costs of incarceration, this would be a fiscal and political impossibility. Moreover, if the devotees of compliance law enforcement systems for business crimes are even partially right, a policy of consistent administration of just deserts to convictable offenders would undermine compliance and jeopardize more lives and cost millions of dollars. Equal retributive justice would have been achieved over the bodies of victims of those white collar crimes that cause physical harm (the very white collar crimes toward which the community is most punitive).

Thus, the white collar crime literature implies that if equitable retributivist philosophies are to be relevant to moral choices in the real world, they must be tempered with utilitarian considerations. including those of crime control and fiscal restraint. Retributivists can reject this, as von Hirsch has done, by denying these conclusions from the white collar crime literature—by denying that white collar crime is subjectively and objectively more serious than common crime, by disputing that white collar crime is more pervasive than common crime, by scoffing at suggestions that consistent, proportional punishment could be less effective in preventing crime than compliance or mixed compliance/deterrence law enforcement systems.[88] How these differing streams of white collar crime literature develop should have important implications for those who seek a philosophy of punishment that can be equitably implemented in the real world, rather than in some possible or impossible world.

THE WHITE COLLAR CRIME LITERATURE AND PUBLIC POLICY

The first two sentences of the 1949 edition of *White Collar Crime* read, "This book is a study of the theory of criminal behavior. It is an attempt to reform the theory of criminal behavior, not to reform anything else."[89] Sutherland's book did not reform the theory of criminal behavior; its significance in the way it influenced people like Ralph Nader was more profound than its impact on any criminological theorist.

It has already been speculated that there may have been an element of self-defeating prophecy in Sutherland's observation about "the unorganized resentment of the public toward white collar crimes."[90] Without the impact Sutherland has had on criminological and legal education, one wonders whether governments would be under pressure in the Western democracies to "do something" about at least the most visible kinds of white collar crime. In some measure, governments have responded. Pointing to examples like Abscam, some would even argue they have overreacted.[91] Under the Carter administration, the crusade against white collar crime, with high profile endorsement by the President, reached the point where the FBI to some degree downgraded efforts to solve offenses such as bank robbery in order to concentrate more intensively on fraud, corruption, and other white collar crime.[92] Much of this, though not all, has changed under the Reagan administration. Coffee recently pointed out that 17% of the criminal cases handled by the US Attorney's office in 1981 were classified by the Attorney as "White Collar Crimes." Another 8 percent were classified either as "Government Regulatory Offenses" or "Official Corruption."[93] This of course means that considerably more than 25 percent of federal prosecutorial resources were involved because white collar cases are more complex than average. Admittedly, the bulk of these numbers consist of small-time white collar criminals. So numerous have been the corruption convictions of New York politicians that one study found members of the state legislature during the 1970s to have four times the probability of a criminal record as other citizens.[94]

Sutherland would be surprised to see the appearance since his death of agencies such as the Environmental Protection Agency, the Consumer Product Safety Commission, the Occupational Safety and Health Administration, the Office of Surface Mining Reclamation and Enforcement, and the Mine Safety and Health Administration.

The number of fatalities from coal mining accidents is today less than a tenth of its level earlier in the century for the United States, United Kingdom, Australia, France, and Japan.[95] In Japan, where criminal pollution convictions number over 6,000 a year, the rate of noncompliance with water quality standards for lead, cyanide, cadmium, arsenic, and PCBs by 1980 was at a tenth of the levels prevailing at the beginning of the 1970s.[96] Even in the United States[97] and Britain,[98] with their less rigorous environmental enforcement, the fish are returning to many rivers that were once heavily polluted.[99] Modest consumer product safety enforcement in the United States during the 1970s produced a 40 percent drop in ingestion of poisons by children, a halving of crib deaths of babies, and virtual elimination of children's sleepwear as a cause of flameburn injuries.[100]

In a recent work, I have become persuaded that reforms whereby governments give bargaining clout to regulatory agencies, and companies give top management backing to internal compliance groups, can reduce and have substantially reduced white collar crime.[101] Interestingly, Ralph Nader, the world's most celebrated cynic on regulatory agencies, has also experienced some transition in view. His organization recently reviewed the evidence of the hundreds of thousands of lives saved by the Occupational Safety and Health Administration, Environmental Protection Agency, National Highway Traffic Safety Administration, Food and Drug Administration, and the Consumer Product Safety Commission.[102]

As Chambliss has argued, white collar criminals are among the most deterrable types of offenders because they satisfy two conditions: they do not have a commitment to crime as a way of life and their offenses are instrumental rather than expressive. White collar criminals are also more deterrable than working class criminals because they have more of those things that can be lost by criminal conviction or informal means of stigmatization—status, respectability, money, a job, a comfortable home and family life.[103] This view is supported by some quasi-experimental time series and interview studies, which suggest that white collar offenders are deterred by prosecution.[104]

Indeed, Geis and I have argued that not only deterrence, but also two other discredited doctrines of traditional criminology—rehabilitation and incapacitation—are effective when applied to white collar crime.[105] Incapacitation of criminal doctors or mine managers can be achieved by withdrawing their license to practice their profession or stopping production at a work site rather than by imprisonment; rehabilitation does not occur on the psychiatrist's couch, but at the hands of the management consultant. State-imposed rearrangements of criminogenic organizational structures are easier to effect than state-imposed rearrangements of individual psyches.

On the other hand, the literature also supports the view that proving the guilt of white collar suspects is more difficult, particularly because of the complexity of the evidence and the capacity of wealthy defendants to mobilize legal talent.[106] This reality is a major plank of those who argue for compliance over deterrence law enforcement systems.

Empirical observation of organizational crimes also indicates considerable scholarly agreement on a few additional matters of policy relevance. With large corporations, rarely do the boards of directors become involved in preventing, participating in, or even knowing about corporate offenses.[107] This raises doubts about the Ralph Nader proposal of public interest directors for major corporations as a white collar crime countermeasure.

Case studies of crimes committed on behalf of large organizations repeatedly document either orchestrated or negligent communication blockages that prevent knowledge of white collar crime from reaching the desks of top management.[108] This can be functional for the organization; it allows top management to say to underlings, "I want you to achieve this result, but I don't want to know how you do it," and it protects the corporation as a legal person from the taint of knowledge necessary to prove corporate crime. It can also be dysfunctional in depriving top management of knowledge of white collar crimes pursued to achieve subunit goals or personal ambitions that are at odds with the overall goals of the organization. Governmentally mandated compliance auditing and reporting, corporate ombudsmen and other free routes of communication to the top, staff rotation and laws to protect whistle blowers are among the policy options that have been suggested by this strand of the literature.

Finally, interview research with company executives consistently elicits the view that it is top management attitudes, most particularly those of the chief executive, which determine the level of compliance with the law in a corporation.[109] Moreover, middle managers are frequently reported as squeezed by a choice between failing to achieve targets set by top management and attaining the targets illegally.[110] In other words, while it is middle management who perpetrate the criminal acts, it is top management which set the expectations, the tone, the corporate culture that determines the incidence of corporate crime. These findings again imply reforms to ensure that top management will be tainted with knowledge of illegalities, as well as reforms to facilitate prosecution of chief executives who are willfully blind to the creation of criminogenic corporate cultures.[111]

PUTTING WHITE COLLAR CRIME ON
A SOUNDER CONCEPTUAL FOOTING

Some of the deficiencies of white collar crime as a concept have become clear in this review. But what are the alternatives? Many Marxists, following the tradition of Taylor, Walton, and Young, would have us abandon the laws of capitalist societies for defining our domain.[112] Yet by accepting the laws of the capitalist state, sociologists hardly legitimate ruling class interests when they deal with that subset of laws that criminalize predominantly the behavior of the ruling class. Survey data show that the critical criminologists of the 1970s were essentially wrong in arguing that there is no consensus around the laws of capitalist societies.[113]

If it is false consciousness which drives working class people toward this consensus, then it is an odd sort of false consciousness which, inter alia, consensually supports draconian penalties against ruling class crimes. Liberal and Marxist sociologists alike should feel no embarrassment at taking the considerable progressive democratic support for laws prohibiting white collar crime as the basis for their research. Those who choose to study violations of "politically defined human rights,"[114] or some other imaginative definition of deviance, will deserve to be ignored for indulging their personal moralities in a social science that has no relevance for those who do not share that morality.

The alternative influential definition of white collar crime was formulated by Edelhertz as "an illegal act or series of illegal acts committed by non-physical means and by concealment or guile, to obtain money or property, to avoid the payment or loss of money or property, or to obtain business or personal advantage."[115] The first drawback of this alternative is that it turns attention away from white collar crimes that do physical harm to persons, which, as we have seen, are the kinds of crime that arouse greatest concern in the community. Second, the Edelhertz definition deletes the Sutherland requirement that the offenses be perpetrated in the performance of occupational roles. The practical consequences for empirical research have been that most white collar criminals end up having blue collars.[116] This is because the offenders who use concealment or guile to obtain money illegally and who are most likely to be convicted by courts are welfare cheats. A white collar crime literature dominated by studies of welfare offenders would require a very different theoretical orientation than that which has developed. On the other hand, as Edelhertz and Rogovin point out, a definition which is neutral concerning the social standing of the offender is imperative for public policy because it is unacceptable for the state to target enforcement that is contingent on the status of the offender.[117]

Bloch and Geis, seeking clearly homogeneous types of offenses, suggested the following distinctions: offenses committed by (1) individuals as individuals, (2) employees against their employers, (3) policymaking officials for the corporation, (4) agents of the corporation against the general public, and (5) merchants against customers.[118] A variety of such classifications have been proposed, none of them with the force to command an authoritative partition of the field.[119]

The most influential partition has been that of Clinard and Quinney which divides white collar crime into occupational and corporate crime. "Occupational crime consists of offenses committed by individuals for themselves in the course of their occupations and the offenses of employees against their employers." Note that this brings in many "blue collar" occupational crimes. Corporate crime, in contrast, is defined as "the offenses committed by corporate officials for the corporation and the offenses of the corporation itself."[120] A variation is Schrager and Short's definition of "organizational crime"; this has the advantage over corporate crime of making it clearer that crimes committed on behalf of public as well as private organizations are within the ambit of the concept.[121]

Probably the most sensible way to proceed with organizing work in this area is first to stick with Sutherland's definition. This at least excludes welfare cheats and credit card frauds from the domain. Second, following Clinard and Quinney, occupational crimes should be separated from corporate or organizational crime.

Corporate crime, as the core area of concern, is then left as a broad but reasonably homogeneous domain for coherent theorizing. While useful theories of white collar crime have proved elusive, influential corporate or organizational crime theory is a possibility. Occupational crime is a much less homogeneous category—employees who offend against employers engage in a very different activity from doctors who rip off their patients. General theories of occupational crime might be as difficult as theories of white collar crime. Progress here might be confined to studies of specific types of occupational crime.[122]

Notes

1. Willem A. Bonger, *Criminality and Economic Conditions*. Boston: Little, Brown, 1916.
2. Edward A. Ross, *Sin and Society: An Analysis of Latter-Day Iniquity*. Boston: Houghton Mifflin, 1907.
3. Ida M. Tarbell, *The History of the Standard Oil Company*. New York: Macmillan, 1904.
4. Lincoln Steffens, *The Shame of the Cities*. New York: McClure, Phillips, 1904.
5. Frank Norris, *The Pit*. New York: Doubleday, 1903.
6. Upton Sinclair, *The Jungle*. New York: Doubleday and Page, 1906.
7. Edwin H. Sutherland, "White-Collar Criminality," *American Sociological Review*, 5 (1940):1–12.
8. Edwin H. Sutherland, *White Collar Crime*. New York: Dryden, 1949.
9. Edwin H. Sutherland, *White Collar Crime: The Uncut Version*. New Haven: Yale University Press, 1983.
10. *Ibid.*, p. 7.
11. Jay Albanese, "Corporate Criminology: Explaining Deviance of Business and Political Organizations," *Journal of Criminal Justice*, 12 (1984):11–19.

12. Victoria L. Swigert and Ronald A. Farrell, "Corporate Homicide: Definitional Processes in the Creation of Deviance," *Law and Society Review,* 15 (1980–81):161–182.

13. Marshall B. Clinard, "Criminological Theories of Violations of Wartime Regulations," *American Sociological Review,* 11 (1946):258–270.

14. Robert Sherwin, "White-Collar Crime, Conventional Crime, and Merton's Deviant Behavior Theory," *Wisconsin Sociologist,* 2 (1963):7–10.

15. William B. Waegel, M. David Ermann, and Alan M. Horowitz, "Organizational Responses to Imputations of Deviance," *Sociological Quarterly,* 22 (1981):43–55; Swigert and Farrell, *op. cit.*

16. Ezra Stotland, "White-Collar Criminals," *Journal of Social Issues,* 33 (1977):179–196; John Monahan and Raymond W. Novaco, "Corporate Violence: A Psychological Analysis." In Paul Lipsitt and Bruce Sales, eds., *New Directions in Psychological Research.* New York: Van Nostrand Reinhold, 1980, pp. 3–25.

17. Christopher Stone, *Where the Law Ends: The Social Control of Corporate Behavior.* New York: Harper & Row, 1975; John C. Coffee, Jr., "Beyond the Shut-Eyed Sentry: Toward a Theoretical View of Corporate Misconduct and an Effective Legal Response," *Virginia Law Review,* 63 (1977):1099–1278. But note important sociological contributions: Albert K. Cohen, "The Concept of Criminal Organization," *British Journal of Criminology,* 17 (1977):97–111; Laura S. Schrager and James F. Short, Jr., "Toward a Sociology of Organizational Crime," *Social Problems,* 25 (1978):407–419; M. David Ermann and Richard J. Lundman, "Deviant Acts by Complex Organizations: Deviance and Social Control at the Organizational Level of Analysis," *Sociological Quarterly,* 19 (1978):55–67; Edward Gross, "Organizational Crime: A Theoretical Perspective." In Norman Denzin, ed., *Studies in Symbolic Interaction.* Greenwich, CT: JAI Press, 1978, pp. 55–85.

18. Gilbert Geis and Colin Goff, "Introduction." In Edwin H. Sutherland, *White Collar Crime: The Uncut Version, op. cit.,* pp. xi-xii.

19. Sutherland, *White Collar Crime: The Uncut Version,* p. 51.

20. Paul W. Tappan, "Who Is the Criminal?" *American Sociological Review,* 12 (1947):96–102. See also Ernest W. Burgess, "Comment," *American Journal of Sociology,* 56 (1950):34; Leonard Orland, "Reflections on Corporate Crime: Law in Search of Theory and Scholarship," *American Criminal Law Review,* 17 (1980):501–520.

21. Marshall B. Clinard, *The Black Market: A Study of White-Collar Crime.* New York: Holt, Rinehart & Winston, 1952.

22. Donald R. Cressey, *Other People's Money: The Social Psychology of Embezzlement.* New York: The Free Press, 1953.

23. Gilbert Geis, "Toward a Delineation of White-Collar Offenses," *Sociological Inquiry,* 32 (1962) :160–171; Geis, "The Heavy Electrical Equipment Antitrust Cases of 1961." In Marshall B. Clinard and Richard Quinney, eds.,

Criminal Behavior Systems. New York: Holt, Rinehart & Winston, 1967, pp. 139–150; Geis, ed., *White-Collar Crime: The Offender in Business and the Professions.* New York: Atherton, 1968; Herbert Edelhertz, *The Nature, Impact, and Prosecution of White Collar Crime.* Washington, DC: National Institute of Law Enforcement and Justice, 1970.

24. David Shichor, "Corporate Deviance and Corporate Victimization: A Review and Some Elaborations," *International Journal of Victimology,* 1 (1989):67.

25. Sutherland, *White Collar Crime: The Uncut Version, op. cit.,* p. 240.

26. Ronald Wraith and Edgar Simpkins, *Corruption in Developing Countries.* London: Allen & Unwin, 1963; James C. Scott, *Comparative Political Corruption.* Englewood Cliffs, NJ: Prentice-Hall, 1972.

27. Albert J. Reiss, Jr., and Albert Biderman, *Data Sources on White-Collar Law-Breaking.* Washington, DC: U.S. Department of Justice, 1980.

28. John M. DeMichiei, John F. Langton, Kenneth A. Bullock, and Terrance C. Wiles, *Factors Associated with Disability Injuries in Underground Coal Mines.* Washington, DC: Mine Safety and Health Administration, 1982; John Braithwaite, *To Punish or Persuade: The Enforcement of Coal Mine Legislation.* Albany: State University of New York Press, 1985a.

29. Robert E. Lane, "Why Businessmen Violate the Law," *Journal of Criminal Law, Criminology, and Police Science,* 44 (1953):151–165.

30. Barry M. Staw and Eugene Szwajkowski, "The Scarcity-Munificence Component of Organizational Environments and the Commission of Illegal Acts," *Administrative Science Quarterly,* 20 (1975):345–354.

31. Jacob Perez, *Corporate Criminality: A Case Study of the One Thousand Largest Industrial Corporations in the U.S.A.* Ph.D. dissertation, University of Pennsylvania, 1978, p. 124; Marshall B. Clinard, Peter C. Yeager, Jeane Brissette, David Petrashek, and Elizabeth Harris, *Illegal Corporate Behavior.* Washington, DC: Government Printing Office, 1979, p. 304.

32. Marshall B. Clinard and Peter C. Yeager, *Corporate Crime.* New York: The Free Press, 1980, pp. 50–51.

33. John Lynxwiler, Neal Shover, and Donald A. Clelland, "Determinants of Sanction Severity in a Regulatory Bureaucracy." In Ellen Hochstedler, ed., *Corporations as Criminals.* Beverly Hills: Sage, 1984, pp. 147–165.

34. Aristotle, *Politics,* trans. J. E. C. Weldon. London: Macmillan, 1932, Book II, p. 65.

35. Sutherland, *White Collar Crime: The Uncut Version, op. cit.;* Clinard and Yeager, *op. cit.*

36. Cressey, *Other People's Money, op. cit.*

37. Gwynn Nettler, "Embezzlement without Problems," *British Journal of Criminology,* 14 (1974):70–77.

38. Michael Levi, "Giving Creditors the Business: The Criminal Law in Inaction," *International Journal of the Sociology of Law,* 12 (1984):321–333.

39. See, for instance, W. G. Carson, *The Other Price of Britain's Oil: Safety and Control in the North Sea.* New Brunswick, NJ: Rutgers University Press,

1982; Phillip Knightley, Bruce Page, James Evans, and Elaine Potter, *Suffer the Children: The Story of Thalidomide.* New York: Viking, 1979; Alan Doig, *Corruption and Misconduct in Contemporary British Politics.* Harmondsworth: Penguin, 1984; David Boulton, *The Grease Machine: The Inside Story of Lockheed's Dollar Diplomacy.* New York: Harper & Row, 1978; Kermit Vandiver, "Why Should My Conscience Bother Me?" In M. David Ermann and Richard J. Lundman, eds., *Corporate and Governmental Deviance: Problems of Organizational Behavior in Contemporary Society.* 2d. ed. New York: Oxford University Press, 1982, pp. 102–122; Christopher Stone, "A Slap on the Wrist for the Kepone Mob," *Business and Society Review* (Summer 1977):4–11; Donn B. Parker, *Crime by Computer.* New York: Scribner's, 1976; James A. Waters, "Catch 20.5: Corporate Morality as an Organizational Phenomenon," *Organizational Dynamics* (Spring 1978): 3–19.

40. Michael Levi, *Phantom Capitalists: The Organisation and Control of Long-Firm Fraud.* London: Heineman Educational, 1981.

41. Leon Sheleff, "International White-Collar Crime." In Peter Wickman and Timothy Dailey, eds., *White-Collar and Economic Crime.* Lexington, MA: Lexington Books, 1982, pp. 39–57; Mireille Delmas-Marty, "White-Collar Crime and the EEC." In Leonard H. Leigh, ed., *Economic Crime in Europe.* New York: St. Martin's Press, 1980, pp. 78–105; Herbert Edelhertz, "Transnational White-Collar Crime: A Developing Challenge and a Need for Response," *Temple Law Quarterly,* 53 (1980) :1114–1126; Delmas-Marty and Klaus Tiedemann, "La Criminalité, le droit pénal et les multinationales," *La Semaine Juridique* 2935 (March):21–28.

42. For a review of such studies, see John Braithwaite, "Paradoxes of Class Bias in Criminal Justice." In Harold E. Pepinsky, ed., *Rethinking Criminology.* Beverly Hills: Sage, 1982, pp. 71–75.

43. Note: "Structural Crime and Institutional Rehabilitation: A New Approach to Corporate Sentencing," *Yale Law Journal,* 89 (1979):353–375; "Developments in the Law—Regulating Corporate Behavior through Criminal Sanctions," *Harvard Law Review,* 92 (1979):1227–1375; John C. Coffee, Jr., "Corporate Criminal Responsibility." In Sanford H. Kadish, ed., *Encyclopedia of Crime and Justice.* New York: The Free Press, 1984, vol. 1, pp. 253–264; Christopher Stone, "The Place of Enterprise Liability in the Control of Corporate Conduct," *Yale Law Journal,* 90 (1980):1–77; Brent Fisse, "The Social Policy of Corporate Criminal Responsibility," *Adelaide Law Review,* 6 (1978):361–412; Fisse, "Reconstructing the Corporate Criminal Law: Deterrence, Retribution, Fault, and Sanctions," *Southern California Law Review,* 56 (1983):1141–1246; Fisse, "The Duality of Corporate and Individual Criminal Liability." In Ellen Hochstedler, ed., *Corporations as Criminals.* Beverly Hills: Sage, 1984, pp. 69–84; Leonard H. Leigh, "The Criminal Liability of Corporations and Other Groups," *Ottawa Law Review,* 9 (1977):246–302; Charles B. Schudson, Ashton P. Onellion, and Ellen Hochstedler, "Nailing an

Omelet to the Wall: Prosecuting Nursing Home Homicide," in Hochstedler, ed., *Corporations as Criminals*. Beverly Hills: Sage, 1984, pp. 131–145.

44. Diane Vaughan, *Controlling Unlawful Organizational Behavior: Social Structure and Corporate Misconduct.* Chicago: University of Chicago Press, 1983.

45. W. Michael Reisman, *Folded Lies: Bribery, Crusades and Reforms.* New York: The Free Press, 1979.

46. Lee P. Strobel, *Reckless Homicide: Ford's Pinto Trial.* South Bend, IN: And Books, 1980; Ronald C. Kramer, "Corporate Crime: An Organizational Perspective." In Peter Wickman and Thomas Dailey, eds., *White-Collar and Economic Crime.* Lexington, MA: Lexington Books, 1982, pp. 75–94; Francis T. Cullen, William J. Maakestad, and Gray Cavender, "The Ford Pinto Case and Beyond: Corporate Crime, Moral Boundaries, and the Criminal Sanction." In Ellen Hochstedler, ed., *Corporations as Criminals.* Beverly Hills: Sage, 1984, pp. 107–130.

47. Jack D. Douglas and John M. Johnson, eds., *Official Deviance: Readings in Malfeasance, Misfeasance, and Other Forms of Corruption.* Philadelphia: Lippincott, 1977.

48. Anthony E. Simpson, *The Literature of Police Corruption.* New York: John Jay, 1979; Lawrence Sherman, *Scandal and Reform: Controlling Police Corruption.* Berkeley: University of California Press, 1978.

49. M. David Ermann and Richard J. Lundman, eds., *Corporate and Governmental Deviance.* 2d ed. New York: Oxford University Press, 1984, pp. 144–154.

50. Christopher Stone, "Corporate Vices and Corporate Virtues: Do Private/Public Distinctions Matter?" *University of Pennsylvania Law Review,* 130 (1982): 1459–1460.

51. Maria Los, "Crime and Economy in the Communist Countries." In Peter Wickman and Thomas Dailey, eds., *White-Collar and Economic Crime.* Lexington, MA: Lexington Books, 1982, pp. 121–138.

52. Gross, *op. cit.,* p. 72.

53. Sherman, *op. cit.*

54. Alan Dershowitz, "Increasing Community Control over Corporate Crime," *Yale Law Journal,* 71 (1961):281–306; Sandra S. Evans and Richard J. Lundman, "Newspaper Coverage of Corporate Price-Fixing," *Criminology,* 21 (1983):529–541; Chrisje H. Brants and T. de Roos, "Pollution, Press, and the Penal Process: The Case of UNISER in the Netherlands," *Crime and Social Justice,* 21/22 (1984):128–145.

55. Arthur F. Matthews, "Recent Trends in SEC Requested Ancillary Relief in SEC Level Injunctive Actions," *Business Lawyer,* 31 (1976):1323–1352; Lewis D. Solomon and Nancy Stein Nowak, "Management Restructuring: Prospects for a New Regulatory Tool," *Notre Dame Lawyer,* 56 (1980): 120–140.

56. Brent Fisse and John Braithwaite, *The Impact of Publicity on Corporate Offenders.* Albany: State University of New York Press, 1983.

57. Don E. Waldman, *Antitrust Action and Market Structure*. Lexington, MA: Lexington Books, 1978; Waldman, "Economic Benefits in the IBM, AT&T, and Xerox Cases: Government Antitrust Policy in the 70s," *Antitrust Law and Economics Review*, 12 (1980):75–92.

58. Fisse and Braithwaite, *op. cit.*, pp. 204–212.

59. Paul J. Quirk, *Industry Influence in Federal Regulatory Agencies*. Princeton: Princeton University Press, 1981; Peter J. Freitag, "The Myth of Corporate Capture: Regulatory Commissions in the United States," *Social Problems*, 30 (1983):480–491. See also Suzanne Weaver, *Decision to Prosecute: Organization and Public Policy in the Antitrust Division*. Cambridge: MIT Press, 1977.

60. Robert Kagan, *Regulatory Justice: Implementing a Wage-Price Freeze*. New York: Russell Sage Foundation, 1978; Ross Cranston, *Regulating Business: Law and Consumer Agencies*. London: Macmillan, 1979; Genevra Richardson, Anthony Ogus, and Paul Burrows, *Policing Pollution: A Study of Regulation and Enforcement*. Oxford: Clarendon Press, 1982; W. G. Carson, "White-Collar Crime and the Enforcement of Factory Legislation," *British Journal of Criminology*, 10 (1970):383–398; Neal Shover, Donald A. Clelland, and John Lynswiler, *Developing a Regulatory Bureaucracy: The Office of Surface Mining Reclamation and Enforcement*. Washington, DC: National Institute of Justice, 1983; Neil Gunningham, *Safeguarding the Worker: Job Hazards and the Role of Law*. Sydney: Law Book, 1984. See also Robert A. Katzman, *Regulatory Bureaucracy: The Federal Trade Commission and Antitrust Policy*. Cambridge: MIT Press, 1980; Weaver, *op. cit.*

61. Keith Hawkins, *Environment and Enforcement: Regulation and the Social Definition of Pollution*. Oxford: Clarendon, 1984, p. 3. See also Eugene Bardach and Robert A. Kagan, *Going by the Book: The Problem of Regulatory Unreasonableness*. Philadelphia: Temple University Press, 1982.

62. Peter G. Schrag, "On Her Majesty's Secret Service: Protecting the Consumer in New York City," *Yale Law Journal*, 80 (1971):1529–1603.

63. Albert J. Reiss, Jr., "The Policing of Organizational Life." In Maurice Punch, ed., *Control in the Police Organization*. Cambridge: MIT Press, 1983, pp. 93–94; See also Reiss, "Selecting Strategies of Social Control over Organizational Life." In Keith Hawkins and John M. Thomas, eds., *Enforcing Regulation*. Boston: Kluwer-Nijhoff, 1984, pp. 23–35.

64. Albert E. McCormick, Jr., "Rule Enforcement and Moral Indignation: Some Observations on the Effects of Criminal Antitrust Convictions upon Societal Reaction Processes," *Social Problems*, 25 (1977):30–39.

65. Joseph DiMento, *Getting Compliance: Environmental Law and American Business*. New York: Plenum, 1986.

66. Quoted in Paul H. Weaver, "Regulatory Social Policy and Class Conflict." In Donald P. Jacobs, ed., *Regulating Business: The Search for an Optimum*. San Francisco: Institute for Contemporary Studies, 1978, pp. 193–218.

67. Braithwaite, *To Punish or Persuade, op. cit.*

68. Neal Shover, John Lynxwiler, Stephen Groce, and Donald Clelland,

"Regional Variation in Regulatory Law Enforcement: The Surface Mining Control and Reclamation Act of 1977." In Keith Hawkins and John M. Thomas, eds., *Enforcing Regulation.* Boston: Kluwer-Nijhoff, 1984, pp. 121–146.

69. Steven Kelman, *Regulating America, Regulating Sweden: A Comparative Study of Occupational Safety and Health Policy.* Cambridge: MIT Press, 1981.

70. Reiss, "The Policing of Organizational Life," *op. cit.,* p. 81.

71. Susan P. Shapiro, *Wayward Capitalists: Target of the Securities and Exchange Commission.* New Haven: Yale University Press, 1984.

72. Clifford D. Shearing and Philip C. Stenning, "Modern Private Security: Its Growth and Implications." In Michael Tonry and Norval Morris, eds., *Crime and Justice: An Annual Review.* Chicago: University of Chicago Press, 1981, pp. 193–245.

73. Harold C. Barnett, "Wealth, Crime and Capital Accumulation," *Contemporary Crises,* 3 (1979):171–186; William G. Shepherd, *The Treatment of Market Power.* New York: Columbia University Press, 1975; Colin H. Goff and Charles E. Reasons, "Organizational Crimes against Employees, Consumers, and the Public." In Brian D. McLean, ed., *The Political Economy of Crime: Readings for a Critical Criminology.* Scarborough, Ont.: Prentice-Hall, 1986, pp. 204–231.

74. Michael Levi, "The Powers of the Revenue Agent: An Overview," *British Tax Review,* 1 (1982):37; Harold C. Barnett, "Tax Evasion by Proxy: The Gray Market in Welfare Capitalism," *Contemporary Crises,* 8 (1984):107–123. See also Susan Long, "Growth in the Underground Economy?: An Empirical Issue." In Philip Wickman and Thomas Dailey, eds., *White-Collar and Economic Crime.* Lexington, MA: Lexington Books, 1982, pp. 95–120.

75. Barnett, "Wealth, Crime and Capital Accumulation," *op. cit.,* p. 184.

76. Richard Quinney, *Critique of the Legal Order: Crime Control in Capitalist Society.* Boston: Little, Brown, 1974, p. 52.

77. See, for instance, William Chambliss and Robert B. Seidman, *Law, Order, and Power.* Reading, MA: Addison-Wesley, 1971; Patrick O'Malley, "Theories of Structural versus Causal Determination: Accounting for Legislative Change in Capitalist Societies." In Roman Tomasic, ed., *Legislation and Society in Australia.* Sydney: Allen & Unwin, 1980, pp. 50–65.

78. See also Andrew Hopkins, "Class Bias in the Criminal Law," *Contemporary Crises,* 5 (1981):385–394.

79. Murray J. Edelman, *The Symbolic Uses of Politics.* Urbana: University of Illinois Press, 1964; Joseph Gusfield, *Symbolic Crusade.* Urbana: University of Illinois Press, 1967; W. G. Carson, "Symbolic and Instrumental Dimensions of Early Factory Legislation: A Case Study in the Social Origins of Criminal Law." In Roger Hood, ed., *Crime, Criminology, and Public Policy.* Glencoe, IL: The Free Press, 1975, pp. 107–138; O'Malley, *op. cit.;* Andrew Hopkins and Nina Parnell, "Why Coal Mine Safety Regulations in Australia Are Not

Enforced," *International Journal of the Sociology of Law,* 12 (1984): 179–184.

80. Edelman, *op. cit.*

81. John Hagan, "The Corporate Advantage: A Study of the Involvement of Corporate and Individual Victims in a Criminal Justice System," *Social Forces,* 45 (1982):993–1022.

82. Laureen Snider, "Traditional and Corporate Theft: A Comparison of Sanctions." In Peter Wickman and Thomas Dailey, eds., *White-Collar and Economic Crime.* Lexington, MA: Lexington Books, 1982, pp. 235–258.

83. John Hagan, Ilene Nagel, and Celesta Albonetti, "The Differential Sentencing of White-Collar Offenders in Ten Federal Courts," *American Sociological Review,* 45 (1980):802–820; Stanton Wheeler, David Weisburd, and Nancy Bode, "Sentencing the White-Collar Offender: Rhetoric and Reality," *American Sociological Review,* 47 (1982):641–659.

84. Wheeler et al., *op. cit.* See further Gilbert Geis, "White-Collar and Corporate Crime." In Robert F. Meier, ed., *Major Forms of Crime.* Beverly Hills: Sage, 1984, pp. 137–166.

85. Goff and Reasons, *op. cit.;* Sutherland, *White Collar Crime: The Uncut Version, op. cit.;* Miriam Saxon, *White Collar Crime: The Problem and the Federal Response.* Washington, DC: Congressional Research Service, 1980; Clinard and Yeager, *op. cit.;* Robert F. Meier and James F. Short, Jr., "The Consequences of White-Collar Crime." In Herbert Edelhertz and Thomas D. Overcast, eds., *White-Collar Crime: An Agenda for Research.* Lexington, MA: Lexington Books, 1982, pp. 23–49.

86. James Frank, Francis T. Cullen, and Lawrence F. Travis, III, "Sanctioning Corporate Crime: Public Support for Civil and Criminal Intervention." Paper presented to Midwest Criminal Justice Association, 1984; Frank T. Cullen, Bruce G. Link, and Craig W. Polanzi, "The Seriousness of Crime Revisited: Have Attitudes toward White-Collar Crime Changed?" *Criminology,* 20 (1982):83–102; Cullen, Gregory A. Clark, Richard A. Mathers, and John B. Cullen, "Public Support for Punishing White-Collar Crime: Blaming the Victim Revisited?" *Journal of Criminal Justice,* 11 (1983):481–493; Luis Salas, Sonia Navarro Solano, and Ana Isabel Garita Vilchez, "Comparative Study of White Collar Crime in Latin America with Special Emphasis on Costa Rica," *Revue Internationale de Droit Pénal,* 53 (1982):505–521; and earlier studies reviewed in John Braithwaite, "Challenging Just Deserts: Punishing White-Collar Criminals," *Journal of Criminal Law and Criminology,* 73 (1982): 731–742.

87. Robert F. Meier and James F. Short, Jr., "Crime as Hazard: Perceptions of Risk and Seriousness." *Criminology,* 23 (1985):389–399.

88. Andrew von Hirsch, "Desert and White-Collar Criminality: A Reply to Dr. Braithwaite," *Journal of Criminal Law and Criminology,* 73 (1982): 1164–1175; see also Ernest van den Haag, "Comment on 'Challenging Just Deserts: Punishing White-Collar Criminals,'" *Journal of Criminal Law and*

Criminology, 73 (1982):764–769; van den Haag, "Reply to Dr. John Braithwaite," *Journal of Criminal Law and Criminology,* 73 (1982):794–796.

89. Sutherland, *White Collar Crime, op. cit.,* p. v.

90. Sutherland, *White Collar Crime: The Uncut Version, op. cit.,* p. 59.

91. Gary T. Marx, "Who Really Gets Stung?: Some Issues Raised by the New Police Undercover Work," *Crime and Delinquency,* 28 (1982):165–193.

92. Geis and Goff, *op. cit.,* p. xxxi.

93. John C. Coffee, Jr., "The Metasis of Mail Fraud: The Continuing Story of the 'Evolution' of a White-Collar Crime," *American Criminal Law Review,* 21 (1983):24.

94. Jack Katz, "The Social Movement against White-Collar Crime." In Egon Bittner and Sheldon Messinger, eds., *Criminology Review Yearbook.* Beverly Hills: Sage, 1980, vol. 2, p. 162.

95. Braithwaite, *To Punish or Persuade, op. cit.* For the more skeptical views on the impact of occupational safety enforcement, see Robert S. Smith, "The Impact of OSHA Inspections on Manufacturing Injury Rates," *Journal of Human Resources,* 14 (1979):145–170; W. Kip Viscusi, *Risk by Choice: Regulating Health and Safety in the Workplace.* Cambridge: Harvard University Press, 1983.

96. Japanese Environmental Agency, 1981. Unpublished data available from the author on request.

97. Liz Roman Gallese, "Connecticut's Naugatuck River Became a Sewer; Now Even its Polluters Are Cheering the Cleanup," *Wall Street Journal,* July 16, 1982, pp. 36–37; Bardach and Kagan, *op. cit.,* p. 94.

98. David J. Storey, "Has Economics of Environmental Law Enforcement or Has the Prosecution of Polluters Led to Cleaner Rivers in England and France?" *Environmental Planning* 11 (1979):897–918.

99. See Paul W. MacAvoy, *The Regulated Industries and the Economy.* New York: W. W. Norton, 1979; Harold C. Barnett, "Corporate Capitalism, Corporate Crime," *Crime and Delinquency,* 27 (1981):4–23.

100. Douglas M. Costle, "Innovative Regulation," Economic Impact, 28 (1979):8–14. For an estimate of five million disabling injuries prevented by the Consumer's Product Safety Commission, see Consumer's Federation of America, *On the Safe Track: Deaths and Injuries Before and After the Consumer Product Safety Commission.* Washington, DC: Consumer's Federation of America, 1983.

101. John Braithwaite, *Corporate Crime in the Pharmaceutical Industry.* London: Routledge & Kegan Paul, 1984: Braithwaite, *To Punish or Persuade, op. cit.* See also Vaughan, *op. cit.*

102. Mark Green and Norman Waitzman, *Business War on the Law: An Analysis of the Benefits of Federal Health/Safety Enforcement.* Washington, DC: Ralph Nader, 1981.

103. William J. Chambliss, "Types of Deviance and the Effectiveness of Legal Sanctions," *Wisconsin Law Review* (Summer 1967):703–719.

104. Andrew Hopkins, "The Anatomy of Corporate Crime." In Paul R. Wilson and
      John Braithwaite, eds., *Two Faces of Deviance: Crimes of the Powerless and
      the Powerful.* Brisbane: University of Queensland Press, 1978, pp. 214–231;
      P. A. Holland, "The Effectiveness of Prosecutions under the Environment
      Protection Act," *Environmental Paper No. 2.* Melbourne: Graduate School of
      Environmental Science, Monash University, 1982; Michael S. Lewis-Beck
      and John R. Alford, "Can Government Regulate Safety?: The Coal Mine
      Example," *American Political Science Review,* 74 (1980):745–756; Charles
      S. Perry, *Safety Laws and Spending Save Lives: An Analysis of Coal Mine
      Fatality Rates 1930–1979.* Department of Sociology, University of Kentucky,
      1981; Ezra Stotland, Michael Britnall, André L'Heureux, and Eva Ashmore,
      "Do Convictions Deter Home Repair Fraud." In Gilbert Geis and Stotland,
      eds., White-*Collar Crime: Theory and Research.* Beverly Hills: Sage, 1980,
      pp. 252–265; Michael K. Block, Frederick C. Nold, and Joseph G. Sidak,
      "The Deterrent Effect of Antitrust Enforcement," *Journal of Political Econ-
      omy,* 89 (1981):429–445; Dennis Epple and Michael Visscher, "Environmen-
      tal Pollution: Modeling Occurrence, Detection, and Deterrence," *Journal of
      Law and Economics,* 27 (1984):29–60. See also Paul Jesilow, Gilbert Geis,
      and Mary Jane O'Brien, "Is My Battery Any Good? A Field Test of Fraud in
      the Auto Repair Business," *Journal of Crime and Justice,* 8 (1985):1–20.
105. Braithwaite and Geis, *op. cit.*
106. Levi, *The Phantom Capitalists, op. cit.;* Adam Sutton and Ronald Wild, "Cor-
      porate Crime and Social Structure." In Paul R. Wilson and John Braithwaite,
      eds., *Two Faces of Deviance: Crimes of the Powerless and Powerful.* Bris-
      bane: University of Queensland Press, 1978, pp. 177–198; Barry Rider and H.
      Leigh Ffrench, *The Regulation of Insider Trading.* Dobbs Ferry, NY: Oceana,
      1979; Robert W. Ogren, "The Ineffectiveness of the Criminal Sanction in
      Fraud and Corruption Cases: Losing the Battle against White-Collar Crime,"
      American Criminal Law Review, 11 (1973):959–988; Mark Green, *The Other
      Government: The Unseen Power of Washington Lawyers.* New York: Norton,
      1978.
107. U. S. Senate, Banking and Urban Affairs Committee, *Report of the Securities
      and Exchange Commission on Questionable and Illegal Corporate Payments
      and Practices.* 94th Cong., 2d Sess., 1976; Deborah A. De Mott, "Reweaving
      the Corporate Veil: Management Structure and the Control of Corporate
      Information," *Law and Contemporary Problems,* 41 (1977):182–221; Coffee,
      "Beyond the Shut-Eyed Sentry," *op. cit.;* Melvin A. Eisenberg, "Legal Mod-
      els of Management Structure in the Modern Corporation: Officers, Directors,
      and Accountants," *California Law Review,* 63 (1975):363–439; Myles L.
      Mace, *Directors: Myth and Reality.* Boston: Harvard Business School Divi-
      sion of Research, 1971.
108. Geis, "The Heavy Electrical Equipment Antitrust Cases," *op. cit.;* Stone,
      Where the Law Ends, op. cit.; John E. Conklin, "Illegal but not Criminal."
      Englewood Cliffs, NJ: Prentice-Hall, 1977; Coffee, "Beyond the Shut-Eyed

Sentry," *op. cit.;* Jack Katz, "Concerted Ignorance: The Social Construction of Cover-Up," *Urban Life,* 8 (1979):295–316.

109. Marshall B. Clinard, *Corporate Ethics and Crime: The Role of Middle Management.* Beverly Hills: Sage, 1983; Steven N. Brenner and Earl A. Molander, "Is the Ethics of Business Changing?" *Harvard Business Review,* 55 (January–February 1977):57–71; Raymond C. Baumhart, "How Ethical Are Businessmen?" *Harvard Business Review,* 39 (August 1961):6–19, 156–176; Donald R. Cressey and Charles A. Moore, *Corporation Codes of Ethical Conduct.* New York: Peat, Marwick and Mitchell Foundation, 1980. See also Thomas C. Shelling, "Command and Control." In James W. McKie, ed., *Social Responsibility and the Business Predicament.* Washington, DC: Brookings, 1974, pp. 79–108.

110. George Getschow, "Some Middle Managers Cut Corners to Achieve High Corporate Goals," *Wall Street Journal,* November 6, 1979.

111. Brent Fisse, "Responsibility, Prevention, and Corporate Crime." *New Zealand Universities Law Review,* 5 (1973):250–279; Larry C. Wilson, "The Doctrine of Wilful Blindness," *University of New Brunswick Law Journal,* 28 (1979):175–194.

112. Ian Taylor, Paul Walton, and Jock Young, *The New Criminology: For a Social Theory of Deviance.* London: Routledge & Kegan Paul, 1973.

113. See the fifteen studies cited in John Braithwaite, "Challenging Just Deserts," *op. cit.,* but note the methodological caveats in Terrance D. Miethe, "Public Consensus on Crime Seriousness: Normative Structure of Methodological Artifact?" *Criminology,* 20 (1982):515–526, and Cullen et al., "Consensus in Crime Seriousness," *op. cit.*

114. Herman Schwendinger and Julia Schwendinger, "Defenders of Order or Guardians of Human Rights?" In Ian Taylor, Paul Walton, and Jock Young, eds, *Critical Criminology.* London: Routledge & Kegan Paul, 1975, pp. 113–146.

115. Edelhertz, *op. cit.*

116. See, for instance, Hagan et al., *op. cit.*

117. Herbert Edelhertz and Charles Rogovin, eds., *A National Strategy for Containing White-Collar Crime.* Lexington, MA: Lexington Books, 1980, p. 3.

118. Herbert A. Bloch and Gilbert Geis, *Man, Crime and Society.* 2d ed. New York: Random House, 1970, p. 307.

119. Shichor, *op. cit.*

120. Marshall B. Clinard and Richard Quinney, *Criminal Behavior Systems: A Typology.* 2d ed. New York: Holt, Rinehart & Winston, 1970. The Clinard and Quinney position is now supported by Gilbert Geis, *On White-Collar Crime.* Lexington, MA: Lexington Books, 1982, p. x; Ronald C. Kramer, "Corporate Criminality: The Development of an Idea." In Ellen Hochstedler, ed., *Corporations as Criminals.* Beverly Hills: Sage, 1984, pp. 13–38; and Peter N. Grabosky, "Corporate Crime in Australia: An Agenda for Research," *Australian and New Zealand Journal of Criminology,* 17 (1984):97–105.

121. Schrager and Short, *op. cit.*
122. See, for instance, Richard Quinney, "Occupational Structure and Criminal Behavior: Prescription Violations by Retail Pharmacists," *Social Problems,* 11 (1963):179–185; Henry N. Pontell, Paul D. Jesilow, and Gilbert Geis, "Policing Physicians: Practitioner Fraud and Abuse in a Government Medical Program," *Social Problems,* 30 (1982):117–125.

PART II

Corporate and Professional White-Collar Crime

Introduction to Part II

There are striking pressures that promote white-collar crime in business. The decline of the laissez-faire ethic has imposed contradictory conditions on business operations. On the one hand, there is an espousal of the doctrine of fierce competition, while on the other hand, as Michael Conant has observed with regard to antitrust conspiracies in the motion picture industry, businesses "search for security—for protection against market uncertainty."[1] The eminent economist John Kenneth Galbraith has noted sarcastically: "Restraints on competition and the free movement of prices, the principal source of uncertainty to business firms, have been principally deplored by university professors on lifetime appointments. Such security of tenure is deemed essential for fruitful and unremitting thought."[2] Similarly, the sociologist John Finley Scott points out that "the most exceptional characteristic of the professor's status is security. . . . Professors fail to see how moral commitment erodes in less secure men [and women] when they are faced with strong, fortuitous temptation."[3]

Nonetheless, corporations possess enormous power, and they often operate primarily in terms of the bottom line—the profit associated with a given course.

Obviously, no business can long exist if it consistently brings in less than it expends. But it is at least arguable that some ruthless actions to protect shareholders' investments and, probably more important, executives' incomes and positions, are morally acceptable behaviors and ought to be tolerated under law. Relocating a plant to a site, perhaps overseas, where labor is cheaper, may boost corporate income, but it can wreak havoc on the community that is deserted. In the realm of lawbreaking, the kinds of things depicted in the articles in this section offer an unsavory portrait of what can happen when human life and social interests are relegated to a place far behind the drive for financial reward.

Corporations, as we noted in the Introduction to this book, are often viewed with suspicion by the public and humanists. The moral philosopher C. S. Lewis has expressed that concern as well as anybody:

> The greatest evil is not now done in those sordid "dens of crime" that Dickens loved to paint. It is not done even in concentration camps and labor camps. In those we see the final result. But it is conceived and ordered (moved, seconded, carried and minuted) in clean, carpeted, warmed and well-lighted offices, by quiet men with white collars and cut fingernails and smooth-shaven cheeks who do not need to raise their voices. Hence, naturally enough, my symbol for Hell is . . . the offices of a thoroughly nasty business concern.[4]

Note that Lewis's idea of Hell was shared much earlier by the medieval Italian poet, Dante, who assigned those who had engaged in fraud to the lowest levels of the devil's realm because "fraud . . . more displeases God."[5]

The review of Sutherland's work in terms of the heavy electrical equipment antitrust case, undertaken in the first paper in this section, finds many of his ideas strikingly on target, while others are said to be awry, though both the unique nature of the particular case and the passage of time since Sutherland wrote must be noted. The author of the article calls for additional case studies before venturing too far theoretically; in essence, he takes his stand with Huntington Cairns that "the history of social theory is too largely a record of generalizations wrung from insufficient facts."[6] Sutherland himself indicated in his textbook that "the most important thing to know about crime is the mechanism by which it is produced, and . . . such knowledge can be secured better by individual case studies."[7]

The heavy electrical equipment antitrust violations show the atmosphere within which the offenses were committed, and the kinds of rationalizations violators employ to justify their behavior after they are apprehended. Most white-collar offenders resort to tactics whereby normative boundaries may be "neutralized."[8] Note, for instance, the plaint of W. E. Laite, a former Georgia state legislator, sent to prison for several violations committed while he was running a construction company:

> I felt wrong, mistreated—here I was going into custody several years after the offense had *allegedly* [our emphasis] occurred. The punishment seemed unrealistic and severe. I felt I had been punished enough already—by publicity and the harassment, by the financial drubbing that left my family economically drained.[9]

Laite adds in self-pitying terms: "I was—or had been—a respected citizen. The closest I'd ever been to a jail cell was as an official visitor. I was young—thirty-five—and a prominent citizen." Then he asks: "What was I doing here with what I considered to be foul-mouthed, sadistic riff-raff. I had an unreasoning impulse to get up, very calmly, walk to the door, and leave."[10] Given the lack of severity of the judicial response to the offenses, the unorganized nature of the public's reaction, and the general "invisibility" of the offenses, businessmen usually do not have a difficult time excusing their illegal behavior and maintaining a self-conception as "honest" people.

The following six articles depict specific instances of white-collar crime. "Fire in Hamlet" by Judy Root Aulette and Raymond Michalowski carefully connects the drive by politicians in North Carolina to obtain business with the tragic outcome of a fire that killed 25 workers in a food-processing plant. The state offered financial lures and, particularly important in this case, unconscionably abated safety inspections so that companies would not have to spend their money in order to meet regulations designed to protect workers.

The portrait of the Dalkon Shield tragedy by Morton Mintz, an investigative reporter with the *Washington Post,* illustrates, in his word, how a "few men with little on their minds except the pursuit of megabucks exposed millions of women to serious infection, sterility, and even death." Mintz opens up an area of inquiry that only recently has begun to be adequately explored, that involving the victimization of women by white-collar crime. Earlier, about all that was common knowledge was that auto repair shops tended to overcharge women for real or imagined work on their cars on the assumption that they were less likely than men to understand mechanical matters, an assumption much less well founded these days.

Kitty Calavita and Henry Pontell, in the following article, provide details about the savings and loan scandals, which represented a welfare scheme for the rich. These offenses have been labeled "collective embezzlement" by the authors, who note that they represent a hybrid of organizational and occupational crime—crime *by* the corporation *against* the corporation.[11]

The article by Elizabeth Szockyj, a criminology professor at Southern Illinois University, portrays a small-time insider trading episode in which the owner of a chain of fast food restaurants allegedly passed on to his children information about a pending fall in the company's stock price. The case study provides a wealth of detailed information on matters often more abstractly addressed in overviews of white-collar crime. Questions can be raised about the motives of the regulatory agency in bringing the case in the first place, and particularly about its inability to gain a conviction of the only person it prosecuted criminally.

The final two articles deal with professional white-collar crime. In many respects, there is no crime more difficult to explain. Professionals, supposedly by definition, are oriented toward the needs of others—clients, patients, students, penitents, and others. They are not supposed to be motivated by self-interest; they are expected to help, not to hurt.

The distinction between professional and nonprofessional activity is reflected in the relationships characteristic of each. Customers come to businesses for their own interests; they wish an item offered by the business. Businesses interact with customers to satisfy the customers' desires, and, in so doing, to satisfy their own desire. In the end, the business is not so much interested in satisfying the customer as in satisfying itself. Selling the product is merely the means to this end.

Professionals, on the other hand, are expected to be interested in the needs, interests, and desires of their client. While businesses offer mainly goods, professionals more often offer only services. Clients come to professionals with legal, medical, educational, psychological, or religious needs. They come without expectation of a guarantee, for professionals alone do not guarantee the out-come of their services: acquittal, health, brilliance, or heaven. Professionals, then, are supposed to approach their work without the expectation of overriding personal benefit; their outlook is to be toward others. How, then, can we explain the self-interest acts that constitute white-collar crime by professionals? The reader should ask this question in regard to the concluding two articles in this section.

Doctors have come to be prosecuted criminally for a whole range of offenses that only came into being as the government began to fund medical programs. Doctors face conflicts between their professional and their business roles, and some find it irresistible to take x-rays without film or diagnose more serious ill-nesses than those presented, while others fiddle the system. Sir William Osler, himself a preeminent physician, suggested that the private practice of medicine also tends to breed arrogance in those who carry it on:

> No class of men needs friction so much as physicians; no class gets less. The daily round of a busy practitioner tends to develop an egoism of a most intense kind, to which there is no antidote. The few setbacks are for-gotten, the mistakes are often buried, and ten years of successful work tends to make a man touchy, dogmatic, intolerant of correction, and abom-inably self-centered.[12]

Attorneys, now undergoing public criticism so intense that it has gained its own designation—lawyer-bashing—are the subject of the final article in this section, written by Bruce Arnold and John Hagan. They find that complaints of misconduct are most likely to be directed against inexperienced lawyers in solo practice. They believe that this is brought about in part because of the relative powerlessness of these lawyers to defend themselves, especially during periods of economic recession.

Professionals, despite the occasional public prosecution, use their own sanc-tioning bodies to deal with deviants so that they often are able to avoid airing their dirty business in public. These considerations prevail for them not only in the regard to white-collar crime, but also in regard to more traditional offenses. Doctors caught using narcotics, for instance, generally are punished by having their prescription-writing privileges revoked for a period of time; the underclass addict is likely to go to prison.

Notes

1. Michael Conant, *Antitrust in the Motion Picture Industry.* Berkeley: University of California Press, 1972, p. 1.
2. John Kenneth Galbraith, *The Affluent Society.* Boston: Houghton Mifflin, 1958, p. 84.
3. John Finley Scott, *Internalization of Norms: A Sociological Theory of Moral Commitment.* Englewood Cliffs, NJ: Prentice-Hall, 1971, p. 31.
4. C. S. Lewis, *The Screwtape Letters and Screwtape Purposes.* New York: Macmillan, 1961, p. viii.
5. Dante, *Inferno,* Canto 11.
6. Huntington Cairns, *Law and the Social Sciences.* New York: Harcourt, Brace, 1935, p. 20.
7. Edwin H. Sutherland, *Criminology.* Philadelphia: Lippincott, 1924, p. 86.
8. Gresham M. Sykes and David Matza, "Techniques of Neutralization: A Theory of Delinquency," *American Sociological Review,* 22 (1957):664–670.
9. W. E. Laite, Jr., *The United States vs. William Laite.* Washington, DC: Acropolis Books, 1972, p. 23.
10. *Ibid.,* p. 11.
11. Kitty Calavita and Henry N. Pontell, " 'Other People's Money' Revisited: Collective Embezzlement in the Savings and Loan and Insurance Industries," *Social Problems,* 38 (1991):94–112.
12. Quoted in Harvey Cushing, *The Life of Sir William Osler.* London: Oxford University Press, 1940, p. 447.

8

The Heavy Electrical Equipment Antitrust Cases of 1961

Gilbert Geis

An inadvertent bit of humor by a defense attorney provided one of the major criminological motifs for "the most serious violations of the antitrust laws since the time of their passage at the turn of the century."[1] The defendants, including several vice presidents of the General Electric Corporation and the Westinghouse Electric Corporation—the two largest companies in the heavy electrical equipment industry—stood somberly in a federal courtroom in Philadelphia on February 6, 1961. They were aptly described by a newspaper reporter as "middle-class men in Ivy League suits—typical businessmen in appearance, men who would never be taken for lawbreakers." Several were deacons or vestrymen of their churches. One was president of his local chamber of commerce; another, a hospital board member; another, chief fund-raiser for the Community Chest; another, a bank director; another, director of the taxpayer's association; another, organizer of the local Little League.

The attorney for a General Electric executive attacked the government's demand for a jail sentence for his client, calling it "cold-blooded." The lawyer insisted that government prosecutors did not understand what it would do to his client, "this fine man," to be put "behind bars" with "common criminals who have been convicted of embezzlement and other serious crimes."[2]

The difficulty of defense counsel in considering antitrust violations "serious crimes," crimes at least equivalent to embezzling, indicates in part why the 1961 prosecutions provide such fascinating material for criminological study. Edwin H. Sutherland, who originated the term "white-collar crime" to categorize offenders such as antitrust violators, had lamented that his pioneering work was handicapped by the absence of adequate case histories of corporate offenders. "No first-hand research from this point of view has ever been reported."[3] Sutherland noted, and,

Reprinted from Marshall Clinard and Richard Quinney (eds.), *Criminal Behavior Systems* (New York: Holt, Rinehart & Winston, 1967), pp. 139–150. Copyright © 1967 by Holt, Rinehart & Winston, Inc. Reprinted by permission of Holt, Rinehart & Winston, Inc.

lacking such data, he proceeded to employ prosaic stories of derelictions by rather unimportant persons in small enterprises upon which to build an interpretative and theoretical structure for white-collar crime.

To explain corporate offenses and offenders, Sutherland had to rely primarily upon the criminal biographies of various large companies, as these were disclosed in the annals of trial courts and administrative agencies. In the absence of information about human offenders, the legal fiction of corporate humanity, a kind of economic anthropomorphism, found its way into criminological literature. Factual gaps were filled by shrewd guesses, definitional and semantic strategies, and a good deal of extrapolation. It was as if an attempt were being made to explain murder by reference only to the listed rap sheet offenses of a murderer and the life stories and identification data of several lesser offenders.[4]

Sutherland was writing, of course, before the antitrust violations in the heavy electrical equipment industry became part of the public record. Though much of the data regarding them is tantalizingly incomplete and unresponsive to fine points of criminological concern, the antitrust offenses nonetheless represent extraordinary case studies of white-collar crime, that designation which, according to Sutherland, applies to behavior by "a person of high socioeconomic status who violates the laws designed to regulate his occupational activities"[5] and "principally refers to business managers and executives."[6] In particular, the antitrust cases provide the researcher with a mass of raw data against which to test and to refine earlier hunches and hypotheses regarding white-collar crime.

FACTS OF THE ANTITRUST VIOLATIONS

The most notable characteristic of the 1961 antitrust conspiracy was its willful and blatant nature. These were not complex acts only doubtfully in violation of a highly complicated statute. They were flagrant, criminal offenses patently in contradiction to the letter and the spirit of the Sherman Antitrust Act of 1890, which forbade price-fixing arrangements as restraints upon free trade.[7]

The details of the conspiracy must be drawn together from diverse second-hand sources, because grand jury hearings upon which the criminal indictments were based were not made public. The decision to keep the records closed was reached on the ground that the traditional secrecy of grand jury proceedings took precedence over public interest in obtaining information about the conspiracy and over the interest of different purchasers in acquiring background data upon which to base civil suits against the offending corporations for allegedly fraudulent sales.[8]

The federal government had initiated the grand jury probes in mid-1959, apparently after receiving complaints from officials of the Tennessee Valley Authority concerning identical bids they were getting from manufacturers of highly technical electrical equipment, even though the bids were submitted in sealed envelopes.[9] Four grand juries were ultimately convened and subpoenaed 196 persons, some of whom obviously revealed the intimate details of the price-fixing procedures. A package of twenty indictments was handed down, involving forty-five individual defendants and twenty-nine corporations. Almost all of the corporate defendants pleaded guilty; the company officials tended to enter pleas of *nolo contendere* (no contest) which, in this case, might reasonably be taken to indicate that they did not see much likelihood of escaping conviction.

The pleas negated the necessity for a public trial and for public knowledge of the precise machinations involved in the offenses. At the sentencing hearing, fines amounting to $1,924,500 were levied against the defendants, $1,787,000 falling upon the corporations and $137,000 upon different individuals. The major fines were set against General Electric ($437,500) and Westinghouse ($372,500). Much more eye-catching were the jail terms of thirty days imposed upon seven defendants, four of whom were vice presidents; two, division managers; and one, a sales manager.

The defendants sentenced to jail were handled essentially the same as other offenders with similar dispositions. They were handcuffed in pairs in the back seat of an automobile on their way to the Montgomery County Jail in Norristown, Pennsylvania, fingerprinted on entry, and dressed in the standard blue denim uniforms. During their stay, they were described as "model prisoners," and several were transferred to the prison farm. The remainder, working an eight-hour day for 30 cents, earned recognition from the warden as "the most intelligent prisoners" he had had during the year on a project concerned with organizing prison records. None of the seven men had visitors during the Wednesday and Saturday periods reserved for visiting; all indicated a desire not to be seen by their families or friends.

Good behavior earned the men a five-day reduction in their sentence. Toward the end of the year, the remaining defendants, who had been placed on probation, were released from that status, despite the strong protests of government officials. The judge, the same man who had imposed the original sentences, explained his action by noting that he "didn't think that this was the type of offense that probation lent itself readily to or was designed for." Supervision was seen as meaningless for men with such clean past records and such little likelihood of recidivism, particularly since the probation office was already "clogged to the gunwales"[10] with cases.

The major economic consequences to the corporations arose from civil suits for treble damages filed against them as provided in the antitrust laws. The original fines were, of course, negligible: For General Electric, a half-million dollar loss was no more unsettling than a $3 parking fine would be to a man with an income of $175,000 a year. Throughout the early stages of negotiations over the damage suits, General Electric maintained that it would resist such actions on grounds which are noteworthy as an indication of the source and the content of the rationale that underlay the self-justification of individual participants in the price-fixing conspiracy:

We believe that the purchasers of electrical apparatus have received fair value by any reasonable standard. The prices which they have paid during the past years were appropriate to value received and reasonable as compared with the general trends of prices in the economy, the price trends for materials, salaries, and wages. The foresight of the electrical utilities and the design and manufacturing skills of companies such as General Electric have kept electricity one of today's greatest bargains.[11]

By 1962, General Electric was granting that settlements totaling between $45 and $50 million would have to be arranged to satisfy claimants. Municipalities and other purchasers of heavy electrical equipment were taking the period of lowest prices, when they assumed the price-rigging was least effective, using these prices as "legitimate," and calculating higher payments as products of the price conspiracy. The initial General Electric estimate soon proved untenable. A mid-1964 calculation showed that 90 percent of some 1,800 claims had been settled for a total of $160 million, but General Electric could derive some solace from the fact that most of these payments would be tax-deductible.

TECHNIQUES OF THE CONSPIRACY

The modus operandi for the antitrust violators shows clearly the awareness of the participants that their behavior was such that it had better be carried on as secretly as possible. Some comparison might be made between the antitrust offenses and other forms of fraud occurring in lower economic classes. It was one of Sutherland's most telling contentions that neither the method by which a crime is committed nor the manner in which it is handled by public agencies alters the essential criminal nature of the act and the criminal status of the perpetrator.[12] Selling faucet water on a street corner to a blind man who is led to believe that the product is specially prepared to relieve his ailment is seen as no different from selling a $50 million turbine to a city which is laboring under the misapprehension that it is purchasing the product at the best price possible from closed competitive bidding. The same may be said in regard to methods of treatment. Tuberculosis, for example, remains tuberculosis and its victim a tubercular whether the condition is treated in a sanitarium or whether it is ignored, overlooked, or even condoned by public authorities. So too with crime. As Miss Stein might have said: A crime is a crime is a crime.

Like most reasonably adept and optimistic criminals, the antitrust violators had hoped to escape apprehension. "I didn't expect to get caught and I went to great lengths to conceal my activities so that I wouldn't get caught," one of them said.[13] Another went into some detail concerning the techniques of concealment:

It was considered discreet to not be too obvious and to minimize telephone calls, to use plain envelopes if mailing material to each other, not to be seen together on traveling, and so forth . . . not leave wastepaper, of which there was a lot, strewn around a room when leaving.

The plans themselves, while there were some slight variations over time and in terms of different participants, were essentially similar. The offenders hid behind a camouflage of fictitious names and conspiratorial codes. The attendance roster for the meetings was known as the "Christmas card list" and the gatherings, interestingly enough, as "choir practice."[14] The offenders used public telephones for much of their communication, and they either met at trade association conventions, where their relationship would appear reasonable, or at sites selected for their anonymity. It is quite noteworthy, in this respect, that while some of the men filed false travel claims, so as to mislead their superiors regarding the city they had visited, they never asked for expense money to places more distant than those they had actually gone to—on the theory, apparently, that whatever else was occurring, it would not do to cheat the company.

At the meetings, negotiations centered about the establishment of a "reasonable" division of the market for the various products. Generally, participating companies were allocated essentially that part of the market which they had previously garnered. If Company A, for instance, had under competitive conditions secured 20 percent of the available business, then agreement might be reached that it would be given the opportunity to submit the lowest bid on 20 percent of the new contracts. A low price would be established, and the remainder of the companies would bid at approximately equivalent, though higher, levels. It sometimes happened, however, that because of things such as company reputation or available servicing arrangements, the final contract was awarded to a firm which had not submitted the lowest bid. For this, among other reasons, debate among the conspirators was often acrimonious about the proper division of spoils, about alleged failures to observe previous agreements, and about other intramural matters. Sometimes, depending upon the contract, the conspirators would draw lots to determine who would submit the lowest bid; at other times, the appropriate arrangement would be determined under a rotating system that was conspiratorially referred to as the "phase of the moon."

EXPLANATIONS OF THE CONSPIRACY

Attempts to understand the reasons for and the general significance of the price-fixing conspiracy have been numerous. They include re-examination of the antitrust laws,[15] as well as denunciations of the corporate ethos and the general pattern of American life and American values.[16] A not inconsiderable number of the defendants took the line that their behavior, while technically criminal, had really served a worthwhile purpose by "stabilizing prices" (a much-favored phrase of the conspirators). This altruistic interpretation almost invariably was combined with an attempted distinction among illegal, criminal, and immoral acts, with the offender's expressing the view that what he had done might have been designated by the statutes as criminal, but either he was unaware of such a designation or he thought it unreasonable that acts with admirable consequences should be considered criminal. The testimony of a Westinghouse executive during hearings by the Senate Subcommittee on Antitrust and Monopoly clearly illustrates this point of view:

COMMITTEE ATTORNEY: Did you know that these meetings with competitors were illegal?
WITNESS: Illegal? Yes, but not criminal. I didn't find that out until I read the indictment. . . . I assumed that criminal action meant damaging someone, and we did not do that. . . . I thought that we were more or less working on a survival basis in order to try to make enough to keep our plant and our employees.

This theme was repeated in essentially similar language by a number of witnesses. "It is against the law," an official of the Ingersoll-Rand Corporation granted, but he added: "I do not know that it is against public welfare because I am not certain that the consumer was actually injured by this operation." A Carrier Corporation executive testified that he was "reasonably in doubt" that the price-fixing meetings violated the antitrust law. "Certainly, we were in a gray area. I think the degree of violation, if you can speak of it that way, is what was in doubt." Some of these views are gathered together in a statement by a former sales manager of the I-T-E Circuit Breaker Company:

One faces a decision, I guess, at such times, about how far to go with company instructions, and since the spirit of such meetings only appeared to be correcting a horrible price level situation, that there was not an attempt to actually damage customers, charge excessive prices, there was no personal gain in it for me, the company did not seem actually to be defrauding, corporate statements can evidence the fact that there have been poor profits during all these years. . . . So I guess morally it did not seem quite so bad as might be inferred by the definition of the activity itself.

For the most part, personal explanations for the acts were sought in the structure of corporate pressures rather than in the avarice or lack of law-abiding character of the men involved. The defendants almost invariably testified that they came new to a job, found price-fixing an established way of life, and simply entered into it as they did into other aspects of their job. This explanatory scheme fit into a pattern that Senator Philip A. Hart of Michigan, during the subcommittee hearings, labeled "imbued fraud."[17]

There was considerable agreement concerning the manner in which the men initially became involved in price fixing. "My first actual experience was back in the 1930s," a General Electric official said. "I was taken there by my boss . . . to sit down and price a job." An Ingersoll-Rand executive said, "[My superior] took me to a meeting to introduce me to some of our competitors . . . and at that meeting pricing of condensers was discussed with the competitors." Essentially the same comment is repeated by witness after witness. A General Electric officer said, "Every direct supervisor that I had directed me to meet with competition. . . . It had become so common and gone on for so many years that I think we lost sight of the fact that it was illegal." Price fixing, whether or not recognized as illegal by the offenders, was clearly an integral part of their jobs. "Meeting with competitors was just one of the many facets of responsibility that was delegated to me," one witness testified. . . .

What might have happened to the men if, for reasons of conscience or perhaps through a fear of the possible consequences, they had objected to the "duty" to participate in price-fixing schemes? This point was raised only by the General Electric employees, perhaps because they alone had some actual evidence upon which to base their speculations. In 1946, General Electric had first issued a directive, number 20.5, which spelled out the company's policy against price fixing in terms stronger than those found in the antitrust laws. A considerable number of the executives believed, in the words of one, that the directive was only for "public consumption," and not to be taken seriously. One man, however, refused to engage in price fixing after he had initialed the document forbidding it. A witness explained to the Senate subcommittee what followed:

[My superior] told me, "This fellow is a fine fellow, he is capable in every respect except he was not broad enough for his job, that he was so religious that he thought, in spite of what his superiors said, he thought having signed that, that he should not do any of this and he is getting us in trouble with competition.

The man who succeeded the troublesome official, one of the defendants in the Philadelphia hearing, said that he had been told that he "would be expected to do otherwise" and that this "was why I was offered that promotion to Philadelphia because this man would not do it." At the same time, however, the General Electric witnesses specified clearly that it was not their job with the company that would be in jeopardy if they failed to price-fix, but rather the particular assignment they had. "If I didn't do it, I felt that somebody else would," said one, with an obvious note of self-justification. "I would be removed and somebody else would do it."

Westinghouse and General Electric differed considerably in their reactions to the exposure of the offenses, with Westinghouse electing to retain in its employ persons involved in the conspiracy, and General Electric deciding to dismiss the employees who had been before the court. The reasoning of the companies throws light both on the case and on the relationship between antitrust offenses and the more traditionally viewed forms of criminal behavior.

Westinghouse put forward four justifications for its retention decision. First, it declared, the men involved had not sought personal aggrandizement—"While their actions cannot in any way be condoned, these men did not act for personal gain, but in the belief, misguided though it may have been, that they were furthering the com-

pany's interest"; second, "the punishment incurred by them already was harsh" and
"no further penalties would serve any useful purpose"; third, "each of these individuals is in every sense a reputable citizen, a respected and valuable member of the
community and of high moral character"; and fourth, there was virtually no likelihood that the individuals would repeat their offense.[18]

General Electric's punitive line toward its employees was justified on the ground
that the men had violated not only federal law but also a basic company policy and
that they therefore deserved severe punishment. The company's action met with
something less than whole-hearted acclaim; rather, it was often interpreted as an
attempt to scapegoat particular individuals for what was essentially the responsibility of the corporate enterprise and its top executives. "I do not understand the holier-
than-thou attitude in GE when your directions came from very high at the top,"
Senator Kefauver said during his committee's hearings; while Senator John A. Car-
roll of Colorado expressed his view through a leading question: "Do you think you
were thrown to the wolves to ease the public relations situation . . . that has developed since these indictments?" he asked a discharged General Electric employee.
The witness thought that he had.

Perhaps most striking is the fact that though many offenders quite clearly stressed
the likely consequences for them if they failed to conform to price-fixing expectations, not one hinted at the benefits he might expect, the personal and professional
rewards, from participation in the criminal conspiracy. It remained for the sentencing judge and two top General Electric executives to deliver the harshest denunciations of the personal motives and qualities of the conspirators to be put forth during
the case.

The statement of Judge J. Cullen Ganey, read prior to imposing sentence,
received widespread attention. In it, he sharply criticized the corporations as the
major culprits, but he also pictured the defendants in a light other than that they
chose to shed upon themselves:

> They were torn between conscience and an approved corporate policy, with
> the rewarding objective of promotion, comfortable security, and large salaries.
> They were the organization, or company, man; the conformist who goes along
> with his superiors and finds balm for his conscience in additional comforts and
> security of his place in the corporate set-up.[19]

The repeated emphasis on "comfort" and "security" constitutes the basic element
of Ganey's view of the motivations of the offenders. Stress on passive acquiescence
occurs in remarks by two General Electric executives viewing the derelictions of
their subordinates. Robert Paxton, the retired company president, called antitrust
agreements "monkey business" and denounced in vitriolic terms one of his former
superiors who, when Paxton first joined General Electric, had put him to work
attempting to secure a bid on a contract that had already been prearranged by a
price-fixing agreement. Ralph Cordiner, the president and board chairman of General Electric, thought that the antitrust offenses were motivated by drives for easily

acquired power. Cordiner's statement is noteworthy for its dismissal of the explanations of the offenders as "rationalizations":

> One reason for the offenses was a desire to be "Mr. Transformer" or "Mr. Switchgear"* . . . and to have influence over a larger segment of the industry. . . . The second was that it was an indolent, lazy way to do business. When you get all through with the rationalizations, you have to come back to one or the other of these conclusions.

There were other explanations as well. One truculent offender, the sixty-eight-year-old president of a smaller company who had been spared a jail sentence only because of his age and the illness of his wife, categorically denied the illegality of his behavior. "We did not fix prices," he said. "I can't agree with you. I am telling you that all we did was recover costs." Some persons blamed the system of decentralization in the larger companies, which, they said, placed a heavy burden to produce profit on each of the relatively autonomous divisions, particularly when bonuses—"incentive compensation"—were at stake; others maintained that the "dog-eat-dog" business conditions in the heavy electrical equipment industry were responsible for the violations. Perhaps the simplest explanation came from a General Electric executive. "I think," he said, "the boys could resist everything but temptation."

PORTRAIT OF AN OFFENDER

The highest-paid executive to be given a jail sentence was a General Electric vice president, earning $135,000 a year—about $2,600 every week. The details of his career and his participation in the conspiracy provide additional insight into the operations of white-collar crime and white-collar criminals.

The General Electric vice president was one of the disproportionate number of Southerners involved in the antitrust violations. He had been born in Atlanta and was forty-six years old at the time he was sentenced to jail. He had graduated with a degree in electrical engineering from Georgia Tech and received an honorary doctorate degree from Siena College in 1958; he was married and the father of three children. He had served in the Navy during World War II, rising to the rank of lieutenant commander; he was a director of the Schenectady Boy's Club, on the board of trustees of Miss Hall's School, and, not without some irony, he was a member of Governor Rockefeller's Temporary State Committee on Economic Expansion.

Almost immediately after his sentencing, he issued a statement to the press, noting that he was to serve a jail term "for conduct which has been interpreted as being in conflict with the complex antitrust laws." He commented that "General Electric,

---

* Earlier, a witness had quoted his superior as saying: "I have the industry under my thumb. They will do just about as I ask them." This man, the witness said, "was known as Mr. Switchgear in the industry."

Schenectady, and its people have undergone many ordeals together and we have not only survived them, but have come out stronger, more vigorous, more alive than ever. We shall again." Then he voiced his appreciation for "the letters and calls from people all over the country, the community, the shops, and the offices . . . expressing confidence and support."[20]

The vice president was neither so sentimental about his company nor so certain about the complexity of the antitrust regulations when he appeared before the Kefauver committee five months later. "I don't get mad, Senator," he said at one point, referring to his behavior during a meeting with competitors; but he took another line when he attempted to explain why he was no longer associated with General Electric:

> When I got out of being a guest of the government for thirty days, I had found out that we were not to be paid while we were there [A matter of some $11,000 for the jail term], and I got, frankly, madder than hell.

Previously, he had been mentioned as a possible president of General Electric, described by the then president, as "an exceptionally eager and promising individual." Employed by the company shortly after graduation from college, he had risen dramatically through the managerial ranks, and passed that point, described by a higher executive, "where the man, if his work has been sufficiently promising, has an opportunity to step across the barrier out of his function into the field of general management." In 1946, he had his first contact with price fixing, being introduced to competitors by his superior and told that he "should be the one to contact them as far as power transformers were concerned in the future."

The meetings that he attended ran a rather erratic course, with numerous squabbles between the participants. Continual efforts had to be made to keep knowledge of the meetings from "the manufacturing people, the engineers, and especially the lawyers," but this was achieved, the witness tried to convince the Kefauver committee, because commercial transactions remained unquestioned by managerial personnel so long as they showed a reasonable profit. The price-fixing meetings continued from 1946 until 1949. At that time, a federal investigation of licensing and cross-patent activities in the transformer industry sent the conspirators scurrying. "The iron curtain was completely down" for a year, and sales people at General Electric were forbidden to attend gatherings of the National Electrical Manufacturers' Association, where they had traditionally connived with competitors.

Meetings resumed, however, when the witness's superior, described by him as "a great communicator, a great philosopher, and, frankly, a great believer in stabilities of prices," decided that "the market was getting in chaotic condition" and that they "had better go out and see what could be done about it." He was told to keep knowledge of the meetings from Robert Paxton, "an Adam Smith advocate" and then the plant works manager, because Paxton "don't understand these things."

Promoted to general manager in 1954, the witness was called to New York by the president of General Electric and told specifically, possibly in part because he had a reputation of being "a bad boy," to comply with the company policy and with the antitrust laws and to see that his subordinates did so too. This instruction lasted as long as it took him to get from New York back to Massachusetts, where his superior there told him, "Now, keep on doing the way that you have been doing but just . . . be sensible about it and use your head on the subject." The price-fixing meetings therefore continued unabated, particularly as market conditions were aggravated by overproduction which had taken place during the Korean War. In the late 1950s, foreign competition entered the picture, and lower bids from abroad often forced the American firms to give up on particular price-fixing attempts.

In 1957, the witness was promoted to vice president, and again brought to New York for a lecture from the company president on the evils of price fixing. This time, his "air cover gone"—he now had to report directly to top management—he decided to abandon altogether his involvement in price fixing. He returned to his plant and issued stringent orders to his subordinates that they were no longer to attend meetings with competitors. Not surprisingly, since he himself had rarely obeyed such injunctions, neither did the sales persons in his division.

The witness was interrogated closely about his moral feelings regarding criminal behavior. He fumbled most of the questions, avoiding answering them directly, but ultimately coming to the point of saying that the consequences visited upon him represented the major reason for a reevaluation of his actions. He would not behave in the same manner again because of what "I have been through and what I have done to my family." He was also vexed with the treatment he had received from the newspapers: "They have never laid off a second. They have used some terms which I don't think are necessarily—they don't use the term 'price fixing.' It is always 'price rigging' or trying to make it as sensational as possible."[21] The taint of a jail sentence, he said, had the effect of making people "start looking at the moral values a little bit." Senator Hart drew the following conclusions from the witness's comments:

HART: This was what I was wondering about, whether absent the introduction of this element of fear, there would have been any re-examination of the moral implications.

WITNESS: I wonder, Senator. That is a pretty tough one to answer.

HART: If I understand you correctly, you have already answered it. . . . After the fear, there came the moral re-evaluation.

All things said, the former General Electric vice president viewed his situation philosophically. Regarding his resignation from the company, it was "the way the ball has bounced." He hoped that he would have "the opportunity to continue in American industry and do a job," and he wished some of the other men who had been dismissed a lot of good luck. "I want to leave the company with no bitterness and to go out and see if I can't start a new venture along the right lines." Eight days later, he accepted a job as assistant to the president in charge of product research in a large corporation located outside of Philadelphia. Slightly more than a month after that, he was named president of the company, at a salary reported to be somewhat less than the $74,000 yearly received by his predecessor.

A SUMMING-UP

The antitrust violations in the heavy electrical industry permit a reevaluation of many of the earlier speculations about white-collar crime. The price-fixing behavior, flagrant in nature, was clearly in violation of the criminal provisions of the Sherman Antitrust Act of 1890 which had been aimed at furthering "industrial liberty." Rather, the price-fixing arrangements represented attempts at "corporate socialism," and in the words of Senator Kefauver to a subcommittee witness:

> It makes a complete mockery not only of how we have always lived and what we have believed in and have laws to protect, but what you were doing was to make a complete mockery of the carefully worded laws of the government of the United States, ordinances of the cities, rules of the REA's [Rural Electrification Administration], with reference to sealed secret bids in order to get competition.

The facts of the antitrust conspiracy would seem clearly to resolve in the affirmative any debate concerning the criminal nature and the relevance for criminological study of such forms of white-collar behavior,[22] though warnings regarding an indefinite and unwarranted extension of the designation "crime" to all acts abhorrent to academic criminologists must remain in force. Many of Sutherland's ideas concerning the behavior of corporate offenders also receive substantiation. His stress on learning and associational patterns as important elements in the genesis of the violations receives strong support;[23] so too does his emphasis on national trade conventions as the sites of corporate criminal conspiracies.[24]

Others of Sutherland's views appear to require overhaul. His belief, for example, that "those who are responsible for the system of criminal justice are afraid to antagonize businessmen"[25] seems less than totally true in terms of the electrical industry prosecutions. Sutherland's thesis that "the customary pleas of the executives of the corporation . . . that they were ignorant of and not responsible for the action of the special department . . . is akin to the alibi of the ordinary criminal and need not be taken seriously"[26] also seems to be a rather injudicious blanket condemnation. The accuracy of the statement for the antitrust conspiracy must remain moot, but it would seem important that traditional safeguards concerning guilty knowledge as a basic ingredient in criminal responsibility be accorded great respect. Nor, in terms of antitrust data, does Sutherland appear altogether correct in his view that "the public agencies of communication, which continually define ordinary violations of the criminal code in a very critical manner, do not make similar definitions of white-collar crime."[27]

Various analytical schemes and theoretical statements in criminology and related fields provide some insight into elements of the price-fixing conspiracy. Galbraith's caustic observation regarding the traditional academic view of corporate price-fixing arrangements represents a worthwhile point of departure:

> Restraints on competition and the free movement of prices, the principal source of uncertainty to business firms, have been principally deplored by university professors on lifelong appointments. Such security of tenure is deemed essential for fruitful and unremitting thought.[28]

It seems apparent, looking at the antitrust offenses in this light, that the attractiveness of a secure market arrangement represented a major ingredient drawing corporate officers to the price-fixing violations. The elimination of competition meant the avoidance of uncertainty, the formalization and predictability of outcome, the minimization of risks. It is, of course, this incentive which accounts for much of human activity, be it deviant or "normal," and this tendency that Weber found pronounced in bureaucracies in their move from vital but erratic beginnings to more staid and more comfortable middle and old age.[29]

For the conspirators there had necessarily to be a conjunction of factors before they could participate in the violations. First, of course, they had to perceive that there would be gains accruing from their behavior. Such gains might be personal and professional, in terms of corporate advancement toward prestige and power; they might be vocational, in terms of a more expedient and secure method of carrying out assigned tasks. The offenders also apparently had to be able to neutralize or rationalize their behavior in a manner in keeping with their image of themselves as law-abiding, decent, and respectable persons.[30] The ebb and flow of the price-fixing conspiracy also clearly indicates the relationship, often overlooked in explanations of criminal behavior, between extrinsic conditions and illegal acts. When the market behaved in a manner the executives thought satisfactory or when enforcement agencies seemed particularly threatening, the conspiracy desisted. When market conditions deteriorated, while corporate pressures for achieving attractive profit-and-loss statements remained constant, and enforcement activity abated, the price-fixing agreements flourished.

More than anything else, however, a plunge into the elaborate documentation of the antitrust cases of 1961 and an attempt to relate them to other segments of criminological work points up the considerable need for more and better monographic field studies of law violators and of systems of criminal behavior, followed by attempts to establish theoretical guidelines and to review and refine current interpretative viewpoints. There have probably been no more than a dozen, if that many, full-length studies of types of criminal (not delinquent) behavior in the past decade. The need for such work seems overriding, and the 1961 antitrust cases represent but one of a number of instances, whether in the field of white-collar crime, organized crime, sex offenses, personal or property crimes, or similar areas of concern, where we are still faced with a less than adequate supply of basic and comparative material upon which to base valid and useful theoretical statements.

Notes

1. Judge J. Cullen Ganey, in *Application of the State of California,* 195 F.Supp. 39 (E.D. Pa. 1961).
2. *New York Times,* February 7, 1961.
3. Edwin H. Sutherland, *White Collar Crime.* New York: Dryden Press, 1949, p. 240.
4. For an elaboration of this point, see Gilbert Geis, "Toward a Delineation of White-Collar Offenses," *Sociological Inquiry,* 32 (1962):160–171.
5. Edwin H. Sutherland, *The White Collar Criminal."* In Vernon C. Branham and Samuel B. Kutash, eds., *Encyclopedia of Criminology.* New York: Philosophical Library, 1949, p. 511.
6. Sutherland, *White Collar Crime, op. cit.,* p. 9, fn. 7.
7. *United States Statutes,* 26 (1890), p. 209; *United States Code,* 15 (1958), l, 2.
8. Note, "Release of the Grand Jury Minutes in the National Deposition Program of the Electrical Equipment Cases," *University of Pennsylvania Law Review,* 112 (1964):1133–1145.
9. John Herling, *The Great Price Conspiracy.* Washington, DC: Robert B. Luce, 1962, pp. 1–12; John G. Fuller, *The Gentleman Conspirators.* New York: Grove, 1962, pp. 7–11.
10. Telephone interview with Judge Ganey, Philadelphia, August 31, 1964; *New York Times,* December 20, 1961.
11. *New York Times,* February 7, 1961.
12. Edwin H. Sutherland, "White-Collar Criminality," *American Sociological Review,* 5 (1940):1–12.
13. U.S. Senate, Subcommittee on Antitrust and Monopoly, Committee on the Judiciary, 87th Cong., 2d Sess., 1961, "Administered Prices," *Hearings,* pts. 27 and 28. Unless otherwise indicated, subsequent data and quotations are taken from these documents.
14. Richard Austin Smith, "The Incredible Electrical Conspiracy," *Fortune,* 63 (April 1961):132–137, and 63 (May 1961):161–164ff.
15. See Leland Hazard, "Are Big Businessmen Crooks?" *Atlantic,* 208 (November 1961):57–61.
16. See Anthony Lewis, *New York Times*, February 12, 1961.
17. *Hearings,* pt. 27, *op. cit.,* p. 16773.
18. Sharon, Pa., *Herald,* February 6, 1961.

19. *New York Times*, February 7, 1961.
20. Schenectady, N.Y. *Union-Star,* February 10, 1961.
21. *Hearings,* pt. 27, *op. cit.*, p. 17076. A contrary view is expressed in Alan J. Dershowitz, "Increasing Community Control over Corporate Crime," *Yale Law Journal,* 71 (1961):289–306.
22. See Edwin H. Sutherland, "Is 'White-Collar' Crime Crime?" *American Sociological Review,* 10 (1945):132–139.
23. Sutherland, *White Collar Crime, op. cit.*, pp. 234–257.
24. *Ibid.*, p. 70.
25. *Ibid.*, p. 10.
26. *Ibid.*, p. 54.
27. *Ibid.*, p. 247.
28. John Kenneth Galbraith, *The Affluent Society.* Boston: Houghton Mifflin, 1958, p. 84.
29. Max Weber, *The Theory of Social and Economic Organization,* trans. A. M. Henderson and Talcott Parsons. New York: Oxford University Press, 1947, pp. 367–373.
30. See Donald R. Cressey, *Other People's Money: The Social Psychology of Embezzlement.* New York: The Free Press, 1953; Gresham M. Sykes and David Matza, "Techniques of Neutralization," *American Sociological Review,* 22 (1957):664–670.

9

Fire in Hamlet

A Case Study of State-Corporate Crime

Judy Root Aulette and Raymond Michalowski

O n September 3, 1991, an explosion and fire at the Imperial Food Products chicken processing plant in Hamlet, North Carolina, killed 25 workers and injured another 56. This human disaster, which devastated the small working-class community of Hamlet, immediately became the subject of both controversy and investigation. Shortly after the fire there was speculation that Imperial might face felony manslaughter charges in the deaths because fire doors that would have led the workers to safety were deliberately kept locked. According to a number of workers at the plant, fire doors were "routinely locked to keep employees from stealing chicken nuggets."[1] Subsequent inquiry indicated that not only did the company lock the fire doors, one of which displayed the bloody footprints of workers who tried to batter it open before they died, but also that an interwoven pattern of regulatory failure on the part of several state and federal agencies played a significant role in creating the conditions that led to the tragedy. This regulatory failure was facilitated by the State of North Carolina through its refusal to fund and support the state's Occupational Safety and Health Program even to the limits of *available* Federal monies. In 1990, a year before the Imperial plant fire, the State of North Carolina returned $453,000 in unspent OSHA money to the Federal government, even though its OSHA program was "underfunded and overwhelmed" and state safety inspections had fallen to their lowest level in 16 years.[2]

The fire at the Imperial Food Processing plant and the regulatory environment that made it possible underscore the importance of the interplay between corporations and government in the production of life-threatening criminal conduct by businesses. The *technical cause* of the Imperial plant fire was the rupture of a hydraulic line near a deep fryer. This resulted in an explosion and a fireball that not only destroyed the plant and the lives of 25 workers, but also shattered the social make-

Reprinted from Kenneth D. Tunnell, ed., *Political Crime in Contemporary America: A Critical Approach.* New York: Garland Publishing, 1993, pp. 171–206.

up of an entire town. Those who died or were injured in the Hamlet fire, however, were the victims of much more than a simple mechanical breakdown. They were the victims of a series of *social decisions* made by a broad array of institutions. These include Imperial Food Products, the U.S. Occupational Safety and Health Administration, the U.S. Food and Drug Administration, the legislature and governor of the State of North Carolina, the North Carolina Occupational Safety and Health Administration, and, finally, local agencies responsible for building inspection and fire protection. These organizational units pursued a pattern of actions and relations that made it possible and routine that workers in the Imperial chicken processing plant would be denied adequate escape routes in case of fire. This pattern does not represent an aberrant moment in North Carolina labor history. Rather, we argue, it is only a current reflection of North Carolina's long-standing commitment to a development policy based on attracting industry by offering low taxation and, particularly relevant in the immediate case, a lax regulatory environment.

In this chapter we will examine the ways in which the interplay of government and business interests in North Carolina culminated in the disastrous fire at the Imperial chicken processing plant. Specifically, we will argue that the deaths and injuries in Hamlet represent an example of what Kramer and Michalowski term *state-corporate crime,*[3] and we will explore three nested contexts—the societal context, the organizational context, and the control context—that shaped the conditions which produced 25 new graves in Hamlet, North Carolina, in the fall of 1991.

STATE-CORPORATE CRIME IN CONTEXT

In his 1939 Presidential Address to the American Sociological Association, Edwin Sutherland introduced the concept of *white-collar crime,* which later served as the basis for his pioneering book by the same title. Although Sutherland was primarily concerned with the social class positions of "white-collar" offenders as *individuals,* the data he actually analyzed consisted of violations charged against corporations and businesses as *organizations.*[4] This contradiction in Sutherland's work ultimately led to the study of what has become known as "corporate crime." The study of corporate crime focuses on deviant organizational patterns rather than on the deviance of individuals.[5] This approach has resulted in an important insight and an important oversight. The *insight* is that corporate crime is a form of organizational deviance.[6] Insofar as corporations are formal organizations, the study of corporate crime can and should incorporate the theoretical and substantive insights of organizational research.[7] The *oversight* is the failure to recognize that since the modern corporation emerged as the basic unit of economic activity within private-production systems in the late 19th century, corporations and governments have been functionally interdependent. The modern corporation in the United States could not have developed, nor could it currently function, without the legal, economic, and political infrastructure provided by government.[8] Governments in private-production systems, in turn, depend upon corporations and other economic organizations to supply necessary goods and services, to provide the economic base in the form of individual salaries and/or corporate profits upon which governments must depend for their revenues, and to make possible the fulfillment of government development policies.[9]

Despite its ubiquity, the relationship between corporations and governmental units has been peripheral to the study of corporate crime. Instead, two nearly independent bodies of research have developed. Theory and research in the area of corporate crime has concentrated primarily on organizational deviance *within* private business corporations. Parallelling corporate crime research, but seldom intersecting with it, others have examined crimes and malfeasance by governments, what Chambliss terms "state-organized crime."[10] These latter are crimes or socially injurious actions that result as governmental organizations pursue goals that cannot be attained, or cannot be attained easily, within the boundaries of the government's own laws.[11]

Our argument here is that many injurious events, such as the killing fire at the Imperial chicken processing factory, are generated at the interstices of corporations and governments. Kramer and Michalowski have defined these state-corporate crimes as follows:

> State-corporate crimes are illegal or socially injurious actions that occur when one or more institutions of political governance pursue a goal in direct cooperation with one or more institutions of economic production and distribution.[12]

This definition appears to give particular weight to the ways in which governments utilize businesses in order to achieve *government* goals, and in their initial work on the subject Kramer and Michalowski offer the explosion of the space shuttle Challenger as their prototype for state-corporate crime. In another context Kauzlarich and Kramer utilize the concept of state-corporate crime as a device to examine the relationship between the U.S. government and weapons manufacturers in the production of a nuclear arsenal, again emphasizing the central role of the government in organizing a cooperative activity involving both government and business.[13] The case at hand, however, suggests a different kind of relationship, one where government omissions permit private businesses to pursue illegal and potentially injurious courses of action which, *in a general way,* facilitate the fulfillment of certain state policies.

The relationship between the overarching government policies and the specific goals of business and industry is well illustrated by North Carolina's labor history. Since the late 19th century the political leadership of North Carolina has pursued a policy of industrial development through, among other things, limiting unionization and blocking the power of regulatory agencies. This pursuit of industrial development is a more general and less delimited goal than the specific pursuit of such things as a space program or nuclear weapons production. By contrast, the Imperial Food Processing company, like most industries, had a very specific goal of profit maximization through (among other things) worker discipline. This goal and the methods used to attain it, however, dovetailed nicely with the state's general concern with industrial development through (among other things) creating a climate within which businesses were not burdened with either unions or extensive safety regulation.

Like the state-corporate crimes examined by Kramer and Michalowski, and Kauzlarich and Kramer, the Imperial plant fire depended on the *interaction* between the pursuit of government and corporate goals. Thus, we think the general framework state-corporate crime is appropriate for the task at hand. We would, however, modify the definition of state corporate crime to read:

> State-corporate crimes are illegal or socially injurious actions that result from a mutually reinforcing interaction between (1) policies and/or practices in pursuit of the goals of one or more institutions of political governance and (2) policies and/or practices in pursuit of the goals of one or more institutions of economic production and distribution.

State-corporate crimes occur within a capitalist economy when two or more organizations, at least one of which is in the civil sector and one of which is in the state sector, pursue goals that intersect in such a way as to produce some form of social injury.

The following discussion of the Imperial plant fire as state-corporate crime is divided into three parts. First, we establish the *societal context* in which the Imperial fire occurred by examining the history of industrial regulation in North Carolina as it relates to the state's overall development policy. Second, we will construct the *institutional context* for the disaster by examining the specific pattern of industrial relations characteristic of the Imperial Food Processing company. And lastly, we will examine the *control context* within which the fire occurred by exploring the ways in which the activities of regulatory agencies intersected with the activities of Imperial in a way that resulted in the disastrous fire of September 3, 1991.

THE SOCIETAL CONTEXT

Political-Economic History of North Carolina

The societal context within which the Hamlet fire occurred is characterized by a set of political economic arrangements that have historically centered around broad, state-supported latitude for investors, and extensive state-enforced or state-permitted controls over labor.[14] The overall climate in North Carolina, since the end of the Civil War, has been one in which state policies toward both development and labor have been breathtakingly tilted in favor of capital accumulation and away from advancements in wages or work conditions for labor.[15] The result has been a history of economic growth without real economic development. As Tomaskovic-Devey observes:

Economic growth is a process of economic change which leads to increased employment and production activity. Economic development, on the other hand, is a growth process which leads to increased standards of living for the people in a region.[16]

North Carolina's recent economic history has certainly produced economic growth, but development, in the form of improved living standards for the mass of the state's industrial workers, has lagged behind substantially. Between 1976 and 1986 nonagricultural employment in the South overall grew by 44 percent, as compared to only 10 percent in the Northeast,[17] and North Carolina enjoyed a substantial share of this growth explosion in the so-called "Sunbelt." By 1987, the state was ranked first among all the states in the number of new manufacturing plants opened, and the North Carolina Department of Commerce boasted that businesses had invested nearly $5.4 billion dollars in new and expanded industrial facilities with the subsequent creation of 76,600 jobs. Yet, at the same time the state retained its long-standing position as last among the fifty states in average manufacturing wage, as well as attaining the highest infant mortality rate of any state in the United States, and being only 44th in median family income.[18]

Since the emergence of the "New South" at the end of the 19th century, North Carolina's ability to attract capital investment in industry has been linked to the state's ability to offer what state officials like to refer to as an "attractive business environment." In practice this meant high rates of return due to lower production costs, preferential tax policies for industry, and most importantly, extremely low rates of unionization which, in turn, meant both a lower wage bill for investors, and a limited ability of workers to press for improvements in working conditions.

The pro-business/anti-labor characteristics of the North Carolina political economy are not the outcome of simple market forces. They are the fruits, first, of a war on progressive political organizations in the late 19th century, and then, of a concerted battle against unionization throughout the 20th century.[19] Regarding the destruction of 19th-century political movements that might have developed as a force for the protection of the industrial and agricultural labor force in North Carolina, Tomaskovic-Devey says:

The only effective challenge to capitalist elite rule occurred during the populist period in which black and white farmers created a populist party, the Farmers Alliance. The Populist and Republican parties created a fusion alliance in the 1890s, in 1894 won two-thirds of the seats in the General Assembly, and in 1896 elected a reformist Republican Governor [Crow, 1984]. The Democrats, the party of the planter-industrialist elites, countered with a violent white supremacy campaign, successfully institutionalizing Jim Crow legislation and disenfranchised blacks and many poor whites and led to nearly complete conservative pro-business, anti-labor Democratic control of the state for the entire twentieth century.[20]

The destruction of populist parties, although setting the stage for North Carolina's 20th-century labor policy, was not the final struggle. Throughout the 20th century business and political leaders in North Carolina struggled against unionization, an effort that was punctuated by a number of bitter and often bloody labor battles in which the police powers of the state, and the state-supported moral authority of dominant religious institutions, usually weighed in heavily on the side of capital, and against labor.[21]

The consequences of this political history have been a pattern of economic development in contemporary North Carolina characterized by low wages, violent discouragement of unionization by the state officials as well as employers, enduring racial inequalities, little protective legislation for workers, transfer payments to the poor lower than the national averages, and fewer controls over business activity than found in many other states.

The political apparatus of the State of North Carolina has not only allowed this pattern to develop, it has also played an active role in creating and maintaining it. As Wood argued, the government of North Carolina

> played a decisive role in attracting "external" capital by providing the social, political and economic conditions required to facilitate exploitation and capital accumulation; by containing class conflict; and by limiting the possibility of "external" intervention either in the form of the unionization of the state's workers, or in the form of Federal social and economic regulation.[22]

These conditions created a labor force that in some ways offers the benefits of industrial investment in Third World countries, but without Third World liabilities. As Robert C. Holland, a business consultant and President of the Washington, D.C.–based Committee for Economic Development explained:

> I see the Southeast as the major area for business relocations. Labor and land are cheap in this region, and the uncertainties about government instabilities are not found here.[23]

In recent years, in pursuit of investment, North Carolina's state government has developed a wide number of agencies, divisions, departments, and programs whose purpose is to attract "external" capital to the state by publicizing North Carolina as a "promised land" for high-yield capital investment. The Industrial Development Division of the State of North Carolina, which was established in the late 1970s, employed sixteen full-time industrial recruiters whose role was to "sell" North Carolina to corporate executives outside the state. Wood argues that these recruiters are not pursuing *all* industries, but specifically those that would be best suited to and attracted by North Carolina's labor climate—that is, labor intensive, low-wage industries seeking to escape unionization, labor market competition, and higher wages in other regions.[24]

It is important to note that the kinds of industries that fit this description, and which North Carolina has actively recruited and attracted, are most heavily concentrated in the competitive sector of the economy. Industries in this sector find it more difficult to pass on every increase in wages, taxes, or regulatory costs to consumers as easily as businesses in the oligopolistic sector such as automobiles, metals, rubber, and petroleum production. Thus, competitive-sector industries frequently operate on a narrow margin of profitability. For this reason they are particularly attracted to states that can promise reduced labor, regulatory, and tax costs. As a relatively small, family-run operation, Imperial Foods was an ideal target for North Carolina's industrial recruitment. In 1980, Imperial responded to the attraction of a nonunionized labor force that enjoyed few labor market options, and that would consequently be willing to accept low wages and marginal working conditions, by moving its operation from Pennsylvania to North Carolina.

North Carolina's public industrial policy is not merely a passive one, promising a hands-off attitude toward business and business regulation. The state is also proactive in providing businesses special benefits. North Carolina state laws allow local city and county governments to issue revenue bonds to finance branch plant recruitment, and allow counties to negotiate property tax abatements with potential industrial recruits.[25] As one example of the extremes to which the state will go to attract low-wage industry, in 1989 John Martin, Governor of North Carolina, eliminated the inventory tax on *all* manufacturers in order to lure a *single* cookie plant to the state.[26]

Altogether, these forces have produced a form of growth with only limited benefit for workers. Wood, however, suggests that there were two key institutions that might have placed pressure on North Carolina's political establishment in ways that would have resulted in a closer linkage between economic growth and economic advancement for workers.[27] The first of these is unionization, and the second is Federal regulation. Both of these mechanisms for improving wage and working conditions, however, have been effectively blocked by the political-economic arrangements within North Carolina.

Blocking Worker Organization

The most consistent specific vehicle by which unions have been undercut in North Carolina is the state's right-to-work law. This law hinders the ability of unions to organize, and legally limits the strength of unions by outlawing union shops. Under the right-to-work law, which is more appropriately named a "right-not-to-unionize law," if a union wins the right to represent a plant, only those workers who wish to join the union, pay union dues and abide by union decisions, such as a strike vote, do so. In states without such laws, when a union wins recognition, all of the workers in the plant must join the union, pay dues and abide by union decisions.

Because it is a right-to-work state, even a unionized plant in North Carolina may have up to 49 percent of its work force who are not union members. Consequently, the economic strength of the union is diminished because not all workers pay dues, and its bargaining strength is substantially weakened because employers know that even if there is a strike vote, only the union members will walk out. Thus, while strikes may be an inconvenience, in many plants they do not threaten a total shut-down of operations. Moreover, in a plant that is significantly split between union-ized and nonunionized workers, managers have to employ far fewer strike breakers in order to maintain near-full levels of operation than they would if they were faced by a union-shop strike.

When right-to-work laws are coupled with the willingness of North Carolina's government to use the police power of the state to arrest or otherwise control striking workers, the ability of workers to improve their bargaining position through strikes—which in the final analysis are the basis of organized labor's power—has been seriously damaged. One of the most notorious modern examples of this was the 1958 strike at the Harriet-Henderson mills in Henderson, North Carolina. One of the longest and most violent strikes in U.S. history, this struggle involved over one thousand workers, open violence against the strikers, including the bombing of workers' homes, and at times, nearly one-fifth of the state's entire police force.

> The state police and units of the National Guard, reinforced on occasion by regular army units, maintained fixed bayonets and were given authority by the state legislature to arrest without warrant, to protect strikebreakers imported from Virginia, and to enforce injunctions against picketing. In addition, a spe-cial judge and prosecutor were sent to establish a strike court at which union-ists and sympathizers were sentenced to hard labor on road gangs and to heavy fines.[28]

The Henderson strike provides a dramatic example of direct state action against workers' organizations in the postwar period, but it is far from the only one.[29] "Intimidation of strikers by sheriffs, local police, and state troopers remains a char-acteristic of North Carolina's strikebreaking apparatus."[30]

In North Carolina not only are unions kept from organizing by the combined efforts of state government and industry, but already organized companies are kept out by a similar constellation of forces. In order to insure North Carolina remains an employers' paradise, members of the business community have often actively worked to discourage investment that they felt might raise the value of labor by cre-ating too many job opportunities, or by establishing a higher wage scale, particularly if the industry seeking relocation to North Carolina was a unionized one. In one instance, in 1976 the owners of Cannon Mills sought to keep a Philip Morris plant from being built in their county because they feared it would create competition for workers and would drive up the price of labor.[31] In another instance, the Raleigh Chamber of Commerce has a written policy against recruiting companies that do not agree to resist unionization, and throughout the 1970s and 1980s they have rejected companies such as the Miller Brewing Company, Brockway Glass, and Xerox because they would bring union jobs.[32] In yet another case: "As recently as 1991 groups of businessmen actively discouraged United Airlines from locating a major maintenance facility in Greensboro, North Carolina, for fear that the 1,500 unionized high skill jobs would drive up wages and increase unionization."[33]

This climate of state-sponsored or state-tolerated opposition to unionization and intimidation of already unionized workers in North Carolina was part of the experience of workers at the Imperial plant in Hamlet. After the fire, Valerie Ervin, an organizer for the United Food and Commercial Workers who had been working in North Carolina, said she had never feared for her life before she came to Hamlet. After the fire, workers were threatened with reprisals for speaking out about unsafe conditions at the plant. Ervin said:

> The toughest state I've ever worked is in North Carolina. . . . People are afraid for us to come to their homes. They feel that there's going to be violence.[34]

As a result of this political-economic history, North Carolina has, despite its demonstrable economic growth, failed to provide significant advancement for the majority of the industrial labor force that has been the backbone of this growth.

In recent years a new problem has emerged, the problem of sustaining the rate of growth the state enjoyed throughout the Sunbelt boom of the 1970s and 1980s. Some authors have likened the attraction of outside investment into the state to a great buffalo hunt. As one report observed:

> The stampede of plants to the South is definitely over—especially for the rural areas that lack a skilled workforce, transportation, infrastructure, and cultural amenities.[35]

This slow-down of economic growth has been reflected in lessened growth in state revenue. Among other things, this has meant that the state has had to make cutbacks in its already low level of public service, and has felt a need to intensify its pro-business/anti-labor stance in order to compete for the remaining few domestic industries that might relocate to North Carolina.

What all of this means for industrial workers, as well as other working people in North Carolina, is that they operate in a societal context hostile to worker protection, a context created by a state that has actively blocked the ability of workers to make their collective voices heard through effective labor organization, and which additionally is now facing a fiscal crisis that threatens to exacerbate these conditions.

Blocking Worker Safety: The Case of NC-OSHA

The second factor Wood suggests might be an avenue for North Carolina workers to improve their situation is through Federal regulation.[36] In the case of workplace safety, a relatively strong Federal law has been in place since 1970 in the form of the Occupational Safety and Health Act. The Act's stated goal is "to assure as far as possible every working man and woman in the Nation safe and healthful working conditions." The Act requires that each employer furnish each employee "a place of employment which is free from recognized hazards that are causing or likely to cause death or serious physical harm" to employees.[37]

The law gives impressive rights to American workers. First it obliges companies to reduce the risks in the workplace. While other labor laws limit businesses from preventing efforts by workers to make improvements in the safety of their workplace, the OSH Act not only allows workers to fight for safety and health, it places the burden of responsibility on the employer, demanding that the company take action to improve the workplace in ways that benefit the worker. The second way in which the Act is impressive is in its breadth of coverage compared to other protective legislation. Public-sector employees are the only group of workers who are not protected by the Act. The OSH Act also differs from all previous worker health and safety legislation because it gives employees the right to participate in agency inspections.[38]

Despite its positive potential for American workers, the OSH Act is not as progressive as similar legislation in other countries. For example, U.S. employers, unlike those in some other nations, are not required to establish health and safety committees, nor are they required to involve workers in decision making about health and safety issues. In addition, some property rights of the employer are protected through an appeal system that facilitates employer challenges to cited violations.[39]

The establishment of OSHA, nevertheless, threatens the interests of investors because it can make inroads into profits. In order to maintain profit levels employers need to either keep their production costs low, or be able to pass on any increase in costs to consumers. Profit pressures can inhibit the development of a safe workplace because minimizing costs usually means forgoing the establishment of safety measures that absorb workers' time or the company's money. The OSH Act, which insists that safe practices be implemented, even if they have a negative impact on profits, is particularly threatening to competitive-sector industries, which as previously mentioned, are less able to pass on the cost of a safe workplace to consumers.

The OSH Act potentially restructures the relations between workers and managers of capital by insisting that profits are not the only standard by which businesses will be judged. It creates new rights to health and safety for employees and empowers the Federal government to enforce them.

Many employers have seen the OSH Act as an unwelcome intrusion on the rights of investors in a private production system, have fought vigorously against its implementation, and in many cases sought to circumvent its requirements. Especially after the economic downturn of the mid-1970s, investors and capital managers have worked particularly hard to neutralize the effects of the OSH Act. Employers have found support for these efforts in the Federal executive branch.

Every president since the mid-1970s has sought support from the business community by backing their demands that economic costs be weighed when any new worker safety or health standards are considered. This includes, for example, supporting the right of employers to claim economic hardship as an acceptable reason for not implementing health and safety standards.

In addition, Congress sought to appease states'-rights advocates by allowing states to create their own version of OSHA that was to be controlled by the state rather than the Federal government. In a last minute compromise during the passage of the bill, state governments successfully lobbied for this joint program. By establishing the North Carolina Occupational Safety and Health Administration (NC-OSHA) in 1974, North Carolina become one of 23 states with their own OSHA program. Of these 23, ten have only been conditionally approved because they are not in compliance with Federal OSHA regulations. North Carolina is one of these ten on probation. No state OSHA, however, has ever been decertified and placed under Federal control because of non-compliance, regardless of its performance record, and no specific criteria have been established to determine whether or not a state should be decertified.[40]

If a state chooses to establish its own OSHA operation, it has the option of setting its own penalties and priorities. NC-OSHA has used this prerogative to minimize the effect of penalties for violations of safety and health standards. In 1991, for instance, North Carolina increased the fines for OSHA violations for the *first time* since the establishment of NC-OSHA in 1974. The current maximum fine in North Carolina (and by no means the most common one) is $14,000, just a fraction of the Federal maximum fine of $70,000.[41]

Workers in North Carolina, like other American workers could be protected by Federal regulation under the OSH Act. The implementation of the OSH Act, however, has been diluted at the Federal level by the executive branch. In addition, the option of states' rights has allowed the state of North Carolina to organize its own version of OSHA, one that is even less effective than the Federal version. In this way, the potential for protection of North Carolina workers by Federal regulation has been successfully blocked in North Carolina by the mutual efforts of business and government in North Carolina.

INSTITUTIONAL CONTEXT

The history of North Carolina's political economy reveals a state in which workers have been most often blocked in their efforts to control their work environment by a business-government coalition favoring a relatively *laissez-faire* industrial policy. But this political-economic climate alone does not explain the complex dynamics that led to the fire at Hamlet. Word *could* have reached authorities about the unsafe practices in the plant, and NC-OSHA *did have* the legal authority to unlock the doors. What then kept these things from happening? This question is partially answered by examining the institutional context in which the fire took place, and by delineating the specific pattern of industrial relations among Imperial's management, workers and NC-OSHA.

By the late 1980s Imperial Foods was under considerable pressure because of the general economic decline and because of specific fiscal problems within the corporation. Even before the fire in Hamlet, it appears that Emmett Roe, the owner of Imperial Foods, was facing financial difficulty. In 1990 he had closed a plant in Alabama without giving his employees proper notice. The courts had awarded the laid-off workers $250,000 in severance pay, although by the time of the fire no payments on this obligation to the Alabama workers had been made. Roe was facing suits for $350,000 in debts owed to his creditors and a $24,000 bill for unpaid taxes.[42] The financial difficulty which Roe faced may have increased the likelihood of decisions that placed profitability ahead of the health or safety costs to workers. This interpretation would be consistent with the findings of Clinard and Yeager which suggest that the greater the financial strain faced by businesses, the greater the likelihood that they will engage in regulatory violations.[43]

Regardless of what decisions Roe's financial pressures or management policies may have provoked, NC-OSHA could have intervened in a way that would have ultimately protected the workers in Hamlet. What were the factors that disrupted the ability of NC-OSHA to regulate the conditions at Hamlet? Two issues stand out. First, there is some evidence to suggest that workers who recognized hazards at the plant found it difficult to make their concerns for a safe workplace heard. Second, NC-OSHA failed to effectively regulate Imperial's safety practices because it was not adequately funded, and because, at least according to some observers, it was not efficiently organized.

Unheeded Warnings

In order for workers to be protected from dangerous work environments, at least in any work environment where they are not empowered to alter their own work conditions, someone must recognize the problems and make them known to those who *do have* the power to alter the hazardous conditions. There is evidence that the workers at the Hamlet plant were aware of safety problems and that they attempted to make their voices heard.

At the hearings on the fire, Mr. Bobby Quick, an employee at the plant, was asked if any fellow employee had made a complaint about the locked doors. Mr. Quick said his immediate co-workers knew about the problem although they had not gone to management:

> The maintenance [workers] talked about it amongst ourselves. We never took it to the office. We said amongst ourselves we hope a fire doesn't break out.[44]

Among other departments in the plant, however, people did complain to management, although their efforts apparently did not lead to any changes in the hazardous conditions. Quick testified that:

A lot of people talked about it catching on fire and killing people. I recall one day Brad [plant supervisor and the son of its owner Emmett Roe] was there. I think it was a white lady who told him, it was the day that it smoked up. She said "This thing is going to kill somebody." Brad did not pay her no attention. He was always rushing the maintenance men to fix something so they would not lose money and product. All they cared about was the product, getting it out.[45]

At the Congressional hearings, representatives asked why more people did not question the safety of the plant, or why they were not more persistent in their complaints. Mr. Quick was asked if people were fearful of making a complaint. He answered by saying:

If you try to make a statement to Brad he did not want to hear it. What you said did not matter. He was running the show. If you keep making a stink, he will fire you, you know.[46]

The threat of firing in response to voicing concerns about safety was also revealed in the testimony of North Carolina's governor before the Hearings Committee. Governor Martin referred committee members to Alfred Anderson whose wife had died in the fire. Martin said that prior to the fire Mr. Anderson had accompanied his wife to talk to her boss about conditions at the plant. She was reprimanded for taking her complaint outside of the plant, even to her husband.[47]

And another witness, Dr. Fred McQueen, a local physician who examined the 25 bodies, indicated that Mrs. Anderson's experience was not unusual. Dr. McQueen said that a system should be designed to allow workers to make anonymous complaints. He wrote:

Many workers present me, a physician, with complaints but do not want to follow through with their complaints because of the fear of losing their jobs.[48]

Overall, the testimony that has come forth in this case suggests that there were workers who recognized safety hazards in the plant and in its method of operation, and who did try to have them remedied. Their expressions of concerns, however, did not result in any changes. Additionally, the evidence suggests that many other workers at Imperial felt they inhabited a chilling climate when it came to suggesting safety problems to management. The perception among workers that there are costs attached to making complaints regarding job safety, perhaps costs as high as losing one's job, represents a critical institutional flaw in any work setting where the only power workers have to rectify unsafe conditions is through appeals to management. In the case of Imperial, this flaw was a significant factor in the loss of 25 lives.

The Failure of OSHA

Had the concerned workers at Imperial chosen to contact OSHA instead of bringing their complaints directly to the plant's management, they, like many other workers in North Carolina, would not likely have met with success. First of all, they would have been informed by a poster in the plant to call an 800 number. Three-fourths of the 160,000 workplace posters publicizing the phone number for safety complaints, including the posters at Imperial, listed a number that had been disconnected. with no forwarding number. Thus, the basic requirement of being able to contact the safety agency could not be met. Certainly, a highly motivated worker, familiar with the process of hunting through a bureaucratic tangle of phone numbers and disconnected lines, might have reached OSHA. But the more likely response of the average worker who called the NC-OSHA number only to be told it was disconnected would be to conclude that the office was no longer in operation. At the very least, the incorrect posters, and the failure to replace them with correct ones, constituted a serious limitation on the accessibility of OSHA to the workers at Imperial and elsewhere in North Carolina

The incorrect posters and other problems faced by NC-OSHA reflect in part the organization's inadequate level of funding. Nationally, OSHA is seriously underfunded, and NC-OSHA is comparatively even less well funded. North Carolina Governor James Martin testified before Congress that although a minimum of 64 safety inspectors were required to be working in the state according to Federal OSHA guidelines, the legislature had authorized only 34. He went on to say that in January of 1991 he attempted to have 19 more inspectors authorized, but that the legislature had denied his request. Even if Martin's request had been granted, however, North Carolina would have remained 11 short of the minimum number of required OSHA inspectors. Only nine states in the United States have fewer inspectors than is recommended by Federal OSHA regulations. Of these nine, North Carolina falls the farthest below the recommended number, funding only 53% of the total number of inspectors required. As a consequence, for instance, although North Carolina has 83 poultry plants, only half of them have ever been inspected since the inception of NC-OSHA.

In 1980 North Carolina had 1.9 million workers and 47 OSHA safety inspectors. Ten years later, when North Carolina's work force had grown by 37 percent, to a total of 2.6 million, the number of OSHA inspectors had declined by 12 percent, to 42 inspectors. According to the Bureau of Labor Statistics, between 1977 when John Brooks, Commissioner of the Department of Labor and head of the NC-OSHA, first took office, and 1988, the number of North Carolina workplace injuries grew from 120,000 a year to 177,300.[49] This rate of growth in workplace injuries outstripped the growth in the actual number of workers, suggesting that between 1977 and 1988 North Carolina actually lost ground in workplace safety despite the fact that the purpose of the OSH Act was to ensure just the opposite. The record of NC-OSHA in improving worker safety in North Carolina is not commendable.

In addition to the inadequate numbers of inspectors, Brooks reported to the Congressional committee that until late in 1991 the inspectors NC-OSHA did have were able to work in the field only four days a week because the department lacked sufficient travel funds. Since then they have been able to work in the field only three days a week because of further cuts in NC-OSHA funding. Brooks also noted that even if he hired additional staff there would be difficulty training them because the closest training center is in Chicago and it is constantly booked up.[50]

At the Congressional hearings on the fire it was also revealed that $453,000 which could have been used for salaries for OSHA inspectors in North Carolina was returned to the Federal government in 1991.[51] Moreover, this was not a one-time budgetary aberration. According to testimony, in five of the six years preceding the Imperial fire, Federal OSHA money had been returned to Washington by NC-OSHA. These funds were returned to the Federal government because in order to accept them, the state would have been required to match them. For example, in 1991, because the state legislature was unwilling to provide the state OSHA with $243,000, they were unable to accept the matching $453,000 from the Federal government.[52]

Brooks also explained that another reason the money was not accepted is because it was stipulated for salaries only. Because there is a hiring freeze on state jobs in North Carolina, according to Brooks, it would be illegal to spend the money to hire additional safety inspectors.[53] This particular explanation seems somewhat disingenuous because it is not true that under the state hiring freeze no one is ever hired. Cases are often made that certain positions are of such crucial importance that they must be filled. Insofar as we have personally witnessed continued hiring in universities in North Carolina while the state was under a "hiring freeze," it is difficult to believe that had there been significant political will to bring NC-OSHA up to standards it could not have been done. But then that is the point, since the inception of NC-OSHA, there has been little political will in North Carolina to make it a powerful agency actually capable of protecting workers to the full extent envisioned by the Federal OSH Act. NC-OSHA has been budgetarily strangled and bureaucratically stymied since its inception, a pattern that is consistent with the goal of North Carolina's political leadership of ensuring a business investment climate relatively unimpeded by so-called "burdensome regulation."

In the final analysis, the lack of personnel and funding resulted in a seriously inadequate state-run OSHA program in North Carolina. This conclusion is perhaps best demonstrated by Representative Kildee's (D. Michigan) detailing of an evaluation made by Federal OSHA of the OSHA program in North Carolina. He said:

I am looking at your evaluation of North Carolina OSHA Mr. Scannel, and I read, "North Carolina OSHA conducted only five general schedule health inspections during 1990, all of which involved trenching." That means, no inspections were conducted to identify worker overexposure to toxic substances. Later it says, "North Carolina OSHA does not inspect in response to complaints within a reasonable time frame, no imminent danger complaints, and fewer than 10 percent of serious complaints are inspected within OSHA's recommended time frames." In North Carolina when workers report safety problems, it may be 2 years before an inspection occurs. North Carolina has complaints from 1984 that have not yet been inspected.[54]

FAILURE OF CONTROLS IN CONTEXT

A competitive economy dominated by profit-seeking investors, a government committed to offering an attractive profit-making climate and consequently far from aggressive in protecting the health and safety of workers, and workers with very limited ability to shape the safety and health conditions of their work place, all contributed to the fire in Hamlet. These things alone, however, did not cause the tragedy at Imperial. In order to understand how these things interacted to produce the outcome they did, it is important to examine the ways in which the activities of government regulatory agencies intersected with the activities of the management of Imperial. The fire and the locked doors may have resulted from actions taken by management at Imperial, but those actions were made possible by the failure of several control agencies.

Kramer and Michalowski suggest that state-corporate crime can be understood as the result of an interaction between elements of government and elements of the private-production system. They offer the destruction of the space shuttle Challenger as a prototypical example of state-corporate crime, emphasizing the relationship between several governmental units (NASA, Congress, and the Administration), and a private corporation, Morton Thiokol, the builder of Challenger's rocket motors.[55] We argue that the Hamlet fire was likewise a case of state-corporate crime. But unlike the prototype offered by Kramer and Michalowski, the events leading to the Hamlet fire were more the consequences of socially injurious omissions on the part of governmental agencies, rather than direct consequences of the pursuit of specific goals, as was the case with governmental actions surrounding the building and launching of the ill-fated Challenger.

In the case of the Hamlet disaster, the critical intersections were between a private business, Imperial Foods, and several government agencies at the Federal level (US-OSHA and the USDA), at the state level (NC-OSHA, the office of the governor, and the state legislature), and at the local level (the county building inspectors and the city of Hamlet fire department). For a variety of reasons each of these agencies, by omission—that is, by failing to perform the control functions assigned to them—made possible the continuation of the hazardous conditions at the Imperial plant in Hamlet that led to the deaths of 25 workers. To unravel this skein of ultimately destructive decisions and omissions we will first examine the specifics of the fire and then discuss the ways in which each of the controls failed within the specific context of Imperial's operation in Hamlet.

The Imperial Fire

The accumulated evidence in the Hamlet fire indicates that the single most important factor leading to the 25 deaths was the lack of readily accessible routes to safety. All but one of the 25 deaths resulted from smoke inhalation. Only one person died of extensive burns.[56] The fire itself and the heat it produced was not large enough within the 30,000 square foot building Imperial occupied to kill the number of people it did. Rather, people died because they could not escape the smoke the fire produced. Particularly telling is the fact that a number of the dead were found in a large freezer where they had retreated to escape the fire. Once inside the freezer they were protected from the heat and fire, but unfortunately they were unable to close the door tightly enough to keep out the toxic smoke.[57] Considering that these workers had sufficient time to reach the freezer, in all likelihood they would also have had sufficient time to escape the building, *if* there had been adequate pathways to safety. This point is underscored by the example of one woman who survived because, although she could not get out of a blocked door, she was able to put her face out of the door where a friend who was outside fanned away the smoke with his baseball cap.

"There were eight entrances to the building. Four were locked from the outside and one other was probably locked from the outside. Three doors were not locked. One was the main plant entrance which is where most of the employees who did escape exited, and which was the only door marked with an exit sign. One door was blocked by the fire. And one door, that could only be reached by walking through a freezer, was unmarked and unknown to most employees because they were not allowed in the freezer unless that was their work station.[58]

Workers testified that most employees assumed that the doors were not locked because of fire laws.[59] And in fact that is the law. The OSHA law reads, "Every exit must be well lit. Door passages and stairways that might be mistaken for access should be so marked. Doors should be unobstructed so that employees can always get out."[60]

There were two reasons given for why the doors were locked; one was that it was to keep the flies out, and one was that it was to keep the employees from stealing the chicken.

Approximately a dozen current and former plant workers told news reporters that doors were routinely locked to keep employees from stealing chicken nuggets. Police records show the company reported employee thefts three times in recent years. "Hamlet police records show Imperial employees stole chicken valued at between $24 and $245.[61] If the theft of chicken was, in fact, the reason for locking the doors, it suggests that Imperial management operated according to a frightening calculus wherein preventing the theft of several hundred dollars worth of chicken parts justified risking human lives by cutting off what would be escape routes in case of fire, and doing so in violation of the law. It is also disturbing that in all of the discussion and reportage about the locking of the doors, there appears little evidence that the simple solution of installing fire doors with alarms that sound whenever the door is opened, a commonplace installation in many buildings and a solution that would have both insured safe exits *and* minimized the use of these doors for illicit commerce, was ever seriously considered.

In addition to locked doors, exits were unmarked and employees were not made aware of where exits were and whether they were locked or not. There had never been a fire drill in the plant nor any fire safety instruction of employees.

The fire itself started because of the unsafe practice of repairing hoses carrying hydraulic fuel while continuing to maintain cooking temperatures with gas flames under large vats of oil. To minimize down-time, Imperial Food Products routinely left its gas-fired chicken fryer on while repairing adjacent hoses carrying flammable hydraulic fluid, a maintenance worker testified.[62] Bobby Quick testified at the Congressional hearings that on the day of the fire he heard Brad Roe tell a maintenance worker to hurry repairs to the line in order to avoid down-time.[63]

The vats of oil are 27 feet by 4 feet and are kept at 390–405 degrees. The flash point of cooking oil is 460 degrees.[64] On the day of the fire, repairs were being made on hoses carrying hydraulic fuel to the cooking vats. The cooking was not stopped as the repairs were made. The insurance department of the state of North Carolina filed a report describing how the fire started.

> The cause of the fire was determined to be the ignition of hydraulic oil from a ruptured line only a few feet from a natural-gas-fueled cooker used in preparation of the chicken. Investigators determined that during a repair operation, the incoming hydraulic line separated from its coupling at a point approximately 60 inches above the concrete floor and began to discharge the fluid at high pressure. This high pressure and subsequent flow resulted in the hydraulic fluid being sprayed against the floor and onto the nearby cooker. Ignition of the fuel was immediate; likely from the nearby gas burners. . . . The intense fire also impinged upon a natural gas regulator (located directly above the ruptured hydraulic line) on the supply line to the burners which soon failed and added to the fuels being consumed.[65]

To make matters worse, there were no automatic cutoffs on the hydraulic or gas lines, there was only one fire extinguisher in the plant, and there were no working telephones to call the fire department when the fire broke out. An employee had to drive several blocks to the fire station to inform them that there was a serious fire at the plant.[66]

How did these conditions come about, and what were the acts of omission on the part of governmental agencies that helped make it possible?

Omission by the Federal Government

Two Federal agencies failed the workers at Hamlet in important ways. The first of these is OSHA. OSHA was statutorily responsible for insuring the quality of services provided by state-run NC-OSHA. As previously discussed, while Federal OSHA had known for quite some time about the inadequacy and ineffectiveness of the North Carolina agency's operations, no effective effort was taken to remedy the situation, except to file a report.

The second agency that could have acted, but did not, to prevent the disaster in Hamlet came as a surprise to most people—the United States Department of Agriculture (USDA). Because Imperial Foods in Hamlet is a meat-processing plant, a USDA agent visited the plant *daily* in order to make sure that the meat was being handled properly.

Kenneth Booker, the regular inspector for the USDA, told a congressional panel that he knew about the locked doors because workers had complained to him, and that he had talked with plant managers about the problem. He did not do anything further because he believed he lacked authority, and because Imperial management told him the door could be quickly unlocked in an emergency.[67] Booker's failure to pursue the matter is yet another omission that helped make the Hamlet tragedy possible. USDA's involvement in the deaths at Hamlet, however, is not limited to Booker's inaction. A USDA agent also was responsible for the locking of at least one of the doors in question.

The summer before the fire, on June 19, 1991, Grady Hussey, a USDA inspector, who sometimes substituted for the regular inspector, Booker, cited Imperial Foods for allowing flies to enter the plant and for leaving two doors open to a trash bin. An Imperial official, Joseph Kelly, responded to the citation writing on it that he had solved the problem stating, "Inside door closed and outside door closed and locked. Outside door to this area will be locked at all times unless for an emergency." Hussey signed his name on the citation noting that "corrective action has taken place."[68]

The USDA claimed that it had no responsibility in the case. Carol Foreman, former assistant U.S. Agriculture secretary who supervised meat and poultry inspections from 1977 to 1981, disagreed stating, "Every USDA inspector is a law enforcement officer, they carry a badge and they are sworn to uphold all laws of the United States." She said the inspector should have noticed locked doors. "This inspector had time to pick up a telephone and call the N.C. Department of Labor and say there's a serious hazard here. If the inspector saw somebody get raped or murdered in that plant, would he say that wasn't his responsibility too?"[69] Again, it appears that the simple solution of requiring automatically closing doors, rather than signing off on the solution of locking the door, a patently illegal option, was not considered by either the USDA inspector or by Imperial management. As in the case of the other doors, the simplest and least costly option—locking the doors—was the route taken.

The Failure of North Carolina State Government

Three components of the state government in North Carolina contributed to the circumstances that led to the fire and deaths at the Imperial plant. First of all, the state legislature refused to match funds with the Federal OSHA. The actual decision-making process of the individual legislators who voted not to fund OSHA to the required level is difficult to know for sure. The general political climate of North Carolina suggests, however, that probably some combination of four views on worker safety—(1) expanding NC-OSHA would contradict the interests of key constituents in the business community, (2) mandatory safety inspections are an unacceptable intrusion of the state into the rights of private enterprise, (3) inspections are not worth the money they would cost in the light of North Carolina's budget crisis, or (4) expanding NC-OSHA would give the wrong signal to industries that might relocate in North Carolina—played a role in the history of the North Carolina legislature's refusal to adequately fund NC-OSHA. Not only did the legislature fail to fund NC-OSHA's inspector staff to required levels, but it even failed to provide adequate travel and training funds for the limited number of NC-OSHA inspectors it did authorize. In addition, the state legislature was apparently quick to interpret the state's hiring freeze as an absolute barrier to the expansion of NC-OSHA's staff of inspectors, when exceptions to this freeze were allowed in other areas deemed "critical." Additionally, the Governor appeared to be reluctant to use the weight of his office to pressure the legislature toward expanding the number of NC-OSHA inspectors. While the Governor did request funds from the legislature in 1991 for additional inspectors, this was the first time in six years he had done so. In the previous five years of his tenure in office he took no lead in attempting to bring NC-OSHA up to Federal standards.

The internal operations of NC-OSHA itself may have also contributed to the situation in Hamlet in ways that are not entirely attributable to the lack of financial support NC-OSHA received from the state. While the underfunding of NC-OSHA was undoubtedly the critical factor in limiting its effectiveness, employees of NC-OSHA have also suggested that the management style of John Brooks, its director, may have been a contributing factor. Four current safety inspectors and five recent retirees from NC-OSHA discussed Brooks with news reporters. All expressed frustration with the department's performance over the past 10 years. "A lot of people have come in, seen what was going on, and left," said Bryan McGlohon, who retired in 1987 after 14 years as a safety inspector and consultant. McGlohon said he left in part because of Brooks' "lack of skill in human resources. I can't put up with bureaucracy and inefficiency." Each of the other eight inspectors said he knew of at least one person he considered qualified rejected by Brooks for a job in the past few years.[70] It is difficult to know to what extent internal management difficulties further limited NC-OSHA's effectiveness, or to what extent these difficulties were themselves the consequence of the stress resulting from an inadequate budget, but the testimony of current and former NC-OSHA workers suggests that the organization may not have been functioning as effectively as it might have, even in the face of its limited budget.

Taken together, these factors suggest that the State of North Carolina, for a variety of reasons, simply did not take the issue of worker health and safety seriously, or at least did not take them seriously enough to insure that NC-OSHA was adequately funded and effectively run.

Local Government

The operations of local government agencies also played their part in contributing to the Hamlet fire. Hamlet is located in Richmond County, which is responsible for regularly conducting inspections to identify unsafe or unlawful buildings in the county. According to the North Carolina Insurance Department, the Hamlet plant was in violation of building codes because it did not have a sprinkler system, did not have enough doors, workers had to walk more than the allowable 150 feet to exit the building, one door opened to the inside, four doors were locked, and there were no exit signs. Some of these violations were a result of Imperial management having made changes in the building without requesting inspections and without obtaining building permits.

Another issue regarding local inspection concerns the question of whether or not the building code violations at Imperial were inappropriately "grandfathered" as permissible under Richmond county law. According to this law the Building Code Council cannot require existing buildings to meet new and tougher codes unless the building is substantially renovated. In 1983 a new $125,000 roof was put on the building after a fire damaged the plant, an expenditure that could have been viewed as a substantial renovation. The Richmond County inspector, under the wide latitude provided by the building code, however, chose to conclude that despite the new roof, the Imperial plant had not been substantially renovated, and that it did not have to bring the entire building up to code.[71]

Richmond building inspector Jack Thompson examined the new roof put on in 1983 but not the building. "I just figured the roof wouldn't be more than 50 percent of the property's value." He said he did not check property value records and only guessed at Imperial's worth. "I did look around but as far as digging around looking to see what was holding the building up, I didn't do that. Didn't nothing stand out to me that wouldn't meet the code."[72] What can be said of Thompson's testimony is that it is relatively clear he did not take a proactive stance toward building safety. This minimalist approach to building safety inspections is consistent with the climate of business regulation in North Carolina generally, and in industry-hungry

Richmond county in particular, and is another example of the velvet-glove treatment given to industry in North Carolina.

The other local government agency that played a role in the deaths of the 25 workers, although perhaps a minor one, was the Hamlet Fire Department. Here the story takes a racial twist. The town of Hamlet is predominately white, and its fire department is all white. Although Hamlet is a small town, it has a suburb—the town of Dobbins—which, as a reflection of the continuing patterns of residential racial segregation in North Carolina, is predominately black and has a black fire department. When the fire at the plant started, the Dobbins Fire Department arrived at the scene. They were not, however, allowed to assist in the rescue and were asked to leave. Members of the Dobbins Fire Department claim they were asked to leave for racial reasons. Specifically, they contend that members of the Hamlet Fire Department believe that because the members of the Dobbins Fire Department are black, they are not qualified fire fighters.[73] It will never be known for sure whether or not the added aid of the Dobbins Fire Department might have saved additional lives, but the simple fact that they were not allowed to assist in the rescue raises serious questions about the relative priorities that guided the Hamlet Fire Department in attempting to assist the workers trapped inside the Hamlet plant.

CONCLUSION

The fire in Hamlet was caused by an array of actors, actions, omissions, and social circumstances that surrounded the workers in concentric circles from the closest supervisors and owners to local, state and Federal agencies, and finally to the organization of both the North Carolina and the U.S. political economy itself. Like a noose, these concentric circles closed around Hamlet and interacted in a way that brought about the death of 25 workers. When the list of factors arrayed against worker safety in North Carolina are tallied, it is surprising that there are not more workplace disasters such as the one at Imperial. It also suggests that many other industrial employees in North Carolina work on the fine edge of potential disaster. The Hamlet fire was not an aberration. It was almost predictable. In fact, it had been predicted by some workers.

In the final analysis, what is particularly disturbing and particularly telling is that *so many* components of the system designed to protect the health and safety of workers, from Federal OSHA, to NC-OSHA, to local inspectors *had to fail* in order for this killing fire to have occurred. The deaths in Hamlet are clear evidence that laws alone are not sufficient to protect worker safety. They require political will for their effective enforcement. Without this will, they become more symbolic than real. The Hamlet fire constitutes a clear instance of state-corporate crime precisely because it was the absence of this *political will* and the omissions on the part of *politically constituted agencies* that enabled the management of Imperial to continue violating basic safety requirements at the plant in its pursuit of private profit.

Notes

1. John Drescher and Ken Garfield, "Workers: Doors Kept Locked," *Charlotte Observer,* September 12, 1991, P. A1.
2. Jennifer Parker, Joseph Menn, and Kevin O'Brien, "North Carolina Inspection Program Ranks Last in U.S.," *Charlotte Observer,* September 5, 1991, p. 1.
3. Ronald Kramer and Raymond Michalowski, "State-Corporate Crime." Paper presented at the American Society of Criminology meetings, 1990.
4. Edwin H. Sutherland, "White-Collar Criminality," *American Sociological Review,* 5 (1940):1–12.
5. Marshall B. Clinard and Peter Yeager, *Corporate Crime.* New York: The Free Press, 1980; Ronald C. Kramer, "Corporate Crime: An Organizational Perspective." In Peter Wickman and Timothy Dailey, eds., *White-Collar and Economic Crime.* Lexington, MA: Lexington Books, 1982, pp. 75–94.
6. John Hagan, *Structural Criminology.* Cambridge, MA: Polity Press, 1988, p. 3; Clinard and Yeager, *op. cit.*, p. 17.
7. Diane Vaughan, *Controlling Unlawful Organizational Behavior: Social Structure and Corporate Misconduct.* Chicago: University of Chicago Press, 1983.
8. Martin J. Sklar, *The Corporate Reconstruction of American Capitalism, 1890–1916.* New York: Cambridge University Press, 1988.
9. Claus Offe and Volker Ronge, "Theses on the Theory of the State." In Anthony Giddens and David Held, eds., *Classes, Power and Conflict.* Berkeley: University of California Press, 1982, pp. 249–256.
10. William Chambliss, "State-Organized Crime," *Criminology,* 27 (1989):183–208.
11. M. David Ermann and Richard J. Lundman, eds., *Corporate and Governmental Deviance: Problems of Organizational Behavior in Contemporary Society.* 3d ed. New York: Oxford University Press, 1987; Julian Roebuck and Stanley Weber, *Political Crime in the United States.* New York: Praeger, 1978; David R. Simon and D. Stanley Eitzen, *Elite Deviance.* 3d ed. Boston: Allyn and Bacon, 1990.
12. Kramer and Michalowski, *op. cit.*
13. David Kauzlarich and Ronald C. Kramer, "State-Corporate Crime in the US Nuclear Weapons Production Complex," *Journal of Human Justice,* 5 (1993):4–28.
14. Phillip Wood, *Southern Capitalism: The Political Economy of North Carolina, 1880–1980.* Durham, NC: Duke University Press, 1986.
15. Michael Myerson, *Nothing Could be Finer.* New York: International Publishers, 1982.
16. Donald Tomaskovic-Devey, *Sundown on the Sunbelt? Growth without Development in the Rural South.* Raleigh: North Carolina State University Press, 1991, p. 2.

17. Southern Women's Employment Coalition, *Women of the Rural South: Economic Status and Prospects.* Lexington, KY: SWEC, 1986.
18. Tomaskovic-Devey, *op. cit.*, p. 27.
19. Valdimer O. Key, *Southern Politics in State and Nation.* New York: Knopf, 1950; Jeffrey J. Crow, "Cracking the Solid South: Populism and the Fusionist Interlude." In Lindley S. Butler and Alan D. Watson, eds., *The North Carolina Experience: An Interpretative and Documentary History.* Chapel Hill: University of North Carolina Press, 1984, pp. 333–354; Jack Bloom, *Class, Race and the Civil Rights Movement.* Bloomington: Indiana University Press, 1987; Paul Luebke, *Tar Heel Politics: Myths and Realities.* Chapel Hill: University of North Carolina Press, 1990.
20. Tomaskovic-Devey, *op. cit.*, p. 20.
21. Liston Pope, *Millhands and Preachers.* New Haven: Yale University Press, 1942.
22. Wood, *op. cit.*, p. 1.
23. Quoted in Southern Women's Employment Coalition, *op. cit.*, p. 11.
24. Wood, *op. cit.*, p. 164.
25. Tomaskovic-Devey, *op. cit.*, p. 15.
26. *Ibid.*, p. 16.
27. Wood, *op. cit.*
28. *Ibid.*, pp. 160–161.
29. Barbara Koeppel, "Something Could Be Finer Than to Be in Carolina," *Progressive,* 40 (June 1976): 21–22.
30. Wood, *op. cit.*, p. 161.
31. Luebke, *op. cit.*
32. Wood, *op. cit.*, p. 163.
33. Tomaskovic-Devey, *op. cit.*, p. 24.
34. Quoted in Greg Trevor, "Work-Safety Advocates Buck Anti-Union Sentiment," *Charlotte Observer,* October 27, 1991, p. B1.
35. MDC, *Shadows in the Sunbelt: Development in the Rural South in an Era of Economic Change.* Chapel Hill: MDC, Inc., 1986.
36. Wood, *op. cit.*
37. Quoted in Charles Noble, *Liberalism at Work: The Rise and Fall of OSHA.* Philadelphia: Temple University Press, 1986, p. 3.
38. *Ibid.*
39. *Ibid.*
40. U.S. House of Representatives, Committee on Education and Labor, *Hearing on H.R. 3160. Comprehensive OSHA Reform Act, and the Fire at the Imperial Food Products Plant in Hamlet, North Carolina.* Series No. 102-47. Washington, DC: Government Printing Office, 1991, p. 104.
41. Parker et al., *op. cit.*
42. James Greif and Ken Garfield, "Debt Dogged Imperial's Owner—Then the Fire," *Charlotte Observer,* September 15, 1991, pp. A1, 12.
43. Clinard and Yeager, *op. cit.*

44. U.S. House, *op. cit.*, p. 55.
45. *Ibid.*
46. *Ibid.*
47. *Ibid.*, p. 122.
48. *Ibid.*
49. Joseph Menn, "North Carolina Official Puts Blame on Legislature," *Charlotte Observer,* September 6, 1991, p. A1.
50. U.S. House, *op. cit.,* p. 168.
51. *Ibid.*, p. 129.
52. *Ibid.*, p. 223.
53. *Ibid.*, p. 225.
54. *Ibid.*, p. 222.
55. Kramer and Michalowski, *op. cit.*
56. U.S. House, *op. cit.*, p. 233.
57. *Ibid.*, p. 118.
58. *Ibid.*, p. 102.
59. *Ibid.*, p. 52.
60. *Ibid.*, p. 100.
61. Drescher and Garfield, *op. cit.,* pp. A1, 11.
62. Greg Trevor and Paige Williams, "Workers: Repairers Left Fryer On," *Charlotte Observer,* September 10, 1991, p. A1.
63. Trevor and David Perlmutt, "Workers to Testify on Order to Rush Repair," *Charlotte Observer,* September 12, 1991, pp. A1, 10.
64. U.S. House, *op. cit.*, p. 49.
65. *Ibid.*, p. 112.
66. *Ibid.*, p. 57.
67. Matthew Davis, "Inspector: Managers Were Warned," *Charlotte Observer,* November 13, 1991, p. A6.
68. John Drescher, "USDA Inspector OK'd Locked Door in Hamlet Plant," *Charlotte Observer,* November 13, 1991, p. A1.
69. John Drescher and David Perlmutt, "Hamlet Plant Violated Code," *Charlotte Observer,* November 15, 1991, p. A1.
70. Menn, *op. cit.*
71. John Drescher, "In Hamlet Fire Government Safety Nets Gave Away," *Charlotte Observer,* September 22, 1991, p. A1.
72. Paige Williams and John Drescher, "Plant Not Inspected as Authorized," *Charlotte Observer,* September 21, 1991, p. C1.
73. "Firefighters Near Plant Not Called: Chief Cites Racism," *Charlotte Observer,* September 6, 1991, p. 4A.

10

Corporate Greed, Women, and the Dalkon Shield

Morton Mintz

In January 1971, the A. H. Robins Company began to sell the Dalkon Shield, promoting it as the "modern, superior," "second generation," and, most important, "safe" intrauterine device for birth control. Robins, a major pharmaceutical manufacturer in Richmond, Virginia, distributed 4.5 million of the IUDs in eighty countries before halting sales in the mid-1970s. There followed a catastrophe without precedent in the annals of medicine and law.

The story of the Dalkon Shield lays bare the perils inherent in contemporary business practices and in corporate law, in a system that allows corporations to profit even if they put human beings at risk. The Shield created a disaster of global proportions because a few men with little on their minds except the pursuit of megabucks made decisions, in the interest of profit, that exposed millions of women to serious infection, sterility, and even death. To be sure, the same pursuit finally led Robins, in August 1985, to seek reorganization under Chapter 11 of the Bankruptcy Code. For the uncompensated victims, this may be yet another blow because, critics fear, reorganization could let the company put them at the end of a line of lenders, suppliers, and other creditors.

The problem at the core of such conduct is not simply that corporations have no conscience, but that they are endowed by law with rights beyond those allowed to individuals. Corporations too often act without compassion and, no matter what damage they cause, without remorse. Even worse, they cannot be held accountable, as people can be. You cannot lock up a corporation, or sentence it to hard labor or to the electric chair. And too often the law fails to look behind the corporate veil, to prosecute the individuals who make decisions and act in the name of the corporation.

A human being who would not harm you on an individual face-to-face basis, who is charitable, civic-minded, loving, and devout, will wound or kill you from behind the corporate veil. He may do this without qualm because he has been conditioned to drop a curtain between his private moral and religious self and his corporate

Reprinted from *The Progressive,* 49 (November, 1985), pp. 20–25.

immoral and irreligious self. Society at large accepts and, if only by its silence, *validates* such compartmentalization.

Worldwide, the seriously injured victims of the Dalkon Shield could number in the tens of thousands. Nearly all suffered life-threatening forms of the infections known as pelvic inflammatory disease (PID). In the United States alone, PID killed at least eighteen women who had been wearing Shields. Most of the infections impaired or destroyed the women's ability to bear children.

Not only was the Shield unsafe, it was surprisingly ineffective. The number of wearers who became pregnant with the devices in place was on the order of 110,000, or 5 per cent, a rate nearly five times the one falsely claimed in advertising and promotion to physicians and women, and a rate sharply higher than that for many other IUDs. The exaggerated and bogus claims led women to reject more effective birth control in favor of the Shield, and this led directly to consequences far worse than unwanted pregnancies.

An estimated 60 per cent of the U.S. women who conceived with Shields in place lost their unborn, or about 10,000 more than would have done so had they been wearing other IUDs. Some of these women had elective abortions. Others suffered the previously rare miscarriages called *spontaneous abortions.* Others, in the fourth to sixth months of pregnancy, experienced the still rarer infected miscarriages, or *septic spontaneous abortions.* By the count of the Food and Drug Administration (FDA), 248 women, just in this country, endured this dangerous, Shield-related complication. For fifteen of them, these septic abortions were fatal.

Hundreds of women throughout the world who conceived while wearing the Shield gave birth prematurely, in the final trimester, to children with grave congenital defects, including blindness, cerebral palsy, and mental retardation. No one can pinpoint the exact number of such women, partly because no one knows how many times women or their doctors failed to make a proper connection between the Shield and the premature birth of a defective baby.

Robins distributed about 2.86 million Shields in the United States, and doctors implanted them, by the company's estimate, in 2.2 million women. Abroad, Robins distributed about 1.71 million Shields, and in June 1974 it estimated that 800,000 to one million were implanted.

In 1974, increasing and alarming numbers of Shield-related spontaneous septic abortions became known to the FDA, and the agency asked Robins to suspend Shield sales in the United States. It did so on June 28, 1974.

In 1975, a year after the suspension of Shield sales here, Martina Langley was a volunteer at a family-planning clinic in El Salvador. Now a lawyer in Austin, Texas, she recalls that the only IUD the clinic's doctors were inserting was the Shield, and that some clinics in El Salvador continued to implant Shields until 1980.

"Sometimes the doctor would say to the patient, 'This is from the United States and it's very good,' " Langley told David Phelps, a Washington correspondent for the *Minneapolis Star and Tribune.* Then, she said, the doctor would motion toward her and tell the woman, "She is from the United States and people [there] use it." Figures are simply unavailable from most of the countries where the Shield was used. My guess is that Shield-related PID killed hundreds—possibly thousands—of women outside of the United States.

Dr. Richard P. Dickey, a former member of the Food and Drug Administration's obstetrical and gynecological devices advisory panel, has seen first-hand the conditions faced by a woman who suffers PID. An infected Shield wearer "where there are no doctors, no antibiotics, she's going to die," he told me.

Today, more than a decade after Shield sales officially ended in the United States, its legacies of death, disease, injury, and pain persist. Even women who have had the Shield removed are not out of danger. Because PID is commonly not an affliction that is simply treated and is then over and done with, large numbers of Dalkon Shield wearers suffer chronic pain and illness, sometimes requiring repeated hospitalization and surgery. Many have waged desperate battles to bear children despite severe damage to their reproductive systems.

More cheerless news came last April from two studies funded by the National Institutes of Health. They showed that childless IUD wearers who have had PID run a far higher risk of infertility if their devices were Shields than if they were other makes. Not even women who still wear the Shield with no apparent problem are safe: They run the risk of suddenly being stricken by life-threatening PID. In the words of Miles W. Lord, who retired recently as Chief District Judge for Minnesota, they are wearing "a deadly depth charge in their wombs, ready to explode at any time."

The exact number of women still wearing the Shield is unknown. By early 1983, some FDA officials and gynecologists were confident that few American women, probably only hundreds, still used it. Other qualified observers, however, were estimating the figure to be much higher, anywhere from 80,000 to more than half a million.

Certainly the response to Robins's own call-back campaign of October 1984 suggests the higher figures are closer to the mark. By February 1, 1985. a $4 million advertising drive, which urged women still wearing the Shields to have them removed at Robins's expense, had drawn more than 16,000 telephone calls on toll-free hotlines; by the end of March, 4,437 women had filed claims for Shield removals. The claims were flowing in at the dramatic rate of more than 100 a week.

Mary Beth Kornhauser, a screenwriter in West Hollywood, California, was thirty-one when I interviewed her last December. In its essentials, her story is similar to that of countless other women whose quest for safe and effective birth control led them to trust their physicians, who in turn trusted the manufacturer.

Mary was first fitted with a Shield when she was eighteen. She began having dangerous, extremely painful, and recurring pelvic infections. From the start, her misfortune was compounded by physicians whose incompetent diagnoses, such as that she was experiencing a nervous breakdown, destroyed her chances for a full and swift recovery.

In October 1972, one physician pronounced her seriously infected and removed her Shield; he did not properly treat the infection and intimated that she had gotten it because of a promiscuous life style. After seven terrible years of misdiagnosis and illness she was finally deprived of her ability to bear a child. Here is her description of the events directly preceding the "total hysterectomy" she suffered at age twenty-five:

"In 1978, I started getting sick cramps, vomiting, high fever, the same spells that had come up periodically. I went to a doctor, and he gave me oral antibiotics, which didn't work. So I went back to the University of California at Los Angeles Medical Center, where a doctor recommended me to . . . Dr. Charles E. Hamrell in Santa Monica, and he immediately put me in the hospital.

"I was very infected with tubo-ovarian abscesses, one the size of a grapefruit, one the size of an orange. I was apparently about ready to explode. To try to control the infection to prevent it from spilling into the abdominal cavity, Dr. Hamrell put me in Santa Monica Hospital for serious intravenous antibiotic therapy, by which I mean that three different antibiotics were pumped into me, one each hour."

After eight days in the hospital, Mary returned to her apartment, sensing that she was only having a reprieve: Hamrell had prepared her for the possibility of a radical hysterectomy. She took antibiotics orally and was cared for by her sister, who flew in from the Midwest, and her mother, who came from Maryland. Two weeks later, Hamrell had to operate. It was February 15, 1979—one day less than seven years after her Dalkon Shield had been inserted.

Mary filed suit against Robins in November 1979. When her lawyer, John T. Baker, prepared a "statement of facts," she said, "it read like Watergate, except that this was my life. You know, charges such as reckless disregard of truth, fraud. The reality of seeing this in print, it was staggering. But the real truth was that what they did was criminal, and that criminal charges should have been brought against the persons responsible.

"That there was a conspiracy by Robins executives to hide the truth is what got me. The fact that Americans, especially in pharmaceutical companies, would so knowingly ravage women, and get away with it, was staggering. . . . You'd think that when people deal in pharmaceutical medicine, they'd be honorable people. . . .

"It's worse than abortion. They took away the right of someone to decide to have children. Losing the ability to choose whether I wanted a family—that was the hardest thing for me to get over."

Robins sent her pretrial interrogatories, but did not move to take her deposition.

"They went right to trying to settle, because, I believe, I had a strong case," she said. At the same time, Mary said she did not want to go to trial. She found herself unable to bear the prospect of litigating for two to five more years, "never able to put the pain behind me, wondering when I would have to completely relive the experience in a trial situation. . . . I had had enough pain caused by them. . . .

"A lot of things had been blown apart by the hysterectomy; it was an intensely painful period in my life. I was not emotionally stable because of it and its ramifications. I had lost ten pounds in two days. I wanted to heal myself and I knew I couldn't if I had to dredge everything up. I had already waited two years for the setting of a trial date. Money's fine, but were they going to give me my ovaries back?

Like, yes, Your Honor, ladies and gentlemen of the jury, are you going to give me a boy child and a girl child? Maybe for that I would have waited for trial."

In February 1982, Mary settled out of court.

Peggy J. Mample, thirty-two years old when I interviewed her in February, is one of several hundred mothers who conceived while wearing a Dalkon Shield and gave birth prematurely, in the third trimester, to a child with a grave birth defect. She was nineteen when she had Melissa, who has cerebral palsy and will be in a wheelchair for life. "Melissa is very intelligent," she told me. "Her only disability is that she can't walk." At home, the child moves about by crawling, but she attends regular classes in a public elementary school.

Peggy Mample is also among the hundreds of mothers who were themselves physically unharmed, or not seriously harmed, by the Shield while, unknown to them, it attacked their unborn children.

She learned she was pregnant in February 1972. At the time, the medical profession was divided as to the wisdom of removing an IUD from a pregnant woman, and her obstetrician was among the physicians who believed the odds were fifty-fifty that removal of the Shield would induce a miscarriage.

The Robins Company, which had made no studies at that time of the IUD's potential to induce premature births or of the possible consequences of such births, was making a soothing promotional claim that it would abandon two years later. As the fetus grew, Robins claimed, the Dalkon Shield would be "pushed gently aside" and no harm would befall either the fetus or the mother. The obstetrician's advice was to leave the Shield in place and go to term, and Peggy agreed. She then gave birth prematurely to Melissa on July 22, 1972.

She had no basis for implicating the Shield until almost nine years later. On April 19, 1981, when she was living in Seattle, the CBS investigative news program "60 Minutes" included a scorching segment on "the disaster of the Dalkon Shield." A friend who saw the television program called to tell her about it and to ask if the IUD she had worn was a Shield. This led her to consult a lawyer and, shortly after, to sue Robins.

Peggy Mample's lawyers, Jane I. Fantel and John J. Davids, argued to the jury that the cerebral palsy was the ultimate result of Robins's false effectiveness claims, of its failure to do studies on the Shield's potential to cause premature births, and of its related failure to investigate the consequences of such births.

Checking around the country before and during the trial, Fantel and Davids found thirty more children of Shield wearers who had been born prematurely in the third trimester with major congenital defects. They told me that Robins initially resisted their demands for data on such children, but finally confirmed the number.

Actually, according to trial testimony by Dr. David A. Eschenbach of the University of Washington, an expert on the adverse effects of IUDs, the total number of such children in the United States was 200 to 300.

The jury awarded $125,000 to Mrs. Mample, but nothing to Melissa, holding that a causal relation had not been established between the Shield and her premature birth and cerebral palsy. Mample then filed a new lawsuit for damages for Melissa. In June 1984, when Melissa was almost twelve, a second jury returned a verdict for her. Although the sum is secret, it was well above an initial offer by Robins to settle for $1.4 million.

Mample now lives in Boise, Idaho. She is still enraged when speaking about the company. "I just think it's absolutely incredible that a large corporation can do this to the American public, using us as guinea pigs," she says. "Needless to say, I don't buy Robins's products any more. . . . I just experienced so many emotions—the anger, the shock, of knowing what large corporations, what *this* corporation, did to my child. . . . It's absolutely incredible that the American public puts up with it, that they don't do something about it."

The anger of the Shield's victims has been fueled by Robins's consistent stone-walling and professions of innocence and ignorance. In the face of several thousand settlements, multimillion-dollar court awards of punitive damages, and its own Shield removal campaign, the claims of innocent ignorance seem incredible, but persist. At a series of depositions taken in 1984 by plaintiffs' lawyer Dale Larson, E. Claiborne Robins swore that he was unable to recall ever having discussed the Shield with his son, E. Claiborne Robins Jr., the company's chief executive officer and president.

"You certainly knew, when you started marketing this device. that pelvic inflammatory disease was a life-threatening disease, did you not?" Larson asked. "I don't know that," Robins testified. "I have never thought of it as life-threatening." Did he know it could destroy fertility? "Maybe I should, but I don't know that," he swore. "I have heard that," he added. "I am not sure where."

Larson drew similar answers from Carl Lunsford. Since 1978, when he became senior vice president for research and development, Lunsford has been in charge of the company's medical department and thus the highest-ranking executive with specific jurisdiction over the Shield's safety. He is a chemist whose involvements with the Shield date back to the premarketing year of 1970.

Lunsford swore he recalled no "expressions of concern" by any company official about PID, and did not remember having "personally wondered" about the toll it was taking. He had not tried to find out how many users died. He had not "personally reviewed" any studies of the Shield's safety or effectiveness in preventing conception. Did he have "any curiosity" about why the company, a few months before, had paid $4.6 million, mostly in punitive damages, to settle seven Shield lawsuits? The answer was "no."

In February 1977, extremely few of the more than 800,000 American women believed to be wearing the Shield had the faintest notion that the devices were becoming more hazardous with each passing day. But Bradley Post, a leading plaintiff's lawyer, did know of the danger, and so he wrote a letter to the company. He asked that Robins mail a corrective "Dear Doctor" letter, partly to urge "immediate removal of devices in use."

Upon receiving no response, Post sent a second letter. He wrote that he had just learned of deaths of two young women, that the circumstances were clearly causally related to their Shields, and that he was concerned about how many more fatalities and serious injuries would have to occur before Robins would take preventive action. No response came to this plea, either.

Four years later, a sequence of deaths began to be reported among long-time Shield users who were not pregnant. The first, in November 1981, was a Los Angeles woman; the second, in April 1983, was Eugenie Standeford, thirty-four, of New Orleans. Ten months later, on February 29, 1984, Judge Lord pleaded for a recall in an instantly famous courtroom reprimand to three senior company officers. He told E. Claiborne Robins Jr., the company's chief executive officer; Carl Lunsford, the senior vice president, and William A. Forrest Jr., the vice president and general counsel:

> The only conceivable reasons you have not recalled this product are that it would hurt your balance sheet and alert women who already have been harmed that you may be liable for their injuries. . . . If this were a case in equity, I would order that your company make an effort to locate each and every person who still wears this device and recall your product. But this court does not have the power to do so. I must therefore resort to moral persuasion and a personal appeal to each of you. . . . You are the corporate conscience. Please, in the name of humanity, lift your eyes above the bottom line. . . . Please, gentlemen, give consideration to tracing down the victims and sparing them the agony that will surely be theirs.

Robins contended, however, that no campaign was needed, because the Shield was no more hazardous than rival IUDs.

Eighteen days after Judge Lord's appeal, Christa Berlin, forty-one, was admitted to the Los Angeles County–University of Southern California Medical Center with lower abdominal pain and fever. The diagnosis was a pelvic abscess. Antibiotics in high doses were injected into her, but her condition worsened, requiring drastic surgery including a hysterectomy. After the operation her condition improved for a time, only to deteriorate again.

"Despite intensive care and cardiorespiratory support," said Dr. Charles M. March, the chief gynecologist, in a letter to the company, "she expired on the eighteenth postoperative day." He pointed out that Berlin had worn a Shield for many years. In October 1984, six months after she died, Robins finally announced a recall campaign. It is reasonable to suggest that Eugenie Standeford, Christa Berlin, and other women might not have died, and that thousands of other women would not have suffered pain and agony, if Robins had acted earlier. But Robins consistently claimed—and continues to claim—that the Dalkon Shield was safe and effective when "properly used." Robins executives insist that they did not know of any special hazard. But they did know, and they chose to do nothing—until it was much too late.

What does the Dalkon Shield catastrophe teach us? Not that the A. H. Robins Company was a renegade in the pharmaceutical industry. Yes, Robins knowingly and willfully put corporate greed before human welfare; suppressed scientific studies that would ascertain safety and effectiveness; concealed hazards from consumers, the medical profession, and government; assigned a lower value to foreign lives than to American lives; behaved ruthlessly toward victims who sued, and hired outside experts who would give accommodating testimony. Yet almost every other major drug company has done one or more of these things, some have done them repeatedly or routinely, and some still continue to do so.

Nor does the Shield catastrophe teach that the pharmaceutical industry is unique. Cigarette companies profit from smoking, the single greatest cause of preventable disease and death. Knowingly and willfully, automobile manufacturers have old cars that would become rolling incinerators in rear-end collisions; chemical companies have sold abroad carcinogenic pesticides that are banned here; makers of infant formula have, in impoverished Third World countries, deprived babies of breast milk, the nearly perfect food; assorted industries have dumped poisonous wastes into the environment; coal companies have falsified records showing the exposure of miners to the particles that cause black lung disease; military contractors have supplied defective weapons to the armed services.

No, the lesson of the Dalkon Shield catastrophe is not that Robins alone behaved in an immoral or unexpected fashion, but that, first, the corporate structure itself—oriented as it is toward profit and away from liability—is a standing invitation to such conduct; second, the global scale of contemporary marketing has made hazardous corporate activities more perilous to ever larger numbers of people, and, third, all the deterrents and restraints that normally govern our lives—religion, conscience, criminal codes, economic competition, press exposure, social ostracism—have been overwhelmed.

Government provides insufficient and erratic protection, in part because it is subject to political pressure from both Congress and the corporations themselves, and in part because of the lethargy of entrenched bureaucracy. Thus, despite evidence produced by trial lawyers that rotting tail strings put large numbers of women at risk, the Food and Drug Administration did nothing to protect Shield wearers for nine years, from the time the Shield went off the market in 1974 until 1983, when a study by the Centers for Disease Control incriminated the device.

The FDA never acted on a petition filed by the National Women's Health Network in April 1983 for a recall, to be paid for by Robins, to ensure retrieval of the Shield "from all women who currently wear it" and for imposition of criminal penalties. I am not suggesting that we should abandon Government regulation, but only that we must recognize its limitations. As it stands now, it often provides the illusion, but not the substance, of adequate protection.

Modern society cannot function without the large organization. It manages our great endeavors; it brings us great good. The need today is to stop the individuals who run corporations from inflicting harm. This will not be done by weakening or eliminating existing deterrents and restraints, such as Federal regulators; our hopes lie in strengthening them and adding new ones.

For the foreseeable future, there is no prospect of enacting legislation embodying the powerful moral command in Leviticus 19:16: "Neither shalt thou stand idly by the blood of thy neighbor." Not so long as Ronald Reagan is President. Not so long as the likes of George Bush may succeed him. Not so long as Congress allows special interests to control election financing. And not so long as Americans remain content to live with the paradoxical proposition that harm knowingly and willfully inflicted on them is to be punished, even by death, if done for personal reasons, but is to be unpunished, not even by a day in jail, if done for corporate reasons.

But even in today's political climate, growing numbers of Americans have awakened to the paradox. They have become aware, in part through the repercussions of the Shield disaster, of the impossibility of reconciling personal responsibility with corporate immunity; they know that the proposition is fraudulent. As the public mood becomes more receptive to efforts to hold individuals accountable for corporate actions, we can expect prosecutors, governors, and legislators in many states to make such efforts, and to earn public approval for doing so.

Only last summer in Illinois, three former executives of Film Recovery Systems, Inc., in Elk Grove Village were successfully prosecuted for murdering a sixty-one-year-old Polish immigrant who had inhaled cyanide used to recover silver from used X-ray film. The murder charges, brought by Cook County prosecutors, were said to be the first in a work-related death. Circuit Judge Ronald J. P. Banks sentenced the executives to twenty-five years in prison and $10,000 fines. Such prosecutions must proliferate, and state office-holders and candidates must make passage of tougher laws an issue. The press and clergy, too, will have to take the stand that a person's criminal and immoral conduct is criminal, period, and that no ethical counterargument exists.

Judge Lord saw the absurdity of condemning what a man did in a bedroom but not in a boardroom when he said: "We still haven't grasped that the man who assaults women from an office chair is as grave a sinner as the man who assaults a woman in an alley." Surely the time has come to extend the definition of immoral conduct into the boardroom and the corporate office.

11

"Heads I Win, Tails You Lose"

Deregulation, Crime, and Crisis in the Savings and Loan Industry

Kitty Calavita and Henry N. Pontell

I n the winter of 1989, reports of the biggest set of white-collar crimes ever uncovered hit the news. According to the reports, some savings and loan operators across the United States had brought their institutions to financial ruin while pocketing untold millions of dollars in personal profits, passing the tab on to the American taxpayer.

The savings and loan crisis provides an important opportunity for the study of white-collar crime. First is its mere size. Official estimates of the cost of the rescue effort to bail out insolvent savings and loans are placed at $200 billion over the next decade, and range from $300 billion to $473 billion by the year 2021.[1] Government reports suggest that criminal activity was a central factor in 70 to 80% of these insolvencies.[2] Second, the case brings into sharp relief the mechanisms of the production and reproduction of white-collar crime and the role of the state in those processes.

This article investigates the factors facilitating savings and loan crime and traces the responses of regulators and other state officials to evidence of this crime over time. Drawing on a wide variety of sources, including General Accounting Office (GAO) reports, Congressional Hearings and debates, and media accounts, the study highlights the central role played by deregulation in the generation of thrift fraud. In this respect it confirms the conclusions of previous analyses of white-collar crime that emphasize the pressures associated with competition as important causal factors.[3] More important, however, it is argued that the advance of finance capitalism has set the context for what is called here "collective embezzlement" or "looting," the examination of which may lead to a more precise understanding of how various types of business crime are generated within distinct economic structures.

The article is organized as follows. First a brief overview of the savings and loan system and the current crisis in the industry is provided as background for the dis-

Reprinted from *Crime & Delinquency,* 36 (July 1990), pp. 309–341.

cussion of thrift fraud. Next three types of crime that permeate the savings and loan industry are identified and their respective causal and facilitating factors are discussed. The article then examines the regulation and enforcement process focusing on the ideological, political and structural forces that have constrained regulators and have contributed to the epidemic of crime in the industry. Finally it concludes with a discussion of the possibility that the structure of finance capitalism as distinct from the industrial capitalism upon which most previous analyses of white-collar crime have been based both provides the incentives and opportunities for new types of white-collar crime and inhibits the state from responding effectively.

DESCRIPTIVE BACKGROUND
Underpinnings of the Crisis

The federally insured savings and loan system was established in the early 1930s both to promote the construction of new homes during the depression and to protect financial institutions against the kind of devastation that followed the panic of 1929. The Federal Home Loan Bank Act of 1932 established the Federal Home Loan Bank Board (FHLBB) whose purpose was to create a reserve credit system to ensure the availability of mortgage money for home financing and to oversee federally chartered savings and loans. Two years later, the second principal building block of the modern savings and loan industry was put in place when the National Housing Act of 1934 created the Federal Savings and Loan Insurance Corporation (FSLIC) to insure deposits in savings and loan institutions.

The FHLBB has been (until the 1989 reform, to be discussed later) the primary regulatory agency responsible for federally chartered savings and loans. It is an independent executive agency made up of a Chair and two members appointed by the President. This agency oversees 12 regional Home Loan Banks that serve as the conduit to the individual savings and loan institutions that comprise the industry. It is the function of these regional district banks to provide a pool of funds for their member institutions at below market rates, in order to disburse loans and cover withdrawals. In 1985, the FHLBB delegated to the district banks the task of examining and supervising the savings and loans within their regional jurisdiction. Thus, although the FHLBB is formally responsible for promulgating and enforcing regulations, agents of the district banks oversee the thrifts' operations and have discretion to initiate corrective measures and/or to notify the Bank Board of savings and loan misconduct. As will be shown, this dual role of the district banks and the Bank Board to both promote *and* regulate the savings and loan industry is a potentially critical factor in explaining their curiously complacent response to ongoing indications of fraud in the industry.

The National Housing Act of 1934 provided for federal insurance on savings and loan deposits through the FSLIC, also under the jurisdiction of the FHLBB. In exchange for this protection, thrifts were regulated both geographically and in terms of the kinds of loans they could make, essentially being confined to the issuance of home loans within fifty miles of their home office. The 1960s brought a gradual loosening of these restraints—for example extending the geographical area in which savings and loans could do business and slowly expanding their lending powers— yet did not significantly alter the protection/regulation formula.

A confluence of economic factors in the 1970s radically changed both the fortunes of the savings and loan industry and ultimately the parameters within which they were to operate. Most important, "stagflation" hit the savings and loan industry particularly hard, as the "double whammy" of high interest rates and slow growth squeezed the industry at both ends. Locked into relatively low-interest fixed mortgages from previous eras, limited by regulation to pay no more than 5.5% interest on new deposits, and with inflation at 13.3% by 1979, the industry suffered steep losses. Not surprisingly, thrifts found it difficult to attract new money when inflation outpaced the meager 5.5% return on deposits. Even worse, the new Money Market Mutual Funds allowed middle-income investors to buy shares in large denomination securities at high money market rates, triggering "disintermediation," the euphemism for massive withdrawals from savings and loans.

In 1979, Paul Volker, head of the Federal Reserve Board, tightened the money supply in an effort to break the back of inflation, sending the interest rate up to its highest levels in this century, and ultimately contributing to a serious recession. Faced with defaults and foreclosures resulting from the recession, combined with increasing competition from high-yield investments given the new hikes in the interest rate, savings and loans were doomed. The net worth of the industry fell from $16.7 billion in 1972 to a *negative* net worth of $17.5 billion in 1980, with 85% of the country's savings and loans losing money.[4]

Deregulation: The Cure that Killed

Coinciding with these economic forces, a new ideological movement was afoot. Since the early 1970s, policymakers had been considering significantly loosening the restraints on savings and loans so that they could compete more equitably for new money and invest in more lucrative ventures. However, it was not until the deregulatory fervor of the early Reagan administration that this strategy gained political acceptance as a solution to the rapidly escalating savings and loan crisis. Throwing caution to the wind and armed with the brashness born of overconfidence, the deregulators undid most of the regulatory infrastructure that had kept the thrift industry together for four decades.

The conviction of deregulators was that the free enterprise system works best if left alone, unhampered by perhaps well-meaning but ultimately counterproductive government regulations. The bind in which the savings and loan industry found itself seemed to confirm the theory that government regulations imposed an unfair handicap in the competitive process. The answer then was to return the industry to what these policymakers saw as the self-regulating mechanisms of the free market. In 1980, the Depository Institutions Deregulation and Monetary Control Act began to do just that, phasing out restrictions on interest rates paid by savings and loans. It is important to point out, however, that the move to the free market model was incomplete and accompanied by a decisive move in the *opposite* direction. For, at the same time that the law unleashed savings and loans to compete for new money, it bolstered the federal protection accorded these "private enterprise" institutions, increasing FSLIC insurance from a maximum of $40,000 to $100,000 per deposit.

The 1980 law was followed by devastating losses in the industry. In the first place, it triggered an even more pronounced "negative rate spread." Savings and loans did attract more new money at the higher interest rates they could now offer, but the discrepancy between the high rates they had to pay to attract short-term deposits and the low rates at which they had invested in long-term home mortgages widened. The law's primary effect was to precipitate larger losses on more money.

When these deregulatory measures did not work, Congress prescribed more of the same. In 1982, the Garn-St. Germain Depository Institutions Act did away with the differential between permissible interest rates for commercial banks and savings and loans, and accelerated the phase-out of the ceiling on interest rates initiated in the 1980 law. Probably more important, it dramatically expanded the investment powers of savings and loans, moving them farther and farther away from their traditional role as a provider of home mortgages. They were now authorized to increase their consumer loans, up to a total of 30% of their assets; make commercial, corporate or business loans; and invest in nonresidential real estate worth up to 40% of their total assets. Furthermore, the Garn-St. Germain Act allowed thrifts to provide 100% financing, requiring no down payment from the borrower, in an apparent effort to attract new business to the desperate industry.

Industry regulators soon joined Congress in the deregulation. In 1980, regulators removed the 5% limit on "brokered deposits," allowing thrifts access to unprecedented amounts of cash. Brokered deposits were placed by middlemen who aggregated individual investments that were deposited as "jumbo" certificates of deposit (CDs). Since the maximum insured deposit was $100,000, these brokered deposits were packaged as $100,000 CDs, on which the investors could command high interest rates. So attractive was this system to all concerned—brokers who made hefty commissions, investors who received high interest for their money, and thrift operators who now had almost unlimited access to funds—that between 1982 and 1984, brokered deposits as a percentage of total assets increased 400%.[5] These brokered deposits turned out to be a critical factor both in creating pressure to engage in misconduct and in providing unprecedented opportunities for fraud.

In 1982, regulators dropped the requirement that thrifts have at least 400 stockholders, with no one owning more than 25% of the stock, opening the door for a single entrepreneur to own and operate a federally insured savings and loan. Furthermore, single investors could now start thrifts with noncash assets, such as land or real estate. Presumably hoping that the move would halt the dying off of savings and loans as innovative entrepreneurs bought them up, the deregulators seemed unaware of the disastrous potential of virtually unlimited new charters in the vulnerable industry.

The deregulatory process was complicated and accelerated by the fact that federal and state systems of regulation coexisted and not infrequently overlapped. State-chartered thrifts were regulated by state regulatory agencies and governed by their regulations, but could be insured by FSLIC if they paid the insurance premiums, which most did. (By 1986, 92.6% of the country's savings and loans—holding 98.5% of the industry's assets—were insured by FSLIC.)[6] This dual structure, which had operated smoothly for almost fifty years, had disastrous consequences within the context of federal deregulation. Because the funding for state regulatory agencies was provided in large part from "member" institutions, state agencies that were perceived by savings and loans as more rigorous or enforcement-oriented than the federal system risked losing their funding. The experience of the California Department of Savings and Loan serves as a good example of the effect of the regulatory competition that resulted.

Beginning in 1975, the California Department of Savings and Loan had been staffed by no-nonsense regulators who imposed strict rules and tolerated little deviation. The California thrift industry complained bitterly, and when federal regulations were relaxed in 1980, they switched en masse to federal charters.[7] With the exodus, the California Department lost over half of its funding and more than half of its staff. In July 1978, the California agency had 172 full time examiners; by 1983, the number of examiners had shrunk to 55.[8]

It seemed that California policymakers had learned the hard way that if the state's Department of Savings and Loan was to survive (and if California state politicians were to continue to have access to the industry's lobbying dollars), they had to make it more likable. On January 1, 1983, the Nolan Bill passed with only one dissenting vote, making it possible for almost anyone to charter a new savings and loan, and virtually eliminating any limitations on investment powers. Similar state legislation around the country followed the federal initiative, as state legislatures and regulators deregulated for their survival. Some states—Texas, for example—already had thrift guidelines that were even more lax than the new federal regulations, but those that did not quickly enacted "me-too" legislation.[9]

At the same time as this deregulation zeal gained momentum, Congress passed a Joint Current Resolution in 1982, putting the full credit of the U.S. government behind the savings and loan industry. Although by law, the federal government is not obligated to rescue the FSLIC to cover insured deposits, Congress acted with this joint resolution to appease the fears of depositors. Once again, the free market deregulators had applied their principles selectively, setting in place the ultimately fatal formula of deregulation and protective insurance.

Losses continued to mount. In 1982, the FSLIC spent over $2.4 billion to close or merge insolvent savings and loans, and by 1986 the federal insurance agency was itself insolvent.[10] As the number of insolvent and ailing thrifts climbed, the FSLIC, knowing that its resources were inadequate to cope with the financial disaster, began to slow the pace of closures. Hoping against hope that windfall profits or an innovative buyer might reverse the decline of these institutions, the fateful decision compounded the crisis. In 1988, the FSLIC closed or sold 220 defunct savings and loans, and 300 other insolvent institutions were waiting in the wings.[11] In the first six months of 1988, the industry lost an unprecedented $7.5 billion.[12]

MAJOR FORMS OF THRIFT CRIME
AND THEIR CAUSAL STRUCTURE

In 1987, the Federal Home Loan Bank Board referred 6,205 savings and loan cases to the Justice Department for possible criminal prosecution, and an additional 5,114 cases were referred in 1988 (testimony before the Senate Committee on Banking, Housing and Urban Affairs).[13] It has been estimated that crime or misconduct played a significant role in 80% of the insolvent savings and loans destined to be bailed out by the U.S. government.[14] A GAO study of 26 of the nation's most costly thrift failures found evidence of "numerous and sometimes blatant violations of laws and regulations" in every one of the thrifts in the sample.[15] Furthermore, the GAO concluded that criminal activity was the central ingredient in the collapse of all of these institutions. By October, 1988, the FSLIC had sued the officers or directors of 51 failed thrifts for misconduct and estimated that these cases alone had cost the government over $8 billion.[16]

The Federal Home Loan Bank Board, in a report to Congress in 1988 defined fraud as it relates to the savings and loan industry:

> Individuals in a position of trust in the institution or closely affiliated with it have, in general terms, breached their fiduciary duties; traded on inside information; usurped opportunities or profits; engaged in self-dealing; or otherwise used the institution for personal advantage. Specific examples of insider abuse include loans to insiders in excess of that allowed by regulation; high-risk speculative ventures; payment of exorbitant dividends at times when the institution is at or near insolvency; payment from institution funds for personal vacations, automobiles, clothing, and art; payment of unwarranted commissions and fees to companies owned by a shareholder; payment of "consulting fees" to insiders or their companies; use of insiders' companies for association business; and putting friends and relatives on the payroll of the institutions.[17]

The varieties and possible permutations of criminal activity perpetrated by thrift operators are seemingly endless. By and large, however, fraud in the savings and loan industry falls into three general categories, classified here as "unlawful risk-taking," "looting," and "covering up." Although these categories of fraud are analytically distinct in their makeup and in terms of the incentives, pressures, and facilitating factors that produce them, in practice they are often found as interacting parts of the same complex money machine.

Unlawful Risk-Taking

The GAO, in its study of 26 insolvent savings and loans, found that "All of the 26 failed thrifts made nontraditional, higher-risk investments and in doing so . . . violated laws and regulations and engaged in unsafe practices."[18] Deregulation made it legal for thrifts to invest in "nontraditional, higher-risk" activities, but regulations and laws were often broken in the process, either by extending these investment activities beyond permissible levels or by compounding the level of risk by, for example, inadequate marketability studies or poor supervision of loan disbursements. In order to explain the prevalence of this unlawful risk-taking, it is important to understand the new deregulated environment in which it was taking place, the pressures that this environment exerted, and the opportunities that it accorded. Two related thrift activities—brokered deposits and Acquisition, Development, and Construction (ADC) loans—were an integral part of this environment and will serve as good examples of both the incentive to commit fraud and the disastrous consequences for the industry.

The deregulation of savings and loans' investment powers unleashed an escalating competitive process in which brokered deposits were a key ingredient. Overnight, ailing savings and loans could obtain huge amounts of cash to stave off their impending insolvency. But the miracle drug had a downside. Like a narcotic, the more these institutions took in brokered deposits, the more they depended on them, and the more they were willing to, and had to, pay to get them. As brokerage firms shopped across the country for the best return on their money, thrifts had to offer ever-higher interest rates to attract them. And, like a drug, the most desperate institutions needed the most and paid the highest interest rates. In a perverse contortion of the theory of the survival of the fittest to which the free market deregulators subscribed (and tenaciously clung in spite of all the contrary evidence), in this environment it was the weakest thrifts that grew the fastest.

By 1984, Edwin Gray, Chair of the FHLBB, was so alarmed over the rate of growth of brokered deposits that he attempted unsuccessfully to reregulate the handling of these accounts. Referred to in the business as "hot money," brokered deposits often entail huge sums, at high rates for the short term—not infrequently passing through an institution in twenty-four hours, then moving on to the next highest bidder. Institutions whose survival depends on such jumbo deposits are clearly vulnerable to the effects of unexpected withdrawals. But the problems associated with brokered deposits go far beyond this simple vulnerability factor.

The FHLBB today claims that "a large influx of brokered savings" is an "abuse flag," in recognition of the high probability of misconduct related to dependence on these deposits.[19] Given the addictive quality of brokered deposits and the high cost of obtaining them, it should not be surprising that they are associated with what is called here "unlawful risk-taking." Not only do the large cash infusions facilitate risky speculative ventures, but conversely and more importantly, long-shot investments with the potential for high payoff are undertaken by desperate institutions to offset the costs of high-interest deposits.

Among the most popular of the high-risk strategies used in conjunction with brokered deposits are Acquisition, Development, and Construction (ADC) loans. The power of federally chartered savings and loans to invest in commercial real estate projects was expanded with the deregulation of 1982, so that thrifts could invest up to 40% of their total assets in such ventures. Increasingly, high-risk loans were made to developers to acquire and develop projects for commercial use, more than tripling such loans between 1980 and 1986.[20] As long as high-risk ADC loans remained within the 40% limit stipulated by federal regulation, they did not, by themselves, constitute misconduct. The problem was that, given the competitive pressure exerted on thrifts by the new deregulation and the proliferation of high-interest brokered deposits that it triggered, some thrifts exceeded the federal ceiling on ADC loans and/or committed misconduct in handling them.

Because these high-risk loans have the potential (although are unlikely) to be very profitable in the long run, and because they provide a desperately needed cash flow in the short run (in the form of "points" paid up front), they are an extremely attractive source of investment for the brokered money to which faltering savings and loans increasingly turned in the early and mid-1980s. But it was the "no-risk," federally insured, nature of these "high-risk" investments that ensured their proliferation and abuse. For, should developers default on these loans, they suffered no personal liability, and deposits were protected by FSLIC insurance. William Black, the San Francisco regional counsel for the newly created Office of Thrift Supervision, referring to the enormous cash flow generated by such loans, observed that "it was as simple as 'ADC.' "[21] The short-term and long-term potential of these ADC loans, in combination with their low risk for the investor, triggered a scramble among savings and loans to enter the world of speculative development (particularly in Texas and other states where no ceiling existed for ADC lending).

The scramble was often accompanied by inadequate marketability studies of project potential, violations of the loans-to-one-borrower limitations, and other such regulatory misconduct. The GAO concluded that of the 26 failed institutions it examined, 19 engaged in ADC lending, and two-thirds of these performed either no marketability studies or inadequate studies, in violation of federal regulations.[22]

In some cases, thrift operators dropped any pretense of caution. Tyrell Barker, owner and operator of State Savings and Loan in Texas, who has since pleaded guilty to misapplication of bank funds, told speculators in Dallas in the early 1980s, "You bring the dirt, I bring the money. We split 50-50."[23] When one Barker-backed speculator was asked how he determined which property to buy, he replied flippantly "Wherever my dog lifts his leg I buy that rock and all the acreage around it." So common are such arrangements that they have come to be known colloquially in the industry as "cash-for-dirt" loans. With the caution of a state official and the clarity of overdue hindsight, the U.S. Attorney for the Central District of California described the motive: "It appears that there have been institutions . . . that have been sufficiently desperate for income in the competitive arena for loan money that they have become less conscious and vigilant than one would like."[24]

The House Committee on Government Operations concludes that in some cases "normally honest bankers (including thrift insiders) have resorted to fraud or unsafe and unsound practices in efforts to save a battered institution. In those cases an incentive existed to turn an unhealthy financial institution around by garnering more deposits and then making even more speculative investments hoping to 'make it big.' "[25] The Commissioner of the California Department of Savings and Loan described the pressure to engage in fraud in the competitive environment dominated by brokered deposits: "If you have got a lot of money, high-cost money pushing you, and you have to make profits, you have to put it out awful fast."[26] FHLBB Chair M. Danny Wall described the bind of thrift operators on a "slippery slope of a failing institution trying to save probably their institution first and trying to save themselves and their career."[27] But, the words of an unidentified witness best summed up the formula that produced an epidemic of unlawful risk-taking in the thrift industry: "If you put temptation and the opportunity and the need in the same place you are asking for trouble."[28]

Deregulation was heralded by its advocates as a free market solution to the competitive handicap placed on thrifts by restraints on their investment powers and interest rates. But the "cure" turned out to be worse than the disease. Deregulation itself triggered an ever-escalating competition for deposits, and pressed some thrift operators into high-risk, often unlawful, loan arrangements. Dennis Fitzpatrick, Chair of Beverly Hills Savings and Loan in the early 1980s, told the Congressional Committee investigating wrongdoing at the thrift whose insolvency cost the FSLIC almost $1 billion (apparently with no irony intended), "We could not survive if we continued to do business in the traditional fashion."[29]

As deregulation lifted the ceiling on interest rates and intensified competition, it provided a primary incentive for fraud, and by opening up investment powers, it provided the opportunity; by simultaneously deviating from the free market model upon which these moves were ostensibly based, and increasing the level of protective FSLIC insurance, would-be "deregulators" added the irresistible force of temptation.

In many respects, the factors that generate this unlawful risk-taking are similar to those highlighted in other analyses of white-collar crime. Most obviously, Sutherland, Farberman, Geis, Hagan, and others, have cited the importance of the force of competition in the profit-making enterprise as a major incentive to commit corporate crime.[30] According to these analyses, the corporate criminal violates laws and regulations in the pursuit of the maximization of profits within the context of a competitive economy. Thus executives at Ford Motor Company in the 1970s decided to design and build the Pinto with a defective rear assembly, in spite of their knowledge that even minor rear-end collisions would cause death, injury, and burned vehicles. Spending the $11 per vehicle that it would cost to correct the defect, they reasoned, would cut into profits and impair their competitive position.[31] At about the same time, the president of General Motors explained his refusal to use safety glass in Chevrolets: "You can say perhaps that I am selfish, but business is selfish. We are not a charitable institution—we are trying to make a profit for our stockholders."[32] How similar is the refrain of a Houston savings and loan consultant and developer, explaining regulatory violations in the thrift industry: "If you didn't do it, you weren't just stupid—you weren't behaving as a prudent businessman, which is the ground rule. You owed it to your partners, to your stockholders, to maximize profits. Everybody else was doing it."[33]

In addition, the opportunity structure has been cited as a facilitating factor in the commission of corporate crime. Some analyses, for example, have emphasized the ease with which these crimes can be committed as complementary to the profit motive in the production of such crime.[34] The infamous electrical company conspiracy of the 1940s and 1950s, in which employees of the heavy electrical manufacturing industry engaged in price-fixing, is exemplary.[35] Clearly, the reduction of competition and the maximization of profits were the motives for the price-fixing, but the relatively small number of very large companies such as General Electric and their domination of the industry (in a sense, the relative *lack* of competition) provided the opportunity structure for, and facilitated, the criminal conspiracy.

But the unlawful risk-taking in the savings and loan industry described here is distinct from such corporate crimes in a number of very important ways. Probably most fundamental is the way in which the savings and loan industry itself resembles the gambling casinos that they financed so heavily in the early 1980s. Whereas corporate crime in the industrial economy virtually automatically "pays off" in increased profits and long-term liquidity for the company, unlawful risk-taking in the thrift industry is a gamble—and one with very bad odds. It should not be surprising, then, that unlike more traditional corporate crimes in the manufacturing sector, these financial crimes often result in the bankruptcy of the firm.

Furthermore, although the logic of the economic structure (i.e., the inexorable drive for profits in a competitive economy) is primarily responsible for traditional corporate crime, in the case of thrift crime, the state itself has in large part set in place the generating components, in the form of deregulation, enhanced competition, and cushioned losses. The following discussion of "collective embezzlement"—a crime unique to the economic structure of finance capitalism—underscores the opportunities and temptations that this peculiar mix of deregulation and protectionism produces, the seemingly endless variety of scams devised to capitalize on it, and the havoc that it unleashes on the thrift industry.

Collective Embezzlement or Looting

In its report on crime and fraud in financial institutions, the House Committee on Government Operations concluded, "Usual internal controls do not work in this instance."[36] Elaborating, the Committee quoted the Commissioner of the California Department of Savings and Loans: "We built thick vaults; we have cameras; we have time clocks on the vaults; we have dual control—all these controls were to protect against somebody stealing the cash. Well, you can steal far more money, and take it out the back door. *The best way to rob a bank is to own one.*"[37]

"Collective embezzlement," also called here "looting," refers to the siphoning off of funds from a savings and loan institution for personal gain, at the expense of the institution itself *and with the implicit or explicit sanction of its management.* This "robbing of one's own bank" is estimated to be the single most costly category of crime in the thrift industry, having precipitated a significant number of the thrift insolvencies to date.[38] In characteristic understatement, the GAO reports that of the 26 insolvencies it studied, "almost all of the 26 failed thrifts made transactions that were not in the thrift's best interest. Rather, the transactions often personally benefited directors, officers, and other related parties."[39]

In discussing various forms of white-collar lawbreaking, Sutherland noted that "the ordinary case of embezzlement is a crime by a single individual in a subordinate position against a strong corporation."[40] Cressey, in his landmark study, *Other People's Money,* developed an explanatory model of the behavior of the lone white-collar embezzler, stealing from his or her employer.[41] Traditionally, then, embezzlement has been considered an isolated act of individual employees. The "collective embezzlement" described here is a relatively new form of corporate crime that has yet to be closely studied. Previous analyses have differentiated between corporate crime (in which fraud is engaged in *by* the corporation *for* the corporation) and embezzlement (in which crime is committed *against* the corporation), but the "collective embezzlement" discussed here is a hybrid—perhaps "crime *by* the corporation *against* the corporation."

In some cases, thrift embezzlement takes the form of "buying sprees,"[42] in which thrift operators and others with inside access to thrift funds, purchase luxury goods and services and charge them to the institution. Examples abound. When Erwin Hansen took over Centennial Savings and Loan in California at the end of 1980, one of the industry's most expensive shopping sprees began. "Erv" Hansen threw a Centennial-funded, $148,000 Christmas party for 500 friends and invited guests that included a 10-course sitdown dinner, roving minstrels, court jesters, and pantomimes. Hansen and his companion Beverly Haines, a senior officer at Centennial, traveled extensively around the world in the thrift's private airplanes, purchased antique furniture at the thrift's expense, and "renovated" an old house in the California countryside at a cost of over $1 million, equipping it with a gourmet chef at an annual cost of $48,000. A fleet of luxury cars was put at the disposal of Centennial personnel, and the thrift's offices were adorned with art from around the world.[43] Hansen died before he could be formally charged, but Haines was convicted of having embezzled $2.8 million. Centennial's inevitable insolvency cost the FSLIC an estimated $160 million.[44]

Don Dixon similarly operated Vernon Savings and Loan in Texas as if it were his own personal slush fund. He and his wife Dana divided their time between a luxury ski resort in the Rocky Mountains and a $1 million beach house north of San Diego, commuting on one of two Vernon jets that cost the thrift $100,000 apiece to operate. They went on luxury vacations across Europe, in one case running up a bill of $22,000, paid for with Vernon funds. Dixon bought a 112-foot yacht for $2.6 million, with which he wooed Congressmen and regulators on extravagant boating parties. In March, 1987, Vernon Savings and Loan was declared insolvent; it was estimated that the Vernon debacle would cost FSLIC $1.3 billion. Regulators argued in court that Dixon and others connected with Vernon had "wrongly extracted" up to $40 million from the thrift's coffers.[45]

Other more subtle forms of collective embezzlement include a variety of schemes to obtain "excessive compensation" for the institution's directors and officers.[46] As defined by the General Accounting Office, "compensation includes salaries as well as bonuses, dividend payments, and perquisites for executives."[47] Although a federal regulation limits permissible compensation for thrift personnel to that which is "reasonable and commensurate with their duties and responsibilities," the GAO found instances of excessive compensation in 17 of the 26 failed thrifts they studied.[48]

At one thrift, the chairman of the board of directors resigned his formal position in January 1985, whereupon he arranged a "services agreement" with the institution to carry on all his previous responsibilities. According to this agreement, he was to be paid $326,000 plus a percentage of profits in the form of a bonus. Six months later, the thrift paid him a bonus of $500,000 in "special employee compensation," even though it reported a loss of approximately $23 million during the course of 1985.[49]

The most widespread techniques of looting discovered thus far, however, involve an array of "special deals." For example, in "nominee loan" schemes,[50] a "straw borrower" outside of the thrift obtains a loan for a third person, who is usually affiliated with the thrift from which the loan is received. Such nominee loans are a popular device for disguising violations of the regulation which limits unsecured commercial loans to "affiliated persons" to $100,000. Don Dixon, of Vernon, was particularly adept at this, setting up an intricate network of at least 30 subsidiary companies for the express purpose of making illegal loans to himself.

A related system for violating the loans-to-affiliated-persons regulation is "reciprocal loan arrangements."[51] Hearings before the House Subcommittee on Commerce, Consumer, and Monetary Affairs in 1987 described four investigations in Wyoming that "revealed a pattern of complex activities . . . [which] include reciprocal loans in which the insiders from one bank authorize loans to the insiders of another bank in return for similar loans."[52] The scam resulted in losses to taxpayers of $26 million when the loans defaulted and the institutions failed.

So-called "land flips" use real estate deals as the mechanism for looting.[53] Land flips are defined as "transfers of land between related parties to fraudulently inflate the value of the land. The land is used as collateral for loans based on the inflated or fraudulent valuation. Loan amounts typically greatly exceed the actual value of the land."[54] Hansen of Centennial Savings and Loans, his friend and high financier Sid

Shah, and Dutch investor Neik Sandmann, regularly used this technique to mutual advantage. According to reporters Pizzo et at., the three "flipped" one property worth $50,000 back and forth in the early 1980s until it reached the inflated value of $487,000, upon which they received a loan from Atlas Savings, the "sucker" institution of choice for Hansen.[55]

Similarly, loan broker J. William Oldenburg bought a piece of property in Richmond, California, in 1979 for $874,000. Two years later, after a number of "flips," he had the land appraised at $83.5 *million*. After buying State Savings and Loans in Salt Lake City for $10.5 million, he sold the property to the newly acquired thrift for $55 million.[56] In 1985, the ill-fated thrift went under, leaving the FSLIC responsible for $416 million in outstanding deposits.

"Linked financing," or "daisy chains" as they are known in the industry, is perhaps the most subtle and complex of the "special deals" used for embezzling. Linked financing is "the practice of depositing money into a financial institution with the understanding that the financial institution will make a loan conditioned upon receipt of the deposits."[57] It often involves large brokered deposits, made by a deposit broker who then receives a generous loan from the bank or thrift for his business. The brokers can then default on their loans, essentially obtaining free cash (these are called "drag loans," because the borrower simply drags away the loan, with no intention of repayment); middlemen obtain a generous "finder's fee"; and thrift operators record hefty deposits and inflated assets, which spell extra bonuses and dividends for thrift executives.

Looting is not confined to inside operators of thrifts. More often than not, the scheme requires intricate partnerships with those outside the industry, usually in real estate or loan brokerage.[58] In some cases the outsiders themselves initiate the fraud by identifying weak thrifts as "easy targets" that are "ripe for the plucking."[59] In one infamous deal, loan broker Charles J. Bazarian, Jr., engaged in fraudulent real estate transactions that contributed to the insolvency of two large California thrifts—Consolidated Savings Bank of Irvine and American Diversified Savings Bank of Costa Mesa. According to charges brought against Bazarian, in one instance he borrowed more than $9.5 million from Consolidated, putting close to $5 million of it into a partnership in which the owner of the thrift, Robert Ferrante, had a direct interest. The same year, Bazarian arranged a reciprocal transaction with American Diversified in which the thrift bought $15 million of "worthless" investor notes from Bazarian's brokerage firm, in exchange for Bazarian's purchase of $3.85 million in promissory notes and two pieces of real estate from the thrift. When federal regulators finally closed the two thrifts, together they registered close to $200 million in losses.[60]

"Daisy chains," "dead cows for dead horses," "land flips," "cash for trash," "cash for dirt," "kissing the paper," "white knights"—their playful jargon reflects the make-believe, candy-store mentality of this new breed of white-collar criminal and belies the devastating consequences of their actions. In Arkansas, where one-third of all thrifts have collapsed since 1986, taking with them $4 billion in deposits (a sum which is more than the state's annual budget), local residents have developed a jargon of their own. "S&L" they say, stands for "Squander and Liquidate."[61]

As looters were shoplifting goods and pilfering cash out the back door of thrifts, more shady characters were being welcomed in the front door. Increasingly, the word spread that deregulation of thrifts had offered up a money machine to the unscrupulous. At the federal level, new charters, which had averaged 45 a year in the 1970s, shot up to an average of 96 per year in the 1980s.[62] In states such as Texas and California where regulations were especially lax, the number of new charters increased even more sharply. In California, 235 applications for new thrift charters were received by the California Department of Savings and Loan in a little over a year between 1982 and 1984, and most were quickly granted.[63]

Summarizing the looting epidemic, the House Committee on Government Operations lamented the opportunities opened up for the con artist: "We have even got organized crime types taking a look at thinly capitalized institutions which are candidates for takeover and then using [various specified fraud schemes] . . . to create a paper financial asset which they can pull the plug on after a year-and-a-half or two, and leave the FDIC or FSLIC, i.e., the taxpayers, holding the bag."[64]

Deregulation and subsequent intense competition had produced the incentive for those on the "slippery slope of a failing institution" to try to save that institution via unlawful, but in the end not very "risky," risk-taking. As deregulation had thus opened the doors to gambling risk-free with depositors' money, it simultaneously opened them to crooks and swindlers whose intention was to embezzle funds. Not infrequently, the gamblers and swindlers were the same people. Whether the motive was to keep the doors open for further sport, or to get in and out with as much of the pot as possible, the game was the same: "Heads I win. Tails you lose."

Covering up

As savings and loans teetered on the brink of bankruptcy, broken by negligent loan practices on one hand and outright looting on the other, their operators struggled to hide both the insolvency and the fraud through a manipulation of their books and records. This "covering up" was, and is, perhaps the most widespread criminal activity of thrift operators. Of the alleged 179 violations of criminal law reported in the 26 failed thrifts that the GAO studied, 42 were for such covering-up activity, constituting the largest single category of fraud.[65] Furthermore, every one of the 26 failed thrifts had been cited by regulatory examiners for "deficiencies in accounting."[66]

In some cases, the cover-up comes in the guise of deals similar to those discussed above—the difference being that the primary purpose of the transactions is to produce a misleading picture of the institution's state of health. Most important, thrifts are required to have on hand a specific amount of capital, as well as a given capital-to-assets ratio; when they fail to meet these standards, they are subject to enforcement actions. U.S. Attorney Anton R. Valukas describes a number of cover-up deals and the motivation for them:

> In the prosecuted cases of Manning Savings and Loan, American Heritage Savings and Loan of Bloomingdale and First Suburban Bank of Maywood, when the loans ("nominee loans") became non-performing the assets were taken back into the institution, again sold at inflated prices to straw purchasers, financed by the institution, in order to inflate the net worth of the bank or savings and loan. The clear purpose was to keep the federal regulatory agencies . . . at bay by maintaining a net worth above the trigger point for forced reorganization or liquidation.[67]

In some cases, deals can be arranged that include a built-in cover-up. For example, in cases of risky insider or reciprocal loans, a reserve account can be included in the original loan to be used to pay for the first few months (or years) of interest. Thus if a real estate developer, or for that matter a straw borrower, wants to borrow $500,000, he can be extended $750,000, putting the additional $250,000 into a special account from which the interest payments can be drawn. The effect is to make a loan appear current whether or not the real estate project has failed or was phony in the first place.

Probably most common, however, is simply adjusting the books to shield the thrift from regulatory action. At one savings and loan studied by the GAO, three irreconcilable sets of records were kept—two on two different computer systems and one manually.[68] At another, $21 million of income was reported in the last few days of 1985 in transactions that were either fabricated or fraudulent, allowing the thrift to report a net worth of $9 million, rather than its actual worth of negative $12 million.[69] Noting the prevalence of such cover-up devices, the president of one savings and loan testified in Congressional hearings that, "instead of attempting to remedy the problems which were so apparent, they [industry operatives] spent all of their efforts in proposing intricate schemes which . . . would appear to aid in maintaining the equity at a proper level."[70]

Having perpetrated fraud and brought their institutions to ruin, thrift operators had to cover their tracks, both to protect themselves from prosecution and to keep their money machine running. Ironically, they were aided and, some would say, encouraged in their efforts by the same agencies from which they were presumably hiding. The Federal Home Loan Bank Board set in place a number of bookkeeping strategies during the deregulatory period that simultaneously provided the industry with the tools to juggle their books to present themselves in the best possible light, and implicitly relayed the message that in trying to keep afloat, "anything goes."

Most important, in 1981 the FHLBB devised and encouraged the use of new accounting procedures known as "regulatory accounting procedures" (RAP). The new procedures entailed a complex formula that allowed for the understating of assets and the overstating of capital.[71] The sole purpose of the new RAP techniques was to inflate an institution's capital-to-assets ratio, thereby bolstering its image of financial health, and warding off reorganization, which the FSLIC increasingly could not afford. Not only did the procedures supply the industry with a "gray area" within which they could commit fraud with little chance of detection, but it sent the message that the Bank Board itself promoted deceptive bookkeeping.

In addition, the Bank Board in the early 1980s sent a more general message that it condoned discretionary reporting by thrifts. The GAO, for example, cites the Board's failure to provide appropriate guidelines for recording ADC transactions until 1985, thereby implicitly encouraging accounting treatments that inflated thrifts' net worth. ADC transactions can be classified as loans or investments; "Thus, a thrift could possibly forestall regulatory action by using whichever classification resulted in the most favorable portrayal of its financial condition."[72] Nonetheless, the Bank Board issued no guidelines for the recording of these important transactions. One district bank official who sought advice from the Board as to how these transactions should be reported "was told that the Bank Board was not going to act on this issue."[73]

Deregulation, based on a free market model of capitalism, had provided the economic pressure and the opportunity for thrift operators and their partners to make a fortune fast. But the free market model was by no means uniformly applied. As deregulators busily dismantled restrictions on thrifts, protections were not only left intact, but were increased, providing a risk-free environment for the white-collar heist of the century. In the following section, we address the question asked pointedly by one of the most prolific of thrift embezzlers, Charles Bazarian: "So where were the regulators?"[74]

SAVINGS AND LOAN ENFORCEMENT: IDEOLOGY, NETWORKS OF INFLUENCE, AND STRUCTURAL FACTORS

Deregulation Ideology and Limited Resources

According to the House Committee on Government Operations "serious deficiencies" exist in the way the federal banking regulators and the Justice Department have handled fraud in the banking and thrift industry.[75] The Committee Report points out that in the early 1980s, many thrifts were able to avoid timely examination altogether,[76] and that those that were found to be violating the law, were treated too leniently to offer any deterrence.[77] The Committee faults the "graduated response" strategy of enforcement, describing the system as follows:

An agency uncovers abuse and issues a directive or letter; the abuse continues and becomes worse, and the agency then issues a MOU [Memorandum of Understanding] or a supervisory agreement; and then, as the situation worsens, the agency issues one or more supervisory directives, and possibly a C&D [Cease and Desist] order or removal [of management], but by then the institution is failing. This committee specifically criticized this practice in its 1984 report. With certain exceptions, the agencies' approach has not changed.[78]

Both the House Committee and the GAO report a general lack of "formal enforcement actions" against even the most serious offenders. One GAO study[79] examined 424 "Significant Supervisory Cases," that is, thrifts that both have serious internal control problems and are in imminent danger of insolvency, and found that formal actions had been taken by regulators in fewer than 50% of the cases; in most of these cases the formal actions involved placing the thrift into receivership *after* it had become insolvent. Another GAO report[80] concludes that "numerous safety and soundness problems" had been documented by examiners in 26 of the nation's most costly insolvencies over the course of five years or more. Despite the examiners' notes that these thrifts required "urgent and decisive corrective measures," in most cases nothing substantive was done before it was too late.[81] The House Committee on Government Operations[82] reports that enforcement actions, which they had argued in a 1984 report[83] were already too rare to constitute a deterrent, declined further after 1986.

Not only did thrift fraud go relatively undetected by regulators, and was generally not dealt with through formal actions, but those offenders who were prosecuted typically received lenient sentences. According to the report of the House Committee cited above, "The message to culpable insiders and outsiders is: 'Crime does pay.' "[84] Every U.S. Attorney who testified before the Committee complained of the light sentences handed down in financial fraud cases. The U.S. Attorney for Southern California reported that in his district since January 1986, 60% of the convictions under the bank fraud statutes have brought sentences of probation; 10% received less than a year in custody; and fewer than 5% of the defendants were given five years or more in prison.[85] The House Subcommittee on Commerce, Consumer, and Monetary Affairs conducted its own examination of the sentences of 38 serious offenders in 28 thrifts and found that 16 received probation, and that only 8 of these were ordered to pay significant restitution.[86] As one U.S. Attorney put it, responding to such lenience, "If someone had walked in the door of the bank with a note saying this is a robbery . . . and walked out with $1500, I dare say he would have received 5 to 10 years in prison."[87]

The lack of meaningful enforcement in the savings and loan industry in the 1980s is partly the result of ideological imperatives in the deregulatory era. In the first place, deregulators believed wholeheartedly in the intrinsically healthy nature of intense competition and in the healing power of entrepreneurial innovation. Regulators themselves had invented and encouraged the use of Regulatory Accounting Procedures that would camouflage thrifts' actual state of declining health. The perpetrators of thrift fraud were, in a sense, only carrying this message of the deregulators to an extreme. Second, having deregulated the thrift industry, policymakers and industry regulators were undoubtedly reluctant to intervene while the new deregulated thrift environment was presumably working its magic and revitalizing the industry. If a few thrift operators were getting carried away, and their institutions were on the brink of insolvency, this was merely a transitional period on the road to a reinvigorated industry.

Related to these ideological imperatives of deregulation, inadequate resources compounded the problem. The size of the examination staff of the FHLBB remained constant for almost 20 years, despite dramatic increases in workload. In 1966, when the total assets of thrift institutions were $133.8 billion, FHLBB had a field examination staff of 755 persons; by 1985, when total assets had soared to $1 trillion, the examination staff stood at 747. The House Committee on Government Operations remarks on this shortage of inspectors: "No one questions that this contributed to untimely detection of misconduct in numerous institutions which subsequently failed."[88]

Despite repeated requests by the FHLBB for budget increases commensurate with the growth of the industry, the Office of Management and Budget (OMB) was determined to maintain existing low levels of funding in the first half of the 1980s. Citing OMB's "disdain for the examination process," the former deputy director of the FSLIC told the House Subcommittee on Commerce, Consumer, and Monetary Affairs that OMB budgetary policies were directly responsible for the lack of supervision in the thrift industry.[89] In July 1985, the FHLBB decentralized its examination process in the quasi-independent FHL District Banks, thereby taking it outside the budgetary control of OMB. As a result, the examination staff doubled in two years.[90]

Networks of Influence

The increase in budget and enforcement personnel after 1985 proved insufficient to offset the impact of political influence and favor-trading that dictated against strict enforcement. A revolving door between the state and federal regulatory agencies and the thrift industry itself provides one dimension of these networks of influence. For example, it is commonly understood that the U.S. League of Savings Associations, a powerful lobbying group of thrift executives, had virtual veto power on the nomination of the head of the FHLBB, and that members of the regulatory board are drawn almost entirely from the industry itself.[91] Richard Pratt, head of the FHLBB at the time, in a moment of candor told his subordinates at an agency conference that the Bank Board was "perhaps too closely allied to the industry that it regulates."[92] At the lower levels, it is not uncommon for thrifts to woo examiners and regulators with job offers in the industry.[93] Journalists Pizzo et al. put it bluntly, describing the strategy of "Erv" Hansen, owner and embezzler of Centennial Savings and Loan: "Hansen had his own way of appeasing regulators. He'd hire them." Hansen, for example, hired Pat Connolly, former deputy commissioner of the California Department of Savings and Loan, making him an executive vice president of the thrift and doubling his $40,000 a year government salary.[94]

In one of the most infamous cases of personal intrigue in the savings and loan crisis, it has been charged that M. Danny Wall, head of the FHLBB at the time, met personally with Charles Keating, owner of Lincoln Savings and Loan, and intervened on behalf of Keating to ward off FHLBB regulators in the San Francisco district who were investigating the thrift.[95] Wall managed to move the investigation from the San Francisco office to Washington and to delay closure of the insolvent thrift for two years—a delay that is estimated to have cost the FSLIC insurance fund $2 billion.[96] Once the investigation had been moved to Washington, according to Congressional testimony, Rosemary Stewart, head of the enforcement office in Washington, signed a "memo of understanding" with Lincoln. This "understanding" was bitterly referred to by examiners in the San Francisco office as "Rosemary's Baby," because it essentially permitted Lincoln to continue its high risk-taking and misconduct for a full year before it was finally closed.[97]

Similar networks of influence have been documented between members of Congress and the thrift industry, with significant repercussions on enforcement. For example, just before the Lincoln case was moved to Washington, five U.S. Senators (Cranston, Glenn, DeConcini, McCain, and Riegle) who had received campaign and other contributions from Charles Keating, called San Francisco regulators to Washington to discuss their prolonged examination of Lincoln.[98] According to a racketeering lawsuit brought against accountants in the Lincoln case, the intervention of the Senators "protracted the examination process and afforded [operators] additional time in which to exacerbate their frauds."[99]

In other well-publicized cases, former House speaker Jim Wright and former Democratic Whip Tony Coelho have been linked to the savings and loan industry in Texas, intervening on behalf of Dixon's Vernon Savings and Loan, and attempting to devise more "flexible" regulatory policies.[100] Republicans are by no means exempt from the maneuverings. According to one report, the Republican National Committee put together an exclusive group of high financiers and named them the "Team 100." A prominent member of this group, and one who donated heavily to the Bush campaign in 1988, was Texas billionaire Trammel Crow. Crow has managed the Texas real estate repossessed by the FSLIC for years. As thrift failures have increased, Crow and other members of the "Team" have been offered the insolvent S&Ls at bargain-basement prices, suggesting a link between thrift failures in Texas and the financial fortunes of the Republicans' "Team 100."[101]

Structural Conflicts and Enforcement

Besides these networks of personal influence and corruption, more general structural forces sabotaged regulation. According to the GAO, a "basic structural flaw" permeated the FHLBB system. This structural flaw consisted of the complex division of labor and overlapping responsibilities of thrift regulators and, related to this, the "conflicting responsibilities for promoting the thrift industry while at the same time regulating and insuring it."[102] Prior to the reform of 1989, the FHLBB regulatory system included the following layers: the 12 district banks' examiners, to whom primary field-level responsibility was delegated in 1985; the Office of

Regulatory Activity (ORA), established in 1986 to oversee these district bank examiners; the Office of Enforcement (OE) within the central FHLBB in Washington, DC, to whom the district examiners made recommendations for formal enforcement actions; the three-member Federal Home Loan Bank Board itself; and, finally, the FSLIC, which had ultimate responsibility for liquidating or reorganizing insolvent thrifts.

In addition to the potential for overlapping responsibilities inherent in this system, the structural problems were two-fold. First, the FSLIC, which insured the thrifts and had to pay the tab for insolvencies, had no legal authority to monitor or supervise the institutions and had to receive approval from the Bank Board before it could take any final action. Making matters worse, a "fundamental conflict" existed in the Bank Board and district banks' "roles in both promoting and regulating the industry."[103] The Bank Board was responsible for chartering new thrifts and promoting the general welfare of the savings and loan system, yet at the same time was the main thrift regulator. The district banks, whose field examiners had to uncover any potential problems or misconduct, had as their primary role the provision of banking services to the member institutions and depended on these institutions for their livelihood. The thrift industry executives who made up the vast majority of district bank board members[104] were the personal embodiment of this symbiotic relationship between the district banks and the thrift industry that they were supposed to regulate. Previous analyses have used the concept of "captive agencies" to refer to regulatory agencies that are subordinate to, and cater to, the industries they are charged with regulating.[105] The dual functions of the FHLBB effectively *institutionalized* the "captive agency" syndrome.

But there are other, even more fundamental, structural problems. First, not only was the FSLIC dependent on the Bank Board for approval for its actions, but the insurers faced a catch-22 situation: The worse the crisis in the thrift industry, the less likely it was that the FSLIC could respond. This dilemma has plagued the insurers for years, but by the mid-1980s it paralyzed them. By 1986, the FSLIC itself was insolvent (its liabilities exceeded its assets by an estimated $3 billion to $7 billion), drained of its resources by the epidemic of thrift failures.[106]

Throughout the 1980s, the FHLBB had extended "forbearance" to ailing thrifts, forestalling their closure or reorganization, "either because it believed the thrift to be capable of recovery" in the new deregulated environment, or "because the regulators desired to postpone using insurance fund reserves."[107] When the fund itself became insolvent in 1986, forbearance became a matter of necessity. As the FSLIC stopped closing insolvent thrifts, not only did the final costs escalate, but fraud—which in many cases had contributed to the insolvency in the first place—went undeterred. With nothing to lose, careless risk-taking and looting permeated the brain-dead institutions until they were finally, mercifully, put out of their misery.

Finally, and perhaps most importantly, a contradiction inherent in the structure of finance capitalism underlies the inability of regulators to respond effectively to the widespread fraud in the thrift industry. Clues as to the nature of this contradiction occasionally surface in government reports on the crisis. For example, the U.S.

Attorney for the Southern District of Texas testified before the House Subcommittee on Commerce, Consumer, and Monetary Affairs that "the public's faith in the security and integrity of their banking institutions is considered so vital to the continued viability of the banking system that Congress has promulgated laws to prevent people from even starting rumors about a bank's solvency or insolvency."[108] Although the official concluded from this that the state must act quickly to deter crime and restore public confidence in the banking system, quite a different conclusion could be drawn. In fact, the House Committee on Government Operations reports that "Although every other Federal regulatory agency discloses final enforcement actions, the banking agencies continue to refuse to routinely disclose the existence or a summary of final civil enforcement orders taken against individuals or institutions."[109] The FHLBB argument against the "adverse publicity" that such disclosure would generate is that it would damage public confidence in the institution, worsening its condition. The Committee points out that this reluctance of the agency to act decisively and openly, in the interest of protecting the banking industry, has exacerbated thrift misconduct.[110]

An essential characteristic of finance capitalism is that its product is illusory—based on collectively agreed upon, but fundamentally arbitrary, values and shared faith. In this context, the "market" works so long as all of the players agree to pretend. Alan Webber, managing editor of the *Harvard Business Review,* points to this make-believe quality of our "soap-bubble" economy and explains, "That's why the slightest whiff of smoke can so easily spook the crowd to rush for the exits."[111] The banking industry is a clear and simple example of the importance of the collective agreement to have faith, since its success, indeed its very survival, depends on our illusion that banks in fact can pay off their debts (our deposits). Any "whiff of smoke" to the contrary sets off a run on the bank. For the regulator caught between sending up this smoke and shattering the collective illusion, or ignoring fraud and insolvency, the name of the game may be "Heads I Lose, Tails You Win."

DISCUSSION

The House Committee on Government Operations summed up the testimony of senior Justice Department officials on the topic of bank fraud, reporting "(a) that financial institution fraud has reached epidemic proportions, [and] (b) that the number of criminal cases is increasing at an alarming rate."[112] Federal Bureau of Investigation figures reveal that Financial Institution Fraud and Embezzlement (FIF & E) cases make up 45.2% of all white-collar crime convictions or pretrial diversions, and that more than 80% of these involve insider fraud.[113]

The argument presented here has been that the epidemic of financial fraud in the thrift industry can be traced in large part to state policies and related ideologies of the 1980s that set in place a formula of deregulation and protectionism that unleashed unprecedented incentives and supplied tempting opportunities to commit fraud. Furthermore, it has been shown that the economic structure of the deregulated and protected thrift industry has generated a new breed of white-collar crime, called here "collective embezzlement," in which the systematic embezzlement of company funds is *company policy.*

But a more general point is implicit in this analysis: Both this new hybrid of white-collar crime—crime by the corporation against the corporation—and the role of the state in its generation and proliferation, are products of a new economic structure. French economist and Nobel prize winner, Maurice Allais, has called finance capitalism in the United States a "casino" economy.[114] Profits in this economy are made from speculative ventures designed to bring windfall profits from having placed a clever bet. In contrast to industrial capitalism where profits are dependent on the production and sale of goods and services, profits in finance capitalism increasingly come, as one commentator has put it, from "fiddling with money."[115] Corporate takeovers, currency trading, loan swaps, land speculation, futures trading—these are the "means of production" of finance capitalism. Only one thing is missing: Nothing is being produced but capital gains.

Maurice Allais underlines the magnitude of this shift from an economy based on the circulation of goods to one circulating money itself, by pointing out that "more than \$400 billion is exchanged every day on the foreign exchange markets, while the flow of commercial transactions is only about \$12 billion."[116] Nothing epitomizes the new financial era like the junk bond. The irony of its name should not be lost. The device transforms debt into wealth, and "junk" into "one of the greatest fortunes in Wall Street history."[117]

The advent of finance capitalism has clearly created new opportunities for fraud, because the amount that can be reaped from financial crime is confined only to the limits of one's imagination. Furthermore, as we have seen, state policies in the form of deregulation multiplied the opportunities in the savings and loan industry. But there is a way in which the new economic structure more generally encourages fraud, or at least fails to discourage it. A number of analysts have delineated the constraints placed on entrepreneurs in industrial or manufacturing capitalism, focusing on the contradiction between the simultaneous need to maximize surplus value and to minimize labor unrest and other forms of economic and political instability.[118] Weinstein, for example, explains Progressivism in the early 20th century as the product of capitalists' pressing need for stability dictated by long-term investments in the costly infrastructure of capitalist production versus the potential instability of an escalating class struggle.[119] Industrial capitalism clearly presents incentives and opportunities for serious crime, as several generations of students of white-collar crime have documented. Nonetheless, these corporate criminals are generally pressed into crime to *advance* their corporation and are constrained by a vested interest in its long-term survival. By contrast, perpetrators of financial fraud in the thrift industry and throughout the "casino" economy, have little to lose by their reckless behavior. With no long-term investment in the infrastructure of production and no labor relations (since there are no workers in this "production" process) to inhibit them, the casino capitalists' main concern is to get in and out of the "house" with as much of the pot as possible. The effect of their crimes on the health of the casino, or even its long-term survival, are unimportant to these financial gamblers. Not surprisingly, then, the repercussions of these crimes, unlike more traditional white-collar crimes, have the potential to extend far beyond their direct costs to wreak havoc throughout the economy.

The structure of finance capitalism not only has contributed to the unprecedented proportions and far-reaching consequences of savings and loan and other financial fraud, but has limited the state's ability to respond to it effectively. One reason for this paralysis of the state in treating thrift fraud has to do with outdated assumptions and ideologies that were the product of industrial capitalism, but which are anachronistic in the new economic environment. Most important is the notion that individual profit-making activity is intrinsically beneficial to the general economy, and that the spillover will eventually "trickle down" to the public at large in the form of increased jobs, better wages, and an overall improved standard of living. Thus, in 20th century America, it became a truism that "What's good for General Motors is good for the country." There was a certain, albeit limited, logic to this trickle-down axiom within the framework of early 20th century capitalism. State actions calculated to provide conditions favorable to capital accumulation, while exacting brutal sacrifices from workers, at least had the *potential* to pay a return on those sacrifices in the form of an expanded economy. Given the right conditions (a strong and active labor movement being a central one), trickle-down theory could, and sometimes did, work.

This trickle-down ideology born of industrial capitalism has had direct implications for the treatment of corporate crime. Policymakers and regulators have reasoned that an overly punitive approach to corporate crime is counterproductive if it cuts into profits or discourages aggressive business practices. Theorists of the state have thus noted a structural contradiction between the need of the capitalist state to encourage the maximization of profits versus the threat to profit maximization entailed in, for example, the rigorous enforcement of occupational safety and health standards.[120]

But the logic of finance capitalism is such that capital gains based on speculative ventures are, at best, irrelevant to the welfare of the general population. Unlike the production of goods and services, "fiddling with" money produces few new jobs and no consumer goods. Policies based on outdated assumptions about the intrinsically beneficial nature of entrepreneurial activity tend to exacerbate the situation. Thus, for example, deregulation—rooted in notions of the inherent desirability of profit maximization—within the context of the new casino economy not only did not solve the thrift crisis, but compounded it by condoning fraud as simply aggressive business practices that would eventually stimulate recovery. In the case of savings and loans, the abstract theory of "trickle down" yielded the harsh reality of "trickle up," as taxpayers foot the bill for the casino extravaganza.

As policymakers are mired in the old ideologies of a past era, a new contradiction adds to the paralysis. As we have seen, a fundamental contradiction between profit maximization and enforcement of standards and regulations permeates industrial capitalism and limits the state's ability to respond to corporate crime. The logic of finance capitalism contains its own set of contradictions, with even more disastrous consequences. The new economy is built on "soap-bubbles" and illusion, where prosperity is based on debt, and the collective agreement to ignore the emperor's nakedness not only staves off collapse but is the very motor that drives the economy. In this context, the role of the state is not to establish optimal conditions for productive activity, as it was in industrial capitalism, but to shore up the illusion and minimize the potential for panic. Thus it makes sense that the same deregulators who dismantled all restrictions on the savings and loan industry in the name of the free market deviated so dramatically from their own convictions and *increased* deposit insurance. The contradiction underlying the thrift debacle, then, is that the casino economy is based on illusion but that that illusion must be preserved at all costs. As losses were covered by federal insurance, and regulators were discouraged from publicizing fraud and insolvencies, the state response to the thrift crisis and financial fraud inevitably contained within it the seeds of its own destruction.

The future is likely to bring more of the same, because the savings and loan reform act passed by Congress in August, 1989, leaves untouched the major causal factors in both the thrift crisis and the crime that contributed to it. The Financial Institutions Reform, Recovery, and Enforcement Act of 1989 (FIRREA), among other things, raises the capital-to-assets ratio required of thrifts, reorganizes the regulatory apparatus by creating a new Office of Thrift Supervision, and sets up the Resolution Trust Corporation to manage and sell an estimated $500 billion worth of assets from failed thrifts. However, the deregulation and protectionism that in the early 1980s provided the unprecedented incentives and opportunities for white-collar crime in the thrift industry, and the underlying contradictions upon which these policies were based, remain fundamentally unchanged. Having been bailed out with huge subsidies from taxpayers and their coffers replenished, the savings and loan casino is once again open and ready for business.

Notes

1. U.S. Congress, House Comm. on Ways and Means, "Budget Implications and Current Tax Rules Relating to Troubled Savings and Loan Institutions," *Hearings,* February 22, March 2, and March 15, 1989; U.S. Congress, Senate Comm. on Banking, Housing and Urban Affairs, "Problems of the Federal Savings and Loan Insurance Corporation (FSLIC)," *Hearings,* March 3, 7–10, 1989.
2. U.S. General Accounting Office [GAO], "Thrift Failures. Costly Failures Resulted from Regulatory Violations and Unsafe Practices," *Report to the Congress,* 1989; U.S. Congress, House Comm. on Government Operations, "Combatting Fraud, Abuse, and Misconduct in the Nation's Financial Institutions," 1988, p. 51.

3. Edwin H. Sutherland, *White Collar Crime.* New York: Dryden, 1949; Harvey Farberman, "A Criminogenic Market Structure: The Automobile Industry," *Sociological Quarterly,* 16 (1975):438–457; Stanton Wheeler and Mitchell Rothman, "The Organization as Weapon in White-Collar Crime," *Michigan Law Review,* 80 (1982):1403–1426.
4. Stephen Pizzo, Mary Fricker, and Paul Muolo, *Inside Job: The Looting of America's Savings and Loan.* New York: McGraw-Hill, 1989, p. 11.
5. GAO, "Thrift Industry Restructuring and the Net Worth Certificate Program," *Report to Congress,* 1985, p. 7.
6. Federal Home Loan Bank System, *A Guide to the Federal Home Loan Bank System.* Washington, DC: Federal Home Loan Bank System Publishing, 1987, p. 11.
7. U.S. Congress, House Comm. on Government Operations, Subcomm. on Commerce, Consumer, and Monetary Affairs, "Fraud and Abuse by Insiders, Borrowers, and Appraisers in the California Thrift Industry," *Hearings,* June 13, 1987.
8. U.S. Congress, House, *op. cit.,* 1988, p. 62.
9. GAO, "Troubled Thrifts, Bank Board Use of Enforcement Actions," *Briefing Report,* 1989, p. 25.
10. U.S. Congress, House Comm. on Banking, Finance and Urban Affairs, Subcommittee on Financial Institutions Supervision, Regulation and Insurance, "Financial Institutions, Reform, Recovery, and Enforcement Act of 1989 (H.R. 1278)," *Hearings,* March 8, 9, 14, 1989, p. 286.
11. GAO, "Failed Thrifts. Internal Control Weaknesses Create an Environment Conducive to Fraud, Insider Abuse and Related Unsafe Practices," 1989, p. 2.
12. Ned Eichler, *The Thrift Debacle.* Berkeley: University of California Press, 1989, p. 119.
13. GAO, "Failed Thrifts," *op. cit.,* p. 11.
14. U.S. Congress, House, 1988, *op. cit.,* p. 51.
15. GAO, "Failed Thrifts," *op. cit.,* pp. 51–52.
16. U.S. Congress, House, 1988, *op. cit.,* pp. 4–5.
17. GAO, "Thrift Failures," *op. cit.,* p. 22.
18. *Ibid.,* p. 17.
19. U.S. Congress, House, 1988, *op. cit.,* p. 41.
20. U.S. Congress, House, "Fraud and Abuse by Insiders," *op. cit.,* p. 265.
21. *Los Angeles Times,* October 28, 1989b, p. Dl.
22. GAO, "Failed Thrifts," *op. cit.,* p. 27.
23. Pizzo et al., *op. cit.,* p. 191.
24. U.S. Congress, House, "Fraud and Abuse by Insiders," *op. cit.,* p. 334.
25. U.S. Congress, House, 1988, *op. cit.,* p. 34.
26. U.S. Congress, House, "Fraud and Abuse by Insiders," *op. cit.,* p. 13.
27. U.S. Congress, House, 1988, *op. cit.,* p. 46.
28. U.S. Congress, House, "Fraud and Abuse by Insiders," *op. cit.,* p. 9.
29. Eichler, *op. cit.,* p. 108.

30. Sutherland, *op. cit.*; Farberman, *op. cit.*; Gilbert Geis, "The Heavy Electrical Equipment Antitrust Cases of 1961." In Marshall Clinard and Richard Quinney, eds., *Criminal Behavior Systems: A Typology.* New York: Holt, Rinehart & Winston, 1967, pp. 140–151; John Hagan, *Modern Criminology.* New York: McGraw-Hill, 1985.

31. Mark Dowie, "Pinto Madness." In Jerome Skolnick and Elliot Currie, eds., *Crisis in American Institutions.* 4th ed. Boston: Little, Brown, 1979, pp. 26–34.

32. Morton Mintz and Jerry Cohen, *Power, Inc.: Public and Private Rulers and How to Make them Accountable.* New York: Viking, 1976, p. 110.

33. Curtis J. Lang, "Blue Sky and Big Bucks," *Southern Exposure,* 17 (1989):20–25.

34. Wheeler and Rothman, *op. cit.*, p. 21.

35. Geis, *op. cit.*

36. U.S. Congress, House, 1988, *op. cit.*, p. 34.

37. *Ibid.* (emphasis in original).

38. *Ibid.*, p. 41.

39. GAO, "Thrift Failures," p. 19.

40. Edwin Sutherland, *White Collar Crime: The Uncut Version.* New Haven: Yale University Press, 1983, p. 231.

41. Donald Cressey, *Other People's Money: The Social Psychology of Embezzlement.* Glencoe, IL: The Free Press, 1953.

42. Pizzo et al., *op. cit.*, p. 36.

43. *Ibid.*, pp. 25–27.

44. U.S. Congress, House, 1988, *op. cit.*, p. 38.

45. Pizzo et al., *op. cit.*, p. 193.

46. GAO, "Thrift Failures," p. 21.

47. *Ibid.*

48. *Ibid.*

49. *Ibid.*

50. U.S. Congress, House, 1988, *op. cit.*, p. 41.

51. *Ibid.*

52. United States Congress, House Comm. on Government Operations, Subcomm. on Commerce, Consumer, and Monetary Affairs, "Adequacy of Federal Efforts to Combat Fraud, Abuses, and Misconduct in Federally Insured Financial Institutions," *Hearings,* November 19, 1987, pp. 79–80, 129–130.

53. U.S. Congress, House, 1988, *op. cit.*, p. 41.

54. *Ibid.*, p. 42.

55. Pizzo et al., *op. cit.*, p. 46.

56. *Ibid.*, p. 177.

57. U.S. Congress, House, 1988, *op. cit.*, p. 42.

58. U.S. Congress, House, 1987, "Fraud and Abuse by Insiders," *op. cit.*, p. 332.

59. U.S. Congress, House, 1988, *op. cit.*, p. 12.

60. *Los Angeles Times,* September 19, 1989, pp. A3, A23.

61. Eric Bates, "Outrage in Little Rock," *Southern Exposure,* 17 (1989):16–18.
62. Federal Home Loan Bank Board, *Savings & Home Financing Source Book.* Washington, DC: Federal Home Loan Bank Board, 1987, p. A29.
63. U.S. Congress, House, 1987, "Fraud and Abuse by Insiders," *op. cit.*, p. 18.
64. U.S. Congress, House, 1988, *op. cit.*, pp. 5–6.
65. GAO, "Thrift Failures," *op. cit.*, p. 51.
66. *Ibid.*, p. 40.
67. U.S. Congress, House, 1987, "Adequacy of Federal Efforts," *op. cit.*, pp. 99–100.
68. GAO, "Thrift Failures," *op. cit.*, p. 41.
69. *Ibid.*, pp. 44–45.
70. U.S. Congress, House, "Fraud and Abuse by Insiders," *op. cit.*, p. 546.
71. Eichler, *op. cit.*, pp. 72, 78.
72. GAO, "Thrift Failures," *op. cit.*, p. 42.
73. *Ibid.*
74. Pizzo et al., *op. cit.*, p. 14.
75. U.S. Congress, House, 1988, *op. cit.*, p. 8.
76. *Ibid.*, p. 69.
77. *Ibid.*, pp. 16, 34–39.
78. *Ibid.*, p. 16.
79. GAO, "Troubled Thrifts," *op. cit.*
80. GAO, "Thrift Failures," *op. cit.*, p. 4.
81. GAO, "Troubled Thrifts," *op. cit.*, p. 4.
82. U.S. Congress, House, *op. cit.*, pp. 75–77.
83. U.S. Congress, House Comm. on Government Operations, "Federal Response to Criminal Misconduct and Insider Abuse in the Nation's Financial Institutions," *Report,* 1984.
84. U.S. Congress, House, *op. cit.*, p. 35.
85. *Ibid.*, p. 36.
86. U.S. Congress, House, "Financial Institutions," *op. cit.*, pp. 982–1014.
87. U.S. Congress, House, "Adequacy of Federal Efforts," *op. cit.*, pp. 110–111.
88. U.S. Congress, House, 1988, *op. cit.*, p. 69.
89. U.S. Congress, House, "Fraud and Abuse by Insiders," *op. cit.*, p. 175.
90. U.S. Congress, House, 1988, *op. cit.*, p. 15.
91. Eichler, *op. cit.*, p. 131.
92. Federal Home Loan Bank Board, *op. cit.*, p. 46.
93. *Los Angeles Times,* September 1, 1989, sec. 4, p. 1.
94. Pizzo et al., *op. cit.*, p. 47.
95. *Los Angeles Times,* October 21, 1989, p. Dl.
96. *Ibid.*, October 25, 1989, p. D2.
97. Ibid., October 26, 1989, p. Dl.
98. Pizzo et al., *op. cit.*, pp. 392–404.
99. *Los Angeles Times,* September 21, 1989, sec. 4, p. 3.
100. *U.S. News and World Report,* June 12, 1989, pp. 21–22.

101. Lang, *op. cit.*, p. 24.
102. GAO, "Failed Thrifts," *op. cit.*, p. 80.
103. *Ibid.*
104. *Ibid.*, p. 81.
105. Theodore Lowi, *The End of Liberalism.* New York: Norton, 1969; Francis E. Rourke, *Bureaucracy, Politics, and Public Policy.* Boston: Little, Brown, 1969.
106. GAO, "Thrift Industry Forbearance for Troubled Institutions, 1982–1986." *Briefing Report,* 1987, p. 3.
107. *Ibid.*, p. 1.
108. U.S. Senate, House, "Adequacy of Federal Efforts," 1987, *op. cit.*, p. 126.
109. U.S. Congress, House, 1988, *op. cit.*, p. 17.
110. *Ibid.*
111. *Los Angeles Times,* October 18, 1989, p. B7.
112. U.S. Congress, House, 1988, *op. cit.*, p. 5.
113. U.S. Congress, House, "Adequacy of Federal Efforts," pp. 991–992, 592–593.
114. *Los Angeles Times,* October 26, 1989, *op. cit.*
115. *Ibid.*, October 4, 1989, sec. 2, p. 7.
116. *Ibid.*, October 26, 1989, *op. cit.*
117. James Grant, "Michael Milken, Meet Sewell Avery," *Forbes,* 400 (October 23, 1989):60–64.
118. Ralph Miliband, *The State in Capitalist Society.* New York: Basic Books, 1969; James Weinstein, *The Corporate Ideal in the Liberal State, 1900–1919.* Boston: Beacon, 1968; Robert H. Wiebe, *The Search for Order, 1877–1920.* New York: Hill and Wang, 1967.
119. Weinstein, *op. cit.*
120. Daniel M. Berman, *Death on the Job, Occupational Health and Safety Struggles in the United States.* New York: Monthly Review Press, 1978; Patrick Donnelly, "The Origins of the Occupational Safety and Health Act of 1970," *Social Problems,* 30 (1982):13–25; Lisa Stearns, "Fact and Fiction of a Model Enforcement Bureaucracy: The Labor Inspectorate of Sweden," *British Journal of Law and Society,* 6 (1979):1–23.

12

Insider Trading
The SEC Meets Carl Karcher

Elizabeth Szockyj

C orporate officers and major shareholders are restricted as to when and on what grounds they may trade company stock, but insider trading is not illegal in the United States. On the contrary, allowing officers and directors of corporations to own and to deal in stock in their company is supported in order to reward past performance and to supply an incentive for future profitability. What is illegal is when an insider trades on information that is confidential or not available to the general public, such as advance knowledge regarding a new product or unanticipated profits or losses. Trading on nonpublic information, or tipping other people who then trade, is said to undermine "the fair and honest operation of our securities markets."[1]

In 1988, the California office of the Securities and Exchange Commission (SEC) filed a civil insider trading action against Donald Karcher, the president, and Carl Karcher, the founder of Carl Karcher Enterprises (CKE), a fast-food chain, and against 13 members of the Karcher family. Before the case was over, the head of the CKE accounting department, Alvin DeShano, was prosecuted criminally by the Department of Justice for alleged illegal insider trades. After much publicity, negotiation, and expense, the Karcher family members settled with the SEC. DeShano was acquitted of criminal charges by a jury whose members felt uncomfortable convicting him on the basis of entirely circumstantial evidence.

Both the civil and criminal nature of insider trading are illustrated in this case. The civil suit reveals the motivations, on the part of all parties, for pursuing a settlement, the most frequent method of disposal of insider trading cases. By not forcing the defendants to admit to committing the offense, that is, by allowing them to settle without admitting or denying guilt, the SEC is able to assess penalties that the court might deny, while the defendants may be better off financially and emotionally by avoiding possible higher fines, additional legal fees, disruption to the corporate functioning, psychological stress, and potential adverse publicity.

Reprinted from the *Annals of the American Academy of Political and Social Science,* 525 (January 1993), pp. 46–58.

The criminal trial in this case depicts the subtleties of a jury trial for a white-collar offense. The jury's shift from an initial stance favoring guilt to an acquittal of the defendant reveals the dynamics of the jury deliberation process, particularly when a respectable defendant is being tried. The uncertainty of proving criminal intent based on circumstantial evidence has haunted attempts to prosecute insider traders. Set in a time when insider trading had became a household word and when penalties from the newly passed Insider Trading Sanctions Act of 1984 (ITSA) could be applied, the Karcher case takes the reader from the circumstances surrounding suspect securities trades to the discovery of possible illegality and then to a final resolution.

DISCOVERY OF SUSPICIOUS TRADES

Aroused by unusual trading activity, the computer in the Washington offices of the National Association of Securities Dealers (NASD) red-flagged shares trading in Carl Karcher Enterprises, Inc. Heavy selling of stock on 22 October 1984 resulted in a fourfold increase in volume from the previous day, with a jump from 21,250 to 107,620 shares. On 23 October the volume rose to 182,000 shares after CKE released its startling profit expectations, under the wire service headline "Carl Karcher Said Third Quarter Net Could Be Off by 50%." NASD, now alerted, surveyed the brokers involved in the trades to determine the individuals who had bought and sold CKE stock. By January 1985, NASD, whose suspicions of illegal insider trading appeared confirmed, turned its findings over to the SEC for further investigation and possible official action.[2]

The stock under scrutiny was fairly new to the over-the-counter market. The company, CKE, had gone public in 1982 after decades of nurturing by its founder, Carl Karcher. From his humble beginnings in Los Angeles in 1941, with a small hot dog stand purchased for $326, Carl Karcher had watched his investment grow into a chain of 449 restaurants spanning four states.[3]

PRECURSORS TO THE 1984 NEWS RELEASE

As the three-and-a-half-year SEC investigation progressed, the events of the days prior to the news release regarding the drop in CKE earnings were revealed. Due to some poor business ventures, primarily an ill-fated national expansion attempt, as well as a slump in the Los Angeles fast-food industry following the 1984 summer Olympics, the CKE earnings for the fiscal period ending 5 October 1984 were approximately 83 percent lower than for the same period the previous year, as stated in the SEC charges; the Department of Justice estimated the decline at 65 percent. These reduced period-nine earnings had a strong impact on CKE earnings for the third quarter ending 2 November 1984.

DeShano, the director of general accounting for the corporation, received the preliminary report for period nine on Friday, 12 October. Between that Friday and

Tuesday, 16 October, DeShano, the controller, and staff members adjusted and corrected the information in the report. On 16 and 17 October the final report was distributed to the CKE executives. Donald Karcher, the president of the corporation, was notified in Europe of the period-nine results. Not only were the results devastating news for the company, but Donald was scheduled to speak at a conference on 23 October and there were certain to be questions regarding the economic status of CKE. At a meeting of company executives on Saturday, 20 October, it was decided that in lieu of releasing the customary report of earnings in November, a special press notice would be issued just prior to Donald Karcher's speaking engagement. CKE had never before made a midquarter announcement. The release was transmitted Tuesday morning, 23 October, over the Dow Jones newswire. That day the CKE stock opened at 21½, declined to a low of 16½, and closed at 17¼.

In a flurry of activity before the time of the press release, stocks and debentures were sold by several of Carl Karcher's children, relatives of Donald Karcher, and Alvin DeShano. Sales by the Karcher family members accounted for 27.5 percent of the total trading volume of CKE common stock for 22 October 1984.[4] It was these trades, which occurred after the preliminary report but before the press release, that were of concern to the SEC; it was during this time that nonpublic information that would affect the price of the stock was in the hands of Donald and Carl Karcher.

THE SEC INDICTMENT

Insider trading was at this time a well-known priority for the SEC. With increased sanctions for insider trading legislated just months before by the ITSA, the SEC was moving full-steam ahead. On the East Coast, the agency made media headlines in 1984 and 1985 with insider trading charges against Paul Thayer, the Deputy Secretary of Defense to President Reagan, and against *Wall Street Journal* reporter R. Foster Winans.

In 1984, when Irving Einhorn arrived in Los Angeles to head the regional SEC office, he found the branch "in an embarrassing state of disarray."[5] What the office needed was the successful prosecution of a major securities-fraud case. With the Karcher case, the office was guaranteed national exposure. Because of the sheer number of possible defendants—16 in all—this was the largest insider trading case the Los Angeles SEC had encountered.

After countless interviews with CKE officials, traders, and family members, and after tracing telephone conversations and stock reports, the SEC announced, on 14 April 1988, three and a half years after the relevant events, its charges against a number of Karcher family members and the CKE accountant. According to the SEC, Carl Karcher and his wife, Margaret,[6] had conveyed information regarding the impending decline in profits to three daughters, a son, and two sons-in-law. Karcher had assumed the role of advising his children in their financial affairs; and all the children charged were heavily in debt from stock margin accounts.[7] Donald Karcher and his wife, Dorothy, were also charged with relaying confidential information to four relatives.

The complaint claimed that the 10 relatives avoided a total of $310,000 in losses by trading on the confidential information before the public announcement of 23 October. Neither Donald nor Carl Karcher was accused of selling CKE stock himself, only of tipping the others.

Finally, both the accountant, Alvin DeShano, and Carl Karcher's son and vice president of manufacturing and distribution, Carl Leo Karcher, were said to have been aware of the drastic decline in earnings because of their position. DeShano was accused of selling all of his 1725 shares of CKE stock, thereby avoiding losses of $9367—the Department of Justice estimated this sum at $7107—while it was alleged that Carl Leo Karcher avoided approximately an $8000 loss through his sale of stock.

In the complaint, the SEC sought, for all defendants, a permanent injunction from engaging in insider trading violations. For those guilty of trading illegally, disgorgement of the avoided loss, to be paid to the stockholders defrauded, and fines up to triple the amount disgorged—in accordance with the ITSA—were requested. The individuals charged with passing the information would be responsible for damages up to triple the amount of the losses avoided by those they allegedly tipped. Under these stipulations, Carl Karcher would be required to pay close to $1 million in fines.

A DETERMINATION OF GUILT

Carl Leo Karcher, a vice president of the company at the time in question, was aware of the period-nine report by virtue of his position. At the monthly meeting of company officers, he was startled to see the drastic period-nine drop in earnings and the dismal third-quarter profit expectations. Two days later, Carl Leo instructed his broker to sell 75 debentures. He hoped to reduce his $836,000 debt to his brokerage firm, thereby avoiding a margin call.

In testimony before the SEC, Carl Leo stated that after he had made the phone call to his broker, the chief financial officer for CKE warned him not to sell the debentures until after the public announcement on the third-quarter earnings. Upon receiving this information, Carl Leo canceled his order, but 50 debentures already had been sold. He did not attempt to reacquire these debentures. Within an hour after the earnings news release, he sold another 50 debentures.

The SEC charged Carl Leo with trading on inside information to avoid potential losses estimated at $8000. During testimony before the SEC, Carl Leo admitted to receiving and acting on the confidential earnings information, stating that at the time he believed that as long as he was selling at a loss, this act would not be considered insider trading. Carl Leo explained, "I had a legal right to sell the debentures because the sale would result in a loss to me."[8]

With this evidence in hand, the SEC asked that Carl Leo be found guilty and fined without a trial. Carl Leo proved to be the only defendant to admit to using the inside information to trade. In the summary proceedings that took place on 12 September 1988, the defense argued that Karcher had not intended to defraud, deceive, or manipulate but had simply made a mistake. Los Angeles Federal Court Judge Edward Rafeedie found that there was enough evidence without a trial to convict the former vice president of insider trading. Carl Leo's personal knowledge of the law was not relevant to his guilt.[9]

Armed with the ITSA, which allows civil penalties of up to three times the amount gained or avoided, the SEC requested that Carl Leo pay $10,500, including interest, for the losses that he avoided, plus up to $34,500 in civil penalties. The judge granted the $10,500 disgorgement and enjoined Carl Leo from committing future securities violations, but he refused to impose the treble penalty. Judge Rafeedie felt that the provision should be used for "a more egregious case." He continued, "This involved a single trade [and] is not the type of case that has been in the headlines involving . . . secret transactions [referring to the Levine-Boesky-Siegel insider trading cases]."[10]

The Carl Leo Karcher case, one of the first that attempted to use the triple-damages provision in the ITSA, dealt a blow to SEC enforcement ambitions.[11] Ironically, the standard SEC settlement incorporates a civil penalty equal to the profit obtained or loss avoided, which is more stringent than the civil court sentence handed down in the Carl Leo case. This is contrary to the normal plea-bargaining assumption that one will receive a more lenient sentence by waiving the trial alternative. As discussed later in this article, the remainder of the Karchers settled with the SEC by agreeing to pay a penalty equal to the amount disgorged.

THE DESHANO TRIAL

The only criminal charge in the Karcher episode was laid in March of 1989 against the head accountant, Alvin DeShano. This was a case where the link between the confidential period-nine report and the sale of CKE stock was direct. Since neither Carl nor Donald Karcher sold his own stock, the government would have to show that the brothers first had access to the nonpublic report and then relayed the information to their families and that thereafter the relatives charged sold the stock based on that knowledge. In the accountant's case, the government did not have the difficult task of proving the middle step.

A long-time employee of CKE, DeShano, who turned 55 during the course of the trial, was depicted as an unsophisticated investor, an honest man whose major fault was that he procrastinated. The defense claimed that DeShano had intended to sell the stock long before the preliminary ninth-period report was compiled but never quite got around to doing so.

Held in Los Angeles federal court from 23 May to the final jury verdict on 5 June 1989, the DeShano criminal trial demonstrated the difficulty of litigating insider trading cases. For the defense, there was the presupposition of guilt in the jurors' minds to be overcome. For the prosecution, a case based on circumstantial evidence is always risky.

The judge's instruction to the jury had explicated the elements that constitute insider trading. Essentially, the jurors were required to find, beyond a reasonable doubt, that the defendant (1) was a corporate insider, (2) was in possession of non-public material information, (3) used and relied on that information, and (4) intended to defraud. It was primarily the third and fourth elements that led the jurors to reach a verdict of not guilty.

When DeShano took the stand, he denied that he sold his stock because of the unfavorable preliminary report; instead, he claimed that he had intended to sell weeks before but had procrastinated. It was argued by the defense that DeShano was a numbers cruncher; he was not in a position to step back and view the entire picture, nor was he able to forecast the drastic decline in the stock price from the limited information he possessed. One of the jurors countered this position with his own analysis of the situation:

My argument against that was . . . that he could have almost done it in his head. You can look at your checkbook and you don't have to run it all the way through to know that you've got a lot less money than you had a month ago at this time, not right to the dollar amount, but you know.[12]

In his summation to the jury, the defense attorney, David Wiechert, explained that the case is "as complicated as the human mind. You have to determine what he [DeShano] was thinking when he sold his stock."[13] The jury took this advice to heart.

One of the jurors, who originally had voted for guilt, reflected:

I relented only because one of the elements that the judge had instructed us on, as a prerequisite for a guilty finding, was something that couldn't possibly be reached. It was asking us for a smoking gun and there was no such thing possible. . . . In the instructions to the jury, Judge Tashima pointed out that we would have to conclude he [DeShano] had used it [the preliminary report) in his decision to sell. And, of course, that's an impossibility. I mean how can we presuppose what went on in his mind?[14]

The same juror later added, "The last element, of course, was that he did in fact use it in determining whether to sell his stock. And that was the one that stopped everybody, because, like I say, you can't delve into the man's mind."[15]

The consensus appeared to be that the circumstantial evidence presented was not sufficient to judge that DeShano had a guilty mind. Another juror stated, "Nobody saw him [DeShano]. Nobody knew what he was thinking. That's what broke the jurors down."[16] The acquittal, my interviews indicated, was the result of the jury's inability to determine positively that DeShano was aware of the drastic fiscal implications of the preliminary report and that he used this information in his decision to sell.

This ambivalence on the part of the jury is significant particularly in light of a statement made by the judge in *Herman and MacLean v. Huddleston:*

> The proof . . . required in fraud cases is often a matter of inference from circumstantial evidence. If anything, the difficulty of proving the defendant's state of mind supports a lower standard of proof [lower than a preponderance of the evidence]. In any event, we have noted elsewhere that circumstantial evidence can be more than sufficient.[17]

This and other court decisions allow intent to be liberally inferred from the circumstantial evidence presented,[18] but the jury in the DeShano case chose not to do so.

Often, nonlegal characteristics of the offender, such as socioeconomic status, moral character, and severity of the possible sentence, may induce juror sympathy and leniency. The finding on whether socioeconomic status has an effect on juror judgment is inconclusive,[19] however, juror responses indicate that DeShano's class was noted. One juror described the defendant's appearance in court as follows: "[DeShano] was well presented, [a] calm, serene individual. . . . He was likable. Both he and his wife presented themselves as a very nice mid-aged couple. I think that impressed everybody."[20]

The moral character of the defendant also was raised by the jurors in the interviews. Studies have found that a defendant's emotional demeanor is influential in a judgment of conviction; those who suffer or appear remorseful may be treated more leniently.[21] An example of this sentiment was expressed by a juror who stated, "I think justice being done in this world, if it ever is, I think it was done in this case because I really think that Al DeShano is the kind of person that suffered . . . over this thing."[22] Moreover, at least one juror may have had sympathy for the defendant because he could picture himself in a similar situation. One of the jurors, commenting on the attitude of another juror, explained, "He made it look like it was okay for [DeShano] to do that because he was a white-collar worker and he might do it, too. He might have done it."[23]

Finally, the five-year maximum prison term that DeShano possibly faced may have swayed some individuals. Krupa has shown that jurors are less likely to convict where the prosecutorial evidence was weak, the prescribed punishment severe, and the final sentence outside of their control.[24] A juror commented:

> We talked about that in the jury room . . . what would they do to him in a case like this. We couldn't possibly see a prison sentence, for instance. I think perhaps that may have been uppermost in the minds of some of those who were [for] not guilty in the beginning, who just couldn't see [giving him] a strong life-changing kind of punishment [that would cause a] loss of a job and all the

rest of it. I think they were thinking more along the lines of the punishment situation.[25]

The jury was able to justify its decision to acquit based on the evidence presented. They did not feel the prosecutor established beyond a reasonable doubt that DeShano used the information in the preliminary report in his decision to sell the stock. Yet, factored into the conversion toward an acquittal were several extralegal variables: the socioeconomic status of the defendant, his demeanor at the trial, and the length of the potential prison sentence.

MOTIVATIONS FOR PROSECUTING DESHANO

There are several factors the SEC considers before it decides to pursue a case. In her analysis of SEC docket investigations, Shapiro lists the following elements, among others: (1) recurrence of the offense, (2) recency, (3) nature of the offense, (4) amount of money involved, (5) culpability, and (6) strength of evidence. Shapiro found that the prior record of investigated offenders was unrelated to the likelihood of SEC prosecution.[26] The Karcher case exemplifies these findings; the extent of the illegal activity, the total of 16 persons charged, and the sum of money involved, $314,000, amounted to sufficient reason for the SEC to devote three years of resource-intensive labor to the case. An added incentive was the publicity that the Karcher name guaranteed.

The SEC generally refers cases to the Department of Justice for consideration of criminal charges. Such was the situation with DeShano. He was the only individual in the case not connected to the Karcher family by blood or marriage. There was no denial that DeShano had access to the confidential preliminary report and that he had read it. Einhorn, the regional administrator of the SEC, stated that DeShano "had the books in front of him and he acted on that information. The rest who traded are either tippees or tippers, and they aren't company employees."[27] DeShano himself perceived the strength of the case against him, stating, "They [the SEC] thought that it would be a good lead case because it was different. They thought because I actually sold they had more [of an] ability to prove that I was guilty."[28] But he also added that both he and the Karchers felt "all along that I was being used as a scapegoat to get to them [the Karchers]. . . . No one knows me, but they sure know his [Carl Karcher's] name."[29] The defense counsel, a former assistant U.S. attorney, reflecting on why the Department of Justice brought the criminal case against DeShano, stated, "They wanted to bring an insider trading case. It's a high priority. There haven't been many in the office."[30]

When taken on its own merit, out of the context of the Karcher family trades, the DeShano case appeared petty and inconsequential. Here was a man who was depicted by witnesses as honest and loyal, who, by all appearances, had never traded on inside information before, and whose loss avoided amounted to only $7107. Small cases such as this may be advantageous from a deterrence standpoint, conveying the message to the community that the district attorney will prosecute small-time offenders. But, as one of DeShano's defense attorneys remarked,

> if you want to use that as a goal of the prosecution, the deterrence aspect, then you've got to pick a case that's a strong case because if you lose it then you may have the opposite effect. The word may go out that you can't even win the little one.[31]

The jurors did not view this case as particularly strong; there was no eyewitness testimony as to DeShano's intent. They could only infer it from the circumstantial evidence presented in court. A juror remarked:

> It was a case that I wondered why the government brought in the first place.... I think everybody should be prosecuted ... [when there is] sufficient evidence to bring a case. But I don't think that, in this case for instance, they were wisely using the taxpayers' money to bring this case unless they had something more to go on than they did.[32]

The Department of Justice believed it had a strong case. Circumstantial evidence, such as that presented in this case, had been sufficient in the past to return a guilty finding. DeShano was an insider who sold stock after he received the preliminary report. But, when there is only circumstantial evidence, the jury must infer the thought process of the defendant based solely on the timing of the stock trade and the information he had available. Although arguably the strongest case, taken by itself, out of the context of the Karcher family trades, the DeShano trade appeared insignificant. In light of the blatant abuse of inside information by individuals such as Boesky, the case against DeShano made the jury question the prudence of the government's decision to prosecute.

SETTLEMENTS WITH THE SEC

The Karcher family civil trial was set for May of 1989. Numerous defense motions had been filed, including one to have the case dismissed and another to try each Karcher separately. The motions served to tie up SEC resources and undoubtedly enriched the Karcher attorneys. As the trial date approached, two of the three lawyers of the SEC's litigation department were devoting their full attention to the case. But there was no trial.

Donald Karcher and those he allegedly tipped settled the civil charges with the SEC in February of 1989. The six defendants agreed to pay a total of $187,560 to settle their portion of the case. This included disgorgement of the loss avoided by those trading, with fines of the same amount, and a fine of $62,520 for Donald and his wife: All the defendants consented to an injunction from future securities violations.

The cases against the other Karchers were based primarily on circumstantial evidence: Carl had talked with his children during this time frame and they all sold their securities around the same time. An SEC lawyer later stated, after an unsuccessful defense motion to dismiss charges against the family, "They've never been able to explain what it was that triggered those sales. It's a little too much to believe that they coincidentally all decided to dump their stock on the same weekend."[33] The Karcher children claimed that they had personal financial reasons for selling more than $1 million worth of stock in the days before the announcement.

On 2 May 1989, the day the Karcher trial was to begin and more than a year after the complaint had been first filed by the SEC, headway was being made toward a settlement. Wes Howell, Carl Karcher's attorney, explained:

> The money we're talking about is not going to make an enormous amount of difference [to Karcher]. [But] he was seeing his whole family being swept up. . . . He was seeing his company, with all of the principal executives, being subpoenaed. . . . And I couldn't promise him that he'd win.[34]

Before the SEC settlement could be completed, however, Karcher wanted assurance that the Department of Justice would not later file criminal charges. In July, the final settlement was reached, and it was formalized in August 1989. Karcher and the remaining family members neither admitted nor denied guilt. The stipulations in the consent agreement included an injunction from violating the insider trading regulations, disgorgement from the tippees of a total of $332,122 in profit, in addition to fines totaling the same amount, and $332,122 in fines for Carl Karcher. An SEC attorney pointed out that this settlement was fairly standard for insider trading cases.[35]

A *Los Angeles Times* interview with Karcher's attorney, Thomas Holliday, revealed that, "by settling the case, Karcher chose to avoid both the emotional and financial costs of a trial. . . . 'We had a winnable case,' Holliday said, 'but the monetary cost, in terms of lawyers and personal impact on the family, far outweighed the desire to win' at trial."[36]

Alvin DeShano formally settled the SEC civil charges against him in August of 1989. While neither admitting nor denying guilt, he agreed to an injunction against future insider trading infractions and consented to a disgorgement of $12,386, the amount he saved, plus interest, by selling the stock, in addition to a fine for the same amount.

CONCLUSION

The Karcher case study sheds light on the difficulties encountered when prosecuting either a civil or criminal white-collar crime. It was through the computer surveillance program at NASD that the Karcher trades were initially discovered. The case was then turned over to the SEC, which decided to investigate and file a complaint against those involved. Proactive market surveillance is one of the most frequently used insider trading detection techniques, but, at the same time, it has the greatest inaccuracy rate.[37] Approximately 0.6 percent of the initial inquiries made by self-regulatory organizations, such as the New York Stock Exchange or NASD, into anomalies detected by their surveillance strategies were referred to the SEC for the fiscal years 1985 and 1986. Of these 468 insider trading referrals, only 45, approximately 10 percent, resulted in SEC enforcement actions.[38] The Karcher case was one of the few that made it to the final stage of the process.

As affluent, prominent members of the community, the Karchers were able to engage the SEC in numerous pretrial motions. In the end, Carl Karcher was not prosecuted criminally, and, like most white-collar defendants, agreed to the sentence without admitting or denying guilt. By settling the case, both the SEC and the defendants avoided the time-consuming, resource-draining alternative of a trial. Yet, because of the reluctance of the trial judge in the Carl Leo Karcher case to use the treble penalties available under the ITSA, the defendants who settled with the SEC were financially penalized to a greater extent than the only defendant sentenced by the court.

The criminal prosecution of DeShano, in which his stock sale was examined by itself and not in the context of the other Karcher trades, appears trivial and insignificant when compared to more heinous criminal offenses. Ordinarily, though, a theft of approximately $7000 by a street criminal would be considered egregious. The average loss from robbery in 1987, for instance, was $447, with only 6 percent of the completed robberies involving property valued at more than $1000.[39]

Unlike a bank robbery, however, where the offense is not debated, the prosecutor in insider trading cases must prove that an offense was indeed committed. The complexities of the definition of the offense and the reliance on circumstantial evidence are common problems that prosecutors of white-collar crime must overcome. What looked like the strongest case for the government resulted in a not-guilty finding, leaving jurors questioning the wisdom of allocating resources to the prosecution of this offense.

Notes

1. U.S. Congress, House Committee on Energy and Commerce, *Insider Trading and Securities Fraud Enforcement Act of 1988,* 100th Congress, 2d Sess., 1988, p. 8.
2. Eric Shine, "A Little Bell Set Carl Karcher Probe in Motion," *Los Angeles Times,* April 15, 1985.
3. Mary Ann Galante, "Karcher: Cloudy Chapter in Horatio Alger Success Story," *Los Angeles Times,* April 15, 1988.

4. Gary G. Lynch et al., "Recent SEC Enforcement Developments." In *Insider Trading, Fraud, and Fiduciary Duty under the Federal Securities Laws.* Washington, DC: American Law Institute, American Bar Association, 1 (1989):508.
5. David A. Vise and Steve Coll, *Eagle on the Street.* New York: Scribner's, 1991, p. 260.
6. Charges against Margaret Karcher were dropped in March 1989.
7. A margin account allows investors to buy securities on credit as long as they maintain a minimum amount of equity in their account. If the securities in the account drop in value, the brokerage firm may request that the investor provide more equity; this is known as a margin call.
8. Declaration of Carl Leo Karcher to the Securities and Exchange Commission, filed August 9, 1988.
9. Mary Ann Galante, "Judge Rules Karcher Son Violated Stock Sale Laws," *Los Angeles Times,* September 13, 1988.
10. *Ibid.*
11. Theodore A. Levine, Arthur F. Mathews, and W. Hardy Callcott, "Current Legal Developments Affecting Insider Trading Enforcement Actions and Litigation 1988–1989," *Insider Trading, Fraud, and Fiduciary Duty,* 1 (1989):5.
12. Personal interview with juror.
13. *Ibid.*
14. *Ibid.*
15. *Ibid.*
16. *Ibid.*
17. 459 U.S. 375, 384 (1983).
18. See John W. Bagby, "The Evolving Controversy over Insider Trading," *American Business Law Journal,* 24 (1986):571, 606–607.
19. Francis C. Dane and Lawrence S. Wrightsman, "Effects of Defendants' and Victims' Characteristics on Jurors' Verdicts." In Norbett L. Kerr and Robert M. Bray, eds., *The Psychology of the Courtroom.* New York: Academic Press, 1982.
20. Personal interview with juror.
21. Dane and Wrightsman, *op. cit.*
22. Personal interview with juror.
23. *Ibid.*
24. Martin F. Kaplan, "Cognitive Processes in the Individual Juror." In Kerr and Bray, *The Psychology of the Courtroom, op. cit.*
25. Personal interview with a juror.
26. Susan P. Shapiro, *Wayward Capitalists: Target of the Securities and Exchange Commission.* New Haven, CT: Yale University Press, 1984.
27. Mary Ann Galante, "Carl's Jr. Chief Accountant Charged with Stock Fraud," *Los Angeles Times,* February 17, 1989.
28. Personal interview with Alvin DeShano.
29. *Ibid.*
30. *Ibid.*

31. Personal interview with one of DeShano's defense attorneys.

32. Personal interview with a juror.

33. David Greenwald, "Karcher Denies Telling His Children to Sell Their Stock," *Orange County Register,* March 21, 1989.

34. Mary Ann Galante, "Tentative Settlement in Suit against Karchers," *Los Angeles Times,* March 21,1989.

35. Personal interview with an SEC attorney.

36. Mary Ann Galante, "Karchers Settle Insider-Trading Case with Fine," *Los Angeles Times,* July 25, 1989.

37. Shapiro, *op. cit.*

38. U.S. General Accounting Office, *Securities Regulations: Efforts to Detect, Investigate, and Deter Insider Trading.* Washington, DC: General Accounting Office, 1988.

39. U.S. Department of Justice, Bureau of Justice Statistics, *Special Report: Robbery Victims.* Washington, DC: Department of Justice, 1987.

13

Medicaid Fraud

Gilbert Geis, Henry N. Pontell, and Paul D. Jesilow

The present article examines fraud and abuse in Medicaid, the program for the poor, where it is believed to be significantly more extensive than in Medicare, which serves the needs of the aged. Undoubtedly, a major reason for the higher level of violation in Medicaid, presuming that common understanding is accurate, lies in the considerably lower levels of payment accorded doctors under Medicaid. Physicians treating Medicare patients are paid 80% of what the government determines is a reasonable fee: They can collect the remaining 20% and any other unreimbursed charges directly from patients. Medicaid, state-operated with federal subsidy, typically pays physicians about 77% of what they might expect to collect from Medicare for the same procedures, and they cannot assess patients additional amounts. States employ one of two systems to set physicians' fees under Medicaid: fee schedules or fee profiles. A fee schedule assigns a value for each medical procedure. A fee profile is based on the distribution of charges for a particular procedure by physicians in the area. States using the second approach generally compare a physician's actual charge against the level determined by the profile and pay whichever amount is lower.

Abuses of Medicaid also may be more extensive than those of Medicare because of attitudes held by some physicians toward welfare clients, and because the behavior of such clients sometimes irritates physicians. This view comes across pointedly in a statement by an obstetrician-gynecologist working in a metropolitan hospital:

> I like patients who are intelligent, responsible people, and I hate patients who are irresponsible slobs. The Medi-Cal [California's name for Medicaid] patients—the people on welfare—are the worst of the bunch. Since the government is paying for it, they just don't care about what's going on. They don't show up for appointments, and they never call to tell you. They don't take their medicine. They call you Saturday night, three in the morning, with a problem that could have been taken care of on Wednesday afternoon.
>
> Half of the problems these people have could have been avoided by just minimal precautions. Abortions, infections, venereal diseases, and all their

Reprinted from Joseph E. Scott and Travis Hirschi, eds., *Controversial Issues in Crime and Justice*, Newbury Park, CA: Sage Publications, 1988, pp. 17–39.

complications. It's irritating to have to take care of people when they don't make the slightest effort to take care of themselves.[1]

Pay and prejudice by no means exhaust the roster of explanations for fraud by physicians against Medicaid. Medicaid is also notoriously vulnerable to fiscal exploitation, and the likelihood of being apprehended and punished for fraud and abuse appears to be extremely low. Investigators of Medicaid violations point out that the only malefactors they are likely to catch are "the fish who jump into the boat," and "the dopes." But with better resources, they believe there is so much law-breaking that nabbing violators would be "like catching fish in a barrel."

The fact that Medicaid is federally authorized and subsidized, but state-operated, also complicates enforcement efforts. In addition, the uneasy relationship between government forces and private medical practitioners and their extraordinarily powerful lobby handicaps control of fraud and abuse in the Medicaid program.

The practice of medicine is both a professional calling and a business enterprise, and any attempt to understand it exclusively as one or the other is to miss the point. For ages, doctors have traded services (of real or imagined utility) fundamental to human survival in a manner combining altruism and aggressive fiscal self-interest. The London College of Physicians was founded in 1523 primarily "to entrench a monopoly of medical practice in the hands of the few medical graduates that lived there": The motives of its founders, it has been noted, "were largely selfish."[2] In Puritan New England, Cotton Mather berated the only licensed doctor practicing in Boston during the 1721 smallpox epidemic for his failure to support inoculation. The doctor replied that he thought it "more natural to begin by reducing my small-pox accounts into bills and notes for the improvement of my purse" than to translate his medical notes into an agenda for the improvement of humankind.[3] It should be remembered that the Hippocratic oath gives top priority to the payment and support of a doctor's teacher and his family, and not to the requirements of the patient.[4]

Difficulties in Medicaid enforcement associated with attempts to deal with doctors solely as commercial entrepreneurs, however, have been noted in a California study:

> Most of the procedures involved in the detection and recovery of inappropriate Medi-Cal expenditures are highly invasive of the traditional professional roles of physicians, hospital administrators, pharmacists, and other providers. Even though these techniques may be justified in terms of recovery of inappropriate payments, they also have the effect of driving providers—physicians in particular—out of the Medi-Cal program.[5]

Such observations are reminiscent of Bentham's principle that punishment should never be so severe that its consequences outweigh the good derived from it. Bentham recommended, in such terms, that a foreign diplomat not be prosecuted for a petty offense if such a prosecution would antagonize his government.[6] Doctors cheating Medicaid, unlike other thieves, find themselves in the position of being able to unnerve enforcers, who fear that their perceived heavy-handedness might drive these and other practitioners out of the benefit program in which their voluntary participation is essential. But what is particularly novel today is that doctors have been afforded an extraordinary opportunity to engage in one of the least traumatizing forms of fraud: stealing from an impersonal and faceless bureaucracy.[7]

SOURCES OF DATA

The primary source of data for the present article is from interviews with officials seeking to discover abuses of the Medicaid program. More than 50 such interviews were held, primarily in New York and California—the two largest Medicaid programs—and also in Florida, Illinois, and Indiana. Beyond this source, we have used an extensive literature on Medicaid fraud and abuse compiled by federal agencies, and numerous reports of Congressional committees.

Our aim is to identify crucial issues in the enforcement of the laws and regulations concerned with fraud and abuse in the Medicaid program. If Pies is correct, inadequate control has restricted expansion of health services, and has allowed loss of funds that might otherwise have been used for legitimate treatment of persons requiring such services.[8] Our concentration on physicians does not imply that they are the worst Medicaid offenders. There is ample evidence of widespread fraud by pharmacists, ambulance companies, and every other group associated with Medicaid. Hospital expenses in particular have driven medical care costs beyond the fiscal tolerance of the government, and there is widespread belief that a significant portion of these expenses is legally unwarranted and, at times, criminally fraudulent. Physicians, however, stand at the heart of the medical treatment system; they are the linchpins of most Medicaid services. What Winsten has noted about Medicare applies equally well to Medicaid:

> The doctor is the key decision maker recommending hospitalization and surgery, ordering laboratory tests, deciding when a patient is discharged and influencing adoption of new techniques. Typically, the physician is a private entrepreneur who mobilizes hospital resources yet bears no financial responsibility for the ensuing costs. In no other industry are senior decision makers so unaccountable for the economic consequences of their actions.[9]

CONTROLLING FRAUD AND ABUSE

The original legislative blueprints for Medicaid did not closely attend to questions of fraud and abuse. Passage of the law was so fraught with difficulty that any hint of distrust of physicians' behavior would have scuttled its hopes. For that matter, there was no warning from private insurance schemes, such as Blue Cross, that exploitation would prove to be a problem. There were two reasons for this: First, as programs based on actuarial calculations, systems such as Blue Cross were only pass-ingly concerned about expenses since, at least within broad limits, premiums could readily be adjusted to cover payments; and second, a large segment of the private insurance field was controlled by the medical profession, which has been chroni-cally disinterested in monitoring the business behavior of its members.

The guidelines for Medicaid in regard to fraud and abuse, as set out in the origi-nal act, noted that states must "provide such methods of administration . . . as are found by the Secretary to be necessary for the proper and efficient operation of the plan." Federal regulations later spelled out in more detail requirements that states were obligated to meet with respect to fraud and abuse. In practice, the precise delineation of violative actions, particularly the distinction between "fraud" and "abuse," would prove difficult. Some investigators would come to take a hard-nosed position: "I don't recognize the word 'abuse' as it applies to this. It's either fraud or it's not. You tell me what abuse is." Other commentators would make the effort to distinguish the categories:

Fraud is generally defined as intentional deception or misrepresentation, with the intent of receiving some unauthorized benefit. In the health area, examples of fraud may include: billing for services not rendered, kickbacks, deliberate duplicated billing, and false or misleading entries on cost reports. Providers engaged in fraudulent activities are subject to criminal penalties. Program abuse is less clearly defined and includes activities wherein providers, practi-tioners, and suppliers of services operated in a manner inconsistent with accepted, sound medical or business practices resulting in excessive cost to Medicare or Medicaid. Included in the area of abuse are the provision of unnecessary health services and the provision of unnecessary care in unneces-sarily costly settings.[10]

Two circumstances drew particular attention to fraud and abuse as the Medicaid program developed. The first was the stunningly rapid rise in the program's cost. Total federal expenditures rose from $3.45 billion in 1968 to $8.71 by 1973. By 1978, the cost had climbed to $17.6 billion.[11] By 1985, the program involved expen-diture of about $23 billion. Such huge increases were deemed unacceptable by offi-cials faced with a huge deficit and a commitment to continuing heavy spending on the military.[12]

In addition, not long after Medicaid was established, Congress began to concen-trate on what became widely publicized hearings about "Medicaid mills,"[13] "small, for-profit welfare clinics that proliferate in the ghettos of our cities" with work involving "a conspiracy of several practitioners and the introduction of assembly-line methods to defraud the government."[14] Some Medicaid mills employed "hawk-ers" to round up customers. Several catered to drug traffic.[15] Colorful terms were invented to describe their practices, including (1) pingponging—referring patients from one practitioner to another within the facility, though no medical need dictated such a procedure, (2) ganging—billing for multiple service to members of the same family on the same day, generally involving a mother and accompanying children, (3) upgrading—billing for a service more extensive than the one actually provided, and (4) steering—directing a patient to a particular pharmacy, in violation of the patient's freedom of choice.[16]

Undercover Congressional investigators visited about 85 Medicaid mill practitioners, usually pretending to be suffering from a cold. They underwent 18 electrocardiograms, eight tuberculosis tests, four allergy tests, as well as hearing, glaucoma, and electroencephalogram tests. Only once during the four months of investigation did a physician tell an investigator, "Get out of here, there's nothing wrong with you."[17] More typical was the following summary of an investigator's experience:

His "head cold" was diagnosed as "sinusitis," he was given a general physical, an EKG, a TB test, told he had a severe heart murmur and that he probably had had rheumatic fever as a child. In addition, the doctor ordered a series of x-rays of the patient's sinuses and chest, and referred him to the heart specialist—all in the space of three minutes.[18]

The U.S. Senate committee, following its investigation and a review of other sources, concluded that Medicaid was "not only inefficient, but riddled with fraud and abuse."[19] Control of Medicaid fraud and abuse was seen as severely handicapped by the view that the agencies administering the programs thought of themselves as no more than "bill payers," with a "lamentable inability" to do anything about fraud and abuse.[20] This was deemed by the Senate review committee as a consequence of their "hierarchy of priorities," which placed the delivery of services and the payment of providers and recipients in the preeminent position.[21] Congress ultimately concluded that investigative, audit, and legal functions for Medicaid had to be combined in a separate office and that the office that conducted the investigations also would have to take responsibility for prosecutions. Creation of such agencies—Medicaid Fraud Control Units (MFCUs)—was authorized in 1981 by Public Law 95-142. Congress provided 90% matching funds for the initial years, but gradually cut back to 75%. Without federal subsidies, states were regarded as likely to be reluctant to mount effective enforcement efforts, since sums recovered largely went into federal coffers.

The law called for MFCUs to be part of the state attorney general's office or another department of government that possessed statewide criminal prosecuting authority, and to have formal procedures for the referral of cases to prosecutors, if the state constitution did not provide the attorney general or another department of government with statewide criminal prosecuting authority. The MFCUs also were mandated to establish a formal relationship with the state attorney general and to institute procedures for referring cases to that office. Today, 30 states as well as the District of Columbia have MFCUs certified by the federal government. States not enrolled in the program primarily insist that they desire to retain their fraud control work within the state Mcdicaid agency. A Congressional report has been sharply critical of the failure of those states to form MFCUs. "The primary reason the 20 states have not applied for 90% funding," it noted "is the resistance of state Medicaid administrators who do not want to share their powers or have them taken away from them. . . . Political jealousies have interfered with the establishment of a viable national network and a national commitment to detect and prosecute those who commit Medicaid fraud." A number of states also had maintained that they were not interested in establishing a fraud control unit because they believed that few Medicaid violations existed in their jurisdiction, while others thought that investigative agencies already in place were perfectly capable of dealing with the issue.[22]

In 1982, a staff study by the U.S. House of Representatives' Select Committee on Aging was sharply critical of the work of the MFCUs to that date. The report assumed that the Medicaid program was "fraught with fraud" and that virtually all such fraud was perpetrated by providers and not by recipients. The states were castigated for being "happy to accept federal funds [for enforcement], but not the responsibility to police Medicaid." The number of convictions for fraud was declared to be "infinitesimal" compared to the presumed extent of such behavior. States were said to be having difficulty obtaining funds for their enforcement units from their legislatures, despite the fact that whatever sum was appropriated would be matched on a 9-to-1 ratio by the federal government. The staff report also deplored the number of states whose units did not have independent subpoena power, but noted that most states, with the notable exception of California, had granted authority to use Medicaid cards for "shopping" potential violators. During 1980, there had been 197 convictions for Medicaid fraud, with 13 resulting in prison sentences—the longest term, involving a physician, was for 2½ years. The average fine imposed on violators was $1,000. MFCUs indicated in a questionnaire response that they had identified fraud and overpayments equal to about 40% of their own funding.[23]

In addition, the staff report faulted the Medicaid Management Information System (MMIS), a computer program that had been heralded as the precursor to more efficient detection of fraudulent practices. The computer could readily pinpoint aberrant billings, such as performing a hysterectomy on a male, but the staff report found that its promised benefits had not been achieved, and that there were "very real problems in the system." In all, the tone of the staff report was one of disappointment. "Convictions and jail sentences are the only hope the system has of deterring further fraud," it noted.[24]

THE EXTENT OF FRAUD

The precise amount of fraud and abuse associated with Medicaid is a matter of uncertainty. Each year about 200 physicians are suspended from participation in Medicare and Medicaid because of fraudulent or abusive practices. Most of these acts take place in connection with Medicaid. A portrait of the violators through 1983 showed that family and general practitioners accounted for the greatest number (27%), followed by psychiatrists (18%), general surgeons (11%), and obstetricians and gynecologists (7%).[25] Except for psychiatrists, these percentages roughly represent the portion of each specialty in the practice of medicine. Psychiatrists are apparently apprehended disproportionately more often because their violations are easier to detect and prove: Only they (and anesthesiologists) charge for time rather than for services. Surveillance can readily determine, for instance, that a psychiatrist is seeing a patient for 15 minutes but billing the government for 40 minutes of therapy.[26] Blacks and foreign medical school graduates also were overrepresented in the ranks of violators, probably because they form a relatively large portion of the staff in inner-city Medicaid mills, where enforcement tends to be stringent.[27] Two statements appear to go hand-in-hand regarding the extent of infractions in Medicaid. First, there is a seemingly reflexive tribute to the general honesty of the medical profession as a whole: Almost invariably it is said that violations are the acts of an aberrant minority. The most impressive evidence of the possible truth of this point comes from a California fraud investigator who noted that before the advent of the MFCUs, "we would just kind of open the phone book and point and do random samples because we weren't set up yet for complaints and we needed to get going." Those included in this random audit process "usually came out clean," in contrast to the cases that had been initiated by a complaint, where "we found stuff."

Second, there are numerous speculations that the amount of Medicaid fraud is extremely extensive. "I would not be surprised that 85, 90% of all practitioners nickel and dime from time to time," a highly knowledgeable federal official maintained. There is widespread belief among enforcement personnel that physicians routinely "overutilize," that is, that they perform services that are not required. This sometimes is done to try to avoid malpractice actions—a strategy outside Medicaid guidelines. In appraisals that may be driven more by cynicism than facts, enforcers presume that numerous doctors calculate the likelihood of being discovered in a violation and, finding the risk virtually nonexistent if the act is done with even slight care and discretion, choose to pick up extra income from the government. The anecdotal information is difficult to interpret. One enforcement official maintained that "in the early days, the program was wide open and there was so much the providers could get away with and they certainly were getting away with it," implying a direct relationship between increasing enforcement energy and, perhaps, a less egregious level of violation. At the same time, another official insisted that since enforcement nets only the most blatant offenders, the program continues to be bled to death by overutilizers.

When a number is attached to the presumed amount of Medicaid fraud, it tends to be 10%[28] or 25%.[29] No evidence that we have been able to locate permits the slightest credence to be accorded either figure. The most forthright statement on the issue was that of the Director of the Congressional Budget Office when she was asked in 1977 to comment on the financial implications related to the establishment of MFCUs. "The unknown magnitude of fraud and abuse presently extant in the programs," she wrote, "makes it impracticable for the CBO to project the actual cost impact of this measure at this time."[30] Estimates of the extent of Medicaid fraud undoubtedly have been influenced by the extraordinary, often bizarre nature of some of the violations. In Illinois, for instance, a psychiatrist was found to have billed Medicaid for 4,800 hours, or almost 24 hours each workday.[31] Other doctors have been caught billing for services on persons who were dead at the time the alleged work was done. An optometrist sold patients cataract glasses for $35 and charged the government $180 for reading glasses. A California doctor billed Medicaid for $3,000 for a time period when he was in Africa on a safari. An opthalmologist performed unnecessary eye operations that left 14 persons with impaired vision in a scheme that defrauded the state of $14,000, while a psychiatrist in California charged Medicaid for sexual liaisons with a patient, claiming that he had submitted the bills for professional services so that his wife would not become suspicious.

Another doctor billed for abortions on women who were not pregnant, including one who had had a hysterectomy. In 48 separate instances, he billed Medicaid for performing two abortions within a month on the same patient. Perhaps the most unusual case arose in Florida in the early days of the program. A physician was identified as the top biller in the state and was found to be requesting payments for such matters as treating a 22-year-old for diaper rash. Ultimately, the doctor received a 20-year sentence for fraud. Later, a life sentence was added when she was convicted of hiring someone to attempt to kill her partner to keep him from testifying in the Medicaid case.[32]

THE PROCESS OF DETECTION

The roster of cases noted in the previous section indicates one criterion by which fraud and abuse are detected: Physicians who engage in blatantly aberrant practices are marked for investigation. They cannot defend themselves by insisting that what they did involved medical judgment: No such judgment will justify bills for a 36-hour day or for extraction of more teeth than those contained in the human mouth.

The MMIS computer system is programmed to flag unusual practices. Further cases are generated by EOMBs (Explanation of Medical Benefits) and by patient referrals. On very rare occasions, a doctor will complain about a colleague; more often, office personnel or a disgruntled wife or lover is apt to tell enforcement authorities about illegal practices. Of employees, an investigator notes: "This happens because the doctor is too cheap to cut them in on the loot. They're doing the phony stuff for the guy and they're being underpaid, he's cheating them, too. That tends to breed a certain disloyalty." Of patients sexually involved, the same person says: "It's jim-dandy for a while, as they are flattered and impressed by it, but after a while they begin to feel cheapened and used and when that happens, they come in voluntarily. We filed on one guy and all of a sudden a couple more gals came in and told." Investigators also develop a sense of the patterns that represent cheating. A California investigator, for instance, notes: "I simply choose patients from the computer printouts. I look for common surnames. If I see four or five members of a single family being billed for one hour individually on the same day, I'm pretty sure it isn't happening."

As in other police work, the attitude of the person under suspicion plays a significant role in the reaction of those carrying out the inquiry. If a doctor says: "I didn't know that was what my billing clerk was billing—we'll change it right away," the enforcers note that they are apt to be indulgent. Truculence and hostility generate tougher enforcement responses. Investigations may be impaired, agents point out, because patients sometimes do not make good witnesses. "If you're talking about psychiatry-type cases, most of your patients are going to be borderline competent anyway. If they need psychiatric treatment, there's something wrong with them anyway. I maybe shouldn't say that, but they're not the best witnesses." Elderly patients, another investigator observed, "are a little forgetful like I am," and occasionally what appears to be fraud is a case of faulty memory.

"Patients, believe it or not," says a New York investigator, "have pretty good memories about when they went to the doctor and when they didn't." Many of them write their appointments on calendars, and some have to rely on calling a taxicab in order to get to the doctor, so that there is the possibility of a record check. Another agent thought physicians tended to be careless because they underestimated the intelligence of their Medicaid patients:

They think that welfare patients are stupid, and I think that's their biggest mistake because there are a lot of bright people on public assistance and we go out and interview those people.

There are, in addition, structural barriers that inhibit the enforcement of the laws regulating Medicaid work. A Florida agent, for instance, pointed out that he is not regarded as a law enforcement officer and, therefore, under state law he cannot carry a weapon, has no arrest authority, and cannot use electronic wiretapping or carry a body bug. In this connection, one investigator noted that juries had been "spoiled" by the Abscam cases, and that they now were more apt to look askance at evidence that does not include a videotape of the charged behavior. Investigators also feel hamstrung in many jurisdictions by their inability to obtain information from private insurers. They maintain that if they could put together private and Medicaid billing patterns, they could more expeditiously obtain a complete picture of a physician's practice and more easily pinpoint violations.

To obtain records from private insurers involves issues of privacy and confidentiality and often requires a grand jury subpoena. Confidentiality questions bring into conflict two highly regarded values: that of the government to police the ways in which its funds are expended, and that of the physician to bar access to information revealed to him or her by patients. At times, agents have obtained the permission of patients to provide them access to a doctor's records, but their efforts often are thwarted by court rulings that insist either that medical confidentiality takes precedence over government attempts to detect fraud or that the government's mission could equally well be carried out by the use of other tactics.[33] Investigators feel frustrated because they believe that physicians sometimes use the cloak of confidentiality to camouflage wrong-doing, and they find it hypocritical and offensive to be confronted with high-minded defenses of mean-spirited behavior.

PROSECUTING MEDICAID CASES

The most common complaint of Medicaid investigators concerns the difficulty they experience getting prosecutors to go forward with cases they have developed. The law creating MFCUs insisted that the agencies be placed in a government niche that provided its own prosecutorial resources. Nonetheless, investigators must persuade attorneys to give precedence to their cases, which tend to be complicated and often hinge on proof of intent. One investigator noted cynically some of the difficulties in this connection:

> We can't prove intent for a number of reasons. One, no one would suspect this upstanding pillar of the community of any fraudulent intent. He has a tremendous education, makes a great appearance. He is in that social order that is making the decision whether he is right or wrong—judges, prosecutors, etc.

The major complaint, however, is that prosecutors are concerned with glory-grabbing, and that they will not be bothered with low-profile matters such as Medicaid fraud. Several interview quotations convey the strength of the agents' views on this matter:

> White-collar crime calls for a lot of patience and most of the young attorneys want to go into a courtroom with John Dillinger by the nape of the neck. It just doesn't work that way.

An agent in Florida made these observations:

> These smaller circuits, all they're doing is rapes, robberies, murders, B-and-Es. You can try a good murder case in probably three or four days, whereas a white-collar crime could be taking three or four weeks. You can walk in with a wheelbarrow full of documentary evidence. They're apprehensive about trying them. They're complex, take a lot of time, a lot of preparation.

A federal official echoed several of the foregoing remarks:

> Most prosecutors are young people, relatively new out of school, and they break, you know, cut their teeth on gun cases and buy or bust drug cases.

You're trying to build your record around the community as a good lawyer, and you go off on a two-year investigation, and people don't know you're around anymore. That's the down side of doing fraud cases.

The most common criterion for moving forward with a Medicaid case is the amount that the alleged fraud has involved. Federal officials believe that it's very difficult to get a U.S. Attorney to take a case that involves less than $20,000, so that "a lot of cases fall between the cracks."

Prosecutorial strategy generally involves selecting the easiest charges rather than placing all possible violations before the jury: "You don't list as a basis for a charge every single rotten thing the guy did, because you would bore the court and the jury to death." Similarly, the statute of limitations—generally five years—delimits the audit period. At the same time, there is some pressure upon physicians to plead guilty. "They don't want too much embarrassment, and they know they'll get light sentences."

PUNISHING MEDICAID FRAUD

There is a considerable behavioral science literature that insists that punishment of white-collar offenders is apt to be notably effective, both in deterring them from further illegal acts and in deterring others like them who might otherwise have been likely to commit such acts.[34] Essentially, such conclusions are based on two suppositions: first, that white-collar offenders, such as physicians, have a great deal to lose by prosecution and therefore will be much more disinclined than street offenders to take the risk if they suspect that they will be caught; and second, that white-collar offenses, such as Medicaid fraud, are essentially rational behaviors and therefore are much more susceptible than many street crimes, particularly acts of violence, to utilitarian calculations on the part of those who might engage in them. The response of physicians to the Surgeon General's report on smoking provides inferential support for these theses. Well before the public had reduced its cigarette smoking, members of the medical profession showed a decline in usage. The probability that a physician was continuing to smoke related directly to the distance of his or her specialty from the lungs. Physicians dealing with lung cancer were quite unlikely to be smokers; so too were radiologists.[35]

A supervisor of New York investigators maintains that he has observed that "doctors' earnings go down when they realize they're being investigated," but this, at best, is only an intuition and could well represent, if accurate, prudence rather than a move toward law-abiding behavior: Both speeders and those traveling within the speed limit are apt to slow down when they spy a patrol car in their rear view mirror. Most investigators bewail the failure of courts to impose jail or prison sentences on convicted Medicaid offenders, and they believe that professional associations are notoriously indulgent of persons against whom Medicaid fraud has been proven.

The associations rarely suspend the right to practice, and commonly regard such behavior as merely business-related and not a reflection of professional competence. A California doctor working with a licensing agency summarized the situation:

> Unless a guy has been blatant about his fraud, he usually doesn't lose his license. What we usually do is to put him on probation, restitution to the Department of Health. One of the most important terms in probation is an imposition of community free medical care and in some needed area, for a number of years, maybe for six to eight hours a week.

Even this seemingly straightforward resolution has not been without sardonic twists. In the same state, another official told about clinics billing the state for services provided by physicians who had been sentenced to provide free care at them.

Prison terms are believed to be exceedingly difficult to obtain from judges against doctors convicted of Medicaid fraud. In some instances, the physician is seen as providing a vital service that cannot readily be replaced, especially in small communities. In other instances, the incongruity of regarding doctors as "real" criminals appears to protect them from incarceration. In Memphis, one investigator noted, "a doctor . . . was convicted of a hundred and some odd counts of Medicaid fraud, and it was his second conviction, and he still got no jail time." On the other hand, like many other white-collar criminals, physicians proceeded against for Medicaid violations suffer from adverse effects that are not commonly associated with prosecution for street offenses. Their reputation is an integral aspect of their continuance in their profession and, as an official noted, "you put his nose on the front page of the article as a thief . . . you've destroyed him." The common tactic of excluding convicted doctors for a period of time—usually a few years—from further participation in Medicaid and Medicare seems to be a relatively benign consequence, though for doctors dependent on the programs for their livelihood the deprivation could be hurtful until or unless other sources of income are located.

The original Medicaid legislation provided only for recovery of overpayments and not for suspension. Suspension, however, became automatic in 1977 if a physician was convicted in a federal, state, or local court for defrauding the system. A legal notice of suspension must be published in a local newspaper (and in a Spanish-language newspaper, where appropriate) after a letter of notification is sent to the provider. The first claim received from a beneficiary who goes to a suspended doctor is paid, but a notice is sent to the beneficiary indicating that no further claim involving the particular provider will be honored. Most enforcement people—though they appear to be strongly in favor of tough penalties, and especially jail and prison terms, for Medicaid fraud perpetrators—have concluded that such outcomes are very unlikely except for the most flagrant offenses. Instead, the enforcement focus has begun to concentrate heavily on the recovery of monies and the imposition of further fines. In 1981, a civil money penalty intended to discourage fraud in government health care programs was established.[36] The statute allows the secretary of HHS to impose a civil penalty of up to $2,000 for each fraudulent claim, and to impose an assessment of up to twice the amount of the fraudulent portion of the claim in lieu of damages. But such provisions can also be eviscerated by what investigators regard as overindulgent judges. Note, for instance, the following from a former director of the California MFCU:

> A classic case. We did a complete, comprehensive audit on a lab operator that established without any question $300,000 of bilking the state. We went in and got another one of these gutless judges who said, "Oh, he's a professional man, he's suffered enough having to go through the criminal process and therefore, even though he pleaded guilty, I am going to require him to pay only half of the restitution." So we get $160,000 from this guy, and we were outraged. The rest is profit. Who wouldn't go into crime?

WHICH WAY TO REFORM?

The most common remedial action proposed is a movement from for-service programs to Health Maintenance Organizations (HMOs). HMOs differ from fee-for-service systems in at least three major respects. First, providers are at risk and are not reimbursed for each service they give; second, HMOs must either provide directly or have provided at their expense those services specified in their contract with the patient; and finally, a member of an HMO is not allowed, except under extraordinary circumstances of medical emergency, to seek care from physicians or other providers outside of the plan.[37] Contracts between the government and HMOs for Medicaid services regularize and delimit expenditures, since the HMOs are paid a specified sum for each patient on their roster and any additional expenditure or saving is theirs to keep or bear. Fraud enforcement officials are skeptical about the likelihood that HMOs will reduce fraud notably, though they grant that HMOs might change fraud's form and say it probably will make the detection of fraud even more difficult. In past years, HMOs have been discovered enrolling persons who did not exist, and selecting for their rosters only persons with superior health. A California official told us of one such scam:

> The entrepreneur would send two recruiters to the neighborhood. The first would go through the poor neighborhood where there was going to be a high proportion of Medi-Cal patients. First they would go to the door and say, "We're doing a survey on the health of your family—how many people are there in your family, how healthy are they, have you had any diseases?" Then, if it turned out that this was a person or family that statistically was not likely to produce medical problems, then the next person who came through the neighborhood would sell them on joining the HMO. . . . So they got a higher proportion of well people at the HMO than the payments contemplated. Then, by eliminating the high cost operations, like emergency rooms, weekend ser-

vice . . . and sending these people to other hospitals, they increase the profit by that much more, and then when it began to look as if they were going to get caught, they declared bankruptcy and walked away with it.

Other suggested reforms include a proposal by one investigator for a central clearing source that would allow enforcers to see to it that violators do not migrate from one jurisdiction to another without the awareness of the agents in the second site. A Congressional Committee recommended that the Department of Justice establish a Medicaid strike force, and that a number of U.S. Attorneys be assigned to prosecute persons defrauding government programs.[38] In Hawaii, attorneys in the MFCU are deputized to serve as prosecutors, so that the reluctance of attorneys in other agencies to handle Medicaid cases is overcome.

ASSIGNMENT: THE PHYSICIANS' BLUDGEON?

All law enforcement ultimately depends upon the tacit consent or weakness of the enforcement targets. A notably efficient method for detecting tax fraud—with many thousands more investigators—would probably so infuriate the huge population of cheaters that a government inaugurating such measures would shortly find itself in political difficulty. Airport security can go only so far in hindering the pace of air traffic; and campaigns against theft can employ only a limited repertoire of techniques without running the risk of offending altogether too many persons. This condition is particularly pronounced with Medicaid fraud. Fear that physicians would not participate in the benefit programs was largely responsible for the many concessions granted to practitioners when Medicaid and Medicare were inaugurated: "There was," Marmor notes, "the widespread fear, grounded in the bitter, hostile propaganda of the AMA, that physicians would refuse to provide services under a national health program."[39] Continuing apprehension about such withdrawal constitutes one of the major points of tension in enforcement efforts.

In the early 1980s, one-quarter of all primary care physicians were refusing to accept Medicaid patients, largely because of the low reimbursement rates.[40] Program administrators continually warn investigators, as one of them pointed out, "if you put doctors in jail, pretty soon none of the doctors will be in Medicaid." How reasonable are the fears that enforcement will so alienate Medicaid practitioners that it will become counterproductive? The best evidence seems to be that Medicaid now has become so intricately involved in medical practice that fears of massive physician withdrawal are only meaningless bluffs. In California, for instance, 15% of practicing physicians derive more than a quarter of their incomes from Medi-Cal patients.[41] With competition for patients becoming more intense because of the "overproduction" of doctors in the United States, it seems unreasonable to expect that Medicaid would be abandoned wholesale by doctors because of decent efforts to combat fraud.

CONCLUSION

Physicians continue to enjoy extraordinarily high status in the United States. A 1985 Gallup Poll found them outpacing the clergy, college professors, lawyers, and business executives (in that order) in terms of designation as "very prestigious."[42] At the same time, a Harris Poll indicates that "the major group of concerns that physicians have about the future of medical practice relates to loss of autonomy, mainly as a result of regulatory interference and external intervention." Many physicians were worried about controls on such things as location and specialty. Only about half of the doctors surveyed said that they would recommend the practice of medicine today as highly as they might have 10 years ago, and fewer than half of the physicians were satisfied either with their current incomes or with their financial prospects.[43] Obviously, there is a striking discrepancy between the fiscal self-image of a large number of the physicians and the state of public opinion about their earnings. Typical in our interviews, for instance, was the hostile remark of a federal investigator:

> [Doctors are] causing nursing home patients to lie in their own feces and their own bedsores and all of this good other stuff, because they're taking money that should be paying for food and nursing care and buying yachts and tennis courts.

Monitoring for fraud probably has contributed in some degree to the malaise expressed by physicians with their lot. As a prior condition, of course, the government had to invade the traditionally reserved enclaves of medical practice. It did so because there was a perceived (and real) absence of protection from fiscal disaster for large segments of the population and because sizable numbers of poor persons were unable to afford adequate medical care. It seems naive of doctors to have presumed, if they did, that the virtually open checkbook structure of the early days of the medical benefit programs would persist, especially in the face of escalating health care costs that far exceeded inflation figures. Government officials, traditionally beholden to the medical lobby, nonetheless have priorities that transcend obligations they might feel to a particular constituency: They devoutly desire to continue in office. In terms of Medicaid fraud control, these and other considerations are shaping what seems to be a continuing diminution of medical autonomy and power and a gradual, rather erratic course of toughening enforcement against violators. It will be a complicated process to determine the long-run impact of this process on the health of citizens. In the meantime, it seems clear that doctors have been placed in what is for them an uncommonly discomforting position. That position can be illustrated by an observation gathered during our interviews. Enforcement officers, like the prototypical British servant, come to know their "betters" in ways denied to most outsiders. On the basis of her experience, one investigator carried on the following dialogue with us:

INVESTIGATOR: How do I feel about the medical profession personally? I'm afraid
to go to a doctor. I don't trust any of them.
INTERVIEWER: You're into self cures now?
INVESTIGATOR: No, I'm into being well. I hope I never need a doctor. They scare
me.

Notes

1. Michael Medved, *Hospital: The Hidden Lives of a Medical Center Staff.* New York: Simon & Schuster, 1982.
2. R. S. Roberts, "The Personnel and Practice of Medicine in Tudor and Stuart England, part III," *Medical History* 8 (1964):221
3. Kenneth Silverman, *The Life and Times of Cotton Mather.* New York: Harper & Row, 1984, p. 345.
4. W. H. S. Jones, ed., *Hippocrates, with an English Translation.* London: Heinemann, 1923–1931, pp. 291–301.
5. Rigby Leighton, *Looking for the Monster: Description of the Problem of Medical Costs and Catalog of Cost Containment Strategies.* Sacramento: California Department of Health Services, 1980, pp. 60–61.
6. Jeremy Bentham, *The Works of Jeremy Bentham.* John Bowring, ed. Edinburgh: Tait, 1839.
7. Erwin O. Smigel and H. Laurence Ross, eds., *Crimes against Bureaucracy.* New York: Van Nostrand Reinhold, 1970.
8. Harvey F. Pies, "Control of Fraud and Abuse in Medicare and Medicaid," *American Journal of Law and Medicine,* 3 (1977):321–332.
9. Jay A. Winsten, "Bailing Out Medicare," *New York Times,* May 5, 1983, p A31.
10. U.S. Senate, "Oversight of HHS Inspector General's Effort to Combat Fraud, Waste, and Abuse." Committee on Finance, Special Committee on Aging. 97th Cong., 1st Sess., 1982, p. 5.
11. Kenneth R. Wing, "The Impact of Reagan-Era Politics on the Federal Medicaid Program," *Catholic University Law Review,* 33 (1983):16.
12. Randall R. Bovbjerg and John Holahan, *Medicaid in the Reagan Era: Federal Policy and Stated Choices.* Washington, DC: Urban Institute, 1982, p. xi.
13. See Jerry Cromwell and Janet B. Mitchell, "High Income Medicaid Practices," *Inquiry,* 18 (1981):18–27; Mitchell and Cromwell, "Large Medicaid Practices and Medicaid Mills," *Journal of the American Medical Association,* 244 (1980):2433–2437.
14. U.S. Senate, "Fraud and Abuse among Practitioners in the Medicaid Program." Subcommittee on Long-Term Care, Special Committee on Aging. 94th Cong., 2d Sess., 1976, p. 12.

15. Paul J. Goldstein, *Prostitution and Drugs.* Lexington, MA: Lexington Books, 1982, pp. 42–43.
16. U.S. Senate, "Fraud and Abuse," *op. cit.*, p. 18.
17. *Ibid.*, p. 44.
18. *Ibid.*, p. 26.
19. *Ibid.*, p. 1.
20. U.S. Senate, "Oversight of HHS Inspector General," *op. cit.*, p. 33.
21. *Ibid.*, p. 107.
22. U.S. Comptroller General, *Federal Funding in State Medicaid Units Still Needed.* Washington, DC: Government Printing Office, 1980, p. 4.
23. U.S. House of Representatives, "Medicaid Fraud: A Case Study in the Failure of State Enforcement." Select Committee on Aging. 97th Cong., 2d Sess., 1982, pp. iii, v, 19, 22, 23, 32.
24. *Ibid.*, pp. 66, 101
25. Henry N. Pontell, Gilbert Geis, Mary Jane O'Brien, and Paul Jesilow, "A Demographic Portrait of Physicians Sanctioned by the Federal Government for Fraud and Abuse against Medicare and Medicaid," *Medical Care,* 23 (1985): 1028–1031.
26. Gilbert Geis, Paul Jesilow, Henry N. Pontell, and Mary Jane O'Brien, "Fraud and Abuse of Government Medical Benefit Programs by Psychiatrists," *American Journal of Psychiatry,* 142 (1985):231–234.
27. Pontell et al., *op. cit.*
28. U.S. House of Representatives, "Medicare: A Fifteen-Year Perspective." Select Committee on Aging. 95th Cong., 2d Sess., 1980, p. 78.
29. U.S. Senate, "Oversight of HHS Inspector General," *op. cit.*, p. 10.
30. U.S. Senate, "Medicare-Medicaid Fraud and Abuse Amendments of 1977." Committee on Finance. 95th Cong., 1st Sess., 1977, p. 48.
31. Pawel Horoszowski, *Economic Special-Opportunity Conduct and Crime.* Lexington, MA: Lexington Books, 1978, p. 151.
32. Al Messerschmidt, "Witnesses Dispute Doctor's Claim," *Miami Herald,* January 16, 1982, p. B2; Fred Grimm, "Women Doctor Convicted in Plot to Kill Partner Sentenced to Life," *Miami Herald,* February 4, 1983, p. Bl.
33. See, e.g., Commonwealth v. Kobrin, 395 Mass. 284, 479 N.E.2d 674 (1985).
34. Johannes Andenaes, "Deterrence and Specific Offenses," *University of Chicago Law Review,* 38 (1971):537–553; John Braithwaite and Gilbert Geis, "On Theory and Action for Corporate Crime Control," *Crime and Delinquency,* 28 (1982):292–314; Michael R. Geerken and Walter R. Gove, "Deterrence: Some Methodological Considerations," *Law and Society Review,* 9 (1975):497–513; Franklin E. Zimring and Gordon Hawkins, *Deterrence: The Legal Threat in Crime Control.* Chicago: University of Chicago Press, 1973, pp. 127–128.
35. Richard E. Nisbett and Lee Ross, *Human Inference: Strategies and Shortcomings of Social Judgment.* Englewood Cliffs, NJ: Prentice-Hall, 1980, p. 56.
36. Richard P. Kusserow, "Civil Money Penalties Law of 1961: A New Effort to

Combat Fraud and Abuse in Federal Health Care Programs," *Notre Dame Law Review,* 58 (1983):985–994.

37. Robert J. Price, *Health Maintenance Organizations.* Washington, DC: Library of Congress, Congressional Research Service, 1982, p. 1.

38. U.S. House, "Medicare," *op. cit.*, p. 101.

39. Theodore Marmor, *The Politics of Medicare.* Chicago: Aldine, 1970, p. 15.

40. Stephen M. Davidson, "Physician Participation in Medicaid: Background and Issues." *Journal of Health, Policy and Law,* 6 (1982):703–717.

41. Michael W. Jones and Bette Hamburger, "A Survey of Physician Participation in and Dissatisfaction with the Medi-Cal Program," *Western Journal of Medicine,* 124 (1976):75–83.

42. Gene I. Maeroff, "Polls Say Americans Support Raises and Tests for Teachers," *New York Times* (West Coast ed.), July 2, 1985, p. 10.

43. Louis Harris and Associates, *Medical Practice in the 1980's: Physicians Look at Their Changing Profession.* Menlo Park, CA: Kaiser Foundation, 1984, pp. 70, 74, 96.

14

Careers of Misconduct
Professional Deviance among Lawyers

Bruce L. Arnold and John Hagan

The concept of "career" has a powerful appeal to sociologists who study crime and deviance.[1] Part of this appeal stems from the notion that a deviant career suggests a parallel between activities in illegitimate and legitimate sectors of society.[2] The provocative potential of this parallel is anticipated in the ironic suggestion that "jails are schools of crime." Yet applications of the career concept to the study of crime and deviance have sometimes proved frustrating, as when criminal and deviant acts are found to be isolated events with little organized structure.[3]

One reason for this apparent lack of structure may be that highly structured criminal and deviant careers are more often shaped by the reactions of agents of social control. For example, Tittle argued that the existence of a group of persistent criminal offenders "might reflect stability of police attention to some individuals rather than stable rates of 'offending.' "[4] Hagan and Palloni proposed that the study of criminal careers is better conceptualized using a life-course framework[5] that treats deviant or criminal acts as movements of individuals through positions in a system, with these movements often shaped by the reactions of control agents.[6] We use this perspective to study careers of prosecuted misconduct among lawyers.

THE MODEL OF PROSECUTED MISCONDUCT

Our multidimensional career model is built around Becker's concept of "career contingency,"[7] which refers to the factors that influence movement from one position to another. In the study of occupations, Becker noted that while career contingencies influence the course of individuals who allow legitimate career paths, they can also influence "several varieties of career outcomes," including outcomes defined as deviant. He emphasized that a crucial step in the deviant context is "being caught

Reprinted from *American Sociological Review,* 57 (December 1992), pp. 771–780.

and publicly labeled as a deviant."[8] Our analysis therefore focuses on the prosecution of formal complaints of misconduct among lawyers.

Because legal practice is largely self-regulated, complaints against lawyers are initially monitored within the profession, e.g., by Bar Associations. Although complaints are common, prosecutions are relatively rare. Prosecution of complaints is usually undertaken within the profession, although more serious complaints may be transferred to the criminal justice system. A multidimensional dynamic which structures the process that leads to the prosecution of misconduct among lawyers underlies our model.[9] This model considers dynamic and structural features of prosecuted complaints, including the scale of the organizational setting and the phase of the economic cycle at the time of the complaint. Agencies of social control may be especially sensitive to these influences. Therefore these influences may structure the dynamics of deviant careers through the mediating role of agency interventions.

Although our model recognizes a distinction between the occurrence of behavioral misconduct and its prosecution, we follow labeling theory[10] and conceive of misconduct and its control as a product of interactions between deviant actors and control agents. Like labeling theory, the research literature on lawyer misconduct implies that the prosecutorial process, through selective surveillance and sanctioning, determines much of the existing structure in careers of lawyer misconduct.

For example Carlin's classic study of ethics in the legal profession emphasized that most lawyer misconduct is not prosecuted—he estimated that only 2 percent of lawyers who violate accepted ethical norms are processed, and that less than 1 percent of these cases is officially sanctioned.[11] Carlin concluded that prosecutions have little deterrent effect and that "a more likely function of these formal controls is the forestalling of public criticism of the legal profession."[12] This highly selective process of prosecution is probably not random. Instead prosecution is probably structured by social conceptions and lay theories that guide the surveillance of types of lawyers and conditions of lawyering that are expected to produce unethical behavior, and by the expectations imposed on a system that is obliged to control misconduct and to uphold the profession's public image through selective sanctioning.[13]

Interviews with regulators and a reading of the literature suggest three factors that may influence misconduct among lawyers. The first is inexperience, or more specifically, lack of time in practice. With practice, lawyers gain stability, working knowledge, and resources that help them maintain proper conduct or avoid detection. Handler reported that "the more recently admitted lawyers had lower professional incomes, poorer individual clients, and more unstable clients," and therefore encountered "more pressures and more opportunities to violate than did lawyers who had been in practice longer."[14] Carlin found in New York City that lawyers in these newer offices encountered increased pressures to engage in unethical practices.[15] The challenge of earning a stable livelihood in unstable conditions with insufficient knowledge and inadequate resources is a career contingency conducive to compensatory misconduct. Exaggeration of the problems resulting from inexperience may increase prosecutorial attention to less experienced lawyers, who lack the resources to resist or divert this attention.

A second factor influencing misconduct among lawyers involves the stratification hierarchy of the profession. Although law presents itself formally as a unified profession with a common base of credentials, the legal profession is highly stratified.[16] This stratification can be described in various ways, but the consensus is that solo practitioners are at the bottom of the hierarchy.[17] Solo practitioners are associated with lower court settings and unstable practices in "trouble" specialties, e.g., criminal, personal injury, matrimonial cases. Carlin suggested that "lawyers at the bottom of the status ladder are maximally exposed to pressures to violate,"[18] and Handler concurred that these lawyers are "under great pressure to violate ethical rules."[19] Thus, a second career contingency is an intraoccupational stratification system that places solo practitioners at increased risk of misconduct leading to increased regulatory attention and an increased chance of prosecution for misconduct. Like inexperienced lawyers, solo practitioners may also lack resources to fend off prosecution.

Third, lawyer misconduct is influenced by macroeconomic changes in the society at large. Despite their professional status, lawyers are vulnerable to fluctuations in the economic cycle.[20] Concern with lawyer misconduct may increase during recessionary periods in a manner similar to the moral panics concerning law and disorder in general.[21] Because the self-regulatory responsibilities of the profession include being responsive to surrounding social and economic trends, the prosecution of lawyer misconduct may intensify in response to macroeconomic downturns.

These three career contingencies—inexperience, solo practice, and macroeconomic recession—are not only widely believed to increase lawyer misconduct; they are the source of the relative powerlessness of the individual lawyer to deflect prosecutorial attention.

It is useful to think about the interaction of career contingencies and enforcement agencies in terms of their synchronization.[22] Riley used the principle of "asynchrony" to refer to the poorly coordinated interplay between changes in the lives of individuals and changes in the surrounding social structure. She noted that "lack of synchrony imposes strains on both individuals and society," that "the strains of asynchrony are often overlooked—as in an exclusively individual-level focus on life-course transitions," and that "these strains can ramify through all levels of the system."[23] These effects of asynchrony indirectly highlight the potential multiplicative role of regulatory activity.

Riley's observations coordinate components of our model. Experience and economic conditions may interact in asynchronic ways because each factor changes independently and with its own metric. A classic example is Elder's finding that effects of the Great Depression varied across birth cohorts.[24] In our analysis, Riley's observations suggest that interactions between macroeconomic conditions and time in practice and position in the professional stratification hierarchy may produce deviance-inducing contingencies. Thus, inexperienced solo practitioners may be at a relatively high risk of misconduct during recessionary periods.

However, Riley's observations implicate not only the individuals at risk, but the surrounding system that monitors relevant problems. Under the stresses and strains of a recessionary period, misconduct may be more prone to prosecutorial attention because of its potential damage to the profession's public image and because of the relative powerlessness of inexperienced solo practitioners to defend themselves. It is in this sense that surveillance and sanctioning of misconduct structure the paths of lawyer misconduct.

DATA AND METHODS

The concept of career concerns temporal movement between positions. To analyze deviant careers requires "a model that allows for change through time."[25] Event history analysis formally models this kind of change in terms of transition rates that consider the pace of movement between events, e.g., between a complaint against a lawyer and the hazard of subsequent prosecution for misconduct.[26]

Our data come from an eight-year sampling frame of lawyers (from January 1, 1979 to December 31, 1986) against whom complaints of misconduct were lodged with the Law Society of a Canadian province. (The Law Society in Canada is analogous to a state Bar Association in the United States.) We selected a response-based sample,[27] based on whether complaints against lawyers resulted in prosecution during this period. The sample includes all lawyers for whom a complaint resulted in prosecution between the above dates (N = 639), and a random sample of a similar number of lawyers against whom complaints were registered during the same period, but who were not prosecuted (N = 635). We examined each lawyer's history for prior complaints and recorded a complete, dated complaint history for each of the 1,274 lawyers from their entry into practice up through December 31, 1986. Spells between successive complaints, from entry into practice up to and including their "current" complaint (i.e., the complaint between 1979 and 1986) are the units for the event history analysis. For lawyers with more than one complaint, the first spell is the time from entry into practice to the date of their first complaint. A first spell may also be one in which the current complaint is the only complaint since being called to the bar.

We are interested in the timing of events that lead to a decision to formally prosecute lawyers for misconduct. The effect of the timing of events on a formal prosecution for misconduct is conceptualized in event history analysis as a hazard. Although event history analysis usually involves single-spell models of rates of transition to events that occur once or only a few times (e.g., marriage), some social events, like lawyer misconduct, can occur repeatedly. The lawyers in our sample experienced an average of 14 complaints during their time in practice; 85 lawyers experienced a single complaint while several had more than 60.[28] Following Allison,[29] we use Cox's[30] proportional hazards model to estimate rates of transition between successive complaints. This requires rearranging our data so that all intervals between complaints are treated as separate observations, with successive complaints about a particular lawyer associated in a nonindependent fashion.[31] This transforms our sample of 1,274 lawyers into 9,092 units or spells, of which 3,892 are censored in our initial analysis. Spells were censored because they did not end in a prosecution.

An advantage of the event history models we present is that they take into account information from these censored cases.[32] These censored cases are also analyzed separately.

Our response-based sample is stratified on the dependent variable—a formal prosecuted complaint—and includes successive, nonindependent events. Our event history analysis minimizes effects of nonindependence among units by including variables (experience, prior complaints, and prior prosecutions) that control for common sources of variance.[33]

MEASURES

Table 14.1 describes the independent variables in our model. Dummy variables identify position in the professional stratification hierarchy. Although our focus is on solo practitioners, we include other positions in the professional hierarchy:[34] partners in large firms (firms with 30 or more lawyers); partners in medium-sized firms (10 to 29 lawyers); partners in small firms (2 to 9 lawyers); solo practitioners; associates in firms; and lawyers employed by the government, corporations, or other organizations. There is little movement between firm practice, solo practice, and the corporate and government sectors of the profession.[35] Associates and employed lawyers are lower in the professional hierarchy than partners, so their experiences are of interest.

Economic recession is represented by a dummy variable, coded 1 if a complaint of misconduct was filed with the Law Society from 1981 to 1986. Although we cannot identify the period of the recession precisely, Canadian macroeconomic indicators suggest that it began in the early 1980s and continued through 1986. The number of prosecuted formal complaints against lawyers in our sample began to move upward in 1981, peaked in 1982, and fell to a low in 1984. By 1986, prosecuted complaints were somewhat higher than in 1979 and 1980. For this analysis, then, the effects of the Canadian recession probably extended from 1981 through 1986.

Inexperience is measured as years in practice prior to the "current" complaint of misconduct. The relationship between complaints and years in practice is nonlinear, especially for solo practitioners. Rather, among solo practitioners (and to a lesser degree among the other positions) complaints peak at about five years of legal practice, then decline slowly. The curve for solo practitioners is much like the curve observed in research on the relation between age and crime.

The apparent nonlinearity of the relationship between years in practice and complaints suggests that a discrete measure of experience is appropriate. To capture the nonlinear effects of experience, we coded experience into three categories: 1 through 4 years experience; 5 through 9 years experience; and 10 or more years. Allison noted that the effects of nonindependent events in models that express the hazard rate as a function of the time since a prior event are reduced by including an experience measure.[36] Three control variables characterize the offenses mentioned in the complaints: their presumed seriousness, the financial harm to clients, and violations of real estate or trust accounts. These variables probably increase the transition rate between complaints and the likelihood of being prosecuted, and our concern is to control for their association with the variables of interest. All these offense variables involve a violation of trust, and trust plays a central role in professional deviance and its sanctioning.[37] We distinguished serious offenses (coded 1) by asking the Law Society's discipline lawyers to rate the complaints filed against the lawyers. The following offenses were most commonly ranked as serious: misappropriation, counseling false evidence, conduct unbecoming, and failing to account to the Law Society. Law Society records were used to establish financial harm to the complainant (coded 1) and whether a real estate or trust violation was alleged (coded 1). Controls also were introduced for aspects of the lawyer's prior history that would increase the transition rate for lawyers being prosecuted. These variables

Table 14.1
PERCENTAGE OF LAWYERS WITH SELECTED CHARACTERISTICS: CANADIAN PROVINCE, 1979–1986

Characteristic	Percentage
Position in Professional Hierarchy	
Partner in large firm (> 30)	1.3
Partner in medium-size firm (10–29)	1.4
Partner in small firm (2–9)	21.1
Solo practitioner	62.1
Associate in firm	6.0
Employee (government or corporate)	8.1
Recession (1981–1986 = 1)	78.7
Experience	
1 to 4 years	13.5
5 to 9 years	28.7
10+ years	57.8
Offense	
Serious offense	48.3
Financial harm to client	11.2
Violation of real estate/trust account	51.1
History	
Past complaints (mean)	
(s.d. = 9.61)	13.7
Prior prosecution (= 1)	14.9
Sex (male = 1)	94.5
Number of Lawyers	1,274

include the total number of prior complaints filed against the accused and whether the accused was previously prosecuted (coded 1). Inclusion of these variables removes spurious and intervening sources of variation when estimating the direct effects of the labeling variables. The history variables also minimize the consequences of including nonindependent events in our models.

Finally, gender is included in the analysis (male = 1). Approximately 95 percent of the sample is male.

RESULTS

Models of transition to the hazard of prosecution for misconduct showed that solo practitioners have the highest rates of transition to prosecution for complaints of misconduct. (Partners in small firms are the omitted category.) Taking the antilog of the coefficient for solo practitioners ($e^{383} = 1.467$), we see that, net of all other variables in the model, solo practitioners move to prosecution at a rate about 47 percent faster than the rate for partners in small firms. Associates in firms and employees of government and corporations are also more likely to be prosecuted (about 18 and 24 percent more likely, respectively) than are partners in small firms.

The coefficient for recession introduces the main and direct effect of macrolevel change in the economy. The recession of the early 1980s has a significant effect on rates of prosecution for misconduct: Complaints move to prosecution at a rate about 26 percent faster during the recession compared to nonrecession complaints.

The coefficients for years of experience introduce the main effects of microlevel change, i.e., personal experience. Rates of transition to prosecution for experienced lawyers are much lower than those for lawyers with less experience: The two dummy variables representing less than 10 years' experience have strong positive effects on transactions to prosecution. Complaints involving lawyers with 1 through 4 years in practice are prosecuted at a rate more than 118 percent higher than are complaints involving lawyers with 10 or more years' experience, while for lawyers with 5 through 9 years of experience, the rate is increased by about 65 percent. In the context of our model, then, prosecution is most likely during the earliest years of practice.

Thus, all three hypothesized factors—low professional position, economic recession, and legal inexperience—have the expected main effects of increasing the hazard of prosecution for misconduct. These are direct causal effects, as the control variables of type of offense, prior history, and gender are included in the model. Serious offenses and offenses involving the violation of a real estate or trust account both have large and statistically significant effects. Both variables tap the significance of violations of trust emphasized by Shapiro.[38] These variables increase the rate of transition to prosecution by about 75 and 67 percent respectively. Complaints involving financial loss to the client have only a slightly higher rate of prosecution. A previous prosecution as well as a relatively large number of prior complaints also increase the rate of transition to prosecution.

We found that solo practitioners have higher rates of transition to prosecution for misconduct during the recession, and solo practitioners with 5 through 9 years of experience have higher rates of transition. Although the least experienced lawyers (1 through 4 years of experience) should have been even more vulnerable to prosecution, these findings are consistent with Riley's observations and our theoretical model, that macrolevel and microlevel sources of change have multiplicative as well as additive effects.[39]

A model adding two three-way interactions involving solo practitioners, the recession, and years of experience shows one significant interaction that the highest rates of transition during the recession involve the least experienced solo practitioners. Lawyers with this combination of career contingencies are prosecuted for misconduct at a rate nearly 5 times higher than other lawyers in our sample.

Although the findings presented to this point are consistent with multilevel labeling theory, they may simply reflect the motivation involved in deviant behaviors that are not influenced by prosecutorial intervention and labeling. The models have minimized this possibility by including measures of offense seriousness and complaint history as control variables and by utilizing the capacity of event history methods to incorporate information from censored observations, in this case the unprosecuted complaints. Behavioral differences among lawyers should be screened through these statistical controls.

If the variables in our models structure the hazard of a complaint apart from the influence of prosecutorial attention, then these variables should operate on unprosecuted complaints as well as prosecuted complaints. The model for prosecuted complaints excludes information from the censored unprosecuted complaints, which are modeled separately. Nonetheless, the model of prosecuted complaints produces results similar to, though somewhat less robust than, those found for the total sample. However, the model for unprosecuted complaints is less coherent: Only the number of past complaints, an offense involving financial harm to the client, and inexperience increase the hazard of current unprosecuted complaints. In other words, results from unprosecuted complaints are more random and reveal less structure than results for prosecuted complaints.

DISCUSSION AND CONCLUSION

Our research blends a sociological interest in careers with a labeling perspective on deviance. These concepts are highly relevant to understanding the prosecuted misconduct of lawyers. The focus on movement over time and between positions is consistent with the repeated involvement of lawyers in careers of misconduct—these careers are clearly structured by predictable contingencies that are associated with movement to prosecution. Riley's principle of asynchrony, which focuses on the consequences of life cycle changes for precariously positioned actors and the systems in which these actors are located, evokes connections between labeling studies and career themes.[40]

The cross-level emphasis of research on careers and the life course encourages a consideration of the needs of regulators to respond to deviant actors who, in turn, are poorly positioned to fend off prosecutorial intervention. Riley's observations suggest that these perceived pressures may intensify institutional responses by amplifying the threat to institutional stability. The notion of asynchrony adds a crucial multiplicative dimension to our understanding of careers of misconduct by suggesting that microlevel and macrolevel changes be brought together through interaction effects.

Our analysis of the prosecution of lawyers for complaints of misconduct supports a multiplicative, multilevel integration of a labeling perspective on professional deviance among lawyers within a career framework. The additive effects of inexperience, solo practice, and economic recession lead to increased prosecution of misconduct. Furthermore, these factors interact with one another to increase the hazard of prosecution so that, for example, inexperienced solo practitioners are prosecuted for professional misconduct at a higher rate during economic recession.

Our interpretation involves elements of *both* deviant behavior and agency response, i.e., we do not assume that prosecuted lawyers are passive innocents. Prosecuted lawyers are simply the offending lawyers whose behaviors have been singled out for prosecutorial attention, and this attention structures their careers. Such interdependence of action and reaction is the essence of Becker's notion of "pure deviance"[41] and Lemert's conception of a "dynamic of exclusion."[42] The focus of event history analysis on the structure of successive events is uniquely suited to capture the dynamics of a self-regulating system in which deviant behavior and its control move in an interdependent fashion.

If, as Carlin suggested, the observed pattern of prosecution is intended to forestall public criticism of the legal profession,[43] it is important to understand what justifies this policy and what the implications of the policy are. One justification for the policy is its deterrent effect: Because inexperienced solo practitioners are thought to have a higher risk of misconduct in a recessionary environment, it could be argued that such offenders should be singled out for deterrent sanctions. However, our empirical findings lend little support to such a policy. Although the results for unprosecuted complaints reveal somewhat greater involvement of inexperienced lawyers, it is only with prosecution that solo practitioners and the recession are involved. Furthermore, a past prosecution increases the movement to a current prosecution, which is the opposite of a deterrent effect. These effects on prosecution hold despite the inclusion of information on unprosecuted cases and explicit controls for past and present behavioral differences among the prosecuted lawyers. The evidence supports a labeling model of deviant careers in which inexperienced solo practitioners are placed at heightened risk of surveillance and sanctioning during a recessionary period. It is regulatory attention more than pre-existing behavioral differences that structures these deviant careers.

In general, our findings reflect generic social processes that are relevant to an understanding of similarities and differences between deviant and conventional careers. Pursuit of a common explanatory framework is part of the appeal of the application of the career concept to the study of social deviance. Future research will determine whether this common agenda can be advanced by application of the career concept to other kinds of deviance.

Notes

1. Howard Becker, *Outsiders: Studies in the Sociology of Deviance.* New York: Free Press, 1963.
2. Richard Cloward and Lloyd Ohlin, *Delinquency and Opportunity: A Theory of Delinquent Gangs.* New York: Free Press, 1960.
3. Michael R. Gottfredson and Travis Hirschi, "Science, Public Policy, and Career Paradigm," *Criminology,* 26 (1988):37–55.
4. Charles Tittle, "Two Empirical Regularities (Maybe) in Search of an Explanation: Commentary on the Age/Crime Debate," *Criminology,* 26 (1988):76.
5. John Hagan and Alberto Palloni, "Crimes as Social Events in the Life Course: Reconceiving a Criminological Controversy," *Criminology,* 26 (1988):87–100; Hagan, "The Social Reproduction of a Criminal Class in Working Class London, Circa 1950–1980," *American Journal of Sociology,* 96 (1990):265–299; See also Robert Sampson and John Laub, "Crime and Deviance in the Life Course," *American Sociological Review,* 18 (1992):63–84.
6. Glenn H. Elder, Jr., *Life Course Dynamics.* New York: Cornell University Press, 1985.
7. Becker, *op. cit.*, p. 24.
8. *Ibid.*, p. 31.
9. Matilda W. Riley, "On the Significance of Age in Sociology." In Matilda W. Riley, ed., *Social Structures and Human Lives.* Beverly Hills: Sage, 1988, pp. 24–45; Morris Rosenberg, "Disposition Concepts in Behavioral Science." In Robert K. Merton, James S. Coleman, and Peter H. Rossi, eds., *Qualitative and Quantitative Social Research.* New York: Free Press, 1979, pp. 245–260; Paul F. Lazarsfeld, "Latent Structure Analysis." In Sigmund Koch, ed., *Psychology: A Study of a Science.* New York: McGraw-Hill, 1959, pp. 476–543 .
10. Becker, *op. cit.*; John Kitsuse and Aaron Cicourel, "A Note on the Use of Official Statistics," *Social Problems,* 11 (1963):131–139.
11. Jerome Carlin, *Lawyers' Ethics: A Survey of the New York City Bar.* New York: Russell Sage Foundation, 1966. See also Joel Handler, *The Lawyer and His Community.* Madison: University of Wisconsin Press, 1967.
12. Carlin, *op. cit.*, p. 170.
13. Aaron Cicourel, *The Social Organization of Juvenile Justice.* New York: Wiley, 1968.
14. Handler, *op. cit.*, p. 127.
15. Carlin, *op. cit.*

16. John P. Heinz and Edward O. Lauman, *Chicago Lawyers: The Structure of the Bar.* New York: Russell Sage Foundation, 1982; Howard Erlanger, "The Allocation of Status within Occupations: The Case of the Legal Profession," *Social Forces,* 58 (1980):882–903; John Hagan, Marie Huxter, and Patricia Parker, "Class Structure and Legal Practice: Inequality and Mobility among Toronto Lawyers," *Law and Society Review,* 22 (1988):9–56.

17. Jack Ladinsky, "Careers of Lawyers: Law Practice and Legal Institutions," *American Sociological Review,* 28 (1963):47–54.

18. Carlin, *op. cit.*, p. 168.

19. Handler, *op. cit.*, p. 116.

20. Marc Galanter, "Larger than Life: Mega-Law and Mega-Lawyering in the Contemporary United States." In Robert Dingwall and Philip Lewis, eds., *The Sociology of the Professions: Lawyers, Doctors, and Others.* London: Macmillan, 1983, pp. 152–176; Sally S. Simpson, "The Decomposition of Antitrust: Testing a Multi-Level, Longitudinal Model of Profit-Squeeze," *American Sociological Review,* 51 (1986):859–875.

21. Stanley Cohen, *Folk Devils and Moral Panics.* London: MacGibbon and Kee, 1972.

22. Elder, *op. cit.*

23. Riley, *op. cit.*, pp. 38–39

24. Elder, *op. cit.*

25. Becker, *op. cit.*, p. 22.

26. Nancy B. Tuma and Michael T. Hannan, *Social Dynamics: Models and Methods.* New York: Academic Press, 1984; Paul D. Allison, *Event History Analysis: Regression for Longitudinal Event Data.* Newbury Park: Sage, 1984.

27. Yu Xie and Charles F. Manski, "The Logit Model and Response-Based Samples," *Sociological Methods Research,* 17 (1989):283–302.

28. The power and responsibility of the provincial Law Society to investigate and discipline lawyers derive from parliamentary acts. In our data, 32 different types of misconduct were mentioned in complaints against lawyers. The most serious (as indicated by staff lawyers) included misappropriation of funds; conduct unbecoming a lawyer; failure to account/report transactions; misleading clients/others; counseling false evidence; illegal borrowing of funds; failure to reply to, cooperate with, follow, or adhere to Law Society Requirements; mental incompetence; fraud; and forgery. The sanctions for misconduct include issuing a reprimand, a reprimand plus costs, restrictions or suspension of practice, directed resignation, and disbarment.

29. Allison, *op. cit.*, chap. 6; See also Alfred Hamerle, "Multiple Spell Regression Models for Duration Data," *Applied Statistics,* 38 (1989):127–138.

30. David R. Cox, "Regressions Models and Life Tables," *Journal of the Royal Statistical Society, Series B,* 34 (1972):187–202.

31. Allison, *op. cit.*, p. 51.

32. Alberto Palloni and Aage Sorenson, "Methods for the Analysis of Event History Data: A Didactic Overview." In Paul Baltes, David Featherman, and

Richard Lerner, eds., *Life Span Development and Behavior, Volume 10.* Hillsdale, NJ: Lawrence Erlbaum Associates, 1988, pp. 291–323.

33. Allison, *op. cit.*, p. 54.
34. Hagan and Palloni, *op. cit.*
35. Carlin, *op. cit.*; Heinz and Lauman, *op. cit.*
36. Allison, *op. cit.*, p. 55.
37. Susan Shapiro, "Collaring the Crime Not the Criminal: Reconsidering the Concept of White-Collar Crime," *American Sociological Review,* 55 (1990): 346–365.
38. *Ibid.*
39. Riley, *op. cit.*
40. *Ibid.*
41. Becker, *op. cit.*
42. Edwin Lemert, "Paranoia and the Dynamics of Exclusion," *Sociometry,* 25 (1962):2–20.
43. Carlin, *op. cit.*, p. 170.

PART III

Enforcement and Sentencing

Introduction to Part III

A 1992 news report on the prison activities of "celebrity wrongdoers," persons such as onetime junk bond king Michael Milken, former Lincoln Savings and Loan president Charles Keating, evangelist Jim Bakker, ex-hotel queen Leona Helmsley, and onetime California State Senator Joseph Montoya, is symbolic of the tougher enforcement surge against white-collar criminals. Milken, it was noted, was to join with his fellow inmates at the Federal Correctional Institution in Pleasanton, California, for a meal of baked ham, mashed potatoes, rice, salad, and rolls. Helmsley was to receive either a coffee cup, earmuffs, or a $5 fruit pack as a holiday present at the Federal Prison Camp in Danbury, Connecticut.[1]

This banal human interest newspaper story reflects significant developments in regard to the punishment of white-collar criminals. There has been a rise in concern about white-collar crime in the media as well as among the public, legislators, and the authorities who investigate, prosecute, and sentence white-collar offenders. Opinion polls consistently register growing citizen hostility to white-collar criminals such as environmental polluters and to corporations responsible for the illegal dumping of toxic wastes.

In addition, tougher and innovative approaches to the punishment of white-collar crime have been put into place. These include the Racketeering and Corrupt Influence Act (RICO), which was aimed at organized crime, but has proven to be a powerful weapon against white-collar crime as well, and the provisions regarding organizations in the guidelines promulgated by the United States Sentencing Commission.

White-collar crimes are believed to be notably responsive to tough sanctions, particularly criminal sanctions. This supposition rests on the idea that white-collar offenders behave rationally, that they estimate with some care the possible consequences of their acts. Being conformists often is what brought them their success; therefore, they will be influenced by the grim contemplation of notoriety for wrongdoing, humiliating appearances in criminal court, and a mortifying and fiscally disabling sentence to prison.

Statements by individuals caught in the web of white-collar crime prosecutions indicate considerable anguish regarding the process. Some explicitly mourn that had they known what would happen they would never have done what they did. "I would starve before I would do it again," said one of the executives sentenced to jail in the heavy electrical equipment antitrust case.[2] Oliver North, deeply involved in the Iran-Contra crimes, told a Congressional investigating committee in 1987: "I never in my wildest dreams or nightmares envisioned that we would end up with criminal charges. It was beyond my wildest comprehension."[3] Later, North made the same point with different words. He had anticipated, he said, that he would "go quietly" as the "scapegoat" whose silence and destruction of evidence would protect his superiors. But when he learned that his fate included possible criminal charges, North said, "my mind set changed considerably."[4]

A major difficulty in establishing ideal deterrent conditions is that the likelihood of being apprehended for white-collar crime is quite low (we will never know the true extent of such behavior, of course), and that the degree of peril is impossible to ascertain for a person thinking about committing a white-collar crime. In-depth interviews with business executives and managers suggest that formal sanction possibilities are rarely considered when illegal conduct is contemplated, though stigmatic costs (that is, threats to reputation and future employment) are salient concerns.[5]

Potential offenders also must weigh the risk of being caught by enforcement agents against the usually more pronounced risks associated with failure to meet explicit or implicit organizational demands. Then, too, most executives have been cold-bloodedly familiar with what were the likely inconsequential outcomes of illegal behavior, even if they were caught. They appreciated that until recently (and to some extent continuing today) only the most egregious wrongdoing was likely to propel them into a criminal court. As one executive bluntly stated: "It's cheaper to pay claims than it is to control fluorides."[6]

It is largely to combat such attitudes that tougher penalties have been applied to white-collar crimes. Developments in environmental law enforcement typify this trend. For many years, governmental agencies primarily used civil penalties to punish violators. "These agencies now feel that the mere imposition of fines is largely ineffective," Eva Fromm notes. Today, "the threat of possible incarceration for violations of environmental statutes has terrorized many environmental managers and commanded their previously unattainable respect."[7] Not only have tougher penalties been established, but an array of other federal statutes increasingly are being used to deal with white-collar crime: statutes such as those outlawing conspiracy, false statements, mail and wire fraud, and aiding and abetting.

Typical of the puny amounts once levied against offending corporations was the $25,000 assessed against Eli Lilly, the pharmaceutical manufacturer, after a guilty plea to a misdemeanor charge for failing to inform the government of four deaths and six illnesses related to Oraflex, an arthritis drug that Lilly marketed. Oraflex was linked to at least 26 deaths in the United States and even more overseas.[8] In their comprehensive study of the offenses of Fortune 500 companies, Marshall Clinard and Peter Yeager learned that two-thirds of what they regarded as serious offenses and four-fifths of moderately serious offenses were handled by administrative means rather than prosecuted criminally.[9]

Things have changed considerably. In 1988, the stockbrokerage firm of Drexel Burnham Lambert pled guilty to six counts of mail, wire, and securities fraud and agreed to pay $650 million in fines and penalties. In another landmark case, late in 1991, liquidators for the Bank of Credit & Commerce (BCCI) agreed to forfeit all of the company's assets in the United States, valued at more than $550 million, as part of a guilty plea. Penalties against individual white-collar offenders also have escalated. Risk arbitrageur Ivan Boesky paid the government $100 million as part of a negotiated settlement on insider trading charges.

The two major vehicles for enhanced prosecution of white-collar crime are found in RICO and in the Sentencing Commission guidelines. RICO imposes criminal and civil liability on persons and groups engaged in certain "prohibited activities" which have a connection to "a pattern of racketeering activity." The law defines "racketeering activity" as "any act or threat" involving designated state crimes or any act indictable under specified federal statutes. A pattern of such activity is deemed to be "at least two acts of racketeering activity" within a ten-year period.

Businesses have fought with only limited success to distinguish their way out of the meshes of RICO. Congress has refused to legislate them out and, absent such a signal, the courts have refused to exempt businesses when what they have done squares with conduct proscribed under RICO.

Guidelines recommended by the U.S. Sentencing Commission to apply to organizations were adopted in November 1991. They provide fiercely higher fine levels for corporate offenders and also authorize the use of adverse publicity, paid for by the offender, as part of the arsenal of sanctioning weapons. The guidelines also allow the courts to intrude directly into the management of an offending organization. Probation terms can mandate corrective internal measures by a corporation and provide for the external monitoring of such measures for up to five years. A corporation also can be required to provide regular financial reports to the courts and to submit to unannounced audits of its books and interrogation of officers involved in activities of interest to the probation officer. The corporation on probation also could be ordered to secure a judge's approval to pay dividends, obtain new financing, or enter into a merger with another corporation.[10]

The four articles in this section address various aspects of the enforcement and sentencing procedures directed toward white-collar crime. The Ford Pinto case, detailed by Francis Cullen, William Maakestad, and Gray Cavender in the first reading, was the first major prosecution of a national corporation for homicide. Victoria Swigert and Ronald Farrell have pointed out that focusing on the actual burn victims rather than the more nebulous social harm, enabled the prosecution to secure a grand jury indictment.[11]

Ford executives knew that their product was dangerous because the gas tank was likely to explode on impact, but they elected to market the product and risk losing some civil suits that they estimated would cost them less than a major recall and repair campaign. The homicide case probably was filed because Indiana law permitted recovery for damages for minors only until they came of age; therefore, the amounts that the victims' survivors could have gained civilly was very limited. The case against Ford was lost for a number of reasons. For one thing, the company brought to bear an impressive array of legal talent for its defense. For another, the case itself was not strong. The victims may have contributed to their fate by having left their gas cap at a service station when last they filled the tank. The jury also undoubtedly was impressed by upper-echelon Ford executives who had purchased Pintos for their children, an indication that they had confidence in the vehicle's safety.

Pharmaceutical companies, John Braithwaite's extensive field research indicates, often falsify drug tests in order to hustle their product onto the market, sometimes with dire results. Braithwaite visits the headquarters of organizations that he studies, rather than relying on material such as Congressional and media reports; at one corporate interview, he learned that the company he was visiting jokingly referred to an executive as "the vice president in charge of going to jail"—or, put another way, the person who would protect the chief executive officer from having criminal knowledge of lawbreaking.

Braithwaite has conducted pathbreaking research on transnational white-collar crime. In the pharmaceutical industry, he found that some companies dump products that cannot meet domestic standards onto third-world nations. On the other side, he learned that third-world markets sometimes gain because pharmaceutical companies will sell them a product on which considerable sums have been spent to meet the toughest safety requirement to be found anywhere in the world. They do so, he found, both for moral reasons and because they believe that sooner or later the sites with inadequate standards will elevate them.

Michael L. Benson uses interviews with 30 convicted white-collar offenders to assess their response to their situation. He found that, in addition to shame and embarrassment, they felt anger and rage, and in the article seeks to assess the implications of these feelings as they bear on the utility of the punishment process.

The article by John Hagan and Patricia Parker is part of a series of pioneering research contributions by different writers addressing the question of whether white-collar offenders are sentenced with greater leniency than other criminals appearing in the court. Studies by Hagan, Ilene Nagel, and Celesta Albonetti[12] and by Stanton Wheeler, David Weisburd, and Nancy Bode[13] both reported that white-collar offenders received more severe sentences than those with lesser standing or charged with other kinds of offenses. Critics suggested that the broad definition of who constituted white-collar offenders was in part responsible for these conclusions. Subsequently, Michael Benson and Esteban Walker found a contrary result, using essentially the same definition, and suggested that either the passage of time or the different courts that they studied may have been an important distinguishing factor.[14] Thereafter, Robert Tillman and Henry Pontell's research on persons convicted of Medicaid violations supported the intuitive view that the higher the offenders' status the more likely they were to receive a better deal from the courts.[15] The Hagan and Parker work, employing a research design that addresses many of the earlier objections, also concludes that those with occupational clout receive lighter punishment than those without such power.

Notes

1. "Celebrity Inmates Get Homey Comforts for the Holidays," *Orange County (CA) Register,* December 26, 1992, p. A22.
2. Gilbert Geis, "Criminal Penalties for Corporate Criminals," *Criminal Law Bulletin,* 8 (1972): 279.
3. Oliver North, *Taking the Stand.* New York: Bantam Books, 1987, p. 207.
4. *Ibid.,* p. 337.
5. Sally S. Simpson, "Corporate-Crime Deterrence and Corporate-Control Policies: Views from the Inside." In Kip Schlegel and David Weisburd, eds., *White-Collar Crime Reconsidered.* Boston: Northeastern University Press, 1992, pp. 289–305.
6. Reynolds Metal v. Lampert, 324 F.2d 465, 466 (9th Cir. 1963).
7. Eva M. Fromm, "Commanding Respect: Criminal Sanctions for Environmental Crimes," *St. Mary's Law Journal,* 21 (1990): 822.
8. Amitai Etzioni, "The U.S. Sentencing Commission on Corporate Crime: A Critique," *Annals of the American Academy of Political and Social Science,* 525 (1993):147–156.
9. Marshall B. Clinard and Peter C. Yeager, *Corporate Crime.* New York: The Free Press, 1980.

10. William S. Lofquist, "Organizational Probation and the U.S. Sentencing Commission," *Annals of the American Academy of Political and Social Science,* 525 (1993):157–169.

11. Victoria Lynn Swigert and Ronald A. Farrell, "Corporate Homicide: Definitional Processes in the Creation of Deviance," *Law and Society Review,* 15 (1980–1981):161-182.

12. John Hagan, Ilene Nagel, and Celesta Albonetti, "The Differential Sentencing of White-Collar Offenders in Ten Federal District Courts," *American Sociological Review,* 45 (1980):802–820.

13. Stanton Wheeler, David Weisburd, and Nancy Bode, "Sentencing the White-Collar Offender: Rhetoric and Reality," *American Sociological Review,* 47 (1982):641–659.

14. Michael Benson and Esteban Walker, "Sentencing the White-Collar Offender," *American Sociological Review,* 53 (1988):294–302.

15. Robert Tillman and Henry Pontell, "Is Justice 'Collar-Blind?' Punishing Medicaid Provider Fraud," *Criminology,* 30 (1992):401–428.

15

The Ford Pinto Case and Beyond
Moral Boundaries and the Criminal Sanction

Francis T. Cullen, William J. Maakestad, and Gray Cavender

In 1968 the President's Commission on Law Enforcement and Administration of Justice concluded that "the public tends to be indifferent to business crime or even to sympathize with the offenders who have been caught."[1] Now some might question the accuracy of the commission's assessment; indeed, it appears that the public has never been quite so sanguine about white-collar crime as governmental officials and academicians have led us to believe.[2] Nevertheless, it would be too much to assert that the commission's evaluation of the views of the American citizenry was fully without empirical referent. For if the commission underestimated the willingness of the public to punish criminals of any sort, it was perhaps more correct in sensing that citizens had yet to define white-collar and corporate criminality as anything approaching a social problem.

By contrast, few social commentators today would seek to sustain the notion that the public considers upperworld illegality as "morally neutral conduct."[3] To be sure, there are now and undoubtedly will continue to be calls for citizens both to sharpen their awareness of the dangers posed by the lawlessness of the rich and to demand that the state take steps to shield them from this victimization. Nonetheless, public awareness of white-collar and corporate crime has reached the point where the concept has become part of the common vernacular. Further, survey data indicate that the public judges such criminality to be more serious than ever before, is quite prepared to sanction white-collar offenders, and is far more cognizant of the costs of upperworld crime than had been previously imagined.[4]

In light of the events of the past decade and a half, the finding that upperworld crime has emerged as an increasingly salient social issue is not surprising. Indeed, during this time we have witnessed what Katz[5] has termed "the social movement against white collar crime."[6] Thus, with Watergate and Abscam representing the

Reprinted from Ellen Hochstedler, ed., *Corporations as Criminals.* Beverly Hills: Sage, 1984, pp. 107–130.

more celebrated examples, prosecutions for political corruption have climbed markedly.[7] Similarly, consumer groups have scrutinized corporate activities and asked what officials planned to do in order to put a halt to "crime in the suites."[8] Meanwhile, investigative news reporters and news shows such as "60 Minutes" have told us much about improprieties ranging from kickbacks to the illegal dumping of chemical wastes that endanger lives.[9] Mistrust has run so deep that physicians are now suspected of fraudulent Medicaid schemes, and hence states have moved to establish enforcement agencies to combat this possibility.[10] In 1977 the notion that white-collar crime is a serious problem received further reification when U.S. Attorney General Griffin Bell remarked that he would make such illegality his "number 1 priority."

It is clear, then, that consciousness about upperworld lawlessness rose, perhaps substantially, since the President's Commission on Law Enforcement and Administration of Justice characterized public opinion about such matters as essentially disinterested.[11] However, it is equally important to be sensitive to the particular content that this consciousness came to assume. On the one hand the social movement Katz speaks of alerted people to the enormous costs incurred by white-collar crime.[12] Yet it did much more than this: It provided the additional message that the rich and powerful could exact these harms with impunity. Consequently, questions of justice and moral right were immediately suggested. The matter was thus not merely one of preventing victimization but of confronting why crime allows "the rich to get richer and the poor to get prison."[13] As Katz has observed:

> The demand supporting the movement to date has been much more than a utilitarian concern for the efficient deterrence of antisocial conduct. . . . In order to understand the expansion of "white collar crime," we must understand the demand that unjust enrichment and unjustly acquired power be made criminal; not just that it be made unprofitable but that it be defined officially as abominable, that it be treated as qualitatively alien to the basic moral character of society.[14]

In short, a core element of the movement against white-collar crime was to assert that the harms committed by the more and less advantaged be subject to the same moral mandates, particularly within our courts. Of course the very attempt to reshape moral boundaries is itself a manifestation of broader changes in the social context of any historical era.[15] While a complicated matter, two circumstances would appear to have done much to encourage and structure the nature of the attack on upperworld criminality that has emerged in recent times.

First, the unfolding of the civil rights movement focused attention on the intimate link between social and criminal justice. Pernicious patterns of racism and class discrimination were thus seen to be reproduced within the legal system. In turn it became incumbent upon political elites to explain why such inequities were allowed to prevail in our courts. Significantly, a second circumstance made answering this charge of perpetuating injustice an essential task for those in government: the "legitimacy crisis" facing the state.[16] Indeed such poignant happenings as Attica, Kent State, Vietnam, and Watergate, as well as the failure of the "Great Society" programs to fulfill promises of greater distributive justice, all combined to shake people's trust in the benevolence of the government.[17] In response, elected officials (like Jimmy Carter) felt compelled to campaign on their integrity and to claim that they would not show favor to criminals of any class. That is, political elites, under the press of the call for "equal justice," were placed in the position of having to publicly support the notion that the harms of the rich be brought within the reach of the criminal law. And as Piven and Cloward have demonstrated, when necessity moves political elites to define existing arrangements as unfair, the possibility of a social movement to refashion the social order is greatly enhanced.[18] It would thus appear that, at least in part, elite definitions lent legitimacy and helped give life to the movement against white-collar crime.

Now in this social climate the behavior of corporations took on new meaning. The world of big business was seen to suffer, in Durkheim's terms, from "chronic anomie," a breakdown of any sense of ethical regulation.[19] It was thus common to encounter articles which first asked, "How lawless are big companies?" and then answered that "a surprising number of them have been involved in blatant illegalities."[20] What is more, these infringements of existing legal and administrative standards not only involved enormous and ostensibly intentional harm, but also were seen to be greeted only rarely with the full force of the criminal law. Corporate actors were thus depicted as readily sacrificing human well-being for unjustly acquired profits with little worry over paying any real price; meanwhile those who had the misfortune of stealing lesser amounts through more customary means could anticipate no immunity from state sanction.

Notably, such imagery helped to precipitate not only public discussion and popular accounts about corporate malfeasance,[21] but a proliferation of scholarship on the topic as well.[22] Typically these academic writings followed a pattern of initially identifying the large costs of corporate illegality and lamenting the failure of existing enforcement strategies to diminish this pressing problem. The commentary would then turn to a consideration of whether such activity should be brought under the umbrella of the criminal law. In particular, two issues were debated: (1) Should corporations and their executives be held responsible for unlawful acts just as street criminals are? (2) Will efforts to use criminal sanctions really result in a reduction of corporate illegality?

These latter concerns as well as those discussed previously furnish a context for understanding both the very occurrence and importance of Ford Motor Company's prosecution for reckless homicide by the State of Indiana. It appears that the Ford Pinto case was very much a child of the times; succinctly stated, it is doubtful that Ford would have been brought to trial during a previous era. Yet if the case is best seen as a manifestation of the broad movement against white-collar crime—and, in particular, against corporate crime—it is also unique in the legal precedent it set, the publicity it received, and in the opportunity it provides to examine how more theoretical insights on corporate responsibility and control are shaped by the realities of the courtroom.

With these issues in mind the current endeavor attempts to present a case study of Ford's prosecution. To be more exact, four matters are discussed below: Why was an indictment brought against Ford in Indiana? Why did the courts permit a corporation itself to be tried for a criminal offense? What transpired at the trial? And what will be the meaning of the case in the time ahead?

ASSESSING BLAME

On August 10, 1978, Judy and Lyn Ulrich and their cousin visiting from Illinois, Donna Ulrich, set out to play volleyball at a church some twenty miles away. While on U.S. Highway 33 in northern Indiana, the yellow 1973 Pinto they were driving was struck in the rear by a van. Within seconds their car was engulfed in flames. Two of the teenagers, trapped inside the vehicle, died quickly; the driver, Judy, was thrown clear of the blazing Pinto with third-degree burns on more than 95 percent of her body. Though conscious following the accident, she died at a hospital eight hours later.[23]

As might be anticipated, the accident stunned those who witnessed the aftermath of the crash and soon sent shock waves throughout the local community of Elkhart. Yet like many other fatal collisions, this might have been defined exclusively as a tragedy. Or, if wrongdoing was involved, law enforcement officials might have prosecuted the driver of the van. Indeed, as a 21-year-old who had just recently reacquired a suspended license and who was driving a van which was labeled "Peace Train" and contained half-empty beer bottles as well as the remains of marijuana cigarettes scattered on the floor, he would have made a likely candidate to take the rap.

However, both the particulars of the accident and the tenor of the times led the blame to be placed elsewhere. In particular the observations of State Trooper Neil Graves were crucial in determining that this was not a "normal crime."[24] After arriving at the scene of the crash, Graves discovered that gasoline had somehow soaked the front floorboard of the car. He found as well that the van had sustained only minor damage, and its driver, Richard Duggar, was only mildly injured. By contrast, the Ulrichs' Pinto was viciously crushed in the rear and, of course, badly charred. This oddity was made even more poignant when eyewitnesses reported that the van was not speeding and that it looked initially like the accident was going to be nothing more than a fender-bender.[25]

These inconsistencies might have been set aside had it not been that Trooper Graves recalled reading an exposé about Pinto some months before. This piece, written by Mark Dowie and entitled "Pinto Madness," alleged that the placement of the gas tank on the Pinto constituted a lethal hazard. Specifically, Dowie noted that the location of the tank adjacent to the rear bumper made it highly susceptible to puncture by the fender's bolts during a rear-end collision. In turn this meant that the Pinto would experience considerable fuel leakage and hence fires when hit even at low speeds.[26]

Yet this is not all that Dowie claimed. Far more controversial was his assertion that Ford was fully aware of this problem in the initial stages of production but chose not to fix the Pinto's defect because it was not cost efficient. To bolster this conclusion, he presented secret Ford memoranda which revealed that the financial loss of a recall exceeded the loss incurred as the result of injuries and fatalities "associated with crash-induced fuel leakage and fires." In the name of profit, Dowie believed, "for seven years the Ford Motor Company sold cars in which it knew hundreds of people would needlessly burn to death."

Sensitized to the potential dangers of the Pinto, Graves was thus aware that the blame for the accident might rest with Ford. This sentiment was reinforced when he began to receive calls from news reporters around the country inquiring about the crash and the possibility that the fuel tank defect may have been responsible for the deaths of the three teenagers. Meanwhile, Michael A. Cosentino, Elkhart County's State's Attorney, was apprised of the accident. When he had an opportunity to review photographs of the crash, he too was troubled by the discrepancy between the minimal damage to the van and the wreckage of the Ulrich girls' Pinto. And then there was the emotional, human side to the incident: the pictures of the charred remains of the victims and the reality that three teenagers had suffered a terrible death.[27]

As a 41-year-old conservative Republican county prosecutor, Cosentino was an unlikely candidate to try to bring Ford Motor Company within the reach of the criminal law. Like many people at this time, he had heard about the problems associated with the Pinto and about the recall of the car that Ford had begun earlier in the summer. However, he had not read Dowie's article, and he was not inclined to attack corporations because of an ideological persuasion that they constituted a menace to society. Indeed even now Cosentino is convinced that the civil law should be used to deal with "99 percent" of all cases involving alleged corporate misbehavior.[28]

Yet in light of the facts surrounding the accident and of conversations with Neil Graves (who by this time had called and talked with Mark Dowie), Cosentino could not easily put the matter aside. He was aware as well that Indiana's revised criminal code, which had become effective on October 11, 1977, less than a year before the accident, contained a provision for the offense of "reckless homicide." Section 35-42-1-5 of the Indiana Code thus read: "A person who recklessly kills another human being commits reckless homicide." Taken together, these considerations led Cosentino to wonder whether the Ford Motor Company could or should be criminally prosecuted. Because of the novelty of the case, the power of Ford, and the difficulty of piercing the corporate veil, Cosentino did not seriously consider prosecuting individual Ford executives.[29]

Cosentino, however, did not want to act precipitously. Therefore, he set out to explore whether Ford could in fact be prosecuted under Indiana law. Since Section 35-41-1-2 of the penal code included "corporation" under its definition of "person," his staff reported that a prosecution was legally permissible. This conclusion was corroborated by William Conour of the Indiana Prosecuting Attorney's Office, who had been involved in drafting the reckless homicide statute.[30]

But even though the potential for prosecution seemed to exist, the question remained whether Ford really should be charged with a criminal offense. Research conducted by Cosentino and his staff suggested that it should be. Particularly influential were the conversations with and documents supplied by those involved in civil judgments against Ford. The prosecutor was in contact, for example, with automobile experts who had testified against Ford in civil hearings and with Mark Robinson, who was the lawyer in the Alan Grimshaw case.[31] As the evidence from these varied sources who had been close to the Pinto scene accumulated, it became clear that Ford knew that its Pinto was defective and chose to risk human life by not moving quickly to fix it. Thoughts of criminal culpability did not seem out of place in this context.[32]

It is important to note here that, without the mounting attention concerning Ford's handling of the Pinto, it would have been unlikely that Cosentino would have come to blame Ford for the deaths of the three teenagers. Had the accident occurred several years before, he might have been forced, perhaps reluctantly, to put aside the peculiarities of the crash and move on to other cases. Yet now the social climate worked against this option and, alternatively, made a criminal prosecution seem plausible, if not obligatory. By August of 1978 the attack against Ford and its Pinto had emerged as a "symbolic crusade,"[33] a movement aimed at showing that Ford, like other powerful corporations, felt comfortable in operating outside accepted moral boundaries in its irresponsible pursuit of profit. Ford's handling of the Pinto thus came to symbolize what was wrong with corporate America.

In general terms Dowie's "Pinto Madness" article, its release trumpeted at a press conference sponsored by Ralph Nader, signaled the beginning of the "crusade" against Ford.[34] With concern over corporate crime running high, Dowie's article earned national exposure. In February of 1978 the movement intensified still further with the announcement of the exorbitant financial damages awarded in the Grimshaw civil case. At the same time the National Highway Traffic Safety Administration (NHTSA), a federal regulatory body, had undertaken tests on the Pinto. In May of 1978 NHTSA notified Ford that there had been "an initial determination of the existence of a safety-related defect."[35] Denying any wrongdoing but faced with pressure on all sides, Ford subsequently issued a recall of all Pintos manufactured from 1971 to 1976 and all 1975 to 1976 Bobcats, a total of 1.5 million cars.[36] As might be expected, this series of events sparked a marked escalation in the focus placed by the media on Pinto issues.[37] Indeed, it was clear that reporters had come to view the Ford Pinto matter as a fascinating and eminently newsworthy upperworld scandal.

Thus it is significant that Mike Cosentino confronted the Ulrichs' tragic accident in the midst of a general crusade against Ford, for in several ways this necessarily shaped what the case could and did come to mean to him. First, unlike the traffic fatalities he had processed in the past, the numerous calls that his office and Neil Graves received from reporters across the nation alerted him, if only vaguely at the start, to the fact that any Pinto crash was potentially of national concern. Second, the movement against Ford, while certainly informal and unorganized, nevertheless created invaluable informational networks. This meant that in a matter of days Cosentino acquired revealing documents and expert feedback from parties who harbored strong sentiments against Ford. Under normal circumstances such material would have either been unavailable or taken months to uncover, a task beyond the resources of a county prosecutor. Third, the ideological framework of the Pinto crusade provided the conservative state's attorney with a vocabulary about the case that encouraged a response by the criminal law. As Swigert and Farrell have demonstrated, accounts of the Pinto appearing at this time increasingly characterized Ford as willfully and without repentance inflicting harm on innocent citizens. In a sense, then, Ford was being designated as a sociopath which knew no social responsibility.[38]

In short Cosentino quickly learned that the death of the Ulrich girls was not a local or isolated occurrence and that Ford, like the worst of criminals, endangered its victims not inadvertently but intentionally. He was aware as well that evidence existed that made a prosecution feasible. Taken together these considerations personally convinced Cosentino that Ford had acted recklessly and should be prosecuted. Again he did not wish to initiate a campaign calling for the use of criminal sanctions to deal with all corporate wrongdoing. However, it was manifest to him that Ford had been largely unaffected by traditional forms of control; after all, Ford's conduct surrounding the Pinto had already triggered nearly every legal response possible other than criminal prosecution: civil cases involving compensatory damages, civil cases involving both compensatory and punitive damages, and federal administrative agency actions. In the absence of effective regulation and where corporate behavior is so outrageous as to affront moral sensibilities, Cosentino could see the application of the criminal law as appropriate. And from what he knew of the Pinto case, it seemed that this was just such an instance, where justice demanded that a corporation be held criminally responsible for its behavior.[39]

However, the very novelty of this idea caused Cosentino to exercise caution. While he believed that Ford should be indicted and that he possessed the authority to do so, he was not certain that the community would support such a prosecution. Consequently, he convened a grand jury to consider an indictment under the reckless homicide statute. From the beginning of the hearing, Cosentino consciously made every effort not to sway the grand jury one way or the other.[40] Nevertheless, after entertaining testimony from both Ford officials and safety experts who had previously served as witnesses in civil cases against Ford, the grand jury unanimously returned indictments against Ford Motor Company for three counts of reckless homicide. In essence the six-member panel agreed with Cosentino that there was sufficient evidence to believe that Ford had acted with moral irresponsibility. Swigert and Farrell captured this point when they wrote:

The indictment against Ford may be viewed as an attempt on the part of the state to assert moral integrity in the face of enemy deviation. In its decision to contest civil suits, the corporation refused to recognize that moral boundaries had been transgressed. This opened the way to a definition of the manufacturer as a force against whom the power of the law must be directed.[41]

GETTING TO TRIAL

Word of Ford's indictment immediately received front-page attention in newspapers across the nation. It now appeared that Ford Motor Company, at that moment the fourth-largest corporation in the world,[42] would go to trial for reckless homicide. While a guilty verdict would bring only a $30,000 fine ($10,000 on each count), company officials viewed the prospect of a trial with considerable consternation. With Pinto sales already down 40 percent due to the recent recall, a lengthy, highly publicized criminal case could only serve to erode still further consumer confidence in the car and, more generally, in the corporation. Equally troubling was that a prosecution could encourage State's Attorneys elsewhere to bring criminal charges against the company and alert other Pinto victims (or surviving families) to the fact that Ford should be held civilly liable for burn injuries occurring in rear-end collisions.[43] Moreover, executives realized that a criminal conviction would be powerful evidence of Ford's culpability in any subsequent civil suits. With the potential costs of a prosecution running high, Ford thus quickly mobilized to see that the case would never come before a jury.

The task of preventing a trial was given to the prestigious Chicago law firm of Mayer, Brown, and Platt. With a ten-member team assigned to the case, the result of the firm's efforts was a 55-page motion which argued that the criminal indictment should be dismissed on both conceptual and constitutional grounds. In fashioning a response to this attack, Cosentino and his small staff realized that they could well benefit from additional assistance. However, all such help would have to come from volunteers. Cosentino had asked Elkhart County for a special fund of $20,000 to try the case, and he had promised not to request any additional moneys. This figure would have to be stretched far in the fight against Ford; in fact, Cosentino would eventually spend money of his own to defray expenses.[44] Yet given the prevailing social context, finding law professors to join the prosecution's team did not prove overly difficult. After all, corporate liability and the criminal law was a "hot topic," and the Pinto case obviously possessed both important national and legal ramifications. Again, whether a local prosecutor could have so readily acquired such expert assistance in a previous decade or on a different case is questionable. Bruce Berner, one of the two law professors who worked full time on the case, wrote that "originally, of course, I got involved because of the novel legal questions presented by the indictment." However, it should also be realized that, after agreeing to become part of the prosecution's staff, the appeal of legal novelties was not all that sustained the commitment of volunteers to the case. There was also and always the reality of the horrible deaths of the Ulrich girls. In Berner's words:

It was only after I became involved that I saw the photographs [of the girls following the crash] and met the families of the girls. It is nevertheless hard for me to separate the motivating force of the legal issues from that of the personal aspect of the tragedy. . . . Part of what we were saying is that a corporation like all other persons must be forced at all times to look at the very personal tragedies it causes. It seems to me that Ford's whole effort in keeping the pictures of the girls out of evidence, including the pictures of them while they were alive, was in part a way to disconnect themselves from what they had wrought to some very nice people. All I can say about the "Car Wars" photos was that they made me ill and that I cannot, to this day, get them out of my head.[45]

While numerous arguments were voiced in the debate over whether Ford could be brought to trial, the continued vitality of the indictment hinged on two central issues.[46] To begin with, Ford's legal brief contended that conceptually the reckless homicide statute could not be applied to corporate entities. For one thing the statute defines the offense as "a person who recklessly kills another human being." Ford claimed in turn that the meaning of "another" was "one of the same kind." Consequently, since the victim is referred to as "another human being," it followed that the perpetrator of the crime must also be human.[47] For another thing the brief asserted that the use of the word "person" in other places in the criminal code clearly is not meant to apply to corporations. Conceptual consistency thus would preclude corporations from being charged with violently oriented offenses like reckless homicide. Quoting Ford's memorandum:

There are numerous examples in the Criminal Code where the legislature has used the word "person" to refer exclusively to human beings. See, e.g., the section prohibiting rape. . . . ("A person who knowingly or intentionally has sexual intercourse with a member of the opposite sex. . . .") Thus, although corporations may generally be covered by the definition of "persons," there are clearly crimes—essentially crimes of violence against other human beings—where it is irrational to read the statutes as applying to corporations.

In response to this line of reasoning, the prosecution initially turned to the penal code itself. First, it observed that the code distinguishes between a "person" ("a human being, corporation, partnership, unincorporated association, or governmental entity") and a "human being" ("an individual who is born and alive"). Because the statute defines reckless homicide as a "person who recklessly kills another human being," rather than as a "human being who recklessly kills another human being," it is evident that the legislative intent here is to encompass corporate behavior. Second, the prosecution noted that the Indiana criminal code explicitly reads that a corporation "may be prosecuted for any offense . . . if it is proved that the offense was committed by its agent within the scope of his authority." Finally, the state's brief dismissed the idea that "corporations" cannot physically commit violent crimes like rape and homicide by emphasizing the realities of the corporation as a legal fiction:

> The major premise that "person" cannot include corporation in the rape statute is simply incorrect. This argument patently exploits the corporate fiction. It attempts to show corporate inability to commit rape. . . . Of course. a corporation cannot itself engage in sexual intercourse; a corporation cannot itself do anything. As it is a fictional person, it can act only through its natural-person agents. A corporation has no genitals, to be sure, but neither does it have a trigger finger, a hand to forge a check, an arm to extend a bribe nor mind to form an intent or to "consciously disregard" the safety of others. Nevertheless, a corporation is liable for all crimes of its agents acting within their authority. The unlikelihood of corporate rape liability is because sexual intercourse by its agents will almost always be outside the scope of their authority—not because the crime is definitionally ridiculous.

Apart from conceptual considerations Ford maintained that there were two constitutional barriers to its being brought to trial. First, there was the matter that the National Traffic and Motor Vehicle Safety Act had already created a federal apparatus to supervise the automobile industry. Consequently, Ford argued, Congress intended that this system would preempt any state, including Indiana, from regulating the same field. In rebuttal, the prosecution argued that the federal measure was not invoked to deprive states of their police power, and they observed that Ford was unable to cite "a single case where a traditional, general criminal statute was found to have been preempted by a federal regulatory scheme."

Yet there was a second, more serious constitutional matter raised by Ford's lawyers: the ex post facto provision of both the Indiana and U.S. Constitutions. As may be recalled, the revised Indiana code which contained the new reckless homicide crime category became law only on October 1, 1977. Moreover, it was not until July 1, 1978—41 days prior to the Ulrichs' crash—that the reckless homicide offense was amended to include acts of omission as well as commission. Significantly, it is the amended version of the statute which was employed to indict Ford. In light of these two dates, Ford reminded the court that it was being charged with recklessly designing and manufacturing a car that was a 1973 model. It was thus being prosecuted for an act that had transpired several years before enactment of the very law under which it was being charged. Even if its acts were reckless, such ex post facto application of the law constitutionally barred prosecution.

The prosecution assaulted Ford's logic on two fronts. First, issue was taken with Ford's interpretation of when its offense occurred. Contrary to Ford's assertions, the prosecution argued that it is the date the offense is completed, not the date of the first element of the crime, that determines whether ex post facto provisions have been violated. Thus, since the accident postdated the reckless homicide law, the company was potentially subject to criminal sanction. Second, the prosecution maintained that the defendant's omissions in regard to its obligation to either repair the Ulrichs' 1973 Pinto or warn them of the car's hazards were important elements of the offense. That is, Ford was being charged with reckless homicide not only for an act of commission (building a dangerous vehicle), but for an act of omission (ignoring its duty to protect owners from the Pinto's known dangers). The prosecution then went on to propose that once either proscribed acts or omissions are shown to have taken place after a criminal statute is enacted, all of the defendant's prior acts and omissions can properly and constitutionally be considered by the court.

On February 2, 1979, Judge Donald W. Jones succinctly rendered his decision: "There are substantial factors in this case for which there are no precedents. The indictment is sufficient. I therefore deny the motion to dismiss."[48] In large part Judge Jones embraced the prosecution's reasoning, agreeing that Indiana law does permit a corporation to be charged for reckless homicide and that federal regulatory statutes did not in this instance preempt the state's rights to seek retributive and deterrent goals unique to the criminal sanction. However, he was only partially persuaded by the prosecution's thoughts on the ex post facto aspects of the case, and thus he attempted to clarify exactly what Ford could and could not be tried under.

In essence Jones's ruling declared that since the vehicle was marketed in 1973, Ford could not be charged for recklessly designing and manufacturing the Pinto. Instead, its actions with regard to the actual production of the Pinto were relevant only to the extent that they constituted antecedents for Ford's alleged recklessness in repairing the vehicle. Alternatively, Ford could be charged with failure to fulfill its obligation to repair, because such recklessness could potentially have occurred in the 41 days between the enactment of the omission amendment to the reckless homicide statute on July 1 and the Ulrich girls' deaths on August 10.

The problems surrounding the ex post facto issue clearly complicated the prosecution's case. At least in theory it would no longer be sufficient to convince the jury that Ford had recklessly assembled the Pinto. To be sure, this much would have to be proven in order to show that Ford knew its product was unsafe and thus had a duty to warn its customers, including the Ulrichs, of this fact. However, Ford could now only be convicted if it could also be revealed that the company had recklessly ignored its duty to inform the Ulrichs of the Pinto's dangers in the period following July 1.

In sum, with the help of law professors and other volunteers, Cosentino had succeeded in getting Ford to trial. However, the legal constraints on his case, the realities of the courtroom, and the resources at his opponent's disposal would make getting a conviction another matter.

TRYING FORD

Ford's failure to quash the indictment taught the company that their foes were perhaps more formidable than initially imagined. It was now manifest that nothing could be spared in order to avert the shame of a criminal stigmatization. In particular

Ford's lawyers would be given a blank check; they would be free to craft the best defense money could buy.

For Ford two orders of business were immediately at hand. First, there was the crucial matter of whom to select to head the defense team. The choice proved to be a wise, if expensive, one: James J. Neal, a former special prosecutor during Watergate.[49] The second pressing concern was to move Cosentino off his home turf by securing a change of venue. Based on evidence gathered from a survey of Elkhart residents about the case (commissioned by Ford) and the testimony of $1000-a-day consultant Hans Zeisel (co-author with Harry Kalven of *The American Jury*), Ford argued that it could not receive a fair trial in Elkhart. Judge Jones agreed, and the case was moved to Winamac, a town of 2450 located in Pulaski County some 55 miles southwest. Sixty-year-old Judge Harold Staffeldt would preside over the trial.[50]

The move to Winamac and the additional living expenses this entailed further strained the prosecution's budget; Cosentino himself would shoulder much of this new burden. However, as would become evident throughout the trial, there appeared to be no limit to the resources that Ford was able and willing to devote to its defense. The cost of the survey employed to justify the change of venue itself approximated the entire Cosentino budget. Other facts are equally revealing. For instance, after the place of the trial became known Ford quickly made an attractive offer to and succeeded in retaining a local Winamac lawyer who was a close friend of Judge Staffeldt and who had practiced with the judge for 22 years. Similarly, the bill for housing the Ford defense team, which at times reached 40, ran to $27,000 a month. Later they would undertake additional crash tests on Pintos at a cost of around $80,000. Importantly, they were also able to purchase daily transcripts of the trial at $9 a page, with the total expenditure for the trial transcripts being $50,000.[51] Since the complexity and length of the trial meant that a private firm supplied the court stenographers and thus that the transcripts were not available free to the prosecution, budgetary constraints precluded Cosentino from having access to this material. In his opinion the inability to review previous testimony (e.g., to prepare for cross-examination) was one of the largest disadvantages plaguing the prosecution.[52] In the end it is estimated that Ford may have spent anywhere from $1.5 million to $2 million on its defense.

In launching its case, the prosecution wanted to impress upon the members of the jury that they were not merely dealing with statistical casualties; like other homicide cases, they were being asked to assess whether Ford should be held responsible for the horrible burn deaths of three vibrant teenagers. James Neal, however, fully realized that it would be important to neutralize this emotional factor. In a skillful maneuver he thus submitted a document which first admitted that the Ulrich girls had died as a result of burns and then declared that there was no need for the jury to see the grotesque pictures of or hear testimony about the girls' charred bodies. The prosecution countered that Neal was endeavoring to "sanitize" the girls' deaths and that it is common practice to present evidence on cause of death in a homicide trial. Somewhat amazingly, Judge Staffeldt agreed with Neal and prevented the jury from seeing or hearing about what the reality of the crash entailed. Stymied on this front, the emotional advantage of the prosecution was largely confined to the remarks of the victims' mother, Mrs. Mattie Ulrich, who told the court that she would have gotten rid of the Pinto had she known of its dangers. She then remarked that she had in fact received notice of the Pinto recall; however, it came to her house in February of 1979, several months after the crash in which her two daughters and niece had perished.[53]

Despite this setback the prosecution remained optimistic. After all, the foundation of its case was not erected upon the angle of playing on the jurors' sympathies. Instead, Cosentino felt that he had sufficient evidence to prove that Ford knew early on that the Pinto had a defective fuel tank placement. This material included internal Ford memos and documents commenting on the Pinto's safety as well as the results of crash tests on 1971 and 1972 models, conducted by Ford and the government, showing that the vehicle exploded in flames at low impact speeds. These tests would be crucial, Cosentino reasoned, because they revealed that in planning the production of the 1973 Pinto, Ford had concrete evidence of the car's defects, yet chose not to rectify them. Moreover, Cosentino did not have crash tests at low speeds for the 1973 model, and his tight budget precluded his conducting them at this stage.

Recognizing the damaging nature of this evidence, Neal moved quickly to challenge the admission of any testimony or tests that were not directly related to the 1973 Pinto, the model year of the Ulrichs' car. In a series of rulings over the course of the trial, Judge Staffeldt concurred with Neal and barred nearly all materials that predated 1973. Needless to say, this had the result of seriously undermining the state's case. In the end, only a small percentage, perhaps as low as 5 percent, of the documents the prosecution had compiled were admitted as evidence.[54]

The judge's reluctance to permit the jury to consider the totality of the prosecution's case points up the difficulty of transporting what has traditionally been a product liability case from civil into criminal court. To a large extent it appears that the rural judge was never fully comfortable in knowing how this was to be done. Indeed his grabbing onto 1973 as his evidentiary standard reveals that he either did not fully comprehend the logic of the prosecution's case or did not embrace the legal theory on which it was based. It seems that he wished to treat the 1973 Pinto as he would any other weapon in a homicide case: Since it was this weapon that caused the crime, evidence on other weapons was irrelevant. Of course at the heart of the prosecution's case was the understanding that Ford's recklessness with regard to the 1973 Pinto was intimately contingent on what the corporation had done in its product development of the car line in the previous years. Whether rightly or wrongly, Judge Staffeldt failed to appreciate this distinction between the recklessness of corporate decision making and that involved in more traditional forms of criminality.

Now with much of its case set aside, the prosecution presented two major lines of argument to the jury. First, it called in auto safety experts, including a former Ford executive who testified that the fuel tank on the Pinto was placed in a potentially lethal position. Second, Cosentino relied upon eyewitnesses to prove that Duggar's van was traveling at 50 miles per hour or less, and that the Ulrichs' Pinto was still moving when hit from behind. Taken together, these facts indicated that the speed differential at the moment of impact was around 30. In turn, establishing this low differential was crucial to the prosecution's case because it explained both why so little damage was done to the van and why the girls died from their burns but not from injuries sustained in the crash, as would be expected in a high-velocity collision. Most importantly, however, it showed that the Pinto the girls were driving exploded despite being hit at a relatively low speed. The implication was thus clear: Because of Ford's reckless construction of the Pinto, three girls died in an accident that should have been little more than a fender-bender.

Having done much to diminish the force of the prosecution's case, James Neal began Ford's defense by vigorously rejecting the claim that the Pinto was an unsafe vehicle. For instance, Neal brought his own automotive experts before the jury to testify that the 1973 Pinto met prevailing federal automotive standards and was just as safe as comparable subcompacts manufactured at that time. He also produced Ford executives who testified that they had such faith in the car that they had purchased Pintos for members of their own families. Neal then challenged the prosecution's version of the speed differential between the van and the Ulrichs' Pinto. Crucial in this regard were the dramatic accounts of two surprise witnesses; both claimed that prior to her death in the hospital Judy Ulrich had said that her car was stopped on the highway. If so, the speed at impact would have been 50 miles per hour, a collision that no small car could have withstood. This reasoning was given added credence when Ford presented newly conducted crash tests which showed that at 50 miles per hour a van would sustain only minimal damage despite the large crushing effect it exerted on the rear of the Pinto. Neal thus concluded from this that the small front-end wreckage of Duggar's van was not evidence of a low-impact accident but rather was normal, even at speeds exceeding 50.[55]

The defense also took pains to remind the jurors that Ford itself had voluntarily agreed to recall the Pinto two months before the Ulrich accident and thus during all 41 days following the enactment of the omission amendment to the reckless homicide statute. Ford employees testified that during this period the company had pressured them to contact Pinto owners about the recall as quickly as possible. To accomplish this task, workers were given overtime pay, and airplanes were used to hurry recall kits across the nation. With 1.5 million customers it was not surprising, though of course terribly regrettable, that the Ulrichs' notification did not arrive until February 1979. Indeed, Ford had done everything feasible to warn Pinto owners: it certainly had not been reckless in this duty.[56]

After four days of exhausting deliberations, the jurors returned their verdict: not guilty. The initial vote was 8–4 to acquit. Twenty-five ballots later, the final holdout changed his mind and joined the majority. Some on the jury felt that the hazards of the Pinto were basically inherent in all small cars and that owners took certain risks when they chose a vehicle that was less costly and consequently less sturdy. A number of other jurors, however, were convinced that Ford had marketed a defective automobile, but that the prosecution simply had not proven that the corporation was reckless in its recall efforts during the 41 days in which it was criminally liable.[57] Regardless, the ten-week Ford Pinto trial was now over. As might be anticipated, there was much jubilation and relief at Ford headquarters in Dearborn, Michigan.[58] Meanwhile, Cosentino and his staff were left to contemplate the bitterness of an unsuccessful crusade and to wonder what might have occurred had a different judge presided over the case and the prosecution not been burdened by a tight budget and ex post facto considerations.

CONCLUSION: BEYOND THE FORD PINTO CASE

The Ford Pinto trial was regularly hailed in the media as "one of the most significant criminal court trials in American corporate history."[59] This notoriety clearly signifies the uniqueness of the case. While Ford's prosecution was not totally devoid of legal precedents,[60] it was certainly the most poignant example of a corporation being brought within the reach of the criminal law for allegedly visiting violence upon innocent citizens.[61] In this light it thus provided a rare and concrete glimpse of the power that corporations can bring to bear in order to avoid conviction. Similarly, it revealed that prosecution of corporations for offenses of a product liability type will necessarily involve legal theories with which participants in the criminal justice system are only vaguely familiar and perhaps find inappropriate for their arena. Indeed, from an ideological standpoint, the potential for irony here is pronounced: We can expect conservative jurists now to be inclined to look favorably on the rights of the defendant (the corporation), and their more liberal brethren to furnish a more generous interpretation of the prerogatives enjoyed by the state. Finally, the very fact of prosecution is notable not merely for its role in bolstering formal legal precedent but in breaking psychological barriers. The legal community is now sensitized to the possibility that companies that recklessly endanger the physical well-being of the public may, even by a local state's attorney, be held criminally responsible for their conduct.

Yet the special character of the Pinto case should not mask the realization that Ford's prosecution was very much a social product. As argued earlier, the more general crusade against the Pinto, itself a manifestation of a broader movement attacking corporate crime that sought to question the appropriate moral boundaries of corporate behavior, was integral in creating the opportunity for Cosentino to prosecute Ford. In turn this perspective suggests that the ultimate, long-range meaning of the Pinto trial may depend less on the legal precedent that has been set and more on the nature of the social context that comes to prevail. That is, will the time ahead sustain the movement against corporate crime and thus encourage attempts to build upon the Pinto prosecution, or will concern with upperworld illegality diminish and interest in criminally sanctioning corporations commensurately decline?

At present the answer to the question is by no means certain. To be sure, the Reagan Administration has moved to reinterpret the moral character of corporate America and to officially clarify what "real" crime is.[62] Thus Reagan's loosening of regulatory controls on business has been accompanied by a renewed concern over violent street crimes and the trafficking of drugs; meanwhile, white-collar and corporate criminality has been placed on the back burner.[63] Notably, like many of his other social policies, Reagan's crime control agenda is informed by his implicit view of human nature; the productive respond to incentives (opportunities for profit), while the unproductive respond to punishments, thus the need for harsh sanctions for the crimes of the poor.[64]

However, these policies and the sentiments that underlie them may very well have the unanticipated consequence of fueling the public's concern over upperworld lawlessness. The ostensible failure of the president's domestic programs to effect promised benefits for working people has made his administration susceptible to charges of injustice, an image that Democrats across the nation are constantly trying to make more salient. In this climate sensitivity to collusion between government and big business, as in the EPA incident involving the dumping of chemical wastes, should run high.[65] Corporate conduct should thus remain a matter of continuing public concern, and in turn it will be difficult for the state to retain legitimacy if it chooses to ignore flagrant affronts to existing moral boundaries. If this analysis is correct, we should see additional, if only intermittent, criminal prosecutions within the immediate future of corporations who persist in recklessly endangering the public's well-being.

Notes

1. President's Commission on Law Enforcement and Administration of Justice, *The Challenge of Crime in a Free Society.* New York: Avon, 1968, p. 84.
2. See John Braithwaite, "Challenging Just Deserts: Punishing White-Collar Criminals," *Journal of Criminal Law and Criminology,* 73 (1982):732–733.
3. Sanford Kadish, "Some Observations on the Use of Criminal Sanctions in Enforcing Economic Regulations," *University of Chicago Law Review,* 30 (1963):423–449.
4. Francis Cullen, Bruce Link, and Craig Polanzi, "The Seriousness of Crime Revisited: Have Attitudes toward White-Collar Crime Changed?" *Criminology,* 20 (1982):82–102; Francis Cullen, Richard Mathers, Gregory Clark, and John Cullen, "Public Support for Punishing White-Collar Crime: Blaming the Victim Revisited?" *Journal of Criminal Justice,* 11 (1983):481–493.
5. Jack Katz, "The Social Movement against White-Collar Crime." In Egon Bittner and Sheldon Messinger, eds., *Criminology Review Yearbook,* vol. 2. Beverly Hills: Sage, 1980, pp. 161–184.
6. See also Marshall Clinard and Peter Yeager, "Corporate Crime: Issues in Research," *Criminology,* 16 (1978):255–272. Clinard and Yeager, *Corporate Crime.* New York: The Free Press, 1980.

7. Katz, *op. cit.*, pp. 161–164.
8. Ralph Nader and Mark Green, "Crime in the Suites: Coddling the Corporations," *New Republic,* 166 (April 29, 1972), p. 18.
9. Michael Brown, *Laying Waste: The Poisoning of America by Toxic Chemicals.* New York: Pantheon, 1980.
10. See Henry Pontell, Paul Jesilow, and Gilbert Geis, "Policing Physicians: Practitioner Fraud and Abuse in a Government Medicaid Program," *Social Problems,* 30 (1982):115–125.
11. President's Commission, *op. cit.*
12. John Conklin, *"Illegal but Not Criminal": Business Crime in America.* Englewood Cliffs, NJ: Prentice-Hall, 1977; Laura S. Schrager and James F. Short, Jr., "Toward a Sociology of Organizational Crime," *Social Problems,* 25 (1978):407–419.
13. Jeffrey Reiman, *The Rich Get Richer and the Poor Get Prison.* New York: Wiley, 1979.
14. Katz, *op. cit.*, pp. 178–179.
15. Kai Erikson, *Wayward Puritan.* New York: Wiley, 1966; Joseph Gusfield, "Moral Passage: The Symbolic Process in Public Designations of Deviance," *Social Problems,* 15 (1967):175–188; Ronald Farrell and Victoria Swigert, *Deviance and Social Control.* Glenview, IL: Scott, Foresman, 1982.
16. David Friedrichs, "The Law and Legitimacy Crisis: A Critical Issue for Criminal Justice." In R. Iacovetta and Dae Chang, eds., *Critical Issues in Criminal Justice.* Durham, NC: Carolina Academic Press, 1979.
17. David Rothman, "The State as Parent: Social Policy in the Progressive Era." In Willard Gaylin, David Rothman, Steven Marcus, and Ira Glasser, *Doing Good: The Limits of Benevolence.* New York: Pantheon, 1978, pp. 67–96.
18. Frances Piven and Richard Cloward, *Regulating the Poor: The Functions of Public Welfare.* New York: Pantheon, 1971; Piven and Cloward, *Poor People's Movements: Why They Succeed, How They Fail.* New York: Pantheon, 1977.
19. Emile Durkheim, *Suicide.* New York: The Free Press, 1951.
20. Irwin Ross, "How Lawless Are Big Companies?" *Fortune,* 102 (December 1, 1980), pp. 56–64.
21. See e.g., Kermit Vandivier, "The Aircraft Brake Scandal," *Harper's Magazine,* 244 (April 1972):45–52; Gerald Stern, *The Buffalo Creek Disaster.* New York: Vintage, 1976; Harry Caudill, "Manslaughter in a Coal Mine," *Nation,* 224 (April 23, 1977):492–497; Mark Dowie, "The Corporate Crime of the Century," *Mother Jones* (November 1979):23–38, 49; J. Patrick Wright, *On a Clear Day You Can See General Motors: John Z. De Lorean's Look inside the Automotive Giant.* New York: Avon, 1979.
22. See e.g., Brent Fisse, "The Use of Publicity as a Criminal Sanction against Corporations," *Melbourne University Law Review,* 8(1971):107–150; Bruce Coleman, "Is Corporate Criminal Liability Really Necessary?" *Southwestern Law Journal,* 29 (1975):908–927; Christopher Stone, *Where the Law Ends: The Social Control of Corporate Behavior.* New York: Harper & Row, 1975;

James Elkins, "Corporations and the Criminal Law: An Uneasy Alliance," *Kentucky Law Journal,* 65 (1976):73–129.

23. Lee Strobel, *Reckless Homicide? Ford's Pinto Trial.* South Bend, IN: And Books, 1980.

24. David Sudnow, "Normal Crimes: Sociological Features of the Penal Code in a Public Defender's Office," *Social Problems,* 12 (1965) :255–276.

25. Strobel, *op. cit.*

26. Mark Dowie, "Pinto Madness," *Mother Jones* (September–October 1977): 18–32.

27. Strobel, *op. cit.*; Michael Cosentino, telephone interview, February 1983.

28. Cosentino, *ibid.*

29. *Ibid.*

30. Strobel, *op. cit.*

31. In this latter instance, Grimshaw, who had undergone over 50 operations to correct burn injuries suffered during a Pinto crash-turned-inferno, was awarded $2.8 million in compensatory damages and $125 million in punitive damages. The award was reduced to a total of $6.6 million two weeks after the trial.

32. William Maakestad, "State v. Ford Motor Co.: Constitutional, Utilitarian, and Moral Perspectives on the State of Indiana v. Ford Motor Company," *Saint Louis University Law Journal,* 27 (1983):857–880.

33. Gusfield, *op. cit.*

34. Dowie, *op. cit.*

35. Strobel, *op. cit.*, p. 23.

36. *Ibid.*

37. Victoria Swigert and Ronald Farrell, "Corporate Homicide: Definitional Processes in the Creation of Deviance," *Law and Society Review,* 15 (1980–81):161–182.

38. *Ibid.*

39. Cosentino, *op. cit.*; Maakestad, *op. cit.*

40. Cosentino, *op. cit.*

41. Swigert and Farrell, *op. cit.*, p. 180.

42. Clinard and Yeager, *op. cit.*, p. 3.

43. Strobel, *op. cit.*

44. *Ibid.*

45. Bruce Berner, Letter to the Author, February 21, 1982.

46. William Maakestad, "A Historical Survey of Corporate Homicide in the United States: Could It Be Prosecuted in Illinois?" *Illinois Bar Journal,* 69 (1981):2–7.

47. Glenn Clark, "Corporate Homicide: A New Assault on Corporate Decision-making," *Notre Dame Lawyer,* 54 (1979):911–924.

48. Strobel, *op. cit.*, p. 55.

49. Neal's salary in other cases is reputed to have been as much as $800,000 (Strobel, *op. cit.*, p. 60).

50. *Ibid.*

51. *Ibid.*
52. Cosentino, *op. cit.*
53. Strobel, *op. cit.*
54. Douglas S. Anderson, "Corporate Homicide: The Stark Realities of Artificial Beings and Legal Fiction," *Pepperdine Law Review,* 8 (1981):370.
55. Strobel, *op. cit.*
56. *Ibid.*
57. *Ibid.*
58. "Three Cheers in Dearborn," *Time* (March 24, 1980), p. 24.
59. "Ford's Pinto: Not Guilty," *Newsweek,* 95 (March 24, 1980), p. 74.
60. Maakestad, *op. cit.*
61. Anderson, *op. cit.*
62. Reiman, *op. cit.*
63. Diana Gordon, *Doing Violence to the Crime Problem: A Response to the Attorney General's Task Force.* Hackensack, NJ: National Council on Crime and Delinquency, 1980; Francis Cullen and John Wozniak, "Fighting the Appeal of Repression," *Crime and Social Justice,* 18 (1982):23–33.
64. Frances Piven and Richard Cloward, *The New Class War: Reagan's Attack of the Welfare State and Its Consequences.* New York: Pantheon, 1982, p. 39.
65. "Superfund, Supermess," *Time* (February 21, 1983), pp. 14–16.

16

Transnational Regulation of the Pharmaceutical Industry

John Braithwaite

In 1984, I published a book on the serious and rather widespread nature of corporate crime in the international pharmaceutical industry.[1] Since that book was published, there has been some improvement in the social control brought to bear against some of the problems I identified. The nature of this progress will be discussed in the present article. The interesting thing is that there has been little progress with criminal enforcement, which remains exceedingly rare in all nations of the world in spite of the fact that serious criminal conduct seems more common in the pharmaceutical industry than in perhaps any industrial sector in the world economy.[2] Implications of this situation for a legal-pluralist approach to the control of international corporate crime will be discussed. First, however, the nature of the problem must be described.

THE PROBLEM

In *Corporate Crime in the Pharmaceutical Industry,* I concluded that bribery is probably a larger problem in the pharmaceutical industry than in almost any other industry.[3] Of the 20 largest American pharmaceutical companies, 19 had been embroiled in bribery problems during the decade before the publication of the book. There was evidence of almost every conceivable type of actor who could strategically affect the interests of pharmaceutical companies receiving bribes from them: health ministers, government price control officials, purchasers for government pharmaceutical benefits systems, tax officials, police, customs officers, hospital administrators, health inspectors, physicians—and so the list went on. Product-safety offenses such as the sale of impure, overstrength, out-of-date, or nonsterile products were also shown to be widespread.[4] Antitrust offenses kept some of the postwar wonder drugs financially out of the reach of most of the world's population

Reprinted from the *Annals of the American Academy of Political and Social Science,* 525 (January 1993):12–30.

for many years, causing countless lives to be lost needlessly.[5] Misrepresentations in printed advertising and by word of mouth by sales representatives were common offenses in the pharmaceutical industry, with particularly serious consequences.[6] The pharmaceutical industry also had its share of tax offenders and fraudsters who duped shareholders and creditors.[7] But the most serious corporate crimes in the pharmaceutical industry were, and still are, in the safety testing of drugs.

Cases were documented of rats and monkeys in drug trials developing terrible symptoms like tumors and blindness and being replaced by healthy animals.[8] Cases of reincarnated rats were documented—rats that died reappeared later in the data as living animals. There were also many cases involving physicians who were paid handsomely to do clinical trials on humans for new drugs. Some had terrible misfortunes on the eve of Food and Drug Administration (FDA) audits of the quality of the data they had collected in support of new drug applications. For example, Dr. James Scheiner of Fairfax, Virginia, who did experiments for Johnson and Johnson, had his office vandalized the night before an FDA audit—the mindless vandals dumping the records relating to the studies to be audited into a whirlpool bath. Dr. Francois Savery, who had earned a fortune testing drugs for Hoffman-La Roche and other leading companies, suffered the catastrophe of accidentally dropping his data overboard while out in a rowboat. Unfortunately, a U.S. court did not believe him; he was sentenced to five years' probation for felony fraud. Regrettably, however, safety-testing fraud remains a serious problem, with new allegations involving leading companies and leading researchers continuing to emerge repeatedly.

THE TRANSNATIONAL NATURE OF THE PROBLEM

The internationalized nature of corporate crime in the pharmaceutical industry makes criminal convictions difficult to obtain. The offenses we are discussing are complex to start with, before one adds the problem of international jurisdictional tangles. There is the complexity of the books—paper trails through the finances and the raw scientific data that are difficult to follow. Then there is the scientific complexity of cutting-edge technology. Not many of us are capable of understanding it, certainly not many Federal Bureau of Investigation officers. Then there is organizational complexity: everyone in the organization has a story as to why the slipups in the system were someone else's responsibility. All of these complexities are to some extent inherent in an international high-technology industry. But pharmaceutical industry informants have explained to me how the complexity is more contrived than inherent. For example, companies generally can get clearly defined internal accountability for things that matter to them. They define accountability clearly for internal purposes on matters like product quality, while setting forth a smokescreen of diffused and confused accountability for projection to the outside world. Three of the U.S. companies I visited a decade ago had "vice presidents responsible for going to jail." Incumbents in these positions explained to me how lines of accountability for purposes of official presentation to the outside world were drawn so that if a head had to go on the chopping block, it would be theirs. After a period of faithful service as the vice president responsible for going to jail, they would be rewarded with promotion sideways to a safe vice presidency.

International complexity is also both inherent and contrived. The bribe from a U.S. company to a Latin American health minister can be arranged so that it is paid in a third country by an intermediary from a fourth country through a Swiss (fifth country) bank account. This is using jurisdictional complexity to make lawbreaking harder to discover and punish. The more fundamental and insidious way that international jurisdictional complexity is used, however, is to evade laws instead of breaking them. International law evasion strategies have reached a high level of sophistication in the pharmaceutical industry.

The paradigmatic law evasion strategy is transfer pricing or profit shifting to avoid tax. A transnational corporation has massive intracorporate sales. Tax liabilities can be avoided by pricing low for intracorporate sales from a subsidiary located in a high-tax country to a subsidiary in a low-tax country and by pricing high when sales are from a low-tax to a high-tax nation. There have been cases where pharmaceutical transnationals have managed to run their worldwide operations at a loss except for a single obscure tax haven, in which massive profits are recorded.[9]

International law evasion in the pharmaceutical industry comes in both cruder and more sophisticated variants than profit shifting. An example of a cruder form of evasion is an impure or understrength product that is forbidden from sale in one country being dumped in another nation with looser laws.[10] With products where there is reason to believe that risks could be high during the experimental stage, initial testing can be done on Third World populations without a practical capacity to sue or to stir up public opinion in the firm's home country.[11] This strategy is often an element of a much more sophisticated international law evasion strategy whereby the firm develops an integrated plan of where it will do the early testing and where it will do its final testing; where it will seek marketing approval first, second, third, penultimately, and ultimately; and where it will locate manufacturing of the new product. While a remote jungle clinic may be ideal for initial testing, sophisticated final testing will have to be done by internationally reputable clinicians in the First World if the U.S. FDA is to be impressed. As far as marketing is concerned, after the initial testing in a Third World market, an Organization for Economic Cooperation and Development country with permissive standards for approval might be the next choice; Belgium was such a country at the time of my research a decade ago. Belgian approval might then be used to justify entry to a number of large Third World markets such as Brazil. The first manufacturing plant could be located in Belgium, so that Belgium could issue the certificate of free sale required by most Third World nations these days—a certificate indicating that the product is approved for marketing in the country of manufacture.[12] Then the firm might work its way up through First World markets with progressively more demanding registration requirements, using evidence from the safe and efficacious use of the products in the less sophisticated markets to gain entry to more sophisticated markets.

Hence using people in the Third World as guinea pigs is part of a rather complex totality. It is a complexity that manifests the rationality of the transnational corporation in finding the line of least resistance to early marketing through the complex jungle of the international regulatory nonsystem. Transnationals use system against nonsystem. While the transnational's worldwide goals are coherent, the goals of the regulatory agencies of the world are conflicting. So the transnational plays one off against the others. Corporations exploit the fact that regulatory goals have coherence only at a national level while corporate coherence is transnational. Transnational corporations also sometimes use—or turn a blind eye to—intermediaries who smuggle a product into countries where marketing approval has not been obtained. But such blatant lawbreaking is not the main game. In fact, it is a rather unimportant one for the transnational pharmaceutical corporation. The main game is the more subtle business of computer-assisted strategizing to find the path of least legal resistance through the international regulatory thicket. Instead of one nation's laws being viewed as an obstacle to be broken through by law violation, compliance with these laws becomes a resource for getting around the spirit of another nation's laws. In other domains of regulatory failure, we see the same paradigm of an international evasion strategy. The Bank of Credit and Commerce International (BCCI) used the laws of each country in which it operated to set itself up in such a way that it was effectively offshore in every country where it operated.[13] Compliance with the letter of some national laws can be used to avoid the spirit of all national laws.

SOME SOLUTIONS

When criminologists discover the great subtlety, sophistication, and power that enable transnational corporations to achieve their objectives with international law evasion strategies, the tendency is to evince a policy analysis of despair. National governments will be outmaneuvered every time by an adversary with a coherent international strategy in a game that is played in an international market. The alternative of an international regulatory agency is pie in the sky, so effective regulation in the public interest is hopeless.

This despair is warranted only if one's vision is restricted to national states as the sole regulators who matter. I will attempt to move to a legal-pluralist model of regulation that helps us to understand why prospects for protecting the public interest from exploitation by pharmaceutical transnationals are actually improving. My contention will be that we must view intervention to protect the public interest in safe and efficacious drugs as possible at a number of levels: national regulatory enforcement, regional regulatory cooperation, international regulatory coordination, intrafirm regulation through both individual executive consciences (for example, professional values) and organizational consciences (internal compliance groups), interfirm self-regulation through national and international industry associations as well as through the work of reforming individual firms, and private regulation by product liability suits and consumer activism.

National Regulatory Enforcement

Criminal law enforcement to deal with the problems of corporate crime in the pharmaceutical industry has been practically nonexistent in every country in the world. This is a result of the technological, jurisdictional, legal, and organizational complexities discussed earlier. Given these realities, consistent criminal enforcement against known corporate lawbreaking is an impossible aspiration. An attraction of a legal-pluralist policy analysis is that the belief that there are constructive ways of solving problems of lawbreaking and evasion without recourse to the criminal law means that we can harbor our criminal enforcement resources for the rather small number of cases where criminal prosecution is the best way to have an impact on the problem. Policymakers who believe that the 100 criminal cases they know about should be investigated and prosecuted with an eye to criminal sanctions set themselves an impossible goal in the domain of complex corporate crime. Policymakers who believe that there are better ways of dealing with 99 out of 100 corporate crimes than taking them to court leave themselves with a superior capacity to concentrate their enforcement resources on the 1 case in 100 that they think is best handled by a criminal prosecution. Then when they score a major enforcement success by concentrating their scarce litigation resources on that 1 case in 100, this success strengthens their hand with the more negotiated approach they adopt toward the other 99 cases.[14]

Within the sphere of national criminal enforcement, there is a capacity for sanctioning that contains a rather more international reach than existing practice has. Brent Fisse and I develop this approach in a book we have almost completed on reforming corporate criminal law.[15] The book offers an approach to the problem of the limits of national law for dealing with conduct in international markets. The approach would force corporate offenders to use their private justice systems to take remedial action. Our accountability model proposes that, having proved the *actus reus* of the offense—for example, that the corporation distributed nonsterile products—the court would invite the corporation to prepare, perhaps with outside consultants, a report indicating the reasons for the offense, those responsible for its execution, the organizational reforms to be taken to prevent recurrence, and the disciplinary measures to be taken against those responsible. If the package of measures proposed by the corporation in its self-investigation report is unsatisfactory to the court, the judge can allow the ax he or she has been holding over the corporate head to fall. If the package of measures is satisfactory to the needs of justice and community protection, then corporate sanctioning is withheld.

I will not attempt a detailed treatment of all the problems with the proposal and how these can be addressed. Instead, I want to emphasize one advantage of this approach that is relevant to the concern of this article—the limits of national enforcement for dealing with internationalized lawbreaking or law evasion. While the court or a regulatory agency cannot act directly against misconduct beyond its jurisdictional authority, our proposal allows it to hold a national threat over the head of an international corporation, which can use its private justice system to exert some international control. For example, if one reason for an offense occurring in the United States is certain actions of French executives at a French manufacturing plant, the self-investigation report to the U.S. court could recommend disciplinary action by the corporation against the French executives. While our accountability model does not enable an American court to put the French executives behind bars, it can lever private justice measures that cost them their jobs or their annual bonuses or can interrupt their career paths. These are not inconsequential levers, and national courts could use them against offenses that involve multiple offshore offenders within the employ of a transnational corporation.

There are many other measures that can be taken to improve national regulatory enforcement, but since I have discussed a number of these at length in the earlier book,[16] I shall not dwell upon them here. Rather, the purpose of this article is to show how this is only one of many control options from the perspective of a legal pluralist.

Regional Regulatory Cooperation

National governments do not have to harmonize their laws perfectly to prevent transnational corporations from playing one country's set of laws off against another's. Indeed, the practical economic constraints of law evasion are often such that a country that sets higher regulatory standards can effectively impose its higher standards on all other countries in a region. This is particularly so when the country is a large and powerful one such as the United States. But strategic government intervention even by small countries can change lowest-common-denominator regulation into highest-common-factor regulation. For example, a Central American regional director for a transnational pharmaceutical company explained to me that when Costa Rica banned a suspected carcinogenic additive in one of its products, the company took the additive from all products being distributed in all Central American countries, since the cost of special production runs for the Costa Rican market was prohibitive. Similarly, Costa Rica has long ruled that all disclosures and warnings made on the drug packages and inserts in the country of origin should be identically made in Costa Rica. The same executive explained, "From our point of view, that means they all have to say what we say in [our home country] because the cost of having different packaging for the different Central American countries is too great."

Again, though, because of the capacity of the transnational to shift its activities around the world, there are limits to how high Costa Rica can push up all Central American standards. The same executive noted:

Let me put it this way. It would not be in our interests to locate more of our manufacturing in the United States. For [one of the company's main products], our literature in Europe, Africa, Australia, South America, and so on claims some 10 indications for the product. In the U.S., the FDA approves only 3. We don't want to be forced by Costa Rica and others to suggest only three indications worldwide when we believe in 10.

Even though Costa Rica did not push this European company's standards up to those of the United States, the interesting thing is that they can push them up to some degree across the whole of Central America. Where international conventions fail, little Costa Rica can succeed in harmonizing minimum standards upward.

The Costa Rican situation illustrates the fact that within a region of the world, harmonization is possible. There are costs for transnationals in playing the international law evasion game—shuffling operations, product, and money around the world is never frictionless. A progressive nation does not always have to bring the whole world with it to defeat international law evasion in its region. The European Community and the European Free Trade Association provide various examples of this, though they also provide examples of nations with higher regulatory standards being pegged back to a regional norm.[17] The Benelux countries (Belgium, the Netherlands, Luxembourg) and the Andean Pact (Peru, Ecuador, Bolivia, Colombia, and Venezuela) both have made progress toward establishing some uniformity in drug regulation within their regions. The United States, like many other nations, has signed a number of bilateral memoranda of understanding. These memoranda bind the FDA and the foreign regulator to common standards for good laboratory practices and preclinical testing.[18]

Overall, the regional harmonization game can be a win-win game for the industry and its consumers. While harmonization cuts down possibilities for international law evasion by industry, having a single uniform set of regulatory requirements also reduces the costs of compliance. Even if consumers in some countries some of the time get products meeting lower standards under harmonized rules, they also get improved protection against products designed to meet much lower standards creeping into their market. And as we have seen, consumers in a lot of countries a lot of the time will get products that meet higher standards. This is because in regional regulatory forums, a captured or corrupt bureaucrat who wants to set standards well below the international average tends to be less persuasive than a crusading bureaucrat from a country that, because of a history of special problems with the product in his or her homeland, wants to get standards well above the international average.

International Regulatory Cooperation

The United Nations, preeminently the World Health Organization (WHO), provides a forum where more ambitious harmonization of laws is facilitated to thwart international law evasion strategies.[19] WHO's international drug adverse-reaction-reporting scheme does not work wonderfully well, but it effects some opening up of regulatory exposure in sophisticated markets for companies who test and dump in unsophisticated markets. The exposure is limited, however, because the unsophisticated markets are precisely those where problems are not reported into the scheme.

Advocacy groups, as we will see later, have targeted their windows of exposure more effectively on these unsophisticated markets. The Certification Scheme on the Quality of Pharmaceutical Products Moving in International Commerce is a successful harmonization project of the WHO. The large number of participating countries certify on request from another participant country that specified pharmaceutical exports meet the Good Manufacturing Practices Standards set down under the scheme, that the plants are subject to periodic inspection, and that the product is authorized for sale in the exporting country. Good Laboratory Practices are now becoming increasingly internationalized, thereby increasing the auditability of data from other countries and bringing the problem of fraud in the international safety testing of drugs under somewhat improved control. International regulatory cooperation on such matters under the auspices of the WHO and other international agencies has no panaceas to offer in a complex world, but it can effect limited improvements in international regulatory capability.

Professionalism and Self-Regulation

One of the analytical mistakes that scholars of white-collar crime repeatedly make is to assume that when an executive works for a criminogenic corporation, the executive's corporate identity is the only identity that matters to him or her. The 131 interviews I conducted with executives in the international pharmaceutical industry demonstrated clearly how executives have plural identities and multiple loyalties to multiple organizations. The Lilly research executive may have a loyalty to her research team that is more profound than the more remote loyalty to Lilly as a corporation. She may have a loyalty to her profession, to her patients if she is a doctor, and so on. The identity "Lilly executive" is just one of many identities.

An important conclusion from my earlier study was that the consumers of the world receive more protection from the higher standards that these competing identities bring into the firm than from enforcement of the law. This is particularly true with regard to the Third World. As many have demonstrated, drug companies have double and triple standards when it comes to marketing drugs in the Third World.[20] It is also true, however, that most, if not all, transnational pharmaceutical companies set much higher standards in the least regulated Third World markets than they are required to meet by the laws of those countries. They set higher standards because it would simply be intolerable to the professional standards of the people who work for them to stoop to the levels allowed by lax laws. There are other reasons that we will get to later. But in my fieldwork, and in my work as a consumer advocate, I have encountered many instances of responsible professionals within transnational corporations exposing the unethical conduct of certain of their own executives to the professional disapproval of their peers within the firm, and this in the firms that are among the worst lawbreakers in an industry with an unusually bad record for lawbreaking.[21]

Those in the best position to know about corporate wrongdoing are within the corporation. Those in the best position to understand whether organizationally and technologically complex corporate conduct actually amounts to wrongdoing are those imbued with an understanding of the organization, its technology, and the potential effects of that technology. The actors in the best position to mobilize informal sanctioning and disapproval that wrongdoers will care about are peers with whom they share a daily professional life. These are reasons why intracorporate self-regulation by employees with consciences is the form of regulation that almost certainly saves the greatest number of lives. If transnational pharmaceutical companies really did meet the minimum standards in the law of all the countries in which they operated, and never performed above those legal standards, the death toll from prescription drugs would be horrific. This observation points to the fundamental limitation of state law enforcement as a control strategy.

In all firms, there are constituencies that are supportive of the intent of regulatory laws. In pharmaceutical companies, the office of the medical director and the quality assurance group are often such constituencies, and in some cases the general counsel's office is a constituency that also pushes for compliance with the law. Effective self-regulation depends to a considerable extent on strengthening the hand of such offices. An example is the strategy, now widespread throughout the industry, of allowing decisions of quality control on batches of drugs to be overruled only by the signature of the chief executive. This eliminates much of the day-to-day nullifying of quality control by production managers who insist on meeting production targets when they deem attainment of specifications to be good enough. Such a management policy strengthens the hand of a pro-regulation internal constituency enormously.

Interfirm Self-Regulation

Interfirm regulation is one of the things that can constitute the intrafirm self-regulation that I concluded was so important in the last section—but so can it be constituted by state regulation, such as law requiring the signature of the chief executive when quality control is overruled, or by consumer activism. Interfirm regulation can occur at a number of levels. National industry associations can write and enforce self-regulatory codes, as can international industry associations. Then there is the work of single firms seeking to upgrade the standards of their corporate peers. Each of these levels of interindustry regulation will now be illustrated.

An example of national industry association self-regulation is the Australian Pharmaceutical Manufacturers' Association Code of Conduct.[22] The code relates primarily to the promotion of prescription drugs. Throughout the 1980s, I was a highly public advocate, along with leaders of the Australian consumer movement, of the view that self-regulation was not the way to go for the control of pharmaceutical advertising, that tougher government regulation was needed. I still believe that in principle this is an area in which government regulation ought to be more effective and efficient than self-regulation. In the aftermath of the total failure of such regulation during the 1970s and 1980s, however, the government decided to give a rejuvenated self-regulation scheme a three-year trial beginning in 1988. It turned out that self-regulation during this period was more effective in improving the integrity of pharmaceuticals' promotion than the limp government regulation of the previous decade had been.[23] While Australian consumer activists such as myself who have been involved in a hands-on way with this issue do not doubt the finding that self-regulation worked better than the feeble government regulation that it replaced, we still believe that inappropriate marketing practices are widespread and unremedied. Nevertheless, improvement is improvement, and it warrants the concession that historical circumstances arise that result in self-regulation's working better than government regulation even in an area where in principle the reverse should be true. The reasons for the success of this scheme were contingent; they included a substantial industry investment in prepublication monitoring of advertisements for compliance with the code, repeated postpublication surveys of the percentage of ads that complied that were conducted independently by the Australian Society of Clinical and Experimental Pharmacologists,[24] and knowledge that the self-regulation scheme would be evaluated by the Trade Practices Commission to determine if it should be replaced by government regulation.

This case illustrates that consumer advocates and regulatory strategists must avoid myopic rejection of strategies on the basis of theoretical dogma. Where self-regulation does outperform government regulation, pragmatism is needed to give credit where credit is due, rewarding improved protection for consumers in a plural regulatory order, so that improved protection may be achieved.

The International Federation of Pharmaceutical Manufacturers' Association (IFPMA) has also been in the business of self-regulation. Indeed, the Australian Pharmaceutical Manufacturers' Association code, discussed in the last two paragraphs, received part of its impetus from pressure for increased self-regulation from the IFPMA.[25] In turn, the fear of de facto international and national regulation by the WHO in conjunction with Third World governments in order to implement the WHO list of essential drugs—that is, to eliminate nonessential drugs from the market so that scarce health budgets could be concentrated on lifesaving products—prompted the IFPMA in 1982 to start supplying essential drugs to a few pilot countries.[26] In countries such as Gambia and Sierra Leone, the initiative seems to have been responsible for some improvement in primary health care and in the availability of lifesaving drugs.[27] By and large, however, one would have to say that the IFPMA efforts at self-regulation have been tokenistic and that it is only in a few countries such as Australia that they have been taken seriously because of extra pressure from professional and consumer constituencies.

An interesting more recent development in interfirm regulation has been at the level of a single firm—the Swiss giant Ciba-Geigy—that has sought to persuade its corporate peers to upgrade self-regulatory standards voluntarily. Ciba-Geigy was a pariah firm until the late 1980s as far as the international consumer movement was concerned.[28] It had done terrible things in product testing, such as spraying Third World agricultural workers with experimental chemicals from the air without their consent and aggressively marketing products such as clioquinol that had disastrous side effects, which were covered up. Ciba-Geigy also persisted in the marketing of products in the Third World after they had been demonstrated to be unsafe and had been withdrawn from First World markets. Cynics will say that it was the public relations setbacks associated with the consumer movement perception of Ciba-Geigy as a killer corporation, combined with the threat of an international consumer boycott, that caused the corporation to change its spots. Greater cynics will say that Ciba-Geigy has not altered its spots at all. My view is that Ciba-Geigy has changed, if not completely changed. At the end of 1986, the company initiated a program called the Risk Assessment of Drugs—Analysis and Response (RAD-AR). RAD-AR's goal is to get leading companies to be more open about the risk factors associated with their products and to foment a more constructive dialogue about the risks and benefits of particular pharmaceuticals, a dialogue in which industry critics take part.[29] RAD-AR's success has been patchy, varying from one part of the world to another. Representatives of many companies have attended RAD-AR seminars, but not many have acted to make their safety and efficacy data more genuinely open to their competitors and their critics. The U.S. company G. D. Searle, formerly a prominent practitioner of reincarnated rat research, is one organization that has moved significantly in the direction of greater openness about its products.[30] It is both interesting and theoretically significant that the companies that have taken the most determined steps toward greater openness and dialogue about the risks of an industry that markets tamed poisons have been those such as Ciba-Geigy and Searle that have been subjected, with good reason, to some of the strongest consumerist vilification.

Consumer Activism

The interplay between interfirm regulation and consumer activism became clear in the last section. National and international industry associations have stepped up their self-regulatory activities when they have been put under pressure from consumer groups. The individual firms that have been preeminent in leading the industry in the direction of a more responsible regulatory culture[31] in recent decades have been firms that have been effectively targeted by the consumer movement. This self-regulatory improvement is in considerable part an attempt to fend off strengthened state and international regulation. And the threatened state and international regulation is itself a threat largely, or at least partly, because of the lobbying of national and international consumer groups. Another threat the industry fears is strengthened consumer product liability laws and class action legislation. Where this strengthening has occurred, it largely has been through consumer movement activism. This in turn brings in another level of analysis to a legal-pluralist examination of the social control of drug risks, that concerned with private consumers punishing corporations in the courts for taking unjustified risks with their bodies. All these levels are interconnected, and very often interconnected in a way that suggests that an initial impetus from consumer movement activism was crucial. The industry itself recognizes this. Consequently, a new tactic in its appeals for partial deregulation of drug safety testing has been to work with gay and lesbian groups concerned about red tape holding up new drugs to combat acquired immune deficiency syndrome (AIDS).

In the United States, Ralph Nader's organization, Sidney Wolfe and the Health Research Group, and the Consumers' Union all have been important players in the drug regulation game, working hand in hand with sympathetic journalists such as Morton Mintz of the *Washington Post* and sympathetic legislators such as Edward Kennedy and Howard Metzenbaum. Internationally, the preeminently important group has been Health Action International, an arm of the International Organization of Consumers' Unions. These two groups now have a regional office structure that puts them on the battlefront of the worst abuses of the industry in the Third World.

In Australia, professional groups with strong links to the consumer movement have been particularly important in effecting change in industry practices. Dr. Ken Harvey has been a leading activist from the medical profession in promoting peer guidelines for the appropriate use of different drugs. Use of the guidelines within Australian hospitals has both reduced irrational prescribing and cut drug costs. The most interesting group in Australia has been the Medical Lobby for Appropriate Marketing (MLAM). The MLAM strategy has been relatively simple. Dr. Peter Mansfield, the inspiration behind MLAM, writes to a large number of doctors who are MLAM members around the world with information about a product that is being marketed inappropriately by a particular company in a particular country. These medical professionals then write to the company—generally at its world headquarters or in the country where the offense occurred or in their own country—demanding an explanation for the alleged inappropriate marketing practice. A naive strategy, hard-bitten advocates of state deterrence might say. Not really. It is a strategy that works enough of the time to make it an extremely cost-efficient method of social control for activists with scarce resources. Writing letters is cheap. Moreover, it is a decent method of social control based on a reasoned appeal to corporate and medical responsibility.[32] Sometimes MLAM decides that it wrongly assessed a situation and writes back to the company with an apology. Pharmaceutical executives, even some of the very worst of them, do have a better side, a responsible side, to which appeals to professional and corporate responsibility can be made. They have multiple selves that make it worth considering a strategy that encourages them to put their best self forward. When that does not work, there are other strategies available to advocacy groups—muckraking in the media and calls for state enforcement, for example, and in extreme cases threats of consumer or professional boycotts.

In addition to corporate executives having a socially responsible self that can, surprisingly, often be brought to the fore, pharmaceutical companies have self-interested reasons to listen and respond seriously to rising ground swells of professional concern about their marketing practices. Pharmaceutical companies survive in the marketplace by persuading physicians to prescribe their products. In other words, they depend for success on convincing health care professionals that they are trustworthy. Sometimes they make the judgment that the best way to promote their long-term success is to actually be trustworthy, to admit a mistake and put it right. Five of 17 MLAM letters between January 1988 and June 1989 resulted in an agreement by the targeted company to alter claims or withdraw the product in question.[33] This strike rate increased to 5 of 9 for the period from July 1989 to June 1990.[34]

CONCLUSION

State regulation is very important for controlling corporate crime in the pharmaceutical industry. But inappropriate state regulation can deter innovation and push up the costs of drugs that are desperately needed in many parts of the world.[35] In this article, I have said very little about these crucial issues because they always are the focus in debates on the regulation of the pharmaceutical industry. Here I have sought to decenter the state. My argument has been that while the state is very important, its importance to market ordering and regulation of abuse is overrated. Underrated sources of regulation of abuse are market ordering by international organizations, mobilization of community disapproval by consumer and professional groups, intrafirm self-regulation at the level of individual executive professionalism, and interfirm self-regulation mobilized by national and international industry associations and individual firms, such as Ciba-Geigy.

All these forms of social control may seem weak, but their weakness can be overstated if we fail to realize that their strength comes from the way they are interrelated. Pharmaceutical companies are not exactly enmeshed in a Foucauldian carceral archipelago,[36] but they are surrounded by a web of controls that must be taken more seriously than any single strand of that web. Consumer groups might seem disorganized and weak. But when they can mobilize media assaults, sow seeds of professional distrust of the industry, foment consumer cynicism about the products the industry sells, heighten the threat of government regulation, nurture industry self-regulation to fend off the latter threat, and initiate mass tort litigation, the entire web of influences can change industry conduct. Most crucially, advocates engaging in a critical public dialogue with the industry flush out sympathizers within the industry. The pharmaceutical industry has within it thousands of public citizens who believe in corporate responsibility, who care about human health, and who have standards of professional integrity. In a pinch, some of these executives with a conscience will blow the whistle; at the drop of a hat, a good number of them will discreetly provide useful information to industry critics. Because the industry cannot exile its huge fifth column of responsible professionals, to a certain extent it actually listens to them and responds to their internal critiques. This is why intracorporate self-regulation is the main game. But it is a main game that gets a lot of its power from outside forces—consumerist critics, scientific journals, the popular media, professional societies, the professional socialization practices of universities, and, yes, criminal law. Criminal law must be seen, therefore, in proper perspective as one of the critical outside forces that empowers a web of market-ordering mechanisms. Criminal law is too clumsy and costly a device to be the frontline assault weapon that routinely strikes the blows that are decisive for winning the battle. Rather, criminal law has enormous importance as heavy artillery that provides the backing to push the front-line troops forward into hand-to-hand combat with the mercenaries.[37]

The United States is the country that is the heaviest user of criminal law as a control mechanism for regulatory problems in the pharmaceutical industry. Even so, criminal law is used in U.S. pharmaceuticals regulation with extreme rarity.[38] All nations should be using criminal law much more against the worst corporate crimes of the pharmaceutical industry. Although all nations have in common the fact that criminal law is rarely or never used against pharmaceutical transnationals, countries vary enormously in the levels of unwarranted risk that drug companies take with consumers' lives. A quick visit to a pharmacy in Guatemala and one in Sweden, neither country being one that uses criminal law against pharmaceutical companies, immediately communicates the enormous difference in the risk that consumers confront in these two societies. What accounts for the differences in drug morbidity and mortality is the total fabric of the web of controls I have outlined previously. Criminologists who eschew a legal-pluralist analysis will never get to the bottom of what really protects the lives of consumers from corporate crime.

A policy analysis of despair is no longer warranted in the face of the reality of international law evasion strategies, as deep and deadly as the problem remains. International harmonization efforts are slowly moving forward, particularly in a European Community that is increasingly setting the international agenda. Guarded support for these harmonization moves is coming from the industry and many national regulators and consumer and professional groups who see some prospect for win-win change. More striking, there is a new view gaining momentum in the industry that the international law evasion game is not the way to go. This view is succinctly summarized in the advice of Harvard Business School guru Michael Porter in his paradigm-shattering book, *The Competitive Advantage of Nations.*

Establish norms exceeding the toughest regulatory hurdles or product standards. Some localities (or user industries) will lead in terms of the stringency of product standards, pollution limits, noise guidelines, and the like. Tough regulatory standards are not a hindrance but an opportunity to move early to upgrade products and processes.[39]

Find the localities whose regulations foreshadow those elsewhere. Some regions and cities will typically lead others in terms of their concern with social problems such as safety, environmental quality, and the like. Instead of avoiding such areas, as some companies do, they should be sought out. A firm should define its internal goals as meeting, or exceeding, their standards. An advantage will result as other regions, and ultimately other nations, modify regulations to follow suit.[40]

Firms, like governments, are often prone to see the short-term cost of dealing with tough standards and not their longer-term benefits in terms of innovation. Firms point to foreign rivals without such standards as having a cost advantage. Such thinking is based on an incomplete view of how competitive advantage is created and sustained. Selling poorly performing, unsafe, or environmentally damaging products is not a route to real competitive advantage in sophisticated industry and industry segments, especially in a world where environmental sensitivity and concern for social welfare are rising in all advanced nations. Sophisticated buyers will usually appreciate safer, cleaner, quieter products before governments do. Firms with the skills to produce such products will have an important lever to enter foreign markets, and can often accelerate the process by which foreign regulations are toughened.[41]

Here we have an intriguing emerging international dynamic. Firms that have upgraded their safety standards early because of their location in states that are early movers to higher standards have an interest in getting other states to follow the lead. There is thus a connected strategy for those of us who are active in the international consumer movement. It is to persuade targeted national governments to be first movers to upgrade regulatory standards through the argument that they can actually benefit their national economy by doing so. Porter supplies many examples of nations that constructed important competitive advantages by being first to establish tougher health and safety standards. Then home-base transnationals from those first nations can be recruited to support upgrading standards in other nations, thus setting back their competitors from laggard nations.

Porter's way of thinking about the constitution of competitive advantage is gaining wider acceptance in business and regulatory communities. Pharmaceutical companies can see that it is actually a competitive disadvantage to have as a home base an Eastern European country that might have cheap labor costs and minimal regulatory standards. The absence of demanding regulators and demanding consumer groups gives companies from these countries totally inadequate preparation for competing in sophisticated markets.

What is it that is generating this shift among some industry strategists from an interest in seeking the lowest possible standards to finding the highest standards? It is "sophisticated buyers . . . [who] . . . appreciate safer . . . products before governments do." To the sophisticated buyers we might add sophisticated health care professionals, sophisticated corporate insiders, and sophisticated industry association leaders. Shifts toward a search for the highest standards are caused by the web of influences that has been the subject of this article. Increasingly one does meet pharmaceutical industry executives who are actively committed to shooting for the highest regulatory standards in the way Porter commends. Shifts away from lowest-common-denominator regulation in the world system toward highest-common-factor regulation can be a result of the web of interconnections among regulatory, self-regulatory, and consumerist actors in a plural international ordering of markets. Comparatively poorly resourced players of the regulatory game, such as consumer groups, need not be powerless actors if they are smart. To be smart, they must have an internationalist strategy that recognizes and works with the plural sources of market ordering.[42]

Notes

1. John Braithwaite, *Corporate Crime in the Pharmaceutical Industry.* London: Routledge & Kegan Paul, 1984.
2. *Ibid.*, pp. 14–17.
3. *Ibid.*, pp. 11–50.
4. *Ibid.*, pp. 110–158.
5. *Ibid.*, pp. 159–203.
6. *Ibid.*, pp. 204–244.
7. *Ibid.*, pp. 279–289.
8. *Ibid.*, pp. 51–109.
9. *Ibid.*, p. 285.
10. See David A. Bryan, "Consumer Safety Abroad: Dumping of Dangerous American Products Overseas," *Texas Tech Law Review,* 12 (1981):435–458.
11. Braithwaite, *op. cit.*, p. 266.
12. Rosemary P. Wall, "International Trends in New Drug Approval Regulation: The Impact of Pharmaceutical Innovation," *Rutgers Computer and Technology Law Journal,* 10 (1984):129.
13. Albert J. Reiss, Jr., "Detecting, Investigating and Regulating Business Law-Breaking." In Peter Grabosky and John Braithwaite, eds., *The Future of Regulatory Enforcement in Australia.* Canberra: Australian Institute of Criminology, 1993.
14. See further Ian Ayres and John Braithwaite, *Responsive Regulation: Transcending the Deregulation Debate.* New York: Oxford University Press, 1992, chap. 2.
15. Brent Fisse and John Braithwaite, *Corporations, Crime and Accountability.* New York: Cambridge University Press, 1993.
16. Braithwaite, *op. cit.*, pp. 290–383.
17. Wall, *op. cit.*, p. 334.
18. *Ibid.*, p. 335.
19. Ellen N. Cohn, "International Regulation of Pharmaceuticals: The Role of the World Health Organization," *Virginia Journal of Transnational Law,* 23 (1983):331–361.
20. See, for example, Charles Medawar, *Insult or Injury?* London: Social Audit, 1979; Maurice N. G. Dukes and Barbara Swartz, *Responsibility for Drug-Induced Injury.* Amsterdam: Elsevier, 1988; Milton Silverman, Philip R. Lee, and Mia Lydecker, *Prescriptions for Death.* Berkeley: University of California Press, 1982.
21. Marshall B. Clinard and Peter C. Yeager, *Corporate Crime.* New York: The Free Press, 1980, pp. 119–122.
22. Australian Pharmaceutical Manufacturers' Association, *Code of Conduct of the*

Australian Pharmaceutical Manufacturers' Association, Inc. North Sydney: APMA, 1990.

23. See Trade Practices Commission, *Report by the Trade Practices Commission on the Self-Regulation of Promotion and Advertising of Therapeutic Goods.* Canberra: Trade Practices Commission, 1992.

24. Lindon M. H. Wing and Robert Moulds, "Drug Advertising," *Medical Journal of Australia,* 150 (1989):410–411.

25. See IFPMA, *IFPMA Code of Pharmaceutical Manufacturing Practices.* Geneva: IFPMA, 1987.

26. Cohn, *op. cit.*, p. 352.

27. Andrew Chetley, *A Healthy Business? World Health and the Pharmaceutical Industry.* London: Zed Books, 1990, pp. 133–134.

28. See Olle Hansson, *Inside Ciba-Geigy.* Penang: International Organization of Consumers' Unions, 1989.

29. An important forum for this discussion is the periodical *RAD-AR Report.*

30. Chetley, *op. cit.*, p. 139.

31. Regulatory culture includes firms, regulators, and public interest groups. I see regulatory culture as a very useful concept; see Errol Meidinger, "Regulatory Culture: A Theoretical Outline," *Law and Policy,* 9 (1986):355–386.

32. See Clifford Shearing, "A Constitutive Conception of Regulation," in Grabosky and Braithwaite, *op. cit.*

33. Victoria A. Wade, Peter R. Mansfield, and Peter J. McDonald, "Drug Companies' Evidence to Justify Advertising," *Lancet,* 8674 (November 25, 1989):1261–1264.

34. Peter R. Mansfield, "Classifying Improvements to Drug Marketing and Justification for Claims of Efficacy," *International Journal of Risk and Safety in Medicine,* 2 (1991):171–184. Of course, with such data one can never be certain that the company would not have changed its marketing practices without the pressure from MLAM.

35. See, for example, Robert I. Chien, *Issues in Pharmaceutical Economics.* Lexington, MA: Lexington Books, 1979.

36. Michel Foucault, *Discipline and Punishment: The Birth of the Prison,* trans. Alan Sheridan. London: Allen Lane, 1977.

37. See Ayres and Braithwaite, *op. cit.*, chap. 2

38. Braithwaite, *op. cit.*

39. Michael Porter, *The Competitive Advantage of Nations.* London: Macmillan, 1990, p. 585.

40. *Ibid.*, p. 588.

41. *Ibid.*, pp. 648–649.

42. For a sophisticated discussion of the theoretical foundations for a pluralistic analysis of market ordering, see Shearing, *op. cit.*

17

Emotions and Adjudication

Status Degradation among White-Collar Criminals

Michael L. Benson

Few events produce stronger emotions than being publicly accused of a crime. Especially for the individual who has a stake in maintaining a legitimate persona, the prospect of being exposed as a criminal engenders "deep emotions"[1]: shame, humiliation, guilt, depression, and anger. During adjudication, judgments about an offender's moral integrity may be publicized throughout the individual's social world and thus may strike deeply at the offender's sense of self and reputation in the community. The potential negative impact of conviction on community standing presumably deters those contemplating crimes.

Because of their extensive social reputations, white-collar criminals are assumed to have a special sensitivity to criminal adjudication.[2] Supposedly, white-collar offenders experience significantly more humiliation and shame during the adjudicatory process than ordinary offenders. Indeed, some observers have suggested that the significance of stigma for white-collar offenders' relationships with others may bring them special consideration in the justice system.[3] Yet as with so many other aspects of our understanding of white-collar offenders and offenses, the idea of special sensitivity is based largely on speculation and anecdotal data. In view of the supposed deterrent effects of shame and embarrassment on white-collar criminals, it is surprising that little systematic attention has been given to the processes by which such emotions are produced in these individuals. Indeed, little is known about the reality of white-collar crime.[4]

This article describes the emotional experiences of a small sample of white-collar offenders. It focuses on the major emotion-producing features of the adjudicatory process and argues that contemporary criminal justice practices have potentially

Reprinted from *Justice Quarterly,* 7 (September 1990), pp. 515–527.

dysfunctional effects. The process of criminal adjudication may provoke as well as deter antisocial attitudes and behavior.

THE STUDY

The study was conducted under the auspices of a federal probation office located in a major urban center. For the purposes of this study, white-collar offenders were those convicted of economic offenses committed through the use of indirection, fraud, or collusion.[5] In collaboration with probation officers, I identified a sample of 78 potential subjects and reviewed their case files to gather data on the offenders and their crimes. I notified the subjects by mail, telling them that a study investigating the effects of conviction on white-collar offenders was under way, and I asked them for interviews. Of those receiving the letter, 30 offenders agreed to be interviewed. All were men; the two women in the sample refused to participate.

The sampled offenders had been convicted of a wide variety of white-collar crimes, such as embezzlement, securities and exchange violations, antitrust violations, postal and wire fraud, and income tax evasion. In general, before their convictions, they had had respectable careers as lawyers, dentists, stockbrokers, and businessmen.

Because the sample was essentially self-selected, the results of the interview analysis must be viewed as provisional. The interviewed persons varied greatly in their occupations, offenses, and demographic characteristics, but I found no systematic differences between those who agreed to be interviewed and those who refused. Nevertheless, the interviewees may differ psychologically from the nonrespondents. Conceivably, those who refused to be interviewed may have been more sensitive to the embarrassment of being convicted. If this is true, the study may underestimate the sense of stigmatization experienced by white-collar offenders.

Most of the interviews were tape recorded and later were transcribed for analysis. The questions were open-ended; subjects were encouraged to focus on the aspects of their experience that concerned them most strongly. Among other matters, the interviews dealt with how offenders felt during and after their involvement with the criminal justice system. These sections of the interviews form the basis of the descriptions and analyses presented below.

In analyzing the interviews, I looked for certain emotional descriptors—embarrassment, degrading, shock, humiliation, shame, angry, and the like—and then noted the context in which they occurred. I also noted how offenders described people and events. Where they spoke in stronger or more descriptive language, referring to physical experiences or using obscenities, I inferred that these events and people were associated with emotional experiences for the offender. This procedure has shortcomings, however. Emotions are located temporally and spatially, whereas this study is based on retrospective descriptions of emotions and experiences. It is unlikely that the reports given during the interviews capture the full complexity and depth of the subjects' "lived reality."[6] In addition, we must acknowledge the possibility that in describing their feelings, subjects may be work-ing on and managing them.[7] Nevertheless, the interviews provide a rare glimpse of the subjective reactions of white-collar offenders who have passed through the jus-tice system.

DEGRADATION CEREMONIES, CRIMINAL JUSTICE, AND EMOTIONS

When a person is accused of a crime, he or she is caught up in degradation cere-mony.[8] In the criminal justice system, this ceremony is conducted through grand jury hearings, indictments, plea negotiations, and trial. The news media also play a role in this process through their publication of the crime and their presentation of the offender.

The object of a degradation ceremony is to redefine and debase the subject's gen-eral identity. Such an undesirable status passage[9] produces deep emotions in those who attach significance to community membership and community standing. White-collar criminals have a material and symbolic stake in the prevailing social order. They have benefited from the generalized perception that they are trustworthy mem-bers of society. Indeed, it is widely assumed, though it rarely has been studied, that separation from the community means more to them than to street criminals.

Status degradation occurs through characterizations of the offense and the offender made by the prosecutor and the news media. As Garfinkel described in his seminal article, offense and offender are presented in black-and-white terms: they are made into caricatures of evil. The offense and the offender are *linked,* so that the offense is used to reveal the offender's "true" character.[10] The interviews show that two tech-niques are used to accomplish this end: magnification of the crime and selective attention to the offender's identities.

Magnification of the Crime

A general feature of criminal justice processing as a degradation ceremony is the social construction of the crime. The process of social construction is especially dif-ficult for white-collar offenders to accept because of the way in which they interpret their behavior. Unlike street criminals, white-collar offenders frequently deny the criminality of what they did, claiming that the action should not have been criminal-ized in the first place. They see their actions as justifiable or excusable.[11] In contrast, street criminals are more likely to accept the wrongfulness of their actions,[12] though some may feel that in their particular situations crime was the only option.[13]

The facts of a criminal event and of a person's role in that event are malleable. As with any event, the facts can be shaped and arranged to fit a particular line.[14] It is a difficult experience for the offender when the line being presented is not what he or she intended to present; in a sense, one's past is fictionalized before one's eyes. Facts are reported, but their meaning and significance for the offender are misconstrued and arranged to make a new context in which to judge the offender. This socially constructed interpretation shocks and degrades the white-collar offender.

> The prosecutors, they plant all kinds of things in the newspapers. Some of those newspaper articles that came out were an abomination. They would seize on little key phrases and you could see how it was all planted by the prosecutors (Businessman convicted of antitrust violations).

The presentation of the offender and the offense in the media is not necessarily wrong factually; more likely it is one-sided, magnifying the disreputable aspects of the offender's crime and personal history. Cases are presented in this way in part because local newspapers and television news programs often must rely upon prosecutors and police for information about crimes and offenders. Hence their reports tend to portray events from the official criminal justice perspective.[15]

Publicity exposes one's involvement in a shameful activity. Naturally, this exposure is embarrassing, but the type of publicity given to white-collar and other offenses does much more than merely expose the offender. The anger and bitterness reported by offenders toward newspapers and television stem from the particular type of treatment given the event, not merely from the fact of exposure.

> [The press] blew it all out of proportion. When I saw it on TV that was really tough. You'd have thought I was the worst criminal that ever lived, that I stole this twenty-eight million dollars (Banker convicted of misapplication of funds).

A lawyer involved in an illegal adoption scandal and eventually convicted of income tax evasion described his feelings towards the newspapers in this manner:

> The only one I am bitter at is the newspapers, as many people are. They are unfair, because you can't get even. They can say things that are untrue ... They wrote an article on me that was so blasphemous, that was so horrible. They painted me as an insidious, miserable creature, wringing out the last penny (Lawyer convicted of income tax evasion).

Even if the offender's personal history has admirable qualities, these can be presented in such a manner as to increase his culpability. Thus, what ordinarily would be construed as reflecting well on an individual suddenly becomes evidence that his crime is more serious and more blameworthy.

> As far as the newspapers are concerned, they did a job on me that I wouldn't want anybody to go through. I can see why politicians and so on really get fed up with the papers ... I really think that to some extent they write something just to make it; you know they can't write the facts because the facts really aren't much fun to read, so they have to embellish it. I was brought up on the North Side of Chicago, so they did a job like Little Lord Fauntleroy gets caught with his hand in the cookie jar. You don't need that shit (Banker convicted of embezzlement).

The news reporter's interest lies in whatever is exceptional. Hence the news media emphasize the out-of-the-ordinary aspects of a case. The more exceptional a case can be made to appear, the more newsworthy it is. Thus, by focusing on the defendant's high social status or the large amount of money allegedly involved, news reporters fulfill one of the conditions of a successful degradation ceremony: they make the event stand out of the ordinary.[16] In carrying out their professional responsibilities, they automatically become denouncers in the process of degradation regardless of their intent.

An extreme example of social construction involved an electrical inspector who worked for the city and who was convicted of extorting money from contractors. The offender denied being an extortionist; he claimed that the money he received was for services he performed in helping contractors to meet code requirements for their work. His case was made unusual by his assertion that he donated the money to various charities in which he had a personal interest. As this claim was publicized through the trial, the offender was ridiculed in a newspaper by a well-known columnist, who called him an "extortionist with a heart." Another offender described his trial as "a circus, an oratorical contest among the assistant U.S. attorneys to see who could say the worst things about me." Through the process of social construction, the crime is magnified and the offender is made into an object worthy of society's punishment and unworthy of its sympathy.

Selective Attention

Selective attention is analogous to the process of retrospective interpretation used to assign deviant statuses to marginal or powerless individuals.[17] It differs, however, in that the offender's past actions are not placed in a new scheme of interpretation as much as they are ignored. Only selected acts receive attention. The amputation of these acts from the rest of the offender's life produces feelings of anguish, shame, and rage, especially when this new interpretation of self is publicized.

Not all white-collar offenders are pillars of the community,[18] but even garden-variety white-collar offenders typically have at least some socially esteemed identities. They have careers or families. They are members of community, business, political, or religious organizations. They may do charitable work and act as good neighbors. These identities are important in their social worlds, but they are ignored during the process of status degradation. At least they appear to be ignored from the white-collar offender's point of view.

You get the feeling—some in the federal government but more from the newspapers—they never mention any of the good things you have done in your life. It's one bad thing that is splattered and splattered ... A thousand good deeds and things that you've done in your life are never mentioned. This is one of the things that kind of hurts (Lawyer convicted of income tax evasion).

The white-collar offender's feelings about selective attention are ironic when we consider how most criminologists view white-collar justice. The very attributes that criminologists claim arouse sympathy in judges and prosecutors are those which white-collar offenders claim are ignored or twisted by the media.

Normally we do not need to attend closely to our different identities; we have the illusion that we are always and everywhere the same. Adverse publicity can expose this illusion to the offender along with the multiplicity of his or her identities. Ironically, as this previously unperceived condition of life is revealed to the offender, its existence is ignored at the same time by the denouncers in the degradation process. Only one of the offender's many identities is considered. The offender, like all of us, understands the diversity and complexity of his or her personality and is aware of its many sides. He or she is one person in one situation and a different person in another, but during adjudication this variety of identities is ignored. From among many different identities, one is selected during the denunciatory process and is held up as indicative of the offender's entire personality. The offender believes, however, that the act in question is only one facet of his or her life. Anguish comes when one is judged on the basis of a single action, even though not all of oneself was in that action.

> They never said anything about my turning myself in. Only once in one article did it mention that I ever got a medal in the Marine Corps. I mean it was all negative. There was never a discussion about what the guy did. You know (I did) some social work in the Cabrini area. (I) worked at pulling a hospital that was in trouble out of trouble. I was spending all kinds of time there. Got a medal in the Marine Corps, etc., etc. They didn't write any of that. Just here's a guy that had good schooling . . . (Banker convicted of embezzlement).

As with magnification of the crime, selective attention is practiced by the news media as well as the justice system. Indeed, selective attention is a standard technique of news reporting. Reporters seek to develop angles on events that will emphasize their newsworthiness.[19] This style of reporting selects, organizes, and presents information according to certain standard formats, which transform mundane occurrences into news in the form of easily understood mini morality plays.[20] One such format used to report white-collar cases tells how the high and mighty have fallen. Another tells how the seemingly trustworthy have turned out to be untrustworthy after all. To give thematic unity to these stories, reporters often emphasize two themes known to strike responsive chords in viewers and readers: abuse of privilege and just deserts. Thus information is selected and organized to show that privileges were abused and that whatever deserts may follow are justified.

In today's complex and diversified urban society individuals play many roles: this multiplicity increases opportunities for embarrassment. When one is brought into simultaneous contact with others who know him or her in different roles, the resulting conflict in expectations can be embarrassing.[21] College professors, for example, sometimes experience discomfort when they accidentally run into students in bars or at the laundromat. Most of us avoid these awkward encounters by compartmentalizing our lives and segregating the salient audiences for each of our many roles. Except for chance meetings, audience segregation ordinarily prevents a breakdown in role compartmentalization. In everyday interaction, failures in audience segregation usually last for only a short time and are limited in scope. One can walk away from the embarrassing moment.

For the person accused and convicted of a crime, however, such an easy escape is not possible. Because of publicity the white-collar offender cannot walk away from a breakdown in audience segregation. The offender loses control over the presentation of self and finds prima facie disreputable acts attached to his or her identity. To make matters worse, the offender has no way of knowing how others perceive this new identity, or even whether they know about it. A dentist convicted of Medicaid fraud reported feeling embarrassed when he attended professional meetings after his name appeared in the paper, even though his colleagues at the meetings did not mention his involvement in the offense. Many other offenders reported worrying about what their friends, neighbors, or business associates were thinking, but none reported being confronted or ridiculed by others. Thus their shame and embarrassment appeared to be self-imposed as they imagined how others saw them. The offenders appeared to assume that they would be viewed by others as they were treated by the news media and criminal justice personnel. Offenders assume that friends, neighbors, and business associates gossip about them and their troubles.

Unequal Power Relationships

Some offenders do not receive extensive media attention. They may be indicted on a day when other, more newsworthy events take place, or they may quietly plead guilty rather than go to trial. They do not thereby avoid stressful emotions, however. They still experience a key emotion-producing aspect of criminal justice processing: inability to present one's definition of the situation.

Criminal adjudication occurs in a context of unequal power relationships. Throughout the process of investigation, prosecution, and trial a ritualized silence is imposed on the offender. The prosecutor and other members of the criminal justice system dominate the proceedings. They have the power to command the offender's presence at various meetings and hearings. They also frame the questions and issues that are to be considered, always interpreting the offender's actions from the narrow perspective of the law's prescriptions and not allowing alternative moral frameworks to be introduced. The successful degradation ceremony allows no room for alternative definitions; if the process is to be effective, all ambiguity must be removed. Therefore the offender must be prevented from presenting his or her definition of the situation. For white-collar offenders, this ritualized silence is especially difficult to accept.

Within the bureaucracy of justice, the accused is nearly powerless to speak on his or her behalf. Many white-collar offenders are accustomed to wielding power and authority in their occupations; they are used to being in command and having others respond to their perspective. Now, however, they find themselves in an institutional context where their authority and power are deliberately not recognized—hence the complaint, "They treated me like just another criminal." Even the most powerful business tycoon cannot command a forum in the justice system from which to proclaim, *in his or her own manner,* a definition of the situation. The accused cannot simply tell a story without interruption. Even if offenders are allowed by their lawyers to take the stand (a rare event), they must respond to questions that are framed by others; their answers are required to fit the sometimes-narrow criterion of legal relevance.

> You can never say anything in your defense on the record, because it can be used against you by some third party in a suit. I never got to say one word in my defense. It's like being put in a meat grinder and coming out as sausage on the other end. This government can just crush you, and you can't say anything (Contractor convicted on antitrust violations).

Ironically, the smart offender keeps quiet in a system based upon public adversarial proceedings. Defense attorney and prosecutor negotiate; if the case goes to trial, the offender avoids taking the stand. Although the defendant's silence may make good legal strategy, it prevents him or her from contributing to the definition of reality. Most important, it prevents the offender from explaining his or her reasons for committing the crime. Being forbidden to explain is difficult for white-collar offenders because their reasons for their actions are more important to them than the fact that those actions violated the law. If they could present their reasons, the impact of conviction on identity could be mitigated. The offender could show how the offense is not indicative of his or her true character.

> I don't think I ever had a really full chance to explain everything . . . I felt personally that if I had an opportunity to explain things much more thoroughly—it's very complex, too; it's not just cut and dried about billing and whatnot—that it would have been justified (Dentist convicted of Medicaid fraud).
>
> Eventually, I probably believed that were I to get on the witness stand, I don't think I'd have been guilty. And my lawyers feel the same way. But the fact that I couldn't get on the stand, everybody said, "Why in hell doesn't he get up there and defend himself?" (Advertising agent convicted of mail fraud).

Unequal power relationships and one-sided reality construction are inherent in the adjudicatory process. They produce powerful and conflicting emotions in the offender: shame and rage, embarrassment and hostility. The offender perceives that a reality is being constructed in which his or her status and reputation are discredited. Significantly, however, the offender is also aware of powerlessness to prevent or repair the damage.

THE WHITE-COLLAR
OFFENDER'S ANGER

Prosecution and conviction involve the white-collar offender in a loss of status, and loss of status leads to anger directed at those responsible for the loss.[22] For white-collar criminals loss of status is particularly significant because it occurs on both vertical and horizontal dimensions. Conviction lumps the white-collar offender with other offenders, typically of the lower class; thus he or she is taken down a notch in the status hierarchy. At the same time, during the offender's fall from upstanding citizen to lawbreaker, other status-giving identities are ignored as his or her case is typified by the media and the prosecutor. Roles and activities that lent prestige to the offender in his or her social world, such as occupational position or organizational membership, have little or no relevance in the bureaucracy of justice. Such secondary statuses take on an inverse relevance in the media politics of status degradation; they are used to amplify blameworthiness and to promote righteous indignation about the crimes of the rich.

Yet in viewing the anger felt by white-collar offenders as a function of status loss and one-sided interactions, one may overlook the role of emotion management and self-interactions in generating these emotional experiences. Hochschild argues that emotions are managed or worked upon. Because of their occupations, middle- and upper-class individuals must do more emotion work than lower-class individuals. Thus they gain skill at adopting emotionally usable frames of reference.[23] This skill in managing emotions in the workplace may carry over into the white-collar offenders' dealings with the criminal justice system.

The person subject to criminal prosecution faces a conflict between what he or she thinks ought to be felt (guilt or shame), even if this thought is only momentary, and what he or she wants to feel (self-respect). The interviews suggest that this conflict can be resolved in the individual's favor. The emotions that social rules tell the individual ought to be felt are suppressed in favor of what the individual wants to feel. Thus, as a person goes through the degradation process, he or she may experience a series of emotions: first guilt and shame, as culturally prescribed, but then anger and rage.

White-collar offenders may evoke feelings of rage and hostility in order to work through or manage feelings of embarrassment and shame. The latter emotions are socially useful and are important means by which society achieves social control.[24] From the individual's perspective, however, they are paralyzing. They are not useful because they detract from the individual's ability to act and interact; thus rage and hostility may represent survival mechanisms used by offenders to overcome the paralysis of shame. These emotions, then, may arise not only because of the sense of loss that accompanies status degradation, but also because they are useful for the individual. The degradation process destroys the offender's character completely; therefore the offender must reject it in order to maintain a useful sense of self.

DYSFUNCTIONS OF ADJUDICATION

Having thus described the experiences of white-collar offenders, I do not wish to suggest that these offenders deserve any special consideration. The hardships they endure pale in comparison to those undergone by many ordinary street criminals. White-collar offenders, for example, typically await their trials at home rather than under pretrial detention. Nevertheless, the interviews illustrate certain troubling features of the justice process, which have broader implications for crime control in general.

Underlying the criminal law and justice system are ideologically based rules that structure the emotions which these institutions are meant to produce in the individual. We are supposed to feel bad when we break the law and even worse when we are caught. White-collar offenders do feel bad; they do experience shame and embarrassment. Significantly, however, they also feel anger; that is, they appear to experience emotions that violate the emotional rules which society, for reasons of social control, would want to be followed.

Although anger may be advantageous for offenders, it has potential disadvantages for society. Feelings of anger fuel techniques of neutralization, such as condemning the condemners, which in turn weaken the morally binding force of law. When offenders feel anger toward a society that stigmatizes them, they also may feel less respect for the legitimacy of law. This feeling in turn may strengthen the cohesion of subcultures of noncompliance in the business world.[25] That is, it may provoke rather than deter antisocial attitudes in white-collar offenders.

It is particularly troubling that white-collar offenders feel this way because we assume that they willingly accept the law's legitimacy and the principles of responsible behavior. In view of their commitment to the social order, these are the offenders who we assume would be most likely to feel repentant about their crimes. If the justice process has the effects described above on these offenders, what effects does it have on offenders who have little or no stake in conformity? Is it likely that the justice process promotes feelings of repentance?

The available evidence on these questions suggests that the justice process is equally alienating to other offenders. On the basis of interviews with ordinary street criminals, Casper concludes that they learn from the system only that it does not care much for them. Interaction with the legal system merely reinforces the street offender's image of himself as an outsider.[26]

Following Braithwaite,[27] I suggest that offenders lack a sense of repentance because of the punishment-oriented and stigmatizing nature of our adjudicatory system. The American approach to criminal justice emphasizes what Braithwaite calls "disintegrative shaming"—that is, shaming in which a deviant characteristic is assigned to a person as a master status. In other words, the offense and the offender are linked inextricably; one's true nature is revealed through the degradation process. To be convicted of a crime makes one a criminal and *nothing but* a criminal. By this stigmatization society rejects offenders, making them outsiders. Disintegrative shaming is counterproductive, however. Rather than making offenders feel repentant, it provokes anger and resentment as offenders attempt to maintain a morally acceptable view of self.

Yet there is another type of shaming, which Braithwaite calls "reintegrative shaming." This form of shaming attends to the wrongfulness of the act rather than dramatizing the evil of the actor. The act is criticized and the offender is shamed for having engaged in it, but these expressions of community disapproval are followed by gestures of reacceptance by the community.[28] Rather than casting offenders out, reintegrative shaming attempts to bring them back into the community and to induce them to recommit themselves to community standards. It places less emphasis on fear and more on moral suasion to induce responsible behavior in individuals. With the recognition that offenders need a sense of self-respect, reintegrative shaming offers a moral escape hatch. Offenders who demonstrate their worthiness to be community members by accepting the wrongfulness of their actions are accepted back into the community. The central feature of degradation ceremonies is avoided; the offense is not taken to indicate the offender's "true" character.

The American approach to justice emphasizes punishing wrongful behavior rather than inducing responsible behavior; we conduct degradation ceremonies to stigmatize offenders. We stigmatize offenders because in doing so we make them different from us and hence deserving of punishment. The stigmatization justifies the punishment. Yet we must ask ourselves whether this approach exacerbates the very problems it is designed to solve. For white-collar criminals the justice process, as currently conducted, encourages rejection rather than acceptance of the law's legitimacy. It does not appear to make offenders acknowledge their responsibilities toward the community. It seems unlikely that the process works any more effectively with nonwhite-collar criminals.

Notes

1. Norman K. Denzin, "A Note of Emotionality, Self, and Interaction," *American Journal of Sociology,* 89 (1983):402–409.
2. Kenneth Mann, Stanton Wheeler, and Austin Sarat, "Sentencing the White-Collar Offender," *American Criminal Law Review,* 17 (1980):479–500.
3. John E. Conklin, "Illegal But Not Criminal": Business Crime in America. Englewood Cliffs, NJ: Prentice-Hall, 1977; Paul Jesilow, Henry Pontell, and Gilbert Geis, "Medical Criminals: Physicians and White-Collar Offenses," *Justice Quarterly,* 2 (1985):149–165.
4. Jack Katz, *Seductions of Crime.* New York: Basic Books, 1988, pp. 318–321.
5. Susan Shapiro, *Thinking about White-Collar Crime: Matters of Conceptualization and Research.* Washington, DC: United States Government Printing Office, 1980.

6. Norman K. Denzin, *On Understanding Emotion.* San Francisco: Jossey-Bass, 1984.

7. Arlie R. Hochschild, "Emotion Work, Feeling Rules, and Social Structure," *American Journal of Sociology,* 85 (1979):551–575.

8. Harold Garfinkel, "Conditions of Successful Status Degradation Ceremonies," *American Journal of Sociology,* 61 (1956):420–424.

9. Barney Glaser and Anselm Strauss, *Status Passage.* Chicago: Aldine, 1971.

10. Garfinkel, *op. cit.*

11. Michael Benson, "Denying the Guilty Mind: Accounting for Involvement in a White-Collar Crime," *Criminology,* 23 (1985):583–607: James Coleman, *The Criminal Elite.* New York: St. Martin's Press, 1985; Gilbert Geis, "The Heavy Electrical Equipment Antitrust Cases of 1961." In Marshall Clinard and Richard Quinney, eds., *Criminal Behavior Systems.* New York: Holt, Rinehart & Winston, 1967, pp. 139–150.

12. Jonathan D. Casper, *American Criminal Justice: The Defendant's Perspective.* Englewood Cliffs, NJ: Prentice-Hall, 1972, pp. 145–151.

13. Lonnie H. Athens, *Violent Criminal Acts and Actors.* Boston: Routledge & Kegan Paul, 1980; Donald Black, "Crime as Social Control," *American Sociological Review,* 48 (1983):34–45; Katz, *op. cit.*, pp. 12–51.

14. Erving Goffman, *The Presentation of Self in Everyday Life.* Garden City, NY: Doubleday, 1959.

15. David L. Altheide, *Creating Reality.* Beverly Hills: Sage, 1976.

16. Garfinkel, *op. cit.*

17. Erving Goffman, *Asylums.* Garden City, NY: Anchor, 1961; John Lofland, *Deviance and Identity.* Englewood Cliffs, NJ: Prentice-Hall, 1966; Edwin Schur, *Labelling Deviant Behavior.* New York: Harper and Row, 1971.

18. Stanton Wheeler, David Weisburd, Elin Waring, and Nancy Bode, "White Collar Crimes and Criminals," *American Criminal Law Review,* 25 (1988): 331–357.

19. Altheide, *op. cit.*, pp. 73–83.

20. David L. Altheide, *Media Power.* Beverly Hills: Sage, 1985.

21. Erving Goffman, *Interaction Ritual.* Garden City, NY: Anchor, 1967.

22. Theodore D. Kemper, "Social Constructionist and Positivist Approaches to the Sociology of Emotions," *American Journal of Sociology,* 87 (1981): 336–362.

23. Hochschild, *op. cit.*

24. Susan Shott, "Emotions and Social Life: A Symbolic Interactionist Analysis," *American Journal of Sociology,* 84 (1979):1317–1334.

25. John Braithwaite, *Crime, Shame and Reintegration.* Sydney: Cambridge University Press, 1989.

26. Casper, *op. cit.*, pp. 165–166.

27. Braithwaite, *Crime, Shame, op. cit.*; John Braithwaite, "Criminological Theory and Organizational Crime," *Justice Quarterly,* 6 (1989):333–359.

28. Braithwaite, *Crime, Shame, op. cit.*, p. 55.

18

White-Collar Crime and Punishment
Class Structure and Legal Sanctioning of Securities Violations

John Hagan and Patricia Parker

G ibbons accurately observes that, "in many other areas of sociology, it is possible to list a considerable number of important contributors..., but in criminology, Sutherland stands virtually alone."[1] Sutherland's contributions occurred at the micro- and macrostructural levels reflected in his concepts of differential association and differential social organization.[2] The coordinating premise was that differential social organization structures the differential association of people and the definitions learned from them. Sutherland applied his concepts most provocatively to the explanation of white-collar crime, arguing that "businessmen are not only in contact with definitions which are favorable to white collar crime but also ... are isolated from and protected against definitions which are unfavorable to such crime."[3]

However, the full structural implications of Sutherland's work remain undeveloped. This may in part result from his much debated definition of white-collar crime as "crime committed by a person of *respectability* and high social *status* in the course of his occupation."[4] While Sutherland implied much more, status today is understood as a social-psychological concept which refers to the perceived relative position of an individual in a hierarchy of respect. This gradational conception has caused confusion in the study of white-collar crime and its sanctioning,[5] and recently has led to the unexpected finding by Wheeler et al. that higher-status white-collar offenders receive more severe sentences than lower-status white-collar offenders.[6]

But do studies so conceived actually get to the core of what concerned Sutherland?[7] Geis suggests they do not, reasoning that, "Sutherland, for all his definitional uncertainty, was particularly concerned about the use of positions of power and influence in the corporate, professional, and political world to abuse and even

Reprinted from *American Sociological Review,* 50 (June 1985), pp. 302–316.

exploit others. Neither education nor income nor even status, which Sutherland stressed—actually cut to the scientific-ideological essence of the concept."[8] The problem is that a contemporary understanding of the concept of status glosses over what is potentially most salient in Sutherland's attention to differential social organization: the differential power that derives from structural location in the social organization of work.

Sutherland probably would have agreed, for he noted that "although the concept of 'status' is not entirely clear, it seems to be based principally upon power."[9] He was also explicit. about the power that derives from forms of business organization,[10] and insisted further that "white collar crime is organized crime."[11] This emphasis has resulted in important efforts to distinguish between crimes committed by individuals acting alone and those committed throughout occupational and organizational roles.[12]

However, the above efforts have not yet formed the basis of a structural theory of white-collar crime and punishment. The class structure of these organizational crimes has not been articulated, and a structural theory of white-collar crime and punishment that incorporates the role of power has neither been explicitly formulated nor subjected to empirical test.

In this paper we outline and test a structural theory that begins with a *relational* conception of class.[13] The need for such a conception is linked directly to Sutherland's observation that the most flagrant white-collar crime is also organized crime, in the sense that these crimes make use of organizational positions and resources. It is not gradational status, but rather structural position in the social organization of work that makes such forms of organized crime possible. Relational conceptions of class penetrate to the heart of this matter by locating individuals in structural terms. The relational indicators we use in this paper, ownership and authority, locate individuals in class positions that are directly relevant to the perpetration of white-collar crime as organized crime. We develop this point further, after introducing the substantive focus of our study.

SECURITIES VIOLATIONS AS WHITE-COLLAR CRIMES

We focus in this paper on the class structure and legal sanctioning of securities violations in the Province of Ontario (Canada). Securities markets are among the preeminent institutions of modern capitalist societies,[14] and their manipulation is therefore a preeminent white-collar crime with national and international implications. The latter point has particular relevance to the data we analyze. The Province of Ontario plays a primary role in regulating the Toronto Stock Exchange, Canada's busiest securities market. This market is second only in its volume on this continent to the New York Stock Exchange. The United States is the largest trading partner of Canada, and the Toronto Exchange is a focal point in the interpenetration of the two economies. It is difficult to miss the element of power in this relationship and its implications for securities regulation.

"Throughout its history," writes Clement, "Canada has conformed to the pressures of external demands and internal opportunism.[15] Prior to World War I, the source of these demands was British, after World War I, they were increasingly American. In both cases, Canada encouraged and facilitated resource extraction as a source of foreign capital and as a base for industrialization. The result was an unequal alliance in which the United States became the "extractive power," dominating much of Canada's industry and its resource markets. Through most of this century, therefore, Canada has been much more concerned with stimulating than restricting capital investment, much of which was foreign, but some of which was domestic. Predictably, the regulation of securities was of low priority during this period, and the manipulation of securities was common.[16]

So common that by the mid-1960s Canada had earned an unfavorable international reputation for securities manipulation that itself posed a threat to investment.[17] Reestablishing "investor confidence" and the "credibility of the marketplace" became prominent concerns. This led to a strengthening of enforcement efforts, including passage of the Ontario Securities Act of 1966.[18] These efforts have in the last year included an investigation by the Ontario Securities Commission (OSC) of Conrad Black, Chairman of the giant Argus Corporation and reputedly the most powerful corporate entrepreneur in Canada,[19] as well as an investigation of the multinational participants in a set of real-estate transactions involving the block sale of over 10,000 Toronto apartments eventually valued at over a half billion dollars. Although neither of these investigations has led to a criminal conviction, both have attracted the attention of the national and international press and helped stimulate the current research.[20]

The structure and enforcement of Canadian securities legislation offers a unique opportunity to explore definitional issues raised by Sutherland, but never since explored empirically. Sutherland noted that many white-collar law violations are prosecuted under noncriminal statutes, but that these statutes and the violations specified nonetheless are criminal in the sense of including two necessary elements: "legal description of acts as socially injurious and legal provision of a penalty for the acts."[21] These criteria, rather than a strict reliance on criminal-code constructions,[22] were what Sutherland used in selecting cases for his classic study. Although Sutherland's position on this definitional issue today prevails in theoretical discussions of white-collar crime,[23] empirical studies since Sutherland have been restricted to samples of persons convicted under criminal statutes.[24]

In Canada, securities violations are prosecuted under both kinds of statutes: the Ontario Securities Act and the Criminal Code. Both statutes describe socially injurious offenses and specify fines and imprisonment as penalties.[25] It is commonly asserted that "criminal code prosecution will be undertaken where the conduct of the accused has been flagrant or persistent, or is clearly indicative of malice."[26] Sutherland, and a structural theory of white-collar crime and punishment, cast doubt on such assumptions, asserting that power as well is at least part of the equation.[27] We already have made the point that power was not meaningfully operationalized in past studies. To this is now added the further problem that since Sutherland, only persons convicted under criminal statutes have been sampled for study. The empirical implications of this problem are made explicit in Table 18.2, where we have cross-classified the statute of proscution and the disposition of cases prosecuted in the Province of Ontario from 1966 to 1983. Since Sutherland, only cases of the type found in cell four (which comprise little more than a third of the cases) of this table have been studied. This may constitute a severe form of sample selection bias. However, before addressing this issue further, we describe our data in greater detail, and elaborate the theory, concepts and indicators to be used in this study.

THE DATA AND THE THEORY

The sampling frame for this study consists of all cases referred for prosecution under the Securities Act or the Criminal Code in Ontario from 1966 to 1983. Rather than rely exclusively (as have past studies) on case file data, we interviewed investigators from provincial agencies about the cases they developed during this period. All investigators (whether currently employed by the agencies or not) who could be located were interviewed about their cases, resulting in a sample of 203 cases which are considered in this analysis.[28] The interviews were tape-recorded and transcribed, with excerpts reproduced below. The interview method allowed us to collect information on the class position, organizational involvement, and other aspects of the suspects' cases not included in official case files and therefore not considered in previous research.

Information collected from the above interviews and case files forms the basis of our test of a structural theory. The fundamental premise of such a theory is that class position influences involvement in white-collar criminal *behavior* as well as the *punishment* of this behavior. Indeed, it is our argument that the latter cannot be understood fully without consideration of the former. This is because the punishment of white-collar crime is not simply a function of class position, but also of the kinds of organized white-collar criminal behavior that certain class positions make possible. To make these points, we must identify the classes we will consider. First, however, we must justify using the kind of data we have collected for the study of white-collar criminal behavior and its punishment.

Our data consist of cases referred for prosecution, and thus may not be a random sample of behaviors. Our justifications for using these cases to study white-collar criminal behavior as well as punishment are three-fold. First, the most commonly assumed source of nonrandomness is that the "bigger fish," for various reasons, get away. However, Wheeler and Rothman make a compelling case against this assumption:

> The simple fact is that we really don't know, in the case of common crime, simple white-collar crime, or complex white-collar crime what the relationship is between the magnitude of the take and the likelihood of getting caught. We see no reason in principle for that relationship to differ greatly across types of crime, and we rather imagine that in both simpler and more complex

offenses law enforcement officials must trade off their estimated likelihood of conviction against the magnitude of the take. The same felt need to maintain a winning record, to favor cases that will conclude expeditiously with negotiated pleas of guilt, will obtain regardless of the form the illegality takes.[29]

Of course Wheeler and Rothman are correct in saying that we really don't know what the forms of these biases might actually be. However, beyond their own cogent reasoning we offer, as the second justification for our use of the data chosen, that these data start at an earlier stage, referral for prosecution, than any other empirical study of these issues we have found. Third, lacking some involvement of authorities, such as referral for prosecution, there is a problem of establishing a basis for the assumption that crimes actually have taken place for study. Referral for prosecution is the first decisive commitment to the proposition that a crime has occurred. While the above justifications individually may not be determinative, in combination we believe they weigh heavily in favor of the kind of sample we have selected.

Our analysis considers occupants of four class positions: employers, managers, the petty bourgeoisie, and workers. Note that our interest is in the structural location of individuals in these class positions rather than in the individuals themselves. The positions are defined in the relational (i.e., structural) terms summarized in Table 18.1. This operationalization derives from the Marxist work of Wright,[30] but is adapted to the criminal population involved.[31] Thus the first indicator derives from a question which asks whether the accused is involved in a legitimate or illegitimate occupation. This indicator locates the individual in the legitimate or illegitimate economic sector. The second indicator taps ownership of the means of production by asking whether the individual owns a business. The third indicator measures authority in the workplace by asking whether the individual has one or more levels of subordinates beneath him/her.

Employers work in the legitimate sector, own a business, and have subordinates; they comprise 27.09 percent of our sample. *Managers* also work in the legitimate

Table 18.1
CRITERIA FOR CLASS CATEGORIES

Class	Economic Sector	Ownership of Means of Production	Authority in Workplace	Distribution
Employers	Legitimate	Owner	Has Subordinates	27.09% (55)
Managers	Legitimate	Nonowner	Has Subordinates	19.70% (40)
Petty Bourg.	Legitimate	Owner	No Subordinates	9.36% (19)
Workers	Legitimate or Illegitimate	Nonowner	No Subordinates	43.85% (89)

sector and have subordinates, but they do not own a business; they make up 19.70 percent of our sample. The *petty bourgeoisie* work in the legitimate sector and own a business, but have no subordinates; they constitute 9.36 percent of our sample. (The petty bourgeoisie are usually identified as a dying class, and therefore excluded from Marxist analyses.[32] However, such entrepreneurs, operating "paper" or "shell companies," are a more lively group in the securities area, and we therefore include them in our analysis.) The above three classes are treated as dummy variables, with *workers* designated as the comparison or omitted category. Workers are located in the illegitimate *or* legitimate sector, they are not owners of legitimate businesses and they have no subordinates; they make up 43.85 percent of our sample. A measure of prior record (none/one or more prior convictions) is considered simultaneously with the preceding class variables in our analysis. This is the most frequently included control variable in studies of sanctioning. Additional control variables were included at several stages of our analysis, but eliminated for lack of effect, as discussed further below.

The structural theory we are proposing assumes that employers, managers, and the petty bourgeoisie are more likely than workers to engage in organized forms of white-collar crimes that are more extensive in their scope. Offenses may be organized informally by affiliated individuals, or they may occur through the use of formal organizations including, most notably, businesses. As Sutherland notes, "criminals perfect an organization and with organization their crimes increase in frequency and seriousness."[33] Our theory is premised on the assumptions that organizations, especially formal business organizations, make resources available for the perpetration of grander crimes than is otherwise the case, and that organizations also frequently provide effective covers for the commission of these crimes. Measures of the form and scope of white-collar crimes are therefore required. A key requirement of the measure of the form of the offense is that it effectively indicate whether the crime was organized in an informal and/or formal way. Our measure of the organization of the offense is derived from Wheeler and Rothman[34] and is based on information obtained from investigators as to whether the offense was committed (a) by a single individual; (b) by an individual acting with one or more affiliated persons; or (c) by an individual acting through an organized association, business organization, partnership or family business. (In thirteen cases during the period of our study an organization rather than an individual was charged; these cases are not included in this analysis.) The joint variation of this measure of the organization of the offense with the preceding measures of class position will allow us to explore the class structure of white-collar crime as organized crime.

Both class position and organization of the offense are expected to influence the scope of white-collar crimes. However, difficulties in measuring the scope of securities crimes became apparent as we began to ask for dollar estimates of losses. An example of this problem is provided in the following response of an investigator when asked about the dollar loss in a specific case:

Well, I don't know. It would be a guesstimate, and a bad one at that. People want to know how much money is involved in a scheme like this. Well, the only thing you can allege is how much money was lost by a total number of victims .... You know bloody well that _____ took in, over four or five years of operating on Bay Street, something in those days approaching if not exceeding several million dollars. ... We alleged a loss of ten million dollars, or something like that, and that was done by multiplying the number of shares sold by the top market price of the unit that was reached on a given day by the number of shareholders, or something like this, and we ended up with some grand glorious figure. ... I don't think it was done fairly ... but in order to respond to it they had to make a few admissions and it was done for that very purpose.

To deal with this kind of problem of accuracy, we asked investigators to estimate in each case broad categories of dollar loss (none, hundreds, thousands, millions), number of victims (none, less than a hundred, thousands, many thousands, millions), and the geopolitical spread of the crime (none, local, national, international). When assigned ordinal ranks and summed, these items form a scale, called "scale of offense," with an alpha reliability coefficient of .63. Further analysis revealed that the measure of dollar loss correlated least with the other items, and when it was excluded from the scale the alpha coefficient increased to .72. Use of either scale produces similar substantive results in the analysis that follows; the latter two-item scale is the basis of results presented below.

Our attention shifts next to the prosecution of these white-collar crimes. Here we consider the strength of the evidence in the case, whether plea negotiation was involved, and the type of charge placed against the offender. Investigators ranked the evidence in their cases as strong, uncertain or weak; indicated whether or not plea negotiation occurred; and case files were used to indicate whether the offense was prosecuted under the Securities Act or the Criminal Code. Although conviction under the Securities Act can result in imprisonment, the maximum penalties allowed are lower than under the Criminal Code, and the stigma of a *criminal* conviction is avoided. A structural theory of white-collar crime and punishment therefore predicts that persons located in positions of power will be less likely to be prosecuted under the criminal code. Yet we noted above that seriousness of the offense and malice of motive conventionally are assumed to increase the likelihood of criminal prosecution. The issue, then, is not simply whether powerful persons are more likely than others to benefit from securities convictions, but rather whether this benefit applies with scope of the offense (our measure of seriousness) and strength of evidence (which must include a consideration of intent, and therefore malice) taken into account.

The dependent variable for our analysis is the severity of sentence imposed. The relationship between type of charge and actual sentence imposed is of particular concern. We have already indicated that "sentence exposure" is greater under the Criminal Code than under the Securities Act. Nonetheless, type charge and actual sentence severity are independent events in that exposure under the Criminal Code and the Securities Act overlap, with neither specifying statutory minimum sentences and both allowing commitments to prison, albeit for differing maximum lengths of time. Empirically, more than half (57%) of the persons convicted under the Criminal Code receive sentences of less than one year in prison, the maximum term allowed under the Securities Act. However, as we report further below, the relationship between type of charge and sentence severity is strong. The implication is that the two statutes encourage differential sentence severity, without requiring this outcome by statutory definition.

We present results based on several measures of sentence severity below. The most familiar of these measures is an adapted eleven-point scale widely used in the sentencing literature[35] to reflect variation in the punitiveness of sentences in an approximate interval form.[36] This scale recently has received criticism in the sentencing literature, with the argument being that sentence severity is a discrete rather than a continuous variable.[37] We demonstrate below that the level of measurement assumed makes little substantive difference for the purposes of this study. The substantive interest of a structural theory of white-collar crime and punishment is in how positions of power influence sentencing, with the assumption being that the bias is in the direction of leniency.

A final exogenous variable included in our analysis is the year in which the case was processed. We noted above that beginning in 1965 there was an increasing emphasis on securities enforcement in Ontario. Ontario probably is not unique in this regard. Katz speaks of a "social movement against white-collar crime" that began in the United States in the late 1960s, and public-opinion data documents an increasing concern with the occurrence of such crimes.[38] Wheeler et al. suggest that the status effects found in their data may result from the aftermath of Watergate, but they are unable to test this hypothesis because their data come only from the post-Watergate period.[39] Canada experienced a major political scandal, dubbed "Harbourgate,"[40] that resulted in similar calls for stricter treatment of white-collar criminals. The interesting issue for a structural theory of white-collar crime and punishment is whether such "movements" have the kinds of effects conventionally assumed. The structural theorist is skeptical. By including year in our analysis, we will be able to explore this issue.

A final set of control variables were incorporated at several points in the data analyses presented in this paper. These variables included the age of the defendant, whether the defendant was represented by private counsel, the cooperativeness of the defendant with investigators and prosecutors, and the defendant's prior reputation in the community.[41] These variables had no causal significance for the sanctioning decisions that interest us. The results of including these variables are therefore not presented, but are available on request. There were only five women in our data, so the effects of gender could not be analyzed.

METHODS

Below we explore a causal model of white-collar crime and punishment that incorporates the variables, save the last group, described above. These variables were presented in an assumed logical-temporal sequence that is consistent with the structural theory we wish to explore. Clearly, this theory is not sufficiently developed to allow a deductive model-testing approach. Instead, a series of equations is used inductively to determine causal linkages between variables. However, before doing so, it is necessary that we address the issue of selection bias noted above.

Recall that our dependent variable is sentence and that past studies of the sanctioning of white-collar offenders have dealt only with offenders *convicted* of white-collar *crimes:* cell four of Table 18.2. Yet decisions to charge with noncriminal rather than criminal statutes, and to acquit, dismiss or withdraw charges rather than convict, may result in a highly selected pool of offenders to be sentenced. Parameter estimates based on such samples may be biased and inconsistent.

We address this problem of selection bias in two ways. First, as indicated above, we adopt Sutherland's strategy and include persons charged with Securities Act as well as Criminal Code violations. Second, we conceptualize sentencing as a two-stage process, involving first a decision as to whether to convict, and subsequently, if conviction occurs, a decision as to sentence severity.[42] Heckman outlines a procedure that allows us to combine information from these two decisions in a meaningful way. This procedure involves two equations: the first is a probit equation that estimates whether an accused person is convicted, and the second is an OLS equation for sentence severity that is corrected for selection bias.

The first equation is:

$$\text{Probit } (P_1) = X_1 B^* \qquad (1)$$

where P_1 is the probability of the ith accused person being convicted; X_1 is a row

Table 18.2
THE SELECTION PROBLEM: CROSS-CLASSIFICATION
OF CHARGE BY DISPOSITION[a]

Type of Charge		Unconvicted			Convicted		Row
					Disposition		
Securities	(1)	Unconvicted	35.6	(2)	Convicted	64.4	
		Securities	41.3		Securities	43.8	42.9
		Defendants	15.3		Offenders	27.6	
		(31)			(56)		(87)
Criminal	(3)	Unconvicted	37.9	(4)	Convicted	62.1	
		Criminal	58.7		Criminal	56.3	57.1
		Defendants	21.7		Offenders	35.5	
		(44)			(72)		(116)
Column		(75)	36.9		(128)	63.1	(203)

[a] Percentaged by row, column, and cell, respectively, with cell frequencies in parentheses.

vector of covariates; and $\overset{*}{B}$ the corresponding volume vector of parameters. The second equation is:

$$Z_1 = A_1\upsilon + \Phi_0\lambda_1 + E_1 \qquad (2)$$

where Z_1 is sentence severity; $A_1\upsilon$ is a set of explanatory variables and parameters; λ_1 is a regressor (a new covariate) derived from equation (1) and defined as the "hazard" or risk that the ith offender will be convicted, with Φ_0 as its regression coefficient (i.e., the estimator of the covariance between the errors in the equation predicting conviction and the errors in the equation predicting sentence severity); and E_1 is an error term.

The above strategy allows us to include information from cases in all four cells of Table 18.2. Including securities as well as criminal cases, and treating type of charge as an endogenous variable, will allow us to explore the effects of selection through charging practices. Comparison of Ordinary Least Square [an estimation procedure in regression analysis] (OLS) sentence equations that do and do not include the correction factor derived from the Heckman procedure will allow us to explore the effects of selection through conviction.[43]

THE ANALYSIS

We begin with the probit model of determinants of conviction used to create the correction factor described above. Probit estimates for this model are presented in Table 18.3, along with the correlations of the predictor variables with the correction factor

Table 18.3
PROBIT ESTIMATES OF DETERMINANTS OF CONVICTION AND CORRELATIONS WITH (CORRELATION FACTOR)

	Estimate	Standard Error	Correlation with
Year	−.092†	.026	.320
Petty Bourgeoisie	.028	.384	−.105
Managers	−.225	.303	.107
Employers	−.037	.279	−.008
Prior Record	.805*	.358	−.342
Organization of Offense	.062	.139	−.116
Scope of Offense	.019	.077	−.062
Strength of Evidence	1.068†	.181	−.631
Plea Negotiation	.472	.272	−.174
Type Charge	−.232	.215	.131
Constant = 5.341			

* Significant at the .05 level.
† Significant at the .001 level.

(λ). As one might hope, strength of evidence is the strongest predictor of conviction, and therefore the strongest correlate of the correction factor.[44] Prior record and year are also significantly related to conviction and are the next strongest correlates of the correction factor. (The signs of the significant correlates of conviction are reversed as correlates of the correction factor; since the correction factor is a control variable with no substantive significance in itself, the direction of these correlations is irrelevant.)

The consequences of including the correction factor in our analysis are indicated in Table 18.4, which presents the results of estimating sentence equations containing our independent variables, first without and then with the correction factor included. This table makes clear the importance of type of charge to sentence severity. In both the uncorrected (b = 3.307) and corrected (b = 3.542) equations, charge is the only significant ($p < .001$) predictor: persons charged under the Criminal Code receive much more severe sentences. The important implication of our analysis thus far is that type of charge is crucial to sentence severity. This suggests the necessity of a causal model approach that treats type of charge as an intervening variable in the sentencing of white-collar offenders. On the other hand, there is little evidence that looking only at convicted offenders will bias our analysis. Reestimating the corrected sentence equation makes little difference substantively. We proceed, then, by estimating a causal model of sentencing decisions that considers only convicted offenders. Later in the analysis we return to the full sample of convicted and unconvicted offenders to provide a further check on our results. Before turning to our

Table 18.4
UNCORRECTED AND CORRECTED SENTENCE EQUATIONS

Variables	Uncorrected Equation			Corrected Equation		
	b	B	SE	b	B	SE
Year	−.084	−.167	.051	.020	.040	.092
Petty Bourgeoisie	−.348	−.041	.674	−.354	.041	.672
Managers	−.198	−.030	.588	.170	.025	.656
Employers	.164	.028	.546	.150	.026	.545
Prior Record	.439	.064	.510	−.358	−.052	.812
Organization of Offense	.072	.024	.272	.019	.006	.277
Scope of Offense	.050	.029	.149	.037	.021	.149
Strength of Evidence	−.132	−.024	.440	−1.607	−.285	1.250
Plea Negotiation	−.456	−.080	.442	−.983	−.171	.608
Type Charge	3.307*	.629	.402	3.542*	.674	.443
λ				−2.905		2.306
R^2	.429			.437		
Constant	8.625			5.136		

* Significant at the .001 level.

causal model, we will make a few further points about the coding of sentence sever-ity in these analyses.

When the sentence-severity scale described above is used as the dependent vari-able in the uncorrected OLS sentence equation estimated in Table 18.4, the standard-ized effect of type of charge on sentence is .629. Above we noted a criticism of this scale; that it obscures discrete differences in types of sentences imposed. To explore this issue we estimated separate probit equations that modeled the likelihood of offenders receiving fine, probation, and jail sentences. These equations contained the identical independent variables as the uncorrected sentence equation estimated in Table 18.4. Again in each of these equations, only type of charge was significant in its effect. These equations revealed that persons charged under the Criminal Code were much less likely than those charged under the Securities Act to receive fines (B = 2.175, ρ < .05); they were about equally likely to receive probation (B = 2.30, ρ > .10), and much more likely to be imprisoned (B = 2.304, ρ < .05). We also assigned sentences ordinal ranks of three for imprisonment, two for probation, and one for fines, and regressed this scale on the independent variables on an OLS equa-tion. We use this coding in the causal model presented below, and the results of using this coding are presented in the last column of the Appendix. The result again is that only type of charge is significant in its effect, with a standardized coefficient of .701. So regardless of the measure used, it is clear that type of charge is crucial to sentence severity.

We proceed now to our causal model. The metric and standard form results of estimating equations for the full model are presented in the Appendix.[45] Paths less than .10 in significance or weaker than .10 in strength were deleted from the model, and the equations were then reestimated. Metric coefficients are indicated in Figure 18.1 (in parentheses) next to the standard-form path coefficients. This model further clarifies the importance of type of charge in the sentencing of white-collar offenders. Thus while as noted above only charge exerts a direct effect (B = .656) on sentence severity, a number of other variables influence sentence indirectly through type of charge. As conventionally assumed, the greater the scope of the offense (B = .290), the more likely the person is to be charged with a criminal offense. However, with scope of offense and other variables held constant, there are also two important class effects: compared to workers, managers (B = .259) are *more* likely, and employers (B = −.172) *less* likely, to be charged under the Criminal Code.

To understand further the role of class position in our model, we consider next the influence of organization of the offense. Recall that our organizational measure has three values that represent individuals acting alone (31.8%), with affiliated oth-ers (18.2%), and through formal organizations (50%), most notably business organi-zations. So informally organized offenses are the least frequent in our sample, with formally organized offenses most frequent. In our preliminary analyses, we created dummy variables to measure separately the impact of the informal and formal orga-nization of offenses on their scope. Offenses committed with formal (B = .528, ρ < .001) and informal (B = .517, ρ < .001) organization were about equal in scope, with both kinds of offenses much broader in scope than unorganized offenses. Recall, however, that formally organized offenses were much more frequent than informally organized offenses. Furthermore, employers were more likely to be involved in formally than informally organized offenses. (A separate probit analysis of the effects of class position on organization of offense revealed that employers are much less likely than workers to act alone [B = .904, ρ < .05], about equally likely to commit their offenses with informally affiliated others [B = .221, ρ > .05], and much more likely to commit their offenses through formal organizations [B = .849, ρ < .05]). In other words, it appears that employers make good use of the formally organized business resources available to them. This is, of course, consistent with the structural theory we propose.

The three-valued version of the organizational variable is used in the causal model presented. Again in this model, scope of offense is in large part determined by its organization: organized offenses are bigger (B = .325). Beyond this, it is employers who are particularly likely to perpetrate organized offenses (B = .223). Again, our structural theory assumes that this is because employers are best positioned to use organizational resources in committing white-collar crimes. A structural theory of white-collar crime and punishment is therefore unsurprised to find that the correlation between being an employer and scope of offense is significant

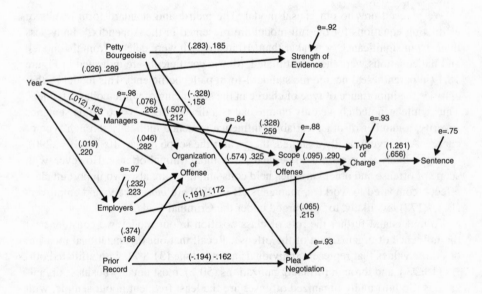

Figure 18.1
Causal Model of White-Collar Crime and Punishment

and positive (r = .164); that the effect of employer position on scope of offense is largely indirect through organization of offense (.223 × .325 = .073); and that the correlation between being an employer and sentence severity is negligible and non-significant (r = .002). Given the scope of employer offenses, the weakness of the latter correlation is suggestive of an inequality of outcomes, made possible in part by a reduced likelihood of employers being charged with criminal offenses.

Thus far, our account of the model estimated in Figure 18.1 suggests that managers are treated with disproportionate severity, and employers with disproportionate leniency. However, the model becomes even more interesting when we take into account the year in which the case was processed. This part of the model indicates a shift over time toward the prosecution of what would commonly be regarded as more important cases. Year of the case exerts a positive direct effect (B = .262) on scope of the offense, and a positive indirect effect on scope of the offense through organization of the offense (.282 × .325 = .092). Over time, managers (B = .163) and employers (B = .220) were more likely to be prosecuted than workers.

The prominence of the above year effects made us wonder if there might be evidence of a "Watergate" or "Harbourgate" effect. More specifically, we wondered if it could have been the increased charging of employers over time that led to a reduced proscution of employers under the Criminal Code. To answer this question we first reestimated the type-of-charge equation, including an interaction term formed by multiplying year, coded first as an interval and then as a binary variable, times the employer variable. With year coded as an interval variable, the interaction effect is significant (t = 1.716, ρ < .05, one-tailed). With year coded as a binary variable, the interaction effect remains marginally significant (t = 1.526, ρ < .10, one-tailed).

Table 18.5 further clarifies the above findings by presenting the results of estimating the type-of-charge equations in the before- and after-Watergate periods. Before Watergate, the effect of being an employer on being charged under the Criminal Code was positive and nonsignificant (b = .214, ρ > .10). After Watergate, this effect is significantly negative (b = −.316, ρ < .05). In other words, it is only after Watergate, and the increased prosecution of employers, that the apparent leniency in the use of Securities Act charges with employers occurs. Recall that managers were also more likely to be prosecuted after Watergate. However, before (b = .406, ρ < .10) and after Watergate (b = .356, ρ < .05), managers are *more* likely than workers to be charged under the Criminal Code (between periods, t = .232, ρ < .10).

Two final concerns remain. The above equations were estimated using the sample of convicted offenders and OLS regression. The concerns are whether using only the convicted sample and using OLS regression with a binary dependent variable bias our results. Since we are not directly concerned with sentencing in this part of the analysis, we can again use the full sample, and we can use probit in place of OLS regression.

The results are presented in Table 18.6.[46] These results confirm that it was only after Watergate that employers were significantly less likely than workers (B = −.797, ρ < .05) to be charged under the Criminal Code (t = 3.25, ρ < .01). On the

Table 18.5
OLS ESTIMATES OF DETERMINANTS OF TYPE OF CHARGE
BY TIME PERIOD

Variables	1966–1973 (N = 54)			1974–1983 (N = 72)		
	b	B	SE	b	B	SE
Year	.045	.154	.042	.027	.158	.020
Petty Bourgeoisie	−.120	−.086	.227	.277	.145	.234
Managers	.406	.236	.286	.356*	.324	.148
Employers	.214	.160	.282	−.316*	−.313	.140
Prior Record	.045	.032	.222	.210	.172	.150
Organization of Offense	−.105	−.184	.117	.025	−.038	.079
Scope of Offense	.100*	.316	.052	.135†	.360	.044
Strength of Evidence	−.053	.126	−.063	.073	.041	.208
Plea Negotiation	−.291	−.227	.185	.014	.132	.014
R^2	.218			.243		
Constant	−2.557			2.154		

* Significant at the .05 level.

† Significant at the .01 level.

other hand, we also find that after (B = .517, ρ < .10) as well as before Watergate (B = 1.340, ρ < .10), managers were significantly more likely than workers to be charged with Criminal Code offenses. This effect declines, but not significantly, after Watergate (t = 1.145, ρ > .10). More generally, the effect of year within the second time period (B = −.083, ρ < .10) and the above class effects suggest that the increased prosecution of managers and employers after Watergate was offset by a reduced use of criminal charges. For our purposes, the most important conclusion is that in this period, employers were particularly unlikely to be charged under the Criminal Code. Indeed, occupants of this class position were in this period the least likely in the sample to be charged as criminal offenders. Meanwhile, members of the managerial class continued to be the persons most vulnerable to these charges.

DISCUSSION AND CONCLUSIONS

We have proposed a structural theory of white-collar crime and punishment. This theory urges that a relational conception of class replace earlier considerations of socioeconomic status. Sutherland might well have seconded this change, for it allows a more direct consideration of the role of power that he also emphasized. Empirical results of our work suggest that the substitution of class for status measures is crucial.

Table 18.6
PROBIT ESTIMATE OF DETERMINANTS OF TYPE OF CHARGE
BY TIME PERIOD

Variables	1966–1983 (N = 203)		1966–1973 (N = 81)		1974–1983 (N = 123)	
	Estimate		Estimate		Estimate	
	(B)	SE	(B)	SE	(B)	SE
Year	−.005	.021	.215*	.103	−.083†	.049
Petty Bourgeoisie	−.743*	.344	−.686	.569	−.408	.483
Managers	.524†	.278	1.340†	.814	.517†	.328
Employers	−.464†	.256	.324	.501	−.797*	.326
Prior Record	−.250	.275	.282	.579	−.013	.356
Organiz. of Offense	−.031	.127	−.136	.217	.051	.180
Scope of Offense	.187**	.072	.037	.109	.400***	.111
Strength of Evidence	.283†	.148	.150	.233	.416†	.214
Plea Negotiation	−.293	.240	−.978†	.546	−.010	.317
Constant	−.079		−14.74		4.856	

† Significant at the .10 level, one-tailed.

* Significant at the .05 level.

** Significant at the .01 level.

For example, recall Sutherland's concern that white-collar crime is a form of organized crime. Our class-based analysis of securities violations indicates why and how this is the case. Employers are located in positions of power that allow them to use organizational resources to commit white-collar crimes. As might be expected, these organizational crimes are also the largest in scope (measured in terms of numbers of victims and geopolitical spread) in our data. However, persons located in the employer class do not receive sanctions commensurate with these crimes. Our data indicate that in large part this is because employers are less likely than others to be charged under the Criminal Code. Employers are instead more likely to be charged with Securities Act violations that carry less stigma and lower sentence exposure. Subsequent analyses revealed that these patterns were most noticeable following Watergate. This was an era in which the enforcement of securities laws increased, with a new emphasis on large, organized offenses committed by managers as well as employers. Employers apparently were spared some of the consequences of this increased proscution through the use of Securities Act rather than Criminal Code charges.

On the other hand, the post-Watergate attention to securities violations was felt most acutely in the managerial class. The prosecution of members of this class increased over time, and before as well as after Watergate managers were more likely than others to be subjected to Criminal Code charges. The implication is that persons located in this class were scapegoats for the "social movement against white-collar crime" that Katz and others describe. The question is why?[47]

Our answer begins with the uniquely powerful positions that employers occupy in modern capitalist economies.[48] Employers are in positions of power that allow them to be distanced from criminal events and that can obscure their involvement in them. Sutherland made this point in noting the "obfuscation as to responsibility" that accompanies corporate positions of power.[49] Two intriguing studies published in the *Harvard Business Review* suggest that this problem of distance and disengagement is not only large but growing. The latter of these studies reports that the percentage of managing executives who indicate an inability to be honest in providing information to their employers has nearly doubled since the earlier research. About half of those surveyed in the latter study thought that their employers frequently did not wish to know how results were obtained, so long as the desired outcomes were accomplished.[50] Such tendencies, and the indication that they are increasing, may explain the greater liability of managers than employers to criminal sanctioning, particularly in the post-Watergate era when the "failure to know and/or recall" defense became common.

Two further factors compliment the above argument and should be noted with regard to employer-class leniency. The first is the role that the complexity of employers' offenses may play in insulating them from criminal prosecution. Investigators frequently noted in our interviews the difficulty judges had in understanding securities offenses, and the hesitancy judges therefore felt in reaching judgments of guilt in criminal cases:

> The biggest problem is convincing the courts of what their offense was, because the courts don't understand securities frauds. . . . There are only a smattering of provincial court judges that have a knowledge of securities law, and a lot of them will take the easy way out and give accused the benefit of the doubt.

Consider such a judge hearing the following investigator's description of a typical employer-class case:

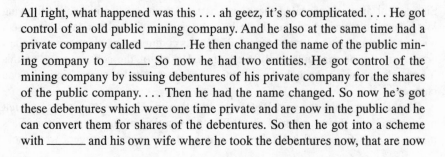

> All right, what happened was this . . . ah geez, it's so complicated. . . . He got control of an old public mining company. And he also at the same time had a private company called _____. He then changed the name of the public mining company to _____. So now he had two entities. He got control of the mining company by issuing debentures of his private company for the shares of the public company. . . . Then he had the name changed. So now he's got these debentures which were one time private and are now in the public and he can convert them for shares of the debentures. So then he got into a scheme with _____ and his own wife where he took the debentures now, that are now

owned by that public company, he took them and put them into _____, a stockbroker, as legitimate bonds. And he arranged with _____ and _____ to buy and sell the bonds because he figured out that as long as you kept a bid on the bonds that give them a price, even though they were worthless, they were convertible debentures due in 1994 or something, you know, they were just, nothing behind them at all, but as long as somebody was willing to put a bid in on them and there was a buy at least once a month, then the deal would go through and the IBM print-out would show a price on the bond. So if he could show a price on the bond then he could get margin on it from the broker. And by using this margin, they were able to buy and sell these Dune shares. . . .

In such complicated cases, it undoubtedly is easier to convince a judge of a more specific securities charge than of a criminal conviction that requires a demonstration of malice.

A related factor is the international scale of many employers' cases. In many such cases the additional cost involved in securing a criminal conviction may explain reliance on the Securities Act. An investigator observes:

The principals in _____ were involved in a tremendous scam that was taking place in Holland and in the Netherlands, the Antilles and in the Bahamian Islands, and places like that, and they [OSC investigators] put a tremendous amount of work in it, spent all sorts of money trying to prove what had gone on and they [the OSC] went to the Attorney General's department and . . . no criminal charges were laid. You know, it was a matter of economics. Because it would have meant bringing witnesses from practically all over the country, all over the world, to give evidence.

The above factors help further explain the reluctance to pursue employer-class cases under the Criminal Code.

We turn finally to the broader implications of our findings. Our findings contrast most noticeably with those of Wheeler et al., who report a linear, additive relationship between socioeconomic status and sentence severity in white-collar cases. They note that this relationship is surprising and controversial, and they encourage further research to evaluate three alternative explanations of their results. The first explanation focuses on the kinds of sample selection problems we have examined; the second on a kind of Watergate effect we have explored; the third on "historical patterns that link greater social obligation with higher social status."[51] Our categorical measure of class suggests a more complicated link between class and court outcomes than is found in the Wheeler et al. study, and our findings are more supportive of the first two explanations of their results than the third. This is important because, as Wheeler et al. note, acceptance of the third explanation would require "modification of most currently held views," including the widely respected views of Sutherland.[52]

Beyond this, Marxists and non-Marxists alike should find our results of interest, for they are relevant to both functionalist and structural Marxist theories of capital formation and law. We noted at the outset Canada's chronic dependence on foreign as well as domestic infusions of capital to extract its resources and develop its industrial base. It is through securities markets that such capitalization must occur. For much of Canada's history these markets were given as free a rein as possible, so as to develop as quickly as possible. When in the 1960s these markets fell into disrepute, a new mandate for enforcement emerged. We have noted that this mandate did not develop in Canada alone, but it was felt particularly acutely in the enforcement of Canadian securities laws. As in the United States (i.e., Canada is culturally as well as economically dominated), this "social movement" reached its peak in the post-Watergate era. There was a felt need to rebuild "investor confidence" and the "credibility of the marketplace." It is in this kind of context that the classic conflict between the desire for free enterprise and the need for government regulation comes most openly into view. Both functionalist and structural Marxist theories have something to say about this.

The laissez-faire functionalist assumption is that freedom from regulation facilitates economic enterprise, at least insofar as the exchanges involved are consensually based. The role of the state is therefore to prohibit and punish unwilling exchanges, while giving due consideration to the potential costs and gains of alternative sanctions.[53] This concern for balance is captured nicely in the observation of the outgoing Chairman of the Ontario Securities Commission that "our role is not solely investor protection, but it is to create an environment which leads to an efficient market place."[54] The goal, of course, is the efficient formation of capital.

Structural Marxist theories of law seek to explain how such goals influence legal behavior. These theories, in contrast with older instrumental Marxisms, acknowledge a "relative autonomy of law," and seek to determine when this autonomy will be observed as well as violated.[55] The tendency after Watergate of employers more than others to be charged under the Securities Act rather than the Criminal Code suggests a violation of autonomy. We have speculated that an increasing distancing and disengagement of employers from unlawful behavior that employers nonetheless implicitly or explicitly encourage among others, namely managers, may account for the above result, and further explain the finding that managers were especially liable to criminal prosecution in the post-Watergate era. These are structural conditions that may protect employers and leave managers more vulnerable to criminal prosecution. Both functionalist and structural Marxist theories of capital formation and law are relevant to the understanding of these conditions. Meanwhile, conceptualization and measurement of such practices as distancing and disengagement will provide the kind of elaboration and specification that a structural theory of law requires to be more fully developed and tested in terms of traditional criteria of causality. Our results indicate that the substitution of class for status measures is a crucial precondition for such developments.

APPENDIX: REGRESSION COEFFICIENTS, MEANS AND STANDARD DEVIATIONS (N = 126)[a]

	Year	Petty Bour- geoisie	Mana- gers	Employ- ers	Prior Record	Organi- zation of Offense	Scope of Offense	Strength of Evidence	Plea Negoti- ation	Charge	Sen- tence (1–11)	Sen- tence (1–3)
Year	.	–.132	.163	.220	.016	.278	.263	.230	.140	.026	–.167	–.048
Petty Bourgeoisie	–.008	.	•	•	•	.218	–.032	.175	–.186	–.065	–.041	–.038
Managers	.012	•	.	•	•	.114	–.056	.050	.074	.269	–.030	–.127
Employers	.019	•	•	.	•	.331	–.008	.157	–.141	–.193	.028	.056
Prior Record	.001	•	•	•	.	.168	.045	.036	–.170	.023	.064	.047
Organization of Offense	.046	.612	.249	.632	.378	.	.341	.085	.023	–.043	.024	.037
Scope of Offense	.076	–.156	–.215	–.029	.178	.603	.	.092	.212	.319	.029	–.129
Strength of Evidence	.020	.268	.060	.162	.044	.046	.028	.	.054	.051	–.024	.093
Plea Negotiation	.012	–.278	.086	–.143	–.204	.012	.064	.053	.	–.136	–.080	–.101
Charge	.003	–.107	.340	–.214	.030	–.025	.110	.055	–.148	.	.629	.701
Sentence (1–11)	–.084	–.348	–.198	.164	.439	.072	.050	–.132	–.456	3.306	.	•
Sentence (1–3)	–.009	–.118	–.308	.120	.119	.042	–.082	.192	–.212	1.346	•	.
Mean	73.952	.103	.190	.278	.175	2.294	2.714	1.786	.294	.556	4.222	1.952
Standard Deviation	5.237	.305	.394	.450	.381	.859	1.517	.467	.457	.499	2.623	.954

[a] Unstandardized and standardized regression coefficients below and above diagonal, respectively.

Notes

1. Don Gibbons, *The Criminological Enterprise.* Englewood Cliffs, NJ: Prentice-Hall, 1979, p. 65.
2. Karl Schuessler, *Edwin H. Sutherland: On Analyzing Crime.* Chicago: University of Chicago Press, 1973, part 1.
3. Edwin Sutherland, *White Collar Crime: The Uncut Version.* New Haven, CT: Yale University Press, 1983, p. 250.
4. *Ibid.*, p. 7 (emphasis added).
5. Gilbert Geis and Robert F. Meier, eds., *White Collar Crime.* New York: Free Press, 1977.
6. Stanton Wheeler, David Weisburd, and Nancy Bode, "Sentencing the White-Collar Offender: Rhetoric and Reality," *American Sociological Review,* 47 (1982): 641–659.
7. See also John Hagan, Ilene Nagel, and Celesta Albonetti, "The Differential Sentencing of White-Collar Offenders in Ten Federal District Courts," *American Sociological Review,* 45 (1980):802–820.
8. Gilbert Geis, "White-Collar and Corporate Crime." In Robert F. Meier, ed., *Major Forms of Crime.* Beverly Hills: Sage, 1984, p. 146.
9. Edwin Sutherland, *White Collar Crime.* New York: Dryden, 1949, p. 224; see also Schuessler, *op. cit.*, pp. 49, 57.
10. Edwin Sutherland, "Crime in Corporations." In Karl Schuessler, ed., *Edwin H. Sutherland: On Analyzing Crime.* Chicago: University of Chicago Press, 1973.
11. Sutherland, 1949, *op. cit.,* chap. 14.
12. Stanton Wheeler and Lewis Rothman, "The Organization as Weapon in White-Collar Crime," *Michigan Law Review,* 80 (1982):641–659; see also John Hagan, "The Corporate Advantage: The Involvement of Individual and Organizational Victims in the Criminal Process," *Social Forces,* 60 (1982): 993–1022.
13. Erik Olin Wright, "Varieties of Marxist Conceptions of Class Structure," *Politics and Society,* 9 (1980):325; John Hagan, A. R. Gillis, and John Simpson, "The Class Structure of Gender and Delinquency: Toward a Power Control Theory of Common Delinquent Behavior," *American Journal of Sociology,* 90 (1985):1151–1178.
14. Wayne Baker, "The Social Structure of a National Securities Market," *American Journal of Sociology,* 89 (1984):775–811.
15. Wallace Clement, *Continental Corporate Power.* Toronto: McClelland and Stewart, 1977, p. 7.
16. Lawrence Kryzanowski, "Misinformation and Security Markets," *McGill Law Journal,* 24 (1978):124.
17. Carol LaPrairie, "The Development of Sanctions for Stock Market Manipulations in Ontario," *Canadian Journal of Criminology,* 21 (1979):275–292.

18. David Johnston, *Canadian Securities Regulations.* Toronto: Butterworths, 1977. Three court cases attracted particular attention during this period. R. v. Jay (1965), 2 Ontario Reports 471; R. v. Lampard (1968), 2 Ontario Reports 470; R. v. MacMillan (1968), 1 Ontario Reports 475. These cases were highly publicized and earned the designation of "scandals," especially the last, which was popularly known as the "Windfall Oil and Mines Affair."

19. Peter C. Newman, *The Establishment Man.* Toronto: McClelland and Stewart, 1982.

20. "Crown Rejects Charges against Norcen," *Toronto Globe and Mail,* June 10, 1983, p. 5. Also, "Financiers Knew Loans Breached Act, Report Says," *Globe and Mail,* June 15, 1983, p. 11; "Investigation of Norcen Is Dropped by Ontario Securities Commission," *Wall Street Journal,* April 14, 1983, p. 6; "Canada Police Probes of Norcen's Hanna Bid Ends without Charges," *Wall Street Journal,* June 13, 1983, p. 18; "Ontario Report Questions Whether Saudis Purchased 11,000 Apartments in Toronto," *Wall Street Journal,* June 20, 1983, p. 4.

21. Edwin Sutherland, "Is 'White Collar Crime' Crime?" *American Sociological Review,* 10 (1945):132.

22. Paul Tappan, "Who Is the Criminal?" *American Sociological Review,* 12 (1947): 96–102.

23. Stanton Wheeler, "Trends and Problems in the Sociological Study of Crime," *Social Problems,* 23 (1976):525–533.

24. Hagan et al., 1980, *op. cit.* See also Wheeler et al., *op. cit.*

25. The Securities Act specifies offenses which for an individual can result in fines up to $2,000 and imprisonment for one year. The act deals specifically with takeover bids, proxies, insider reporting and financial disclosure, and also includes a general offense provision. The Criminal Code specifies offenses which for an individual can result in imprisonment for ten years. These offenses include conspiracy, spreading false news, false pretenses or statements, fraud, false prospectus, fraudulent manipulation of stock exchange transactions, gaming in stocks and merchandise, broker reducing stock by selling his own account (short sales), and breach of trust by public officials.

26. Johnston, *op. cit.*, p. 372.

27. See, e.g., William Chambliss, "White Collar Crime and Criminology," *Contemporary Sociology,* 13 (1984):160–162.

28. The file system of provincial agencies provided our initial enumeration of 226 cases referred for prosecution from 1966 to 1983. When investigators primarily responsible for cases could not be located (this occurred in 43 cases), alternative sources of information were used (news accounts, related case files, and other investigators). In 23 cases this information was eventually judged to be inadequate and these cases were omitted from the analysis presented here. Removal of these cases does not change the structure of the casual model presented, but it does improve the performance of the scope of offense scale described here.

29. Wheeler and Rothman, *op. cit.*, p. 1423.

30. Wright, 1980, *op. cit.* See also: Erik Olin Wright and Luca Perrone, "Marxist Class Categories and Income Inequality," *American Sociological Review,* 42 (1977):32–55; Eric Olin Wright, Cynthia Costello, David Hachen, and Joey Sprague, "The American Class Structure," *American Sociological Review,* 47(1982):709–726.

31. John Hagan and Celesta Albonetti, "Race, Class, and the Perception of Criminal Injustice in America," *American Journal of Sociology,* 88 (1982): 329–355.

32. Wright and Perrone, *op. cit.*, p. 43.

33. Schuessler, *op. cit.*, p. 21.

34. Wheeler and Rothman, *op. cit.*

35. Lawrence P. Tiffany, Yakov Avichai, and Geoffrey W. Peters, "A Statistical Analysis of Sentencing in Federal Courts: Defendants Convicted after Trial, 1967–1968," *Journal of Legal Studies,* 4 (1975):369–390; Shari Seidman Diamond and Hans Zeisel, "Sentencing Councils: A Study of Sentence Disparity and Its Reduction," *University of Chicago Law Review,* 43 (1975):109–149.

36. This scale takes the following values: suspended sentence, without supervision (1); fine (2); probation with supervision to 12 months, with or without fine (3); probation with supervision to 36 months, with or without fine (4); prison to 121 months, with or without fine or probation (6); prison to 24 months, with or without fine or probation (7); prison to 36 months, with or without fine or probation (8); prison to 48 months, with or without fine or probation (9); prison to 60 months, with or without fine or probation (10); prison to 72 months, with or without fine or probation (11).

37. Alfred Blumstein, Jacqueline Cohen, Susan E. Martin and Michael H. Torny, *Research on Sentencing: The Search For Reform.* Washington, DC: National Academy Press, 1983, p. 82.

38. Jack Katz, "The Social Movement against White Collar Crime." In Egon Bittner and Sheldon Messinger, eds., *Criminology Review Yearbook,* vol. 2. Beverly Hills: Sage, 1980; see also Francis T. Cullen, Bruce G. Link, and Craig W. Polanzi, "The Seriousness of Crime Revisited: Have Attitudes toward White-Collar Crime Changed?" *Criminology,* 20 (1982):83–102; Laura Schrager and James Short, "How Serious a Crime?: Perceptions of Organizational and Common Crimes." In Gilbert Geis and Ezra Stotland, eds., *White Collar Crime: Theory and Research.* Beverly Hills: Sage, 1980.

39. Wheeler et al., *op. cit.*, p. 657.

40. "Politicians 'On Take' Dredge Trail Tape Says," *Toronto Star,* June 4, 1975, p. A24.

41. Age was coded in actual years, private counsel as a dummy variable, and cooperativeness and reputation as Likert scales.

42. James J. Heckman, "Shadow Prices, Market Wages, and Labor Supply," *Econometrica,* 42 (1974):679–694; Heckman, "Shadow Prices, Market Wages and Labor Supply Revisited: Some Computational and Conceptual Simplifications and Revised Estimates," Mimeographed paper, University of Chicago,

1975; Heckman, "Sample Selection Bias as a Specification Error," *Econometrica*, 45 (1979):153–161; Richard Berk, "An Introduction to Sample Selection Bias in Sociological Data," *American Sociological Review*, 48 (1983): 386–397.

43. For discussions of possible limitations of the Heckman procedure in correcting for selection bias, see Berk, *ibid.*; See Also Arthur Goldberger, "Linear Regression after Selection," *Journal of Econometrics*, 15 (1981):357–366. We simply note here that the selection equation itself gives little indication that the kinds of class bias that are of concern in the literature on white-collar crime influence our results through the process of conviction.

44. Although there was no indication of this in our interviews with investigators, it is possible that the influence of strength of evidence was exaggerated by the investigators' retrospective knowledge of case outcomes. For this reason, among others, we return below to the full sample of convicted and unconvicted offenders to conduct a final check on our results.

45. We believe that the analysis that follows is free of common technical or specification problems. None of the independent variables are correlated as high as .6, the Durbin-Watson d-statistics for equations estimated below are concentrated between 1.5 and 1.8, scattergrams reveal no outlier problems, and our attempts to incorporate additional exploratory variables do not alter the structure or substance of our results.

46. Douglas A. Smith, "The Organizational Context of Legal Control," *Criminology*, 22(1984), p. 36. Smith points out that the following statistic had a t-distribution and can be used to test for significant differences between pairs of probit coefficients across equations.

47. Katz, *op. cit.*

48. See also Hagan et al., *op. cit.*

49. Sutherland, *op. cit.*, p. 226.

50. Raymond C. Baumhart, "How Ethical Are Businessmen?" *Harvard Business Review*, 39 (1961):51–76. Steven N. Brenner and Earl A. Molander, "Is the Ethics of Business Changing?" *Harvard Business Review*, 55 (1977): 57–71.

51. Wheeler et al., *op. cit.*, pp. 658, 680.

52. *Ibid.*, p. 658.

53. Drew Humphries and David Greenberg, "Social Control and Social Formations: A Marxian Analysis." In Donald Black, ed., *Toward a General Theory of Social Control*. New York: Academic Press, 1984, p. 188.

54. "An Interview with Outgoing Chairman of OSC," *Toronto Globe and Mail*, February 26, 1985, page B1.

55. Isaac Balbus, *The Dialectics of Legal Repression*. New York: Russell Sage Foundation, 1973.

PART IV

Conceptualizations of White-Collar Crime

Introduction to Part IV

The very first paragraph of the presidential address to the American Sociological Society by Edwin H. Sutherland that introduced the concept of white-collar crime called attention to its theoretical implications. His comparison of the crimes of those in business and the professions with the crimes of the lower class was undertaken, Sutherland insisted, "for the purpose of developing theories of criminal behavior, not for the purpose of muckraking or of reforming anything except criminology."[1] Thereafter, Sutherland argued that his theory of differential association offered a set of principles that best interpreted all criminal behavior. He believed that white-collar crime could be most efficiently understood as a form of illegal behavior learned by newcomers from their contact with persons who trained them in the techniques and passed along the attitudes necessary to carry out such offenses. John Barron Mays's critique of differential association seems fair: "It takes us a little way and then abandons us to doubt," he wrote,[2] emphasizing that differential association raises more questions about crime causation than it answers.

Sutherland was particularly harsh on psychiatric explanations of criminal behavior. In a particularly quotable paragraph from a speech that he delivered in the spring of 1948 to the Toynbee Club, a group of sociology majors at DePauw University in Greencastle, Indiana, Sutherland observed:

> We have no reason to think that General Motors has an inferiority complex or that the Aluminum Company of America has a frustration-aggression complex or that U.S. Steel has an Oedipus complex, or that the Armour Company has a death wish or that the DuPonts desire to return to the womb. The distortion of the intellect or the emotions seems to me absurd, and if it is absurd regarding the crimes of businessmen, it is equally absurd regarding the crimes of persons in the lower class.[3]

There are, of course, several difficulties with this broadside. For one thing, Sutherland anthropomorphizes the corporations, treating them as if they were human, a position that fueled the kind of controversy that is discussed in the final three chapters of this section. Besides, of course, the fact that upper-class offenders may not have such pathological disturbances does not disprove the proposition that lower-class offenders may. It is not an illogical proposition, just an unlikely one; and indeed, few, if any, scholars then or now would maintain that all crime was caused by the psychiatric aberrations of those who committed the offenses. Sutherland was giving voice to his strong distaste for psychiatric and psychological interpretations of crime,[4] and, at the same time, pushing his viewpoint that all crime should be explained by a single theoretical formula.

The first three articles in this section address different aspects of the original concern raised by Sutherland with the need for a theoretical understanding of the criminal phenomenon. In the first piece, James William Coleman offers what he calls an "integrated theory of white-collar crime." Criminal behavior, Coleman posits, results from the confluence of appropriate motivation and opportunity. Motivation for white-collar crime, he believes, arises from the structure of industrial capitalism and the culture of competition characteristic of capitalism. Coleman argues that no single theory of motivation would be sufficient to explain the causes of white-collar crime, but that understanding can result from an appreciation of the patterns of opportunities available to persons in positions of power.

The article by Travis Hirschi and Michael Gottfredson is part of their larger thesis that all crime (and many forms of deviance) can best be understood as the consequence of the absence of "self-control" in the perpetrator. Hirschi and

Gottfredson appreciate that white-collar crime has been the stumbling block for theorists whose views may seem sensible regarding lower-class offenses but fall far short when applied to the lives and traits of white-collar offenses. They therefore explicitly seek to show that white-collar offenders exhibit traits similar to those of other lawbreakers, most particularly a deficiency of self-control. The vital importance of definition—that is, of what precisely is said to be white-collar crime—is demonstrated by Darrell Steffensmeier's critique of Hirschi and Gottfredson, in the next article in this section, in which he seeks to show that they have been able to reach their conclusion only by distorting the definition of white-collar crime. A further problem is that to say that white-collar crime results from low self-control and that evidence for such low self-control can be found in the behavior of white-collar offenders is logically suspect. The terms "crime" and "low self-control" are so closely connected as to be parts of the same thing. A satisfactory theory does not explain something merely in terms of the characteristics of that something. There is the further problem of identifying the conditions under which low self-esteem might be expressed in criminal behavior.

The final three articles deal with the possibility of theories that explain corporate crime. Holding institutional entities responsible for lawbreaking not only has aroused the interest of theorists but also poses controversial issues for policy-makers. Some believe that individuals alone should bear the responsibility for criminal actions; that blaming corporations deflects the moral obloquy from a person to an inanimate, unfeeling object. Among the arguments for maintaining corporate criminal liability are these:

1. A corporate body is distinctive from the sum of those persons who make up the organization, and it is more reasonable to pursue the collectivity rather than persons who separately fall short of satisfactorily representing the culpable entity;
2. Punishing individuals rather than the corporate body is not an effective strategy since for employees the risks associated with potential criminal liability will generally be less compelling than those related to failure to meet organizational demands;
3. The shame and moral disgrace associated with criminal conviction will

have a stronger deterrent impact on a corporation than on individual malefactors within it;

4. It is much easier for prosecutors to establish corporate criminal guilt than
   it is to discover and to prosecute guilty individuals;

5. Since the corporation almost invariably possesses much greater assets
   than the individuals who work for it, the opportunity for satisfactory
   redress of the harm inflicted will be enhanced if the corporate resources
   can be attacked instead of those of employees.

Those who disagree with these premises, or believe that other conditions
override them, maintain, among other things, that there is no such thing as a corporation that is different from the sum of its constituent human elements. They
argue that the fear of corporate reprisals if the employee does not violate the law
is no more than the kinds of pressure that all of us have to resist. Nor do they
believe that corporations are more deterrable than humans and they maintain
that by focusing on corporations as defendants prosecutors take the easier path
and neglect the route that is most just and more effective.

That these matters are not merely sterile debating points is indicated by a
number of cases in which judges have been unhappy with prosecutions directed
only at corporations. In one illustrative instance, a persnickety judge refused to
acknowledge a plea bargain between a corporation and the government without
having the (presumptively innocent) chief executive appear before him.

A Seattle courtroom was the initial setting in this 1989 case for what was supposed to be a routine plea bargain between the prosecutor and lawyers for the
Pennwalt Corporation, a Philadelphia-based manufacturer of chemicals and
health products. Pennwalt had been charged with spilling more than 75,000 gallons
of cancer-causing sodium chlorate from a corroded storage tank into Puget Sound.
The company was further accused of trying to hide the spill from state inspectors and then lying to Coast Guard officials about what had been spilled. Three
corporate officials were named in the indictment, but none was a top executive.

The attorney representing Pennwalt told the court that he was very sorry for
the spill, and that his company accepted full responsibility. Federal district judge
Jack E. Tanner, however, refused to accept the plea. "Who is the corporation?"
he asked. "I think the public is entitled to know who is responsible." A month
later, responding to the judge's concern, three top executives of Pennwalt flew to

Tacoma to appear in court, as the company for the second time sought to plead guilty and to agree to pay $1.1 million in penalties in return for a promise from the government to drop four misdemeanor charges and a felony count. The judge again reneged: "I want the top executive here," he said, noting that he sought to deter future environmental crimes by rendering the plea bargain session more dramatic, vivid, and human.[5] Ultimately, Edwin E. Tuttle, Pennwalt's president, did appear before Judge Tanner, and the deal was cut.

The action of the judge was declared by a local constitutional law professor to be "unprecedented, novel, daring, and legally questionable" as well as "a model for the rest of the nation" that could be "extremely effective."[6] Other commentators were less taken with the move. "The notion of public humiliation is something that is increasingly used in white-collar crimes," an official of the National Association of Criminal Defense Lawyers noted. "But to expect that someone who is not specifically charged come forward seems gratuitous."[7]

Are corporations actors, or are we necessarily talking about the human beings within the corporation? Can the law be applied in a meaningful manner to aggregates or is it necessarily limited to specific persons? The implications of the answers to these questions are basic for the conception of corporate crime and its control.

Notes

1. Edwin H. Sutherland, "White-Collar Criminality," *American Sociological Review*, 5 (1940):1.
2. John Barron Mays, *Crime and the Social Structure*. London: Faber and Faber, 1963, p. 87.
3. Edwin H. Sutherland, "Crimes of Corporations." In Albert Cohen, Alfred Lindesmith, and Karl Schuessler, eds., *The Sutherland Papers*. Bloomington: Indiana University Press, 1956, p. 96.
4. John H. Laub and Robert J. Sampson, "The Sutherland-Glueck Debate: On the Sociology of Criminological Knowledge," *American Journal of Sociology*, 96 (1991):1402–1440.
5. Katia Blackburn, "Judge Wants Answer from Pennwalt CEO," *Washington Post*, August 9, 1989, p. D3.
6. Timothy Egan, "Putting a Face on Corporate Crime," *New York Times* (Western edition), July 14, 1989, p. B9.
7. *Ibid.*

19

Motivation and Opportunity

Understanding the Causes of White-Collar Crime

James William Coleman

Over the years, numerous theories have been created to explain the puzzling phenomena of white-collar crime. Most of them focus on either the social psychological forces that motivate individuals to violate the law or on the structural forces that account for the prevalence and distribution of those violations. The objective of this analysis is to explore those two dimensions of white-collar crime and to bring them together in a single theoretical framework. The theory presented here is based on the common-sense notion that two basic factors—motivation and opportunity—must come together in order for any crime to occur. At first, it may appear that this analysis implies a strict division between the social psychological causes (motivation) and the structural causes (opportunity) of white-collar crime, but just the opposite is true. An opportunity must ultimately reach down and become psychologically available to individual actors or it will remain merely a theoretical possibility. And conversely, the roots of the individual motivations for white-collar crime can be traced directly to the culture and structure of industrial society. Motivation and opportunity are inseparably interwoven, and any successful theory of white-collar crime must take that fact into account.

THE MOTIVATION

Because of its great complexity, the problem of motivation will be broken down into four interrelated parts. The first part of this analysis examines the role of individual personality in formulating the original motivation to commit a white-collar crime, and the second part examines the role of cultural factors in general and what I have termed the "culture of competition" in particular. But a mere attraction to the rewards

Adapted by the author from *The Criminal Elite: The Sociology of White-Collar Crime*, New York: St. Martin's Press, 1994, chapter 6.

of criminal behavior is not a sufficient motivation, since society also erects strong ethical barriers to restrain such behavior. The third part, therefore, deals with the ways in which white-collar criminals neutralize those controls. Finally, the role of complex organizations in shaping individual motivation is given separate attention.

The Personality Factor. The public tends to see criminals as a breed apart from "normal" women and men. The deviants among us are branded as insane, inadequate, immoral, impulsive, egocentric, or with any one of a hundred other epithets. In seeing the deviant as a wholly different kind of person from ourselves, we bolster our self-esteem and help repress the fear that under the right circumstances we, too, might violate the same taboos. But this system of facile psychological determinism collapses when applied to white-collar criminals. The embezzling accountant or the corporate functionary involved in an employer's illegal schemes conforms too closely to the middle-class ideals of American culture to be so easily dismissed. Edwin H. Sutherland, the man who invented the term white-collar crime, repeatedly used the belief in the psychological normality of the white-collar criminal as an argument against the psychological explanation of *any* crime But whether or not Sutherland's conclusions are accurate for street crimes, it is generally agreed that personal pathology plays no significant role in the genesis of white-collar crime, and that the white-collar criminals are indeed psychologically normal.[1]

Of course, the fact that most white-collar offenders are free from major psychiatric disorders does not prove that their personality structures played no part in the genesis of their crimes. The handful of studies that have attempted to analyze the personality or personal history of white-collar offenders have reached rather divergent conclusions, but some traits do recur in sufficient numbers to be worthy of mention. All the studies that based their conclusions on the direct research on actual white-collar offenders agree on one point: white-collar offenders are psychologically "normal," if by that term we mean that they are free from the symptoms of major psychiatric disorder (hallucinations, delusions, neurotic compulsions, etc.). In addition, two studies agreed that white-collar criminals were "egocentric," and two characterized white-collar offenders as "reckless." In his study of war crimes such as spying and sabotage, Selling concluded that such offenders were egocentric and antisocial. However, Selling's conclusions, formed from interviews with convicted offenders he encountered in the course of his psychiatric practice, are in many places so obviously prejudiced and ill-conceived as to cast grave doubt about the validity of his entire study.[2] Bromberg's methodology was similar to Selling's in that he examined criminals he happened to encounter in his work at Bellevue Psychiatric Hospital, but despite the obvious flaws in his sampling technique, the moderate tone of his writings at least gives us hope of greater objectivity. Bromberg cites the case of a successful banker, convicted of various illegal financial manipulations, as typical of many white-collar criminals. The banker, Bromberg wrote, "impressed the examiners as a realistic, though relatively uncompromising, individual, independent rather than stubborn, yet unaware of his rather strong tendency toward recklessness. On a deeper level, one could sense in him a certain rigidity of character expressed openly in stubbornness, independence, and lack of compromise. Egocentricity and an unconscious feeling of omnipotence shone through [his] character structure."[3]

In an interview with a sample of thirty white-collar offenders from Leyhill Prison in Great Britain, John Spencer also found a high degree of recklessness. He described the outstanding features of these offenders' personalities as "their ambition, their drive, their desire to mix with people of higher social position than their own, and to give their children an expensive private education, and their willingness to take financial risks in the process." Spencer went on to characterize their behavior as "reckless and ambitious." However, he was more careful to qualify his conclusions than was Bromberg, noting that "it would be a mistake to see the adventurous and ruthless gambler as typical of the white-collar criminal. Such men did not account for more than one-third of the sample."[4] Spencer found that just as many of his subjects were "muddlers and incompetent men" without firm principles who simply drifted into criminal behavior.

Blum's study of industrial spies was the only one to use a control group of non-deviant subjects, but the methodological advantages of this procedure were outweighed by the extremely small sample—only three industrial spies and six controls. Like other psychologically oriented researchers, Blum found the white-collar offenders he studied (and, for that matter, the control group as well) to be "remarkably free from instability or disabling psychopathology."[5] Blum focused his investigation on the life histories of his subjects. The main difference Blum discovered between the two groups was that the offenders reported a far greater number of troubling "life experiences," especially during childhood. The average was only three such experiences for the controls and eleven for the offenders.

Taken as a group, these studies provide scant evidence for the proposition that white-collar criminals have significant psychological differences from other white-collar workers. The empirical evidence on this point is so weak, however, that it would be unwise to disregard the personality factor completely pending the arrival of more conclusive data. One can easily imagine how personality differences could lead one executive to embrace criminal activities, and another similarly placed executive to reject them. It seems likely, however, that a particular personality orientation will facilitate criminal activities in one occupational situation and discourage them in another, so that no single set of characteristics is conducive to crime in all situations. For example, nonconformists might well be more likely to become involved in an occupational crime directed against an employer, but less likely to go along with an organizational crime the employer demanded. A strict conformist might be expected to show the opposite tendencies.

Culture and Motivation. Whether or not the personality of the offender is considered important, conventional wisdom offers an even more popular explanation of the motivation for white-collar crime. White-collar criminals break the law, according to this view, because it is the easiest way for them to make a lot of money. Robert Lane, for example, found that the business and government officials he studied saw the desire for financial gain as the principal cause of white-collar crime: "Most businessmen and most responsible government officers, at least from the

sample interviewed, believe that businessmen run afoul of the law for economic reasons—they may want to 'make a fast buck.' "[6] Those familiar with criminological
theory will recognize these views as an unknowing restatement of the principles of
the classical criminology propounded in the late eighteenth and early nineteenth
centuries by Beccaria and Bentham. According to that school of criminology, people
violate the law because they believe it will bring them more pleasure and less pain
than the other courses of action available to them.

The longevity of this kind of explanation is not hard to understand. Although it
may not provide a very convincing account of the reasons a woman would murder
her husband in a fit of rage, it is very persuasive when applied to rational, calculating crimes. But Lane's formulation is too narrow, for although the desire to "get rich
quick" is certainly a motivating factor in many white-collar crimes, other kinds of
financial motivations are often equally important. Many white-collar offenders are
driven by the fear that they will lose what they already have rather than the desire
for more. For example, when Weisburd, Wheeler, Waring, and Bode examined the
statements of a sample of convicted white-collar criminals made in their presentence
information reports, they found that this "fear of falling" was a central motivating
force for a large group of offenders. Such offenders would have been ". . . reasonably happy with the place they have achieved through conventional means if only
they could keep that place. But the fate of organizational success and failure, or the
changing nature of the economy in their line of work, may put them at least tem-
porarily under great financial pressure, where they risk losing the lifestyle that they
have achieved. . . . The motivation for their crime is not selfish ego gratification, but
rather the *fear of falling*—of losing what they have worked so hard to gain."[7] Of
course, the desire to make more money and the desire to protect what one already
has are two closely related aspects of the same phenomenon, which may be termed
financial self-interest.

But financial self-interest, even in its most general sense, is only part of a larger
motivational complex that is deeply ingrained in white-collar workers. Along with
the desire for great wealth goes the desire to prove oneself by "winning" the competitive struggles that play such a prominent role in our economic system. And this
desire to be "a winner" provides another powerful motivation for white-collar crime
irrespective of any financial gains that may be involved.

The definition of wealth and success as central goals of individual activity is part
of what may be termed the *culture of competition;* a complex of values and beliefs
that is particularly strong in social systems based on industrial capitalism. In addition to giving great importance to wealth and success, the culture of competition
defines the competitive struggle for personal gain as a positive, rather than a negative or selfish, activity. Competition is seen not only to build the character and
endurance of the competitors, but also to produce the maximum economic value for
society as a whole. Not surprisingly, the competitive economic struggles typical of
industrial capitalism are seen by and large as a fair battle in which the most capable
and the hardest-working individuals emerge victorious. This belief in turn becomes
an important legitimation for social inequality, as it implies that the poor deserve

their inferior position because they are lazy or incompetent. The winners, on the other hand, are admired for the ability and drive that made them successful. And this adoration of the rich and successful and the stigmatization of the poor not only provides strong reinforcement for the drive for personal success, but also contributes to the pervasive sense of insecurity and the fear of failure that make up a powerful undercurrent in the culture of competition.

Of course, the culture of competition is only one of the many diverse strains of contemporary culture, and there are other constellations of values that reject or mitigate this kind of orientation. But how, then, do we explain why one individual comes to see the world in a way that is highly conducive to criminal behavior and another does not? Sutherland answered this question with his famous theory of differential association: "The hypothesis of differential association is that criminal behavior is learned in association with those who define such behavior favorably and in isolation from those who define it unfavorably, and that a person in an appropriate situation engages in such criminal behavior if, and only if, the weight of the favorable definitions exceeds the weight of the unfavorable definitions."[8] Sutherland argued that criminal behavior is learned like any other behavior, and that the criminal must learn both the techniques of crime and motivations favorable to criminal behavior.

Sutherland's contention that criminal behavior is learned can hardly be challenged, and his forceful insistence on this point has been of lasting benefit to modern criminology. In other respects, however, his theory is clearly too narrow. The most fundamental problem with Sutherland's theory is his insistence that the construction of personal reality is entirely a product of one's associations with others. Sutherland felt that individuals automatically adopt the definitions of those with whom they have the greatest frequency, duration, and intensity of association. But if that were true, how could those definitions ever change? For that matter, how could they have originated in the first place?

In fact, individuals constantly create new ideas and definitions. Most are quickly discarded because they do not conform to the accepted structure of social reality, but a few have what Weber called an "elective affinity" for the social conditions of a particular group, and so are integrated into its cultural system. Some individuals also persist in maintaining idiosyncratic conceptions of reality with little social support, despite the stigma that may result. Sutherland's view was that all criminals are ultimately conformists, but true deviance does in fact exist. Contemporary society would hardly have been possible without it.

Despite these objections, it still seems fair to say that most of our attitudes, values, and definitions are learned from others. But that doesn't explain the origins of those ideas. To do that, we must look for their structural causes. Anthropological studies of the few remaining hunting and gathering societies indicate that, in general, their people are not acquisitive or competitive. Most of those societies are, moreover, strongly egalitarian, with no social classes or even much in the way of permanent political leadership. The enormous differences between hunting and gathering societies and the industrial societies with which we are familiar can be traced to their relationship to the environment and the economic system it creates. The cooperative, egalitarian ethos of most hunting and gathering societies can be attributed, at least in part, to the fact that such societies produce little surplus wealth. Thus, the economic base cannot support the system of status competition based upon the accumulation of wealth that is found in the industrial societies. Significantly, the Indians living along what is now the Northwest coast of the United States and Canada, whose fishing activities generated a more substantial surplus, were in some important respects less egalitarian and more competitive than other hunting and gathering peoples.

The system of exchange of hunting and gathering societies is generally based upon sharing and reciprocity. For example, Richard Lee found that the bands of !Kung Bushmen in the Kalahari desert share all the available food equally.[9] Each day a group of adults leaves camp and forages for food. When they return, all the food is divided among the members of the band. Everyone receives an equal share whether they have been foraging, hunting, or sleeping. Robert Dentan found similar patterns of distribution among the Semai of Central Malaya.[10] Even a hunter who succeeds in killing a large animal and dragging it back to camp through the dense jungle has no more claim on its meat than any other member of the band. The meat is cut up into equal portions and distributed to all who are hungry. The hunter is not given a special status because of his accomplishments—indeed, he is not even thanked by the other members of the group, for, as Dentan put it, "Saying thank you is very rude, for it suggests first that one has calculated the amount of a gift, and second that one did not expect the donor to be so generous."

The culture of competition that plays such an important role in white-collar crime is rooted in the structure of the industrial economy. Most obviously, the enormous surplus wealth generated through industrial production provides a vast store of material goods to be competed for—a condition largely absent from hunting and gathering societies. A second key factor is the displacement of the open sharing of reciprocal exchange with the calculated self-interest of market exchange. Of course, reciprocal exchange still persists in industrial capitalism, particularly among relatives and close friends, but market exchange is the dominant mode. And that mode of exchange fosters a very different kind of personal outlook from that found among hunters and gatherers. Market exchange is inevitably tied to the notion of profit and loss: the gain of one trading partner often comes at the expense of the other. Thus, as production for market replaces production for immediate consumption, competition and the quest for personal gain replace the more cooperative sentiments fostered in reciprocal exchange.

In addition, the use of money provides an objective, impersonal standard by which to measure profit and loss in industrial society, thus further reinforcing the spirit of competition and the goal of the personal acquisition of wealth. Finally, there is the steady growth of individualism and the tendency for the members of industrial cultures (especially in the West) to define themselves as autonomous actors whose individual needs take precedence over the collective needs of society.

Neutralizing Social Controls. The culture of competition receives strong social support in the industrialized nations, but so do the ethical standards that attempt to restrain it. Schools teach general moral principles at all grade levels, and religious institutions place even greater emphasis upon such values. Newscasts, popular television programs, and the pronouncements of corporate and government leaders frequently proclaim the importance of maintaining high ethical standards, and even the shadiest operators claim to share them. The network of laws based on those values provides them with another powerful support. In addition to the threat of punishment, the law has enormous symbolic importance. It provides official reinforcement for the principles it embodies and creates a stigmatizing label for those who violate its standards—a label that is, moreover, especially repugnant to the respectable business people, politicians, and professionals who comprise the majority of white-collar criminals.

The conflict between the culture of competition and many widely accepted ethical standards is carefully papered over in public. An elaborate pretense is maintained that there is no contradiction, and that unethical behavior is ultimately rewarded with failure and disgrace. In private, of course, the fact that "bending" the rules of the game provides an important competitive advantage is much too obvious to ignore, and other ways must be found to resolve this contradiction. Some people openly reject conflicting ethical standards, while others find nothing appealing in the values of materialism and competition; but most people are attracted by both ideals. One way to construct a personal reality that accommodates both is through the use of what Sykes and Matza have called "techniques of neutralization."[11] A technique of neutralization is essentially a device that enables individuals to violate important normative standards, but to neutralize any definition of themselves as deviant or criminal. Such techniques take many forms, but in essence, they are rationalizations deviants use to justify their actions. For example, a physician may justify claiming Medicaid reimbursements for services that were never performed by telling himself that his actions didn't really harm anyone, while salespeople pass off their deceptive statements on the grounds that "everyone does it."

But techniques of neutralization are not just *ex post facto* rationalizations—they are available to the potential deviant before the offense actually occurs and form part of the motivation for the original act. A physician does not file fraudulent Medicaid claims and then suddenly make up a rationalization to justify her actions. Rather, she is aware from the beginning that her schemes will not cause any direct harm to her patients, and that rationalization makes it psychologically feasible for her to carry out her plans.

Of all types of white-collar criminals, embezzlers have been the subject of the most scientific study, perhaps because so many people have difficulty understanding why trusted, well-paid employees would jeopardize their position by stealing from their employers. Most of the research on embezzlement has attributed the offenders' crimes to their need for money caused by such things as gambling, extravagant living, and costly personal problems. But in itself the fact that embezzlers feel they need more money than they can legitimately earn is hardly a sufficient explanation, for the culture of competition and the advertising that supports it have planted the desire for more money and more possessions in the minds of most people. The question still remains: Why do some individuals embezzle to get that extra money, while others do not?

Donald R. Cressey's detailed study of the motivations for embezzlement was the first to provide an answer to this question.[12] Based on intensive interviews with a sample of incarcerated embezzlers, Cressey concluded that three distinct elements are necessary for embezzlement to occur: the perpetrators must have a nonshareable financial problem, they must have the opportunity and the knowledge necessary to commit an embezzlement, and they must apply a suitable rationalization to "adjust" the contradiction between their actions and society's normative standards. Of these three propositions, the first is the most questionable, for there appears to be no necessary reason why an embezzlement must result from a nonshareable problem instead of from a simple desire for more money. The second proposition was widely accepted before Cressey's work, but his third proposition and his investigation of the specific types of rationalizations embezzlers use to justify their actions helped create a whole new direction for research on white-collar crime.

Most embezzlers, according to Cressey, rationalize their crimes by telling themselves they are just borrowing the money and will soon return it. As one subject put it, "I figured that if you could use something and help yourself and replace it and not hurt anybody, it was all right." Cressey found that his respondents continued to use this rationalization to justify their embezzlement while they became more and more deeply involved in crime. Eventually, they were either caught or realized they would never be able to pay back all the money they had taken and were finally forced to accept the criminal nature of their behavior. Cressey's respondents reported using several other rationalizations as well, but the borrowing rationalization was by far the most common, probably because it is so well suited to neutralize the ethical standards condemning embezzlement.

The borrowing rationalization doesn't work as well for other white-collar crimes. There are numerous studies that examine the rationalizations criminals use to justify other kinds of white-collar crimes. One of the most common is the claim that the crimes do not harm anyone. If one's actions do not hurt other people, the argument goes, then there is nothing unethical about them. When a Westinghouse executive on trial for price fixing was asked if he thought his behavior had been illegal, he responded, "Illegal? Yes, but not criminal . . . I assumed that a criminal action meant damaging someone, and we did not do that." Survey data have shown that the public is more tolerant of theft from large businesses and the government than it is of theft from smaller, more vulnerable organizations—probably because theft from a larger organization is perceived as less harmful to the victim.

Those involved in business crimes frequently justify their behavior by claiming that the law itself is unnecessary or unjust. Business people complain loudly about "government interference" in their affairs, often using the ideology of laissez-faire capitalism to point out what they consider to be inappropriate statutes and regulations. According to such beliefs, it is the law that causes harm to the public and not the illegal activities of business. Given this ideology, a host of business crimes can

easily be justified. Clinard's study of wartime gasoline rationing, for example, concluded that gasoline dealers used the belief that the rationing was unnecessary to
rationalize their violations of the law.[13]

Another common technique of neutralization is the claim that one's criminal
behavior was necessary in order to survive or to achieve vital economic goals. Many
employees use this appeal to necessity to explain why they went along with the illegal activities expected by their employer. Sutherland cited the case of an idealistic
young college graduate who had lost two previous jobs because he refused to
become involved in unethical activities. After taking his third job, this time at a used
car dealership, he found out that they, too, expected him to become involved in
shady business practices. "When I learned these things I did not quit as I had previously. I sometimes felt disgusted and wanted to quit, but I argued that I did not have
much chance to find a legitimate firm. I knew the game was rotten, but it has to be
played—the law of the jungle and that sort of thing." Even representatives of giant
corporations also use this justification, although such firms are unlikely candidates
for economic extinction. The Westinghouse executive quoted earlier went on to justify his involvement in the price-fixing conspiracy by saying, "I thought we were
more or less working on a survival basis in order to try to make enough to keep our
plant and our employees." Another version of this argument of necessity often used
to justify occupational offenses is that the crime was required to help one's friends
or family.

A justification that is often combined with the argument of necessity is the claim
that "everybody else is doing it." As one of Cressey's subjects put it, "In the real
estate business you have to paint a pretty picture in order to sell the property. We did
a little juggling and moving around, but everyone in the real estate business has to do
that. We didn't do anything that they all don't do." This kind of rationalization is frequently used to justify "fudging" on income tax returns, and Benson found it to be
popular among those convicted of criminal tax fraud.[14] According to one respondent:
"Everybody cheats on their income taxes, 95 percent of the people. Even if it's
ten dollars, it's the same principle." Another version of this justification is that
criminal behavior must be some sort of individual choice, and that people are not
responsible for their actions when they are merely conforming to the expectations of
others. Corrupt employees often claim that they haven't done anything wrong,
because they were merely going along with a pattern of behavior accepted among
their peers.

Finally, many occupational crimes are justified on the grounds that the offender
deserves the money. This rationalization is particularly common in cases of
employee theft. In his study of dock workers, Gerald Mars found that pilferage was
defined as a "morally justified addition to wages" or an "entitlement due from
exploiting employers."[15] Lawrence Zeitlin found similar attitudes among employees
who stole from retail stores. One of his subjects felt that the "store owed it to me,"
while another said, "I felt I deserved to get something additional for my work since I
wasn't getting paid enough."[16]

Of course, many other justifications are used to neutralize normative controls, but the rationalizations just discussed seem to be the most common. Before moving on, however, we must explore an important question concerning the origins of such justifications. Cressey argued that individual offenders do not invent their own rationalizations but simply apply existing definitions to their behavior. Although some individuals certainly do construct their own unique justifications based upon individual circumstances or rework previously learned rationalizations to better fit their own experience, most techniques of neutralization are to a large degree learned from others. Of particular importance in this regard are the various occupational subcultures that not only supply their members with a set of appropriate rationalizations, but also help to isolate them from contact with those who would pass harsher judgment on their criminal activities. Police subcultures, for example, often distinguish between "clean" payoff money and "dirty" payoff money, and hold that there is nothing unethical about accepting the former. Then, too, the workers in many factories make clear distinctions between property which is permissible to steal and property which is not, while many politicians learn to see the exchange of political favors for campaign contributions or personal rewards as a normal part of their job. Moreover, such deviant subcultures need not be confined to a single employer or even to a single profession. The business culture that is shared to one degree or another by most business people not only provides incentives for illicit activities but also contains justifications that can be used to neutralize ethical restraints. The common expression that "business is business" reflects the subculture's belief that harsh necessity justifies both the unethical and the illegal activities of the business world. Polls indicate that the "everybody else is doing it" rationalization also has a strong affinity to the attitudes and opinions of the business subculture.

Motivation in Organizations. Up to this point we have been discussing the causes of white-collar crime in general, but now some special attention must be devoted to organizational crime. Although the same process of motivation and rationalization occurs in both individual and organizational crime, the structural demands of formal organizations create unique pressures that require some separate analysis. Modern organizations are, in a sense, machines for controlling human behavior. In order to survive, a large corporation must directly control the behavior of thousands of employees and indirectly influence the activities of much larger groups on the outside. And although organizations may well encounter special problems in persuading employees to engage in illegal activities, the mechanisms for achieving conformity to organizational expectations are much the same whatever the legal standing of the organization's demands.

One of the most powerful techniques to win conformity with organizational expectations is the threat of dismissal. John Z. DeLorean, a former top executive of General Motors and founder of his own unsuccessful automobile firm, gave the following description of the pressure applied to an engineer who objected to dangerous design elements in the notorious Chevrolet Corvair: "Charlie Chayne, vice-president of engineering, along with his staff, took a very strong stand against the Corvair as an unsafe car long before it went on sale in 1959. He was not listened to but told in effect, 'You're not a member of the team. Shut up or go looking for another job.' "[17]

Of course, such threats are seldom made so blatantly, but even so, employees understand what is involved in going against the company's demands.

The fear of losing an important assignment or being passed up for the next promotion is just as much a threat for the achievement-oriented executive as the possibility of dismissal. In the social world of the modern corporation, dedication to the company and conformity to the wishes of one's superiors are seen as essential to success. Regular promotions are an expected part of the climb up the corporate ladder, and overly scrupulous managers are likely to find the promotions they expected going to those who have been more cooperative.

Organizational control nonetheless involves much more than simply handing out sufficient rewards and punishments to ensure employee obedience. A large organization harbors a unique social world all its own, and the subculture embodied in the organization shapes its members' behavior in countless ways; many times without much conscious awareness on the part of the employees. At the most fundamental level, the way an organizational subculture defines the work situation and the role of various employees creates the context for all organizational behavior. The ethos of a corporation also helps shape the moral sensibilities and perspectives of its employees—especially those in managerial positions. Any decision of its members to engage in illegal activity is inevitably affected by the social world sheltered within the organization.

Considerable research shows that one important element of this social world is its "moral tone"—that is, its ethical system and its attitudes toward illegal behavior which many writers attribute largely to the attitudes of top management. But while it is undoubtedly true that top management has a major impact on the moral tone of most companies, those managers' ethical standards are not simply their own personal beliefs. The ethics and outlook of those who come to hold the most powerful positions in an organization are molded and shaped by the same process of socialization that influences other, less successful managers. Indeed, promotion to the highest ranks generally requires a much higher degree of ethical conformity than is expected of lower-level employees. Those who refuse to change personal standards that are incompatible with the demands of their corporate employer seldom reach the top.

Much has been written about the numbing effects modern bureaucracies have upon the moral sensibilities of their employees. Numerous writers have chronicled the growth of what William H. Whyte called the "organization man," who is under such overwhelming pressure to conform that individuality and personal ethical standards must be sacrificed for the sake of a career. The organization man must be a "team player" and not an individualist who allows personal values to interfere with his or her performance. Many sociologists have argued that these amoral functionaries have become so common because they are necessary to bureaucratic organization. One of the principal strengths of a bureaucracy is that individual employees are dispensable—one employee can be replaced by another with a minimum of disruption. But this interchangeability requires that individual employees think and act in a similar fashion, and the existence of widely divergent ethical standards and attitudes among the work force might interfere with the smooth operation of the organization. Thus, the efficient bureaucracy breeds moral conformity, or perhaps more often, a kind of amoral pragmatism.

The process of socialization into the corporate ethic occurs at all levels of the organization, but a particular effort is made to shape aspiring managers according to the corporate image. The transfer is one of the devices commonly used to achieve this goal. By continually moving young executives from one area to another, the firm weakens outside ties that might interfere with their socialization. These transfers make managers more dependent upon the corporation to satisfy their social needs and brings them ever more deeply into its social world. The long hours of work required of up-and-coming executives have a similar effect. The burden of overwork disrupts commitments to family, friends, community, and other interests that might place conflicting pressures upon the manager.

This rigorous process of socialization can produce a kind of "moral numbness" in corporate managers. Well-socialized executives tend to display a narrow, pragmatic approach to their work, acting in the best interests of the corporation with little thought of the moral implications of their behavior. C. Wright Mills held such attitudes to be part of the "structural immorality" of American society. But perhaps the phenomenon can more appropriately be termed "structural amorality," for the well-trained bureaucrat does not oppose or reject popular morality, but he or she is often indifferent to it.

Socialization into a bureaucratic organization does much more than just dull the initiate's ethical sensibilities, however. As numerous sociologically oriented organizational theorists have pointed out, an organization also controls its members through its influence on the definition of the situations they face on the job. The organization provides definitions about what needs to be done, the importance of various tasks, and the effects of those tasks upon the company and the community. The organization defines the goals it is pursuing and the ways those goals are to be achieved. It provides repertoires of actions to be used in response to given situations, and it teaches employees to direct their attention to certain aspects of their environment and to ignore others. This network of definitions often makes unethical or illegal activities appear to be a normal part of the daily routine. Time after time, individuals unlucky enough to have been caught committing corporate crimes have expressed surprise and even shock that their actions were really considered criminal by the world outside their organizations.

The organizational structure of modern bureaucracy greatly facilitates its ability to manipulate employees' definition of their occupational world. The mammoth size of many of these organizations, their labyrinth of organizational units, and the ever-increasing trend toward specialization fragment the responsibility of individual employees. Most employees work on only a small part of a much larger overall operation, and many never see—or choose to ignore—the potential impact of the project as a whole. Employees who question the ethical or legal implications of their work are told to carry out their duties and not to worry about things that are the responsibility of top management.

At the same time, top managers often make an intentional effort to avoid legal responsibility for the illegal activities they encourage. In the heavy electrical equipment price-fixing cases, for example, top management first set quotas and goals that virtually required price fixing to achieve, and then they made it clear that they did not want to hear anything about the criminal activities of their subordinates. Surveys indicate that many middle-level managers are afraid to be honest with their boss, and that the number of managers reporting this problem has steadily increased.

Another factor that facilitates corporate control of its managers is their relative isolation from the outside world. In one of his most well-known works on business administration, Peter Drucker compared the isolation of the executive with that in a monastery. He went on to note that the executive's "contacts outside of business tend to be limited to people of the same set, if not to people working for the same organization. The demand that there be no competing outside interests and loyalty applies to the corporate executive as it does to the army officer. Hence executive life not only breeds a parochialism of the imagination comparable to the 'military mind,' but places a considerable premium on it."[18] This isolation is important, because it insulates the white-collar criminals from the condemnation they would otherwise receive from those outside the social world of their organization, and also because it discourages normal skepticism about attitudes and goals executives learn on the job.

THE OPPORTUNITY

No matter how strong an individual's motivation, by itself it can never provide a complete explanation of criminal behavior. If there is no opportunity, there is no crime. Of course, everyone has the opportunity to commit some kind of crime, and almost all white-collar workers have had the opportunity to commit a white-collar crime. But all opportunities are not equal, and the actors' evaluation of the potential dangers and rewards of each opportunity plays a major role in determining their behavior. The attractiveness of an opportunity is strongly influenced by the individual's perception of how likely he or she is to get caught, how severe the punishment might be, and of course, how big a payoff is expected from the crime. But each opportunity is also judged in comparison to the other available options. The fewer legitimate opportunities an actor has, the more attractive a particular crime is likely to appear.

From a societal standpoint, it is the distribution of attractive criminal opportunities that is most critical to our understanding of the problem of white-collar crime. The remainder of this section therefore summarizes what we know about the way the opportunities for white-collar crime are distributed among different industries, different types of organizations and occupations, and between the genders.

Industries. Clearly, both the distribution of opportunities and their relative attractiveness vary significantly from one industry to another. One question that has created a great deal of interest among scholars is the role that the market structure of an industry plays in corporate crime. Many contradictory claims have been made about which type of market structure has the greatest criminogenic effects. On the one hand, it can be argued that competitive markets in which many different firms struggle to keep afloat are the most likely to have high crime rates because the combatants will use every possible means to survive and prosper. On the other hand, it appears that price fixing and other antitrust conspiracies are far easier in highly concentrated industries. Thus, it would seem that industries with many small, highly competitive firms would be characterized by a high rate of crimes that are intended to improve competitive performance, such as fraud, false advertising, and espionage, and that collusion and antitrust activities would be most common in more concentrated industries. Unfortunately, the empirical research so far has produced highly contradictory findings. As Clinard and Yeager suggested, quantitative research on this topic is extremely difficult, and more sophisticated methodology will be needed before these issues can be resolved.[19]

The case study method, which analyzes the conditions that contribute to particular white-collar offenses in particular industries, has so far produced better results. For example, several studies have concluded that the economic organization of the automobile industry virtually forces individual dealers to engage in shady business practices, because the oligopolistic firms that control the supply of new automobiles pressure their franchises to sell their cars at an extremely low price in order to increase their sales volume, and dealers are therefore forced to make up their losses through repair and service rackets and other fraudulent activities. Similar conditions have been found in the liquor industry. Because distillers impose rigid sales quotas on their distributors, they are often forced to give untaxed, under-the-table incentives to retailers in order to keep their volume up.

Needleman and Needleman have, however, criticized the assumption in such studies that the participants are coerced into criminal activity.[20] They argue that in most cases it is more accurate to talk about "crime facilitative" rather than "crime coercive" systems. Their study of the securities industry, for example, found many conditions that made criminal activities easier but did not actually force individuals to participate. More specifically, the Needlemans found that the legal doctrines limiting the financial risk in handling stolen securities, the strong financial incentives to keep up market flow, and the traditions of trust and professional solidarity in the industry all combine to facilitate securities theft. The wave of convictions for insider trading and fraud that swept Wall Street in the last decade and numerous statements from those familiar with the operations of the stock market and commodity exchanges suggest an extremely high rate of other criminal activities among those involved in financial markets as well. Not surprisingly, Weisburd, Waring, and Wheeler's analysis of convicted white-collar offenders found a higher crime rate in the securities industry than in any of the six other industries they analyzed.[21]

Another variable influencing the opportunity structure within an industry is what Edward Gross called "organizational sets"—groups of similar organizations whose actions are visible to each other.[22] The key point is that these sets tend to have an internal system of stratification with dominant organizations, middle-level organizations, and marginal organizations. The relatively small number of firms at the top of these stratified organizational sets greatly increases the attractiveness of antitrust conspiracies, because it reduces the number of firms that must become involved and thus reduces their chances of being uncovered. Gross also argues that both the tendency for organizations to focus their attention almost exclusively on the activities of other members of their set and the great complexity of relations among participants in different sets make it easier for outsiders to conceal fraudulent schemes that cut across set boundaries.

Variations in the regulatory environment play a major role in determining the opportunity structure in different industries. The more tightly an industry is regulated, the more attractive opportunities are likely to be illegal, and the more white-collar crime we can expect. One of the most important influences shaping an industry's regulatory environment is the type of products it makes. Industries whose products cause serious and clearly identifiable harm to the public or the environment tend to be subject to more stringent regulation than those that do not. Examples include the manufacturers of pharmaceuticals, whose products may mean life or death for their users, the automobile industry, which has been subject to an increasing number of safety and environmental regulations, and the chemical and petroleum industries, which produce a wide variety of hazardous substances often using industrial processes that pose great environmental risks as well. It is therefore not surprising that Clinard and Yeagers's comprehensive study of corporate crime found all these industries to have unusually high crime rates.[23]

Banking is another industry that has traditionally been subject to tight regulation, not because its products are physically dangerous, but because they play such a vital role in the economy. Traditionally, banks and savings and loans were not considered particularly high crime industries (although, of course, the abundant opportunities for embezzlement have always been a problem). But changes occurred during the 1980s that created a virtual explosion of crime and corruption among the nation's thrift institutions. Although many factors were involved, one principal cause was the deregulation of the industry. Deregulation stripped away most of the restrictions that had been imposed on the way these institutions could use funds from publicly insured deposits and helped to create a kind of "casino mentality" among savings and loan operators. Equally important was the fact that in its antiregulatory fervor the Reagan administration refused to support funding for a sufficient number of federal inspectors and auditors, thus leading many savings and loan operators to believe that they could get away with almost any kind of fraudulent activities without fear of detection.

Finally, there is considerable evidence that illegal practices spread from one organization in an industry to another. Some of this tendency can be attributed to the diffusion of motivations and rationalizations discussed earlier, but other processes appear to be involved as well. For one thing, knowledge about the availability of criminal opportunities and the specific techniques necessary to carry them out diffuse within an industry just as rationalizations do. Moreover, the illegal activities of a firm also have a direct impact on its competitors. Seeing a competitor increase its profits by illegal means is likely to enhance the attractiveness of such behavior, while the failure of a competitor's illegal enterprise is likely to have the opposite effect. Profits generated by illegal means may also allow a firm to lower its prices or take other advantages over its competition, thus reducing the attractiveness of the competition's legitimate opportunities and encouraging all the firms in the industry to become involved in similar illegal schemes.

Organizations. The goals an organization pursues are certain to have a major impact on both the type and the amount of its criminal activities, and for private firms producing a profit is obviously one of the most important. Not surprisingly, a very considerable body of research shows firms with declining profitability are more likely than others to break the law. In the words of Clinard and Yeager, "Firms in depressed industries as well as relatively poorly performing firms in all industries tend to violate the law to a greater degree.[24]

Modern corporations are, however, far too complex to operate with only a single goal. A corporation can hardly tell its manufacturing division or sales division that its goal is simply to make profits. Each organizational unit must be given specific subgoals that ultimately contribute to the overall organizational goals. The sales division, for example, might be given a particular quota to reach, while the manufacturing division is told to produce a certain number of items at a particular cost. Corporate managers have little discretion in selecting the primary corporate objective (profitability), but they are responsible for the subgoals. Moreover, the specific targets selected by top management may have an important influence on the decisions of middle-level employees whether or not to stay within the confines of the law. For example, Ronald Kramer argues that the goals set for the Ford Pinto—that it weigh less than two thousand pounds and cost less than $2,000—ultimately caused the safety problems for which it became famous, because such goals led to the rejection of safety modifications that would have increased the weight and cost of the car.[25]

The retired middle managers studied by Marshall Clinard expressed the belief that top management is responsible for setting the overall ethical standards of the corporation. Many of them drew a distinction between "financially oriented" managers and "technical and professional types." The interviewees believed that financially oriented managers were primarily interested in quick profits and personal prestige and were therefore more inclined to criminal activities. Professionally oriented managers were held to be less willing to risk criminal activities and more concerned with the long-term well-being of the corporation.[26]

It would be a mistake, however, to attribute too much independence to those at the top. For one thing, top management is confronted by a complex balance of political forces within the organization that places clear limits on its discretion. Individuals and groups who occupy strategic lower positions within the organization may have great power over certain types of corporate operations. Those at the top often find that they have great power only so long as they use it in the ways that are expected of them. The culture and traditions of an organization have a resilient strength that is difficult for even the most capable leader to overcome. Most upper-level executives have, moreover, been socialized into the same organizational culture as other employees, and that culture plays an important part in determining their decisions.

In addition to those powerful internal forces, top management is also restrained by the external environment of the organization. Many critical definitions, ideas, and beliefs come from the industry in which a firm operates and the general ethos of corporate culture. Government controls and the climate of public opinion place another set of restraints on contemporary corporations, as do the economic realities of the marketplace. Under many circumstances, top management may have little choice but to engage in illicit activities if it is to meet the overriding demand for profits. If, for instance, a competitor is cutting costs by violating pollution and safety standards, it may be impossible to maintain competitive prices without engaging in similar activities.

Many observers have claimed that there is a relationship between the size of a firm and its involvement in illegal activities, but they do not agree on whether large or small firms are most likely to break the law. John Conklin, for example, suggested that the anonymity and impersonality of the large corporations and the way responsibility for important tasks is fragmented among many different employees promote crime in such firms.[27] Others, especially those working for large corporations, have claimed that small firms are more likely to violate the law because they lack the professional expertise to decipher the maze of government regulations that controls business activities. The empirical research on this point is as contradictory as the theoretical claims, and no clear relationship between firm size and criminal conduct has been established.

Occupations. All occupations offer some illicit opportunities, even if only to evade the taxes on the money we earn. These opportunities are, however, unevenly distributed, and some occupations clearly hold far greater possibilities for illicit gain than others. Unfortunately, the great diversity of occupational categories and the paucity of sociological research on this subject make it possible to present only a few basic generalizations and hypotheses. The attractiveness of the opportunities for bribery, for instance, appears to depend on the economic value of the services the holder of a particular job can offer in exchange for corrupt payments. One of the reasons police corruption is most common among officers involved in the enforcement of narcotics and vice laws is that organized criminals are willing to pay those officers large sums of money to look the other way. Other occupations with rich opportunities for corruption include purchasing agents, government inspectors, and politicians.

The opportunities for embezzlement vary with the degree of financial trust placed in the holders of different occupational positions. Accountants, bookkeepers, and clerks have many opportunities for embezzlement, while other employees in the same organizations may have none. Opportunities for fraud and other illegal financial manipulations appear to be greatest in occupations with direct involvement in financial dealings, such as salespeople and upper-level executives. The size of the potential rewards from criminal behavior also varies among different types of occupations. A study by Weisburd, Waring, and Wheeler of federal presentence reports found that managers were convicted of the most serious crimes, the crimes of owners were second, and lower-level employees committed the least serious offenses.[28]

In general, it appears that the opportunities for employee pilferage are more widely dispersed than the opportunities for fraud or embezzlement. Most employees have the opportunity to steal from their employer at one time or another, and a great many actually do. Such opportunities are not, however, evenly distributed throughout the occupational structure. Clark and Hollinger's comprehensive survey found that employees with access to and knowledge about vulnerable targets for theft (e.g., sales clerks in stores, engineers in factories, and nurses and technicians in hospitals) were the most likely to report having actually committed a theft.[29] Occupations also differ in the size of the reward they offer to the potential thief. Whereas the television assemblers in Horning's study usually took small objects of little value,[30] stockbrokers and securities dealers have the opportunity to steal far more valuable items.

One of the most important determinants of the illicit opportunities available to professionals is the financial arrangements determining their payment. Professionals working on a fee-for-service basis have numerous opportunities to persuade their clients to consent to profitable but unnecessary procedures, while those working on salary have little to gain from such activities. Another important factor is the ignorance of clients about what kind of services they really need, and the strong emphasis on mutual trust in the professional-client relationship which leads many clients to an unquestioning acceptance of the professional's judgment. The fact that a substantial portion of medical and dental bills are paid by insurance further decreases the clients' concern about unnecessary services and overcharging, thus decreasing the chances of punishment for such actions.

Occupational subcultures play an important role in facilitating many types of white-collar crime by promoting the spread of the knowledge and techniques necessary to transform a potential course of criminal action into a psychologically available opportunity. Because these subcultures typically have a diverse membership, they provide a source of communication independent of the industry or organization in which an individual works. Accountants, physicians, and lawyers, for example, learn about opportunities for white-collar crime as they learn their profession and are socialized into its subculture. Similarly, the striking parallels in the patterns of corruption found in the New York and Philadelphia police departments in the early 1970s strongly suggest the transmission of criminal techniques through an occupational subculture shared by officers in those two departments. Although subcultures in law, medicine, and the other professions do not directly condone criminal behavior, the sense of mutual solidarity and self-protection make criminal opportunities more attractive by reducing the chances of receiving severe punishment. Occupational subcultures thus serve as part of a network of communication that transmits information about opportunities, techniques, and motivations, as well as a protective shield that reduces the visibility of professional misconduct.

Gender.   Gender is one of the strongest predictors of criminality, and in general, men commit far more crimes than women. A quick examination of the statistics on criminal arrests, however, appears to cast some doubt about the validity of this generalization for white-collar crimes. Although only 18.4 percent of the persons arrested in the United States in 1990 were female, women made up 41.2 percent of those arrested for embezzlement and 44.2 percent of those arrested for fraud (a higher percentage than for any other crime except prostitution and vice).[31] However, Kathleen Daly's analysis of a sample of presentence reports from seven federal court districts indicates that there are indeed very great differences between male and female white-collar offenders.[32] The women in Daly's sample were younger, less educated, and had lower-status positions and lower incomes than the men. She also found that the women made less money from their crimes and were less likely to commit their offenses as part of a group. Although this study included many offenses that do not fall within the normal definition of white-collar crime (welfare fraud, for example), a comparison of the gender differences among specific white-collar offenses produces some interesting results. Women were extremely underrepresented among those charged with the two offenses that are most likely to be corporate crimes. An overwhelming 98 percent of those charged with antitrust and Securities and Exchange Commission violations were male. In contrast, 45 percent of those charged with bank embezzlement were female. However, the women charged with bank embezzlement were more likely to be tellers, while the men were more likely to be bank officers or financial managers. The crimes of these women were also "generally less sophisticated than men's, of shorter duration, and less likely to be carried out with others."

The available research also indicates that men and women tend to use different rationalizations to justify their white-collar crimes. Dorothy Zietz found that the female embezzlers she studied were far more likely to justify their offenses in terms of the needs of their spouse or children than the male embezzlers Cressey studied,[33] and this conclusion was supported by Daly's research as well. The impact of the differences in the distribution of rationalizations among females and males is still unclear, however. For one thing, both genders appear to share many rationalizations. Moreover, the different rationalizations preferred by males and females all appear to provide effective justifications for white-collar crime, and it is difficult to determine if this difference has any impact on the actual incidence of embezzlement or other crimes.

While the issue of motivational differences remains unresolved, differences in the opportunity structure for women and men clearly have a powerful effect on white-collar criminality. Daly's finding that very few women are involved in corporate crimes obviously reflects the gross underrepresentation of women in the higher circles of corporate decision making. Of course, this same pattern of discrimination continues down through the middle and lower levels of the corporate hierarchy and has a similar effect in patterning the distribution of white-collar offenses. The fact that female bank embezzlers are more likely to be tellers, while males have a greater likelihood of holding managerial positions, seems to be an obvious reason why women's crimes were less sophisticated, netted lower returns, and were less likely to be committed by a group of offenders. We cannot, however, assume that men and women in the same occupational position are necessarily presented with the same opportunities for white-collar crime. Steven Box, for example, argues that female workers are more closely supervised than their male counterparts in the same job and, therefore, have fewer criminal opportunities.[34] Research on managerial women also indicates that they are often excluded from the social networks of their male colleagues—another condition that might tend to reduce the availability of criminal opportunity.

CONCLUSIONS

As we have seen, the pattern of etiological factors that generate white-collar crime is indeed a complex one. Although social scientists have tended to focus on either the social psychological or the structural level, a complete understanding of the causes of white-collar crime requires us to recognize the interdependence of those two approaches. Social psychological analysis alone leaves us ignorant of the structural and historical forces that shape all human behavior. But an analysis focused exclusively on structural variables neglects the personal dimension of human behavior and cannot ultimately account for any individual offenses.

Our analysis has shown that white-collar crime is caused by the junction of a compatible motivation with an attractive opportunity. There must be some reason why an individual turns to white-collar crime. In most cases, the motivation is the desire for financial gain, the wish to be seen as a success in the eyes of others, or the fear of losing what one already has. Although many people believe such motivations to be a part of human nature, that is clearly not the case. Rather, the political economy of industrial society, with its enormous economic surplus and reliance on a system of market exchange, has given rise to a culture of competition that fosters these motivations. A second component necessary to formulate a motivation for most white-collar crimes is the neutralization of the society's ethical restraints. On the individual level, this is achieved through the use of various rationalizations that justify the offender's behavior. Oftentimes these rationalizations are learned on the job, but there are many other sources as well. In the case of organizational crime, this process of neutralization is greatly facilitated by the power of large organizations to shape the definitions and rewards that guide the behavior of their employees.

Along with the desire, there must also be an opportunity. A great many people have an opportunity to commit some sort of white-collar crime, but some have far greater and more attractive opportunities than others. Although the existing research is still preliminary and incomplete, the distribution of those opportunities clearly varies greatly among different occupations, organizations, and industries, and between the genders.

Notes

1. Richard Blum, *Deceivers and Deceived*. Springfield, IL: Thomas, 1972, pp. 145–157; Walter Bromberg, *Crime and the Mind: A Psychiatric Analysis of Crime and Punishment*. New York: Macmillan, 1965, pp. 377–400; Lowell S. Selling, "Specific War Crimes," *Journal of Criminal Law, Criminology, and Police Science*, 34 (1944):303–310; John C. Spencer, "White Collar Crime." In Edward Glover, Hermann Mannheim, and Emanuel Miller, eds., *Criminology in Transition*. London: Tavistock, 1965, pp. 233–266.

2. Selling, *op. cit.*

3. Bromberg, *op. cit.*, p. 388.

4. Spencer, *op. cit.*, p. 261.

5. Blum, *op. cit.*, p. 154.

6. Robert E. Lane, *The Regulation of Businessmen: Social Conditions of Government Economic Control*. New Haven: Yale University Press, 1954, p. 90.

7. David Weisburd, Stanton Wheeler, Elin Waring, and Nancy Bode, *Crimes of the Middle Classes: White-Collar Offenders in the Federal Courts*. New Haven: Yale University Press, 1991, p. 224 (emphasis in the original).

8. Edwin H. Sutherland, *White Collar Crime*. New York: Dryden, 1949, p. 234.

9. Richard B. Lee, *The !Kung San: Men, Women, and Work in a Foraging Society*. Cambridge: Cambridge University Press, 1979.

10. Robert K. Dentan, *The Semai: A Nonviolent People of Malaya*. New York: Holt, Rinehart & Winston, 1968.

11. Gresham M. Sykes and David Matza, "Techniques of Neutralization: A Theory of Delinquency," *American Sociological Review*, 22 (1957):667–670.

12. Donald R. Cressey, *Other People's Money: The Social Psychology of Embezzlement*. New York: The Free Press, 1953.

13. Marshall B. Clinard, *The Black Market: A Study of White-Collar Crime*. New York: Holt, Rinehart, 1952, p. 169.

14. Michael L. Benson, "Denying the Guilty Mind: Accounting for Involvement in White-Collar Crime," *Criminology*, 23 (1985):595–607.

15. Gerald Mars, "Dock Pilferage: A Case Study in Occupational Theft." In Paul Rock and Mary McIntosh, eds., *Deviance and Social Control*. London: Tavistock, 1974, p. 224.

16. Lawrence R. Zeitlin, "A Little Larceny Can Do a Lot for Company Morale," *Psychology Today*, 14 (June 1971), p. 22.

17. *Time*, November 19, 1979, p. 85.

18. Peter F. Drucker, *Concept of the Corporation*. Rev. ed. New York: John Day, 1972, p. 88.

19. Marshall B. Clinard and Peter Yeager, *Corporate Crime*. New York: The Free Press, 1980, p. 51.

20. Martin L. Needleman and Carolyn Needleman, "Organizational Crime: Two Models of Criminogenesis," *Sociological Quarterly,* 20 (1979):517–528.

21. David Weisburd, Elin Waring, and Stanton Wheeler, "Examining Opportunity Structures in White Collar Crime: The Roles of Social Status and Structural Position." Paper presented at meeting of American Society of Criminology, 1987.

22. Edward Gross, "Organizational Structure and Organizational Crime." In Gilbert Geis and Ezra Stotland, eds., *White-Collar Crime: Theory and Research.* Beverly Hills: Sage, 1980, pp. 52–77.

23. Clinard and Yeager, *op. cit.*

24. *Ibid.*, p. 129.

25. Ronald C. Kramer, "Corporate Crime: An Organizational Perspective." In Peter Wickman and Timothy Dailey, eds., *White-Collar and Economic Crime.* Lexington, MA: Lexington Books, 1982, pp. 75–94.

26. Marshall B. Clinard, *Corporate Ethics and Crime: The Role of Middle Management.* Beverly Hills: Sage, 1983.

27. John E. Conklin, *"Illegal But Not Criminal": Business Crime in America.* Englewood Cliffs, NJ: Prentice-Hall, 1977, pp. 64–65.

28. Weisburd et al., *op. cit.*

29. John P. Clark and Richard Hollinger, *Theft by Employees in Work Organizations.* Washington, DC: National Institute of Justice, September 1983.

30. Donald N. M. Horning, "Blue Collar Theft: Conceptions of Property, Attitudes toward Pilfering, and Work Group Norms in a Modern Industrial Plant." In Erwin O. Smigel and H. Laurence Ross, eds., *Crimes against the Bureaucracy.* New York: Van Nostrand, 1970, pp. 46–64.

31. U.S. Department of Justice, Bureau of Justice Statistics, *Sourcebook of Criminal Justice Statistics—1991.* Washington, DC: Government Printing Office, 1992, p. 442.

32. Kathleen Daly, "Gender and Varieties of White-Collar Crime," *Criminology,* 27 (1989):769–793.

33. Dorothy Zietz, *Women Who Embezzle or Defraud: A Study of Convicted Felons.* New York: Praeger, 1981.

34. Steven Box, *Power, Crime and Mystification.* London: Tavistock, 1983.

20

Causes of White-Collar Crime

Travis Hirschi and Michael Gottfredson

Nothing in criminology is more secure than the idea of white-collar crime. No textbook, it seems, would be complete without a chapter or set of chapters on the topic. No conference is organized without panels devoted to recent developments in theory and research about crime in the suites. No criminal justice curriculum is constructed without a course on some variant on the theme that much crime is committed by the advantaged class, especially those in positions of economic power. In fact, no topic in criminology can be discussed without the spectre of white-collar crime hanging over it. Theories are constantly tested on the ability of their ideas to comprehend this important portion of the total crime picture. Researchers are regularly faced with the unpleasant fact that the correlates of "crime" they uncover may well be treated as ridiculous examples of the failure of unenlightened criminologists to consider the implications of white-collar crime for traditional work in the area. Outside academia, the notion of white-collar crime has had even more substantial impact, fueling, for example, prosecutorial efforts directed at white-collar offenders, the creation of regulatory agencies, and even redirection of the efforts of the Federal Bureau of Investigation.[1]

Now that white-collar crime is securely established as an important area of inquiry for criminology, now that much research and thinking have gone into it, the costs and benefits of the idea can be more clearly assessed. In this paper we outline a general theory of crime capable of organizing the facts about white-collar crime at the same time it is capable of organizing the facts about all forms of crime. The explicit thesis of this paper is that the distinction between white-collar crime and crime in general should be viewed in the same way as distinctions between any particular type of crime and crime in general, that the usefulness of the distinction for some purposes has been illegitimately generalized to areas where it is inapplicable and therefore inappropriate. The utility of crime-specific analyses for policy purposes[2] is not evidence of the utility of the same distinctions for etiological or research purposes. For example, the fact that vandalism may be reduced by banning the sale of paint in aerosol cans cannot be translated to mean that vandals and muggers are produced by different causes. By the same token, the desire to control white-collar criminals should not be confused with the conclusion that they are

Reprinted from *Criminology,* 25 (1987), pp. 949–971.

products of unique causal processes. In fact, our general theory of crime accounts for the frequency and distribution of white-collar crime at the same time it accounts for the frequency and distribution of all other forms of crime, whether they be rape, vandalism, or simple assault. Given the large literature based on the contrary assumption that white-collar crime poses unique theoretical problems, several conceptual issues must be resolved before our theory can be described.

ORIGINS OF THE CONCEPT OF WHITE-COLLAR CRIME

In classical theory, it was assumed that resort to force or fraud was an ever-present potential in human affairs. Both force and fraud were seen as means of pursuing self-interest, and the distinction between the two was not taken to be of theoretical interest. The classical school gave way to the positivists, with their assumption that crime is evidence of biological, psychological, or social pathology. Since force and fraud were no longer assumed to be natural, some special motive or compulsion was required to explain their use. The major social source of such compulsion in positivistic theory was, from the beginning, low social class, poverty, or inequality. This conception explained the high rate of crime among the poor (and suggested that it was really the fault of the rich and powerful). Unfortunately for some political purposes, it also assumed that the poor really did have a high rate of crime compared to the rich and powerful, who were relatively crime free. In this context, invention of the concept of white-collar crime had two desirable consequences: it falsified poverty-pathology theory and it revealed the criminality of the privileged classes and their impunity to the law.

Those sociological theories that continued to accept the class-poverty-inequality model[3] were able to do so only by remaining essentially silent on the white-collar crime issue. Those sociological theories that accepted the idea of white-collar crime were forced to move in one of two directions: toward a general theory that denied "pathological" causes (for example, differential association) or toward theories tailored to particular crimes or types of crime.[4]

The current popularity of the white-collar crime concept attests as much to its political attractiveness as to its scientific value.[5] We argue, in fact, that the major impact of the idea of white-collar crime has been to complicate the positivistic conception of its dependent variable and to deny the results of positivistic research that does not attend to the idea that crime and its causes are somehow class specific.

EXISTING THEORY OF WHITE-COLLAR CRIME

A major problem facing scholars who study white-collar crime is to determine the claims or assertions implicit in the concept. On its face, the term assumes that white-collar crimes are indeed crimes, that people of high social standing commit real crimes, that the crimes they commit differ from common crimes, that the causes of their law breaking differ from those affecting other people, and that the official response to white-collar crime is different from the official response to common crime. (Not obvious from the term itself, but nonetheless commonly encountered in connection with it, is the view that white-collar crime is actually more serious or more dangerous or more detrimental to social or civic values than is ordinary crime.[6])

At first glance, these assertions do not seem particularly problematic or unreasonable. On reflection, however, it turns out that the concept of "church crime" would permit the same conclusions. The crimes committed by church leaders are undoubtedly real or true crimes, crimes that differ from nonchurch crimes (that is, theft of nontaxable contributions is only possible in a nonprofit organization); the reasons for their crimes may be particular to their culture or economic situation; and, of course, the legal system may respond more leniently or severely to church crime than to crime in other systems.

So, what appears to be a straightforward or useful concept turns out to be a potential source of considerable complexity. If we did not know that "white-collar crime" arose as a reaction to the idea that crime is concentrated in the lower class, there would be nothing to distinguish it from other ways of reminding us that crime may be found in all groups, even in the low rate categories of its causes (for example, intact-home crime; valedictorian crime; female crime; elderly crime; small-town crime). The question is: does the concept of white-collar crime have virtues or uses that distinguish it from the countless alternative ways of classifying crimes by the characteristics of their perpetrators? The search for such virtues or uses of white-collar crime may be facilitated by considering its assumptions one at a time.

Is White-Collar Crime Crime? The question of whether white-collar offending is part of the domain of criminology could not arise in classical theory, which did not attend to the characteristics of the offender, to the form of the crime, or to the likelihood that the crime would be met with legal sanction. Since crimes were attempts to gain personal advantage by force or fraud, they could obviously be committed by the rich and powerful, they could certainly involve force or fraud, and they could clearly be committed without punishment by the state.

Positive criminology made the concept of crime problematic in all respects. Essentially, offenders were people unable to learn civilized behavior, or people compelled to misbehave by forces over which they had little control. As a result, the law and its punishments were themselves concepts or institutions at odds with scientific knowledge of human behavior.

In this sense, the concept of white-collar crime is again a reaction against positivism, an assertion that something must be wrong with a world view that denies the possibility of the obvious, the fact that intelligent, powerful people use force and fraud to secure their own ends.

The evidence, it seems to us, clearly supports this element of white-collar theorizing. There is no good reason to restrict the notion of crime to the lower classes. On the contrary, the evidence suggests that when it comes to the use of force and fraud, crime is possible at all social levels, and white-collar crime is clearly crime.

In fact, we would suggest that any theory of crime that makes claim to generality should apply without difficulty to the crimes of the rich and powerful, crimes committed in the course of an occupation, crimes in which a position of power, influence, or trust is used for the purpose of individual or organizational gain.[7]

Do Persons of High Standing Commit Crimes? According to those promoting it, a major value of the concept of white-collar crime is that it reminds us that actual crime is not restricted to the lower class. "This study has attempted to . . . present evidence that persons of the upper socioeconomic class commit many crimes. . . . [This objective] has been realized in that a sample of large corporations is found to have violated laws with great frequency."[8]

So, not only is white-collar crime crime, white-collar crime does occur. Some doctors commit murder, and doctors sometimes cheat on Medicare;[9] lawyers have been known to misuse funds entrusted to them by their clients; business executives sometimes engage in bid rigging; labor union executives sometimes embezzle funds from pension plans; manufacturers sometimes dispose of toxic chemicals in ways contrary to law.

Obviously, one need not introduce the distinction between people and organizations to conclude that white-collar crime is an empirical reality as well as a conceptual possibility. One also need not introduce motivational elements to distinguish white-collar crime from other forms of crime. As with common crime, the white-collar offender clearly seeks personal benefit. This benefit may come directly to the offender or indirectly to the offender through the group or organization to which he or she belongs. As with other crimes, miscalculation of benefits is not evidence that benefits were not sought. One need not introduce unit of analysis issues (for example, do organizations commit crime?) to document offending by persons of high social standing.

Do White-Collar Crimes Differ from Common Crimes? In order to explore the differences thought to exist between white-collar and common crimes, it is necessary to examine a sample of definitions of white-collar crime and derivative or analogous concepts:

> White-collar violations are those violations of law to which penalties are attached that involve the use of a violator's position of significant power, influence, or trust in the legitimate economic or political institutional order for the purpose of illegal gain, or to commit an illegal act for personal or organizational gain.[10]
>
> . . . crime committed by a person of respectability and high social status in the course of his occupation.[11]
>
> . . . An illegal act or series of illegal acts committed by non-physical means and by concealment or guile, to obtain money or property, to avoid the payment or loss of money or property, or to obtain business or personal advantage.[12]

According to Clinard and Quinney, "occupational crime consists of offenses committed by individuals for themselves in the course of their occupations and the offenses of employees against their employers." According to the same authors, corporate crime is defined as "the offenses committed by corporate officials for the corporation and the offenses of the corporation itself."[13]

Obviously, advocates of the concept of white-collar crime believe they have identified a significant distinction among types of crime and types of criminals. The value of these distinctions must be determined by their usefulness in explaining, predicting, or controlling the behavior of offenders, victims, or officials of the criminal justice system. Without such criteria, analysis and evaluation of these concepts would be difficult or impossible. We therefore ask how white-collar crimes and white-collar criminals differ from other crimes and other criminals in terms relevant to explanation, prediction, and control. We begin with the "criminals" question.

How Do White-Collar Criminals Differ from Other Criminals? One way to approach the white-collar crime issue is to note that it takes a fresh view of the relation between crime and employment. In fact, the white-collar crime notion challenges the traditional assumption that the *absence* of an occupation (unemployment) is conducive to crime and that an occupation (employment) is conducive to noncrime. The traditional assumption (unemployment theory) stresses motivation, suggesting that crime is a consequence of the deprivation resulting from relative poverty; employment theory or "occupation theory,"[14] in contrast, stresses opportunity for crime, suggesting that it is a consequence of on-the-job access to money and goods. Neither view is, however, much concerned with the social status or other properties of the offender. In fact, both suggest that different individuals will respond similarly to the stresses of unemployment and to the opportunities of employment.

Clearly, then, research on the actual impact of employment on crime does not require a distinction between ordinary or common criminals and white-collar criminals. The two views appear to accept the same criminal acts as the focus of inquiry. They differ only on the direction of the predicted impact of a specific independent variable. This difference is consistent with our earlier characterization of "white-collar crime theory" as a reaction to "positivistic" (force or pressure) theory. While research favoring employment theory over unemployment theory would say something about the status of the independent variable, it could not demonstrate the need for a special category of criminal (the white-collar offender). Employment theory can be consistent with the evidence without requiring the notion that crime accompanying employment is the product of distinct causes.

In short, a finding that the employed are more likely to steal because of their employment no more justifies a unique theory of theft (white-collar crime) than a finding that the unemployed are more likely to steal justifies a theory focusing exclusively on the lower class (deprivation or strain theory). Perhaps because the focus on "occupational crime" blurs the distinction between white-collar and other forms of crime, advocates of the white-collar crime concept sometimes favor restricting it to crimes committed by wealthy, high-status, or respectable people in positions of power or trust.[15] With white-collar crime so restricted, the research question becomes more difficult: where do we find an appropriate comparison group for white-collar criminals?

Those adopting this restrictive definition of white-collar criminals traditionally continue to compare them with ordinary offenders and ignore people with low social status who commit white-collar offenses. This allows them to use the same terms to describe common criminals and offenders of high status. For example, Sutherland goes to some length to show that the acts of white-collar criminals are "deliberate," that they often "recidivate," and that they are difficult to "rehabilitate." This comparison also allows expressions of concern about the goodness of high-status, white-collar-crime statistics that are traditionally reserved for ordinary crime statistics. Thus, according to Sutherland, official statistics vastly underestimate the extent of the criminal activities of high-status white-collar offenders, just as they underestimate those of ordinary offenders.[16] According to contemporary scholars, such underestimation and disarray in the relevant white-collar crime statistics continues.[17]

Comparing high-status, white-collar offenders with low-status, ordinary offenders loses a large segment of the criminal population, but it allows description of those in high places using terms usually reserved for people at the bottom of the social ladder (for example, "White collar criminals possess a pimp's mentality").[18] It also allows the suggestion that the revealed rot at the top is only the tip of the iceberg. But it has little else of positive value. In fact, it forces a separate theory of offending by suggesting but not demonstrating that the causes of criminal behavior among the rich and powerful are different from the causes of criminal behavior among the poor and weak. Some other comparison would seem to be required.

One possibility is to compare offenders in high places with nonoffenders in the same positions. Before making this comparison, let us briefly examine its logic. First, one identifies offenders by their social location and then compares them with nonoffenders in the same location. This is analogous to comparing lower-class people who commit crimes with lower-class people who do not or, better, to comparing good students who commit delinquencies with good students who do not (since good students, like white-collar people, may be expected to have low rates of crime). Given that both groups in the comparison share the locational attribute, that attribute cannot account for the difference in their behavior. Therefore, this comparison directs attention away from social location toward microlevel or individual-level attributes such as strain, opportunity, or pathology. Since the same microlevel attributes may account for differences between offenders and nonoffenders among good students *and* among lower-class people, we are once again led to question the unique contribution of the concept of white-collar crime to crime theory. (It is ironic that the concept of white-collar crime, designed to introduce macro level distinctions to crime theory, actually forces the explanation to a lower or psychological level.)

A third mechanism for distinguishing white-collar criminals from other criminals is found in the work of those who favor a focus on corporate crime.[19] According to Braithwaite "corporate crime, as the core area of concern, is . . . a broad but reasonably homogeneous domain for coherent theorizing. While useful theories of white collar crime have proved elusive, influential corporate or organizational crime theory is a possibility."[20] Whatever the potential value of the concept of *corporate* crime, it has not yet generated empirical data that require the concept for their interpretation, nor has it proved useful in identifying an important type of crime that would otherwise be missed. Those suggesting that the unit of study can or should be the organization rather than the individual do not stay long with this idea when it comes to collecting or interpreting their data. Thus, although Sutherland tabulated his crime data on firms (referring to some large portion of them as "habitual criminals") and ridiculed explanations of their behavior based on individual pathology, he continued to explain corporate crime with the theory of differential association, and he consistently equated the behavior of the corporation with the behavior of the people in positions of power within it.[21] Braithwaite's own review of the research on company executives who violate the law reaches the conclusion that "it is top management attitudes, most particularly those of the chief executive, that determine the level of compliance with the law in a corporation. . . . Moreover, middle managers are frequently reported as squeezed by a choice between failing to achieve targets set by top management and attaining the targets illegally."[22] Whatever the validity of these assertions, it seems to us that they take the corporation as a setting in which crimes may or may not occur, but do not treat the corporation as the criminal actor. In this sense, then, white-collar crime is again no different from other crimes that occur in group or organizational settings where those in authority have more to say about what happens than those in subordinate positions—for example, governments, military units, university departments, and, for that matter, delinquent gangs.

It may be, then, that the discovery of white-collar criminals is important only in a context in which their existence is denied by theory or policy. In Sutherland's time, theory did tend to deny, usually implicitly, the existence of crime among the powerful, and social policy was not so highly focused on the area as it is today. Today, neither of these justifications is possible. Some other research comparison is therefore required. Perhaps the theoretical utility of the concept can be found in comparisons of crimes rather than criminals.

How Do White-Collar Crimes Differ from Other Crimes? The question of the difference between white-collar crimes and other crimes can be approached in several ways. First, white-collar crimes can he defined as crimes that can only be committed by persons occupying positions of power and influence. This approach rules out crimes committed by high-status people that can be committed by low-status people as well. In this definition, murder of one's spouse and rape would not be considered white-collar crime, unless they are a consequence of the offender's occupational power and influence. In contrast: bank embezzlement can only be committed by employees of banks; insider trading can only be committed by stockbrokers; Medicaid fraud can only be committed by those who bill their services to the program; only automobile manufacturers can build cars that fail to meet legal standards; income taxes can be evaded only by people who owe taxes.

This approach appears to identify a distinct class of crimes, one that *could* require a unique explanation. What is the theoretical value in distinguishing a pharmacist's theft of drugs from a carpenter's theft of lumber? What is the theoretical value in distinguishing a doctor's Medicaid fraud from a patient's Medicaid fraud? What is the theoretical value of distinguishing a bank manager's embezzlement from a service station attendant's embezzlement'? The white-collar crime concept tends to suggest that the pharmacist's theft is more important or serious than, or the product of different causes from, the carpenter's theft. It suggests that the doctor's fraud is more important (socially damaging?) or serious than the patient's, that the causes of one differ from the causes of the other. And so on for the bank manager and the service station attendant. It strikes us that these suggestions are problematic at best, and really involve two, largely unrelated but often confused questions: (1) Are the causes of various offenses the same? (2) Are the offenses themselves equally serious? White-collar theorists and researchers (in common with many criminologists) often assume that the answer to the second question bears on the answer to the first, that more serious crimes must have causes different from (more powerful than?) those of less serious crimes. Certainly there is no logical requirement that causes of offenses somehow match their seriousness, and as we shall show, there is good empirical evidence that they do not, and good theoretical reasons why they should not.

If there is no obvious theoretical value in distinguishing white-collar crimes from analogous blue-collar crimes, is there such value in the common practice of distinguishing *among* such white-collar crimes as Medicaid fraud, income tax evasion, insider trading, antitrust violations, bid-rigging, and consumer fraud? For some purposes, distinctions among crimes are clearly useful. For example, the expertise required to uncover and prosecute antitrust violations is different from that required to spot Medicaid fraud or insider trading. And legislation or other crime-control efforts may well require attention to specific offense characteristics.[23] But these purposes do not require offender differences across such crimes or unique theories of offending. Students of juvenile delinquency have found no utility in studying specialization in vandalism, arson, rape, or burglary (although they have often been encouraged to do so by ad hoc theories suggesting something special about vandals, arsonists, rapists, and burglars). By extension, there is little reason to think that the idea of specialization in white-collar offenses will bear fruit. On the contrary, there is every reason to think that a single theory will apply to all types of white-collar offenses (and, as we will show, to all other offenses as well). To the extent that this is so, specialized studies of offender motivation for particular offenses (for example, embezzlement, collusion, or air pollution) will be redundant to the extent they overlap and wrong to the extent they do not.

The Connection between Crime Types and Types of Criminals. In an effort to explain the connection between age and crime, we were led back to the distinction between crime and criminality, where the former refers to events and the latter to characteristics of people.[24] Exploration of this distinction led to the conclusion that it makes more sense to talk about types of crime than about types of criminals. Events do have distinct sets of causes (for example, autos are necessary for auto theft, access to other people's money is necessary for embezzlement, other people are required for assault, bid-rigging, and rape). At the same time, the evidence seems reasonably clear that offenders seem to do just about everything, and do not therefore specialize in any particular crime or type of crime. Identifying offenders with offenses is therefore misleading. Robbers may have committed robbery, but, in terms of future offending, they are actually more likely to engage in theft than robbery, and are only very slightly more likely than any other offender to engage again in robbery. If this is so for robbery and rape, which it is, it might also be true for embezzlement, fraud, and forgery. While embezzlement, fraud, and forgery are distinct events, and may therefore have distinct causes, there is no reason to think that offenders committing these crimes are causally distinct from other offenders. A general theory of criminality is therefore not logically precluded by white-collar crime any more than by robbery or any other specific type of crime. The assumption that white-collar criminals differ from other criminals is simply the assumption, in another guise, that offenders specialize in particular crimes, an assumption for which there is no good evidence.

A GENERAL THEORY OF CRIME

We have been developing a general theory of crime designed to account for the distribution of all forms of criminal behavior.[25] This emerging theory starts from a distinction between crimes as events and criminality as a characteristic of people. Whereas traditional positivistic theories begin by looking at offenders, we begin by looking at crime. We conclude that criminal events have properties that must be taken into account in devising explanations of them. That is, there are features of criminal events themselves that are capable of falsifying traditional theories that derive their dependent variable from ordinary disciplinary perspectives. For example, as we have seen, crimes have in common features that make those engaging in any one of them extremely likely to engage in others as well. These common features are not money, success, or peer approval. They are therefore inconsistent with most theories of crime and must be identified by a valid theory of crime. On inspection, most theories of crime assume that offenders specialize in types of crime (an expectation that has found its way into the white-collar crime literature); that they have careers in crime that progress, develop, or change over time; and that each type of crime has its own motives. These assumptions are contrary to the evidence.

Crime. Because the evidence suggests that the essential properties of crimes are not money, success, reduction of frustration, or peer approval (as one or another modern theory would have us believe) and because versatility in offenders is an established empirical fact, all crimes must share other common properties that make them appealing to potential offenders.

A concept of crime that will reveal attractive properties common to diverse acts presupposes a concept of human nature. In our view, the concept of human nature that best organizes the data is that found in the classical assumption that human behavior is motivated by the self-interested pursuit of pleasure and the avoidance of pain. Crimes are events in which force or fraud are used to satisfy self-interest, where self-interest refers to the enhancement of pleasure and the avoidance of pain. Features of events that enhance their pleasure or minimize their pain will be implicated in their causation. To be maximally pleasurable, events should take place immediately; pleasure is therefore enhanced by the *rapidity* with which it is obtained. Force and fraud can often produce more rapid results than alternative means; they are therefore useful in the pursuit of self-interest. To be maximally pleasurable, events should be *certain* in outcome; force and fraud can provide more certain benefit than alternative means, particularly when the benefit sought is short-term and the long-term consequences of the act are of little concern. To be maximally pleasurable, events should require *minimal effort;* force and fraud can provide benefit with less effort than alternative means, especially when the benefit also has the properties of rapidity and certainty.

White-collar crimes satisfy these defining conditions. They provide relatively quick, relatively certain benefit, with minimal effort. Crimes, including white-collar crimes, therefore require no motivation or pressure that is not present in any other form of human behavior.

Since crimes involve goods, services, or victims, they have other constituent properties as well: they all require opportunity, and are thought to result in punishment of the offender if he or she is detected. Such properties cannot account for the general tendency of particular individuals to engage in crime, and they are therefore not central to a theory of criminality.

Criminality. Our conception of the essential features of *crime* provides the basis of a theory of *criminality*. Criminality is the tendency of individuals to pursue short-term gratification in the most direct way with little consideration for the long-term consequences of their acts. (Indicators of such a tendency include impulsivity, aggression, activity level, and lack of concern for the opinion of others.) People high on this tendency are relatively unable or unwilling to delay gratification; they are relatively indifferent to punishment and to the interests of others. As a consequence, they tend to be impulsive, active, and risk-taking.

Work demonstrating consistency in behavior over substantial periods of time is consistent with the concept of criminality as we use it here. For example, it is established that differences in the tendency toward aggression persist from childhood to adulthood;[26] likewise, the evidence is strong that differences in the tendency toward delinquency and crime persist over the same period.[27]

Such tendencies do not lead ineluctably to crime, regardless of the setting in which the individual is located. As indicated, crimes require physical opportunity and immunity from immediate punishment in addition to individual tendencies. Also, many noncriminal acts have the capacity to provide the benefits of crime and are therefore attractive to those with high levels of "criminality"—for example, drug, alcohol, and cigarette use, sex, divorce, job quitting, and fast cars. To complicate things further, these tendencies often affect the settings in which the individuals possessing them are located—for example, the amount of education they attain, the kind of job they have, whether they marry and stay married.

Application of the General Theory to White-Collar Crime. The characteristics described above have implications for the likelihood of criminal acts, but they also have implications for selection into the occupational structure. Ordinary occupations require people to be in a particular place at a particular time. They also require educational persistence, willingness and ability to defer to the interests of others, and attention to conventional appearance. These occupational requirements tend to be inconsistent with the traits comprising criminality. White-collar occupations therefore tend to demand characteristics inconsistent with high levels of criminality. In other words, selection processes inherent to the high end of the occupational structure tend to recruit people with relatively low propensity to crime.

Our theory therefore predicts a relatively low rate of offending among white-collar workers, contrary to the now standard view in the literature.[28] The standard view is based on misleading statistics about the extent of white-collar offending. For one thing, white-collar researchers often take *organizations* as the unit of analysis and do not adjust for their size and complexity when making comparisons with blue-collar *individuals*. For another, the reference period for the organization is often much longer than that applied to individuals.[29] As a consequence, the white-collar crime literature often compares the number of crimes committed by an organization with many thousands of employees over a period of many years with those committed by single individuals in a single year.

When comparable units (for example, individuals with the same crime-relevant characteristics [for example, age, sex, ethnicity]), comparable reference periods (for example, one year), and comparable methods of measurement (for example, self-reports or arrests) are employed, rates of crime among employed white-collar workers should be low compared to those of persons in less structured occupations with similar opportunities, and compared to those outside the occupational structure with similar opportunities.

Note that our distinction between people and events treats white-collar crimes as events that take place in an occupational setting, not as characteristics of people employed in those settings. As a result, it makes problematic the connection between the people and the events and allows the possibility that this connection is less strong than the connection between people in other settings and the criminal events unique to those settings. Obviously, only white-collar workers can commit white-collar crimes, but the fact that they do so cannot be taken as evidence of their criminality unless (1) other people are given the opportunity to commit the same crimes in the same setting, or (2) other settings and crimes are construed, for purposes of comparison, to be equivalent to white-collar crime. The latter solution is the one adopted by the criminal law, and by most compilations of crime statistics.

In law and in crime statistics, embezzlement, fraud, and forgery are defined without reference to the occupational setting in which they occur. As a consequence, it is possible to study the demographic distributions of white-collar crimes and compare them with the same distributions for other crimes. Our general theory of course predicts that differences in the demographic correlates across crimes should be nonexistent given similar opportunity structures.

The Uniform Crime Reports arrest rates for fraud and embezzlement by age show that arrest rates for these white-collar crimes peak in the late teens and early 20s and decline sharply with increasing age. By about age 37, the rate of embezzlement is half the rate at the peak age. By about age 41, the rate of fraud has declined to half its peak value.

The rates of embezzlement in 1981 for males and females are much closer than for most crimes, especially crimes of violence. (In fact, it is widely reported in the literature that the male/female rates of white-collar crimes are converging.) Smaller race differences are found than for ordinary crimes. Although the black/other rates for fraud and embezzlement are higher than those for whites, the differences are not as great as those typically encountered.

The similarity of the age distribution of murder to the age distributions of embezzlement and fraud is remarkable. Actually, fraud arrests are much more common than murder arrests (about 13:1) while embezzlement arrests are even less common than murder arrests (about 1:2). But what is clear is that a major correlate of ordinary crime is similarly correlated with white-collar crime. Neither do age-sex-race differences in opportunity reveal differences in the correlates of white-collar and ordinary crime. On the contrary, they tend to conceal the fact that their correlates are of the same order of magnitude and direction. When opportunity is taken into account, demographic differences in white-collar crime are the same as demographic differences in ordinary crime.

Individual Differences and White-Collar Crime. Research and theory relating characteristics of individuals to involvement in crime are often held up to ridicule on the grounds that individuals involved in white-collar crime have traits "opposite" to those said to cause crime. In fact, the white-collar crime literature in one sense owes its origins to precisely this logic:

> Quite obviously, the hypothesis that crime is due to personal and social pathologies does not apply to white collar crimes, and if it does not explain these crimes such pathologies are not essential factors in crime in general. In contrast with such explanations the hypothesis of differential association and social disorganization may apply to white collar crimes as well as to lower class crimes.[30]

Trait theorists were particularly vulnerable to this criticism, since most of the traits they believed to be conducive to crime (for example, aggressiveness, risk-taking, activity level, mesomorphy, sociability) could also be said to be conducive to business success. (If aggressiveness causes crime, it also causes business success. Therefore, it cannot cause crime. Or, so the logic goes.) The problems with this argument were threefold: (1) It assumed facts not in evidence. There was no empirical reason to believe that "traits" positively correlated with ordinary crime were negatively correlated with white-collar crime. On the contrary, as we have shown, there is good reason to think otherwise. (2) It denied the obvious fact that a single cause (or set of causes) may have differential manifestations. All things equal, an active person may be more likely to succeed in business and more likely to engage in criminal acts. All things equal, an impulsive person may be more likely to shoplift and more likely to embezzle from the firm. (3) It confuses location in the business world with success in business. It assumes that white-collar criminals are successful at white-collar occupations, an assumption exacerbated by the tendency of white-collar crime researchers to rely on anecdote and on particularly notorious cases. Although by definition one must be in the white-collar world to be a white-collar offender, not all white-collar workers enjoy the power, income, and prestige to be found at the top of this world. In fact, most have little power, not much income, and only moderate prestige. However, this erroneous assumption leads to the expectation that the correlates of white-collar crime will be opposite to the correlates of ordinary crime. After all, it takes a while to be successful in the business world, and while this is happening one is growing older, a fact that must reverse the usual negative relation between age and crime; obviously, whites have an advantage over blacks in the white-collar world; therefore, here at least whites should have a higher rate of crime; obviously, intelligence is positively related to white-collar success and therefore should be positively related to white-collar crime. In all cases where data are available, they suggest otherwise.

Experimental tests of our hypotheses could be achieved by distributing credit cards to junior-high-school students or by using banks for prison work-release programs. Without such tests, it is difficult to document the relatively low level of criminality among white-collar workers. Absent such tests, scholars will continue to argue that the criminal justice system favors white-collar workers, that businesses protect them to maintain their own reputations, and that white-collar crimes are relatively easily concealed. A case could be made that these arguments are themselves relics of a bygone age. The Bureau of Justice Statistics reports that, in 1983, the probability of incarceration for white-collar offenders was as high as that for violent offenders. And good research shows that criminal justice system punishments for white-collar offenses are governed by the same criteria governing punishments for other crimes.[31]

The Value of White-Collar Crime for Crime Theory. The concept of white-collar crime is usually seen as incompatible with most theories of crime, particularly theories that focus on differences in the biology, psychology, or social position of offenders and nonoffenders. Other theories have gained considerable advantage from appearing to be peculiarly compatible with the concept. It is universally agreed that the more general a theory, the better, and theories that can encompass white-collar crime along with common crime must, it seems, be very general and therefore superior to theories that deal only with ordinary crime, or, worse, only with "juvenile delinquency." Indeed, the objection most frequently raised to explanatory efforts in criminology is typically phrased something like: "Yes, but what about white-collar crime?"

The theories gaining most from the white-collar crime concept are those focusing on learning, especially those focusing on the learning of cultural values such as Sutherland's own theory of differential association. From the beginning, Sutherland asserted that white-collar crime could only be understood as a consequence or natural extension of ordinary business values.[32] Those socialized within the business world could come to define their criminal activities as required by the needs of profit making and as generally supported in the business community by "neutralizing verbalizations."[33] Additionally, they could there find training in the techniques required to commit crimes of such complexity. Modern variants of this perspective seek to answer similar questions: "In what ways is society organized that it may encourage the very phenomenon it seeks to control?"[34]

The survival of such theories of crime is directly attributable to their apparent generality, to their apparent ability to account for phenomena beyond the reach of theories that focus on individual differences. Ironically, although these theories owe their current popularity and even survival to their connection to white-collar (or organization) crime, white-collar crime has done more for them than they have done for the understanding of white-collar crime.

Consider the causal mechanisms used to understand crime in the cultural theory tradition. In this tradition, the individual learns that crime is condoned by the values of the organization or is required as a natural byproduct of its pursuit of profits. In some versions, the organization creates expectations of performance that may be met only by law violation;[35] in others, the techniques and rationalizations required for white-collar crime are simple extensions of routine business practices. In either case, criminal activity is seen as consistent with rather than contrary to the values of those engaging in it.

The first difficulty encountered by such theories is the relative rarity of white-collar crime. Contrary to the expectations of these theories, white-collar offenses are relatively rare. If the white-collar work force is actually socialized to the virtues of embezzlement, bid-rigging, and fraud, what accounts for the extraordinarily high level of law-abiding conduct among white-collar workers? It is easily shown that crime by partners or employees may increase the cost of doing business to the point that business is no longer profitable. The limits on white-collar crime set by requirements of profits and survival are rarely recognized by white-collar crime theorists. These limits have, however, been noted by students of "organized crime."[36] A second difficulty for such theories is suggested by the routine finding that white-collar offenders tend to receive little support for their criminal activities from the organization or from other white-collar workers. Indeed, the evidence suggests that they are especially concerned with concealing their crimes from co-workers and management.[37] The reasons for such concern are revealing: the victim of white-collar crime is typically the organization itself, not in a direct way the general public. Since white-collar offenders share the general propensity of offenders to pursue self-interest, they naturally take advantage of the most readily available opportunities. By ascribing larger purposes to white-collar criminals, cultural theories tend to mispredict the nature of white-collar victimization.

A third difficulty with the cultural theory of white-collar crime is that it mispredicts the correlates of the phenomena, suggesting that the longer the exposure to the business culture, the higher the level of criminal activity (contrary to the age distribution of white-collar crime), suggesting that opportunity itself is sufficient to overcome ordinary differences in the likelihood of criminal activity (contrary to the sex, race, and age differences reported earlier), suggesting that white-collar crimes are so complicated that unusual training or skill is required for their performance (contrary to evidence showing that most white-collar crime involves such activities as the transfer of funds from one account to another, dumping barrels of chemicals in remote areas, or alteration of routine billing practices,[38] all within a context of belief that such practices are unlikely to be discovered. To say that such practices are consistent with the offender's profit motive (self-interest) is obviously true; to say that they are consistent with the generally accepted values of the business world is wrong.

A fourth difficulty with these theories is frequently noted by students of common crime. They all fail as explanations of ordinary crime and delinquency.[39] The white-collar crime area thus falls prey to its own critique of criminological theories: the generally accepted white-collar crime theories cannot explain ordinary crime and are thus, by their own logic,[40] incapable of explaining crime, whether white-collar or ordinary.

Our theory avoids all of these problems. As indicated above, our general theory of crime predicts variation in rates across social settings, with white-collar crime rates being relatively low, depending on the process of selection into the particular white-collar occupation. Our theory directly disagrees with traditional "white-collar" theory on the rate issue, and thus leads to a directly testable empirical question. Our theory is of course not bothered by the fact that people can pursue criminal activities without social support. On the contrary, it explicitly predicts lack of social support for most white-collar crimes since (1) they are contrary to general social norms and (2) are against the interests of the organization itself. We therefore have a second empirical issue of direct theoretical relevance.

We earlier assert that our general theory expects the properties of those committing crime to be similar regardless of the type of crime. It therefore asserts that the distinction between crime in the street and crime in the suite is an *offense* rather than an *offender* distinction, that offenders in both cases are likely to share similar characteristics. We therefore have a third directly testable distinction between our general theory and the commonly accepted view of white-collar crime.

The fourth difficulty of cultural theories provides another empirical test of the relative value of these competing perspectives. Our theory was constructed with common offenses and offenders in mind. It is meant to predict and explain ordinary crime, juvenile delinquency, drug abuse, serious crime, "organized" crime, status offending, as well as white-collar crime. Since our theory permits no propensity distinctions among types of offenses, it is perfectly general, and is once again directly contrary to cultural theories, with their view that crimes have unique, specific cultural motives.

CONCLUSION

It is time criminology recognized that the typological approach inherent in the concept of white-collar crime is a mistake. One of the causes of this mistake is, we believe, to be found in the enduring tendency of those who study crime to subordinate the topic to the interests of their parent discipline. This tendency is particularly marked among sociologists, who see in white-collar crime an opportunity to save conceptual schemes that have not proved useful with ordinary offenders. It is also present among economists, who see in white-collar crime an opportunity to explicate once again the grand scheme of their discipline. Psychologists, comfortable with the idea of typologies, endlessly divide offenders into groups thought to be "relatively homogeneous" with respect to the meaning of their offenses. And quantitative analysts of all disciplinary persuasions see white-collar crime as one more opportunity to specify a formal model. All of these disciplinary interests are served by acceptance of the received view of "white-collar offending." This paper questions the received view and reasserts the view that crime is a unitary phenomenon capable of explanation by a single theory, a theory that seeks first the features common to all crimes and deduces from them tendencies to criminality in the individual. It is then in position to outline the causes of such tendencies and to consider the differential manifestation of these tendencies. Such differential manifestation is of course a function of the opportunities available to people, of the circumstances in which they find themselves. To think otherwise is to confuse social location with social causation.

Notes

1. Gilbert Geis and Robert F. Meier, eds., *White-Collar Crime*. Rev. ed. New York: The Free Press, 1977, p. 2.
2. See, for instance, Derek Cornish and Ronald Clarke, eds., *The Reasoning Criminal*. New York: Springer-Verlag, 1986.
3. See, for example, Robert K. Merton, "Social Structure and Anomie," *American Sociological Review*, 3 (1938):672–682; Richard Cloward and Lloyd Ohlin, *Delinquency and Opportunity*. New York: The Free Press, 1960; Peter Blau and Judith Blau, "The Cost of Inequality: Metropolitan Structure and Violent Crime," *American Sociological Review*, 47 (1982):114–129.
4. See, for example, Marshall Clinard and Richard Quinney, eds., *Criminal Behavior Systems: A Typology*. 2d ed. New York: Holt, Rinehart & Winston, 1973; Don Gibbons, *Society, Crime and Criminal Careers*. 2d ed. Englewood Cliffs, NJ: Prentice-Hall, 1973; Herbert A. Bloch and Gilbert Geis, *Man, Crime, and Society*. 2d ed. New York: Random House, 1970.

5. Gilbert Geis and Colin Goff, "Introduction." In Edwin H. Sutherland, *White Collar Crime: The Uncut Version.* New Haven: Yale University Press, 1983, pp. ix–xxxiii; John Braithwaite, "White Collar Crime," *Annual Review of Sociology,* 11 (1985d):1–25.

6. Sutherland, *op. cit.* George Will, "Keep Your Eye on Giuliani," *Newsweek,* March 2, 1987, p. 84.

7. Albert J. Reiss, Jr., and Albert Biderman, *Data Sources on White-Collar Law-Breaking.* Washington, DC: U.S. Department of Justice, 1980, p. 4.

8. Sutherland, *op. cit.,* p. 264.

9. Gilbert Geis, Henry Pontell, and Paul Jesilow, "Medicaid Fraud." In Joseph E. Scott and Travis Hirschi, eds., *Controversial Issues in Criminology and Criminal Justice.* Beverly Hills: Sage, 1988, pp. 7–39.

10. Reiss and Biderman, *op. cit.,* p. 4.

11. Sutherland, *op. cit.,* p. 7.

12. Herbert Edelhertz, *The Nature, Impact and Prosecution of White Collar Crime.* Washington, DC: National Institute of Law Enforcement and Criminal Justice, 1970, pp. 19–20.

13. Clinard and Quinney, *op. cit.,* p. 188.

14. *Ibid.*

15. Sutherland, *op. cit.* See also Reiss and Biderman, *op. cit.*

16. Sutherland, *op. cit.,* pp. 227–228.

17. Reiss and Biderman, *op. cit.*

18. August Bequai, "Justice Department Sends Warning to White-Collar Criminals," *Arizona Daily Star,* March 15, 1987, p. F3.

19. Braithwaite, *op. cit.*; M. David Ermann and Richard Lundman, eds., *Corporate and Governmental Deviance: Problems of Organizational Behavior in Contemporary Society.* 2d ed. New York: Oxford University Press, 1982.

20. Braithwaite, *op. cit.,* p. 19.

21. Albert K. Cohen, Alfred Lindesmith, and Karl Schuessler, eds., *The Sutherland Papers.* Bloomington: Indiana University Press, 1956; Geis and Meier, *op. cit.*

22. Braithwaite, *op. cit.,* p. 17.

23. Cornish and Clarke, *op. cit.*

24. Travis Hirschi and Michael Gottfredson, "The Distinction between Crime and Criminality." In Timothy F. Hartnagel and Robert A. Silverman, eds., *Critique and Explanation: Essays in Honor of Gwynne Nettler.* New Brunswick, NJ: Transaction, 1986, pp. 55–69.

25. *Ibid.;* see also Travis Hirschi and Michael Gottfredson, "Toward a General Theory of Crime." In Wouter Buikhuisen and Sarnoff A. Mednick, eds., *Explaining Criminal Behavior: Interdisciplinary Approaches.* Leiden: E. J. Brill, 1987, pp. 8–26. Gottfredson and Hirschi, "A Propensity-Event Theory of Crime," *Advances in Criminology,* 1 (1987):44–53.

26. Leonard Eron, "The Development of Aggressive Behavior from the Perspective of a Developing Behaviorism," *American Psychologist,* 42 (1987):

435–442; Dan Olweus, "Stability of Aggressive Reactions Patterns in Males: A Review," *Psychological Bulletin,* 86 (1979):852–875.

27. Rolf Loeber, "The Stability of Antisocial and Delinquent Child Behavior: A Review," *Child Development,* 53 (1982):1431–1466; Loeber and Thomas Dishion, "Early Predictors of Male Delinquency: A Review," *Psychological Bulletin,* 94 (1983):68–99; Joan McCord, "Some Child Rearing Antecedents of Criminal Behavior in Adult Men," *Journal of Personality and Social Psychology,* 37 (1979):1477–1486; Sheldon Glueck and Eleanor Glueck, *Delinquents and Nondelinquents in Perspective.* Englewood Cliffs, NJ: Prentice-Hall, 1968; Donald J. West and David Farrington, *The Delinquent Way of Life.* London: Heinemann, 1977.

28. See, for example, Jeffrey Reiman, *The Rich Get Richer and the Poor Get Prison.* New York: Wiley, 1979; Sutherland, *op. cit.*

29. Sutherland, *op. cit.*

30. *Ibid.*, p. 264;

31. Stanton Wheeler, David Weisburd, and Nancy Bode, "Sentencing the White-Collar Offender," *American Sociological Review,* 47 (1982):641–659.

32. Sutherland, *op. cit.*, pp. 240–264. See also Donald R. Cressey, "Why Managers Commit Fraud," *Australian and New Zealand Journal of Criminology,* 19 (1986):195–209.

33. Cressey, *op. cit.*, p. 200.

34. Diane Vaughan, *Controlling Unlawful Organizational Behavior.* Chicago: University of Chicago Press, 1983.

35. Braithwaite, *op. cit.*, p. 17; Vaughan, *op. cit.*

36. See Peter Reuter, *Disorganized Crime: The Economics of the Visible Hand.* Cambridge: MIT Press, 1983.

37. Donald R. Cressey, *Other People's Money: The Social Psychology of Embezzlement.* New York: The Free Press, 1953; Vaughan, *op. cit.*; James R. Lasley, "Toward a Control Theory of White-Collar Offending," *Journal of Quantitative Criminology,* 4 (1988):347–362.

38. Vaughan, *op. cit.*

39. Ruth Kornhauser, *Social Sources of Delinquency.* Chicago: University of Chicago Press, 1978.

40. Sutherland, *op. cit.*

21

On the Causes
of "White-Collar" Crime
An Assessment of Hirschi
and Gottfredson's Claims

Darrell J. Steffensmeier

Hirschi and Gottfredson's article, "Causes of White-Collar Crime" is an important contribution to the debate over whether and to what extent criminality (or
deviance) is a unified phenomenon, with various behaviors serving as alternative
manifestations of a more general tendency and with a single explanatory framework
applicable to all forms of crime/deviance (hereafter, crime).[1] Most sociological theories are consistent with the view that criminality is general across different behaviors. Almost any explanation offered for one behavior has been offered for
others—for example, peer influence by Sutherland and social bonds by Hirschi have
been proposed to explain a variety of criminal behaviors. But, while many social
explanations indicate how different criminal behaviors have influences in common,
explanations vary regarding the generality versus specificity of crime and regarding
the degree to which the process causing one criminal behavior will jointly produce
others.[2]

One position is that a general cause (e.g., low self-esteem, subcultural norms,
anomie, weak social bonds) is a *partial* determinant of a range of deviant or criminal
behaviors. This position predicts substantial, but not complete, generality of
deviance, so that it is possible for different deviant behaviors to have some influences in common and some influences that are specific. The alternative position is
that a general cause (e.g., low self-esteem) is a more or less *complete* determinant of
a range of deviant or criminal behaviors. Taking it to its extreme, this position leads
to the conclusion that influences specific to particular forms of deviance not only
would be unimportant, but nonexistent. Given a propensity toward deviance, the

Reprinted from *Criminology*, 27 (1989), pp. 345–358.

specific deviant behaviors in which a person engages at any time would be strictly random.

Hirschi and Gottfredson strongly favor the latter position—that different deviant behaviors are manifestations of a single underlying construct or "thing." This "thing" is criminality, which Hirschi elsewhere defines as "the tendency or propensity of the individual to seek short term, immediate pleasure."[3] In their 1987 *Criminology* article, Hirschi and Gottfredson further articulate their position that the same factors are major sources of all deviant behaviors, that causes specific to any particular form of deviance are essentially nonexistent, and that their version of social control (i.e., absence of social bonds), more so than rival approaches, offers a general theory of crime designed to account for the distribution of all forms of criminal behavior.

In the *Criminology* article, Hirschi and Gottfredson claim that "data relevant to popular images of white-collar crime" are compared with patterns of ordinary crime, and that "several explicit tests of rival explanations" of white-collar crime are presented.[4] They report two major findings: (1) that the demographic distribution (e.g., age, sex, race) of white-collar crime is the same as for ordinary crime and (2) that white-collar crime is a relatively rare phenomenon. They interpret these findings as demonstrating not only that white-collar and ordinary crime are influenced by the same set of factors and are manifestations of the same general tendency, but also that social control theory offers a better explanation of white-collar crime than do traditional explanations, such as Sutherland's differential association.

To stimulate further research on this topic, this article raises several questions about the conclusions Hirschi and Gottfredson have drawn from their data and model. My view is that their "reading" of the Uniform Crime Report (UCR) arrest data is flawed. First, the UCR offense categories of fraud, forgery, and embezzlement are *not* appropriate indicators of white-collar or occupational crime because the typical arrestee in these categories committed a nonoccupational crime. Second, the demographic distribution (age, sex, race) for the three crime categories, regardless of whether they are designated as "white-collar" or some other crime type, is *not* the same as it is for offenses like burglary and larceny, which typically are classified as "ordinary" crimes. Third, the occurrence of these "white-collar" crimes is *not* relatively rare; at least, it is not rarer than other kinds of offending.[5]

CAN THE UCR STATISTICS BE USED AS AN INDICATOR OF WHITE-COLLAR OFFENDING?

Hirschi and Gottfredson assume that arrests for fraud, forgery, and embezzlement are for "white-collar" crimes. But, in fact, the UCR data have little or nothing to do with white-collar crime. The problem arises because the UCR offense categories are broad and are derived from a heterogeneous collection of criminal acts. To put it metaphorically, frauds and forgeries come in a multitude of colors and shapes, from stock fraud to check and credit card fraud to welfare fraud. The question, then, is this: For what kinds of frauds/forgeries are persons arrested within these broad categories? To answer the question, it is necessary to look at information available from sources other than the UCR, such as local police arrest files that permit a breakdown of the specific offenses for which an arrest has been made.

The evidence is quite conclusive—the studies all show that persons arrested for fraud and forgery do not qualify as white-collar criminals, whether that term is used restrictively to refer to crimes committed by persons of high socioeconomic status in the course of their occupation, or if the term is used broadly to refer to crimes committed by any employee—blue-collar or white-collar, business owner, executive, or professional.[6] The evidence indicates that most arrests for fraud or for forgery are not occupationally related but rather involve passing bad checks, credit card fraud, theft of services, falsification of identification, defrauding an innkeeper, fraudulent use of public transport, welfare fraud, and small con games.[7] One recent analysis of 1981 and 1986 police files in a Pennsylvania county found that less than 2% of all arrests for fraud and for forgery (as well as for larceny) were for a white-collar or an occupational crime. (The few "occupational arrests" mainly involved thefts by domestic workers.)[8] Moreover, the typical arrestee for embezzlement apparently fits the broad, but not the narrow, definition of white-collar crime. Meanwhile, the embezzler (who becomes an arrest statistic) is often the club treasurer or the trusted clerk, cashier, teller, or secretary who takes money from his or her organization or employer, and the amount taken is usually small.[9] Moreover, because so few persons are arrested for embezzlement (fewer than for any other crime), the crime is relatively insignificant in terms of overall crime patterns.

In contrast to Hirschi and Gottfredson's treatment, therefore, arrests for fraud or for forgery should not be taken as a measure of participation in white-collar or occupational crime. (Instead, they better approximate ordinary crime.) This observation renders meaningless the remaining "empirical tests" that Hirschi and Gottfredson present in their article. Nonetheless, it is important to examine those tests, because even if we allow for their error of treating the UCR categories of fraud and forgery as if they are "white-collar" offenses, the data still fail to support other claims made by Hirschi and Gottfredson: (1) that the demographic distribution of "white-collar" crime is the same as for ordinary crime and (2) that "white-collar" crime is a relatively rare phenomenon.

DO WHITE-COLLAR AND ORDINARY CRIMES HAVE THE SAME DEMOGRAPHIC DISTRIBUTION?

Hirschi and Gottfredson argue that their general theory of crime (i.e., social control theory) predicts that differences in the demographic correlates across crimes, including white-collar and ordinary crimes, should be nonexistent given similar opportunity structures. As one test of this prediction, they compare the age distribution of arrests for the white-collar crimes of fraud and embezzlement with that for the ordinary crime of homicide. They conclude that the age distributions for the two kinds of offenses—white-collar versus ordinary—are the same. This similarity in the age curves for fraud and homicide has long been recognized in criminological writings.[10] However, criminological writings also recognize that the age curves for fraud and homicide are flatter or "older" than those for many other crimes, in particular, for such crimes as larceny, burglary, and robbery, which traditionally connote what is meant by "ordinary crime."

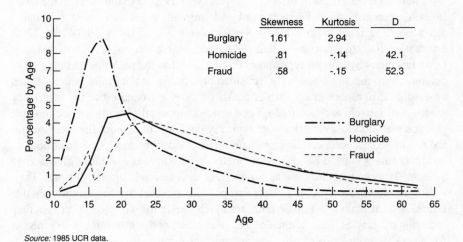

Source: 1985 UCR data.

Figure 21.1
1985 Age Curves for Homicide, Burglary, and Fraud

As is displayed in Figure 21.1, the age curves for fraud and homicide are quite similar, and both differ considerably from the age curve for burglary. The arrest rate for fraud peaks later and declines much more slowly with advancing age than is the case for burglary. The peak age for fraud is 24, the median age is about 30, and it is not until about age 41 that the rate for fraud declines to half its peak value. In contrast, the peak age for burglary is 16, the median age is 17.5, and it reaches one-half its peak value at age 20. The skewness and kurtosis values of fraud and burglary are also very different: for fraud the skewness value is .58 and the kurtosis value is –.15, which compares with 1.61 and 2.94 for burglary, respectively.[11] (These statistical calculations are based on ages 10 to 64.)

Two statistical procedures were used to test whether the age curves for fraud and burglary are homogeneous: the index of dissimilarity and the chi-square test of independence or homogeneity.[12] Both tests confirm that age distributions for the two offenses are quite different. The index of dissimilarity yields a whopping D-value of 51.87 when the age distributions of fraud and burglary are compared. This means that over one-half of all arrests would have to be redistributed to other age groups in order for the two age distributions to match. The p-value yielded from the chi-square test, when the age distributions between burglary and fraud are compared, also shows that the two distributions are significantly different, and strongly so. Thus, the findings from these measures demonstrate rather unequivocally that the age curves are substantially different for "white-collar" and "ordinary" crimes.

The Hirschi and Gottfredson claim about the homogeneity of the age distribution of white-collar and ordinary crimes is an articulation of their more general view, argued elsewhere, that the age distribution of crime is essentially invariant across time and space regardless of offense.[13] Several writers have found Hirschi and Gottfredson's contentions to be overstated and misleading, but the most systematic analysis of the issue is provided by Steffensmeier et al.[14] Using 1940–1980 UCR arrest statistics, they document that the tendency of crime to decline with age is fairly tenacious by offense type and over time, but that the peak age and the rate of decline from the peak age vary considerably. In particular, they conclude that observable differences in age curves across offenses are contrary to the invariancy assertion of Hirschi and Gottfredson and instead support the traditional sociological position that although the crime rate typically declines throughout life after the initial rise in adolescence, certain crimes peak later, or decline more slowly, or both.

Hirschi and Gottfredson also touch briefly on whether sex and race differences in white-collar crime are the same as sex and race differences in ordinary crimes. Their position is ambiguously stated. After first pointing out that there apparently are differences—that male and female rates are much closer for white-collar crimes than for ordinary crimes, like homicide, and that black and white rates, while higher for blacks for both kinds of offenses, are much closer for white-collar than for ordinary crimes, they later write that the demographic correlates (i.e., age, sex, and race) of white-collar and ordinary crime "are of the same order of magnitude and direction."[15] In Figures 21.2 and 21.3 population-adjusted percentages are displayed that compare male-to-female and white-to-black/other arrest levels for fraud, forgery, and embezzlement, along with homicide, burglary, and robbery. I agree with Hirschi and Gottfredson's conclusion that the *direction* of correlate differences is the same across the offenses: whites and females have smaller rates or less proportionate involvement in crime than blacks/other and males for each of the six offenses. But I disagree with Hirschi and Gottfredson's conclusion that these correlate differences are "of the same order of *magnitude*" (italics mine). The percentage of arrests involving whites or females varies considerably across these offenses. The percentage of arrests for whites is about 25 to 30% for the property crimes (fraud, forgery, embezzlement, burglary), but it is only about 10 to 15% for the violent crimes (robbery, homicide).[16] Even more divergent is the size of the sex differences across offenses. The percentage of female arrests varies from 28 to 40% for embezzlement, forgery, and fraud, but it drops off sharply to about 12% for homicide, and is only about 6% for burglary and for robbery.

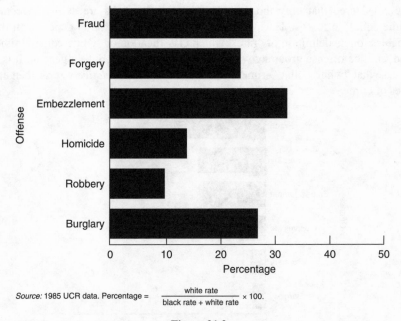

Source: 1985 UCR data. Percentage = $\dfrac{\text{white rate}}{\text{black rate} + \text{white rate}} \times 100.$

Figure 21.2
White Percentage of Arrests, by Offense Type

IS WHITE-COLLAR CRIME RELATIVELY RARE?

Hirschi and Gottfredson also assert that theories such as Sutherland's differential association are seriously flawed because they wrongly predict a high level of white collar crime in our society as an extension of routine business activities that provide for supportive values, techniques, and rationalizations for such criminal activity. In contrast, their social control theory not only explicitly predicts lack of social support for white-collar crimes but correctly predicts relatively low rates of white-collar crime.

As support for their view, Hirschi and Gottfredson display only the rates per 100,000 for embezzlement and note that those rates are very small, as indeed they are. But, because elsewhere in the article Hirschi and Gottfredson define "white-collar" crime as also including fraud and forgery, the pertinent question is this: How rare is "white-collar" crime when offending rates are summed across fraud, forgery, and embezzlement and when this summed rate is compared with rates for other crime types? The answer is presented in Figure 21.4. Note the different ways of calculating the "white-collar" crime rate: by including larceny as a "white-collar" crime[17] and by using either the total U.S. population or the white-collar labor force as the population at risk. The latter method is the one used by Hirschi and Gottfredson in calculating white versus black/other rates of "white-collar" crime because they considered that only those holding white-collar jobs are at risk to commit "white-collar" offenses. Thus, how rare "white-collar" crime is depends on three variables: one's definition of "rare," which classification of "white-collar" crime is used, and the offense grouping with which it is compared. But, in general, it is not the case that "white-collar" crime is rare; at least it is not *relatively rarer* than other types of crime.

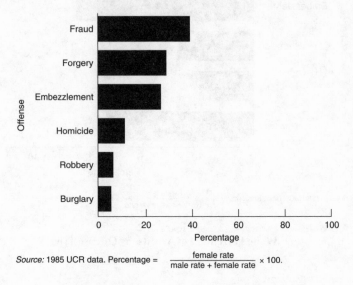

Source: 1985 UCR data. Percentage = $\dfrac{\text{female rate}}{\text{male rate} + \text{female rate}} \times 100$.

Figure 21.3
Female Percentage of Arrests, by Offense Type

Unfortunately, prevalence and incidence statistics on white-collar crime are not available, and one can make any number of claims without fear of being contradicted by "hard evidence." As already noted, UCR statistics are of little use in this regard. A number of studies use organizations as the unit of analysis and conclude that the rate of white-collar offending is fairly high.[18] Hirschi and Gottfredson, with some justification, reject those statistics as misleading.[19] The only study (to my knowledge) that provides useful individual data on the extent of white-collar offending is Hollinger and Clark's survey of workplace deviance, in particular, of employee theft.[20] They found that the taking of company property was self-reported by about one-third of the employees in the three industry sectors surveyed: retail, hospital, and electronics. They also point out that most of the theft reported was not very serious and occurred rather infrequently.[21] A one-third rate of offending is probably high enough to dispute Hirschi and Gottfredson's claim that white-collar offending is rare, but it is also the case that the modal employee did not report any property theft and that not everybody is stealing. (However, the percentage of adults engaging in ordinary crime may be even smaller.)[22]

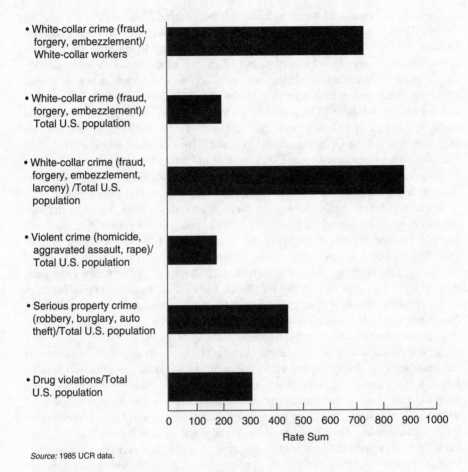

Source: 1985 UCR data.

Figure 21.4
Arrest Rates per 100,000 for Selected Crime Types

CONCLUSION

Hirschi and Gottfredson claim that both white-collar and ordinary crime (and all other forms of crime as well) are manifestations of a single general tendency, and that Hirschi's version of social control better fits the facts of white-collar crime than traditional explanations like differential association. They also claim to present "several explicit tests of rival views," in particular, that the correlates of white-collar and ordinary crime are of the same order of magnitude and direction and that white-collar crime is relatively rare. Both of these "facts," they argue, are consistent with control theory but inconsistent with traditional explanations like differential association.[23]

Students of crime will have to decide whose interpretation of the UCR data is correct, Hirschi and Gottfredson's or mine. I argue that the UCR arrest statistics, particularly for fraud and forgery, have little or nothing to do with white-collar crime. Whatever may be the direction and magnitude of the correlates of white-collar crime, and regardless of whether white-collar crime is a rare or common phenomenon, these issues cannot be decided by the UCR data.[24] Nonetheless, even if one wrongly treats these UCR categories as "white collar" offenses, other assertions made by Hirschi and Gottfredson are still false: (1) the demographic distribution (age, sex, race) of the UCR categories like fraud differs considerably from that of an ordinary crime like burglary and (2) the rate of offending for "white-collar" crimes like fraud and larceny is not relatively rare, at least not according to the UCR data, but is as high or higher than the offending rates for some other types of crime.

There are several implications of my findings and commentary. First, the findings are mixed on the issue of the generality versus specificity of crime. Age, sex, and race do emerge as robust predictors of criminal involvement, but there is considerable variation in the relative magnitude of these correlates across criminal behaviors. This suggests that these correlates are a partial, rather than an absolute, determinant of a range of criminal behaviors, and that each criminal behavior is, in part, a manifestation of a more general tendency and, in part, a unique phenomenon. Nevertheless, the findings reported here should not be taken as a rejection of control theory, much less as a testimonial for differential association.

Second, if the recent debates about the generality versus specificity of crime or the invariancy of the age-crime relationship are to advance our understanding of crime, key concepts (e.g., invariancy, generality) must be stated in an operationally unambiguous manner and the relationships among variables must also be specified unambiguously. It is difficult at times to evaluate Hirschi and Gottfredson's positions because while their assertions are clearly and boldly stated, they vacillate between narrow and broad usages of key terms, and they also vacillate about the criteria for establishing the empirical merit of one position over its alternative. Regarding the stability of the age-crime relationship, for example, Hirschi and Gottfredson neither define "invariancy," nor set forth statistical procedures or criteria for establishing a difference or similarity. Left unspecified, differences in the demographic (e.g., age) distribution of crime across time, space, or offense type can be debated as being trivial rather than meaningful variation. "In the eye of the beholder" becomes the norm, with Hirschi and Gottfredson tending to see similarity where others see a difference.[25]

Third, there is a high-priority need for research offering an exegesis of the UCR arrest statistics, in particular, for localized studies of police files for the purpose of providing a detailed breakdown of the kinds of crime committed by persons within the broad UCR categories. The kind of error made by Hirschi and Gottfredson (i.e., wrongly characterizing the typical arrestee within a particular UCR offense category) is a fairly common one in the writings on crime. Thus, for example, some writers treat arrests for "receiving stolen property" as an indicator of "fencing" or of dealing in stolen goods when, in fact, most persons arrested for receiving are involved in theft, usually burglary.[26] Another example is the use of arrests in the UCR categories of arson and auto theft as indicators of professional arsonists/auto thieves when, in fact, most persons arrested for these offenses are amateurs and the modal age is under 15.

Obviously, there is much to learn about the generality versus specificity of criminality, as well as about which theories can account for meaningful variance in criminal behaviors. The Hirschi and Gottfredson article is a useful contribution in this regard. But significant advances by criminologists on these important theoretical matters are possible only if key concepts are defined in an operationally unambiguous manner, if contrary findings are explicitly acknowledged, and in particular, if the nature and content of official crime statistics (e.g., the UCR arrest data) are carefully appraised. The traditional warnings about the meaning of official statistics are as cogent today as ever, particularly when these data are used, as Hirschi and Gottfredson intended, for "explicit empirical tests of rival views."

Notes

1. Travis Hirschi and Michael Gottfredson, "Causes of White-Collar Crime," *Criminology,* 25 (1987):949–974.
2. See D. Wayne Osgood, Lloyd Johnston, Patrick O'Malley, and Jerald Bachman, "The Generality of Deviance in Late Adolescence and Early Adulthood," *American Sociological Review,* 53 (1988):81–93.
3. Travis Hirschi and Michael Gottfredson, "Delinquent Behavior, Drugs and Alcohol: What is the Relationship?" *Today's Delinquent,* 3 (1984):49–52.
4. Hirschi and Gottfredson, 1987, *op. cit.*, p. 949.
5. Throughout much of this commentary the term "white-collar" is enclosed in quotation marks as a reminder that it is used wrongly by Hirschi and Gottfredson in the 1987 *Criminology* article.
6. The meaning of the term "white-collar crime" is notoriously uncertain: see Gilbert Geis and Robert F. Meier, *White Collar Crime.* New York: The Free Press, 1977. The uncertainty stems from the kinds of crimes and the kinds of people involved. Within the context of the American federal courts, there is some consensus that the following qualify as white-collar crimes: restraint of trade, securities and exchange violations, bribery involving public officials, false claims to the Internal Revenue Service, bank embezzlements, mail fraud, and tax evasion. Also, since white-collar crimes can be committed by persons in all social classes, not all persons who commit white-collar crimes are the kind of persons commonly thought of as white-collar criminals. Thus, some researchers incorporate in their analysis measures of socioeconomic status or ownership and authority in the work place. See John Hagan and Alberto Palloni, " 'Club Fed' and the Sentencing of White-Collar Offenders Before and

After Watergate," *Criminology,* 24 (1986):603–622. Moreover, while the federal court statistics (in contrast to the UCR arrest statistics) do provide at least some data on white-collar offending (i.e., crimes committed by individuals against organizations), even those data are a mixed bag in that many forgeries and some bank embezzlements are closer to ordinary thefts than to white-collar crimes such as securities frauds and antitrust violations. For a good illustration of this, see Stanton Wheeler, David Weisburd, Elin Waring, and Nancy Bode, "White-Collar Crime and Criminals," *American Criminal Law Review,* 25 (1988):331–357.

7. Kathleen Daly, "Gender and White-Collar Crime," paper presented at annual meeting of the American Society of Criminology, Atlanta, 1986; Peggy Giordano, Sandra Kerbel, and Sandra Dudley, "The Economics of Female Criminality: An Analysis of Police Blotters, 1890–1976." In Lee Bowker, ed., *Women and Crime in America.* New York: Macmillan, 1981; Darrell Steffensmeier, "Sex Differences in Patterns of Adult Crime, 1965–77: A Review and Assessment," *Social Forces,* 58 (1980):1080–1108. These studies are prompted in part by the issue of whether increasing numbers of women in the paid labor force were responsible for the increase in female arrests for larceny, fraud, and forgery. In the early 1970's, the media and some students of female crime believed that this was so. While some commentators and some generalists in criminology continue to express this view, female crime specialists do not. There is great consistency among those actually doing research on the matter that the typical female arrestee within these UCR categories is neither a white-collar nor an occupational offender. Instead, she is arrested for more mundane frauds (e.g., bad checks) and larcenies (e.g., shoplifting) that reflect traditional rather than new role patterns. Thus, while in fact there may be more employee theft by women today than yesteryear because there are more women in the paid labor force, that cannot be extrapolated or deduced from the UCR arrest statistics.

8. Steffensmeier, *op. cit.*

9. Federal Home Loan Bank Board, "Fraud and Embezzlement: Increases of 17 Percent Leads Rise in Crimes against Financial Institutions," *Federal Home Loan Bank Board Journal,* 10 (March 1977):19–20; President's Commission on Law Enforcement and Administration of Justice, *Task Force Report: Crime and Its Impact—An Assessment.* Washington, DC: Government Printing Office, 1967.

10. Darrell Steffensmeier, Emilie Allan, Miles D. Harer, and Cathy Streifel, "Age and the Distribution of Crime," *American Journal of Sociology,* 94 (1989): 803–931.

11. A skewness of 0 reflects a symmetrical distribution. Positive values indicate the distribution is skewed to the right, and negative values indicate skewness to the left. A normal distribution has a kurtosis value of 0; negative values indicate the distributions flatter than normal, and positive values indicate a distribution that is more peaked than normal.

12. A D-value of 0 implies perfect congruency or invariance; a D of 100 implies total age variance. The chi-square test is adapted from Leo Goodman, "Criteria for Determining Whether Certain Categories in a Cross-Classification Table Should Be Combined, with Special Reference to Occupational Categories in an Occupational Mobility Table," *American Journal of Sociology*, 87 (1981): 612–652. This chi-square technique is used for testing homogeneity between categories in cross-classification tables. See Steffensmeier et al., *op. cit.*, 1989, for more detail on the application of these procedures to the testing of the similarity of age distributions across time, space, and offense type.

13. Travis Hirschi and Michael Gottfredson, "Age and the Explanation of Crime," *American Journal of Sociology*, 89 (1983):552–584.

14. Steffensmeier et al., 1989, *op. cit.*

15. Hirschi and Gottfredson, 1987, *op. cit.*, pp. 961, 967.

16. My colleagues and I were somewhat surprised at how much higher black/other rates are, even for crimes like fraud and forgery. After further analysis we found that black/other rates are exceptionally high for all UCR categories, except for vandalism, driving under the influence, liquor law violations, and public drunkenness. William Julius Wilson, "The Urban Underclass." In L. Unbar, ed., *Minority Report*, New York: Pantheon, 1984. Wilson noted that there has been little recent systematic research and few cogent explanations of black social dislocations and high rates of black crime. In light of current crime-control policies that account for an ever-increasing rate of black incarceration and execution, it would appear that social scientists can hardly continue to ignore the issue.

17. Rita James Simon, *Woman and Crime.* Lexington, MA: D.C. Heath, 1975.

18. Marshall Clinard and Peter Yeager, *Corporate Crime.* New York: The Free Press, 1980.

19. Hirschi and Gottfredson's rejection of these statistics is somewhat self-serving, however, because they continually confuse crimes against organizations (occupational) crimes with crimes by organizations and because they overlook the common view among criminologists that Sutherland's concept of white-collar crime is not theoretically useful. White-collar crime should be replaced by two distinct subcategories—occupational criminal behavior and organizational/corporate criminal behavior—and not to frame their discussion in terms of the well-accepted Clinard and Quinney definitional dichotomy shows a lack of appreciation for this literature. See Marshall Clinard and Richard Quinney, *Criminal Behavior Systems,* 2nd ed. New York: Holt, Rinehart & Winston, 1973.

20. Richard Hollinger and John Clark, *Theft by Employees.* Lexington, MA: Lexington Books, 1983.

21. Estimates of the employee theft range widely from 10% to 75%, depending on the source of the estimate. The few empirical studies on the incidence of employee theft also yield statistics that vary widely. For example, Ronald Schmidt, in his article "Executive Dishonesty: Misuse of Authority for Per-

sonal Gain." In Sheryl Leininger, ed., *Internal Theft: Investigation and Control.* Los Angeles: Security World, 1975, reports that 76% of the workers who underwent a polygraph examination admitted to employee theft. Robert Tatham, in his article "Employees' Views on the Theft in Retailing," *Journal of Retailing,* 12 (1974):49–55, reports that 50% of employees nonrandomly interviewed admitted taking merchandise from their place of employment without paying for it. Peter Ash, "Screening Employment Applications for Attitudes toward Theft," *Journal of Applied Psychology,* 55 (1971):161–164, reports that both polygraph examinations and preemployment screening lead to the rejection of an average of about 30% of the applicants—many of whom are excluded after admitting to prior theft behavior. A similar level of employee theft is reported by Richard Hollinger in his book *Employee Deviance: Acts against the Formal Work Organization.* Ann Arbor, MI: University Microfilm, 1979. Hollinger reports 28% of a random sample of 339 Midwestern retail employees admitted taking either money or property from their employers.

22. Alan Rowe and Charles Tittle, "Life Cycle Changes and Criminal Propensity," *Sociological Quarterly,* 18 (1977):223–236.

23. Hirschi and Gottfredson, 1987, *op. cit.,* p. 949.

24. In his review of an earlier draft of this paper, Richard Hollinger offered this observation: "The Uniform Crime Reports are virtually useless as a measure of white-collar crime. Study after study has shown that most occupational and corporate crime just does not come to the attention of police agencies. This is precisely why the Hollinger and Clark and Clinard and Yeager studies were funded by the National Institute of Justice in the first place."

25. Alfred Blumstein, Jacqueline Cohen, and David Farrington, "Longitudinal and Criminal Career Research: Further Clarifications," *Criminology,* 26 (1988): 57–74; David Farrington, "Age and Crime." In Michael Torny and Norval Morris, eds., *Crime and Justice, An Annual Review of Research Vol. 7.* Chicago: University of Chicago Press, 1986; Steffensmeier et al., 1989, *op. cit.*

26. Richard Raub, "Effect of Antifencing Operations on Encouraging Crime," *Criminal Justice Review,* 9 (1984):78–83; James Roumasset and John Hadreas, "Addicts, Fences, and the Market for Stolen Goods," *Public Finance Quarterly,* 5 (1977):247–272; Darrell Steffensmeier, *The Fence: In the Shadow of Two Worlds.* Totowa, NJ: Rowman and Littlefield, 1986.

22

Poverty of Theory
in Corporate Crime Research

Donald R. Cressey

During the Watergate scandal and the overseas-payments scandal of the 1970s, executives of most large U.S. corporations wrote or revised codes of conduct for their company managers, officers, and other employees. A study of 119 of these codes found all but one trying to convince readers that the author has good reasons to ask them to behave legally and ethically.[1] Some authors asked for ethical behavior because, they prophesied, the free-enterprise system will go under if business personnel continue to use unethical means for accumulating profits. Other authors asked corporation personnel to be honest because, they said, dishonesty is bad for the reputation of the firm. Still others simply claimed that virtue is its own reward or evoked the authority of Moses, Christ, or Abraham Lincoln in an effort to convince members of their firm that they should be ethical.

Of most relevance to criminological theory about crime causation were admonitions based on the author's assumption that the corporation is a person who, like other persons, has obligations under a social contract. Sheared of its philosophical, political, and sociological complexities, the social-contract principle declares that civilized life exists only because citizens subordinate their personal interests to the interests of the larger society: a social contract or covenant gives each citizen a duty to behave responsibly and ethically toward fellow citizens. In the codes of conduct, as in both popular and professional writings, this principle often is expressed in an analogy with sports, resulting in assertions that "the rules of the game" must be honored in the processes and procedures by which profits are accumulated.[2]

The authors of the conduct codes often expressed the moral of such assertions in terms suggesting that a social contract determines the duties of employee-citizens to the collectivity that is the corporation: each employee has obligations to the corporation and to fellow employees. ("Don't steal from the company or from other workers.") Less commonly, admonitions about following the "rules of the game" were based on the assumption that a social contract puts limits on the methods that the corporation managers, directors, officers, employees and agents can legitimately

Reprinted from *Advances in Criminological Theory,* 1 (1988):31–56.

use to maximize their firm's income. ("Don't commit crime on behalf of the company.")

Of special significance to criminological research and theory pertaining to so-called organizational crime and corporate crime was a third notion, namely, that a social contract ("rules of the game") also limits the behavior of corporations. Here, the social contract is assumed to involve relationships among a society's corporate citizens as well as among its biological ones. That is, the corporation itself, not its personnel, is viewed as the actor. As I just reported, each corporation is considered a person who, like real persons, has ethical and legal obligations to the collectivity. Such anthropomorphism was most clearly expressed in discussions of "corporate social responsibility" and in sentences such as "good corporate citizenship demands business conduct that is both lawful and ethical"[3] A cogent example appeared in a recent letter to the editor of the *Wall Street Journal:* "Adolph Coors Co. is a leader in re-cycling aluminum and certainly wants to be a good corporate citizen in all parts of the country."

Such conceptions of corporations' duties under the social contract are consistent with the legal fiction that a corporation is a person and the concordant legal fiction that this artificial person is capable of committing a crime. Criminologists frequently display deep commitment to the notion that fictitious Americans, like natural ones, should live up to the legal and ethical obligations inherent in the social covenant. They do so when discussing their conceptions of "organizational crime" and "corporate crime," as well as when calling for "corporate social responsibility" and for more severe punishment of corporate wrongdoers. It seems timely to ask whether this commitment is self-defeating because it is based on the erroneous assumption that organizations think and act, thus saddling theoretical criminologists with the impossible task of finding the cause of crimes committed by fictitious persons.

Note that the criminologists who developed the corporate crime and organizational crime concepts, like the corporation executives who characterized corporations as persons in their codes of conduct, have joined the ranks of a wide range of professional personnel, social scientists, and ordinary citizens who make organizations talk, act, think, and otherwise behave just like real people.[5] Nowadays, we accept without question newspaper reports saying that Procter and Gamble has put a new product on the market, or that Exxon is searching for oil in the Santa Barbara Channel. "The White House said today" is heard on the television news almost every evening. Newspapers regularly carry stories saying that corporations and agencies have "decided," "declared," "claimed," and "agreed." Consumers object to form letters saying that the computer made a mistake when it sent the gas bill, but they nevertheless tell their friends that "the gas company" has erred. After the trial of the Ford Motor Company for reckless homicide in 1980, a juror who voted "not guilty" said that he nevertheless thought the Pinto was a reckless automobile.[6]

Consistently, social scientists have written volumes on "organizational behavior." They have done so because it is easy to assume that corporations and other organizations act like humans. Sociologists and experts on business administration say, for example, that corporations and other formal organizations formulate goals and the means to achieve them, just as do human members of committees, teams, and other action groups. Political scientists assert that states, legislatures, and court systems make decisions and seem to have lives of their own. Public administration specialists insist that cities behave, as do their police departments, fire departments, and sewer departments. Historians studying foreign relations treat entire nations as corporations when they analyze actions of "the United States," not of Americans. Anthropologists and sociologists say they can observe the behavior of societies and cultures themselves, not just the behavior of a society's members or of the participants in a culture. And economists, of course, have projected the characteristics of a rational, calculating "economic man" onto many organizations, ranging from mom-and-pop grocery stores to entire nations. To them, the corporation is an ideal "economic man" because it persistently pursues profits and, ideally, lets nothing distract it from that pursuit.

Criminologists, being interdisciplinary, do and say all of these things, and more. For example, a recent review of an important book on controlling white-collar crime anthropomorphized as follows: "Corporations do after all have consciences, and they can be pricked by publicity. That is the conclusion of this first-rate study by two Australian legal scholars."[7] I myself have asserted that juvenile gangs,[8] La Cosa Nostra "families,"[9] and even prisons,[10] as well as corporations[11] and other organizations, behave as units, like persons. More significantly, criminologists rather routinely, unthinkingly, and erroneously assert that corporations have the psychological capacity to be guilty of crime and to suffer from punishment. Assuming such a capacity is what, after all, makes it possible for criminologists to hold that corporations, as corporations, ought to follow ethical and legal "rules of the game," thus displaying social responsibility.

For at least a century, U.S. courts have regarded every corporation as a person. This legal fiction is essential to fairness. For example, if corporations were not assigned the legal characteristics of persons, no one could sue them or make contracts with them. And if corporations were not said to reside in a city, state, and nation—as do persons—they would be "outlaws" in the true sense of the word, for no government would have jurisdiction over them. A citizen could not even be employed by a corporation if the corporation were not viewed as a person who lives somewhere and has a right to make contracts and otherwise conduct business.

But anyone who tries to understand white-collar crime is severely handicapped by the fiction that corporations are disembodied political, social, and economic persons who behave just like ordinary men and women. As Arthur Selwyn Miller, the noted constitutional law scholar, has said, "The corporation is obviously more than a person, however characterized in law."[12] This assertion can be validated by making just two commonsense observations.

In the first place corporations are allowed to do many things persons are not permitted to do. They can buy and sell each other legally, as though the "person" being bought or sold were a slave. (According to the October 4, 1985, issue of the *Wall Street Journal,* "Revlon agreed to go private by selling itself for $56 a share, or about $1.77 billion.") They also can exterminate each other legally by methods resembling those of homicidal maniacs (cutthroat competition).

In the second place the makeup of a corporation is quite different from the makeup of a human being. For this reason, corporations can do things that are not humanly possible: growing from infant to adult in a year, shrinking from giant to midget, merging two or more bodies into one, achieving immortality on earth.

Even more relevant to criminologists is the fact that legal fiction notwithstanding, the corporation is obviously *less* than a person. It cannot learn, contemplate, feel guilty or proud, intend, or decide. For this reason, none of the social machinery— including the social contract—that controls real persons has any effect on corporations. Writing ethical codes, preaching social responsibility, noting the wisdom of the Golden Rule, or even depicting the horrors of hellfire and damnation that await evil persons can have no influence on fictitious persons who do not have the psychological makeup of real ones.

These observations about the nature of the corporation have some counterparts in everyday life. For example, auditors and accountants call corporations "entities," which is another name for "things," not "persons." And even though the language of ordinary citizens endows corporations with human attributes, this language also suggests that everyone knows the difference between a "person" and a "thing." Thus, the gas company is never referred to as "she" or "he." It, like other companies, is always called "it." This usage characterizes legal language too, suggesting that the regulation of corporations might be more effective if corporation codes of ethics as well as regulatory laws pertained to the real persons in charge of inanimate objects, not to the objects themselves.

Everybody knows that automobiles really do not behave, even if "Motor Vehicle Codes" and "Automobile Safety Rules" imply that they do. (Out west, we even have a California Auto Body Association.) Motorists, pedestrians, legislators, police, court officials, jail officials, and criminologists all recognize that the reference in such codes and rules is to drivers and passengers, not to cars. Similarly, a citizen who is indignant about an incorrect gas bill will, sooner or later, attribute the error to humans. "The bastards at the gas company don't know what they are doing," the victim of a bureaucratic snafu is likely to claim. In other bailiwicks, too, people with common sense recognize that "entities" do not behave. Saying that the United States has declared war is recognized as just a shorthand way of saying that the president and a majority of the members of Congress have decided to go to war. Reports stating that the White House has spoken, that the city of New York has made a decision, or that a police department has changed its tactics also are readily recognized as poetic license, as a lazy observer's way of substituting vagueness for needed precision, or as a canny reporter's way of concealing true authorship of the actions.

Although criminologists cannot be expected to crack down on all the poetic license in the world, it is time for them to put their common sense to work when confronting reports indicating that a corporation or other organization has committed a crime. Typical of such reports is a statement recently made by Representative

John D. Dingell. In a five-page letter to Defense Secretary Caspar W. Weinberger, Dingell accused two huge corporations of conspiring to cheat a third organization, the U.S. Air Force:

> General Dynamics knew full well that the Air Force had already paid Westinghouse for the development of these tools. This is not sloppy business practice on the part of General Dynamics—it is fraud. The entire acquisition was clearly double-billed. It is fraud on the part of Westinghouse to plot with General Dynamics. It is also not the finest hour of the Air Force for having allowed this to happen.[13]

In real life, if not in the academic world, criminologists realize that such anthropomorphism is misleading. Firms really do not "know," "plot," and "allow," as the legislator's statement suggests. They are "entities" that are owned, managed, and administered by *people*. Each of these persons talks, decides, intends, agrees, disagrees, deliberates, buys, sells, works, thinks, estimates, errs, and otherwise behaves. Each can be coerced by threats of punishment and persuaded by promise of reward. Except for the few who, due to mental disability, cannot tell right from wrong, each is responsible for individual actions, including violations of the penal code. The corporation itself does not behave. It just sits there. Its so-called actions are but manifestations of actions by real persons, as Hayworth argued years ago,[14] and as the Australian Trade Practices Act, enacted in 1974, makes abundantly clear:

> Any conduct engaged in on behalf of a body corporate by a director, agent or servant of the body corporate or by any other person at the direction or with the consent or agreement (whether express or implied) of a director, agent or servant of the body corporate shall be deemed, for purposes of this Act, to have been engaged in also by the body corporate.[15]

The main criminological complication is this: to say that a real person rather than a corporation made a decision or acted in a certain way is to say that this individual should be held responsible for the costs as well as the benefits of the decision. Under this procedure corporations would commit no crimes—*executives* who commit the crimes now called crimes of corporations would be arrested, prosecuted, and convicted. This seems reasonable in light of the fact that executives and others whose decisions and behavior make money for the corporation, not the corporation itself, are praised and rewarded when total profits soar. On the other side, however, the policy unreasonably asks law-enforcement officers to detect the crimes of executives who are masters at using the corporate form to mask their misbehavior. As Jack Katz has noted, it also unreasonably asks prosecutors to convict managers who skillfully use the corporate entity to make their criminality almost impossible to prove.[16] Finally, a former United States attorney has correctly observed that corporations are often prosecuted because it would be unjust to try to establish the criminal liability of "individuals who, under normal standards of prosecutorial discretion, should not be prosecuted."[17] This is not meant to imply, however, that conviction of corporations is an easy matter, even under strict liability statutes.[18]

Against these practical complications must be weighed the intellectual cost to criminology of the existence of a category of criminal behavior that criminologists' causal theories cannot explain. Although it is possible to find significant correlations between rates of corporate crime and structural variables, such as industry, financial status, and size, it is not possible to go beyond these statistical relationships to statements about causation. Most damaging is the fact that there can be no social psychology of so-called corporate or organizational crime because corporations have no biological or psychological characteristics. I pointed out a quarter of a century ago that an effective model of crime causation must have two parts: a statement about the way crime is distributed in the social order, and a logically consistent statement about the social psychological process by which criminal behavior is manifested.[19] The latter is necessarily missing in explanations of so-called corporation crime or organizational crime. For reasons of expediency, it might be necessary for legislators, prosecutors, and judges to maintain that imaginary persons commit crimes. But it does not make sense for scientists to maintain that these fictitious persons do so because they are in poverty, are frustrated, are labeled as troublemakers, have poor attachments to the social order, or have had an excess of associations with criminal behavior patterns. Clearly, corporate criminality cannot be explained by the same causal principles used to explain the criminality of real persons.

The work of criminological pioneer Edwin H. Sutherland is especially revealing in this regard. Sutherland invented the concept of white-collar crime and introduced criminologists and others to white-collar criminality. He declared that his motive was "to reform the theory of criminal behavior, not to reform anything else."[20] His discovery of white-collar crime, he said, showed that the theories of crime causation that were in favor during the 1930s and 1940s—theories stressing personal and social pathologies—are defective because they pertain, at most, to working-class criminals alone. Accordingly, he developed a new causal theory—differential association and differential social organization—that made sense of the crime of high status persons as well as those of poor people.

It is rather ironic to find, therefore, that Sutherland considered corporations as persons but did not so much as give a hint about how the differential association process, a process of learning, could affect them. There is a great difference between what Sutherland said and what he did.[21] He defined white-collar crime as "a crime committed by a person of respectability and high social status in the course of his occupation," but he studied the crime rates of *corporations,* not of live persons. His writings show that he viewed the executives of corporations as persons who are respectable and of high social status and, thus, as white-collar criminals if they violated the law in the course of their duties as executives. But the same writings show that Sutherland frequently but rather casually treated corporations as high status persons too, just as did the authors of the codes of ethics described earlier.[22]

As Geis pointed out long ago, "The major difficulty in *White Collar Crime* as criminological research lies in Sutherland's striking inability to differentiate between the corporations themselves and their executive and management personnel."[23] For example, Sutherland's demonstration of the relevance of differential association theory to white-collar crime begins with a discussion of documents relating to how businessmen are inducted into illegal behavior by other businessmen.[24] But soon the discussion moves to diffusion of illegal practices, and here the object of inquiry is corporations, not business personnel. Sutherland unthinkingly attributes human capabilities to these corporations: "When one firm devises (an illegal method) of increasing profits, other firms become aware of the method and adopt it, perhaps a little more quickly and a little more generally if the firms are competitors in the same market than if they are not competitors."[25] He never asked the significant theoretical question, "By what process does a firm 'become aware of' and 'adopt' illegal processes?" Had he done so, he would have been reminded that humans behave but entities do not.

Vacillation between concern for the criminality of business personnel and the criminality of anthropomorphized corporations also appears in Sutherland's discussion of the psychological characteristics of offenders. This discussion appears, significantly enough, in a chapter entitled "Variations in the Crimes of Corporations." Sutherland first notes that corporations, being fictitious, obviously cannot suffer from human psychiatric disorders such as feelings of inferiority, regression to infancy, and Oedipus complexes.[26] Then he assaults his own common sense by assuming that as corporations commit crimes they do so without acting through their officers, directors, employees, or agents. This assumption comes as he shows that variations in the crime rates of individual corporations are associated with variations in the positions of these corporations in the economic structure and then argues that the corporations, not their executives, are the significant actors:

> Manufacturing and mining corporations seldom violate laws regarding advertising because they seldom engage in advertising for sales purposes. This variation in practices is related to the position they hold in the economic structure rather than to the personal traits of the executives of the corporations. . . . p. 262. Two facts are especially significant. First, many corporations violate the antitrust law in certain industrial areas and not in others, although the officers and directors are the same in all these areas. . . . That is, behavior as to violations of law varies without variations in persons involved in the behavior. Second, many corporations which violated the antitrust law forty years ago are still violating that law, although the personnel of the corporation has changed completely. That is, variations in persons occur without variations in behavior as to the antitrust law.[27]

Sutherland's materials on the criminal careers of businessmen suggest that a corporation's crimes are but manifestations of the crimes of its executives. In retrospect, it seems incredible that he did not use these materials in his discussions of what is now known as corporate crime or organizational crime. The fact remains, however, that he did not formally attribute similarities and consistencies in law violation among corporations to socialization into criminal behavior of new executives by old ones, as Marilynn Cash Mathews recently did.[28] Such attribution is consistent with the theory of differential association and differential social organization.

It appears that *White Collar Crime* has become an influential criminological classic as much because Sutherland anthropomorphized corporations as because he defined white-collar crime as crime committed by persons of respectability and high social status. The work showed that the prevailing causal theories were incorrect, being based on biased samples, but it really was not much of a theoretical contribution. Thus, as I just indicated, Sutherland neglected to show how differential association or any other social psychological process might possibly work to produce criminal conduct in the fictitious persons called corporations. His macrolevel (sociological, epidemiological) hypothesis that rates of corporate crime are associated with structural conditions, such as position in the economic world (differential social organization), seems reasonable enough. But that is as far as one can go when the object of study is not a human being.

By drawing a distinction between "occupational crime" and "corporate crime," Clinard and Quinney tried to reduce the confusion introduced by Sutherland. The former was defined as "violation of the criminal law in the course of activity in a legitimate occupation," so that, in fact, only some occupational crime is white-collar crime in the Sutherland sense of "crime committed by a person of respectability and high social status in the course of his occupation." Occupational crime differs from corporate crime principally in that it consists of "offenses committed by individuals for themselves in the course of their occupations and the offenses of employees against their employers," and corporate crime consists of "the offenses committed by corporate officials for their corporation and the offenses of the corporation itself."[29] Braithwaite consistently defines corporate crime as "the conduct of a corporation, or individuals acting on behalf of the corporation, that is proscribed by law."[30]

Note that these definitions of corporate crime really show no concern for the differences between corporate crimes committed by persons and crimes committed by organizations. In their recent monumental work, Clinard and Yeager seem to correct this defect by deleting "corporate officials" from the definition: "A corporate crime is any act committed by corporations that is punished by the state, regardless of whether it is punished under administrative, civil, or criminal law."[31] Almost immediately, however, they reintroduce Sutherland's ambiguity by going back to the idea that corporate crime also is perpetrated by real persons:

Corporate and occupational crime can be confused. If a corporate official violates the law in action for the corporation it is corporate crime, but if he gains personal benefit in the commission of a crime against the corporation, as in the case of embezzlement of corporate funds, it is an occupational crime.[32]

This blurring of the distinction between corporate crimes committed by persons and corporate crimes committed by organizations asks theoreticians to use one causal theory to explain both, an impossible task. The meddling is reflected in much of Clinard and Yeager's prose, just as it is in Sutherland's. For instance, in a single paragraph these authors first discuss "corporations whose executives have knowingly concealed" unsafe products or occupational hazards, and then give two examples: (1) "Firestone officials knew that they were marketing a dangerous tire in their radial '500s.' " (2) "Allied Chemical also knew from its own laboratory research that Kepone is a potential carcinogen. It went ahead and marketed the deadly substance anyway." The first example reports on real people, the second on a fictitious person. But then Clinard and Yeager blur the distinction even more by using the plural *their*, not *its*, to refer to a corporation's possessions: "Many workers were subsequently poisoned, and miles of Virginia's James River ruined due to Allied's dumping of their Kepone wastes."[33] This compromise nicely avoids the question of whether the action was that of the corporation or of corporation executives.

Clinard and Yeager's one short reference to organizational crime also blurs the distinction between crimes by persons and crimes by organizations: "Corporate crime actually is *organizational* crime occurring in the context of complex relationships and expectations among board of directors, executives, and managers, on the one hand, and among parent corporations, corporate divisions, and subsidiaries, on the other."[34] Consistently, their chapter on corporate organization and criminal behavior vacillates between the view that the corporation (or parts of it) is a rational actor and the view that so-called corporate actions actually are the actions of managers.[35] When the latter view prevails, causal explanation of executive criminality is stressed, and "the making of a corporate criminal" is said to be a matter of socialization of subordinates by elites (differential association). When the corporation itself is considered the actor, Clinard and Yeager's stress is on explaining crime rates, and variation in them is attributed to organizations' differing economic and political environments. This explanation is not very nourishing: "Economic pressures and other factors operate in a corporate environment that is conducive to unethical and illegal practices."[36]

Sutherland's vacillation between concern for the criminality of business personnel or respectability and high social status and the criminality of anthropomorphized corporations also has been duplicated in the writings of several other sociologists. The most noteworthy of these, perhaps, is Edward Gross, a distinguished scholar who specializes in the study of organizations, not crime. In an attempt to educate criminologists on the subject of organizational crime, Gross asserts that "all organizations are inherently criminogenic." In documenting this theoretical assertion, he shifts back and forth between the notion that organizations commit crimes and the notion that organizational personnel commit them.[37] On the one hand, he says, "there is built into the structure of organizations an inherent inducement for the *organization* itself to engage in crime."[38] On the other hand, he insists that organizations do not behave: "Although organizations are here held to be criminogenic and although courts no longer exhibit much hesitation in charging the organization itself with crime, organizations of course cannot themselves act—they must have agents who act for them."[39]

Once people accept the fiction that organizations behave, they tend to promote it. Gross is no exception. His principal point is one adapted from Hayworth,[40] namely that an organization may be considered as acting when "what is meant is that the organization is *responsible* for the outcome."[41] But a corporation is not responsible, at least in the sense of the criminal law, until the law declares it to be a person. Moreover, even if events represent the outcome of the patterns of activities that make up the "behavior" of this fictitious person, and even if the quality of the outcome "depends minimally on the peculiar qualities of the [biological] persons who make it possible," as Gross put it, the fact remains that biological persons are responsible for establishing and maintaining the patterns and, thus, for the action. "If [a human] were to arrange the workers differently, something different would happen," Gross concedes. But he then argues, in contradiction, that organizations, not humans, commit crimes because they require that persons be able to implement criminal patterns and then socialize them in ways such that they become willing to do so. He attributes all of this to the performance emphasis found in complex organizations, saying that when organizations (not people) face difficulty in meeting their profit goals they resort to crime.[42] His criminological theory, then, is a simple one: poverty causes crime.

After presenting this macrolevel theory, Gross turns to the social psychological processes involved as the "agents" (corporation executives) of organizations come to commit crimes. Again, his key idea is that criminality stems from stress on performance and goal attainment. Ambitious, shrewd, and morally flexible managers are most likely to make it to the top, Gross says, and these are the persons who commit crimes on behalf of corporations.[43] Moral flexibility is especially significant, he continues, because socialization to the attitudes, values, and behavior patterns of successful superiors is the active crime-producing process. But this idea, which is consistent with differential association theory, is soon garbled because, to Gross, the demand for a nondemanding moral code is made by an anthropomorphized organization, not by the corporation executives he has been discussing. Managers are socialized to change their moral beliefs, he says, "so that they match whatever is called for by the organization."[44] But organizations, being only entities, do not make demands; people do.

At the beginning of the follow-up essay Gross seems to correct his error by noting once more that organizations cannot act:

> Although the law has created these "persons," they cannot, of course, act autonomously; agents must act for them. Hence when we speak of corporate "actors" it must be recognized that there are always biological persons who act, in the manner of puppeteers, to put the show on the road.[45]

Still, Gross insists, a theoretical problem of disentangling people and organizations remains.[46] His proposed disentanglement is rather snarled, however, because it includes the legal fiction that corporations are persons and, moreover, that these persons "run afoul of the law" even if they do not deliberately break it.[47] More generally, corporations "take on lives of their own,"[48] and corporate crime follows from their need to create an orderly market,[49] their ways of integrating persons,[50] and their performance emphasis.[51] Consistently, Gross describes Staw and Szwajkowski's study of antitrust law violations[52] and then concludes: "When these organizations faced difficulty in meeting their profit goals, they resorted to crime in order to do so."[53]

Sets of organizations, such as sports leagues, cartels, trusts, industries, and oligopolies, also are clothed with the attributes of people: "The organizations not only know of one another's existence, their own success depends further on a continuous monitoring of one another's behavior."[54] The crime of price fixing, too, is discussed as though it were an arrangement between organizations, not people: "The companies seem to have tacitly recognized that once they get into a battle about prices, they can easily destroy each other."[55] But a U.S. attorney, noting that corporations can act only through their officers, directors, employees, or agents, has come to a more realistic conclusion: "Corporations don't commit crimes, people do."[56] In one famous case illustrating this point, Robert L. Crandall, president and chief operating officer of American Airlines, suggested in a telephone conversation with Howard Putnam, president of Braniff Airways, that price fixing might solve the financial problems that both were experiencing: "I think it's dumb as hell . . . to sit here and pound . . . each other and neither of us making a [word deleted] dime," Crandall said. When Putnam asked, "Do you have a suggestion for me?" Crandall replied, "Yes, I have a suggestion for you. Raise your goddam fares 20 percent. I'll raise mine the next morning. . . . You'll make more money and I will too."[57]

A profound criminological problem is raised by Gross's, Clinard and Yeager's, Sutherland's, and many others' blurring of the distinction between crimes committed by corporations and crimes committed by executives and other managers. This is the problem of intentionality. In courthouses, the rise of the legal fiction that corporations commit crimes gave a severe jolt to the traditional criminal-law principle that performing an outlawed act does not alone make the doer guilty of crime. The actor also must have intended the act to be a crime. The legal fiction also stops theoretical criminologists in their tracks because it undermines every social psychological theory about the causation of crime that has been formulated and every theory that might be formulated in the future. Even if corporations are called persons for purposes of arguments, these juristic persons—unlike real people—cannot have criminal intentions. It is not unreasonable to conclude that the corporation therefore is incapable of committing a crime.[58] But this logical conclusion is not drawn in the criminal courts and, as we have seen, it is not drawn by some criminologists either.

Some people unthinkingly claim that corporations deliberately commit crimes. A science reporter, for example, recently used the following language to describe a case involving the Eli Lilly Company: "According to the Justice Department, Lilly was fully aware of, but delayed telling U.S. authorities about, ten cases in which patients taking Oraflex had suffered fatal or debilitating liver or kidney disease."[59] Sometimes people hold, alternatively, that corporations are guilty of crimes even if they are incapable of formulating criminal intent. For example, the just-quoted reporter also says, "On 21 August, Eli Lilly & Co. wrote to its stockholders to say that it had negotiated an end to a federal investigation that 'puts to rest any speculation regarding intentional misconduct on the part of the company' in the marketing of Oraflex, an arthritis medicine suspected of causing liver and kidney failure. . . . Lilly's strong emphasis [was] on the fact that it was guilty only of 'technical misdemeanors.' "

The Lilly Company could be guilty of "technical misdemeanors" even if no one intended to do wrong because legislatures have enacted statutes which hold persons, including fictitious corporate ones, liable for certain crimes, even if there is no psychological state such as criminal intent or *mens rea*. These strict liability statutes modify the ancient legal principle holding that, by definition. every crime involves an intentional act. Appelate courts have ruled that such statutes are constitutional, despite their radical character.

The best example of a strict liability crime is murder under the felony-murder doctrine of criminal law. Under the rule of strict liability (called "straight liability" in British courts), if someone dies because the defendant committed a felony, the defendant is guilty of murder. For example, a defendant who intentionally committed arson in order to defraud an insurance company is guilty of murder if a firefighter dies trying to knock down the flames. So far as murder is concerned, the defendant's intent is not considered. Another example is so-called statutory rape. If a man has sexual intercourse with a girl who is beneath the age of consent, he is guilty of a crime, even if she eagerly cooperates. He is strictly liable. The fact that he might have believed the girl to be of legal age is not officially considered. Criminal intent or *mens rea* is not an element of statutory rape.

Corporations, not being real persons, cannot intentionally commit crimes such as larceny, murder, or even fraud. Accordingly, most of the crimes said to have been committed by them are, like felony-murder and statutory rape, strict liability offenses. This means that the corporation is held criminally liable for the offense if the offense occurs.

Consider, for example, violations of the Sherman Antitrust Act of 1890, a law that stipulated that "every contract, combination in the form of trust or otherwise, or conspiracy in restraint of trade" is a crime (misdemeanor) punishable by a fine of $5,000. At first federal judges took this statement literally, and corporations were held strictly liable for their violations. But then, as I have shown elsewhere, the "rule of reason" came to replace strict liability: this was a way of insisting that criminal intent must be present before there can be a finding of guilt.[60] For example, what appellate courts were fifty years ago calling a "conscious parallelism" in the pricing of products by "competing" corporation executives was not taken to be evidence of "conspiracy in restraint of trade." The U.S. attorney general at the time (1937) complained that the courts refused to adopt the only practical criterion of restraint of trade—price uniformity and price rigidity—and insisted, instead, on trying to determine whether a fictitious personality has an evil state of mind.

The substitution of an evil intent for strict liability made it difficult to convict corporation executives of violating the Sherman Act, and it made it all but impossible to convict corporations themselves. Probably the substitution was made because, in the cultures of federal courthouses, there was, and is, a sympathetic understanding of corporations and their executives. But it is possible, too, that judges have resisted holding corporations guilty under strict liability statutes because they believe that courts have a duty to defend the traditional principle that an act is not criminal unless the actor intended it. Even today, "monopolizing" in violation of antitrust law must be "nasty monopolizing" to be illegal; "no-fault" (strict-liability) restraint of trade is not enough.[61]

Sutherland's treatment of criminal intent and strict liability is consistent with, but just as confusing as, the fact that he defined white-collar crimes as crimes committed by real, high-status persons but conducted his research on the crimes of fictitious persons called corporations. On the one hand, he argued that corporations or corporation executives (he was not clear about which of these he had in mind) intend at least some fraudulent ("patently false") advertisements: "For example, an advertisement of gum-wood furniture as 'mahogany' would seldom be an accidental error and would generally result from a state of mind which deviated from honesty by more than the natural tendency of human beings to feel proud of their handiwork."[62] On the other hand, he noted that due to strict liability statutes, white-collar crime is like ordinary crime in the sense that a showing of criminal intent is not required in all prosecutions of either kind of crime. "The important consideration here," he said, "is that the criteria which have been used in defining white collar crime are not categorically different from the criteria used in defining some other crimes."[63]

This consideration governed Sutherland's research on the crimes of corporations. He did not acknowledge, in *White Collar Crime* or elsewhere, that most if not all the laws violated by the seventy corporations he studied had strict liability provisions. More important, he did not even speculate about how differential association theory might make sense of criminal behavior that was not intended by a real person, let alone by a juristic one. As already noted, no social psychological theory can make sense of behavior that is not intended, be it an ordinary crime such as felony murder or a white-collar crime such as restraint of trade, false advertising, or unfair labor practices.

Schrager and Short have recently walked in Sutherland's footsteps on this issue.[64] The legal literature teams with discussions of criminal intent, strict liability, and corporate criminal liability.[65] By and large, however, Schrager and Short's discussion of organizational crime ignores the criminological implications of these discussions. They note, clearly enough, that "the white-collar crime perspective does not deal adequately with unintended consequences of organizational behavior," but they do not really remedy this in their discussion of "organizational crimes," defined as "illegal acts committed by an individual or a group of individuals in a legitimate formal organization, which have a serious physical or economic impact on employees, consumers or the general public."[66] This because they first make the puzzling claim that strict liability is rarely used in criminal prosecutions, follow that with an assertion that "lack of intention is typical of organizational offenses having physical consequences,"[67] and then assert further that the law's requirement of criminal intent is met by their definition's stipulation that, to be organizational crime, the action must be committed in accordance with the operative goals of the organization.[68]

There are at least three fuzzy points in their definition and their commentary on it. First, *crime* and *criminal* are technical legal terms. Behavior cannot be a "crime" unless it is in violation of criminal law, meaning that it has been declared to be punishable by the state. And, as I have already noted, if a man does not intend his harmful act and if statute holds him strictly liable for the act, then his behavior is not an "illegal act" or an "offense"—at least not a criminal one—because he is not guilty. Obviously it therefore cannot be an "organizational crime."

Second, the last part of Schrager and Short's definition is gratuitous because no act is a crime unless it does harm of some kind. "Serious physical or economic impact" is a characteristic of all felonies. Schrager and Short seem not to have noticed that violations of occupational health and safety regulations, for example, do not always have a *serious* impact but are crimes nevertheless. The issue is not one of seriousness. It is one of whether the offense is properly called "organizational."

Finally, to discern that an act was performed in accordance with organizational goals—as Schrager and Short's definition of organizational crime requires—is to deal with the legal problem of motivation, not of intent. That this is an error can be made obvious by use of a fictitious, but illustrative, case: Suppose the leaders of a terrorist organization announce that one of their operational organizational goals is to overthrow the government of the nation in which they reside. They agree that they need automatic weapons to do so. Suppose, further, that three members of the organization, hearing of a machine gun for sale, plot a bank robbery in which they will work as a three-person team to pull off the job. Then they harm the bank's investors by robbing them of $23,142.33, and they use the money to buy the gun. Now the *intent* of each of these three members was to rob. The *motive* of each was to acquire some money that could be used for revolutionary purposes, in accordance with the announced operational organizational goals. Each of the three is guilty of robbery and, perhaps, conspiracy, but the motive for the robbery and, perhaps conspiracy, is not what makes them guilty.

To underline the importance of the distinction between intent and motive, suppose that after the robbers in this fictitious case have been arrested, convicted, and sent to prison, they send a note to the editor of *Crime and Social Justice* asserting they are political prisoners. The assertion is based on the fact that their robbery was carried out in accordance with the operative goals of their organization, which are political in nature. At law, however, they are not political criminals or "organizational criminals," for that matter. Their crime was very much unlike the crime of political criminals who have violated laws stating, for example, that "harming the patriotic interests of the people" is punishable by imprisonment. Moreover, their motive (to get money with which to advance their political cause) could not have been officially taken into consideration by the judge or jury deciding their guilt. Instead, a judge or jury necessarily found that their intent was to rob, and a combination of this *mens rea* and a harmful act, prohibited by law, is what got them convicted. If motives were used to determine guilt, as Schrager and Short seem to recommend, then anyone whose motives were not acceptable to judge or jury would be guilty of organizational crime.

It could be argued that all this law talk is beside the point because Schrager and Short are merely saying, in a fuzzy way, that criminological theorists ought to (1) note that organizational crime is an important variety of white-collar crime, itself not a legal category, and then (2) use the organizational criminals' motives ("in accordance with the operative goals of the organization") to explain their behavior. I have been criminology's principal proponent of the notion that this kind of explanation is consistent with differential association theory and ought to be encouraged.[69] But Schrager and Short actually do not use the concept of organizational crime in this social psychological way. This is clear in their discussion of intentionality. They want to shift the focus of inquiry *away* from motives, such as "I kept my mouth shut about the dangerous design of the brakes because I knew the boss would fire me if I didn't," and *toward* the objective characteristics of criminal acts. Significantly, this shift would make organizational crimes into strict liability offenses which are not explainable in differential association terms or in any other social psychological framework:

> In view of the often impenetrable difficulty of evaluating the motives behind illegal organizational actions, the definition shifts the focus of inquiry to the objective characteristics of these actions. The logic is similar to that employed in the legal concept of strict liability, which holds an offender responsible for illegal behavior without regard to the existence or absence of *mens rea* (a guilty mind).[70]

In conclusion, let it be said that it is just as ridiculous for criminologists to try to explain criminal behavior that was not intended as it is for judges to try to determine whether a fictitious person has an evil state of mind. Because corporations cannot intend actions, none of their criminality can be explained in the framework of behavioral theory. It is time for criminologists to eradicate this embarrassment by acknowledging that corporation crimes and organizational crimes are phantom phenomena. Such acknowledgment will not lead to abandoning criminological concern for white-collar offenses and offenders. On the contrary, the strength of this area of criminological research and theory will grow in proportion to the degree to which criminologists first recognize that only real persons have the psychological capacity to intend crimes, and then focus their analytical and theoretical skills on these persons.

Auditors and other accountants have already found an appropriate name for much of the behavior in question: management fraud. This is deliberate deception by managers that injures others through misleading financial statements.[71] Fraud of this kind is by definition perpetrated by corporation executives and other managers rather than by organizations. It is committed on behalf of corporations. not against them. For example, income obtained for firms by means of price fixing, bribery, and false advertising as well as profits obtained for firms by means of industrial pollution of air and water, violations of labor laws, and the manufacture and marketing of dangerous products are all maintained or increased by use of false (and thereby fraudulent) books and records. The techniques that managers use to commit crime on behalf of corporations are the same as those used by embezzlers to commit crimes against corporations. The verbalizations (motives) probably are the same in both cases, too.[72] Robert Elliott and John Willingham, partners in one of the world's largest auditing firms, have noted that there is a practical reason for determining why such behavior is so widespread: "Management frauds are of primary importance in the family of business improprieties because to a large extent the health of the capital markets rests on confidence that financial statements are not fraudulent. Thus, the detection and prevention of fraudulent financial statements goes to the heart of the functioning of the economy."[73]

Despite my emphasis on explaining the criminality of biological persons, not of fictitious ones, I am not here proposing that corporations do not commit crime. Criminologists, like everyone else, must use the only permissible definition of crime, the legal one. This means that criminologists must accept the fact that the criminal law treats corporations as persons and says that these persons commit crimes.

What I am proposing is that criminologists acknowledge that no theory dealing with crime causation can make sense of strict-liability criminality or any other criminality that is not intended. Corporations and organizations, being inanimate, cannot formulate criminal intent. Accordingly, as Geis pointed out a quarter of a century ago, "For the purpose of criminological analysis . . . corporations cannot be considered persons, except by recourse to the same type of extrapolatory fiction that once brought about the punishment of inanimate objects."[74]

It is not reasonable to try to locate the cause of unintentional, accidental, behavior that is called murder under the felony-murder doctrine. By the same token. it is not reasonable to try to identify the cause of crimes that are said to be committed by organizations. These crimes are by definition exceptional to any behavioral theory. Once criminological theoreticians acknowledge that fact they will be able to concentrate more attention, time, and energy on the question of why managers steal for the company as well as from it. As Michael Levi has put it, "There has been much sententious discussion of the need for an organizational perspective in the analysis of corporate crime, but adequate theorizing must mediate organizational norms through individual actors who make decisions. . ."[75]

Notes

1. Donald R. Cressey and Charles A. Moore, *Corporation Codes of Conduct.* New York: Peat, Marwick, Mitchell Foundation, 1980.
2. Milton Friedman, *Capitalism and Freedom.* Chicago: University of Chicago Press, 1962, p. 15.

3. Cressey and Moore, *op. cit.*, p. 22.
4. P. J. Kenney, "Keeping Tabs on Beer Cans," *Wall Street Journal,* May 27, 1986, p. 29.
5. Gilbert Geis, "Toward a Delineation of White-Collar Crime Offenses," *Sociological Inquiry,* 32 (1962):160–171; Marshall B. Clinard and Richard Quinney, *Criminal Behavior Systems: A Typology.* 2d ed. New York: Holt, Rinehart & Winston, 1973; Laura S. Schrager and James F. Short, Jr., "Toward a Sociology of Organizational Crime," *Social Problems,* 25 (1978):407–419; Edward Gross, "Organizational Crime: A Theoretical Perspective." In Norman Denzin, ed., *Studies in Symbolic Interaction,* vol. 2. Greenwich, CT: JAI Press, 1978; Gross, "Organizational Structure and Organizational Crime." In Gilbert Geis and Ezra Stotland, eds., *White-Collar Crime: Theory and Research.* Beverly Hills: Sage, 1980; Marshall B. Clinard and Peter Yeager, *Corporate Crime.* New York: The Free Press, 1980.
6. Clinard and Yeager, *op. cit.*, p. 261.
7. Ian Maitland, Review of Brent Fisse and John Braithwaite, *The Impact of Publicity on Corporate Offenders, Contemporary Sociology,* 15 (1986):380–381.
8. Edwin H. Sutherland and Donald R. Cressey, *Criminology.* 10th ed. Philadelphia: Lippincott, 1978.
9. Donald R. Cressey, *Theft of the Nation: The Structure and Operations of Organized Crime in America.* New York: Harper and Row, 1969.
10. Donald R. Cressey, "Prison Organization." In James G. March, ed., *Handbook of Organizations.* Chicago: Rand-McNally, 1965, pp. 1023–1070.
11. Donald R. Cressey, "Restraint of Trade, Recidivism, and Delinquent Neighborhoods." In James F. Short, Jr., ed., *Delinquency, Crime, and Society.* Chicago: University of Chicago Press, 1976, pp. 209–234.
12. Arthur Miller, *The Supreme Court and American Capitalism.* New York: The Free Press, 1968.
13. Associated Press "Military Contract Fraud Charged," *Santa Barbara News-Press,* November 22, 1985.
14. L. Hayworth, "Do Organizations Act?" *Ethics,* 70 (1959):59–63.
15. Quoted in Andrew Hopkins, "The Anatomy of Corporate Crime." In John Braithwaite and Paul Wilson, eds., *The Two Faces of Deviance.* Brisbane, Australia: University of Queensland Press, 1978, p. 226.
16. Jack Katz, "Concerted Ignorance: The Social Psychology of Cover-up." In Robert K. Elliott and John J. Willingham, eds., *Management Fraud: Detection and Deterrence.* New York: Petrocelli, 1980.
17. John S. Martin, "Corporate Criminals or Criminal Corporation?" *Wall Street Journal,* June 19, 1985.
18. Charles B. Shudson, Ashton B. Onellion, and Ellen Hochstedler, "Nailing an Omelet to the Wall: Prosecuting Nursing Home Homicide." In Ellen Hochstedler, ed., *Corporations as Criminals.* Beverly Hills: Sage, 1984, pp. 131–145.

19. Donald R. Cressey, "Epidemiology and Individual Conduct, A Case from Criminology," *Pacific Sociological Review,* 3 (1960):847–858.
20. Edwin H. Sutherland, *White Collar Crime.* New York: Dryden, 1949, p. v.
21. Cressey, 1976, *op. cit.*
22. Andrew Hopkins, "Controlling Corporate Deviance," *Criminology,* 18 (1980): 198–214.
23. Geis, 1962, *op. cit.*
24 . Sutherland, 1949, *op. cit.*, pp. 234–241.
25. *Ibid.,* p. 241.
26. *Ibid.,* p. 257.
27. *Ibid.,* p. 264.
28. Marilynn Cash Mathews, "Corporate Crime: External v. Internal Regulation," Ph.D. dissertation, Santa Barbara: University of California, 1984.
29. Clinard and Quinney, *op. cit.,* p. 188.
30. John Braithwaite, "Enforced Self-Regulation: A New Strategy for Corporate Crime Control," *Michigan Law Review,* 80 (1982):1466.
31. Clinard and Yeager, *op. cit.,* p. 16.
32. *Ibid.,* p. 18.
33. *Ibid.,* pp. 10–11.
34. *Ibid.,* p. 17.
35. *Ibid.,* pp. 43–73.
36. *Ibid.,* p. 132.
37. Gross, *op. cit.,* p. 56.
38. *Ibid.*
39. *Ibid.,* p. 65.
40. Hayworth, *op. cit.*
41. Gross, *op. cit.,* p. 59.
42. *Ibid.*
43. *Ibid.,* p. 71.
44. *Ibid.,* p. 69.
45. *Ibid.,* p. 54.
46. *Ibid.,* p. 52.
47. *Ibid.*
48. *Ibid.,* p. 58.
49. *Ibid.,* p. 53.
50. *Ibid.,* p. 61.
51. *Ibid.,* p. 64.
52. Barry M. Staw and Eugene Szwajkowski, "The Scarcity-Munificence Component of Organizational Environments and the Commission of Illegal Acts," *Administrative Science Quarterly,* 20 (1975):345–354.
53. Gross, *op. cit.,* p. 64.
54. *Ibid.,* p. 69.
55. *Ibid.,* p 70.
56. Martin, *op. cit.*

57. Dean Rothbart, "American Air, Its President, Get Trust Suit Voided," *Wall Street Journal,* September 14, 1983.

58. Gerhard O. W. Mueller, *"Mens Rea* and the Corporation," *University of Pittsburgh Law Review,* 19 (1957):21–50; Manuel Velasquez, "Why Corporations Are Not Morally Responsible for Anything They Do," *Business and Professional Ethics Journal,* 3 (1983):1–18.

59. Eliot Marshall, "Guilty Plea Puts Oraflex Case to Rest," *Science,* 229 (1985):1079.

60. Cressey, "Restraint of Trade," *op. cit.,* p. 225.

61. Clinard and Yeager, *op. cit.,* pp. 137–138.

62. Sutherland, 1949, *op. cit.,* p. 42.

63. *Ibid.,* p. 41.

64. Schrager and Short, *op. cit.*

65. Jerome Hall, *Law, Social Science, and Criminal Theory,* Littleton, CO: Rothman, 1982.

66. Schrager and Short, *op. cit.,* pp. 111–112.

67. *Ibid.,* pp. 409–410.

68. *Ibid.,* p. 412.

69. Donald R. Cressey, "The Differential Association Theory and Compulsive Behavior," *Journal of Criminal Law, Criminology, and Police Science,* 45 (1954): 49–64.

70. Schrager and Short, *op. cit.,* p. 412.

71. Robert K. Elliott and John J. Willingham, eds., *Management Fraud Detection and Deterrence.* New York: Petrocelli, 1980, p. 4.

72. Donald R. Cressey, "Management Fraud, Accounting Controls, and Criminological Theory." In Elliott and Willingham, *op. cit.,* pp. 117–147.

73. Elliott and Willingham, *op. cit.,* p. viii.

74. Geis, *op. cit.,* p. 163.

75. Michael Levi, "A Criminological and Sociological Approach to Theories of and Research into Economic Crime." In Dan Magnusson, ed., *Economic Crime: Programs for Future Research.* Stockholm: National Council for Crime Prevention, 1985, pp. 32–72.

23

On the Plausibility
of Corporate Crime Control

John Braithwaite and Brent Fisse

T he Australian National University was graced with a lively series of seminars in
1986 in which Donald Cressey presented his latest thoughts on white-collar
crime. The first volume of *Advances in Criminological Theory* published the most
striking contribution from those presentations, "The Poverty of Theory in Corporate
Crime Research." One of us suggested to Cressey in 1986 that we might submit a
critique of his paper to *Advances in Criminological Theory,* in the hope that we
might replicate the stimulating exchange at those Canberra seminars. His tragic
death intervened and we abandoned the idea. Now we suspect this was the wrong
decision.

There is a sense in which "The Poverty of Theory in Corporate Crime Research"
is a critique of the younger Cressey by the older Cressey. In characteristic style,
Cressey catalogued the failings in his earlier work on juvenile gangs, La Cosa Nostra "families," prisons, and corporations. The failing he attributed to his younger self
was that of treating organizations as if they were unitary persons.

Donald Cressey was a great criminologist. He had his influence because he was
majestically contentious, unreservedly iconoclastic. No one revered Edwin Sutherland more than Donald Cressey; yet in "The Poverty of Theory in Corporate Crime
Research," Cressey accuses Sutherland of being "unthinking," "assaulting his own
common sense" by anthropomorphizing corporations. Some insight into this irrever-
ence is revealed in John Laub's oral history, where it is reported that Cressey perceived his influence on criminology as "mostly in getting people going on things. I
like to go in and get something started and stirred up. Then I leave it and let other
people worry about the details."[1]

Cressey was at his provocative best in his last article, in which he delighted in
the mischief of attacking both the younger Cressey and the older Sutherland for
failing to be true to the promise of the younger Sutherland. But if we are to reap
the true harvest of Cressey's intellect, we do not have to take one side or the other;

Reprinted from *Advances in Criminological Theory,* 2 (1990), pp. 15–37.

rather, we must perceive the dialectic between the younger and the older Cressey.

In playing our part to enliven this dialectic, we cannot but be struck by the ironies of Cressey's intellectual history. Sutherland's theory was in important ways a reaction against the psychological ascendancy in criminology during his lifetime. Cressey's great theoretical contribution was to build on differential association in a way that transcended the empty theoretical divisions between psychology and sociology. His masterly presidential address to the Pacific Sociological Association thirty years ago staked out the challenge for criminological theory.[2] This was to develop a theory that explained not only why some individuals engaged in more crime or different kinds of crime from other individuals, but also why some structural contexts show higher crime rates and different crime patterns than others. Cressey was decades ahead of his time in formulating criminology's agenda for integrating micro and macro levels of analysis. He was frustrated in his lifetime by the failure of his criminological peers to pursue integrated micro-macro explanations, and particularly frustrated by the crude methodological holism of most of his sociological contemporaries. This frustration, we suspect, led Cressey to adopt more extremist methodological individualist positions in order to jolt and provoke us. Only Don Cressey could give a speech entitled "Everybody's Wrong."[3] So let us be provoked in the hope that we will ultimately find the individualist-holist synthesis for which Cressey himself yearned.

The thrust of "The Poverty of Theory in Corporate Crime Research" is to call into question seven assumptions that are common in corporate crime research:

1. Corporations are like real persons.
2. Corporations act.
3. Corporations have intentions.
4. Corporations have legal and ethical responsibilities.
5. Corporations can commit crime.
6. Corporations can suffer from punishment.
7. The same theory can be applied to individual and corporate criminals.

It is also important to understand what Cressey did not want to say. As a matter of public policy he did not want to abandon the "legal fiction" that corporations are persons because "this legal fiction is essential to fairness."[4] If corporations were not assigned the legal characteristics of persons, no one could sue them or make contracts with them. He also rather equivocally concedes the practical necessity of holding corporations criminally liable for wrongdoing perpetrated by their executives, given that these executives are "masters at using the corporate form to mask their misbehavior."[5] Our contention will be that corporate criminal responsibility is defensible as more than just an expedient legal fiction. Second, we will defend the position that sound scientific theories can be based on a foundation of corporate action, and that some theories of individual action can also usefully be applied to corporate action.

CORPORATIONS ARE LIKE REAL PERSONS

Cressey's contention here is that "anyone who tries to understand white-collar crime is severely handicapped by the fiction that corporations are disembodied political, social and economic persons who behave just like ordinary men and women."[6] Cressey correctly points out that first, corporations can do many things individuals cannot: "They can buy and sell each other legally, as though the 'person' being sold were a slave."[7] Because the makeup of a corporation is different from that of a human being, it can do things that are not humanly possible, such as growing from infant to adult in a year, securing immortality. Second, in other ways the corporation is less than a person: it cannot feel human emotions.

This much is unexceptionable. Many of us have been guilty of slipping into a forgetfulness of the fundamental differences between corporations and human beings under the seductive influence of the simplifying language of corporate personhood. But this does not mean that there are no ways in which corporations and human beings are similar. What matters is whether there are some theoretically relevant similarities. For some purposes, we can usefully model individual human conduct as rational goal-seeking behavior. For some purposes, we can usefully model corporate conduct as rational goal-seeking behavior.

Some philosophical debates about what the theoretically relevant differences and similarities are between individuals and corporations have been difficult and perplexing. Peter French contends that corporations are moral persons because they manifest intentionality,[8] while many other philosophers contend that much more than a capacity to act intentionally is required for moral personhood.[9] Corporations clearly have a different metaphysical status from individuals; being formed for limited purposes, they do not have the same status as ends in themselves as do human beings.[10] Corporations are not moral persons in the sense of enjoying all of the rights that human beings properly enjoy, such as a right to life.[11] But we do not have to regard corporations as moral persons to hold them responsible for their actions.

The important question for criminological theory is not whether corporations are moral persons but whether corporations are capable of criminal action and whether they can properly be held responsible. A theory of criminal responsibility need not and should not depend on the metaphysical status of moral personhood. Our task is to develop a theory of what it means to be criminally responsible, and then to ask whether corporations are capable of the kind of action that that entails. But first we must ask whether corporations can act at all, something that Cressey called into question.

CORPORATIONS ACT

In adopting the view that corporations do not act, that only individuals act, Cressey not only questions the idea of corporate crime but casts doubt on the whole enterprise of organizational sociology. Cressey shares the methodological individualism that F. A. Hayek formulated as follows: "There is no other way toward an understanding of social phenomena but through our understanding of individual actions directed toward other people and guided by their expected behavior."[12]

Methodological individualism as advocated by Hayek and Popper amounts to an ontology that only individuals are real in the social world, while social phenomena like corporations are abstractions that cannot be directly observed.[13] This ontology is spurious.[14] The notion that individuals are real, observable, flesh and blood, while corporations are legal fictions is false. Plainly, many features of corporations are observable (their assets, factories, decision-making procedures), while many features of individuals are not (for example, personality, intention, unconscious mind).[15] Both individuals and corporations are defined by a mix of observable and abstracted characteristics.

Clifford Geertz contends that "the Western conception of the person as a bounded, unique, more or less integrated emotional and cognitive universe, a dynamic centre of awareness, emotion, judgment, and action organized into a distinctive whole ... is a rather peculiar idea within the context of the world's cultures."[16] Reflecting upon his anthropological fieldwork, Geertz cites Balinese culture, wherein it is dramatis personae, not actors, that endure or indeed exist:

> Physically men come and go, mere incidents in a happenstance history, of no genuine importance even to themselves. But the masks they wear, the stage they occupy, the parts they play, and, most important, the spectacle they mount remain, and comprise not the façade but the substance of things, not least the self. Shakespeare's old-trouper view of the vanity of action in the face of mortality—all the world's a stage and we are but poor players, content to strut our hour, and so on—makes no sense here. There is no make-believe; of course players perish, but the play does not, and it is the latter, the performed rather than the performer that really matters.[17]

The merging of the individual person with the land in Australian aboriginal cultures, where a particular rock can be part of an ancestor or part of oneself, provides another example at odds with the conception of bounded unitary individualism. Even within the Western cultural tradition it is difficult to accept that individuals, unlike corporations, are characterized by a bounded unitary consciousness. As Barry Hindess has pointed out, decisions made by individuals as well as those made by corporations have a diffuse grounding: they represent the product of "diverse and sometimes conflicting objectives, forms of calculation, and means of action."[18] When the sober John Smith expresses remorse at the way John Smith behaves when he is drunk, this disassociation of self illustrates that the individual is not such a unitary self.[19] When scholars speak of defending some of the alleged sins of the younger Cressey against the older Cressey, they can fracture the unitary conception of this individual without questioning that Cressey was capable of action.

The polar opposite to methodological individualism is the methodological holism of the early European sociologists, notably Emile Durkheim. For Durkheim, "the individual finds himself in the presence of a force [society] which is superior to him and before which he bows."[20] From this perspective, the collective will of society is not the product of the individual consciousness of members of society.[21] Quite the reverse: the individual is the product of social forces.

Both the crude methodological individualism of Hayek and the crude methodological holism of Durkheim are unpersuasive. It is just as constricting to see the sailor as the navy writ small as it is to see the navy as the sailor writ large. It is true to say that the activity of the navy is constituted by the actions of individual sailors. But it is also true that the existence of a sailor is constituted by the existence of the navy. Take away the institutional framework of the navy—ships, captains, rules of war, other sailors—and the notion of an individual sailor makes no sense. Institutions are constituted by individuals, and individuals are socially constituted by institutions. To conceive of corporations as no more than sums of the isolated efforts of individuals would be as foolish as to conceive the possibility of language without the interactive processes of individuals talking to one another and passing structures of syntax from one generation to another.

Irving Thalberg and others have suggested that "it would be absurd to say that corporations could act even though all human beings have perished."[22] In fact it is not absurd. If all humankind perished in a nuclear war and preprogrammed missiles of the U.S. Army continued to be launched, why could we not describe their launching as an action of the U.S. Army?[23] Thompson points out that part of the genius of modern organizations is their capacity to perform tasks of spectacular complexity when set against the rather ordinary individual talents of the people involved. This genius can be understood in terms of the composition of these individual talents into a corporate system. To look for the answer as a simple sum of individual genius is to commit a "fallacy of division."[24]

Equally misguided is a sociological determinism that grants no intentionality to individuals, that sees them as wholly shaped by macrosociological forces. Sociological functionalism, as championed by Durkheim, indulges this absurdity. Mesmerized by the achievements of evolutionary theory in biology, the functionalists failed to recognize that human beings are capable of reflecting upon causal laws and engaging in purposive social action that does not conform to those laws or, indeed, that is intended to defeat them. We may readily agree with Durkheim that each kind of community is a thought world that penetrates and moulds the minds of its members, but that is not to deny the capacity of individuals to exercise their autonomy to resist and reshape thought worlds.

All wholes are made up of parts; reductionism can be a near-infinite regress. Psychological reductionists can argue that the behavior of organizations can only be understood by analyzing the behavior of individual members of the organization. Biological reductionists can argue that the behavior of individuals can only be understood by the behavior of parts of the body—firing synapses in the brain, hormonal changes, movement of a hand across a page. Chemical reductionists might argue that these body parts can only be understood as movements of molecules. At all of these levels of analysis, reductionism is blinkered because the whole is always more than the sum of the individual parts; in each case there is a need to build upon reductionism to study how the parts interact to form wholes. In the case of organizations, individuals may be the most important parts, but there are other parts, as is evident from factories with manifest routines that operate to some extent independently of the biological agents who flick the switches. Organizations are "socio-technical" systems,[25] not just aggregations of individuals. More crucially, however, organizations consist of sets of expectations about how different kinds of problems should be resolved. These expectations are a sediment of the individual expectations of many past and present members of the organization. But they are also a product of the *interplay* among individuals' views. The interaction between individual and shared expectations, on the one hand, and the organization's environment, on the other, continually reproduces shared expectations. In other words, an organization has a culture which is transmitted from one generation of organizational role incumbents to the next. Indeed, the entire personnel of an organization may change without reshaping the corporate culture: this may be so even if the new incumbents have personalities quite different from those of the old.

The products of organizations are more than the sum of the products of individual actions; while each member of the board of directors can "vote" for a declaration of dividend, only the board as a collectivity is empowered to declare a dividend. The collective action is thus qualitatively different from the human actions that, in part, constitute it. "Groupthink"[26] and the group risky-shift phenomenon[27] also illustrate how collective expectations can be quite different from the sum of individual expectations. A number of psychological studies suggest that group decision making can make members of the group willing to accept stupid ideas or hazardous risks that they would reject if making the same decision alone.[28]

Cressey underpins his questioning of the concept of corporate criminal liability by suggesting that organizations do not think, decide, or act; these are all things done by individuals. So we are told that it is a crass anthropomorphism to say that the White House decided upon a course of action, or that the United States declared war. Instead we should say that the president decided and that the president and a majority of members of Congress decided to go to war. If saying that "the White House decided" connotes that "the White House" would decide in the same way as an individual person, then we are certainly engaging in anthropomorphism. Yet people who decode such messages understand that organizations emit decisions just as individuals do, but that they reach these decisions in a rather different way. They fully accept that "the White House decided" is a simplification given that many actors typically have a say in such decisions. Nevertheless, it is probably less of a simplification than the statement "the president decided." Indeed, it may be fanciful to individualize a collective product. The president may never have turned his mind to the decision: he may have done no more than waive his power to veto it, or he may have delegated the decision totally.

Similarly, it makes more sense to say that the United States has declared war than to say that the president and a majority of Congress have decided to do so. A declaration of war commits many more individuals and physical resources to purposive social action than the individuals who voted for it; it commits the United States as a whole to war, and many individuals outside the Congress participate or acquiesce in making the commitment:

> A man does not have to agree with his government's acts to see himself embodied in them any more than he has to approve of his own acts to acknowledge that he has, alas, performed them. It is a question of immediacy, of experiencing what the state "does" as proceeding naturally from a familiar and intelligible "we."[29]

The temptation to reduce such decisions to the actions of individuals is widespread, as in the suggestion, once common, that wars be settled by a fistfight or duel between the protagonist heads of state.

The expression "the White House decided" is a social construction; as a matter of social construction, the same organizational output might be expressed as "the president decided" or "the administration decided" or "the United States decided" or "the president gave in to the decision of the Congress." Equally, the concept of "deciding" is a social construct (what amounts to "deciding" for some is "muddling through" or perhaps even "ducking a decision" for others). To talk of individual decisions as real and of collective decisions as fictions, as Cressey does, is to obscure the inevitability of social construction at any level of analysis.

In many circumstances, the social construction "the White House decided" will be a workable one for analytic purposes. This does not mean that we should treat this as the only accurate description of what happened any more than we should accept "the president decided" as the real description of what happened. Indeed, the social control of corporate crime depends on understanding how those involved with a crime socially construct the responsible individuals or collectivity. The key to unlocking the control of corporate crime is granting credibility to multiple social constructions of responsibility, and investigating the processes of generating and invoking these social constructions; as Geertz has explained, "[h]opping back and forth between the whole conceived through the parts that actualize it and the parts conceived through the whole that motivates them, we seek to turn them, by a sort of intellectual perpetual motion, into explications of one another."[30]

Social theory and legal theory are thus forced to stake out positions between individualism and holism. The task is to explore how wholes are created out of purposive individual action, and how individual action is constituted and constrained by the structural realities of wholes. This exploration extends to how responsibility for action in the context of collectivities is socially constructed by those involved as well as by outsiders. Moral responsibility can be meaningfully allocated when conventions for allocating responsibility are shared by insiders and understood by outsiders. Metaphysics about the distinctive, unitary, irreducible agency of individuals tend to obstruct analysis, as do metaphysics about the special features of corporateness. As elaborated in the following section, the moral responsibility of corporations for their actions relates essentially to social processes and not to elusive attributes of personhood; as Surber has indicated, the issue is "more a matter of what we consider moral responsibility to be, rather than what sort of metaphysical entities corporations may turn out to be."[31]

CORPORATIONS HAVE INTENTIONS

Cressey contends that, because corporations are not real persons, they cannot have intentions; intention is something unique to being a person. While it is obviously true that corporations lack the capacity to entertain a cerebral mental state of intentionality, corporations manifest their own special kind of intentionality—corporate policy. Peter French identifies the Corporate Internal Decision Structure of corporations as a license of the sort required to redescribe certain corporate actions as intentional. To be intentional, just one of any number of true redescriptions of the behavior need involve intentionality. Hence, the depositing of money in a bank can be redescribed in a variety of purely mechanical ways, as well as in at least one intentional form. A Corporate Internal Decision Structure involves (1) an organizational system of stations and levels of decision-making, and (2) a set of decision/action recognition rules of two types: procedural and policy. "These recognition rules provide the tests that a decision or action was made for corporate reasons within the corporate decision structure."[32] French applies a Wittgensteinian[33] distinction: the organizational structure supplies a grammar of the corporation's decision making, and the recognition rules provide its logic.

The concepts of corporate policies and procedures do not express merely the intentionality of a company's directors, officers, or employees, but they project the idea of a distinctly corporate strategy:

> It will be objected that a corporation's policies reflect only the current goals of its directors. But that is certainly not logically necessary nor is it in practice true for most large corporations. Usually, of course, the original incorporators will have organized to further their individual interests and/or to meet goals which they shared. [But] even in infancy the melding of disparate interests and purposes gives rise to a corporate long range point of view that is distinct from the intents and purposes of the collection of incorporators viewed individually.[34]

While we accept French's account of a special corporate kind of intentionality that courts can sensibly recognize, one does not have to accept it to be able to hold corporations blameworthy or responsible for their actions. We will turn to this in the next section. But first we must dispense with Cressey's claim that unless behavior is intended, it cannot be explained:

> [I]t is just as ridiculous for criminologists to try to explain criminal behavior that was not intended as it is for judges to try to determine whether a fictitious person has an evil state of mind.[35]
>
> . . . Because corporations cannot intend actions, none of their criminality can be explained in the framework of behavioral theory.[36]
>
> . . . [N]o social psychological theory can make sense of behavior that is not intended, be it ordinary crime such as felony murder or a white-collar crime such as restraint of trade, false advertising, or unfair labor practices.[37]

Yet we know that psychological theories can and do explain behaviors that, instead of being intentional, are negligent or unconscious or a reflex. And if we move from micro to macro levels of explanation, intent as an essential ingredient of social explanation becomes even more suspect. An explanation of the Great Depression is not likely to be found by searching for people who intended it. So we must dismiss out of hand the suggestion that because corporate behavior cannot be intentional, it cannot be explained.

CORPORATIONS HAVE LEGAL AND ETHICAL RESPONSIBILITIES

Cressey considers talk of corporate citizenship, of corporate social responsibility, of a social contract imposing ethical and legal obligations on corporations as anthropomorphism. Good consequences might flow from people being deluded into accepting such fictions, but they are still anthropomorphisms. However, it is not clear why we can only talk of individuals as having responsibilities. Thus, De George, who does not believe that corporations are moral persons, can still argue that corporations are nevertheless subject to moral rules and are to blame for breaking them:

> It suffices to recognize that as human creations which are used by human beings for certain ends and which can be said to act, corporations have the status of moral actors. A moral actor is subject to the moral law and one can correctly evaluate such an actor's actions from a moral point of view.[38]

What, then, is a sensible formulation of corporate moral responsibility or blameworthiness? Blameworthiness requires essentially two conditions: first, the ability of the actor to make decisions; second, the inexcusable failure of the actor to perform an assigned task. Herbert Simon has defined a formal organization as a "decision-making structure."[39] Under this definition, a formal organization has one of the requirements for blameworthiness that a mob, for example, does not have. We routinely hold organizations responsible for a decision when and because that decision instantiates an organizational policy and instantiates an organizational decision-making process that the organization has chosen for itself. A decision made by a rogue individual in defiance of corporate policy (including unwritten corporate policy) to undermine corporate goals, or in flagrant disregard of corporate decision-making rules, is not a decision for which the organization is morally responsible. This is not to say, however, that we cannot hold the organization responsible if the intention of individuals is other than to promote corporate goals and policies. It may be that two individuals, A and B, hold the key to a particular corporate decision. A decides what to support because of a bribe; her intention is to collect the bribe rather than to advance corporate goals. B decides to support the same course of action out of a sense of loyalty to A, who is an important ally and mentor; his intention is formed from a consideration of bureaucratic politics rather than corporate goals. Even though the key individuals do not personally intend to further corporate policy by the decision, it may be that they cannot secure the acquiescence of the rest of the organization with the decision unless they can advance credible reasons as to why the decision will advance corporate policy. If the reasons given are accepted and acted on within the corporate decision-making process, then we can hold the corporation responsible irrespective of any games played by individual actors among themselves. It is not just that corporate intention (the instantiation of corporate policy in a decision) is more than the sum of individual intentions; it may have little to do with individual intentions.

Blameworthiness also requires an inexcusable failure to perform an assigned task. Any culture confers certain types of responsibilities on certain kinds of actors. Fathers have responsibilities not to neglect their children. Doctors bear special responsibilities in the giving of medical advice. Just as fathers and doctors can be held to different and higher standards of responsibility by virtue of role or capacity, so it is possible for corporations to be held to different and higher standards of responsibility than individuals because of their role or capacity as organizations.[40]

It is not a legal fiction for the law to hold corporations responsible for their decisions; in all cultures it is common for citizens to do so. When the law adopts these cultural notions of corporate responsibility, it does more than reflect the culture: it deepens and shapes the notions of corporate responsibility already present in the culture. The law can clarify the content of what we expect corporations to be responsible for. Thus, the law can require large chemical companies to be responsible for an inventory of all hazardous chemicals on their premises, a responsibility not imposed on individual householders. More fundamentally, the law is not only presented with the cultural fact that a corporation can be blamed; the law, more than any other institution in the culture, is constantly implicated in reproducing that cultural fact. Thus, the Roman law tradition of treating corporate persons as fictions and the Germanic realist theory that law cannot create its subjects (that is, that corporations are preexisting sociological persons) both overlook the recursive nature of the relationship between law and culture.[41] Corporations are held responsible for the outcomes of their policies and decision-making procedures partly because organizations have the capacity to change their policies and procedures. Thomas Donaldson has pointed out that, like corporations, a computer conducting a search and a cat waiting to pounce on a mouse are making decisions and are even doing so intentionally.[42] We grant moral agency to the corporation and yet not to the cat or the computer for two reasons, according to Donaldson. First, the corporation, like the individual human being and unlike the cat, can give moral reasons for its decision making. Second, the corporation has the capacity to change its goals and policies and to change the decision-making processes directed at those goals and policies. For these reasons the concept of corporate intentionality defies equation with feline or digital brain waves.

Corporate intentionality does not exhaust the range of relevant fault concepts. We can blame actors for things done deliberately, where the actor does not want or intend harm, but is quite deliberate about being willing to run the risk of harm. In practice, the predominant form of corporate fault is more likely to be corporate negligence than corporate intention. Companies usually are at pains not to display any posture of inattention to legal requirements; on the contrary, compliance policies are de rigueur in companies that have given any thought to legal-risk minimization.[43] Corporate negligence is prevalent where communication breakdowns occur, or where organizations suffer from collective oversight. Does corporate negligence in such a context amount merely to negligence on the part of individuals? It may be possible to explain the *causes* of corporate wrongdoing in terms of particular contributions by managers and employees, but the attribution of *fault* is another matter.[44] Corporate negligence does not necessarily reduce to individual negligence. A corporation may have a greater capacity for avoiding the commission of an offense, and for this reason it may be that a finding of corporate but not individual negligence may be justified. We may be reluctant to pass judgment on the top executives of Union Carbide for the Bhopal disaster (perhaps because of failures of communication within the organization about safety problems abroad), but higher standards of care are expected of such a company given its collective might and resources.[45] Thus, where a corporate system is blamed for criminogenic group pressures, that blame is directed not at individual actors but, rather, at an institutional setup from which the expected standards of organizational performance are higher than the standards expected of any personnel.[46] As Donaldson has observed in the context of corporate intelligence:

> Corporations can and should have access to practical and theoretical knowledge which dwarfs that of individuals. When Westinghouse, Inc. manufactures machinery for use in nuclear power generating plants, it should use its massive resources to consider tens of thousands of possible consequences and be able to weigh their likelihood accurately. Which human errors might occur?

How are they to be handled? How might espionage occur? How should human systems interface with mechanized ones? . . . Good intentions for Westinghouse are not adequate. Westinghouse must have, in addition to good intentions, superhuman intelligence.[47]

Corporations, it may thus be argued, can be blamed and held morally responsible for intentional or negligent conduct. Michael McDonald has gone further by arguing that organizations are paradigm moral agents:

Not only does the organization have all the capacities that are standardly taken to ground autonomy—vis., capacities for intelligent agency—but it also has them to a degree no human can. Thus, for example, a large corporation has available and can make use of far more information than one individual can. Moreover, the corporation is in principle "immortal" and so better able to bear responsibility for its deeds than humans, whose sin dies with them.[48]

Granted, corporations lack human feelings and emotions, but this hardly disqualifies them from possessing the quality of autonomy. On the contrary, the lack of emotions and feelings promotes rather than hinders rational choice, and in this respect the corporation may indeed be a paradigm responsible actor.[49]

There are other difficulties with the view that corporate responsibility amounts to merely an aggregation of individual responsibility. Repeatedly in organizational life, individual actors contribute to collective decision-making processes without being conscious of the totality of that process—each individual actor is a part of a whole, which no one of them fully comprehends. Indeed, even that part that an individual contributes may be unconscious.

Consider the predicament of the campaigner for clearer writing who is concerned about the way children learn an excessive use of the passive voice when they should use the active voice. Our activist wants to allocate blame for the way children leave school with ingrained habits of overusing the passive voice. Empirically, he may find that in general neither students nor teachers have a conscious understanding of what it means to use the passive versus the active voice. Unconsciously, they understand how to choose between them—more precisely, they have "practical consciousness" but not "discursive consciousness" of the choice.[50] The lack of intentional individual action in making these choices makes the blaming of teachers or students problematic. Yet it might be quite reasonable for blame to be directed at the English Curriculum Branch of the Education Department. Conscious awareness of the distinction between the active and the passive voice is widespread throughout the branch because it is, after all, the job of the branch to attend to such matters and to raise the consciousness of teachers and students. It may thus make sense to lay collective blame for social action produced unintentionally, even unconsciously, by all the individual actors. Apart from the justice our campaigner may perceive in blaming the English Curriculum Branch rather than the students or teachers, she might conclude that change is more likely to be effected by collective blame. This raises the issue of collective action and deterrent efficacy, as discussed in the section after next.

CORPORATIONS CAN COMMIT CRIME

If we can accept that corporations have ethical and legal responsibilities, that corporations can act, and that corporations can be held blameworthy for their actions, then corporations can commit crime. We have also argued that corporate intentionality is a coherent idea, having both similarities to and differences from the idea of individual intentionality. But one does not have to believe in corporate intentionality, as Cressey suggests one does, in order to accept that corporations can commit crime. Intention is not the only basis for attributing fault for corporate action; further possible bases of corporate fault include recklessness, negligence, and "willful blindness."[51] There is no novelty in this point. With individuals, mens rea does not mean simply intention: it encompasses a panoply of fault concepts. Similarly, we have argued that it is unnecessary to accept the philosophically controversial idea that corporations are moral persons in order to justify holding corporations criminally responsible. Held puts this position nicely:

> We seem to have some good reasons for conferring personhood on corporations, and some good reasons for denying it. I suggest that we sidestep the problem. It is not necessary to decide whether corporations "are" persons unless we have some unwarranted assumptions that only persons can act, or be responsible, or decide, etc. If what we are interested in is corporate behavior, we can suppose we are talking about an entity which is like a person in some respects and unlike a person in other respects. We can "hold" corporations responsible, in both moral and legal judgments. We can recognize that we need moralities that will recommend guidelines for the actions of corporations as we need guidelines for the actions of individual persons.[52]

Put another way, no modern society can afford a criminal law that communicates the message that, so long as we avoid individual fault, there is no need to worry about corporate fault. Equally, no society can afford a criminal law that communicates the message that, so long as the corporation is kept in the clear, we need not worry about individual fault on the part of actors in corporate roles. What is needed is a criminal law that inculcates both individual and corporate responsibility.

CORPORATIONS CAN SUFFER FROM PUNISHMENT

Cressey's critique here is that "criminologists rather routinely, unthinkingly and erroneously assert that corporations have the psychological capacity to be guilty of crime and to suffer from punishment."[53] It is true that corporations have "no soul to damn, no body to kick." But contemporary social constructions of individual punishment do not generally involve the infliction of pain by causing bodies to bleed, nor do they involve the damning of souls. Rather they tend to involve the identification of individual goals—wealth, security, freedom—and the infliction of punishments that frustrate those goals. For example, the judge assumes that the defendant shares the goal of wealth accumulation when she imposes a fine: she assumes freedom to be desired when she imposes a sentence of imprisonment. From time to time these assumptions will be misplaced. First, there will be individuals who do not care for money or freedom. Second, and more fundamentally, doubt can be cast on the idea that human behavior is all about the pursuit of goals or interests. Equally, it can be about sustaining an identity or nurturing a self-concept as, say, a Christian or a lawyer, even when sustaining that identity is not in the interests of the actor.

Individual behavior can be understood in useful but limited ways both as a process of displaying and sustaining an identity[54] and as the pursuit of goals or interests. Equally, we would contend, corporate behavior can be usefully constructed both as a display of identity and the pursuit of goals. If individual and corporate conduct share in common at least some degree of goal-directedness, then it is just as sensible to seek to punish corporations by interfering with their goal attainment as it is to do so with individuals. Partial account of corporate action though it is, there is reason to believe that corporate crime better fits the model of rational goal seeking than does individual crime.[55]

If corporate behavior is partly about the attainment of collective goals, punishment of individuals alone is bound to fail as a control strategy. We must seek as well a capacity to interfere directly with those collective goals. This is so because if corporations rationally pursue goals, individuals who are deterred from following those goals on behalf of the corporation will be replaced by individuals who will pursue the corporate goals. Adherence to the individualist fallacy of division will have disastrous practical consequences for enforcement policy.

Let us try to make the point more clearly by comparing collective deterrence in the domain of foreign policy. Following Cressey, we could adopt the view that individuals, not nations, decide to go to war. Instead of threatening nuclear or commercial retaliation against a nation should it invade another, we could threaten to find out who the political actors were that lobbied for the invasion and to send assassination squads after them. This policy option is not usually recommended, largely because of an enduring belief in the capacity of groups to replace slain leaders. If collective deterrence is a fiction, it is a fiction on which strategic analysts in the United States and the Soviet Union have based the future of the world.[56]

It is quite possible to deter by damaging collective interests even when individual members of an organization are not personally affected. In an earlier study of seventeen adverse publicity crises experienced by large organizations, we concluded that adverse publicity surrounding allegations of corporate crime was an effective deterrent, but not mainly because of fear of the financial consequences of the publicity.[57] Companies value a good reputation for its own sake, just as do universities, sporting clubs, and government agencies. Individuals who take on positions of power within such organizations, even if they as individuals do not personally feel any deterrent effects of censure directed at their organization, may find that they confront role expectations to protect and enhance the repute of the organization. For example, an academic might be indifferent to the reputation of her university; indeed she might do more to snipe at the incompetence of the administration than to defend it publicly. But, if appointed as dean of a faculty, she confronts new role expectations that she will protect the university's reputation. She may do this diligently, not because of the views she brought to the job as an individual member of the university community, but because she knows what the position requires, and she wants to be good at her task. Thus, in organizations where individuals are stung very little by collective deterrents, deterrence can still work if those in power are paid good salaries on the understanding that they will do what is necessary to preserve the reputation of the organization or to protect it from whatever other kind of collective adversity is threatened.

THE SAME THEORY CAN BE APPLIED TO INDIVIDUAL AND CORPORATE CRIMINALS

Cressey's ultimate concern is that the "blurring of the distinction between corporate crimes committed by persons and corporate crimes committed by organizations asks theoreticians to use one causal theory to explain both, an impossible task."[58] This task is not impossible, though it does require negotiating a mine field of difficulties. In the last section, we concluded that models that conceive that crime is understandable in terms of rational pursuit of goals can have partial validity for both individual and corporate actors. Thus, there is a prospect of rational-choice models accounting for some variance with both types of criminal actors. Corporations can learn, so there is the possibility of learning theory applying to both collectivities and individuals.

Just as individuals can participate in and be influenced by a subculture, so can corporations. Cressey's contribution on criminogenic corporate subcultures of restraint of trade, and the similarities of these to neighborhood subcultures of delinquency, is perhaps the most outstanding contribution to this literature.[59] Corporate offending patterns, like individual offending patterns, may be accounted for by the configurations of legitimate and illegitimate opportunities that actors confront. Rational-choice, learning, subcultural, and opportunity theories doubtless do not exhaust the possibilities for theories that may apply to criminal action by both individual and collective entities. Equally, there are many theories of individual offending that it is difficult to see ever being usefully applied to corporations—such as biological theories of the relation between intelligence, impulsiveness, or race and crime.

The fundamental point is that it is impossible, in advance of a theory being developed and put to the test, to rule out any level of generality in theory application. Before Darwin, the idea that the same theory could account for the origins of both man and amoebas was implausible.[60] Criminology will not progress as a science if its practitioners suffer stultified creativity at the hands of an orthodoxy that theories of a certain scope are, to use Cressey's word, "impossible."

CONCLUSION

Cressey has done a service in his last published work. Sociologists are especially prone to the folly of treating nonactors as actors, as is evident from the sweeping flourishes often made about "the ruling class deciding," when no decision-making structures can be identified within an entity called the ruling class. Cressey's article puts all on guard against such all-too-common Type I errors. Our hope is that it will not also cause criminologists to perpetrate a host of Type II errors, discarding the reality of collective criminal action in favor of an inferior methodological individualism.

Notes

1. John H. Laub, *Criminology in the Making: An Oral History.* Boston: Northeastern University Press, 1983, p. 16.
2. Donald R. Cressey, "Epidemiology and Individual Conduct: A Case from Criminology," *Pacific Sociological Review,* 3 (1960):47–58.
3. Paul Colomy, "Donald R. Cressey: A Personal and Intellectual Remembrance," *Crime and Delinquency,* 34 (1988): 256.
4. Donald R. Cressey, "The Poverty of Theory in Corporate Crime Research," *Advances in Criminological Theory,* 1 (1988):34.
5. *Ibid.,* p. 36.
6. *Ibid.,* p. 34.
7. *Ibid.*
8. Peter A. French, *Collective and Corporate Responsibility.* New York: Columbia University Press, 1984; French, "Principles of Responsibility: Shame and the Corporation." In Hugh Curtler, ed., *Shame, Responsibility and the Corporation.* New York: Haven, 1986, pp. 17–55.
9. Meir Dan-Cohen, *Rights, Persons. and Organizations.* Berkeley: University of California Press, 1986; Richard T. De George, "Corporations and Morality." In Curtler, *op. cit.,* pp. 57–75. John H. Ladd, "Persons and Responsibility: Ethical Concepts and Impertinent Analyses." In Curtler, *op. cit.,* pp. 77–97; Thomas Donaldson, *Corporations and Morality.* Englewood Cliffs, NJ: Prentice-Hall, 1982; Donaldson, "Personalizing Corporate Ontology: The French Way." In Curtler, *op. cit.,* pp. 99–112; Larry May, "Negligence and Corporate Criminality." In Curtler, *op. cit.,* pp. 137–157.

10. De George, *op. cit.*, p. 60.
11. Ladd, *op. cit.*
12. Friedrich A. Hayek, *Individualism and the Economic Order.* Chicago: University of Chicago Press, 1949.
13. Hayek, *op. cit.*; Karl Popper, *The Open Society and Its Enemies.* London: Routledge & Kegan Paul, 1947.
14. Steven Lukes, *Individualism.* Oxford: Blackwell, 1973.
15. See, for example, Michael McDonald, "The Personless Paradigm," *University of Toronto Law Journal,* 37 (1987):212–226.
16. Clifford Geertz, *Local Knowledge.* New York: Basic Books, 1983, p. 59.
17. *Ibid.*, p. 62.
18. Barry Hindess, "Classes, Collectivities, and Corporate Actors." Unpublished manuscript. Canberra: Australian National University, 1988.
19. Erving Goffman, *Relations in Public.* New York: Basic Books, 1971, p. 113.
20. Emile Durkheim, *The Rules of Sociological Method,* trans. Sarah A. Soloway and John H. Mueller. New York: The Free Press, 1938, p. 123.
21. Emile Durkheim, *The Division of Labor in Society,* trans. George Simpson. New York: The Free Press, 1932.
22. Larry May, "Vicarious Agency and Corporate Responsibility," *Philosophical Studies,* 43 (1983): 79–80.
23. See also Dan-Cohen, *op. cit.*; Virginia Held, "Corporations, Persons and Responsibility." In Curtler, *op. cit.*, pp. 159–181.
24. Paul B. Thompson, "Why Do We Need a Theory of Corporate Responsibility." In Curtler, *op. cit.*, p. 117.
25. Fred E. Emery, *Systems Thinking.* Harmondsworth: Penguin, 1969.
26. Irving L. Janis, *Victims of Groupthink.* Boston: Houghton Mifflin, 1972.
27. Michael A. Wallach, Nathan Kogan, and Daryl J. Bem, "Diffusion of Responsibility and Level of Risk Taking in Groups," *Journal of Abnormal and Social Psychology,* 68 (1964):263–274.
28. But see Irving L. Janis and Leon Mann, *Decision Making: A Psychological Analysis of Conflict, Choice, and Commitment.* New York: The Free Press, 1977.
29. Clifford Geertz, *The Interpretation of Cultures.* New York: Basic Books, 1973, p. 317.
30. *Ibid.*
31. Jere Surber, "Individual and Corporate Responsibility: Two Alternative Approaches," *Business & Professional Ethics Journal,* 2 (1983):81.
32. French, "Principles of Responsibility," *op. cit.*, p. 22.
33. Ludwig Wittgenstein, *Philosophical Remarks,* trans. Raymond Hargreaves and Roger White. Oxford: Blackwell, 1975, p. 39.
34. French, *Collective and Corporate Responsibility, op. cit.*, pp. 45–46.
35. Cressey, "Poverty of Theory," *op. cit.*, p. 48.
36. *Ibid.*
37. *Ibid.*, p. 46.

38. De George, *op. cit.*, p. 63.
39. Herbert Simon, *Administrative Behavior.* 2d ed. New York: The Free Press, 1965.
40. Robert E. Goodin, "Apportioning Responsibility," *Law and Philosophy,* 6 (1987):167–185.
41. French, *Collective and Corporate Responsibility, op. cit.*, pp. 35–37.
42. Donaldson, *Corporations and Morality, op. cit.*, p. 22.
43. N. Bruns, "Corporate Preventive Law Programs," *Preventive Law Reporter,* 6 (1987):30–40; J. Sciamanda, "Preventive Law Leads to Corporate Goal of Zero Litigation, Zero Legal Violations," *Preventive Law Reporter,* 6 (1987):3–8.
44. Kelly G. Shaver, *The Attribution of Blame: Causality, Responsibility and Blameworthiness.* New York: Springer-Verlag, 1985.
45. Charles Walter and Edward P. Richards III, "Corporate Counsel's Role in Risk Minimization: Lessons from Bhopal," *Preventive Law Reporter,* 4 (1986): 139–154.
46. David Cooper, "Responsibility and the 'System.' " In Peter A. French, ed., *Individual and Collective Responsibility: The Massacre at My Lai.* Cambridge, MA: Schenckman, 1972, pp. 81–100.
47. Donaldson, *Corporations and Morality, op. cit.*, p. 125.
48. McDonald, *op. cit.*, pp. 219–220.
49. *Ibid.*
50. Anthony Giddens, *Central Problems in Social Theory: Action, Structure, and Contradiction in Social Analysis.* London: Macmillan, 1979; Giddens, *The Construction of Society: Outline of the Theory of Structuration.* Berkeley: University of California Press, 1984.
51. Larry C. Wilson, "The Doctrines of Wilful Blindness," *University of New Brunswick Law Journal,* 28 (1979):175–194.
52. Held, *op. cit.*, p. 178.
53. Cressey, "Poverty of Theory," *op. cit.*, p. 34.
54. Samuel Bowles and Herbert Gintis, *Democracy and Capitalism.* New York: Basic Books, 1986.
55. John Braithwaite and Gilbert Geis, "On Theory and Action for Corporate Crime Control," *Crime and Delinquency,* 28 (1982):292–314.
56. Thomas C. Schelling, *The Strategy of Conflict.* Cambridge: Harvard University Press, 1960; Anthony Kenny, *The Logic of Deterrence.* Chicago: University of Chicago Press, 1985.
57. Brent Fisse and John Braithwaite, *The Impact of Publicity on Corporate Offenders.* Albany: State University of New York Press, 1983.
58. Cressey, "Poverty of Theory," *op. cit.*, p. 40.
59. Donald R. Cressey, "Restraint of Trade, Recidivism, and Delinquent Neighborhoods." In James F. Short, Jr., *Delinquency. Crime and Society.* Chicago: University of Chicago Press, 1976, pp. 209–234.
60. John Braithwaite, "The State of Criminology: Theoretical Decay or Renaissance?" *Advances in Criminological Theory,* 2 (1990):155–166.

24

A Review, Rebuttal, and Reconciliation of Cressey and Braithwaite & Fisse on Criminological Theory and Corporate Crime

Gilbert Geis

This comment is prompted by the disagreements and intellectual jousting in two contributions published earlier in *Advances in Criminological Theory*. Robert Bursik, reviewing the pair of articles, noted the intellectual excitement he gained from the exchange of ideas and called the debate "academic dialectic at its best." Bursik further observed that additional dialogue between the parties "would have been fascinating and theoretically fertile."[1]

The first entry was by Donald R. Cressey in what apparently was the last piece that he wrote before his death. Cressey argued in his usual forceful and feisty manner that it was impossible to formulate a *social-psychological* (the italics are mine) theory of corporate crime. He ridiculed the tendency of students of white-collar crime to anthropomorphize the corporation. "[C]riminologists," Cressey insisted, "rather routinely, unthinkingly, and erroneously assert that corporations have the psychological capacity to be guilty of crime and to suffer from punishment."[2] Along the way, Cressey passed harsh judgment on what he now regarded as his own earlier sloppy thinking, when he had treated La Cosa Nostra families, prisons, juvenile gangs, and corporations as if they were essentially the same as human beings.

John Braithwaite and Brent Fisse, both Australian scholars, took exception to Cressey's ideas. Braithwaite, trained in sociology and psychology at the University of Queensland, and Fisse, law-educated at the University of Canterbury in New Zealand and at the University of Adelaide, with subsequent work at the University of Pennsylvania law school, argued that "sound scientific theories can be based on a foundation of corporate action and ... some theories of individual action can also

Reprinted from *Advances in Criminological Theory*, 8 (1994), pp. 321–350.

usefully be applied to corporate action."[3] Subsequently, they added the rousing, if
not necessarily accurate, concluding dicta that "[c]riminology will not progress as a
science if its practitioners suffer stultified creativity at the hands of an orthodoxy
that theories of a certain scope are, to use Cressey's word, 'impossible.' "[4]

It is, of course, as Braithwaite and Fisse indicate, intellectually irresponsible to
jettison pursuit of an achievable goal. But it would appear feckless and wasteful to
continue to seek, say, an alchemical formula that transmutes base metals into gold.
The question—the one that occupies this chapter—is whether what Cressey declares
to be impossible is impossible, or whether his judgment is flawed on this matter. Can
a social-psychological theory—or any criminological theory, a distinction about
which Cressey is singularly unclear—be rendered in regard to crime by corporations?

Were he still alive, Cressey very likely would have continued the argument: He
delighted in serious intellectual combat. For their part, the Australian duo might well
have pushed their position further after a Cressey response. Braithwaite, for
instance, has done some of his very best work rebutting the views of scholars such
as Charles Tittle,[5] Ernest van den Haag,[6] and criminologist James Coleman[7] in the
pages of prestigious journals such as the *American Sociological Review,* the *American Journal of Sociology,* and the *Journal of Criminal Law and Criminology.* Fisse
too is a rebutter: he took voluminous exception to a note in the *Harvard Law Review*
on corporate crime[8] and, as is the wont of law professors, he used a judicial opinion,
that in the British case of *Tesco Supermarkets Ltd. v. Nattrass,* which sought to specify the necessary status of the perpetrator as a precursor to the criminal liability of a
corporation, as a launching pad to criticize the court's reasoning.[9]

While fate decreed otherwise regarding the continuation of the interchange on
Cressey's part, it nonetheless seems important not to allow the Cressey and Braithwaite-Fisse discussion to lie fallow. This chapter seeks to tease out and to highlight
the essential points of disagreement between the two contributions, to separate the
polemical rhetoric from the core postulates, and, it is hoped, to offer additional ideas
and some resolutions: in short, to coalesce and advance the debate.

Any reluctance that I might have had about immersing myself in others'
ideational bath water (especially when one party is foreclosed from response) is
somewhat reduced by the fact that I (as well as Diane Vaughan) were kindly
acknowledged as having aided and abetted both contributions. This might be
regarded as testament to involvement in the issues that were debated and, perhaps,
can charitably be interpreted as a certain ecumenical impartiality regarding the merits of the positions taken—though it also could signify equivocation and pusillanim-
ity. Further, in a commentary on the subject of corporate crime theory, I was listed as
one of "[a] few criminologists,[10] and even a few prominent organization theorists[11]
[who] have 'resisted' the organizational level of analysis in favor of a more social
psychological approach." Ironically, in the same piece, Cressey[12] was one of two
writers cited to support the position that "most criminologists . . . agree now that
organizations are real, acting entities in their own right."[13]

I can, in short, lay claim to a deep interest in the subject and a long-standing personal and professional attachment to the writers of the articles, as well as to an abiding belief that the theoretical study of white-collar crime sorely needs further airing of the crucial concerns raised by Cressey and thereafter considered by Braithwaite and Fisse.

ON DONALD R. CRESSEY

It does not seem to be without value to set out, briefly, my understanding of characteristic aspects of Cressey's approach to disputation in order to better appreciate nuances of his position on corporate crime. For one thing, Cressey took pleasure in argument, and—like many of us—he was implacably dogmatic when he felt that he was correct. His tone could be acerbic in debate, but he was likely to be sorely puzzled that an antagonist took personal offense, since what he was saying was obviously true, and he had merely sought to enlighten, not to insult. This trait is illustrated in the piece under consideration by his strong attack on what he regarded as Edwin H. Sutherland's unsatisfactory fumbling about in regard to the theoretical implications of corporate crime. Yet, for Cressey, Sutherland was a deeply respected mentor.

In particular, Sutherland was the progenitor of the criminological theory of differential association,[14] to which Cressey clung with a quixotic fanaticism throughout his scholarly career. Differential association is the only theoretical position to which Cressey adverts in his critique of the thinking of those who, he believes, mindlessly regard organizations as entities susceptible to theoretical comprehension. A continuous argument in Cressey's paper is that the association among corporate executives and the indoctrination of neophytes by corporate old-timers illustrates how individual offenses committed within the corporate compound really should be understood.

This loyalty—or pigheadedness, call it what you will—was a strong core of Cressey's personality. The theory of differential association, to my mind, borders perilously close to tautology, presuming it does not pass over the boundary into that territory. The theory also is wildly ambitious in its interpretative reach. The key concept of differential association is that "the specific direction of motives and drives is learned from definitions of legal codes as favorable or unfavorable." Eliminate "legal" from the formulation and you have a painfully inadequate attempt to posit an explanation for all human behavior. Nigel Walker, however harsh, was quite correct when he observed that differential association (as well as many other criminological theories) "begins with the observation of the obvious, generalizes it into a principle, and is eventually reduced again to a statement of the limited truths from which it originated."[15]

There is irony in the fact that the two most uncompromising critical analyses of differential association come from Sutherland, its originator,[16] and Cressey,[17] who was foremost in keeping the theory alive. In the preface to the sixth edition of *Principles of Criminology* Cressey[18] with characteristic frankness granted that the theory had deep flaws, and that it was "highly probable that it would have to undergo revision." He would not undertake such a reformulation until the wave of testing of the theory, "currently in the period of its greatest popularity," was completed and assessed.[19] Exactly the same disclaimer was entered in the seventh edition, 6 years later,[20] as well as in the eighth,[21] ninth,[22] and the final edition revised by Cressey, the tenth in 1978.[23] So for almost two decades Cressey kept postponing the theory revision that in 1960 he had believed necessary. By the eighth edition of the textbook Cressey had begun to suggest that "if considered as a 'principle' rather than as a 'theory' differential association continues to make good sense of most of the phenomena in the delinquency and crime area."[24]

Cressey also insisted that he retained the theory because it had pedagogic value. This was quite true: Since the ideas were virtually impossible to disprove, the cleverest students, who sensed that differential association had a considerable element of the simple-minded in it, rarely were quite able to determine precisely where it erred. And it certainly forcefully conveyed the sociological party line that human interaction best—indeed, exclusively—accounts for illegal behavior.

The essence of Cressey's loyalty—to people and to ideas—can be conveyed by the story of the sociology department faculty member who was concerned that now that Cressey had been named dean at the University of California at Santa Barbara he would bend over backward to appear fair, to the detriment of his own academic unit. "No," the new dean assured him. "I will make a strong effort to see that sociology gets whatever I can reasonably secure for it. There is no point in having power if you can't use it to help your friends."[25]

CRESSEY'S CREDO ON CORPORATE CRIME

A few highlights from Cressey's article offer both the flavor and the essence of his argument. He notes, for instance, that "[c]riminologists frequently display deep commitment to the notion that fictitious Americans [i.e., corporations], like natural ones, should live up to the legal and ethical obligations inherent in the social covenant."[26] I presume that Cressey is not objecting to this, but merely pointing it out: after all, how could it be regarded as linguistically wayward to demand that Iraq behave decently or that the California Angels come to the rescue of their followers by obtaining a top-notch left-handed relief pitcher? His point (the connections and interpolations are my own, not Cressey's) seems to be that this kind of thinking has a tendency to shade over into unacceptable anthropomorphism when criminological theory is on the table: For Cressey this "is self-defeating because it is based on the erroneous assumption that organizations think and act, thus saddling theoretical criminologists with the impossible task of finding the cause of crimes committed by fictitious persons."[27] Corporations do not behave, he insists; their so-called actions are but manifestations of actions by real persons. "[I]t is time," Cressey argues, "for them [criminologists] to put their common sense to work when confronting reports indicating that a corporation or other organization has committed a crime."[28]

Criminological common sense goes by the boards, according to Cressey, because it is "easy to assume that corporations and other organizations act like humans."[29] The corporation, he points out, is "obviously less than a person. It cannot learn, contemplate, feel guilty, or decide."[30] While it is possible to find meaningful correlations between structural variables, such as corporate financial status, and rates of corporate crime, Cressey grants, it is not possible to go beyond such statistical relationships to statements regarding causation.

Cressey drives home his point with the statement that "there can be no social psychology of so-called corporate or organizational crime because corporations have no biological or psychological characteristics."[31] Two items about this sentence are worth noting: first, that it pulls back on—or perhaps only qualifies—Cressey's earlier statement, quoted previously, that it is impossible to find the "cause" of crimes committed by fictitious persons. Now the unattainable goal is a "social psychological" causal theory of corporate crimes. At another point, Cressey will restate his position a bit differently: "Clearly," he writes, "corporate criminality cannot be explained by the same causal principles used to explain the criminality of real persons."[32] This point, a major one in the Braithwaite and Fisse rebuttal, obviously does not preclude the possibility of different causal theories doing the interpretative job.

The second matter, the use of "so-called" before corporate or organization crime, seems to be something of a rhetorical ploy, more in the nature of derogating the subject of concern than in fairly portraying it. Later in his essay Cressey will say categorically, "Criminologists, like everyone else, must use the only permissible definition of crime, the legal one."[33] He goes on to note, "This means that criminologists must accept the fact that criminal law treats corporations as persons and says that these persons commit crimes.[34] In a later section, I will deal with the juridical concept of "corporate crime," particularly in regard to the theoretical implications of a legal system, such as many on the European continent, that does not criminalize corporate behavior, but only that of individuals.[35] For now, it will do merely to call attention to the polemical tactic. Corporate crime is "so-called" only to the extent that anything that is named is "so-called," like the "so-called" Donald Cressey and the "so-called" theory of differential association.

Much of the remainder of Cressey's article takes on one or another of those theorists who believe that an adequate interpretative theory can concentrate on the corporation as criminal. Particularly hard hit is Sutherland: It seems to Cressey "incredible" that Sutherland did not employ his materials on corporate crime as a backdrop for theoretical discussion of the criminal careers of businessmen, that he did not "formally attribute similarities and consistencies in law violation among corporations to socialization into criminal behavior of new executives by old ones."[36] Cressey also points out that while Sutherland defined white-collar crime as offenses committed by human high-status persons, he conducted his research "on the crimes of fictitious persons called corporations."[37]

Thereafter, toward the end of his article, Cressey plunges into a particularly intriguing issue, that concerned with the possibility of a satisfactory criminological theory for strict liability offenses, those in which persons can be convicted even though they were not aware that a crime was being committed. The argument will get careful consideration later; for now, I merely want to record one paragraph that I found confusing. In it, Cressey writes:

> [I]f a man does not intend his harmful act and if statute holds him strictly liable for the act, then his behavior is not an "illegal act" or an "offense"—at least not a criminal one—because he is not guilty. Obviously, it therefore cannot be an "organizational crime."[38]

In a legal sense, this is nonsense. Perhaps Cressey means that the person is not guilty in the philosophical or theological sense because a wrong has not been done deliberately. As do so many other writers, he adverts to statutory rape to illustrate strict liability and thereby (putting aside the puzzling remark quoted above) ties the idea of strict liability into his theme. "[S]trict liability offenses . . . are not explainable in differential association terms or in any other social psychological framework," Cressey notes.[39] Obviously, if a 25-year-old man has sexual congress with a 14-year-old girl, believing her to be 18, and thereby commits the offense of statutory rape, only a theory that can explain such coital behavior, and not one that interprets criminal acts, will be in order. With this material, Cressey shrewdly ties together two points, that of the problem of strict liability offenses with his more arguable discourse on the futility of theorizing socially psychologically about corporate lawbreaking:

> It is just as ridiculous for criminologists to try to explain criminal behavior that was not intended as it is for judges to try to determine whether a fictitious person has an evil state of mind. Because corporations cannot intend actions, none of their criminality can be explained in the framework of behavioral theory. It is time for criminologists to eradicate this embarrassment by acknowledging that corporation crimes and organizational crimes are phantom phenomena.[40]

Finally, in the only bow to those who might desire to know what ground rules Cressey would advocate for criminological theorists if his strictures are adopted, he rather abruptly closes his article with a quote from Michael Levi: "[A]dequate theorizing must mediate organizational norms through individual actors who make decisions."[41]

THE CRESSEY INTERROGATORIES

The contribution by Cressey on the prospects for theory regarding corporate crime raises directly the following questions:

1. Is it possible to construct a social psychological theory of corporate crime?
2. Is it possible to formulate any kind of criminological theory of corporate crime?

3. Can any theory of criminality be rendered that incorporates offenses of strict liability and/or those in which the violator had no criminal intent?

In addition, a number of other interesting questions suggest themselves:

1. If a corporation cannot be prosecuted criminally (as in many continental jurisdictions) what ramifications does this have for theories of corporate crime?
2. What, if anything, can be learned from natural science theories, such as that of gravity, in which no human action is involved, except perhaps that of whatever-whoever created the conditions that make gravity work?
3. What might we learn from situations such as the practice of deodand, which involved the criminal prosecution and forfeiture of animals as well as of inanimate objects that caused death or damage?
4. Is there a reasonable way to interweave into a meaningful criminological theory structural features of the corporate situation with the acts of those who work for the firm and violate the law on its behalf?

ON CORPORATE CRIME

A brief examination of the status in the United States and elsewhere of the legal concept of corporate crime seems important for a considered adjudication of the position of Cressey and that of Braithwaite and Fisse.

Only dim echoes linger today in the jurisprudence of the Anglo-American countries of the once intense debate about whether it is proper to use criminal law to punish a corporation. As one writer notes: "Early decisions in this area evidence a reluctance to convict a corporation of a crime requiring criminal intent, but now it is almost unquestioned that an agent's intent, knowledge or willfulness may be imputed to the corporation."[42] The aim, to quote a Canadian court, has been to rein in organizations that are "more powerful and more materially endowed and equipped than are individuals"; therefore, "if allowed to roam unchecked" they are "potentially more dangerous and can inflict greater harm upon the public than can their weaker competitors."[43]

Since the laws of some countries do not allow criminal penalties to be placed against corporate entities, it may be wondered if the absence of such an arrangement would nullify any attempt to posit a theory of corporate crime. If we take as our guideline Cressey's insistence—presumably accepted by Braithwaite and Fisse, though they do not say so—that the dictates of criminal law are the only declarative definition of criminal behavior, then a theory of corporate crime without the statute book existence of such crime would be out of the question. Therefore, it follows that a fundamental ingredient of a theory of corporate crime has in some manner to be tied to the influence of the law on the perpetrator's actions. If precisely the same concatenation of theoretical ingredients explains antitrust compacts whether or not they are illegal, then we may have a theory of interorganizational price-fixing behavior but not a theory of corporate crime, whether indeed we choose to focus on the individuals involved or on the organizations.

Other rationales for including corporate criminal liability in the statutes, beyond the need to check the power of organizations, include the idea—echoed by Braithwaite and Fisse—that there is something significantly different between a corporate body and the aggregation of individuals employed by that organization. Charles Abbott is one of numerous writers who have insisted on this:

> [A]s has often been noted, it follows that a corporation has a personality of its own distinct from the personalities which compose it, a "group personality" different from and greater than its constituent elements in the sense that the whole is greater than the sums of its parts.[44]

That corporations are something more than what Braithwaite and Fisse and many others call "the sum of their parts" seems to me a misguided piece of metaphysics. The argument is carried only by the choice of terms. Sum up the actions and inputs of individuals in an organization and you most certainly will get something other than what that organization stands for. But if you could but know the diverse contributions of each of the participants—the amalgam, not the sum—then it seems to me that you would derive a perfect understanding of the fonts of the corporate behavior and have a good idea of the various responsibilities of the parties. That this feat is hopeless for any large organization is no more surprising or conclusive for theoretical statements than the idea that you cannot dissociate from any individual action the amalgam of causative inputs—the differential associations—that contributed to it.

There is, of course, no question but that people in groups behave differently than people alone. But the concept of the "group mind,"[45] as one overview notes, has now "slipped ignominiously into the history of social psychology, and by its absence ordained the study of the individual as the prime focus of the field."[46] It may be more sensible to impute to the corporate entity what can be an enormously complicated blend of individual contributions, and it may be possible to shorthand the result for theoretical purposes as the corporation's action, but I would argue that this is only a convenient way of carrying out the business of theorizing, a compromise that may be necessary, but one that ought not be advocated on the ground that it more truly represents reality. A deed cannot belong to someone unless it can be properly said to "issue" from his or her "will," the philosopher Francis H. Bradley wrote more than a century ago.[47] I would endorse that statement and insist that corporations, though they may have policies, do not have wills.

There may be many worthwhile reasons for holding a corporation criminally liable. A corporation may be deterrable, in the sense that those individuals who experience the penalization and shaming of their organization will attempt to see that remedies are taken. Had they themselves or other executives been criminally prosecuted, they might have been dismissed or might even have been lauded by their colleagues, like gang members who defied the authorities. Corporations often also provide easier targets for criminal prosecution than individuals, since locating and charging individual executives or workers is likely to be more "arduous"[48] and "burdensome."[49] The greater assets of the corporation also may make it a more appealing financial target than its employees.

Taking issue with a writer who insists that "it would be absurd to say that corporations could act even though all human beings have perished,"[50] Braithwaite and Fisse offer an example to prove otherwise. "If all humankind perished in a nuclear war and preprogrammed missiles of the U.S. Army continued to be launched, why could we not describe their launching as an action of the U.S. Army?"[51] Of course, we could do so, and we might well have done so when humans were on site. But Braithwaite and Fisse are only restating the argument, not adding to its resolution: Is the corporate army responsible for those missiles, or is some human—or combination of humans—who made the decision that they be launched? The missiles were put in position to fire by human will, though that will has perished. Had they fired by mistake, that is, unplanned and unintended, then neither people nor the U.S. Army presumably would be at fault, either in a moral or a criminal sense, unless the mistake had been brought about by recklessness or negligence. We will postpone then for later in these pages the generic issue that needs to be addressed: Does it make a difference for theoretical purposes whether the missile (or some other act) was knowingly launched against the law or whether it was an act about which the law took no prohibitory position?

What we can firmly fix is that (1) there is such a thing as corporate crime and that therefore (2) it is at least a possible territory for criminological theory. I have also, at least to my own satisfaction, rejected the notion that by some process of transmogrification a corporation can become a distinctive acting unit significantly different from those humans who constitute its present (or past) employees. Nonetheless, even if accurate, the previous point is not dispositive in regard to the likelihood of a theory of corporate crime.

BRAITHWAITE AND FISSE ON CORPORATE CRIME

The article by John Braithwaite and Brent Fisse, spurred by Cressey's polemic, is a much more complicated piece of work than that it seeks to rebut. For one thing, the sources are quite different. Like many writers with an extensive oeuvre, the largest number of Cressey's citations are to his own work (9 of the 47 references), with academic lawyers (Jerome Hall, John C. Coffee), sociological criminologists (Sutherland, Marshall Clinard, Diane Vaughan) and a small sprinkling of philosophers and economists pretty well filling out the roster. For Braithwaite and Fisse, the references represent a much more impressive collage of scholarly talent, past and present, and a much wider disciplinary spread: Emile Durkheim, Clifford Geertz, Anthony Giddens, F. A. Hayek, Irving L. Janis, Karl Popper, Thomas C. Schelling, Herbert Simon, and Ludwig Wittgenstein are among those used to buttress their argument.

The differing reference roster in part reflects the variant aims of the articles.

Cressey seems to draw on his own work so heavily partly out of the conceit that tends to mark social scientists, and partly out of the familiarity that brings it to mind when he seeks to reinforce one or another of his points. In addition, he references other writers whom he attacks; Braithwaite and Fisse, for their part, use their references to lend prestigeful support for their adversarial position. On first reading, I had thought that Cressey was relying more on outdated material, but a check showed that the median date of his 47 references was 1980, while it was 1983 for the 51 references in the article published 2 years later by Braithwaite and Fisse.

For Braithwaite and Fisse, "[t]he important question for criminological theory is . . . whether corporations are capable of criminal action and whether they can properly be held responsible."[52] I am uncertain whether this sentence is meant to be interpreted in legal, sociological, or metaphysical terms; nor am I certain which of these frameworks bears on whether the outcome is "proper." "A theory of criminal responsibility," Braithwaite and Fisse then write, "need not and should not depend on the metaphysical status of moral personhood." There is an analogy to buttress this assertion:

> To conceive of corporations as no more than sums of the isolated efforts of individuals would be as foolish as to conceive of the possibility of language without the interactive processes of individuals talking to one another and passing structures of syntax from one generation to another.[53]

I have earlier taken exception to the idea of a corporation as the "sum" of individual actions. Nor do I find that the analogy offered in the second part of the quoted sentence testifies to the accuracy of the first part. No one has ever accused "language" per se of criminal action nor advocated a theory of linguistic crime.

Cressey's position that it is fruitless to seek a theoretical explanation for acts that do not manifest intentionality is met with several different arguments. As an introduction to the issue, Braithwaite and Fisse maintain that the "moral responsibility" of corporations for their actions is related to "social processes" and not to "elusive attributes of personhood."[54] For them corporate intentionality is manifest in a "special kind" of attribute—corporate policy. These ideas are outlined in a key paragraph:

> Yet we know that psychological theories can and do explain behaviors that, instead of being intentional, are negligent or unconscious or a reflex. And if we move from micro to macro levels of explanation, intent as an essential ingredient of social explanation becomes even more suspect.[55]

This is followed by another analogy: "An explanation of the Great Depression is not likely to be found by searching for people who intended it. So we must dismiss out of hand the suggestion that because corporate behavior cannot be intentional, it cannot be explained."[56]

The concluding sentence of the quoted observation, it might be noticed, deals with but part of the Cressey critique. As I understand him, Cressey was not so much concerned with the absence of intentionality in corporate behavior per se, on the ground that corporations are not human beings, but rather with the prosecution of corporations (and persons in corporate and noncorporate settings as well) for behavior that was not intended. He did not believe it was possible to construct a criminological theory of social psychological content (and perhaps no criminological theory whatsoever) in regard to such behavior. I also have trouble with the term *explained* as used by Braithwaite and Fisse. Most things can be explained in one way or another. I do not believe that explanations are theories, nor that matters that can be explained necessarily can be explained theoretically.

The reference to the Great Depression suggests (and my tone here is amiable, not sarcastic) that Braithwaite and Fisse have never met a phenomenon about which some kind of theory could not be constructed. A depression, like pre–Civil War slavery, the 1908 presidential election, and militant feminism are not acts proscribed by law but rather developments. Whether they can indeed reasonably be interpreted by theories, and, if so, whether this demonstrates in some manner that corporate crimes also can be embraced by criminological theory depends at a minimum on some understanding of what we mean by the concept "theory." Then we should be in a better position to adjudicate what I take to be the key advocacy point in the Braithwaite-Fisse paper: "Social theory and legal theory," they write, "are . . . forced to stake out positions between individualism and holism. The task is to explore how wholes are created out of purposive individual action, and how individual action is constituted and constrained by the structural realities of wholes."[57] Meanwhile, it should be noted that the word *purposive* in the foregoing quotation conflicts with Braithwaite and Fisse's assertion that absence of intentionality in behavior is no barrier to satisfactory theorizing.

To close this section with an issue more directly related to crime than the Great Depression (though there was crime enough involved in it), take the ancient criminal doctrine of deodand, under the terms of which animals and inanimate objects, such as trees, that were deemed to cause death or harm were forfeit to the sovereign. Whether the owner of the object had been at fault was beside the point. Deodand (the word is from the Latin deodandum, meaning "that is to be given to God") was not abolished until 1846.[58] Consider the illustration offered by Oliver Wendell Holmes, Jr.:

> The old books say that, if a man falls from a ship and is drowned, the motion of the ship must be taken to be the cause of death and the ship is forfeited— provided, however, that this happens in fresh water. For if the death took place on the high seas, that was outside the ordinary jurisdiction.[59]

Will any possible criminological theory help us much to comprehend and predict this lawbreaking? Even in the extraordinarily unlikely event that we may puzzle our way to such a formulation, how do we satisfactorily differentiate the drowning in fresh water from that on the high seas? Would Cressey be safe in declaring that an enterprise seeking to incorporate such statutory proscription into a criminological theory was "impossible"?

ON CRIMINOLOGICAL AND OTHER THEORIES

There should be no disagreement that it is essential to try, however inexpertly we may do so, to organize ideas and information into theoretical statements in order to achieve better understanding, to perceive meaningful regularities, and to be able to predict on the basis of such theoretical constructs the likely outcomes of matters of concern.[60] It is not necessary, however, to have a theoretical understanding of the root of matters such as corporate crime in order to deal with it: As pragmatists point out, quinine was employed as a treatment for malaria for centuries before physicians came to appreciate the crucial causal role of the anopheles mosquito in transmitting the disease. Nor does the fact that a phenomenon is denominated and dealt with by the courts, as corporate crime is, prove that there can be a theoretical explanation for it.

The matter of causation as it relates to theory seems to be an unspoken point of dispute between the Cressey and the Braithwaite-Fisse contributions. Theories always imply causality: If the conditions they set forth prevail (all other things remaining equal), then a certain result will ensue.

The question that rarely is addressed directly in criminological theorizing is the level of predictive accuracy required for a theory to be satisfactory. Alfred Lindesmith's theory of analytical induction, used by Cressey in his study of embezzlers,[61] provided that any discovered empirical exception demanded revision of the theory. What then happened was that the theory came to dictate the definition of the subject and in the process semantic maneuvers substituted for definitional integrity. I remember a public interchange I had with Lindesmith in the early 1950s in which I argued against his theory that a "drug addict" was a person who had made the cognitive connection between withdrawal pangs and the absence of the drug.[62] I wanted to know how the theory took account of people who had made such a connection but no longer used drugs. Lindesmith insisted that they were still drug addicts, just as, he said, the adolescent who has intercourse and makes the connection between his physical pleasure and coitus thereafter becomes "addicted to sex," even if he remains abstinent. Lindesmith was an esteemed savant; he swept the laughing audience, appreciative of the earthy illustration, along with him. Half a century later, I still think analytical induction is a frail excuse for a behavioral theory, and that it was doomed to failure because of its implacable refusal to allow any exceptions.

Few persons today insist that a single exception to a criminological theory defeats it totally. The rule that prevails in behavioral science seems to be that any set of propositions that interprets and predicts more of the condition of concern than other precepts will for the moment rule the theoretical roost. Social science theory commonly falls far short of perfect alignment between stipulated precedent factors and an invariant outcome, but in a good causal postulation, the gaps and irregularities are susceptible to empirical inquiry dictated by the theoretical statement. "What we call a cause typically is, and is recognized as being, only a partial cause," John Mackie has noted; but the proposed cause, he further observes, has to be something that makes the difference.[63]

John Stuart Mill suggested that instead of cause we ought to substitute the term *condition.* In a well-known dictum, Mill noted: "Nothing can better show the absence of any scientific ground for the distinction between the cause of a phenomenon and its conditions than the capricious manner in which we select among the conditions that which we denominate the cause." Mill suggests that many conditions play into the production of a phenomenon and that interpreters often select as "the cause" the one that best fits with their personal or political preferences. [64]

Our general understanding is that we have pinpointed a cause if the occurrence of A led to the occurrence of B and that if A had not occurred B would not have happened. In addition to the time sequencing, we use the term cause only when we have some idea of why the occurrence of A leads to the occurrence of B.[65] Philosophical analyses of the meaning of cause pose many intricate problems. Persons of the stature of David Hume, Bertrand Russell, and Karl Popper have been writing on the subject for hundreds of years. Yet in a contemporary survey of "The Concept of Cause" we find the following conclusion: "The epistemology of causation . . . is at present in a . . . state of near chaos. . . . We are far from satisfied with our treatment of it here and find in it no completely satisfying resolution of the major problems of causality."[66]

If there is to be an acceptable theory of corporate crime, it must show how such crime is the product of particular conditions and particular processes. Once these matters are in place, then the criminal acts should be susceptible to accurate prediction. Given the astonishing blindness of all political and organizational theorists about the sudden dismantling of communist regimes in the Soviet Union, Eastern Europe, and East Germany, we may appreciate that the insight and foresight available in the area of organizational behavior seem to be relatively crude. But perhaps they are adequate to predict less cataclysmic consequences such as corporate crime; if so, it seems to me incumbent upon those so proclaiming to demonstrate this point, and before the events as well as retrospectively.

The quest for a theory of corporate crime, if such a theory is possible, clearly is a worthwhile endeavor. A sophisticated theory can organize an enormous amount of isolated information into coherent and impressively informative shapes. Consider, for instance, the theory of gravity, which is able to provide a single explanation for such varied knowledge as the movement of tides, the erect posture of trees, and the difficulty of writing on the ceiling with a ballpoint pen.[67] A primitive person or a child might say that a stone dropped because it "wanted to." A profound thinker in Aristotle's time probably would have said that the stone dropped because it had the property of gravity. But after Newton propounded his theory, we could declare that the stone dropped because it existed in a field of forces of which the most relevant were the mass of the stone, the earth's gravitation pull, and the relative insubstantiality of the intervening medium, in this case air.[68] The theory of gravity allows understanding of the extraordinary demands upon the human body, when standing erect, for blood circulation and explains why some quadrupeds not adapted to the upright position may be killed simply by suspending them vertically.[69]

"The supreme goal of all theory," Albert Einstein has written, "is to make the irreducible basic elements as simple and as few as possible without having to surrender the adequate representation of a single datum of experience."[70] Einstein accomplished that feat of parsimonious explanation for the phenomenon of relativity by representing its essential traits in his $e = mc^2$ formula. It seems impossible that any form of crime ever will be able to be conceptualized in so elegant a manner; but it must be remembered that even for physical phenomena theories are never a precisely accurate statement of exactly what occurs: "Causal hypotheses," as Mario Bunge has noted, "are no more (and no less) than rough, approximate, one sided reconstructions."[71]

There are two other matters of significance before we enter into our attempted adjudication of the claims of Cressey and those of Braithwaite and Fisse about theories of corporate crime. The first is clarity; the second is criticality. There is a tendency among theorists to employ language in ways that camouflage and distort common understanding. At times, this appears to be an occupational disease, a requirement that theorists believe must be met if they are to be taken seriously.

Second, there is the warning by Richard Feynman, a Nobel Prize physicist, that theorists often become so attached to their views, as Cressey did in regard to differential association, that they develop a defensiveness about them. Feynman pointed out that a good theorist ought to be especially diligent in seeking all possible criticisms of his or her position and subjecting it to the best possible logical scrutiny. He further observes:

Details that could throw doubt upon your interpretation must be given, if you know them. You must do the best you can—if you know anything at all wrong, or possibly wrong—to explain it. If you make a theory, for example, and advertise it, or put it out, then you must also put down all the facts that disagree with it. There is also a more subtle problem. When you have put a lot of ideas together to make an elaborate theory, you want to make sure, when explaining what it fits, that those things it fits are not just the things that gave you the idea for the new theory; but that the finished theory makes something else come out right, in addition.[72]

A famous scientist once observed that nothing is more tragic than the murder of a grand theory by a little fact. But he hastened to add that nothing proved more surprising than the way in which a theory will continue to survive long after its brains have been knocked out.[73] Nevertheless, the pursuit of sound theory, if there can be a sound theory of corporate crime, has very strong appeal. William James has outlined his idea of the character and value of theory in words that also need to be kept in mind as we conclude the present discussion:

Investigators have become accustomed to the notion that no theory is absolutely a transcript of reality but that any one of them may from some point of view be useful. Their great use is to summarize old facts and lead to new ones. They are only a man-made language, a conceptual shorthand. . . . in which we write our reports of nature; and languages, as is well known, tolerate much choice of expression and many dialects.[74]

A major problem with interpreting the disagreements between Cressey's essay and the Australian rejoinder is that neither bothers to define what is meant by *theory* in general or *criminological theory* in particular. It seems likely that they have significantly different views of this matter. Obviously, there is a meaningful gap between the tougher demands on theory by physicists Einstein and Feynman and those softer ones by philosopher-psychologist James. For my part, I prefer the position staked out by Feynman, though I am willing to give a little on explanatory elegance for behavioral science formulations as distinguished from those in theoretical physics.

ON STRICT LIABILITY

There is within both the Cressey and the Braithwaite and Fisse articles a point of direct confrontation that not only is relevant to criminological theories of corporate crime, but also cuts to the core of a vitally important—and almost totally neglected—element of all theories of crime. This is the issue of intentionality. Or, as it arises in diverse other forms, the matter of strict liability, *mens rea,* recklessness, knowledge, culpability, willfulness, negligence, and ignorance of the law.

Cressey had pointed out, as we noted, that the only acceptable definition of a crime is that it is an act that violates the criminal law. Later, he observed that many corporate crimes are strict liability offenses; in fact, he seems to believe—quite incorrectly—that all corporate crimes are strict liability violations. Cressey notes that other crimes, such as statutory rape, also allow no excuse beyond the traditional ones such as mental illness and duress. He concludes that there can be no criminological theory seeking to interpret an act that was not intended. In regard to corporate crime theory, this dictate has two components: First, since corporations do not think and cannot legitimately form a criminal intent, their acts cannot be covered by theories of crime; and second, more generally, that when corporate offenses involve strict liability, they fall outside the possible scope of criminological theory. Cressey undoubtedly would have agreed with the judgment of philosopher John Ladd: "For corporations as such cannot be morally culpable, although criminal sanctions may be brought against them to make their conduct socially acceptable."[75] To think otherwise, Ladd maintains, "lends bogus moral support to a conception of corporate decision-making as autonomous and independent of the personal and collective responsibility of managers, stockholders, customers at large, who in the end are the persons responsible for the untoward consequences of corporate undertakings, past, present, and future."[76]

Braithwaite and Fisse dismiss this point with the observation that psychologists have no trouble theorizing (they do not say how satisfactory they regard such efforts) about unconscious, negligent, or reflex acts; presumably, they are arguing therefore that they find no reason to doubt that an adequate criminological theory can be forthcoming to bear upon strict liability offenses, either of the corporate or the individual variety. I do not agree with them. Courts assuredly may convict persons who do not possess knowledge of the law: as the title of a recent law review article noted: "Ignorance Is Not Bliss: Responsible Corporate Officers Convicted of Environmental Crimes . . ."[77] But such criminal convictions are largely a matter of public policy, not of behavior, either human or corporate. As the leading case on strict liability put it:

Balancing relative hardships, Congress has preferred to place it upon those who have at least the opportunity of informing themselves of the existence of conditions imposed for the protection of consumers before sharing in illicit commerce, rather than to throw the hazard on the innocent public who are wholly helpless.[78]

There is sometimes a slight tinge of the idea in court interpretations of strict liability that "responsible corporate officials" (the term usually employed in the decisions) might with greater attention to duty have headed off the criminal offense. If there was indeed willful ignorance ("a conscious purpose to avoid learning the truth" or "deliberate avoidance of positive knowledge,"[79] then such actions conceivably could be embraced by criminological theory. But at the same time, there are criminal convictions for acts in which there is no intentionality in regard to the lawbreaking, where criminal guilt is a function of being the right person in the wrong place at the wrong time. Note, for instance, the words of a recent federal appellate court decision:

A "responsible corporate officer," to be held criminally liable, would not have to "wilfully or negligently" cause a permit violation. Instead, the wilfulness or negligence of the actor would be imputed to him by virtue of his position of responsibility.[80]

I find it difficult to believe that criminological theory can account very satisfactorily for the lawbreaking of corporate officials who did not know what was going on through no act or omission on their own part. The same seems true of a corporation held criminally liable for acts that nobody was aware were against the law. But how about a corporation held responsible for illegal acts committed by a manager whose behavior is not known to others—say, one who offers bribes to overseas purchasers and camouflages the expenditures by inventive accounting procedures? One might in such a case talk about the corporate ethos, or the inadequate oversight procedures, or the poor screening of employees, but it seems to me very doubtful that these themes or others like them are going to offer strong explanatory theses or be powerful predictors. On the other hand, focusing exclusively on the lawbreaking of the manager without appreciating the organizational and business traditions in which it occurred is to be blind to powerful impellents to the criminal act. But it remains the manager who engaged in the bribery, not the corporation.

If the foregoing points are well-taken, then any criminological theory, such as that of Michael Gottfredson and Travis Hirschi, which claims to embrace not only criminal acts but also a variety of perfectly legal "deviant" behaviors,[81] forfeits in large measure, if not totally, the right to be called a theory of crime. This is so because if crime is a violation of the law, then some awareness of the law should constitute, it seems to me, an essential ingredient of a sophisticated criminological theory.

Let's take an example. Suppose the legislature makes it a crime, beginning next January, to ride a motorcycle without a helmet. Prior to January we may have theoretical statements that seek to explain the behavior, or the class of behaviors, that involve riding a motorcycle unhelmeted. Those same models will suffice for cyclists who continue to go unprotected during January because they have not become aware of the new requirement. But a different explanation, I believe, however slight, is necessary for the person who knows about the law and now violates it. That last explanation would be satisfactorily criminological; the earlier one would not, even though presumably it would explain why the behavior was carried out that had, unbeknownst to its perpetrator, been defined as a criminal act. My reservation about denominating the latter explanation as acceptable criminologically therefore is that it will fail to distinguish decently between those who alter their behavior when they learn of the new law and those who ignore its dictates. Whether the explanation reaches a level to deserve the appellation of theory is, of course, a different issue.

I therefore remain unpersuaded that a *criminological* theory that explains criminal behavior without reference to the law—or to the perpetrator's awareness of the law—is either possible or, if possible, is particularly useful, though I remain willing to be shown otherwise. The difficulty I have in moving the foregoing conclusion beyond a tentative judgment inheres in an understanding that awareness of the law, as an offense ingredient, is a yes-no issue jurisprudentially: One either did or did not form a culpable intent. In actual fact, though, such awareness falls along a continuum. Sometimes, as in Dostoyevski's *Crime and Punishment,* the moral guilt (would such guilt be different for homicide if there were no law against it?) seems particularly pronounced and the legal concern very secondary. In other instances, the law's commands seem to be the major ingredient in violations; note, for example, the care that the antitrust violators in the heavy electrical equipment case took to avoid apprehension by enforcement agents.[82]

PENULTIMATE POINTS

There is some discordance between the Cressey contribution and that of Braithwaite and Fisse in terms of the issues they confront directly. Cressey's piece is a rather monochromatic call for abandonment of what he regards as absurd attempts to pretend for the purposes of social-psychological theories of crime that corporations are individuals. The words *social psychology* are not to be found in the response by Braithwaite and Fisse. They do not say so, but they might well have asked what basis Cressey has for suggesting—or declaring—that criminological theory must be social-psychological. On the other hand, Cressey's is a particularly clever bit of argumentative sleight-of-hand since he defined the problem in such a manner—criminological theory must be social-psychological—that had they tried to rebut him on his own grounds Braithwaite and Fisse were doomed to failure—or so I believe. Corporations, as nonhumans, do not possess psychological faculties. To anthropomorphize them—as so many writers do—and to pretend that the actions of individuals within the corporation can be regarded as part of the psychological process of the corporate entity seems to me unconvincing.

In their rebuttal essay, Braithwaite and Fisse grant that they find it difficult to see how some theories of individual offending, such as biological theories about the relation between intelligence, impulsiveness, or race and crime might fruitfully be applied to corporations. It is important to notice here—it is particularly germane to the debate with Cressey—what qualities ideas need to possess to reach the level of "theory" in the minds of Braithwaite and Fisse. Linkages may be established between biology, impulsiveness, intelligence and similar kinds of human attributes and criminal behavior but I would be hard-pressed to grant to such weak kinds of correlations the (for me) exalted status of theories.

Braithwaite and Fisse also declare in passing that existing individualistic theories of crime can be employed to help to explain corporate crime. "Rational-choice, learning, subcultural, and opportunity theories," they note, "doubtless do not exhaust the possibilities for theories that may apply to criminal action by both individual and collective entities."[83] Braithwaite had expanded on this thesis in an earlier paper in which he derived from extant theories hypotheses that appertain to corporate crime.[84] The strongest case is that adapted from Merton's opportunity theory.[85] Braithwaite, appropriating one of its tenets, notes that organizations break the law because they are set certain important goals that they must achieve. Thereafter, two "propositions of a theory of organizational crime" are set forth:

1. Organizational crime is more likely to occur when an organization (or an organizational subunit) suffers major blockages of legitimate opportunities to achieve its goals.
2. Organizational crime is more likely to occur when illegitimate opportunities for achieving the organization's goals are available to organizational actors.[86]

These seem to me to be worthwhile principles, but what I find analytically important is that they are not truly derivative from theories of corporate crime but rather emerge from a theory of individual crime that has a powerful organizational component within it—that is, the stress on material achievement in American society as it triggers human adaptations to its introjection.

Entering the lion's den, Braithwaite also offers eight lines suggesting the relevance of differential association—he calls it a "principle"—to a theory of organizational crime. "The challenge for a theory of organizational crime," he writes, "is to give greater specificity of content to the social conditions in which the stake in compliance will predominate and to the social conditions which tip the balance to a stake in noncompliance."[89] Braithwaite then seeks to demonstrate the value of his ideas about shaming as the catalyst that will allow the congealing of the postulates of differential association into a satisfactory theoretical position.[88] To pursue that discussion lies beyond the bounds of this chapter: my only observation would be that if differential association is tautological in regard to people, transferring it to organizations will not serve to remedy that fatal flaw.

An extended effort by Henry Finney and Henry Lesieur to formulate a theory of corporate crime indicates the problems involved between declaring this a possibility and putting together the promised theoretical statement. Finney and Lesieur maintain that white-collar offenses such as price-fixing, product safety violations, and falsification of product test data "cannot be understood without adopting an organizational level of analysis,"[89] and that such an analysis "can enhance understanding of conflicts between the interests of individual and organization."[90] Then, after maintaining that organizations "do" things such as manufacture products and negotiate contracts, they declare that therefore organizations *can* (their emphasis) commit crimes, a point, of course, that nobody would challenge. "Biologically, of course," Finney and Lesieur write, "only individuals can enact the plans and dictates of organizations; but they do so as its agents, for its sake, to achieve its objectives and according to its constraints."[91] In essence, then, "[o]rganizations harness private energies for organizational purposes, causing them to lose their strictly private and individual nature."[92] They call in the end for the identification of "organizational processes by which organizational requisites and individual values are harmonized,"[93] and offer an extraordinarily complex model of how these matters might be addressed. To be taken into account, among numerous other things, are the conduciveness to crime of the surrounding culture, the internal and external sources of performance pressure, internal social controls, and the societal reactions to organizational crime.

Toward the end of their piece, however, Finney and Lesieur grant that their treatment of organizational crime is a "theory" (their quotation marks) mainly in the sense of "providing a broad paradigm or model for subsequent empirical research. We have tried to draw a map based on earlier piecemeal observations," they write, "others must now test its usefulness."[94]

It has been pointed out by Albert Reiss that there is an organizational matrix for most deviant conduct.[95] This observation also applies, as he noted, to virtually all human behavior. Such behavior reflects the family, the school, the nation, the workplace, and the host of other organized influences that bear upon any social being. Kip Schlegel and David Weisburd have applied Reiss's observation directly to the subject that concerns us:

[I]n white-collar crime the problem of organization most clearly manifests itself. We believe that this fact offers an opportunity for white-collar crime scholars to take a lead in developing and understanding the role of organization in crime. . . . There is no reason why our insights into organization in white-collar crime should not play a role in developing organizational theory for the study of crime generally. Understanding white-collar crime is not enough. We must look at the centrality of organization in white-collar crime as an opportunity for explicating the role of organizations in structuring and facilitating the myriad forms of criminal conduct.[96]

But there is trouble out there. That trouble is captured in the words of Meir Dan-Cohen, who notes about organizational studies that "[t]he field does not even contain a number of competing theories: hardly any of the various statements, research projects, and hypotheses in this field has attained the level of generality or rigor, nor does any of them enjoy the degree of scientific consensus that would merit the appellation 'theory' in any but the most rudimentary sense."[97] If so, the wedding of primitive organizational "theory" with extant criminological theory does not appear to hold out a particularly exalted prospect, which is not to say that it does not have a future.

It seems to me that while Braithwaite and Fisse lose the argument on the possibility of a social-psychological theory of corporate crime, they are correct in their emphasis, if not in all the details of that emphasis, on the need to integrate theoretical ideas about organizations into the mainstream of criminological theorizing. The insight from Reiss and the extended earlier quotation from Schlegel and Weisburd contain for me the essential requirement, long neglected, (and virtually ignored by Gottfredson and Hirschi in their recent stab at a grand theory of all crime) that the superordinate context in which criminal offenses occur should be theoretically integrated into formulations that seek to explain crime. This often is done ex cathedra; as noted, Merton's classic statement that the thrust for fiscal success is a powerful factor in the press to deviance is a perfect illustration of such a compound that could be tested by determining the consequences of other kinds of social emphases and the accompanying organizational crime rates.

For the moment at least (though I believe this will always be true), it seems preferable that theories concentrate on seeking to explain relatively homogeneous criminal behaviors. This is a view offered elsewhere by Braithwaite for occupational crime though not for corporate offenses:

While useful theories of white collar crime have proved elusive, influential corporate or organizational crime theory is a possibility. Occupational crime is a much less homogeneous category [than corporate crime]—employees who offend against employers engage in a very different activity from doctors who rip off patients. General theories of occupational crime might be as difficult as theories of white collar crime. Progress here might be confined to studies of specific types of occupational crime.[98]

I do not find corporate crime nearly as homogenous as Braithwaite apparently does. There are, I believe, theoretically distinctive differences between such things as failure to meet occupational safety and health standards, for example, and antitrust violations as well as between sexual discrimination and the illegal marketing of flammable products.

CONCLUSION

The debate between Donald Cressey and the team of John Braithwaite and Brent Fisse, to my mind, deservedly has been characterized as "academic dialectic at its best."[99] Both contributions deal with complicated and extremely important issues, and both show skilled debaters with agile and sophisticated minds enmeshed in a serious jousting match.

At times, the contributions talk around issues rather than confront them directly. But probably to a greater extent than I have they both largely avoid a major occupational tactic of academic discourse, described by a psychiatrist who claimed he was a master at it: "In this writing," Allen Wheelis notes, "I elliptically assumed as obvious that which was impossible to prove, while proving at length and in detail that which was obvious—a technique for which I claim no credit, it having already been brought to a state of near perfection by some of my colleagues." [100]

To my mind Cressey clearly is correct in his assertion that it is not possible to formulate a social-psychological theory of corporate crime, except by the grossest kind of anthropomorphic thinking. But his victory truly was in place before he galloped into combat; it is a definitional triumph in a semantic sortie and, in my judgment and in terms of issues raised by Braithwaite and Fisse, it is a triumph in a minor skirmish in a much larger and much more significant intellectual encounter.

In terms of that encounter, I am persuaded that in theory there might be postulates about corporate crime that connect various attributes of organizations to various illegal consequences. I find Braithwaite and Fisse particularly on target in their advocacy of the blending of structural matters with human criminal behavior; and in this regard they move constructively forward from Cressey's clarion call which, at its heart, demands retreat with no room for regrouping.[101]

Serendipitously, both contributions brushed against and on occasion tried to resolve by fiat a consideration that I found notably intriguing. This was the matter of strict liability where there is a total absence of intentionality. Can criminological theory cope with this situation? I doubt it; but the issue having been raised (for the first time in any detail as far as I know), I leave it for others for further consideration.

It would be satisfying to be able to say, at the end of this review, that careful analysis showed one contribution to be right on target and the other ill-advised: or, better yet, that I have been able to construct on the basis of the errors in both a new and intellectually exciting approach to deal with the theoretical issues concerned with corporate crime. Neither outcome eventuated. I think that the authors made very important intellectual points and that in many regards both articles were correct. Cressey was correct when he stressed that there is altogether too much of a tendency to treat corporate entities as if they were human beings, that we must constantly be aware that corporations cannot act, that their actions are those of people. To my mind, he was also correct in his declaration that it is not possible to formulate a criminological theory of corporate wrongdoing that is grounded in social psychology. Conditions of corporate existence—such as the press for profits or a piratical corporate ethos—may serve as background that persuades or presses individuals to take certain illegal actions—but those actions are taken by people not by the corporations, however much the actions may be said to be in their name.

For their part, Braithwaite and Fisse move well beyond Cressey's important contribution. In a much more wide-sweeping and eclectic approach, they argue, correctly, that to abandon a focus on the corporation as an essential factor in what the law declares to be corporate crime is to blind oneself to basic elements in that form of lawbreaking.

Notes

1. Robert J. Bursik, Jr., Book Review, *Contemporary Sociology,* 20 (1991):594.
2. Donald R. Cressey, "The Poverty of Theory in Corporate Crime Research," *Advances in Criminological Theory,* 1 (1988):31–56.
3. John Braithwaite and Brent Fisse, "On the Plausibility of Corporate Crime Theory," *Advances in Criminological Theory,* 2 (1990):17.
4. *Ibid.,* p. 35.
5. John Braithwaite, "The Myth of Social Class and Criminality," *American Sociological Review,* 46 (1981):36–57.
6. John Braithwaite, "Reply to Dr. Ernest van den Haag," *Journal of Criminal Law and Criminology,* 73 (1982):790–793.
7. John Braithwaite, "White-Collar Crime, Competition, and Capitalism: Comment on Coleman," *American Journal of Sociology,* 94 (1988):628–632.
8. Brent Fisse, "Reconstructing Corporate Criminal Law: Deterrence, Retribution, Fault, and Sanctions," *Southern California Law Review,* 56 (1983): 1141–1246.
9. Brent Fisse, "Consumer Protection and Corporate Criminal Responsibility: A Critique of *Tesco Supermarkets Ltd v. Nattras." Adelaide Law Review,* 4 (1971):113–129.
10. Herbert A. Bloch and Gilbert Geis, *Man, Crime, and Society.* New York: Random House, 1962, p. 306.
11. James G. March and Herbert A. Simon, *Organizations.* New York: Wiley, 1958.
12. Donald R. Cressey, "Restraint of Trade, Recidivism, and Delinquent Neighborhoods." In James F. Short, Jr., ed., *Delinquency, Crime, and Society.* Chicago: University of Chicago Press, 1976, pp. 209–234.

13. Henry C. Finney and Henry R. Lesieur, "A Contingency Theory of Organizational Crime." In Samuel B. Bacharach, ed., *Research in the Sociology of Organizations,* vol. 1. Greenwich, CT: JAI Press, 1982, pp. 255–299.

14. Edwin H. Sutherland and Donald R. Cressey, *Criminology.* 10th ed. Philadelphia: Lippincott, 1978.

15. Nigel Walker, *Crime and Punishment in Britain.* Edinburgh: Edinburgh University Press, 1965, p. 95.

16. Edwin H. Sutherland, "Critique of the Theory." In Albert Cohen, Alfred Lindesmith, and Karl Schuessler, eds., *The Sutherland Papers.* Bloomington: Indiana University Press, 1956, pp. 30–41.

17. Donald R. Cressey, "Epidemiology and Individual Conduct: A Case from Criminology," *Pacific Sociological Review,* 3 (1960):47–58.

18. Edwin H. Sutherland and Donald R. Cressey, *Principles of Criminology.* 6th ed. Philadelphia: Lippincott, 1960, p. vi.

19. *Ibid.*

20. Sutherland and Cressey, *ibid.,* 7th ed., 1966, p. vii.

21. *Ibid., Criminology,* 8th ed., 1970, p. vii.

22. *Ibid.,* 9th. ed., 1974, pp. vi–vii.

23. *Ibid.,* 10th ed., 1978, pp. vii–viii.

24. *Ibid.,* 8th ed., 1970, p. vii.

25. See further Paul Colomy, "Donald R. Cressey: A Personal and Intellectual Remembrance," *Crime and Delinquency,* 34 (1988):242–262; Ronald L. Akers, "Donald R. Cressey: An Intellectual Portrait of a Criminologist," *Sociological Inquiry,* 59 (1989):423–438.

26. Cressey, "Poverty of Theory," *op. cit.,* p. 32.

27. *Ibid.,* p. 32.

28. *Ibid.,* p. 35.

29. *Ibid.,* p. 33.

30. *Ibid.,* p. 34.

31. *Ibid.,* p. 37.

32. *Ibid.*

33. *Ibid.,* p. 49.

34. *Ibid.*

35. Gerhard O. W. Mueller, *"Mens Rea* and the Corporation," *University of Pittsburgh Law Review,* 19 (1957):21–50.

36. Cressey, "Poverty of Theory," *op. cit.,* p. 45.

37. *Ibid.,* p. 45.

38. *Ibid.,* p. 46.

39. *Ibid.,* p. 48.

40. *Ibid.*

41. *Ibid.,* p. 49; Michael Levi, "A Criminological and Sociological Approach to Theories of and Research into Economic Crime." In Dan Magnusson, ed., *Economic Crime: Programs for Future Research.* Stockholm: National Council for Crime Prevention, 1985, pp. 32–72.

42. Bruce Coleman, "Is Corporate Criminal Liability Really Necessary?" *Southwestern Law Journal,* 29 (1975):908–927.

43. *Regina v. St. Lawrence Corp. Ltd.* 3 C.C.C. 263; 1 O.R. 305, 1969.

44. Charles G. Abbott, *The Rise of the Business Corporation.* Ann Arbor: Edwards Brothers, 1936, p. 2.

45. William McDougall, *The Group Mind, a Sketch of the Principles of Collective Psychology.* New York: Putnam's, 1920.

46. Daniel M. Wegner, Toni Giuliano, and Paula T. Hertel, "Cognitive Interdependence in Close Relationships." In William J. Ickes, ed., *Compatible and Incompatible Relationships.* New York: Springer-Verlag, 1985, pp. 253–271.

47. Francis H. Bradley, *Ethical Studies.* London: H. S. King, 1876, p. 31.

48. Richard M. Carter, "Federal Enforcement of Individual and Corporate Criminal Liability for Water Pollution," *Memphis State University Law Review,* 19 (1981):594.

49. Stephen A. Saltzburg, "The Criminal Control of Corporate Conduct in Organizations," *Boston University Law Review,* 7 (1991):425.

50. Larry May, "Vicarious Agency and Corporate Responsibility," *Philosophical Studies,* 43 (1983):79–80.

51. Braithwaite and Fisse, *op. cit.,* p. 21.

52. *Ibid.,* p. 18.

53. *Ibid.,* p. 21.

54. *Ibid.,* p. 24.

55. *Ibid.,* p. 26.

56. *Ibid.*

57. *Ibid.,* p. 24.

58. Harold Potter, *An Historical Introduction to English Law and Institutions.* London: Sweet & Maxwell, 1932, p. 31.

59. Oliver Wendell Holmes, Jr., *The Common Law.* Boston: Little, Brown, 1881, p. 26.

60. Sections of this discussion have been adopted from Arnold Binder, Gilbert Geis, and Dickson Bruce, *Juvenile Delinquency: Historical. Cultural, Legal Perspectives.* New York: Macmillan, 1988.

61. Donald R. Cressey, *Other People's Money: The Social Psychology of Embezzlement.* New York: The Free Press, 1953.

62. Alfred R. Lindesmith, *Opiate Addiction.* Bloomington, IN: Principia Press, 1947.

63. John L. Mackie, *The Cement of the Universe: A Survey of Causation.* Oxford: Clarendon Press, 1980, p. xi.

64. John Stuart Mill, *A System of Logic.* London: Longmans, Green, 1843, p. 215.

65. Arnold Binder and Gilbert Geis, *Methods of Research in Criminology and Criminal Justice.* New York: McGraw-Hill, 1983, p. 214.

66. Thomas D. Cook and Donald T. Campbell, *Quasi-Experimentation: Design and Analysis Issues for Field Settings.* Chicago: Rand-McNally, 1979, p. 10.

67. Travis Hirschi, "Procedural Rules and the Study of Deviant Behavior," *Social Problems,* 21 (1973):165.
68. Richard Nisbett and Lee Ross, *Human Inference: Strategies and Shortcomings of Human Judgment.* Englewood Cliffs, NJ: Prentice-Hall, 1980, p. 205.
69. George L. Engel, *Fainting.* 2d ed. Springfield, IL: Thomas, 1962, p. 28.
70. Albert Einstein, *On the Method of Theoretical Physics.* New York: Oxford University Press, 1933, pp. 10–11.
71. Mario Bunge, *Causality: The Place of Causal Principles in Modern Science.* Cambridge: Harvard University Press, 1959, pp. 337–338.
72. Richard Feynman, *Surely You're Joking, Mr. Feynman: Adventures of a Curious Character.* New York: W. W. Norton, 1985, p. 341.
73. Helen Thomas, *Felix Frankfurter: Scholar on the Bench.* Baltimore: Johns Hopkins University Press, 1960.
74. William James, *Pragmatism: A New Name for Some Old Ways of Thinking.* New York: Longmans, Green, 1907, pp. 55–58.
75. John Ladd, "Persons and Responsibility: Ethical Concepts and Impertinent Analyses." In Hugh Curtler, ed., *Shame, Responsibility and the Corporation.* New York: Haven, 1986, p. 93.
76. *Ibid.,* p. 93.
77. Lisa Ann Harig, "Ignorance Is Not Bliss: Responsible Corporate Officers Convicted of Environmental Crimes," *Duke Law Journal,* 42 (1992): 145–165.
78. *United States v. Dotterweich.* 320 U.S. 277 (1943).
79. Robin Charlow, "Wilful Ignorance and Criminal Culpability," *Texas Law Review,* 70 (1992):1371.
80. *United States v. Brittain,* 931 F.2d 1413 (10th Cir. 1991).
81. Michael R. Gottfredson and Travis Hirschi, *A General Theory of Crime.* Stanford: Stanford University Press, 1990.
82. Gilbert Geis, "The Heavy Electrical Equipment Antitrust Cases of 1961." In Marshall B. Clinard and Richard Quinney, eds., *Criminal Behavior Systems: A Typology.* New York: Holt, Rinehart & Winston, 1967, pp. 139–150.
83. Braithwaite and Fisse, *op. cit.,* p. 35.
84. John Braithwaite, "Criminological Theory and Organizational Crime," *Justice Quarterly,* 6 (1989a):333–358.
85. Robert K. Merton, *Social Theory and Social Structure.* New York: The Free Press, 1957.
86. Braithwaite, "Criminological Theory," *op. cit.,* p. 338.
87. *Ibid.,* pp. 339–340.
88. *Ibid.* See John Braithwaite, *Crime, Shame and Reintegration.* Sydney: Cambridge University Press, 1989.
89. Finney and Lesieur, *op. cit.,* p. 256.
90. *Ibid.,* p. 259.
91. *Ibid.,* p. 264.
92. *Ibid.*

93. *Ibid.*, p. 275.
94. *Ibid.*, p. 288.
95. Albert J. Reiss, Jr., "The Study of Deviant Behavior: Where the Action Is," *Ohio Valley Sociologist,* 32 (1966):60–66.
96. Kip Schlegel and David Weisburd, eds., *White-Collar Crime Reconsidered.* Boston: Northeastern University Press, 1992, p. 362.
97. Meir Dan-Cohen, *Rights, Persons, and Organizations: A Legal Theory for Bureaucratic Society.* Berkeley: University of California Press, 1986, p. 31.
98. Braithwaite, "White Collar Crime," *op. cit.,* p. 19.
99. Bursik, *op. cit.,* p. 594.
100. Allen Wheelis, *The Seeker.* New York: Signet, 1960, p. 82.
101. See also Diane Vaughan, "The Macro-Micro Connection in White-Collar Crime Theory." In Schlegel and Weisburd, *op. cit.,* pp. 124–145.

Selected Bibliography

The most comprehensive listing of material written on the subject of white-collar crime from 1900 until the date of its publication appears in Hildegard Liebl and Karl-hans Liebl, eds., *International Bibliography of Economic Crime* (Pfaffenweiler: Centaurus-Verlagsgessellschaft, 1985). In the bibliography below only a selection of relevant materials is listed. Computer searches will be useful to discover additional publications concerning specific forms of white-collar crime. In addition, the *American Criminal Law Review* annually publishes a survey of new legal developments in the area of white-collar crime. The most recent editions are cited in this bibliography.

Addison III, Frederick W., and Mack, Elizabeth E. 1991. "Creating an Environmental Ethic in Corporate America: The Big Stick of Jail Time." *Southwestern Law Journal* 44:1427–48.

Akers, Ronald L. 1985. "White-Collar Crime: Crime in Business, Occupations, and Professions." In *Deviant Behavior: A Social Learning Approach,* pp. 227–47. 3d ed. Belmont, CA: Wadsworth.

Albanese, Jay S. 1984. "Corporate Criminology: Explaining Deviance of Business and Political Organizations." *Journal of Criminal Justice* 12:11–19.

_____. 1987. *Organizational Offenders: Understanding Corporate Crime.* Niagara Falls, NY: Apocalypse.

_____. 1992. "What Lockheed and La Cosa Nostra Have in Common: The Effect of Ideology on Criminal Justice Policy." *Crime and Delinquency* 28:211–32.

Albrecht, W. Steve; Howe, Keith R.; and Romney, Marshall B. 1984. *Deterring Fraud: The Internal Auditor's Perspective.* Altamonte Springs, FL: Institute of Internal Auditors Research Foundation.

Arkin, Stanley S. 1985. *Business Crime: The Criminal Liability of the Business Community.* New York: Matthew Bender.

Aubert, Vilhelm. 1952. "White-Collar Crime and Social Structure." *American Journal of Sociology* 58:263–71.

Ayres, Ian, and Braithwaite, John. 1992. *Responsive Regulation: Transcending the Deregulation Debate.* New York: Oxford University Press.

477

Ayres, Kenneth A., Jr., and Frank, James. 1987. "Deciding to Prosecute White-Collar Crime: A National Survey of State Attorneys General." *Justice Quarterly* 4:425–40.

Baker, Donald I. 1978. "To Indict or Not to Indict: Prosecutorial Discretion in Sherman Act Enforcement." *Cornell Law Review* 63:405–18.

Ball, Harry V. 1960. "Social Structure and Rent-Control Violations." *American Journal of Sociology* 65:598–604.

Ball, Harry V., and Friedman, Lawrence M. 1965. "The Use of Criminal Sanctions in the Enforcement of Economic Legislation: A Sociological View." *Stanford Law Review* 17:197–223.

Barnett, Harold C. 1981. "Corporate Capitalism, Corporate Crime." *Crime and Delinquency* 27:4–23.

_____. 1994. *Toxic Debris and the Superfund Dilemma.* Chapel Hill: University of North Carolina Press.

Bastow, Thomas F. 1986. *"This Vast Pollution . . .": United States of America v. Reserve Mining Company.* Washington, DC: Green Fields Books.

Baucas, Melissa S. 1989. "Why Firms Do It and What Happens to Them: A Reexamination of the Theory of Illegal Corporate Behavior." In James E. Post, ed., *Research in Corporate Social Performance and Policy,* vol. 11, pp. 93–118. Greenwich, CT: JAI Press.

Baucas, Melissa S., and Near, Janet P. 1991. "Can Illegal Corporate Behavior Be Predicted? An Event History Analysis." *Academy of Management Journal* 44:9–36.

Benson, Michael L. 1985. "Denying the Guilty Mind: Accounting for Involvement in a White-Collar Crime." *Criminology* 23:583–608.

_____. 1984. "The Fall from Grace: Loss of Occupational Status as a Consequence of Conviction for a White-Collar Crime." *Criminology* 22:573–93.

_____. 1989. "The Influence of Class Position on the Formal and Informal Sanctioning of White-Collar Offenders." *Sociological Quarterly* 30:465–79.

_____. 1985. "White Collar Offenders Under Community Supervision." *Justice Quarterly* 2:429–38.

Benson, Michael L., and Cullen, Francis T. 1988. "The Special Sensitivity of White-Collar Offenders to Prison: A Critique and Research Agenda." *Journal of Criminal Justice* 16:207–15.

Benson, Michael L.; Cullen, Francis T.; and Maakestad, William J. 1990. "Local Prosecutors and Corporate Crime." *Crime and Delinquency* 36:356–72.

Benson, Michael L.; Maakestad, William J.; Cullen, Francis T.; and Geis, Gilbert. 1988. "District Attorneys and Corporate Crime: Surveying the Prosecutorial Gatekeepers." *Criminology* 26:505–18.

Benson, Michael L., and Moore, Elizabeth. 1992. "Are White-Collar and Common Offenders the Same? An Empirical and Theoretical Critique of a Recently Proposed General Theory of Crime." *Journal of Research in Crime and Delinquency* 29:251–72.

Benson, Michael L., and Walker, Esteban. 1988. "Sentencing the White-Collar Offender." *American Sociological Review* 53:294–302.

Bequai, August. 1978. *White-Collar Crime: A 20th-Century Crisis.* Lexington, MA: Lexington Books.

Bernard, Thomas J. 1984. "The Historical Development of Corporate Criminal Liability." *Criminology* 22:3–17.

Biglaiser, Gary, and Horowitz, John K. 1993. "Pollution, Public Disclosure, and Firm Behavior." *Journal of Regulatory Economics* 5:303–15.

Blankenship, Michael B., ed. 1993. *Understanding Corporate Criminality.* New York: Garland.
Frank P. Williams III and Marilyn D. McShane, "Foreword" (ix–x); Michael B. Blankenship, "Understanding Corporate Criminality: Challenges and Issues" (xi–xxiii); Gilbert Geis, "The Evolution of the Study of Corporate Crime" (3–28); Stephen E. Brown and Chau-Pu-Chiang, "Defining Corporate Crime: A Critique of Traditional Parameters" (29–58); B. Grant Stitt and David J. Giacopassi, "Assessing Victimization from Corporate Harms" (57–84); T. David Evans, Francis T. Cullen, and Paula J. Dubeck, "Public Perception of Corporate Crime" (85–114); Sally S. Simpson, Anthony K. Harris, and Brian A. Mattson, "Measuring Corporate Crime" (115–40); Neil Shover and Kevin M. Bryant, "Theoretical Explanations of Corporate Crime" (141–76); Laureen Snider, "Regulating Corporate Behavior" (177–210); Barbara A. Belbot, "Corporate Criminal Liability" (211–38); Colin Goff, "Sanctioning Corporate Criminals" (239–62).

Block, Michael K.; Nold, Frederick C.; and Sidak, Joseph G. 1981. "The Deterrent Effect of Antitrust Enforcement." *Journal of Political Economy* 89:429–45.

Blum-West, Steve, and Carter, Timothy J. 1983. "Bringing White-Collar Crimes Back In: An Examination of Crimes and Torts. *Social Problems* 30:545–54.

Blumberg, Paul. 1989. *The Predatory Society: Deception in the American Marketplace.* New York: Oxford University Press.

Bologna, Jack. 1984. *Corporate Fraud: The Basics of Prevention and Detection.* Boston: Butterworth.

_____. 1993. *Handbook on Corporate Fraud: Protection, Detection, and Investigation.* Boston: Butterworth-Heinemann.

Bologna, Jack, and Lindquist, Robert J. 1987. *Fraud Auditing and Forensic Accounting.* New York: Wiley.

Bologna, Jack; Linquist, Robert J.; and Wells, Joseph T. 1993. *The Accountant's Handbook of Fraud and Commercial Crime.* New York: Wiley.

Boss, Maria S., and George, Barbara C. 1992. "Challenge and Conventional Rules of White-Collar Crime." *Criminal Law Bulletin* 28 (January–February):32–58.

Box, Steven. 1983. *Power, Crime, and Mystification*. London: Tavistock.

Braithwaite, John. 1982. "Challenging Just Deserts: Punishing White-Collar Criminals." *Journal of Criminal Law and Criminology* 73:723–63.

_____. 1984. *Corporate Crime in the Pharmaceutical Industry*. London: Routledge & Kegan Paul.

_____. 1985. "Corporate Crime Research: Why Two Interviewers Are Needed." *Sociology* 19:136–38.

_____. 1989. "Criminological Theory and Organizational Crime." *Justice Quarterly* 6:338–58.

_____. 1981–82. "The Limits of Economism in Controlling Harmful Corporate Conduct." *Law and Society Review* 16:481–504.

_____. 1987. "Negotiation versus Litigation: Industry Regulation in Great Britain and the United States." *American Bar Foundation Research Journal* 2:559–74.

_____. 1985. *To Punish or Persuade: The Enforcement of Coal Mine Legislation*. Albany: State University of New York Press.

_____. 1979. "Transnational Corporations and Corruption: Toward Some International Solutions." *International Journal of the Sociology of Law* 7:125–42.

_____. 1989. "White-Collar Crime, Competition, and Capitalism: Comment on Coleman." *American Journal of Sociology* 94:628–32.

Braithwaite, John, and Fisse, Brent. 1987. "Self-Regulation and the Control of Corporate Crime." In Clifford D. Shearing and Philip C. Stenning, eds., *Private Policing*, pp. 221–46. Newbury Park: Sage.

_____. 1985. "Varieties of Responsibility and Organizational Crime." *Law and Policy* 7:315–43.

Braithwaite, John, and Geis, Gilbert. 1982. "On Theory and Action for Corporate Crime Control." *Crime and Delinquency* 28:292–314.

Braithwaite, John, and Makkai, Toni. 1991. "Testing an Expected Utility Model of Corporate Deterrence." *Law and Society Review* 25:7–39.

Braithwaite, John, and Pettit, Paul. 1990. *Not Just Deserts: A Republican Theory of Criminal Justice*. Oxford: Oxford University Press.

Brickey, Kathleen F. 1982. "Corporate Criminal Liability of Corporate Officers for Strict Liability Offenses—Another View." *Vanderbilt Law Review* 35:1337–81.

_____. 1984. *Corporate Criminal Liability: A Treatise on the Criminal Liability of Corporations, Their Officers and Agents*. Chicago: Callaghan.

Bucy, Pamela H. 1991. "Corporate Ethos: A Standard for Imposing Corporate Criminal Liability." *Minnesota Law Review* 75:1095–1184.

_____. 1989. "Fraud by Fright: White Collar Crime by Health Care Providers." *North Carolina Law Review* 67: 855–937.

_____. 1992. "Organizational Sentencing Guidelines: The Cart before the Horse. *Washington University Law Quarterly* 71: 329–55.

_____. 1992. *White Collar Crime: Cases and Materials.* St. Paul: West.

Burk, James. 1985. "The Origins of Federal Securities Regulation: A Case Study in the Social Control of Finance." *Social Forces* 63: 1010–29.

Calavita, Kitty. 1983. "The Demise of the Occupational Safety and Health Administration: A Case Study in Symbolic Action." *Social Problems* 30:437–48.

_____. 1990. "Employer Sanctions Violations: Toward a Dialectical Model of White-Collar Crime." *Law and Society Review* 24:1041–69.

Calavita, Kitty; DiMento, Joseph; Geis, Gilbert; and Forti, Gabrio. 1991. "Dam Disasters and Durkheim: An Analysis of the Theme of Repressive and Restitutive Law." *International Journal of the Sociology of Law* 19:407–426.

Calavita, Kitty, and Pontell, Henry N. 1991. " 'Other People's Money' Revisited: Collective Embezzlement in the Savings and Loan and Insurance Industries." *Social Problems* 38: 94–112.

_____. 1993. "Savings and Loan Fraud as Organized Crime: Toward a Conceptual Typology of Corporate Illegality." *Criminology* 31:519–548.

Caldwell, Robert G. 1958. "A Re-Examination of the Concept of White-Collar Crime." *Federal Probation* 22 (March):30–36.

Carson, W. G. 1982. *The Other Price of Britain's Oil: Safety and Control in the North Sea.* New Brunswick, NJ: Rutgers University Press.

_____. 1970. "White-Collar Crime and the Enforcement of Factory Legislation." *British Journal of Criminology* 10:383–398.

Cavender, Gray; Jurik, Nancy C.; and Cohen, Albert K. 1993. "The Baffling Case of the Smoking Gun: The Social Ecology of Political Accounts of the Iran-Contra Affair." *Social Problems* 40:152–66.

Chambliss, William J. 1967. "Types of Deviance and the Effectiveness of Legal Sanctions." *Wisconsin Law Review* 1967:703–19.

Chilson, Francis. 1973. "Corporate Ethics and White-Collar Crime." *Drug and Cosmetic Industry Journal* 113:89–90.

Clark, John P., and Hollinger, Richard. 1977. "On the Feasibility of Empirical Studies of White-Collar Crime." In Robert F. Meier, ed., *Theory in Criminology: Contemporary Views,* pp. 129–58. Beverly Hills: Sage.

Clarke, Michael J. 1990. *Business Crime: Its Nature and Control.* New York: St. Martin's Press.

_____. 1987. "Prosecutorial and Administrative Strategies to Control Business

Crimes: Private and Public Roles." In Clifford D. Shearing and Philip C. Stenning, eds., *Private Policing*, pp. 266–92. Newbury Park, CA: Sage.

_____. 1978. "White-Collar Crime, Occupational Crime, and Legitimacy." *International Journal of Criminology and Penology* 6:121–36.

Claybrook, Joan. 1986. "White-Collar Crime: Corporate Misconduct Is More Abusive Than Street Crime," *Trial* 22 (April):32.

Clinard, Marshall B. 1952. *The Black Market: A Study of White-Collar Crime.* New York: Holt, Rinehart & Winston.

_____. 1990. *Corporate Corruption: The Abuse of Power.* New York: Praeger.

_____. 1983. *Corporate Ethics and Crime: The Role of Middle Management.* Beverly Hills: Sage.

_____. 1946. "Criminological Theories of Violations of Wartime Regulations." *American Sociological Review* 11:258–70.

_____. 1968. "White-Collar Crime." *International Encyclopedia of the Social Sciences,* pp. 483–90. New York: Macmillan.

_____, and Quinney, Richard. 1973. *Criminal Behavior Systems: A Typology.* 2d ed. New York: Holt, Rinehart & Winston.

Clinard, Marshall, and Yeager, Peter. 1980. *Corporate Crime.* New York: The Free Press.

_____. 1978. "Corporate Crime: Issues in Research." *Criminology* 16:255–72.

Clinard, Marshall; Yeager, Peter; Brissette, Jeane; Petrashek, David; and Harris, Elizabeth. 1979. *Illegal Corporate Behavior.* Washington, DC: Government Printing Office.

Coffee, John C., Jr. 1977. "Beyond the Shut-Eyed Sentry: Toward a Theoretical View of Corporate Misconduct and an Effective Legal Response." *Virginia Law Review* 63:1099–1278.

_____. 1980. "Corporate Crime and Punishment: A Non-Chicago View of the Economics of Criminal Sanctions." *American Criminal Law Review* 17:419–76.

_____. 1983. "Corporate Criminal Responsibility." In Sanford H. Kadish, ed., *Encyclopedia of Crime and Justice,* vol. 1, pp. 253–64. New York: The Free Press.

_____. 1980. "Making the Punishment Fit the Corporation: The Problem of Finding an Optimal Corporation Criminal Sanction." *Northern Illinois University Law Review* 1:3–36.

_____. 1983. "The Metassis of Mail Fraud: The Continuing Story of the 'Evolution' of a White-Collar Crime." *American Criminal Law Review* 21:1–28.

_____. 1981. " 'No Soul to Damn: No Body to Kick': An Unscandalized Inquiry into the Problem of Corporate Punishment." *Michigan Law Review* 79: 386–459.

Coffee, John C., Jr.; Gruner, Richard; and Stone, Christopher D. 1988. "Standards for Organizational Probation: A Proposal to the United States Sentencing Commission." *Whittier Law Review* 10: 77–102.

Cohen, Albert K. 1977. "The Concept of Criminal Organization." *British Journal of Criminology* 17: 97–111.

_____. 1990. "Criminal Actors—Natural Persons and Collectivities. In School of Justice Studies, Arizona State University, *New Directions in the Study of Justice, Law and Social Control,* pp. 101–25. New York: Plenum Press.

Cohen, Albert K.; Ho, Chih-Chin; Jones, Edward D. III; and Schleich, Laura M. 1988. "Organizations as Defendants in Federal Courts: A Preliminary Analysis of Prosecutions, Convictions, and Sanctions, 1984–1987. *Whittier Law Review* 10:103–23.

Cohen, Albert K.; Lindesmith, Alfred; and Schuessler, Karl, eds. 1956. *The Sutherland Papers.* Bloomington: Indiana University Press.

Cohen, Mark A. 1989. "Corporate Crime and Punishment: A Study of Social Harm and Sentencing Practices in the Federal Courts, 1984–1987." *American Criminal Law Review* 26:605–61.

_____. 1992. "Environmental Crime and Punishment: Legal/Economic Theory and Empirical Evidence on Enforcement of Federal Environmental Statutes." *Journal of Criminal Law and Criminology* 82:1054–1108.

Coleman, Bruce. 1975. "Is Corporate Criminal Liability Really Necessary?" *Southwestern Law Journal* 29:908–27.

Coleman, James William. 1994. *The Criminal Elite: The Sociology of White-Collar Crime.* 3d ed. New York: St. Martin's Press.

_____. 1985. "Law and Power: The Sherman Antitrust Act and Its Enforcement in the Petroleum Industry." *Social Problems* 32:264–74.

_____. 1991. "Respectable Crime." In Joseph F. Sheley, ed., *Criminology: A Contemporary Handbook,* pp. 219–39. Belmont, CA: Wadsworth.

Collins, Judith M., and Schmidt, Frank L. 1993. "Personality, Integrity, and White-Collar Crime: A Construct Validity Study." *Personnel Psychology* 46:295–311.

Comer, Michael J. 1977. *Corporate Fraud.* New York: McGraw-Hill.

Conklin, John E. 1977. *"Illegal But Not Criminal": Business Crime in America.* Englewood Cliffs, NJ: Prentice-Hall. *Communication Monographs,* August 1976.

Conyers, John, Jr. 1980. "Corporate and White-Collar Crime: A View by the Chairman of the House Subcommittee on Crime." *American Criminal Law Review* 17:287–300.

"Corporate and Organizational Crime." 1982. *Michigan Law Review* 80:1377–1528. Diane Vaughan, "Toward Understanding Unlawful Organizational Behavior" (1377–1402); Stanton Wheeler and Mitchell L. Rothman, "The Organization as a

Weapon in White-Collar Crime"(1403–26); Ilene H. Nagel and John L. Hagan, "The Sentencing of White-Collar Criminals in Federal Courts: A Socio-Legal Explanation of Disparity"(1427–65); John Braithwaite, "Enforced Self-Regulation: A New Strategy for Corporate Crime Control"(1466–1507); Leonard M. Leigh, "The Criminal Liability of Corporations and Other Groups: A Comparative View"(1508–28).

Cowan, Andrew. 1992. "Scarlet Letters for Corporations? Punishment by Publicity under the New Sentencing Guidelines." *Southern California Law Review* 65:2387–2420.

Cressey, Donald R. 1961. "Foreword." In Edwin H. Sutherland, *White Collar Crime*, pp. iii–xii. New York: Holt, Rinehart & Winston.

_____. 1953. *Other People's Money: The Social Psychology of Embezzlement.* New York: The Free Press.

_____. 1976. "Restraint of Trade, Recidivism, and Delinquent Neighborhoods." In James F. Short, Jr., ed., *Delinquency, Crime, and Society,* pp. 209–34. Chicago: University of Chicago Press.

_____. 1986. "Why Managers Commit Fraud." *Australian and New Zealand Journal of Criminology* 19:195–209.

Croall, Hazel. 1992. *White Collar Crime: Criminal Justice and Criminology*. Buckingham: Open University Press.

_____. 1989. "Who Is the White-Collar Criminal?" *British Journal of Criminology* 29:157–74.

Crouch, Ben M. 1989. "Mexican Shrimp, Texas Shrimpers, and Maritime Conflict: The Creation of a White-Collar Crime." *Deviant Behavior* 10:211–32.

Cullen, Francis T., and Benson, Michael L. 1993. "White-Collar Crime: Holding a Mirror to the Core." *Journal of Criminal Justice Education* 4:325–47.

Cullen, Francis T.; Clark, Gregory A.; Link, Bruce G.; Mathers, Richard A.; Niedospial, Jennifer Lee; and Sheahan, Michael. 1985. "Dissecting White-Collar Crime: Offense Type and Punitiveness." *International Journal of Comparative and Applied Criminal Justice* 9:16–28.

Cullen, Francis T., and Dubeck, Paula J. 1985. "The Myth of Corporate Immunity to Deterrence: Ideology and the Creation of the Invincible Criminal." *Federal Probation* 49 (September):3–9.

Cullen, Francis T.; Maakestad, William; and Cavander, Gray. 1987. *Corporate Crime under Attack: The Ford Pinto Case and Beyond.* Cincinnati: Anderson.

Cullen, Francis T.; Mathers, Richard A.; Clark, Gregory A.; and Cullen, John B. 1983. "Public Support for Punishing White-Collar Crime: Blaming the Victim Revisited?" *Journal of Criminal Justice* 11:481–93.

Daly, Kathleen. 1989. "Gender and Varieties of White-Collar Crime." *Criminology* 27:769–93.

Denzin, Norman K. 1977. "Notes on the Criminogenic Hypothesis: A Case Study of the American Liquor Industry." *American Sociological Review* 42:905–20.

Dershowitz, Alan M. 1961. "Increasing Community Control over Corporate Crime." *Yale Law Journal* 71:289–306.

"Developments in the Law—Corporate Crime: Regulating Corporate Behavior through Criminal Sanctions." 1979. *Harvard Law Review* 92:1227–1375.

Dickinson, Peter S. 1989. *Civil Rico: A Research Guide to Civil Liability for Business Crime.* Buffalo, NY: Hein.

DiMento, Joseph F. 1989. "Can Social Science Explain Organizational Noncompliance with Environmental Law?" *Journal of Social Issues* 45:109–32.

_____. 1986. *Environmental Law and American Business: Dilemmas of Compliance.* New York: Plenum.

Doerr, Barbara H. 1985. "Prosecuting Corporate Polluters: The Sparing Use of Criminal Sanctions." *University of Detroit Law Review* 62:659–76.

Doig, Jameson W.; Phillips, Douglas E.; and Manson, Tycho. 1984. "Deterring Illegal Behavior by Officials of Complex Organizations." *Criminal Justice Ethics* 3 (Winter–Spring) 27–56.

Douglas, Jack, and Johnson, John, eds. 1977. *Official Deviance: Readings in Malfeasance, Misfeasance, and Other Forms of Corruption.* Philadelphia: Lippincott.

Easterbook, Frank, and Fischel, Daniel R. 1991. *The Economic Structure of Corporate Law.* Cambridge: Harvard University Press.

Eckert, David. 1980. "Sherman Act Sentencing: An Empirical Study, 1971–1979." *Journal of Criminal Law and Criminology* 71:244–54.

Edelhertz, Herbert. 1970. *The Nature, Impact and Prosecution of White Collar Crime.* Washington, DC: National Institute of Law Enforcement and Criminal Justice.

_____. 1983. "White-Collar and Professional Crime." *American Behavioral Scientist* 27:109–28.

Edelhertz, Herbert, and Overcast, Thomas D., eds. 1982. *White-Collar Crime: An Agenda for Research.* Lexington, MA: Lexington Books.
    Herbert Edelhertz, "Introduction"(1–21); Robert F. Meier and James F. Short, Jr., "The Consequences of White-Collar Crime"(23–49); M. David Ermann and Richard J. Lundman, "Corporate Violations Corrupt Practices Act (51–68); Ezra Stotland, "The Role of Law Enforcement in the Fight against White-Collar Crime"(69–98); John M. Thomas, "The Regulatory Role in the Containment of

Corporate Illegality"(99–127); Simon Dinitz, "Multidisciplinary Approaches to White-Collar Crime"(129–52); Edwin H. Stier, "The Interrelationships among Remedies for White-Collar Criminal Behavior"(153–73); Gilbert Geis, "A Research and Action Agenda with Respect to White-Collar Crime"(175–202).

Edelhertz, Herbert, and Rogovin, Charles, eds. 1980. *A National Strategy for Containing White-Collar Crime.* Lexington, MA: Lexington Books.
Herbert Edelhertz and Charles H. Rogovin, "Symposium Background"(11–18); Mark H. Moore, "Notes toward a National Strategy to Deal with White-Collar Crime"(21–46); Marilyn E. Walsh, "The Institutional Challenge of White-Collar Crime"(47–54); Daniel L. Skoler, "White-Collar Crime and the Criminal-Justice System: Problems and Challenges"(57–76); Mary V. McGuire, "The Criminal–Justice System Challenge of White-Collar Crime"(77–82); William A. Morrill, "Developing a Strategy to Contain White-Collar Crime"(85–94); Frederic A. Morris, "Meeting the Challenge of White-Collar Crime: Evolving a National Strategy"(95–102); Herbert Edelhertz and Charles H. Rogovin, "Implementing a National Strategy"(103–111).

Endres, Michael E. 1979. "Social Responses to White Collar Crime." In Dae H. Chang, *Critical Issues in Criminal Justice,* pp. 95–109. Durham: Carolina Academic Press.

Epstein, Samuel S. 1992. "Corporate Crime: Why We Cannot Trust Industry–Derived Safety Studies." *International Journal of Health Studies* 20:443–458.

Ermann, M. David, and Lundman, Richard J. 1982. *Corporate Deviance.* New York: Holt, Rinehart & Winston.

_____. 1978. "Deviant Acts by Complex Organizations: Deviance and Social Control at the Organizational Level of Analysis." *Sociological Quarterly* 19:55–67.

_____. eds. 1992. *Corporate and Governmental Deviance: Problems of Organizational Behavior in Contemporary Society.* 4th ed. New York: Oxford University Press.

Etzioni, Amitai. 1984. *Capital Corruption: The New Attack on American Democracy.* San Diego: Harcourt Brace Jovanovich.

Etzioni-Halevy, Eva. 1989. "Elite Power, Manipulation and Corruption: A Demo-Elite Perspective." *Government and Opposition* 24:215–31.

Evans, Sandra S., and Lundman, Richard J. 1983. "Newspaper Coverage of Corporate Price-Fixing: A Replication." *Criminology* 21:529–41.

Falk, Richard A.; Kolko, Gabriel; and Lifton, Robert Jay. 1971. *Crimes of War.* New York: Vintage.

Farberman, Harvey A. 1975. "A Criminogenic Market Structure: The Automobile Industry." *Sociological Quarterly* 16:438–57.

Farrell, Ronald A., and Swigert, Victoria L. 1985. "The Corporation in Criminology:

New Directions for Research." *Journal of Research in Crime and Delinquency* 22:83–94.

Finney, Henry C., and Lesieur, Henry R. 1982. "A Contingency Theory of Organizational Crime." In Samuel B. Bacharach, ed., *Research in the Sociology of Organizations,* vol. 1, pp. 255–99. Greenwich, CT: JAI Press.

Fiorelli, Paul E. 1988. "Winking through the Blindfold: What Motivates the White-Collar Criminal?" *Akron Law Review* 21:327–35.

Fisse, Brent. 1982. "Community Service as a Sanction against Corporations." *Wisconsin Law Review* 1982:970–1017.

_____. 1971. "Consumer Protection and Corporate Criminal Responsibility: A Critique of *Tesco Supermarkets Ltd v. Nattrass.*" *Adelaide Law Review* 4:113–29.

_____. 1975. "Responsibility, Prevention and Corporate Crime." *New Zealand University Law Review* 5:250–79.

_____. 1983. "Restructuring Corporate Criminal Law: Deterrence, Retribution, Fault, and Sanctions." *Southern California Law Review* 56:1141–1246.

_____. 1986. "Sanctions against Corporations: Economic Efficiency or Legal Efficacy?" In W. Byron Groves and Graeme Newman, eds., *Punishment and Privilege,* pp. 23–54. Albany, NY: Harrow and Heston.

_____. 1978. "The Social Policy of Corporate Criminal Responsibility." *Adelaide Law Review* 6:361–412.

_____. 1971. "The Use of Publicity as a Criminal Sanction against Business Corporations." *Melbourne University Law Review* 8:107–50.

Fisse, Brent, and Braithwaite, John. 1988. "Accountability and the Control of Corporate Crime: Making the Buck Stop." In Mark Findlay and Russell Hogg, eds., *Understanding Crime and Criminal Justice,* pp. 93–127. Sydney: Law Book Company.

_____. 1988. "The Allocation of Responsibility for Corporate Crime: Individualism, Collectivism and Accountability." *University of Sydney Law Review* 11:469–513.

_____. 1993. *Corporations, Crime, and Accountability.* New York: Cambridge University Press.

_____. 1983. *The Impact of Publicity on Corporate Offenders.* Albany: State University of New York Press.

Fisse, Brent, and French, Peter A., eds. 1985. *Corrigible Corporations & Unruly Law.* San Antonio: Trinity University Press.
Fisse and French, "Overview: The Social Control of Corporate Behavior"(3–12); Christopher D. Stone, "Corporate Regulation: The Place of Social Responsibility"(13–38); John Braithwaite, "Taking Responsibility Seriously: Corporate Compliance Systems"(39–62); Gilbert Geis, "Criminological Perspectives on

Corporate Regulation: A Review of Recent Research"(63–84); Tim DeVos, "Toward More Effective Regulation of Corporate Behavior"(85–100); John Byrne and Steven M. Hoffman, "Efficient Corporate Harm: A Chicago Metaphysic"(101–36); Brent Fisse, "Sanctions against Corporations: The Limitations of Fines and the Enterprise of Creating Alternatives"(137–58); Peter A. French, "Publicity and the Control of Corporate Crime: Hester Prynne's New Image"(159–72); Jed S. Rakoff, "The Exercise of Prosecutorial Discretion in Federal Business Fraud Prosecutions"(173–86); Fisse and French, "Corporate Responses to Errant Behavior: Time's Arrow, Law's Target"(187–215).

Foerschler, Ann. 1990. "Corporate Criminal Intent: Toward a Better Understanding of Corporate Misconduct." *California Law Review* 78:1287–1311.

Frank, James; Cullen Francis T.; Travis, Lawrence F. III; and Borntrager, John. 1989. "Sanctioning Corporate Crime: How Do Business Executives and the Public Compare?" *American Journal of Criminal Justice* 13:139–69.

Frank, Nancy. 1984. "Policing Corporate Crime: A Typology of Enforcement Styles." *Justice Quarterly* 1:235–51.

Frank, Nancy, and Lombness, Michael. 1988. *Controlling Corporate Illegality: The Regulatory Justice System.* Cincinnati: Anderson.

Frank, Nancy, and Lynch, Michael J. 1992. *Corporate Crime, Corporate Violence: A Primer.* Rev. ed. Albany, NY: Harrow and Heston.

Freiberg, Arie. 1992. "Confiscating the Proceeds of White-Collar Crime." In Peter Grabosky, ed., *Complex Commercial Fraud,* pp. 174–88. Canberra: Australian Institute of Criminology.

French, Peter A. 1984. *Collective and Corporate Responsibility.* New York: Columbia University Press.

Freyer, Tony. 1992. *Regulating Big Business: Antitrust in Great Britain and America, 1880–1990.* New York: Cambridge University Press.

Fromm, Eva M. 1990. "Commanding Respect: Criminal Sanctions for Environmental Crimes." *St. Mary's Law Journal* 21:821–64.

Gandossy, Robert. 1985. *Bad Business: The OPM Scandal and the Seduction of the Establishment.* New York: Basic Books.

Gardiner, John A., and Lyman, Theodore R. 1978. *Decisions for Sale: Corruption and Reform in Land-Use and Building Regulation.* New York: Praeger.

_____. 1984. *The Fraud Control Game: State Response to Fraud and Abuse in AFDC and Medicaid Programs.* Bloomington: Indiana University Press.

Geis, Gilbert. 1974. "Avocational Crime." In Daniel Glaser, ed., *Handbook of Criminology,* pp. 273–98. New York: Rand-McNally.

_____. 1972. "Criminal Penalties for Corporate Criminals." *Criminal Law Bulletin* 8:277–92.

_____. 1973. "Deterring Corporate Crime." In Ralph Nader and Mark. J. Green, eds., *Corporate Power in America*, pp. 182–97. New York: Grossman.

_____. 1988. "From Deuteronomy to Deniability: A Historical Perlustration on White-Collar Crime." *Justice Quarterly* 5:7–32.

_____. 1982. *On White-Collar Crime.* Lexington, MA: Lexington Books.

_____. 1962. "Toward a Delineation of White-Collar Offenses." *Sociological Inquiry* 32:160–71.

_____. 1981. "Upperworld Crime." In Abraham S. Blumberg, ed., *Current Perspectives on Criminal Behavior,* pp. 114–37. 2d ed. New York: Knopf.

_____. 1975. "Victimization Patterns in White-Collar Crime." In Israel Drapkin and Emilio Viano, eds., *Victimology: A New Focus,* pp. 89–105, vol. 5. Lexington, MA: Lexington Books.

_____. 1984. "White-Collar and Corporate Crime." In Robert F. Meier, ed., *Major Forms of Crime,* pp. 137–66. Beverly Hills: Sage.

Geis, Gilbert, and Edelhertz, Herbert. 1973. "Criminal Law and Consumer Fraud." *American Criminal Law Review* 11:989–1010.

Geis, Gilbert, and Goff, Colin 1987. "Edwin H. Sutherland's White-Collar Crime in America: An Essay in Historical Criminology." In *Criminal Justice History: An International Annual,* pp. 1–31, vol. 7. Westport, CT: Meckler.

_____. 1982. "Introduction." In Edwin H. Sutherland, *White Collar Crime: The Uncut Version,* pp. ix–xxiii. New Haven: Yale University Press.

Geis, Gilbert, and Jesilow, Paul, eds. 1993. "White-Collar Crime." *Annals of the American Academy of Political and Social Science* 225:8–169.
Editors, "Preface"(8–11); John Braithwaite, "Transnational Regulation of the Pharmaceutical Industry"(12–30); Henry N. Pontell and Kitty Calavita, "White-Collar Crime in the Savings and Loan Scandal"(31–46); Elizabeth Szockyj, "Insider Trading: The SEC Meets Carl Karcher"(46–58); Kip Schlegel, "Crime in the Pits: The Regulation of Futures Tradings"(59–70); Michael Levi, "White-Collar Crime: The British Scene"(71–82); Joseph T. Wells, "Accountancy and White-Collar Crime"(83–94); Gary Green, "White-Collar Crime and the Study of Embezzlement"(95–106); Nancy Frank, "Maiming and Killing: Occupational Health Crimes"(107–18); Harold C. Barnett, "Crimes against the Environment: Superfund Enforcement at Last"(119–33); Joseph F. DiMento, "Criminal Enforcement of Environmental Law"(134–46); Amitai Etzioni, "The U.S. Sentencing Commission on Corporate Crime: A Critique"(147–56); William S. Lofquist, "Organizational Probation and the U.S. Sentencing Commission" (157–69).

Geis, Gilbert; Jesilow, Paul; Pontell, Henry; and O'Brien, Mary Jane. 1985. "Fraud and Abuse of Government Medical Benefit Programs by Psychiatrists." *American Journal of Psychiatry* 142:231–34.

Geis, Gilbert, and Meier, Robert. 1979. "The White-Collar Offender." In Hans Toch, ed., *Psychology of Crime and Criminal Justice,* pp. 427–43. New York: Holt, Rinehart & Winston.

Geis, Gilbert, and Stotland, Ezra, eds. 1980. *White-Collar Crime: Theory and Research.* Beverly Hills: Sage.
Geis and Stotland, "Introduction"(7–13); Laura Shill Schrager and James F. Short, Jr., "How Serious a Crime?: Perceptions of Organizational and Common Crimes"(14–31); Marilyn E. Walsh and Donna Schram, "The Victim of White-Collar Crime: Accuser or Accused?"(32–51); Edward Gross, "Organizational Structure and Organizational Crime"(52–76); Diane Vaughan, "Crime between Organizations: Implications for Victimology"(77–97); Neal Shover, "The Criminalization of Corporate Behavior: Federal Surface Coal Mining"(98–125); Charles E. Reasons and Colin H. Goff, "Corporate Crime: A Cross-National Analysis"(126–41); W. G. Carson, "The Institutionalization of Ambiguity: Early British Factory Acts"(142–73); Michael D. Maltz and Stephen M. Pollock, "Analyzing Suspected Collusion among Bidders"(174–98); Donn B. Parker, "Computer-Related White-Collar Crime" (199–220); James E. Sorenson, Hugh D. Grove, and Thomas L. Sorenson, "Detecting Management Fraud: The Role of the Independent Auditor"(221–51); Ezra Stotland, Michael Brintnall, André L'Heureux, and Eva Ashmore, "Do Convictions Deter Home Repair Fraud?"(252–65); Mary V. McGuire and Herbert Edelhertz, "Consumer Abuse of Older Americans: Victimization and Remedial Action in Two Metropolitan Areas"(266–92); Adam C. Sutton and Ronald Wild, "Investigating Company Fraud: Case Studies from Australia"(293–316).

Gerber, Jurg, and Fritsch, Eric J. 1993. "On the Relationship between White-Collar Crime and Political Sociology: A Suggestion and Resource for Teaching." *Teaching Sociology* 21:130–39.

Gerber, Jurg, and Short, James F., Jr. 1986. "Publicity and the Control of Corporate Behavior: The Case of Infant Formula." *Deviant Behavior* 7:195–216.

Gerber, Jurg, and Weeks, Susan L. 1992. "Women as Victims of Corporate Crime: A Call for Research on a Neglected Topic." *Deviant Behavior* 13:325–47.

Giordano, Peggy C. 1982. "Sanctioning the High-Status Deviant: An Attributional Analysis." *Social Psychology Quarterly* 46:319–42.

Glasbeck, Harry J. 1984. "Why Corporate Deviance Is Not Treated as a Crime: The Need to Make 'Profits' a Dirty Word." *Osgoode Hall Law Journal* 22: 393–439.

Glazer, Myron P., and Glazer, Penina M. 1989. *Whistleblowers: Exposing Corruption in Government and Industry.* New York: Basic Books.

Goff, Colin H., and Nason-Clark, Nancy. 1989. "The Seriousness of Crime in Fredericton, New Brunswick: Perceptions toward White-Collar Crime." *Canadian Journal of Criminology* 31:19–34.

Goff, Colin H., and Reasons, Charles E. 1978. *Corporate Crime in Canada: A Critical Analysis of Anti-Combines Legislation.* Scarborough, Ont.: Prentice-Hall.

Goldsmith, Michael. 1993. "Judicial Immunity for White-Collar Crime: The Ironic Demise of Civil RICO." *Harvard Journal on Legislation* 30:1–41.

Goldstein, Abraham S. 1992. "White Collar Crime and Civil Sanctions." *Yale Law Journal* 101:1895–1900.

Gordon, David M. 1973. "Capitalism, Class and Crime in America." *Crime and Delinquency* 19:163–68.

Gordon, Walter. 1983. "Strict Liability, Upper Class Criminality, and the Model Penal Code." *Howard Law Journal* 26:781–99.

Grabosky, Peter. 1988. "Corporate Crime in Australia: An Agenda for Research." *Australian and New Zealand Journal of Criminology* 17:95–107.

_____. 1990. "Professor Advisers and White Collar Illegality: Towards Explaining and Excusing Professional Failure." *University of New South Wales Law Journal* 13:73–96.

Grabosky, Peter, ed. 1992. *Complex Commercial Fraud.* Canberra: Australian Institute of Criminology.

Grabosky, Peter, and Braithwaite, John. 1986. *Of Manners Gentle: Enforcement Strategies of Australian Business Regulatory Agencies.* Melbourne: Oxford University Press.

Grabosky, Peter; Braithwaite, John; and Wilson, Paul. 1987. "The Myth of Community Tolerance toward White-Collar Crime." *Australian and New Zealand Journal of Criminology* 20:45–53.

Grabosky, Peter, and Sutton, Adam, eds. 1992. *Stains on a White Collar: Fourteen Studies in Corporate Crime or Corporate Harm.* Annandale, NSW: Foundation Press.

Green, Gary. 1985. "General Deterrence and Television Cable Crime: A Field Experiment in Social Control." *Criminology* 23:629–45.

_____. 1990. *Occupational Crime.* Chicago: Nelson Hall.

Green, Mark, and Berry, John F. 1985. *The Challenge of Hidden Profit: Reducing Corporate Bureaucracy and Waste.* New York: Morrow.

Green, Mark; Moore, Beverly C., Jr.; and Wasserstein, Bruce. 1972. *The Closed Enterprise System.* New York: Grossman.

Green, Mark; Waldman, Michael; and Massie, Robert Jr., eds. 1983. *The Big Business Reader.* New York: Pilgrim Press.

Gross, Edward. 1978. "Organizational Crime: A Theoretical Perspective." In Norman Denzin, ed., *Studies in Symbolic Interaction,* pp. 55–85. Greenwich, CT: JAI Press.

Gruner, Richard. 1988. "To Let the Punishment Fit the Organization: Sanctioning Corporate Offenders through Corporate Probation." *American Journal of Criminal Law* 16:1–106.

Gunningham, Neil. 1974. *Pollution, Social Interest, and the Law.* London: Martin Robertson.

Hagan, John. 1982. "The Corporate Advantage: A Study of the Involvement of Corporate and Individual Victims in a Criminal Justice System." *Social Forces* 60: 993–1032.

_____. 1992. "White Collar and Corporate Crime." In Rick Linden, ed., *Criminology: A Canadian Perspective,* pp. 451–73. 2d ed. Toronto: Harcourt Brace Jovanovich.

Hagan, John; Nagel, Ilene H. (Bernstein); and Albonetti, Celesta. 1980. "The Differential Sentencing of White-Collar Offenders in Ten Federal District Courts." *American Sociological Review* 45:802–20.

Hagan, John, and Palloni, Alberto. 1986. " 'Club Fed' and the Sentencing of White-Collar Offenders Before and After Watergate." *Criminology* 24:603–22.

Hagan, John, and Parker, Patricia. 1985. "White-Collar Crime and Punishment: The Class Structure and Legal Sanctioning of Securities Violations." *American Sociological Review* 50:302–15.

Hall, Timothy. 1980. *White-Collar Crime in Australia.* Sydney: Harper & Row.

Hanawalt, Barbara A. 1975. "Fur Collar Crime: The Pattern of Crime among the Fourteenth Century English Nobility." *Journal of Social History* 8:1–17.

Hans, Valerie P., and Ermann, M. David. 1989. "Responses to Corporate versus Individual Wrongdoing." *Law and Human Behavior* 13:151–66.

Harig, Lisa Ann. 1992. "Ignorance Is Not Bliss: Responsible Corporate Officers Convicted of Environmental Crimes and the Federal Sentencing Guidelines." *Duke Law Journal* 42:145–65.

Hartung, Frank E. 1953. "White-Collar Crime: Its Significance for Theory and Practice." *Federal Probation* 17 (June):31–36.

_____. 1950. "White-Collar Offenses in the Wholesale Meat Industry in Detroit." *American Journal of Sociology* 56:25–34.

Hawkins, Keith. 1984. *Environment and Enforcement: Regulation and the Social Definition of Pollution.* Oxford: Oxford University Press.

_____, and Thomas, John M. 1984. *Enforcing Regulation: Policy and Practice.* Boston: Kluwer.

Hay, George A., and Kelly, Daniel. 1974. "An Empirical Study of Price-Fixing Conspiracies," *Journal of Law and Economics* 17:13–38.

Heilbroner, Robert, ed. 1972. *In the Name of Profit.* Garden City, NY: Doubleday.

Henning, Peter J. 1993. "Testing the Limits of Investigating and Prosecuting White Collar Crime: How Far Will the Courts Allow Prosecutors to Go?" *University of Pittsburgh Law Review* 54:465–76.

Hill, Charles W. L.; Kelley, Patricia C.; Agle, Bradley R.; Hitt, Michael A.; and Hoskisson, Robert E. 1992. "An Empirical Examination of the Causes of Corporate Wrongdoing in the United States." *Human Relations* 45:1055–76.

Hills, Stuart L., ed. 1987. *Corporate Violence: Injury and Death for Profit.* Totowa, NJ: Rowman & Littlefield.

Hirschi, Travis, and Gottfredson, Michael. 1989. "The Significance of White-Collar Crime for a General Theory of Crime." *Criminology* 27:359–72.

Hochstedler, Ellen, ed. 1984. *Corporations as Criminals.* Beverly Hills: Sage.
Ronald C. Kramer, "Corporate Criminality: The Development of an Idea" (13–37); Nicolette Parisi, "Theories of Corporate Criminal Liability"(41–68); Brent Fisse, "The Duality of Corporate and Individual Liability"(69–84); Nancy Frank, "Choosing between Criminal and Civil Sanctions for Corporate Wrongs" (85–102); Francis T. Cullen, William J. Maakestad, and Gray Cavender, "The Ford Pinto Case and Beyond: Corporate Crime, Moral Boundaries, and the Criminal Sanction"(107–30); Charles B. Schudson, Ashton P. Onellion, and Ellen Hochstedler, "Nailing an Omelet to the Wall: Prosecuting Nursing Home Homicide"(131–45); John Lynxwiler, Neal Shover, and Donald Clelland, "Determinants of Sanction Severity in a Regulatory Bureaucracy"(147–65).

Holland, Robert C. 1984. "Problems in the Investigation of White-Collar Crime: A Case Study." *International Journal of Comparative and Applied Criminal Justice* 8:21–41.

Hopkins, Andrew. 1984. "Blood Money: The Effect of Bonus Pay on Safety in Coal Mines." *Australian and New Zealand Journal of Sociology* 20:30–40.

_____. 1980. "Controlling Corporate Deviance." *Criminology* 18:198–214.

_____. 1978. *Crime, Law and Business: The Sociological Sources of Australian Monopoly Law.* Canberra: Australian Institute of Criminology.

Horoszowski, Pawel. 1978. *Economic Special-Opportunity Conduct and Crime.* Lexington, MA: Lexington Books.

Humphreys, Steven L. 1990. "An Enemy of the People: Prosecuting the Corporate Polluter as a Common Criminal." *American University Law Review* 39:311–54.

Hutter, Bridget. 1988. *The Reasonable Arm of the Law? The Law Enforcement Procedures of Environmental Health Officers.* Oxford: Clarendon.

Jacoby, Neil; Nehemkis, Peter; and Eells, Richard. 1977. *Bribery and Extortion in World Business: A Study of Corporate Payments Abroad.* New York: Macmillan.

Jenkins, Anne, and Braithwaite, John. 1993. "Profits, Pressure, and Corporate Lawbreaking." *Crime, Law and Social Change* 20:221–32.

Jesilow, Paul. 1982. "Adam Smith and White-Collar Crime." *Criminology* 28:317–28.

Jesilow, Paul; Geis, Gilbert; and O'Brien, Mary Jane. 1986. "Experimental Evidence That Publicity Has No Effect in Suppressing Auto Repair Fraud." *Sociology and Social Research* 70:222–23.

_____. 1985. "'Is My Battery Any Good?': A Field Test of Fraud in the Auto Repair Business." *Journal of Crime and Justice* 16:823–32.

Jesilow, Paul; Geis, Gilbert; and Pontell, Henry. 1991. "Fraud by Physicians against Medicaid." *Journal of the American Medical Association* 266:3318–22.

Jesilow, Paul; Geis, Gilbert; Pontell, Henry; and Song, John Huey-Long. 1992. "Culture Conflict Revisited: Fraud by Vietnamese Physicians in the United States." *International Migration* 30:201–24.

Jesilow, Paul; Pontell, Henry; and Geis, Gilbert. 1985. "Medical Criminals: Physicians and White-Collar Offenses." *Justice Quarterly* 2:149–65.

_____. 1986. "Physician Immunity from Prosecution and Punishment for Medical Benefit Program Fraud." In W. Byron Groves and Graeme Newman, eds., *Punishment and Privilege*, pp. 7–22. Albany, NY: Harrow and Heston.

_____. 1993. *Prescription for Profit: How Doctors Defraud Medicaid.* Berkeley: University of California Press.

Johnson, David T., and Leo, Richard A. 1993. "The Yale White-Collar Crime Project: A Review and Critique." *Law and Social Inquiry* 18:63–99.

Johnson, John M., and Douglas, Jack D. 1978. *Crime at the Top: Deviance in Business and the Professions.* Philadelphia: Lippincott.

Johnson, Kirk A. 1986. "Federal Court Processing of Corporate, White-Collar, and Common Crime Economic Offenders over the Past Three Decades." *Mid-American Review of Sociology* 11:25–44.

Josephson, Matthew. 1934. *The Robber Barons: The Great American Capitalists, 1861–1901.* New York: Harcourt Brace.

Kadish, Sanford H. 1963. "Some Observations on the Use of Criminal Sanctions in Enforcing Economic Regulations." *University of Chicago Law Review* 30: 423–49.

Kagan, Robert A., and Scholz, John T. 1984. "The 'Criminology of the Corporation' and Regulatory Enforcement Strategies." In Keith Hawkins and John M. Thomas, eds., *Enforcing Regulation,* pp. 67–95. Boston: Kluwer-Nijhoff.

Katz, Jack. 1979. "Concerted Ignorance: The Social Construction of Cover-Up." *Urban Life* 8:295–316.

_____. 1977. "Cover-up and Collective Integrity: On the Natural Antagonisms of Authority Internal and External to Organizations." *Social Problems* 25:3–17.

_____. 1979. "Legality and Equality: Plea Bargaining in the Prosecution of White-Collar and Common Crimes." *Law and Society Review* 13:431–59.

_____. 1980. "The Social Movement against White-Collar Crime." In Egon Bittner and Sheldon Messinger, eds., *Criminology Review Yearbook,* vol. 2, pp. 161–84. Beverly Hills: Sage.

Katz, Marsha. 1992. "Criminal Liability for Health and Safety: Executives at Risk." *Labor Law Journal* 43:679–83.

Kauzlarich, David, and Kramer, Ronald C. 1993. "State-Corporate Crime in the US Nuclear Weapons Production Complex." *Journal of Human Justice* 5:4–28.

Keane, Carl. 1993. "The Impact of Financial Performance and Frequency of Corporate Crime: A Latent Variable Test of Strain Theory." *Canadian Journal of Criminology* 23:293–308.

Kellman, Herbert. 1976. "Some Reflections on Authority, Corruption, and Punishment: The Social Psychological Contexts of Watergate." *Psychiatry* 39:303–17.

Kennedy, Christopher. 1985. "Criminal Sentences for Corporations: Alternative Fining Mechanisms." *California Law Review* 73:443–82.

Kerbo, Harold R., and Inoue, Mariko. 1990. "Japanese Social Structure and White-Collar Crime: Recruit Cosmos and Beyond." *Deviant Behavior* 11:139–54.

Kerrigan, Laura J.; Berrettini, Caroline W.; Callahan, Melissa L.; et al. 1993. "The Decriminalization of Administrative Law Penalties—Civil Remedies, Alternatives, Policy, and Constitutional Implications." *Administrative Law Review* 45: 367–434.

Knepper, William E., and Bailey, Dan A. 1989. *Liability of Corporate Officers and Directors.* 4th ed. Charlottesville, VA: Michie.

Kornbluth, Jesse. 1992. *Highly Confident: The Crime and Punishment of Michael Milken.* New York: Morrow.

Kramer, Ronald. 1989. "Criminologists and the Social Movement against Corporate Crime." *Social Justice* 16:146–64.

_____. 1984. "Is Corporate Crime Serious? Criminal Justice and Corporate Crime Control." *Journal of Contemporary Criminal Justice* 2(June):7–10.

_____. 1983. "A Prolegomenon to the Study of Corporate Violence." *Humanity and Society* 7:149–78.

Kriesberg, Simeon M. 1976. "Decisionmaking Models and the Control of Corporate Crime." *Yale Law Journal* 85:1091–1129.

Kruttschnitt, Candace. 1985. "Are Businesses Treated Differently? A Comparison of the Individual Victim and the Corporate Victim in the Criminal Courtroom." *Sociological Inquiry* 55:225–38.

Kurczewski, Jacek, and Frieske, Kazimierz. 1977. "Some Problems in the Legal

Regulation of the Activities of Economic Institutions." *Law and Society Review* 11:489–505.

Laite, William E. 1972. *The United States vs. William Laite.* Washington, DC: Acropolis Books.

Lane, Robert E. 1954. *The Regulation of Businessmen: Social Conditions of Government Economic Control.* New Haven: Yale University Press.

———. 1953. "Why Businessmen Violate the Law." *Journal of Criminal Law, Criminology, and Police Science* 44:151–65.

Lann-Kaduce, Lonn. 1980. "Deviance among Professionals: The Case of Unnecessary Surgery." *Deviant Behavior* 1:333–59.

Lansing, Paul, and Hatfield, Donald. 1985. "Corporate Control through the Criminal System—An Alternative Proposal." *Journal of Business Ethics* 4:409–14.

Lasley, James R. 1988. "Toward a Control Theory of White-Collar Offending." *Journal of Quantitative Criminology* 4:347–62.

Lauderdale, Pat; Grasmick, Harold; and Clark, John P. 1978. "Corporate Environments, Corporate Crime, and Deterrence." In Marvin D. Krohn and Ronald L. Akers, eds., *Crime, Law, and Sanctions,* pp. 78–179. Beverly Hills: Sage.

Laufer, William S. 1992. "Culpability and the Sentencing of Corporations." *Nebraska Law Review,* 71:1049–94.

———. 1994. "Corporate Bodies and Guilty Minds." *Emory Law Journal,* 43:647–730.

Lederman, Eliezer. 1985. "Criminal Law, Perpetrator and Corporation: Rethinking a Complex Triangle." *Journal of Criminal Law and Criminology* 76:285–340.

Leigh, Leonard H. 1982. *The Control of Commercial Fraud.* London: Heinemann.

———. 1969. *The Criminal Liability of Corporations in English Law.* London: Weidenfeld & Nicolson.

———, ed. 1980. *Economic Crime in Europe.* New York: St. Martin's Press.
Carlos Viladas Jense, "Business Crime in Spain"(1–14); Leonard Leigh, "Aspects of Economic Crime in the United Kingdom"(15–38); Klaus Tiedemann, "Antitrust Law and Criminal Law Policy in Europe"(39–56); Michael Levi, "The Sentencing of Long–Firm Frauds"(57–77); Mireille Delmas-Marty, "White-Collar Crime and the EEC"(78–105); Leonard Leigh and Susannah Brown, "Crimes in Bankruptcy"(106–208).

Leonard, William N., and Weber, Marvin G. 1970. "Automakers and Dealers: A Study of Criminogenic Market Forces." *Law and Society Review* 4:407–24.

Levi, Michael. 1987. "Crisis? What Crisis? Reactions to Commercial Fraud in the United Kingdom." *Contemporary Crises* 11:207–21.

———. 1991. "Developments in Business Crime Control in Europe." In Frances

Heidensohn and Martin Farrell, eds., *Crime in Europe,* pp. 172–87. New York: Routledge & Kegan Paul.

_____. 1984. "Giving Creditors the Business: The Criminal Law in Inaction." *International Journal of the Sociology of Law* 12:321–33.

_____. 1981. *Phantom Capitalists: The Organisation and Control of Long-Firm Fraud.* London: Heinemann Educational.

_____. 1987. *Regulating Fraud: White-Collar Crime and the Criminal Process.* London: Tavistock.

_____. 1991. "Sentencing White-Collar Crime in the Dark? Reflections on the Guiness Four." *Howard Journal of Criminal Justice* 30:257–79.

_____. 1992. "Policing the Upper World: Towards The Global Village." In David J. Evans, Nicholas R. Fyfe, and David T. Herbert, eds., *Crime, Policing and Place: Essays in Environmental Criminology,* 217–32. London: Routledge.

Levi, Michael, and Suddle, Mohammed Shoaib. 1989. "White-Collar Crime, Shamelessness, and Disintegration: The Control of Tax Evasion in Pakistan." *Journal of Law and Society* 16:489–505.

Lichtenberger, John. 1991. *Readings in White Collar Crime.* Meckler.

Lieberman, Jethro K. 1972. *How the Government Breaks the Law.* New York: Stein and Day.

Litman, Richard C., and Litman, Donald S. 1981. "Protection of the American Consumer: The Muckrakers and Enforcement of the First Federal Food Drug Law in the United States." *Food Drug Cosmetic Law Journal* 36:647–68.

Lofquist, William S. 1993. "Legislating Organizational Probation: State Capacity, Business Power, and Corporate Crime Control." *Law and Society Review* 27:741–83.

Lott, John R., Jr. 1992. "Do We Punish High Income Criminals Too Heavily?" *Economic Inquiry* 30:583–608.

Lynch, Michael J.; Nalla, Mahesh R.; and Miller, Keith W. 1989. "Cross-Cultural Perspectives on Deviance: The Case of Bhopal." *Journal of Research in Crime and Delinquency* 26:7–35.

Magnuson, Jay C., and Levitan, Gareth C. 1987. "Policy Considerations After *People v. Film Recovery Systems, Inc., Notre Dame Law Review* 62:913–39.

Magnuson, Roger J. 1992. *The White-Collar Crime Explosion: How to Protect Yourself and Your Company from Prosecution.* Minneapolis: Dorsey & Whitney.

Magnusson, Dan, ed. 1985. *Economic Crime: Programs for Future Research.* Stockholm: National Council for Crime Prevention.
Lennart Myhlback, "Address of Welcome to the International Research Conferences on Economic Crime"(7–12); Georges Kellens, "Economic Crime: Some Priorities for Research"(13–31); Michael Levi, "A Criminological and Sociologi-

cal Approach to Theories of and Research into Economic Crime"(32–72); Steinar Strom, "Economic Crime"(73–81); Imre Weiner, "Economic Crime from the Jurisprudential Aspect"(118–29); Knut Sveri, "Economic Crime from a Criminological/Sociological Perspective"(130–37).

Maher, Lisa, and Waring, Elin. 1990. "Beyond Simple Differences: White Collar Crime, Gender and Workforce Position." *Phoebe* (February):44–54.

Makkai, Toni, and Braithwaite, John. 1991. "Criminological Theories and Regulatory Compliance." *Criminology* 29:191–220.

_____. 1993. "Pride and Corporate Compliance." *International Journal of the Sociology of the Law* 21:73–91.

Maltz, Michael. 1975. "Policy Issues in Organized Crime and White-Collar Crime." In John A. Gardner and Michael Mulkey, eds., *Crime and Criminal Justice,* pp. 73–92. Lexington, MA: Lexington Books.

Mann, Kenneth. 1985. *Defending White-Collar Crime: A Portrait of Attorneys at Work.* New Haven: Yale University Press.

Mann, Kenneth; Wheeler, Stanton; and Sarat, Austin. 1980. "Sentencing the White-Collar Offender." *American Criminal Law Review* 17:479–500.

Markovits, Richard S. 1990. "The American Antitrust Law on the Centennial of the Sherman Act: A Critique of the Statutes Themselves, Their Interpretation, and Their Operationalization." *Buffalo Law Review* 38:673–776.

Mason, Robert, and Calvin, Lyle D. 1978. "A Study of Admitted Income-Tax Evasion." *Law and Society Review* 13:73–89.

Mathews, M. Cash. 1988. *Strategic Intervention in Organizations: Resolving Ethical Dilemmas.* Beverly Hills: Sage.

McBarnet, Doreen. 1991. "Whiter than White Collar Crime: Tax, Fraud Insurance, and the Management of Stigma." *British Journal of Sociology* 42:323–44.

McCormick, Albert E. 1977. "Rule Enforcement and Moral Indignation: Some Observations on the Effects of Criminal Antitrust Convictions upon Societal Reaction Processes." *Social Problems* 25:30–39.

McVisk, William. 1978. "Toward a Rational Theory of Criminal Liability for the Corporate Executive." *Journal of Criminal Law and Criminology* 69:75–91.

Meeker, James W.; Dombrink, John; and Pontell, Henry N. 1987. "White-Collar and Organized Crime: Questions of Seriousness and Policy." *Justice Quarterly* 4:73–98.

Meier, Robert F., and Geis, Gilbert. 1982. "The Abuse of Power as a Criminal Activity: Toward an Understanding of the Behavior and Methods for Its Control." In Geis, ed., *On White-Collar Crime,* pp. 85–102. Beverly Hills: Sage.

Meyer, John C. 1972. "An Action-Oriented Approach to the Study of Occupational Crime." *Australian and New Zealand Journal of Criminology* 5:35–48.

Meyer, Peter B. 1981. "Communities as Victims of Corporate Crime." In Burt Galaway and Joe Hudson, eds., *Perspectives on Crime Victims,* pp. 33–43. St. Louis: C. V. Mosby.

Michalowski, Raymond J., and Kramer, Ronald C. 1987. "The Space between the Laws: The Problem of Corporate Crime in Transnational Context." *Social Problems* 34:34–53.

Miller, Emmett H. III. 1993. "Federal Sentencing Guidelines for Organizational Defendants." *Vanderbilt Law Review* 46:198–234.

Miller, Jeremy M. 1991. "White Collar Criminal Liability without Mental Fault in the 1990's." *Commercial Law Journal* 96:353–61.

Mintz, Morton. 1985. *At Any Cost: Corporate Greed, Women, and the Dalkon Shield.* New York: Pantheon.

_____. 1992. "Why the Media Cover Up Corporate Crime." 1992. *Trial* (November):72+.

Mokhiber, Russell. 1988. *Corporate Crime and Violence: Big Business Power and the Abuse of Public Trust.* San Francisco: Sierra Club

Moore, Charles A. 1987. "Taming the Giant Corporations? Some Cautionary Remarks on the Deterrability of Corporate Crime." *Crime and Delinquency* 33:379–402.

Moore, Elizabeth, and Mills, Michael. 1990. "The Neglected Victims and Unexamined Costs of White-Collar Crime." *Crime and Delinquency* 36:408–418.

Moore, Mark H. 1986. *Inspectors-General: Junkyard Dogs or Man's Best Friend?* New York: Russell Sage Foundation.

Mueller, Gerhard O. W. 1957. *"Mens Rea* and the Corporation: A Study of the Model Penal Code Position on Corporate Criminal Liability." *University of Pittsburgh Law Review* 19:21–50.

Nader, Ralph. 1972. *The Big Boys: Portraits of Corporate Power.* New York: Pantheon.

_____. 1965. *Unsafe at Any Speed: The Designed-In Dangers of the American Automobiles.* New York: Grossman.

Nader, Ralph, and Green, Mark. 1972. "Crime in the Suites: Coddling the Corporations." *New Republic,* 166 (April 29):17–21.

Nader, Ralph; Green, Mark; and Seligman, Joel. 1976. *Taming the Giant Corporation.* New York: W. W. Norton.

Naftalis, Gary P., ed. 1980. *White Collar Crimes.* Philadelphia: American Law Institute—American Bar Association.

Nagel, Ilene H., and Swenson, Winthrop M. 1993. "The Federal Sentencing Guidelines for Corporations: Their Development, Theoretical Underpinnings, and

Some Thoughts about their Future." *Washington University Law Quarterly* 71:205–59.

"A National Conference on Sentencing of the Corporation." 1991. *Boston University Law Review* 72:189–453.
    John C. Coffee, Jr., "Does 'Unlawful' Mean 'Criminal'?: Reflections on the Disappearing Tort/Crime Distinction in American Law"(193–246); Mark A. Cohen, "Corporate Crime and Punishment: An Update on Sentencing Practice in the Federal Courts, 1988–1990"(247–80); Jonathan R. Macey, "Agency Theory and the Criminal Liability of Organizations"(315–40); Barry D. Baysinger, "Organization Theory and the Criminal Liability of Organizations"(341–76); Michael K. Block, "Optimal Penalties, Criminal Law and the Control of Corporate Behavior"(395–420); Stephen A. Saltzburg, "The Control of Criminal Conduct in Organizations"(421–38).

Needleman, Martin L., and Needleman, Carolyn. 1979. "Organizational Crime: Two Models of Criminogenesis." *Sociological Quarterly* 20:517–28.

Nelkin, David, ed. 1993. *White Collar Crime.* Aldershot, Hants.: Dartmouth.

Newman, Donald J. 1953. "Public Attitudes toward a Form of White-Collar Crime." *Social Problems* 4:228–32.

_____. 1958. "White-Collar Crime: An Overview and Analysis." *Law and Contemporary Problems* 23:735–53.

Noonan, John T. 1984. *Bribes.* New York: Macmillan.

Note. 1979. "Structural Crime and Institutional Rehabilitation: A New Approach to Corporate Sentencing." *Yale Law Journal* 80:353–75.

Ogren, Robert W. 1973. "The Ineffectiveness of the Criminal Sanction in Fraud and Corruption Cases: Losing the Battle against White-Collar Crime." *American Criminal Law Review* 11:959–88.

Orland, Leonard. 1980. "Reflections on Corporate Crime: Law in Search of Theory and Scholarship." *American Criminal Law Review* 17:501–20.

Packer, Herbert L. 1968. *The Limits of the Criminal Sanction,* pp. 345–63. Stanford, CA: Stanford University Press.

Passas, Nikos. 1990. "Anomie and Corporate Deviance." *Contemporary Crises* 14:157–78.

Pearce, Frank. 1973. "Crime, Corporations, and the American Social Order." In Ian Taylor and Laurie Taylor, eds., *Politics and Deviance,* pp. 13–41. Baltimore: Penguin.

_____. 1976. *Crimes of the Powerful: Marxism, Crime, and Deviance.* London: Pluto Press.

_____. 1990. "Responsible Corporations and Regulatory Agencies." *Political Quarterly* 61:415–30.

Pearce, Frank, and Snider, Laureen, eds. 1992. "Crimes of the Powerful," *Journal of Human Justice,* 3:1–124.
David O. Friedrichs, "White-Collar Crime and the Definitional Quagmire: A Provisional Solution"(5–21); John Casey, "Corporate Crime and the Canadian State: Anti-Combines Legislation"(22–35); Mary G. Condon, "Following up on Interests: The Private Agreement Exemption in Ontario Securities Law"(36–55); Doreen McBarnet, "Legitimate Rackets: Tax Evasion, Tax Avoidance, and the Boundaries of Legality"(56–74); Steve Tombs, "Stemming the Flow of Blood? The Illusion of Self-Regulation"(75–92); Harold Barnett, "Hazardous Waste, Distributional Conflict, and a Trilogy of Failures"(93–110); Elizabeth A. Sheehy, "Case Comment: Regulatory Crimes and the Charter: *R. v. Wholesale Travel Inc.*"(111–24).

Pearce, Frank, and Woodiwiss, Michael, eds. 1993. *Global Crime Connections: Dynamics and Control.* Toronto: University of Toronto Press.
Alan A. Block, "Defending the Mountaintop: A Campaign against Environmental Crime"(91–140); Michael Clarke, "EEC Fraud: A Suitable Case for Treatment"(162–86); Frank Pearce and Steven Tombs, "US Capital Versus the Third World: Union Carbide and Bhopal"(187–211); Laureen Snider, "The Politics of Corporate Crime Control"(212–34).

Pelaez, Alfred S. 1980. "Of Crime—and Punishment: Sentencing the White-Collar Criminal." *Duquesne Law Review* 18:823–55.

Pepinsky, Harold. 1974. "From White Collar Crime to Exploitation: Redefinition of a Field." *Journal of Criminal Law and Criminology* 65:225–33.

Pepinsky, Harold, and Jesilow, Paul. 1992. *Myths That Cause Crime,* pp. 54–92. 3d ed. Washington, DC: Seven Locks Press.

Pitt, Harvey L. and Groskaufmanis, Karl A. 1990. "Minimizing Corporate Civil and Criminal Liability: A Second Look at Corporate Codes of Conduct." *Georgetown Law Journal* 78:1559–1654.

Pizzo, Stephen; Fricker, Mary; and Muolo, Paul. 1989. *Inside Job: The Looting of America's Savings and Loans.* New York: McGraw-Hill.

Pontell, Henry N.; Jesilow, Paul D.; and Geis, Gilbert. 1982. "Policing Physicians: Practitioner Fraud and Abuse in a Government Medicaid Program." *Social Problems* 30:115–25.

_____. 1984. "Practitioner Fraud and Abuse in Medical Benefit Programs: Government Regulation and Professional White-Collar Crime." *Law and Policy* 6:405–24.

Pontell, Henry N.; Jesilow, Paul D.; Geis, Gilbert; and O'Brien, Mary Jane. 1985. "A Demographic Portrait of Physicians Sanctioned by the Federal Government for Fraud and Abuse against Medicare and Medicaid." *Medical Care* 23:1028–31.

Pontell, Henry N.; Keenan, Constance; Granite, Daniel; and Geis, Gilbert. 1983. "White-Collar Crime Seriousness: Assessments by Police Chiefs and Regulatory Agency Investigators." *American Journal of Police* 3:1–16.

Pontell, Henry N.; Rosoff, Stephen M.; and Goode, Erich. 1990. "White-Collar Crime." In Erich Goode, ed., *Deviant Behavior,* pp. 289–313. 3d ed. Englewood Cliffs, NJ: Prentice-Hall.

Poveda, Tony G. 1992. "White-Collar Crime and the Justice Department: The Institutionalization of a Concept." *Crime, Law and Social Change* 17:235–52.

President's Commission on Law Enforcement and Administration of Justice. 1967. *The Challenge of Crime in a Free Society,* pp. 102–15. Washington, DC: Government Printing Office.

Quinney, Richard. 1963. "Occupational Structure and Criminal Behavior: Prescription Violations by Retail Pharmacists." *Social Problems* 11:179–85.

_____. 1964. "The Study of White-Collar Crime: Toward a Reorientation in Theory and Research." *Journal of Criminal Law, Criminology, and Police Science* 55:208–14.

Rackmill, Stephen J. 1992. "Understanding and Sanctioning the White-Collar Offender." *Federal Probation* 26 (June):26–33.

Radin, Stephen A. 1983. "Corporate Criminal Liability for Employee-Endangering Activities." *Columbia Journal of Law and Social Problems* 18:39–75.

Rafalko, Robert J. 1989. "Corporate Punishment: A Proposal." *Journal of Business Ethics* 12:917–28.

Randall, Donna M. 1987. "The Portrayal of Corporate Crime in Network Television Newscasts." *Journalism Quarterly* 64:150–53, 250.

Rao, S. Venugopal. 1978. "White Collar Crime: An Adjunct of our Political and Economic System." *Indian Journal of Social Work* 38:399–408.

Raucher, Stephen. 1992. "Raising the Stakes for Environmental Polluters: The *Exxon Valdez* Criminal Prosecution." *Ecology Law Quarterly* 19:147–85.

Reed, John P., and Reed, Robin S. 1974. "Doctor, Lawyer, Indian Chief: Old Rhymes and New on White-Collar Crime." *Australian and New Zealand Journal of Criminology* 7:145–56.

Reichman, Nancy. 1989. "Breaking Confidences: Organizational Influences on Insider Trading." *Sociological Quarterly* 30:185–204.

Reiman, Jeffrey H. 1990. *The Rich Get Richer and the Poor Get Prison: Ideology, Class, and Criminal Justice.* 3d ed. New York: Macmillan.

Reisman, W. Michael. 1979. *Folded Lies: Bribery, Crusades and Reforms.* New York: The Free Press.

Reiss, Albert J., Jr., and Biderman, Albert. 1980. *Data Sources on White-Collar Law-Breaking.* Washington, DC: U.S. Department of Justice.

Richardson, Genevra; Ogus, Anthony; and Burrows, Paul. 1982. *Policing Pollution: A Study of Regulation and Enforcement.* Oxford: Clarendon Press.

Rider, Barry, and Ffrench, H. Leigh. 1979. *The Regulation of Insider Trading.* Dobbs Ferry, NY: Oceana.

Robb, George. 1992. *White-Collar Crime in Modern England: Financial Fraud and Business Morality, 1845–1929.* Cambridge: Cambridge University Press.

Rock, Andrew J. 1982. "The Concept of White-Collar Crime." In Frederick Elliston and Norman Bowie, eds., *Ethics, Public Policy, and Criminal Justice,* pp. 59–72. Cambridge, MA: Oelgeschlager, Gunn & Hain.

Rose-Ackerman, Susan. 1978. *Corruption: A Study in Political Economy.* New York: Academic Press.

Ross, Edward A. 1907. *Sin and Society: An Analysis of Latter-Day Iniquity.* Boston: Houghton Mifflin.

Ross, Irwin. 1980. "How Lawless Are Big Companies?" *Fortune* 102 (December 1):56–62.

Rossi, Peter H.; Waite, Emily; Rose, Christine E.; and Berk, Richard E. 1974. "The Seriousness of Crimes: Normative Structure and Individual Differences." *American Sociological Review* 39:224–37.

Rothman, Mitchell L., and Gandossy, Robert F. 1982. "Sad Tales: The Accounts of White-Collar Offenders and the Decision to Sanction." *Pacific Sociological Review* 4:449–73.

Rubin, Robert L. 1986. "Federal Regulation in Historical Perspective." *Stanford Law Review* 38:1189–1326.

Sargent, Neil. 1989. "Law, Ideology and Corporate Crime: A Critique of Instrumentality." *Canadian Journal of Criminology* 4:39–75.

Saxon, Miriam. 1980. *White Collar Crime: The Problem and the Federal Response.* Washington, DC: Congressional Research Service, Library of Congress.

Schlegel, Kip. 1988. "Desert, Retribution, and Corporate Criminality." *Justice Quarterly* 5: 615–34.

_____. 1990. *Just Deserts for Corporate Criminals.* Boston: Northeastern University Press.

_____. 1989. "Overcoming the Crisis of Legitimacy: Research in White-Collar Crime." *Criminal Justice Review* 13: 69–78.

Schlegel, Kip, and Weisburd, David, eds. 1992. *White-Collar Crime Reconsidered.* Boston: Northeastern University Press.
Kip Schlegel and David Weisburd, "White-Collar Crime: The Parallex View"(3–27); Gilbert Geis, "White-Collar Crime: What Is It?"(31–52); James William Coleman, "The Theory of White-Collar Crime: From Sutherland to the 1990s"(53–77); John Braithwaite, "Poverty, Power, and White-Collar Crime:

Sutherland and the Paradoxes of Criminological Theory"(78–107); Stanton Wheeler, "The Problem of White-Collar Crime Motivation"(108–23); Diane Vaughan, "The Macro–Micro Connection in White-Collar Crime Theory"(124–45); Paul Jesilow, Esther Klempner, and Victoria Chiao, "Reporting Consumer and Major Fraud"(149–68); Michael Levi, "White-Collar Victimization"(169–92); Henry N. Pontell and Kitty Calavita, "Bilking Bankers and Bad Debts: White-Collar Crime and the Savings and Loan Crisis"(195–213); Ronald C. Kramer, "The Space Shuttle *Challenger* Explosion: A Case Study of State-Corporate Crime"(214–43); Nancy Reichman, "Moving Backstage: Uncovering the Role of Compliance Practices in Shaping Regulatory Policy"(244–68); Michael L. Benson, Francis T. Cullen, and William J. Maakestad, "Community Context and the Prosecution of Corporate Crime"(269–86); Sally S. Simpson, "Corporate-Crime Deterrence and Corporate-Control Policies"(289–308): Steve Walt and William S. Laufer, "Corporate Criminal Liability and the Comparative Mix of Sanctions"(309–31); Kenneth Mann, "Procedure Rules and Information Control: Gaining Leverage Over White-Collar Crime"(332–51).

Schneider, Mark W. 1982. "Criminal Enforcement of Federal Water Pollution Laws in an Era of Deregulation." *Journal of Criminal Law and Criminology* 73: 642–74.

Scholz, John. 1984. "Deterrence, Cooperation and the Sociology of Regulatory Enforcement." *Law and Society Review* 18:179–224.

Schrag, Philip G. 1972. *Counsel for the Damned: Case Studies in Consumer Fraud.* New York: Pantheon.

Schrager, Laura S., and Short, James F., Jr. 1978. "Toward a Sociology of Organizational Crime." *Social Problems* 25:407–19.

Scott, Donald W. 1989. "Policing Corporate Collusion." *Criminology* 27:559–82.

Sebba, Leslie. 1983. "Attitudes of New Immigrants toward White-Collar Crime: A Cross-Cultural Exploration." *Human Relations* 36:1091–1110.

Sethi, S. Prakash. 1987. "The Expanding Scope of Executive Liability (Criminal and Civil) for Corporate Law Violations." In Sethi, ed., *Business and Society: Dimensions of Conflict and Cooperation,* pp. 471–506. Lexington, MA: Lexington Books.

Seyhun, H. Nejat. 1992. "The Effectiveness of Insider Trading Sanctions." *Journal of Law and Economics* 35:149–82.

Shapiro, Susan. 1990. "Collaring the Crime, Not the Criminal: Reconsidering the Concept of White-Collar Crime." *American Sociological Review* 55:346–65.

_____. 1987. "Policing Trust." In Clifford D. Shearing and Philip C. Stenning, eds., *Private Policing,* pp. 194–220. Newbury Park: Sage.

_____. 1985. "The Road Not Taken: The Elusive Path to Criminal Prosecution for White-Collar Offenders." *Law and Society Review* 19:179–217.

_____. "The Social Control of Impersonal Trust." *American Journal of Sociology* 93:623–58.

_____. 1980. *Thinking about White-Collar Crime: Matters of Conceptualization and Research.* Washington, DC: Government Printing Office.

_____. 1984. *Wayward Capitalists: Target of the Securities and Exchange Commission.* New Haven: Yale University Press.

Shichor, David. 1989. "Corporate Deviance and Corporate Victimization: A Review and Some Elaborations." *International Journal of Victimology* 1:67–82.

Shover, Neal; Clelland, Donald A.; and Lynxwiler, John. 1986. *Enforcement or Negotiation? Constructing a Regulatory Bureaucracy.* Albany: State University of New York Press.

Shover, Neal; Fox, Greer Litton; and Mills Michael. 1994. "Long-Term Consequences of Victimization by White-Collar Crime." *Justice Quarterly* 11:301–24.

Sigler, Jay A., and Murphy, Joseph E. 1991. *Corporate Lawbreaking and Interactive Compliance: Resolving the Regulation-Deregulation Dichotomy.* New York: Quorum Books.

Simon, David R., and Eitzen, D. Stanley. 1992. *Elite Deviance.* 4th ed. Boston: Allyn and Bacon.

_____, and Swart, Stanley L. 1984. "The Justice Department Focuses on White-Collar Crime: Promises and Pitfalls." *Crime and Delinquency* 30:107–19.

Simpson, Sally. 1987. "Cycles of Illegality: Antitrust Violations in Corporate America." *Social Forces* 65:943–63.

_____. 1986. "The Decomposition of Antitrust: Testing a Multi-Level, Longitudinal Model of Profit-Squeeze." *American Sociological Review* 51:859–75.

_____. 1993. "Strategy, Structure, and Corporate Crime: The Historical Context." *Advances in Criminological Theory.* 4:71–93.

Simpson, Sally, and Koper, Christopher S. 1992. "Deterring Corporate Crime." *Criminology* 30:347–75.

Smigel, Erwin O. 1955. "Public Attitudes toward Stealing as Related to the Size of the Victim Organization." *American Sociological Review* 21:320–27.

Smith, Dwight. 1980. "Paragons, Pariahs, and Pirates: A Spectrum-Based Theory of Enterprise." *Crime and Delinquency* 26:358–86.

Snider, Laureen. 1993. *Bad Business: Corporate Crime in Canada.* Scarborough, Ont.: Nelson Canada.

_____. 1990. "Cooperative Models and Corporate Crime: Panacea or Copout? *Crime and Delinquency* 36:373–90.

_____. 1991. "The Regulatory Dance: Understanding Reform Processes in Corporate Crime." *International Journal of the Sociology of Law* 19:209–36.

_____. 1987. "Towards a Political Economy of Reform, Regulation, and Corporate Crime." *Law and Policy* 9:37–68.

Snyder, Edward A. 1990. "The Effect of Higher Criminal Penalties on Antitrust Enforcement." *Journal of Law and Economics* 33:439–62.

Somers, Leigh E. 1984. *Economic Crimes : Investigative Principles and Techniques.* New York: Clark Boardman.

Soothill, Keith. 1981. "Employing White Collar Ex-Offenders: A Five-Year Criminological Follow-up." *British Journal of Social Work* 11:77–87.

Spaulding, Karla R. 1989. " 'Hit Them Where It Hurts': RICO Criminal Forfeitures and White-Collar Crime." *Journal of Criminal Law and Criminology* 80: 197–292.

Spiegelhoff, Tracey L. 1984. "Limits of Individual Accountability for Corporate Crimes." *Marquette Law Review* 67:604–40.

Staw, Barry M., and Szwajkowski, Eugene. 1975. "The Scarcity-Munificence Component of Organizational Environments and the Commission of Illegal Acts." *Administrative Science Quarterly* 20:345–54.

Stigler, George J. 1985. "The Origin of the Sherman Act." *Journal of Legal Studies* 14:1–12.

Stone, Christopher. 1980. "The Place of Enterprise Liability in the Control of Corporate Conduct." *Yale Law Journal* 90:1–77.

_____. 1975. *Where the Law Ends: The Social Control of Corporate Behavior.* New York: Harper & Row.

Stone, Dan G. 1991. *April Fools: An Insider's Account of the Rise and Collapse of Drexel Burnham.* New York: Warner Books.

Stotland, Ezra. 1981. "Can White Collar Crime Investigators Be Protected from Improper Pressures?: The Case of Israel." *Journal of Criminal Justice* 9:265–88.

_____. 1977. "White Collar Criminals." *Journal of Social Issues* 33:179–96.

Sutherland, Edwin H. 1941. "Crime and Business." *Annals of the American Academy of Political and Social Science* 217:112–18.

_____. 1973. *On Analyzing Crime.* Ed. by Karl Schuessler. Chicago: University of Chicago Press.

_____. 1949. "The White-Collar Criminal." In Vernon C. Branham and Samuel B. Kutash, eds., *Encyclopedia of Criminology,* pp. 511–15. New York: Philosophical Library.

_____. 1949. *White Collar Crime.* New York: Dryden.

_____. 1983. *White Collar Crime: The Uncut Version.* New Haven: Yale University Press.

Sutton, Adam, and Wild, Ronald. 1985. "Small Business: White-Collar Villains or Victims?" *International Journal of the Sociology of Law* 18:247–59.

Swigert, Victoria Lynn, and Farrell, Ronald A. 1980–81. "Corporate Homicide: Definitional Processes in the Creation of Deviance." *Law and Society Review* 15:161–82.

Symposium on White-Collar Crime. 1980. *Temple Law Quarterly* 53:975–1146.
Mark Richard, "Introduction"(975–83); Norman Abrams, "Assessing the Federal Government's 'War' on White-Collar Crime"(984–1008); G. Robert Blakey and Brian Gettings, "Racketeer Influenced and Corrupt Organizations (RICO): Basic Concepts—Criminal and Civil Remedies"(1009–48); Kurt W. Muellenberg and Harvey J. Volzer, "Inspector General Act of 1978"(1049–66); Gilbert Geis and Thomas R. Clay, "Criminal Enforcement of California's Occupational Carcinogens Control Act"(1067–99); Marvin G. Pickholiz, "The Expanding World of Parallel Proceedings"(1100–13); Herbert Edelhertz, "Transnational White-Collar Crime: A Developing Challenge and Need for Response"(1114–26); John Braithwaite, "Inegalitarian Consequences of Egalitarian Reforms to Control Corporate Crime"(1127–46).

Szasz, Andrew. 1986. "Corporations, Organized Crime, and the Disposal of Hazardous Waste: An Examination of the Making of a Criminogenic Regulatory Structure. *Criminology* 24:1–27.

———. 1986. "The Process and Significance of Political Scandals: A Comparison of Watergate and the 'Sewergate' Episode at the Environmental Protection Agency." *Social Problems* 33:202–17.

Szockyj, Elizabeth. 1993. *The Law and Insider Trading: In Search of a Level Playing Field.* Buffalo, NY: Hein.

Talley, Pat. L. 1993. *The Savings and Loan Crisis: An Annotated Bibliography.* Westport, CT: Greenwood.

Thomas, Robert J. 1993. "Interviewing Important People in Big Companies." *Journal of Contemporary Ethnography* 22:80–96.

Thomas, Sari, and LeShay, Steven V. 1992. "Bad Business? A Reexamination of Television's Portrayal of Businesspersons." *Journal of Communication* 42: 95–105.

Thompson, Dennis F. 1993. "Mediated Corruption: The Case of the Keating Five." *American Political Science Review* 87:369–81.

Tigar, Michael E. 1990. "It Does the Crime But Not the Time: Corporate Criminal Liability in Federal Law." *American Journal of Criminal Law* 17:211–34.

Tillman, Robert, and Pontell, Henry. 1992. "Is Justice 'Collar-Blind?' Punishing Medicaid Provider Fraud." *Criminology* 30:401–28.

Tompkins, Dorothy C. 1967. *White-Collar Crime—A Bibliography.* Berkeley: Institute of Governmental Studies, University of California.

Tonry, Michael, and Reiss, Albert J., Jr., eds. 1993. *Beyond the Law: Crime in Complex Organizations*. Chicago: University of Chicago Press.
Reiss and Tonry, "Organizational Crime"(1–10); John Braithwaite, "The Nursing Home Industry"(11–54); Nancy Reichman, "Insider Trading"(55–96); Peter C. Yeager, "Industrial Water Pollution"(97–148); Peter Reuter, "The Cartage Industry in New York"(149–201); Henry Pontell and Kitty Calavita, "The Savings and Loan Industry"(203–46); Franklin E. Zimring and Gordon Hawkins, "Crime, Justice, and the Savings and Loan Crisis"(247–92).

Ts'ai, Lim Wen. 1990. "Corporations and the Devil's Dictionary: The Problem of Individual Responsibility for Corporate Crimes." *Sydney Law Review* 12:311–45.

U.S. Department of Justice, Bureau of Justice Statistics. 1986. *Tracking Offenders: White Collar Crime*.

Vasterling, Gail et al. 1990. "Recent Developments in Corporate and White Collar Crime." *Washington University Law Quarterly* 68:779–818.

Vaughan, Diane. 1983. *Controlling Unlawful Organizational Behavior: Social Structure and Corporate Misconduct*. Chicago: University of Chicago Press.

———. 1981. "Recent Developments in White-Collar Crime Theory and Research." In C. Ronald Huff and Israel L. Barak-Glantz, eds., *The Mad, the Bad, and the Different*, pp. 135–148. Lexington, MA: Lexington Books.

———. 1982. "Transaction Systems and Unlawful Organizational Behavior." *Social Problems* 29: 373–80.

von Hirsch, Andrew. 1982. "Desert and White-Collar Crime: A Reply to Dr. Braithwaite." *Journal of Criminal Law and Criminology* 73:1164–75.

Waegel, William B.; Ermann, M. David; and Horowitz, Alan M. 1981. "Organizational Responses to Imputations of Deviance." *Sociological Quarterly* 22:43–55.

Watkins, John C., Jr. 1977. "White-Collar Crime, Legal Sanctions, and Social Control: 'Idols of the Theatre' in Operation." *Crime and Delinquency* 23:290–303.

Weaver, Suzanne. 1977. *Decision to Prosecute: Organization and Public Policy in the Antitrust Division*. Cambridge: MIT Press.

Webster, William H. 1980. "An Examination of FBI Policy and Methodology Regarding White-Collar Crime Investigation and Prevention." *American Criminal Law Review* 55:346–55.

Weisburd, David; Chayet, Ellen F.; and Waring, Elin J. 1990. "White-Collar Crime and Criminal Careers: Some Preliminary Findings." *Crime and Delinquency* 36:342–55.

Weisburd, David; Waring, Elin; and Wheeler, Stanton. 1990. "Class, Status, and the Punishment of White-Collar Criminals." *Law and Social Inquiry* 15:223–43.

Weisburd, David; Wheeler, Stanton; Waring, Elin; and Bode, Nancy. 1991. *Crimes of the Middle Class: White-Collar Offenders in the Federal Courts*. New Haven: Yale University Press.

Welling, Sarah N. 1993. "White Collar Crime from Scratch: Some Observations on the East European Experience." *William and Mary Law Review* 35:271–78.

Wells, Celia. 1993. *Corporations and Criminal Responsibility.* Oxford: Clarendon Press.

Wells, Joseph T. 1992. *Fraud Examination: Investigative and Audit Procedures.* New York: Quorum Books.

_____. 1990. "Six Common Myths about Fraud." *Journal of Accountancy* 169 (February):82–88.

Wheeler, Stanton. 1993. "The Prospects for Large-Scale Collaborative Research: Revisiting the Yale White-Collar Crime Research Program." *Law and Social Inquiry* 18:101–13.

_____. 1976. "Trends and Problems in the Sociological Study of Crime." *Social Problems* 23:525–34.

_____. 1983. "White-Collar Crime: History of an Idea." In Sanford H. Kadish, ed., *Encyclopedia of Crime and Justice,* vol. 4, pp. 1652–56. New York: Macmillan.

_____. 1992. "White Collar Crime: Some Reflections on a Socio-Legal Problem and on the Problems of Motivation in White Collar Crime." *Tel Aviv University Law Review* 15:435–56.

Wheeler, Stanton; Mann, Kenneth; and Sarat Austin. 1988. *Sitting in Judgment: The Sentencing of White-Collar Criminals.* New Haven: Yale University Press.

Wheeler, Stanton; Weisburd, David; and Bode, Nancy. 1982. "Sentencing the White-Collar Offender: Rhetoric and Reality." *American Sociological Review* 47:641–59.

Wheeler, Stanton; Weisburd, David; Waring, Elin; and Bode, Nancy. 1988. "White-Collar Crime and Criminals." *American Criminal Law Review* 25:331–57.

Wickman, Peter, and Dailey, Timothy, eds. 1982. *White-Collar and Economic Crime: Multidisciplinary and Cross-National Perspectives.* Lexington, MA: Lexington Books.
Gilbert Geis and Colin Goff, "Edwin H. Sutherland: A Biographical and Analytical Commentary"(3–21); Dwight C. Smith, Jr., "White-Collar Crime, Organized Crime, and the Business Establishment: Resolving a Crisis in Criminological Theory"(23–38); Leon Sheleff, "International White-Collar Crime"(39–57); Charles E. Reasons, "Crime and the Abuse of Power: Offenses and Offenders beyond the Reach of the Law"(59–72); Ronald C. Kramer, "Corporate Crime: An Organizational Perspective"(75–94); Susan B. Long, "Growth in the Underground Economy? An Empirical Issue"(95–120); Maria Los, "Crime and Economy in the Communist Countries"(121–37); Michael K. Block, "The Level of Theft and the Size of the Public Sector: Some Empirical Evidence"(139–49); Laureen Snider, "Critical Comments on Michael K. Block's 'The Level of Theft and the Size of the Public Sector: Some Empirical Evidence' "(151–55); Harold C. Barnett, "The Production of Corporate Crime in Corporate Capital-

ism"(157–70); W. G. Carson, "Legal Control of Safety on British Offshore Oil Installations"(173–96); Jerry Parker, "Social Control and the Legal Profession"(197–234); Laureen Snider, "Traditional and Corporate Theft: A Comparison of Sanctions" (235–58); John Hagan, Ilene Nagel, and Celesta Albonetti, "The Social Organization of White-Collar Sanctions: A Study of Prosecution and Punishment in the Federal Courts"(259–75).

Wilson, James Q., ed. 1980. *The Politics of Regulation.* New York: Basic Books.

Wilson, Paul R., and Braithwaite, John, eds. 1978. *Two Faces of Deviance: Crimes of the Powerless and the Powerful.* Brisbane: University of Queensland Press.
John Braithwaite and Paul R. Wilson, "Introduction: Pervs, Pimps, and Power-brokers"(1–12); Adam Sutton and Ron Wild, "Corporate Crime and Social Structure"(177–98); Edward Gross, "Organizations as Criminal Actors"(199–213); John Braithwaite and Barry Condon, "On the Class Bias of Criminal Violence" (232–51).

Wilson, Paul R.; Geis, Gilbert; Pontell, Henry; Jesilow, Paul; and Chappell, Duncan. 1985. "Medical Fraud and Abuse: Australia, Canada, and the United States." *International Journal of Comparative and Applied Criminal Justice* 9:25–34.

Winans, R. Foster. 1984. *Trading Secrets.* New York: St. Martin's Press.

Wray, Christopher A. 1992. "Corporate Probation under the New Organizational Sentencing Guidelines." *Yale Law Journal* 101:2017–42.

Wright, Richard A., and Friedrichs, David O. 1991. "White-Collar Crime in the Criminal Justice Curriculum." *Journal of Criminal Justice Education* 2:95–119.

Yeager, Matthew G. 1984. "Community Redress against the Corporate Offender." *Crime and Social Justice* 21–22:223–27.

———. 1973. "The Gangster as White-Collar Criminal: Organized Crime and Stolen Securities." *Issues in Criminology* 8:49–73.

Yeager, Peter C. 1986. "Analyzing Corporate Offenses: Progress and Prospects." In James E. Post, ed., *Research in Corporate Social Performance and Policy,* vol. 8, pp. 93–120. Greenwich, CT: JAI Press.

———. 1991. *The Limits of Law: The Public Regulation of Private Pollution.* New York: Cambridge University Press.

———. 1987. "Structural Bias in Regulatory Law Enforcement: The Case of the U.S. Environmental Protection Agency." *Social Problems* 34:330–44.

Yeager, Peter C., and Clinard, Marshall B. 1979. "Regulating Corporate Behavior: A Case Study." In Paul J. Brantingham and Jack M. Kress, eds., *Structure, Law, and Power,* pp. 62–82. Beverly Hills: Sage.

Yeager, Peter C., and Kram, Kathy E. 1990. "Fielding Hot Topics in Cool Settings: The Study of Corporate Ethics." *Qualitative Sociology* 13:127–48.

Yellin, David, and Mayer, Carl J. 1992. "Coordinating Sanctions for Corporate

Misconduct: Civil or Criminal Punishment?" *American Criminal Law Review* 29:961–1024.

Yoder, Steven A. 1978. "Criminal Sanctions for Corporate Illegality." *Journal of Criminal Law and Criminology* 69:40–58.

Young, T. R. 1981. "Corporate Crime: A Critique of the Clinard Report." *Contemporary Crises* 5:323–36.

Zey, Mary. 1993. *Banking on Fraud: Drexel, Junk Bonds, and Buyouts.* Hawthorne, NY: Aldine de Gruyter.

Zietz, Dorothy. 1981. *Women Who Embezzle or Defraud: A Study of Convicted Felons.* New York: Praeger.